Praise for the Reformation Commentary on Scripture

"Protestant reformers were fundamentally exegetes as much as theologians, yet (except for figures like Luther and Calvin) their commentaries and sermons have been neglected because these writings are not available in modern editions or languages. That makes this new series of Reformation Commentary on Scripture most welcome as a way to provide access to some of the wealth of biblical exposition of the sixteenth and seventeenth centuries. The editor's introduction explains the nature of the sources and the selection process; the intended audience of modern pastors and students of the Bible has led to a focus on theological and practical comments. Although it will be of use to students of the Reformation, this series is far from being an esoteric study of largely forgotten voices; this collection of reforming comments, comprehending every verse and provided with topical headings, will serve contemporary pastors and preachers very well."

Elsie Anne McKee, *Archibald Alexander Professor of Reformation Studies and the History of Worship, Princeton Theological Seminary*

"This series provides an excellent introduction to the history of biblical exegesis in the Reformation period. The introductions are accurate, clear and informative, and the passages intelligently chosen to give the reader a good idea of methods deployed and issues at stake. It puts precritical exegesis in its context and so presents it in its correct light. Highly recommended as reference book, course book and general reading for students and all interested lay and clerical readers."

Irena Backus, *Professeure Ordinaire, Institut d'histoire de la Réformation, Université de Genève*

"The Reformation Commentary on Scripture is a major publishing event—for those with historical interest in the founding convictions of Protestantism, but even more for those who care about understanding the Bible. As with IVP Academic's earlier Ancient Christian Commentary on Scripture, this effort brings flesh and blood to 'the communion of saints' by letting believers of our day look over the shoulders of giants from the past. By connecting the past with the present, and by doing so with the Bible at the center, the editors of this series perform a great service for the church. The series deserves the widest possible support."

Mark A. Noll, *Francis A. McAnaney Professor of History, University of Notre Dame*

"For those who preach and teach Scripture in the church, the Reformation Commentary on Scripture is a significant publishing event. Pastors and other church leaders will find delightful surprises, challenging enigmas and edifying insights in this series, as many Reformational voices are newly translated into English. The lively conversation in these pages can ignite today's pastoral imagination for fresh and faithful expositions of Scripture."

J. Todd Billings, *Gordon H. Girod Research Professor of Reformed Theology, Western Theological Seminary*

"The reformers discerned rightly what the church desperately needed in the sixteenth century—the bold proclamation of the Word based on careful study of the sacred Scriptures. We need not only to hear that same call again for our own day but also to learn from the Reformation how to do it. This commentary series is a godsend!"

Richard J. Mouw, *President Emeritus, Fuller Theological Seminary*

"Like the Ancient Christian Commentary on Scripture, the Reformation Commentary on Scripture does a masterful job of offering excellent selections from well-known and not-so-well-known exegetes. The editor's introductory survey is, by itself, worth the price of the book. It is easy to forget that there were more hands, hearts and minds involved in the Reformation than Luther and Calvin. Furthermore, encounters even with these figures are often limited to familiar quotes on familiar topics. However, the Reformation Commentary helps us to recognize the breadth and depth of exegetical interests and skill that fueled and continue to fuel faithful meditation on God's Word. I heartily recommend this series as a tremendous resource not only for ministry but for personal edification."

Michael S. Horton, *J. G. Machen Professor of Systematic Theology and Apologetics, Westminster Seminary, California*

"The Reformation was ignited by a fresh reading of Scripture. In this series of commentaries, we contemporary interpreters are allowed to feel some of the excitement, surprise and wonder of our spiritual forebears. Luther, Calvin and their fellow revolutionaries were masterful interpreters of the Word. Now, in this remarkable series, some of our very best Reformation scholars open up the riches of the Reformation's reading of the Scripture."

William H. Willimon, *Professor of the Practice of Christian Ministry, Duke Divinity School*

"The Reformation Scripture principle set the entirety of Christian life and thought under the governance of the divine Word, and pressed the church to renew its exegetical labors. This series promises to place before the contemporary church the fruit of those labors, and so to exemplify life under the Word."

John Webster, *Professor of Divinity, University of St. Andrews*†

"Since Gerhard Ebeling's pioneering work on Luther's exegesis seventy years ago, the history of biblical interpretation has occupied many Reformation scholars and become a vital part of study of the period. The Reformation Commentary on Scripture provides fresh materials for students of Reformation-era biblical interpretation and for twenty-first-century preachers to mine the rich stores of insights from leading reformers of the sixteenth century into both the text of Scripture itself and its application in sixteenth-century contexts. This series will strengthen our understanding of the period of the Reformation and enable us to apply its insights to our own days and its challenges to the church."

Robert Kolb, *Professor Emeritus, Concordia Theological Seminary*

"The multivolume Ancient Christian Commentary on Scripture is a valuable resource for those who wish to know how the Fathers interpreted a passage of Scripture but who lack the time or the opportunity to search through the many individual works. This new Reformation Commentary on Scripture will do the same for the reformers and is to be warmly welcomed. It will provide much easier access to the exegetical treasures of the Reformation and will hopefully encourage readers to go back to some of the original works themselves."

Anthony N. S. Lane, *Professor of Historical Theology and Director of Research, London School of Theology*

"This volume of the RCS project is an invaluable source for pastors and the historically/biblically interested that provides unparalleled access not only to commentaries of the leading Protestant reformers but also to a host of nowadays unknown commentaters on Galatians and Ephesians. The RCS is sure to enhance and enliven contemporary exegesis. With its wide scope, the collection will enrich our understanding of the variety of Reformation thought and biblical exegesis."

Sigrun Haude, *Associate Professor of Reformation and Early Modern European History, University of Cincinnati*

"This grand project sets before scholars, pastors, teachers, students and growing Christians an experience that can only be likened to stumbling into a group Bible study only to discover that your fellow participants include some of the most significant Christians of the Reformation and post-Reformation (for that matter, of any) era. Here the Word of God is explained in a variety of accents: German, Swiss, French, Dutch, English, Scottish and more. Each one vibrates with a thrilling sense of the living nature of God's Word and its power to transform individuals, churches and even whole communities. Here is a series to anticipate, enjoy and treasure."

Sinclair Ferguson, *Senior Minister, First Presbyterian Church, Columbia, South Carolina*

"I strongly endorse the Reformation Commentary on Scripture. Introducing how the Bible was interpreted during the age of the Reformation, these volumes will not only renew contemporary preaching, but they will also help us understand more fully how reading and meditating on Scripture can, in fact, change our lives!"

Lois Malcolm, *Associate Professor of Systematic Theology, Luther Seminary*

"Discerning the true significance of movements in theology requires acquaintance with their biblical exegesis. This is supremely so with the Reformation, which was essentially a biblical revival. The Reformation Commentary on Scripture will fill a yawning gap, just as the Ancient Christian Commentary did before it, and the first volume gets the series off to a fine start, whetting the appetite for more. Most heartily do I welcome and commend this long overdue project."

J. I. Packer, *Retired Board of Governors Professor of Theology, Regent College*

"There is no telling the benefits to emerge from the publication of this magnificent Reformation Commentary on Scripture series! Now exegetical and theological treasures from Reformation era commentators will be at our fingertips, providing new insights from old sources to give light for the present and future. This series is a gift to scholars and to the church; a wonderful resource to enhance our study of the written Word of God for generations to come!"

Donald K. McKim, *Executive Editor of Theology and Reference, Westminster John Knox Press*

"Why was this not done before? The publication of the Reformation Commentary on Scripture should be greeted with enthusiasm by every believing Christian—but especially by those who will preach and teach the Word of God. This commentary series brings the very best of the Reformation heritage to the task of exegesis and exposition, and each volume in this series represents a veritable feast that takes us back to the sixteenth century to enrich the preaching and teaching of God's Word in our own time."

R. Albert Mohler Jr., *President, The Southern Baptist Theological Seminary*

"Today more than ever, the Christian past is the church's future. InterVarsity Press has already brought the voice of the ancients to our ears. Now, in the Reformation Commentary on Scripture, we hear a timely word from the first Protestants as well."

Bryan Litfin, *Professor of Theology, Moody Bible Institute*

"I am delighted to see the Reformation Commentary on Scripture. The editors of this series have done us all a service by gleaning from these rich fields of biblical reflection. May God use this new life for these old words to give him glory and to build his church."

Mark Dever, *Senior Pastor, Capitol Hill Baptist Church, and President of 9Marks.org Ministries*

"Monumental and magisterial, the Reformation Commentary on Scripture, edited by Timothy George, is a remarkably bold and visionary undertaking. Bringing together a wealth of resources, these volumes will provide historians, theologians, biblical scholars, pastors and students with a fresh look at the exegetical insights of those who shaped and influenced the sixteenth-century Reformation. With this marvelous publication, InterVarsity Press has reached yet another plateau of excellence. We pray that this superb series will be used of God to strengthen both church and academy."

David S. Dockery, *President, Trinity International University*

"Detached from her roots, the church cannot reach the world as God intends. While every generation must steward the scriptural insights God grants it, only arrogance or ignorance causes leaders to ignore the contributions of those faithful leaders before us. The Reformation Commentary on Scripture roots our thought in great insights of faithful leaders of the Reformation to further biblical preaching and teaching in this generation."

Bryan Chapell, *Chancellor and Professor of Practical Theology, Covenant Theological Seminary*

"After reading several volumes of the Reformation Commentary on Scripture, I exclaimed, 'Hey, this is just what the doctor ordered—I mean Doctor Martinus Lutherus!' The church of today bearing his name needs a strong dose of the medicine this doctor prescribed for the ailing church of the sixteenth century. The reforming fire of Christ-centered preaching that Luther ignited is the only hope to reclaim the impact of the gospel to keep the Reformation going, not for its own sake but to further the renewal of the worldwide church of Christ today. This series of commentaries will equip preachers to step into their pulpits with confidence in the same living Word that inspired the witness of Luther and Calvin and many other lesser-known Reformers."

Carl E. Braaten, *Cofounder of the Center for Catholic and Evangelical Theology*

"As a pastor, how does one cultivate a knowledge of the history of interpretation? That's where IVP's Reformation Commentary on Scripture and its forerunner, the Ancient Christian Commentary on Scripture, come in. They do an excellent job in helping pastors become more aware of the history of exegesis for the benefit of their congregations. Every pastor should have access to a set of each."

Carl R. Trueman, *Paul Woolley Chair of Church History, Westminster Theological Seminary*

Reformation Commentary on Scripture

New Testament XIII

Hebrews, James

Edited by
Ronald K. Rittgers

General Editor
Timothy George

Associate General Editor
Scott M. Manetsch

IVP Academic
An imprint of InterVarsity Press
Downers Grove, Illinois

For departed family members
and for my mother—my great cloud of
Scripture-loving witnesses

InterVarsity Press
P.O. Box 1400, Downers Grove, IL 60515-1426
www.ivpress.com
email@ivpress.com

InterVarsity Press® is the book-publishing division of InterVarsity Christian Fellowship/USA®, a movement of students and faculty active on campus at hundreds of universities, colleges and schools of nursing in the United States of America, and a member movement of the International Fellowship of Evangelical Students. For information about local and regional activities, visit intervarsity.org.

Design: Cindy Kiple
Images: Wooden cross: iStockphoto
The Protestant Church in Lyon: The Protestant Church in Lyon, called "The Paradise" at Bibliotheque Publique et Universitaire, Geneva, Switzerland, Erich Lessing/Art Resource, NY

ISBN 978-0-8308-2976-7 (print)
ISBN 978-0-8308-8942-6 (digital)

Printed in the United States of America ♾

InterVarsity Press is committed to ecological stewardship and to the conservation of natural resources in all our operations. This book was printed using sustainably sourced paper.

Library of Congress Cataloging-in-Publication Data

A catalog record for this book is available from the Library of Congress.

P 26 25 24 23 22 21 20 19 18 17 16 15 14 13 12 11 10 9 8 7 6 5 4 3 2 1
Y 40 39 38 37 36 35 34 33 32 31 30 29 28 27 26 25 24 23 22 21 20 19 18 17

Reformation Commentary on Scripture
Project Staff

Project Editor
David W. McNutt

Senior Production Manager and Managing Editor
Benjamin M. McCoy

Associate Managing Editor
Elissa Schauer

Copyeditor
Jeffrey A. Reimer

Assistant Project Editors
Andre A. Gazal
Todd R. Hains

Editorial and Research Assistants
David J. Hooper
Ashley Davila

Assistants to the General Editors
Le-Ann Little
Jason Odom

Design
Cindy Kiple

Design Assistant
Beth McGill

Content Production
Richard M. Chung
Maureen G. Tobey
Daniel van Loon
Jeanna L. Wiggins

Proofreader
Travis Ables

Print Coordinator
Jim Erhart

InterVarsity Press

Publisher
Jeff Crosby

Associate Publisher, Director of Editorial
Cindy Bunch

Associate Publisher, Director of IVP Academic
Daniel G. Reid

CONTENTS

ACKNOWLEDGMENTS

This volume has been (too) many years in the making, and I owe a debt of gratitude to many people for helping me bring it to completion. I remain grateful to Timothy George and Scott Manetsch, general editor and associate general editor of the Reformation Commentary on Scripture project, for inviting me to participate in the project a decade ago. Scott has been especially helpful along the way in fielding questions and helping me understand the animating impulse behind the project, which I fully endorse. In nearly all of my scholarly work, I seek to write for both the church and the academy. This volume, which has been quite a different exercise from my previous scholarly monographs, has enabled me to serve the church—especially its clergy—in a new way, even as I hope it will also be of use to the academy. I am most grateful for this opportunity.

The project editors, Joel Scandrett, Michael Gibson, Brannon Ellis, Dan Reid, and David McNutt, have all been most helpful in answering queries, locating sources, and encouraging my progress along the way. A special word of thanks is due to my outstanding research assistant Joel Adeney (and to Scott Manetsch for recommending him). Joel provided the translations of the Latin works from Johannes Bugenhagen, Heinrich Bullinger, Cardinal Cajetan, Johannes Oecolampadius, and Huldrych Zwingli that appear in the Hebrews portion of the volume. Simply put, the volume would not have been possible without his stellar work; I could not have wished for a better research assistant and colaborer on this project.

The research support I receive from the Erich Markel Chair in German Reformation Studies at Valparaiso University has also been crucial in the completion of this project, and I remain grateful to the Kade Foundation for providing the gift that created the chair I am privileged to hold. I wish to thank my dear wife, Jana, and our three sons, Alec, Blake, and Owen, for their support, patience, and understanding as I have worked on this project. In my office at home I have a shelf of Bibles from family members who have since passed on. Each one bears signs of use, in many cases being full of underlined passages and handwritten notes in the margins. These Bibles provide eloquent testimony to the importance of Scripture in my family over the generations. In all of our joys and struggles, triumphs and tragedies, the living and active Word of God (Heb 4:12) has been our source of guidance and solace. I dedicate this volume to my departed great-grandparents, grandparents, and father and stepfather, all of whom, in their own way, taught me to treasure Scripture. I also dedicate it to my mother, Linda Barlow Verman, who continues to teach me this lesson today.

Ronald K. Rittgers

ABBREVIATIONS

ACW	Ancient Christian Writers: The Works of the Fathers in Translation. New York: Newman; Mahwah, NJ: Paulist, 1946–.
ANF	The Ante-Nicene Fathers. 10 vols. Edited by Alexander Roberts and James Donaldson. Buffalo, NY: Christian Literature, 1885–1896. Available online at www.ccel.org.
ASD	Opera Omnia Desderii Erasmi Roterodami. Amsterdam: Elsevier, 1969–.
BoC	*The Book of Concord: The Confessions of the Evangelical Lutheran Church.* Edited by Robert Kolb and Timothy J. Wengert. Translated by Charles Arand et al. Minneapolis: Fortress, 2000.
BRN	*Bibliotheca Reformatoria Neederlandica.* 10 vols. Edited by S. Cramer and F. Pijper. The Hague: Martinus Nijhoff, 1903–1914. Digital copies online at babel.hathitrust.org.
BSLK	*Die Bekenntnisschriften der evangelisch-lutherischen Kirche.* 12th ed. Göttingen: Vandenhoeck & Ruprecht, 1998.
CHB	*Cambridge History of the Bible.* 3 vols. Cambridge: Cambridge University Press, 1963–1970.
CNTC	*Calvin's New Testament Commentaries.* 12 vols. Edited by D. W. Torrance and T. F. Torrance. Grand Rapids: Eerdmans, 1959–1972.
CO	*Ioannis Calvini Opera quae supersunt omnia.* 59 vols. Corpus Reformatorum 29-88. Edited by G. Baum, E. Cunitz, and E. Reuss. Brunswick and Berlin: C. A. Schwetschke, 1863–1900. Digital copy online at archive-ouverte.unige.ch/unige:650.
CRR	Classics of the Radical Reformation. 12 vols. Waterloo, ON, and Scottdale, PA: Herald Press, 1973–2010.
CTS	Calvin Translation Society edition of Calvin's commentaries. 46 vols. Edinburgh, 1843–1855. Several reprints, but variously bound; volume numbers (when cited) are relative to specific commentaries and not to the entire set. Available online at www.ccel.org.
CWE	*Collected Works of Erasmus.* 86 vols. projected. Toronto: University of Toronto Press, 1969–.
DMBI	*Dictionary of Major Biblical Interpreters.* Edited by Donald K. McKim. Downers Grove, IL: IVP Academic, 2007.
DNB	*Dictionary of National Biography.* Edited by Leslie Stephen and Sidney Lee. 63 vols. London: Smith, Elder, 1885–1900. Digital copy online at en.wikisource.org.
EEBO	Early English Books Online. Subscription database, eebo.chadwyck.com.

LB	*Desiderii Erasmi Roterodami Opera Omnia.* 10 vols. Edited by Jean LeClerc. Leiden: Van der Aa, 1704–1706. Reprint, Hildesheim: Georg Olms, 1961–1962. Digital copy online at babel.hathitrust.org.
LCC	Library of Christian Classics. 26 vols. Edited by John Baillie et al. Philadelphia: Westminster, 1953–1966.
LCL	Loeb Classical Library. Edited by Jeffrey Henderson. Cambridge, MA: Harvard University Press, 1911–. Digital copy online at www.loebclassics.com.
LW	*Luther's Works [American edition].* 82 vols. projected. St. Louis: Concordia; Philadelphia: Fortress, 1955–1986, 2009–.
NDB	*Neue Deutsche Biographie.* 28 vols. projected. Berlin: Duncker & Humblot, 1953–.
NPNF	A Select Library of the Nicene and Post-Nicene Fathers of the Christian Church. 28 vols. in two series, denoted as NPNF and NPNF². Edited by Philip Schaff et al. Buffalo, NY: Christian Literature, 1887–1894. Several reprints; also available online at www.ccel.org.
OER	*Oxford Encyclopedia of the Reformation.* 4 vols. Edited by Hans J. Hillerbrand. New York: Oxford University Press, 1996.
r, v	Some early books are numbered not by page but by folio (leaf). Front and back sides (pages) of a numbered folio are indicated by *recto* (r) and *verso* (v), respectively.
RCS	Reformation Commentary on Scripture. 28 vols. projected. Edited by Timothy George and Scott M. Manetsch. Downers Grove, IL: IVP Academic, 2011–.
WA	*D. Martin Luthers Werke, Kritische Gesamtausgabe: [Schriften].* 73 vols. Weimar: Hermann Böhlaus Nachfolger, 1883–2009. Digital copies online at archive.org.
WADB	*D. Martin Luthers Werke, Kritische Gesamtausgabe: Deutsche Bibel.* 12 vols. Weimar: Böhlaus Nachfolger, 1906–1961.
WATR	*D. Martin Luthers Werke, Kritische Gesamtausgabe: Tischreden.* 6 vols. Weimar: Hermann Böhlaus Nachfolger, 1912–1921. Digital copies online at archive.org.

BIBLE TRANSLATIONS

CEB	Common English Bible
ESV	English Standard Version
KJV	King James Version
LXX	Septuagint
NASB	New American Standard Bible
NIV	New International Version
NKJV	New King James Version
NRSV	New Revised Standard Version
Vg	Vulgate

A GUIDE TO USING THIS COMMENTARY

Several features have been incorporated into the design of this commentary. The following comments are intended to assist readers in making full use of this volume.

Pericopes of Scripture

The scriptural text has been divided into pericopes, or passages, usually several verses in length. Each of these pericopes is given a heading, which appears at the beginning of the pericope. For example, the first pericope in this commentary is Hebrews 1:1-4, "God Has Spoken Through His Son." This heading is followed by the Scripture passage quoted in the English Standard Version (ESV). The Scripture passage is provided for the convenience of readers, but it is also in keeping with Reformation-era commentaries, which often followed the patristic and medieval commentary tradition, in which the citations of the reformers were arranged according to the text of Scripture.

Overviews

Following each pericope of text is an overview of the Reformation authors' comments on that pericope. The format of this overview varies among the volumes of this series, depending on the requirements of the specific book(s) of Scripture. The function of the overview is to identify succinctly the key exegetical, theological, and pastoral concerns of the Reformation writers arising from the pericope, providing the reader with an orientation to Reformation-era approaches and emphases. It tracks a reasonably cohesive thread of argument among reformers' comments, even though they are derived from diverse sources and generations. Thus, the summaries do not proceed chronologically or by verse sequence. Rather, they seek to rehearse the overall course of the reformers' comments on that pericope.

We do not assume that the commentators themselves anticipated or expressed a formally received cohesive argument but rather that the various arguments tend to flow in a plausible, recognizable pattern. Modern readers can thus glimpse aspects of continuity in the flow of diverse exegetical traditions representing various generations and geographical locations.

Topical Headings

An abundance of varied Reformation-era comment is available for each pericope. For this reason we have broken the pericopes into two levels. First is the verse with its topical heading. The reformers' comments are then focused on aspects of each verse, with topical headings summarizing the essence of the individual comment by evoking a key phrase, metaphor, or idea. This feature provides a bridge by which modern readers can enter into the heart of the Reformation-era comment.

Identifying the Reformation Authors, Texts, and Events

Following the topical heading of each section of comment, the name of the Reformation commentator is given. An English translation (where needed) of the reformer's comment is then provided. This is immediately followed by the title of the original work rendered in English.

Readers who wish to pursue a deeper investigation of the reformers' works cited in this commentary will find full bibliographic detail for each Reformation title provided in the bibliography at the back of the volume. Information on English translations (where available) and standard original-language editions and critical editions of the works cited is found in the bibliography. The Biographical Sketches section provides brief overviews of the life and work of each commentator, and each confession or collaborative work, appearing in the present volume (as well as in any previous volumes). Finally, a Timeline of the Reformation offers broader context for people, places, and events relevant to the commentators and their works.

Footnotes and Back Matter

To aid the reader in exploring the background and texts in further detail, this commentary utilizes footnotes. The use and content of footnotes may vary among the volumes in this series. Where footnotes appear, a footnote number directs the reader to a note at the bottom of the page, where one will find annotations (clarifications or biblical cross references), information on English translations (where available) or standard original-language editions of the work cited.

Where original-language texts have remained untranslated into English, we provide new translations. Where there is any serious ambiguity or textual problem in the selection, we have tried to reflect the best available textual tradition. Wherever current English translations are already well rendered, they are utilized, but where necessary they are stylistically updated. A single asterisk (*) indicates that a previous English translation has been updated to modern English or amended for easier reading. We have standardized spellings and made grammatical variables uniform so that our English references will not reflect the linguistic oddities of the older English translations. For ease of reading we have in some cases removed superfluous conjunctions.

GENERAL INTRODUCTION

The Reformation Commentary on Scripture (RCS) is a twenty-eight-volume series of exegetical comment covering the entire Bible and gathered from the writings of sixteenth-century preachers, scholars and reformers. The RCS is intended as a sequel to the highly acclaimed Ancient Christian Commentary on Scripture (ACCS), and as such its overall concept, method, format, and audience are similar to the earlier series. Both series are committed to the renewal of the church through careful study and meditative reflection on the Old and New Testaments, the charter documents of Christianity, read in the context of the worshiping, believing community of faith across the centuries. However, the patristic and Reformation eras are separated by nearly a millennium, and the challenges of reading Scripture with the reformers require special attention to their context, resources and assumptions. The purpose of this general introduction is to present an overview of the context and process of biblical interpretation in the age of the Reformation.

Goals

The Reformation Commentary on Scripture seeks to introduce its readers to the depth and richness of exegetical ferment that defined the Reformation era. The RCS has four goals: the enrichment of contemporary biblical interpretation through exposure to Reformation-era biblical exegesis; the renewal of contemporary preaching through exposure to the biblical insights of the Reformation writers; a deeper understanding of the Reformation itself and the breadth of perspectives represented within it; and a recovery of the profound integration of the life of faith and the life of the mind that should characterize Christian scholarship. Each of these goals requires a brief comment.

Renewing contemporary biblical interpretation. During the past half-century, biblical hermeneutics has become a major growth industry in the academic world. One of the consequences of the historical-critical hegemony of biblical studies has been the privileging of contemporary philosophies and ideologies at the expense of a commitment to the Christian church as the primary reading community within which and for which biblical exegesis is done. Reading Scripture with the church fathers and the reformers is a corrective to all such imperialism of the present. One of the greatest skills required for a fruitful interpretation of the Bible is the ability to listen. We rightly emphasize the importance of listening to the voices of contextual theologies today, but in doing so we often marginalize or ignore another crucial context—the community of believing Christians through the centuries. The serious study of Scripture requires more than the latest

Bible translation in one hand and the latest commentary (or niche study Bible) in the other. John L. Thompson has called on Christians today to practice the art of "reading the Bible with the dead."[1] The RCS presents carefully selected comments from the extant commentaries of the Reformation as an encouragement to more in-depth study of this important epoch in the history of biblical interpretation.

Strengthening contemporary preaching. The Protestant reformers identified the public preaching of the Word of God as an indispensible means of grace and a sure sign of the true church. Through the words of the preacher, the living voice of the gospel (*viva vox evangelii*) is heard. Luther famously said that the church is not a "pen house" but a "mouth house."[2] The Reformation in Switzerland began when Huldrych Zwingli entered the pulpit of the Grossmünster in Zurich on January 1, 1519, and began to preach a series of expositional sermons chapter by chapter from the Gospel of Matthew. In the following years he extended this homiletical approach to other books of the Old and New Testaments. Calvin followed a similar pattern in Geneva. Many of the commentaries represented in this series were either originally presented as sermons or were written to support the regular preaching ministry of local church pastors. Luther said that the preacher should be a *bonus textualis*—a good one with a text—well-versed in the Scriptures. Preachers in the Reformation traditions preached not only about the Bible but also from it, and this required more than a passing acquaintance with its contents. Those who have been charged with the office of preaching in the church today can find wisdom and insight—and fresh perspectives—in the sermons of the Reformation and the biblical commentaries read and studied by preachers of the sixteenth century.

Deepening understanding of the Reformation. Some scholars of the sixteenth century prefer to speak of the period they study in the plural, the European Reformations, to indicate that many diverse impulses for reform were at work in this turbulent age of transition from medieval to modern times.[3] While this point is well taken, the RCS follows the time-honored tradition of using *Reformation* in the singular form to indicate not only a major moment in the history of Christianity in the West but also, as Hans J. Hillerbrand has put it, "an essential cohesiveness in the heterogeneous pursuits of religious reform in the sixteenth century."[4] At the same time, in developing guidelines to assist the volume editors in making judicious selections from the vast amount of commentary material available in this period, we have stressed the multifaceted character of the Reformation across many confessions, theological orientations, and political settings.

Advancing Christian scholarship. By assembling and disseminating numerous voices from such a signal period as the Reformation, the RCS aims to make a significant contribution to the ever-growing stream of Christian scholarship. The post-Enlightenment split between the study of the Bible as an academic discipline and the reading of the Bible as spiritual nurture was foreign

[1]John L. Thompson, *Reading the Bible with the Dead* (Grand Rapids: Eerdmans, 2007).

[2]WA 10,2:48.

[3]See Carter Lindberg, *The European Reformations*, 2nd ed. (Malden, MA: Wiley-Blackwell, 2010).

[4]Hans J. Hillerbrand, *The Division of Christendom* (Louisville, KY: Westminster John Knox, 2007), x. Hillerbrand has also edited the standard reference work in Reformation studies, *OER*. See also Diarmaid MacCulloch, *The Reformation* (New York: Viking, 2003), and Patrick Collinson, *The Reformation: A History* (New York: Random House, 2004).

to the reformers. For them the study of the Bible was transformative at the most basic level of the human person: *coram deo.*

The reformers all repudiated the idea that the Bible could be studied and understood with dispassionate objectivity, as a cold artifact from antiquity. Luther's famous Reformation breakthrough triggered by his laborious study of the Psalms and Paul's letter to the Romans is well known, but the experience of Cambridge scholar Thomas Bilney was perhaps more typical. When Erasmus's critical edition of the Greek New Testament was published in 1516, it was accompanied by a new translation in elegant Latin. Attracted by the classical beauty of Erasmus's Latin, Bilney came across this statement in 1 Timothy 1:15: "Christ Jesus came into the world to save sinners." In the Greek this sentence is described as *pistos ho logos,* which the Vulgate had rendered *fidelis sermo,* "a faithful saying." Erasmus chose a different word for the Greek *pistos—certus,* "sure, certain." When Bilney grasped the meaning of this word applied to the announcement of salvation in Christ, he tells us that "immediately, I felt a marvellous comfort and quietness, insomuch as 'my bruised bones leaped for joy.'"[5]

Luther described the way the Bible was meant to function in the minds and hearts of believers when he reproached himself and others for studying the nativity narrative with such cool unconcern:

> I hate myself because when I see Christ laid in the manger or in the lap of his mother and hear the angels sing, my heart does not leap into flame. With what good reason should we all despise ourselves that we remain so cold when this word is spoken to us, over which everyone should dance and leap and burn for joy! We act as though it were a frigid historical fact that does not smite our hearts, as if someone were merely relating that the sultan has a crown of gold.[6]

It was a core conviction of the Reformation that the careful study and meditative listening to the Scriptures, what the monks called *lectio divina,* could yield transformative results for *all* of life. The value of such a rich commentary, therefore, lies not only in the impressive volume of Reformation-era voices that are presented throughout the course of the series but in the many particular fields for which their respective lives and ministries are relevant. The Reformation is consequential for historical studies, both church as well as secular history. Biblical and theological studies, to say nothing of pastoral and spiritual studies, also stand to benefit and progress immensely from renewed engagement today, as mediated through the RCS, with the reformers of yesteryear.

Perspectives

In setting forth the perspectives and parameters of the RCS, the following considerations have proved helpful.

Chronology. When did the Reformation begin, and how long did it last? In some traditional accounts, the answer was clear: the Reformation began with the posting of Luther's Ninety-five

[5]John Foxe, *The Acts and Monuments of John Foxe: A New and Complete Edition,* 8 vols., ed. Stephen Reed Cattley (London: R. B. Seeley & W. Burnside, 1837), 4:635; quoting Ps 51:8; cited in A. G. Dickens, *The English Reformation,* 2nd ed. (University Park, PA: The Pennsylvannia State University Press, 1991), 102.

[6]WA 49:176-77, quoted in Roland Bainton, "The Bible in the Reformation," in *CHB,* 3:23.

Theses at Wittenberg in 1517 and ended with the death of Calvin in Geneva in 1564. Apart from reducing the Reformation to a largely German event with a side trip to Switzerland, this perspective fails to do justice to the important events that led up to Luther's break with Rome and its many reverberations throughout Europe and beyond. In choosing commentary selections for the RCS, we have adopted the concept of the long sixteenth century, say, from the late 1400s to the mid-seventeenth century. Thus we have included commentary selections from early or pre-Reformation writers such as John Colet and Jacques Lefèvre d'Étaples to seventeenth-century figures such as Henry Ainsworth and Johann Gerhard.

Confession. The RCS concentrates primarily, though not exclusively, on the exegetical writings of the Protestant reformers. While the ACCS provided a compendium of key consensual exegetes of the early Christian centuries, the Catholic/Protestant confessional divide in the sixteenth century tested the very idea of consensus, especially with reference to ecclesiology and soteriology. While many able and worthy exegetes faithful to the Roman Catholic Church were active during this period, this project has chosen to include primarily those figures that represent perspectives within the Protestant Reformation. For this reason we have not included comments on the apocryphal or deuterocanonical writings.

We recognize that "Protestant" and "Catholic" as contradistinctive labels are anachronistic terms for the early decades of the sixteenth century before the hardening of confessional identities surrounding the Council of Trent (1545–1563). Protestant figures such as Philipp Melanchthon, Johannes Oecolampadius and John Calvin were all products of the revival of sacred letters known as biblical humanism. They shared an approach to biblical interpretation that owed much to Desiderius Erasmus and other scholars who remained loyal to the Church of Rome. Careful comparative studies of Protestant and Catholic exegesis in the sixteenth century have shown surprising areas of agreement when the focus was the study of a particular biblical text rather than the standard confessional debates.

At the same time, exegetical differences among the various Protestant groups could become strident and church-dividing. The most famous example of this is the interpretive impasse between Luther and Zwingli over the meaning of "This is my body" (Mt 26:26) in the words of institution. Their disagreement at the Colloquy of Marburg in 1529 had important christological and pastoral implications, as well as social and political consequences. Luther refused fellowship with Zwingli and his party at the end of the colloquy; in no small measure this bitter division led to the separate trajectories pursued by Lutheran and Reformed Protestantism to this day. In Elizabethan England, Puritans and Anglicans agreed that "Holy Scripture containeth all things necessary to salvation: so that whatsoever is not read therein, nor may be proved thereby, is not to be required of any man" (article 6 of the Thirty-Nine Articles of Religion), yet on the basis of their differing interpretations of the Bible they fought bitterly over the structures of the church, the clothing of the clergy and the ways of worship. On the matter of infant baptism, Catholics and Protestants alike agreed on its propriety, though there were various theories as to how a practice not mentioned in the Bible could be justified biblically. The Anabaptists were outliers on this subject. They rejected infant baptism altogether. They appealed to the example of the baptism of Jesus and to his final words as recorded in the Gospel of Matthew (Mt 28:19-20): "Go therefore, and make disciples of all nations, baptizing them in the name of the Father, and of the Son, and of the Holy Spirit, teaching them to observe all that I have commanded you." New Testament Christians, they argued, are to follow not only the commands of Jesus in the Great Commission, but also the exact order in which they were given: evangelize, baptize, catechize.

These and many other differences of interpretation among the various Protestant groups are reflected in their many sermons, commentaries and public disputations. In the RCS, the volume editors' introduction to each volume is intended to help the reader understand the nature and significance of doctrinal conversations and disputes that resulted in particular, and frequently clashing, interpretations. Footnotes throughout the text will be provided to explain obscure references, unusual expressions and other matters that require special comment. Volume editors have chosen comments on the Bible across a wide range of sixteenth-century confessions and schools of interpretation: biblical humanists, Lutheran, Reformed, Anglican, Puritan, and Anabaptist. We have not pursued passages from post-Tridentine Catholic authors or from radical spiritualists and antitrinitarian writers, though sufficient material is available from these sources to justify another series.

Format. The design of the RCS is intended to offer reader-friendly access to these classic texts. The availability of digital resources has given access to a huge residual database of sixteenth-century exegetical comment hitherto available only in major research universities and rare book collections. The RCS has benefited greatly from online databases such as Alexander Street Press's Digital Library of Classical Protestant Texts (DLCPT) as well as freely accessible databases like the Post-Reformation Digital Library (prdl.org). Through the help of RCS editorial advisor Herman Selderhuis, we have also had access to the special Reformation collections of the Johannes a Lasco Bibliothek in Emden, Germany. In addition, modern critical editions and translations of Reformation sources have been published over the past generation. Original translations of Reformation sources are given unless an acceptable translation already exists.

Each volume in the RCS will include an introduction by the volume editor placing that portion of the canon within the historical context of the Protestant Reformation and presenting a summary of the theological themes, interpretive issues and reception of the particular book(s). The commentary itself consists of particular pericopes identified by a pericope heading; the biblical text in the English Standard Version (ESV), with significant textual variants registered in the footnotes; an overview of the pericope in which principal exegetical and theological concerns of the Reformation writers are succinctly noted; and excerpts from the Reformation writers identified by name according to the conventions of the *Oxford Encyclopedia of the Reformation*. Each volume will also include a bibliography of sources cited, as well as an appendix of authors and source works.

The Reformation era was a time of verbal as well as physical violence, and this fact has presented a challenge for this project. Without unduly sanitizing the texts, where they contain anti-Semitic, sexist or inordinately polemical rhetoric, we have not felt obliged to parade such comments either. We have noted the abridgement of texts with ellipses and an explanatory footnote.

While this procedure would not be valid in the critical edition of such a text, we have deemed it appropriate in a series whose primary purpose is pastoral and devotional. When translating *homo* or similar terms that refer to the human race as a whole or to individual persons without reference to gender, we have used alternative English expressions to the word *man* (or derivative constructions that formerly were used generically to signify humanity at large), whenever such substitutions can be made without producing an awkward or artificial construction.

As is true in the ACCS, we have made a special effort where possible to include the voices of women, though we acknowledge the difficulty of doing so for the early modern period when for a variety of social and cultural reasons few theological and biblical works were published by women. However, recent scholarship has focused on a number of female leaders whose literary remains show us how they understood and interpreted the Bible. Women who made significant contributions to the Reformation include Marguerite d'Angoulême, sister of King Francis I, who supported French reformist evangelicals including Calvin and who published a religious poem influenced by Luther's theology, *The Mirror of the Sinful Soul*; Argula von Grumbach, a Bavarian noblewoman who defended the teachings of Luther and Melanchthon before the theologians of the University of Ingolstadt; Katharina Schütz Zell, the wife of a former priest, Matthias Zell, and a remarkable reformer in her own right—she conducted funerals, compiled hymnbooks, defended the downtrodden, and published a defense of clerical marriage as well as composing works of consolation on divine comfort and pleas for the toleration of Anabaptists and Catholics alike; and Anne Askew, a Protestant martyr put to death in 1546 after demonstrating remarkable biblical prowess in her examinations by church officials. Other echoes of faithful women in the age of the Reformation are found in their letters, translations, poems, hymns, court depositions, and martyr records.

Lay culture, learned culture. In recent decades, much attention has been given to what is called "reforming from below," that is, the expressions of religious beliefs and churchly life that characterized the popular culture of the majority of the population in the era of the Reformation. Social historians have taught us to examine the diverse pieties of townspeople and city folk, of rural religion and village life, the emergence of lay theologies, and the experiences of women in the religious tumults of Reformation Europe.[7] Formal commentaries by their nature are artifacts of learned culture. Almost all of them were written in Latin, the lingua franca of learned discourse well past the age of the Reformation. Biblical commentaries were certainly not the primary means by which the Protestant Reformation spread so rapidly across wide sectors of sixteenth-century society. Small pamphlets and broadsheets, later called *Flugschriften* ("flying writings"), with their graphic woodcuts and cartoon-like depictions of Reformation personalities and events, became the means of choice for mass communication in the early age of printing. Sermons and works of devotion were also printed with appealing visual aids. Luther's early writings were often accompanied by drawings and sketches from Lucas Cranach and other artists. This was done "above all for the sake of children and simple folk," as Luther

[7]See Peter Matheson, ed., *Reformation Christianity* (Minneapolis: Fortress, 2007).

put it, "who are more easily moved by pictures and images to recall divine history than through mere words or doctrines."[8]

We should be cautious, however, in drawing too sharp a distinction between learned and lay culture in this period. The phenomenon of preaching was a kind of verbal bridge between scholars at their desks and the thousands of illiterate or semiliterate listeners whose views were shaped by the results of Reformation exegesis. According to contemporary witness, more than one thousand people were crowding into Geneva to hear Calvin expound the Scriptures every day.[9] An example of how learned theological works by Reformation scholars were received across divisions of class and social status comes from Lazare Drilhon, an apothecary of Toulon. He was accused of heresy in May 1545 when a cache of prohibited books was found hidden in his garden shed. In addition to devotional works, the French New Testament and a copy of Calvin's Genevan liturgy, there was found a series of biblical commentaries, translated from the Latin into French: Martin Bucer's on Matthew, François Lambert's on the Apocalypse and one by Oecolampadius on 1 John.[10] Biblical exegesis in the sixteenth century was not limited to the kind of full-length commentaries found in Drilhon's shed. Citations from the Bible and expositions of its meaning permeate the extant literature of sermons, letters, court depositions, doctrinal treatises, records of public disputations and even last wills and testaments. While most of the selections in the RCS will be drawn from formal commentary literature, other sources of biblical reflection will also be considered.

Historical Context

The medieval legacy. On October 18, 1512, the degree *Doctor in Biblia* was conferred on Martin Luther, and he began his career as a professor in the University of Wittenberg. As is well known, Luther was also a monk who had taken solemn vows in the Augustinian Order of Hermits at Erfurt. These two settings—the university and the monastery—both deeply rooted in the Middle Ages, form the background not only for Luther's personal vocation as a reformer but also for the history of the biblical commentary in the age of the Reformation. Since the time of the Venerable Bede (d. 735), sometimes called "the last of the Fathers," serious study of the Bible had taken place primarily in the context of cloistered monasteries. The Rule of St. Benedict brought together *lectio* and *meditatio*, the knowledge of letters and the life of prayer. The liturgy was the medium through which the daily reading of the Bible, especially the Psalms, and the sayings of the church fathers came together in the spiritual formation of the monks.[11] Essential to this understanding was a belief in the unity of the people of God throughout time as well as space, and an awareness that life in this world was a preparation for the beatific vision in the next.

[8]Martin Luther, "Personal Prayer Book," LW 43:42-43* (WA 10,2:458); quoted in R. W. Scribner, *For the Sake of Simple Folk: Popular Propaganda for the German Reformation* (Cambridge: Cambridge University Press, 1981), xi.

[9]Letter of De Beaulieu to Guillaume Farel (1561) in *Theodor Beza nach handschriftlichen und anderen gleichzeitigen Quellen*, ed. J. W. Baum (Leipzig: Weidmann, 1851), 2:92.

[10]Francis Higman, "A Heretic's Library: The Drilhon Inventory" (1545), in Francis Higman, *Lire et Découvrire: la circulation des idées au temps de la Réforme* (Geneva: Droz, 1998), 65-85.

[11]See the classic study by Jean Leclercq, *The Love of Learning and the Desire for God* (New York: Fordham University Press, 1961).

The source of theology was the study of the sacred page *(sacra pagina)*; its object was the accumulation of knowledge not for its own sake but for the obtaining of eternal life. For these monks, the Bible had God for its author, salvation for its end and unadulterated truth for its matter, though they would not have expressed it in such an Aristotelian way. The medieval method of interpreting the Bible owed much to Augustine's *On Christian Doctrine*. In addition to setting forth a series of rules (drawn from an earlier work by Tyconius), Augustine stressed the importance of distinguishing the literal and spiritual or allegorical senses of Scripture. While the literal sense was not disparaged, the allegorical was valued because it enabled the believer to obtain spiritual benefit from the obscure places in the Bible, especially in the Old Testament. For Augustine, as for the monks who followed him, the goal of scriptural exegesis was freighted with eschatological meaning; its purpose was to induce faith, hope, and love and so to advance in one's pilgrimage toward that city with foundations (see Heb 11:10).

Building on the work of Augustine and other church fathers going back to Origen, medieval exegetes came to understand Scripture as possessed of four possible meanings, the famous *quadriga*. The literal meaning was retained, of course, but the spiritual meaning was now subdivided into three senses: the allegorical, the moral, and the anagogical. Medieval exegetes often referred to the four meanings of Scripture in a popular rhyme:

> The letter shows us what God and our fathers did;
> The allegory shows us where our faith is hid;
> The moral meaning gives us rules of daily life;
> The anagogy shows us where we end our strife.[12]

In this schema, the three spiritual meanings of the text correspond to the three theological virtues: faith (allegory), hope (anagogy), and love (the moral meaning). It should be noted that this way of approaching the Bible assumed a high doctrine of scriptural inspiration: the multiple meanings inherent in the text had been placed there by the Holy Spirit for the benefit of the people of God. The biblical justification for this method went back to the apostle Paul, who had used the words *allegory* and *type* when applying Old Testament events to believers in Christ (Gal 4:21-31; 1 Cor 10:1-11). The problem with this approach was knowing how to relate each of the four senses to one another and how to prevent Scripture from becoming a nose of wax turned this way and that by various interpreters. As G. R. Evans explains, "Any interpretation which could be put upon the text and was in keeping with the faith and edifying, had the warrant of God himself, for no human reader had the ingenuity to find more than God had put there."[13]

With the rise of the universities in the eleventh century, theology and the study of Scripture moved from the cloister into the classroom. Scripture and the Fathers were still important, but they came to function more as footnotes to the theological questions debated in the schools and brought together in an impressive systematic way in works such as Peter Lombard's *Books of Sentences* (the standard theology textbook of the Middle Ages) and the great scholastic *summae* of the thirteenth

[12]Robert M. Grant, *A Short History of the Interpretation of the Bible* (New York: Macmillan, 1963), 119. A translation of the well-known Latin quatrain: *Littera gesta docet/Quid credas allegoria/Moralis quid agas/Quo tendas anagogia.*

[13]G. R. Evans, *The Language and Logic of the Bible: The Road to Reformation* (Cambridge: Cambridge University Press, 1985), 42.

century. Indispensible to the study of the Bible in the later Middle Ages was the *Glossa ordinaria*, a collection of exegetical opinions by the church fathers and other commentators. Heiko Oberman summarized the transition from devotion to dialectic this way: "When, due to the scientific revolution of the twelfth century, Scripture became the *object* of study rather than the *subject* through which God speaks to the student, the difference between the two modes of speaking was investigated in terms of the texts themselves rather than in their relation to the recipients."[14] It was possible, of course, to be both a scholastic theologian and a master of the spiritual life. Meister Eckhart, for example, wrote commentaries on the Old Testament in Latin and works of mystical theology in German, reflecting what had come to be seen as a division of labor between the two.

An increasing focus on the text of Scripture led to a revival of interest in its literal sense. The two key figures in this development were Thomas Aquinas (d. 1274) and Nicholas of Lyra (d. 1340). Thomas is best remembered for his *Summa Theologiae*, but he was also a prolific commentator on the Bible. Thomas did not abandon the multiple senses of Scripture but declared that all the senses were founded on one—the literal—and this sense eclipsed allegory as the basis of sacred doctrine. Nicholas of Lyra was a Franciscan scholar who made use of the Hebrew text of the Old Testament and quoted liberally from works of Jewish scholars, especially the learned French rabbi Salomon Rashi (d. 1105). After Aquinas, Lyra was the strongest defender of the literal, historical meaning of Scripture as the primary basis of theological disputation. His *Postilla*, as his notes were called—the abbreviated form of *post illa verba textus*, meaning "after these words from Scripture"—were widely circulated in the late Middle Ages and became the first biblical commentary to be printed in the fifteenth century. More than any other commentator from the period of high scholasticism, Lyra and his work were greatly valued by the early reformers. According to an old Latin pun, *Nisi Lyra lyrasset, Lutherus non saltasset*, "If Lyra had not played his lyre, Luther would not have danced."[15] While Luther was never an uncritical disciple of any teacher, he did praise Lyra as a good Hebraist and quoted him more than one hundred times in his lectures on Genesis, where he declared, "I prefer him to almost all other interpreters of Scripture."[16]

Sacred philology. The sixteenth century has been called a golden age of biblical interpretation, and it is a fact that the age of the Reformation witnessed an explosion of commentary writing unparalleled in the history of the Christian church. Kenneth Hagen has cataloged forty-five commentaries on Hebrews between 1516 (Erasmus) and 1598 (Beza).[17] During the sixteenth century, more than seventy new commentaries on Romans were published, five of them by Melanchthon alone, and nearly one hundred commentaries on the Bible's prayer book, the Psalms.[18] There were two developments in the fifteenth century that presaged this development and without which it

[14]Heiko Oberman, *Forerunners of the Reformation* (Philadelphia: Fortress, 1966), 284.

[15]Nicholas of Lyra, *The Postilla of Nicolas of Lyra on the Song of Songs*, trans. and ed. James George Kiecker (Milwaukee: Marquette University Press, 1998), 19.

[16]LW 2:164 (WA 42:377).

[17]Kenneth Hagen, *Hebrews Commenting from Erasmus to Bèze, 1516–1598* (Tübingen: Mohr, 1981).

[18]R. Gerald Hobbs, "Biblical Commentaries," *OER* 1:167-71. See in general David C. Steinmetz, ed., *The Bible in the Sixteenth Century* (Durham: Duke University Press, 1990).

could not have taken place: the invention of printing and the rediscovery of a vast store of ancient learning hitherto unknown or unavailable to scholars in the West.

It is now commonplace to say that what the computer has become in our generation, the printing press was to the world of Erasmus, Luther, and other leaders of the Reformation. Johannes Gutenberg, a goldsmith by trade, developed a metal alloy suitable for type and a machine that would allow printed characters to be cast with relative ease, placed in even lines of composition and then manipulated again and again, making possible the mass production of an unbelievable number of texts. In 1455, the Gutenberg Bible, the masterpiece of the typographical revolution, was published at Mainz in double columns in gothic type. Forty-seven copies of the beautiful Gutenberg Bible are still extant, each consisting of more than one thousand colorfully illuminated and impeccably printed pages. What began at Gutenberg's print shop in Mainz on the Rhine River soon spread, like McDonald's or Starbucks in our day, into every nook and cranny of the known world. Printing presses sprang up in Rome (1464), Venice (1469), Paris (1470), the Netherlands (1471), Switzerland (1472), Spain (1474), England (1476), Sweden (1483), and Constantinople (1490). By 1500, these and other presses across Europe had published some twenty-seven thousand titles, most of them in Latin. Erasmus once compared himself with an obscure preacher whose sermons were heard by only a few people in one or two churches while his books were read in every country in the world. Erasmus was not known for his humility, but in this case he was simply telling the truth.[19]

The Italian humanist Lorenzo Valla (d. 1457) died in the early dawn of the age of printing, but his critical and philological studies would be taken up by others who believed that genuine reform in church and society could come about only by returning to the wellsprings of ancient learning and wisdom—*ad fontes*, "back to the sources!" Valla is best remembered for undermining a major claim made by defenders of the papacy when he proved by philological research that the so-called Donation of Constantine, which had bolstered papal assertions of temporal sovereignty, was a forgery. But it was Valla's *Collatio Novi Testamenti* of 1444 that would have such a great effect on the renewal of biblical studies in the next century. Erasmus discovered the manuscript of this work while rummaging through an old library in Belgium and published it at Paris in 1505. In the preface to his edition of Valla, Erasmus gave the rationale that would guide his own labors in textual criticism. Just as Jerome had translated the Latin Vulgate from older versions and copies of the Scriptures in his day, so now Jerome's own text must be subjected to careful scrutiny and correction. Erasmus would be *Hieronymus redivivus*, a new Jerome come back to life to advance the cause of sacred philology. The restoration of the Scriptures and the writings of the church fathers would usher in what Erasmus believed would be a golden age of peace and learning. In 1516, the Basel publisher Froben brought out Erasmus's *Novum Instrumentum*, the first published edition of the Greek New Testament. Erasmus's Greek New Testament would go through five editions in his lifetime, each one with new emendations to the text and a growing section of annotations that expanded to include not only technical notes about the text but also theological comment. The influence of Erasmus's Greek New

[19]E. Harris Harbison, *The Christian Scholar in the Age of the Reformation* (New York: Charles Scribner's Sons, 1956), 80.

Testament was enormous. It formed the basis for Robert Estienne's *Novum Testamentum Graece* of 1550, which in turn was used to establish the Greek *Textus Receptus* for a number of late Reformation translations including the King James Version of 1611.

For all his expertise in Greek, Erasmus was a poor student of Hebrew and only published commentaries on several of the psalms. However, the renaissance of Hebrew letters was part of the wider program of biblical humanism as reflected in the establishment of trilingual colleges devoted to the study of Hebrew, Greek and Latin (the three languages written on the *titulus* of Jesus' cross [Jn 19:20]) at Alcalá in Spain, Wittenberg in Germany, Louvain in Belgium, and Paris in France. While it is true that some medieval commentators, especially Nicholas of Lyra, had been informed by the study of Hebrew and rabbinics in their biblical work, it was the publication of Johannes Reuchlin's *De rudimentis hebraicis* (1506), a combined grammar and dictionary, that led to the recovery of *veritas Hebraica*, as Jerome had referred to the true voice of the Hebrew Scriptures. The pursuit of Hebrew studies was carried forward in the Reformation by two great scholars, Konrad Pellikan and Sebastian Münster. Pellikan was a former Franciscan friar who embraced the Protestant cause and played a major role in the Zurich reformation. He had published a Hebrew grammar even prior to Reuchlin and produced a commentary on nearly the entire Bible that appeared in seven volumes between 1532 and 1539. Münster was Pellikan's student and taught Hebrew at the University of Heidelberg before taking up a similar position in Basel. Like his mentor, Münster was a great collector of Hebraica and published a series of excellent grammars, dictionaries and rabbinic texts. Münster did for the Hebrew Old Testament what Erasmus had done for the Greek New Testament. His *Hebraica Biblia* offered a fresh Latin translation of the Old Testament with annotations from medieval rabbinic exegesis.

Luther first learned Hebrew with Reuchlin's grammar in hand but took advantage of other published resources, such as the four-volume Hebrew Bible published at Venice by Daniel Bomberg in 1516 to 1517. He also gathered his own circle of Hebrew experts, his *sanhedrin* he called it, who helped him with his German translation of the Old Testament. We do not know where William Tyndale learned Hebrew, though perhaps it was in Worms, where there was a thriving rabbinical school during his stay there. In any event, he had sufficiently mastered the language to bring out a freshly translated Pentateuch that was published at Antwerp in 1530. By the time the English separatist scholar Henry Ainsworth published his prolix commentaries on the Pentateuch in 1616, the knowledge of Hebrew, as well as Greek, was taken for granted by every serious scholar of the Bible. In the preface to his commentary on Genesis, Ainsworth explained that "the literal sense of Moses's Hebrew (which is the tongue wherein he wrote the law), is the ground of all interpretation, and that language hath figures and properties of speech, different from ours: These therefore in the first place are to be opened that the natural meaning of the Scripture, being known, the mysteries of godliness therein implied, may be better discerned."[20]

The restoration of the biblical text in the original languages made possible the revival of scriptural exposition reflected in the floodtide of sermon literature and commentary work. Of even

[20]Henry Ainsworth, *Annotations upon the First Book of Moses Called Genesis* (Amsterdam, 1616), preface (unpaginated).

more far-reaching import was the steady stream of vernacular Bibles in the sixteenth century. In the introduction to his 1516 edition of the New Testament, Erasmus had expressed his desire that the Scriptures be translated into all languages so that "the lowliest women" could read the Gospels and the Pauline epistles and "the farmer sing some portion of them at the plow, the weaver hum some parts of them to the movement of his shuttle, the traveler lighten the weariness of the journey with stories of this kind."[21] Like Erasmus, Tyndale wanted the Bible to be available in the language of the common people. He once said to a learned divine that if God spared his life he would cause the boy who drives the plow to know more of the Scriptures than he did![22] The project of allowing the Bible to speak in the language of the mother in the house, the children in the street and the cheesemonger in the marketplace was met with stiff opposition by certain Catholic polemists such as Johann Eck, Luther's antagonist at the Leipzig Debate of 1519. In his *Enchiridion* (1525), Eck derided the "inky theologians" whose translations paraded the Bible before "the untutored crowd" and subjected it to the judgment of "laymen and crazy old women."[23] In fact, some fourteen German Bibles had already been published prior to Luther's September Testament of 1522, which he translated from Erasmus's Greek New Testament in less than three months' time while sequestered in the Wartburg. Luther's German New Testament became the first best-seller in the world, appearing in forty-three distinct editions between 1522 and 1525 with upward of one hundred thousand copies issued in these three years. It is estimated that 5 percent of the German population may have been literate at this time, but this rate increased as the century wore on due in no small part to the unmitigated success of vernacular Bibles.[24]

Luther's German Bible (inclusive of the Old Testament from 1534) was the most successful venture of its kind, but it was not alone in the field. Hans Denck and Ludwig Hätzer, leaders in the early Anabaptist movement, translated the prophetic books of the Old Testament from Hebrew into German in 1527. This work influenced the Swiss-German Bible of 1531 published by Leo Jud and other pastors in Zurich. Tyndale's influence on the English language rivaled that of Luther on German. At a time when English was regarded as "that obscure and remote dialect of German spoken in an off-shore island," Tyndale, with his remarkable linguistic ability (he was fluent in eight languages), "made a language for England," as his modern editor David Daniell has put it.[25] Tyndale was imprisoned and executed near Brussels in 1536, but the influence of his biblical work among the common people of England was already being felt. There is no reason to doubt the authenticity of John Foxe's recollection of how Tyndale's New Testament was received in England during the 1520s and 1530s:

[21]John C. Olin, *Christian Humanism and the Reformation* (New York: Fordham University Press, 1987), 101.

[22]This famous statement of Tyndale was quoted by John Foxe in his *Acts and Monuments of Matters Happening in the Church* (London, 1563). See Henry Wansbrough, "Tyndale," in *The Bible in the Renaissance*, ed. Richard Griffith (Aldershot, UK: Ashgate, 2001), 124.

[23]John Eck, *Enchiridion of Commonplaces*, trans. Ford Lewis Battles (Grand Rapids: Baker, 1979), 47-49.

[24]The effect of printing on the spread of the Reformation has been much debated. See the classic study by Elizabeth L. Eisenstein, *The Printing Press as an Agent of Change* (Cambridge: Cambridge University Press, 1979). More recent studies include Mark U. Edwards Jr., *Printing, Propaganda and Martin Luther* (Minneapolis: Fortress, 1994), and Andrew Pettegree and Matthew Hall, "The Reformation and the Book: A Reconsideration," *Historical Journal* 47 (2004): 1-24.

[25]David Daniell, *William Tyndale: A Biography* (New Haven: Yale University Press, 1994), 3.

> The fervent zeal of those Christian days seemed much superior to these our days and times; as manifestly may appear by their sitting up all night in reading and hearing; also by their expenses and charges in buying of books in English, of whom some gave five marks, some more, some less, for a book: some gave a load of hay for a few chapters of St. James, or of St. Paul in English.[26]

Calvin helped to revise and contributed three prefaces to the French Bible translated by his cousin Pierre Robert Olivétan and originally published at Neuchâtel in 1535. Clément Marot and Beza provided a fresh translation of the Psalms with each psalm rendered in poetic form and accompanied by monophonic musical settings for congregational singing. The Bay Psalter, the first book printed in America, was an English adaptation of this work. Geneva also provided the provenance of the most influential Italian Bible published by Giovanni Diodati in 1607. The flowering of biblical humanism in vernacular Bibles resulted in new translations in all of the major language groups of Europe: Spanish (1569), Portuguese (1681), Dutch (New Testament, 1523; Old Testament, 1527), Danish (1550), Czech (1579–1593/94), Hungarian (New Testament, 1541; complete Bible, 1590), Polish (1563), Swedish (1541), and even Arabic (1591).[27]

Patterns of Reformation

Once the text of the Bible had been placed in the hands of the people, in cheap and easily available editions, what further need was there of published expositions such as commentaries? Given the Protestant doctrine of the priesthood of all believers, was there any longer a need for learned clergy and their bookish religion? Some radical reformers thought not. Sebastian Franck searched for the true church of the Spirit "scattered among the heathen and the weeds" but could not find it in any of the institutional structures of his time. *Veritas non potest scribi, aut exprimi,* he said, "truth can neither be spoken nor written."[28] Kaspar von Schwenckfeld so emphasized religious inwardness that he suspended external observance of the Lord's Supper and downplayed the readable, audible Scriptures in favor of the Word within. This trajectory would lead to the rise of the Quakers in the next century, but it was pursued neither by the mainline reformers nor by most of the Anabaptists. Article 7 of the Augsburg Confession (1530) declared the one holy Christian church to be "the assembly of all believers among whom the Gospel is purely preached and the holy sacraments are administered according to the Gospel."[29]

Historians of the nineteenth century referred to the material and formal principles of the Reformation. In this construal, the matter at stake was the meaning of the Christian gospel: the liberating insight that helpless sinners are graciously justified by the gift of faith alone, apart from any works or merits of their own, entirely on the basis of Christ's atoning work on the cross. For Luther especially, justification by faith alone became the criterion by which all other doctrines and

[26]Foxe, *Acts and Monuments*, 4:218.

[27]On vernacular translations of the Bible, see *CHB* 3:94-140 and Jaroslav Pelikan, *The Reformation of the Bible/The Bible of the Reformation* (New Haven: Yale University Press, 1996), 41-62.

[28]Sebastian Franck, *280 Paradoxes or Wondrous Sayings*, trans. E. J. Furcha (Lewiston, NY: Edwin Mellen Press, 1986), 10, 212.

[29]BoC 42 (BSLK 61).

practices of the church were to be judged. The cross proves everything, he said at the Heidelberg disputation in 1518. The distinction between law and gospel thus became the primary hermeneutical key that unlocked the true meaning of Scripture.

The formal principle of the Reformation, *sola Scriptura,* was closely bound up with proper distinctions between Scripture and tradition. "Scripture alone," said Luther, "is the true lord and master of all writings and doctrine on earth. If that is not granted, what is Scripture good for? The more we reject it, the more we become satisfied with human books and human teachers."[30] On the basis of this principle, the reformers challenged the structures and institutions of the medieval Catholic Church. Even a simple layperson, they asserted, armed with Scripture should be believed above a pope or a council without it. But, however boldly asserted, the doctrine of the primacy of Scripture did not absolve the reformers from dealing with a host of hermeneutical issues that became matters of contention both between Rome and the Reformation and within each of these two communities: the extent of the biblical canon, the validity of critical study of the Bible, the perspicuity of Scripture and its relation to preaching, and the retention of devotional and liturgical practices such as holy days, incense, the burning of candles, the sprinkling of holy water, church art, and musical instruments. Zwingli, the Puritans, and the radicals dismissed such things as a rubbish heap of ceremonials that amounted to nothing but tomfoolery, while Lutherans and Anglicans retained most of them as consonant with Scripture and valuable aids to worship.

It is important to note that while the mainline reformers differed among themselves on many matters, overwhelmingly they saw themselves as part of the ongoing Catholic tradition, indeed as the legitimate bearers of it. This was seen in numerous ways including their sense of continuity with the church of the preceding centuries; their embrace of the ecumenical orthodoxy of the early church; and their desire to read the Bible in dialogue with the exegetical tradition of the church.

In their biblical commentaries, the reformers of the sixteenth century revealed a close familiarity with the preceding exegetical tradition, and they used it respectfully as well as critically in their own expositions of the sacred text. For them, *sola Scriptura* was not *nuda Scriptura.* Rather, the Scriptures were seen as the book given to the church, gathered and guided by the Holy Spirit. In his restatement of the Vincentian canon, Calvin defined the church as "a society of all the saints, a society which, spread over the whole world, and existing in all ages, and bound together by the one doctrine and the one spirit of Christ, cultivates and observes unity of faith and brotherly concord. With this church we deny that we have any disagreement. Nay, rather, as we revere her as our mother, so we desire to remain in her bosom." Defined thus, the church has a real, albeit relative and circumscribed, authority since, as Calvin admits, "We cannot fly without wings."[31] While the reformers could not agree with the Council of Trent (though some recent Catholic theologians have challenged this interpretation) that Scripture and tradition were two separate and equal sources of divine revelation,

[30]LW 32:11-12* (WA 7:317).

[31]John C. Olin, ed., *John Calvin and Jacopo Sadoleto: A Reformation Debate* (New York: Harper Torchbooks, 1966), 61-62, 77.

they did believe in the coinherence of Scripture and tradition. This conviction shaped the way they read and interpreted the Bible.[32]

Schools of Exegesis

The reformers were passionate about biblical exegesis, but they showed little concern for hermeneutics as a separate field of inquiry. Niels Hemmingsen, a Lutheran theologian in Denmark, did write a treatise, *De methodis* (1555), in which he offered a philosophical and theological framework for the interpretation of Scripture. This was followed by the *Clavis Scripturae Sacrae* (1567) of Matthias Flacius Illyricus, which contains some fifty rules for studying the Bible drawn from Scripture itself.[33] However, hermeneutics as we know it came of age only in the Enlightenment and should not be backloaded into the Reformation. It is also true that the word *commentary* did not mean in the sixteenth century what it means for us today. Erasmus provided both annotations and paraphrases on the New Testament, the former a series of critical notes on the text but also containing points of doctrinal substance, the latter a theological overview and brief exposition. Most of Calvin's commentaries began as sermons or lectures presented in the course of his pastoral ministry. In the dedication to his 1519 study of Galatians, Luther declared that his work was "not so much a commentary as a testimony of my faith in Christ."[34] The exegetical work of the reformers was embodied in a wide variety of forms and genres, and the RCS has worked with this broader concept in setting the guidelines for this compendium.

The Protestant reformers shared in common a number of key interpretive principles such as the priority of the grammatical-historical sense of Scripture and the christological centeredness of the entire Bible, but they also developed a number of distinct approaches and schools of exegesis.[35] For the purposes of the RCS, we note the following key figures and families of interpretation in this period.

Biblical humanism. The key figure is Erasmus, whose importance is hard to exaggerate for Catholic and Protestant exegetes alike. His annotated Greek New Testament and fresh Latin translation challenged the hegemony of the Vulgate tradition and was doubtless a factor in the decision of the Council of Trent to establish the Vulgate edition as authentic and normative. Erasmus believed that the wide distribution of the Scriptures would contribute to personal spiritual renewal and the reform of society. In 1547, the English translation of Erasmus's *Paraphrases* was ordered to be placed in every parish church in England. John Colet first encouraged Erasmus

[32]See Timothy George, "An Evangelical Reflection on Scripture and Tradition," *Pro Ecclesia* 9 (2000): 184-207.

[33]See Kenneth G. Hagen, "'*De Exegetica Methodo*': Niels Hemmingsen's *De Methodis* (1555)," in *The Bible in the Sixteenth Century*, ed. David C. Steinmetz (Durham: Duke University Press, 1990), 181-96.

[34]LW 27:159 (WA 2:449). See Kenneth Hagen, "What Did the Term *Commentarius* Mean to Sixteenth-Century Theologians?" in *Théorie et pratique de l'exégèse*, eds. Irena Backus and Francis M. Higman (Geneva: Droz, 1990), 13-38.

[35]I follow here the sketch of Irena Backus, "Biblical Hermeneutics and Exegesis," *OER* 1:152-58. In this work, Backus confines herself to Continental developments, whereas we have noted the exegetical contribution of the English Reformation as well. For more comprehensive listings of sixteenth-century commentators, see Gerald Bray, *Biblical Interpretation* (Downers Grove, IL: InterVarsity Press, 1996), 165-212; and Richard A. Muller, "Biblical Interpretation in the Sixteenth and Seventeenth Centuries," *DMBI* 22-44.

to learn Greek, though he never took up the language himself. Colet's lectures on Paul's epistles at Oxford are reflected in his commentaries on Romans and 1 Corinthians.

Jacques Lefèvre d'Étaples has been called the "French Erasmus" because of his great learning and support for early reform movements in his native land. He published a major edition of the Psalter, as well as commentaries on the Pauline Epistles (1512), the Gospels (1522), and the General Epistles (1527). Guillaume Farel, the early reformer of Geneva, was a disciple of Lefèvre, and the young Calvin also came within his sphere of influence.

Among pre-Tridentine Catholic reformers, special attention should be given to Thomas de Vio, better known as Cajetan. He is best remembered for confronting Martin Luther on behalf of the pope in 1518, but his biblical commentaries (on nearly every book of the Bible) are virtually free of polemic. Like Erasmus, he dared to criticize the Vulgate on linguistic grounds. His commentary on Romans supported the doctrine of justification by grace applied by faith based on the "alien righteousness" of God in Christ. Jared Wicks sums up Cajetan's significance in this way: "Cajetan's combination of passion for pristine biblical meaning with his fully developed theological horizon of understanding indicates, in an intriguing manner, something of the breadth of possibilities open to Roman Catholics before a more restrictive settlement came to exercise its hold on many Catholic interpreters in the wake of the Council of Trent."[36] Girolamo Seripando, like Cajetan, was a cardinal in the Catholic Church, though he belonged to the Augustinian rather than the Dominican order. He was an outstanding classical scholar and published commentaries on Romans and Galatians. Also important is Jacopo Sadoleto, another cardinal, best known for his 1539 letter to the people of Geneva beseeching them to return to the Church of Rome, to which Calvin replied with a manifesto of his own. Sadoleto published a commentary on Romans in 1535. Bucer once commended Sadoleto's teaching on justification as approximating that of the reformers, while others saw him tilting away from the Augustinian tradition toward Pelagianism.[37]

Luther and the Wittenberg School. It was in the name of the Word of God, and specifically as a doctor of Scripture, that Luther challenged the church of his day and inaugurated the Reformation. Though Luther renounced his monastic vows, he never lost that sense of intimacy with *sacra pagina* he first acquired as a young monk. Luther provided three rules for reading the Bible: prayer, meditation, and struggle *(tentatio)*. His exegetical output was enormous. In the American edition of Luther's works, thirty out of the fifty-five volumes are devoted to his biblical studies, and additional translations are planned. Many of his commentaries originated as sermons or lecture notes presented to his students at the university and to his parishioners at Wittenberg's parish church of St. Mary. Luther referred to Galatians as his bride: "The Epistle to the Galatians is my dear epistle. I have betrothed myself to it. It is my Käthe von Bora."[38] He considered his 1535 commentary on Galatians his greatest exegetical work, although his massive commentary on Genesis

[36]Jared Wicks, "Tommaso de Vio Cajetan (1469-1534)," *DMBI* 283-87, here 286.

[37]See the discussion by Bernard Roussel, "Martin Bucer et Jacques Sadolet: la concorde possible," *Bulletin de la Société de l'histoire de protestantisme français* (1976): 525-50, and T. H. L. Parker, *Commentaries on the Epistle to the Romans, 1532–1542* (Edinburgh: T&T Clark, 1986), 25-34.

[38]WATR 1:69 no. 146; cf. LW 54:20 no. 146. I have followed Rörer's variant on Dietrich's notes.

(eight volumes in LW), which he worked on for ten years (1535–1545), must be considered his crowning work. Luther's principles of biblical interpretation are found in his *Open Letter on Translating* and in the prefaces he wrote to all the books of the Bible.

Philipp Melanchthon was brought to Wittenberg to teach Greek in 1518 and proved to be an able associate to Luther in the reform of the church. A set of his lecture notes on Romans was published without his knowledge in 1522. This was revised and expanded many times until his large commentary of 1556. Melanchthon also commented on other New Testament books including Matthew, John, Galatians, and the Petrine epistles, as well as Proverbs, Daniel, and Ecclesiastes. Though he was well trained in the humanist disciplines, Melanchthon devoted little attention to critical and textual matters in his commentaries. Rather, he followed the primary argument of the biblical writer and gathered from this exposition a series of doctrinal topics for special consideration. This method lay behind Melanchthon's *Loci communes* (1521), the first Protestant theology textbook to be published. Another Wittenberger was Johannes Bugenhagen of Pomerania, a prolific commentator on both the Old and New Testaments. His commentary on the Psalms (1524), translated into German by Bucer, applied Luther's teaching on justification to the Psalter. He also wrote a commentary on Job and annotations on many of the books in the Bible. The Lutheran exegetical tradition was shaped by many other scholar-reformers including Andreas Osiander, Johannes Brenz, Caspar Cruciger, Erasmus Sarcerius, Georg Maior, Jacob Andreae, Nikolaus Selnecker, and Johann Gerhard.

The Strasbourg-Basel tradition. Bucer, the son of a shoemaker in Alsace, became the leader of the Reformation in Strasbourg. A former Dominican, he was early on influenced by Erasmus and continued to share his passion for Christian unity. Bucer was the most ecumenical of the Protestant reformers seeking rapprochement with Catholics on justification and an armistice between Luther and Zwingli in their strife over the Lord's Supper. Bucer also had a decisive influence on Calvin, though the latter characterized his biblical commentaries as longwinded and repetitious.[39] In his exegetical work, Bucer made ample use of patristic and medieval sources, though he criticized the abuse and overuse of allegory as "the most blatant insult to the Holy Spirit."[40] He declared that the purpose of his commentaries was "to help inexperienced brethren [perhaps like the apothecary Drilhon, who owned a French translation of Bucer's *Commentary on Matthew*] to understand each of the words and actions of Christ, and in their proper order as far as possible, and to retain an explanation of them in their natural meaning, so that they will not distort God's Word through age-old aberrations or by inept interpretation, but rather with a faithful comprehension of everything as written by the Spirit of God, they may expound to all the churches in their firm upbuilding in faith and love."[41] In addition to writing commentaries on all four Gospels, Bucer published commentaries on Judges, the Psalms, Zephaniah, Romans, and Ephesians. In the early years of the Reformation, there was a great deal of back and forth between Strasbourg and Basel, and both

[39]CNTC 8:3 (CO 10:404).

[40]*DMBI* 249; P. Scherding and F. Wendel, eds., "Un Traité d'exégèse pratique de Bucer," *Revue d'histoire et de philosophie religieuses* 26 (1946): 32-75, here 56.

[41]Martin Bucer, *Enarrationes perpetuae in sacra quatuor evangelia*, 2nd ed. (Strasbourg: Georg Ulrich Andlanus, 1530), 10r; quoted in D. F. Wright, "Martin Bucer," *DMBI* 290.

were centers of a lively publishing trade. Wolfgang Capito, Bucer's associate at Strasbourg, was a notable Hebraist and composed commentaries on Hosea (1529) and Habakkuk (1527).

At Basel, the great Sebastian Münster defended the use of Jewish sources in the Christian study of the Old Testament and published, in addition to his famous Hebrew grammar, an annotated version of the Gospel of Matthew translated from Greek into Hebrew. Oecolampadius, Basel's chief reformer, had been a proofreader in Froben's publishing house and worked with Erasmus on his Greek New Testament and his critical edition of Jerome. From 1523 he was both a preacher and professor of Holy Scripture at Basel. He defended Zwingli's eucharistic theology at the Colloquy of Marburg and published commentaries on 1 John (1524), Romans (1525), and Haggai–Malachi (1525). Oecolampadius was succeeded by Simon Grynaeus, a classical scholar who taught Greek and supported Bucer's efforts to bring Lutherans and Zwinglians together. More in line with Erasmus was Sebastian Castellio, who came to Basel after his expulsion from Geneva in 1545. He is best remembered for questioning the canonicity of the Song of Songs and for his annotations and French translation of the Bible.

The Zurich group. Biblical exegesis in Zurich was centered on the distinctive institution of the *Prophezei*, which began on June 19, 1525. On five days a week, at seven o'clock in the morning, all of the ministers and theological students in Zurich gathered into the choir of the Grossmünster to engage in a period of intense exegesis and interpretation of Scripture. After Zwingli had opened the meeting with prayer, the text of the day was read in Latin, Greek, and Hebrew, followed by appropriate textual or exegetical comments. One of the ministers then delivered a sermon on the passage in German that was heard by many of Zurich's citizens who stopped by the cathedral on their way to work. This institute for advanced biblical studies had an enormous influence as a model for Reformed academies and seminaries throughout Europe. It was also the seedbed for sermon series in Zurich's churches and the extensive exegetical publications of Zwingli, Leo Jud, Konrad Pellikan, Heinrich Bullinger, Oswald Myconius, and Rudolf Gwalther. Zwingli had memorized in Greek all of the Pauline epistles, and this bore fruit in his powerful expository preaching and biblical exegesis. He took seriously the role of grammar, rhetoric, and historical research in explaining the biblical text. For example, he disagreed with Bucer on the value of the Septuagint, regarding it as a trustworthy witness to a proto-Hebrew version earlier than the Masoretic text.

Zwingli's work was carried forward by his successor Bullinger, one of the most formidable scholars and networkers among the reformers. He composed commentaries on Daniel (1565), the Gospels (1542–1546), the Epistles (1537), Acts (1533), and Revelation (1557). He collaborated with Calvin to produce the *Consensus Tigurinus* (1549), a Reformed accord on the nature of the Lord's Supper, and produced a series of fifty sermons on Christian doctrine, known as *Decades*, which became required reading in Elizabethan England. As the *Antistes* ("overseer") of the Zurich church for forty-four years, Bullinger faced opposition from nascent Anabaptism on the one hand and resurgent Catholicism on the other. The need for a well-trained clergy and scholarly resources, including Scripture commentaries, arose from the fact that the Bible was "difficult or obscure to the unlearned, unskillful, unexercised, and malicious or corrupted wills." While forswearing papal claims to infallibility, Bullinger and other leaders of the magisterial Reformation saw the need for a kind of Protestant magisterium as a check against the tendency to read the Bible in "such sense as everyone shall be persuaded in himself to be most convenient."[42]

Two other commentators can be treated in connection with the Zurich group, though each of them had a wide-ranging ministry across the Reformation fronts. A former Benedictine monk, Wolfgang Musculus, embraced the Reformation in the 1520s and served briefly as the secretary to Bucer in Strasbourg. He shared Bucer's desire for Protestant unity and served for seventeen years (1531–1548) as a pastor and reformer in Augsburg. After a brief time in Zurich, where he came under the influence of Bullinger, Musculus was called to Bern, where he taught the Scriptures and published commentaries on the Psalms, the Decalogue, Genesis, Romans, Isaiah, 1 and 2 Corinthians, Galatians and Ephesians, Philippians, Colossians, 1 and 2 Thessalonians, and 1 Timothy. Drawing on his exegetical writings, Musculus also produced a compendium of Protestant theology that was translated into English in 1563 as *Commonplaces of Christian Religion*.

Peter Martyr Vermigli was a Florentine-born scholar and Augustinian friar who embraced the Reformation and fled to Switzerland in 1542. Over the next twenty years, he would gain an international reputation as a prolific scholar and leading theologian within the Reformed community. He lectured on the Old Testament at Strasbourg, was made regius professor at Oxford, corresponded with the Italian refugee church in Geneva and spent the last years of his life as professor of Hebrew at Zurich. Vermigli published commentaries on 1 Corinthians, Romans, and Judges during his lifetime. His biblical lectures on Genesis, Lamentations, 1 and 2 Samuel, and 1 and 2 Kings were published posthumously. The most influential of his writings was the *Loci communes (Commonplaces)*, a theological compendium drawn from his exegetical writings.

The Genevan reformers. What Zwingli and Bullinger were to Zurich, Calvin and Beza were to Geneva. Calvin has been called "the father of modern biblical scholarship," and his exegetical work is without parallel in the Reformation. Because of the success of his *Institutes of the Christian Religion* Calvin has sometimes been thought of as a man of one book, but he always intended the *Institutes*, which went through eight editions in Latin and five in French during his lifetime, to serve as a guide to the study of the Bible, to show the reader "what he ought especially to seek in Scripture and to what end he ought to relate its contents." Jacob Arminius, who modified several principles of Calvin's theology, recommended his commentaries next to the Bible, for, as he said, Calvin "is incomparable in the interpretation of Scripture."[43] Drawing on his superb knowledge of Greek and Hebrew and his thorough training in humanist rhetoric, Calvin produced commentaries on all of the New Testament books except 2 and 3 John and Revelation. Calvin's Old Testament commentaries originated as sermon and lecture series and include Genesis, Psalms, Hosea, Isaiah, minor prophets, Daniel, Jeremiah and Lamentations, a harmony of the last four books of Moses,

[42]Euan Cameron, *The European Reformation* (Oxford: Oxford University Press, 1991), 120.

[43]Letter to Sebastian Egbert (May 3, 1607), in *Praestantium ac eruditorum virorum epistolae ecclesiasticae et theologicae varii argumenti*, ed. Christiaan Hartsoeker (Amsterdam: Henricus Dendrinus, 1660), 236-37. Quoted in A. M. Hunter, *The Teaching of Calvin* (London: James Clarke, 1950), 20.

Ezekiel 1–20, and Joshua. Calvin sought for brevity and clarity in all of his exegetical work. He emphasized the illumination of the Holy Spirit as essential to a proper understanding of the text. Calvin underscored the continuity between the two Testaments (one covenant in two dispensations) and sought to apply the plain or natural sense of the text to the church of his day. In the preface to his own influential commentary on Romans, Karl Barth described how Calvin worked to recover the mind of Paul and make the apostle's message relevant to his day:

> How energetically Calvin goes to work, first scientifically establishing the text ("what stands there?"), then following along the footsteps of its thought; that is to say, he conducts a discussion with it until the wall between the first and the sixteenth centuries becomes transparent, and until there in the first century Paul speaks and here the man of the sixteenth century hears, until indeed the conversation between document and reader becomes concentrated upon the substance (which must be the same now as then).[44]

Beza was elected moderator of Geneva's Company of Pastors after Calvin's death in 1564 and guided the Genevan Reformation over the next four decades. His annotated Latin translation of the Greek New Testament (1556) and his further revisions of the Greek text established his reputation as the leading textual critic of the sixteenth century after Erasmus. Beza completed the translation of Marot's metrical Psalter, which became a centerpiece of Huguenot piety and Reformed church life. Though known for his polemical writings on grace, free will, and predestination, Beza's work is marked by a strong pastoral orientation and concern for a Scripture-based spirituality.

Robert Estienne (Stephanus) was a printer-scholar who had served the royal household in Paris. After his conversion to Protestantism, in 1550 he moved to Geneva, where he published a series of notable editions and translations of the Bible. He also produced sermons and commentaries on Job, Ecclesiastes, the Song of Songs, Romans and Hebrews, as well as dictionaries, concordances, and a thesaurus of biblical terms. He also published the first editions of the Bible with chapters divided into verses, an innovation that quickly became universally accepted.

The British Reformation. Commentary writing in England and Scotland lagged behind the continental Reformation for several reasons. In 1500, there were only three publishing houses in England compared with more than two hundred on the Continent. A 1408 statute against publishing or reading the Bible in English, stemming from the days of Lollardy, stifled the free flow of ideas, as was seen in the fate of Tyndale. Moreover, the nature of the English Reformation from Henry through Elizabeth provided little stability for the flourishing of biblical scholarship. In the sixteenth century, many "hot-gospel" Protestants in England were edified by the English translations of commentaries and theological writings by the Continental reformers. The influence of Calvin and Beza was felt especially in the Geneva Bible with its "Protestant glosses" of theological notes and references.

During the later Elizabethan and Stuart church, however, the indigenous English commentary came into its own. Both Anglicans and Puritans contributed to this outpouring of biblical studies.

[44]Karl Barth, *Die Römerbrief* (Zurich: TVZ, 1940), 11, translated by T. H. L. Parker as the epigraph to *Calvin's New Testament Commentaries*, 2nd ed. (Louisville, KY: Westminster John Knox, 1993).

The sermons of Lancelot Andrewes and John Donne are replete with exegetical insights based on a close study of the Greek and Hebrew texts. Among the Reformed authors in England, none was more influential than William Perkins, the greatest of the early Puritan theologians, who published commentaries on Galatians, Jude, Revelation, and the Sermon on the Mount (Mt 5–7). John Cotton, one of his students, wrote commentaries on the Song of Songs, Ecclesiastes, and Revelation before departing for New England in 1633. The separatist pastor Henry Ainsworth was an outstanding scholar of Hebrew and wrote major commentaries on the Pentateuch, the Psalms, and the Song of Songs. In Scotland, Robert Rollock, the first principal of Edinburgh University (1585), wrote numerous commentaries including those on the Psalms, Ephesians, Daniel, Romans, 1 and 2 Thessalonians, John, Colossians, and Hebrews. Joseph Mede and Thomas Brightman were leading authorities on Revelation and contributed to the apocalyptic thought of the seventeenth century. Mention should also be made of Archbishop James Ussher, whose *Annals of the Old Testament* was published in 1650. Ussher developed a keen interest in biblical chronology and calculated that the creation of the world had taken place on October 26, 4004 B.C. As late as 1945, the Scofield Reference Bible still retained this date next to Genesis 1:1, but later editions omitted it because of the lack of evidence on which to fix such dates.[45]

Anabaptism. Irena Backus has noted that there was no school of "dissident" exegesis during the Reformation, and the reasons are not hard to find. The radical Reformation was an ill-defined movement that existed on the margins of official church life in the sixteenth century. The denial of infant baptism and the refusal to swear an oath marked radicals as a seditious element in society, and they were persecuted by Protestants and Catholics alike. However, in the RCS we have made an attempt to include some voices of the radical Reformation, especially among the Anabaptists. While the Anabaptists published few commentaries in the sixteenth century, they were avid readers and quoters of the Bible. Numerous exegetical gems can be found in their letters, treatises, martyr acts (especially *The Martyrs' Mirror*), hymns, and histories. They placed a strong emphasis on the memorizing of Scripture and quoted liberally from vernacular translations of the Bible. George H. Williams has noted that "many an Anabaptist theological tract was really a beautiful mosaic of Scripture texts."[46] In general, most Anabaptists accepted the apocryphal books as canonical, contrasted outer word and inner spirit with relative degrees of strictness and saw the New Testament as normative for church life and social ethics (witness their pacifism, nonswearing, emphasis on believers' baptism and congregational discipline).

We have noted the Old Testament translation of Ludwig Hätzer, who became an antitrinitarian, and Hans Denck that they published at Worms in 1527. Denck also wrote a notable commentary on Micah. Conrad Grebel belonged to a Greek reading circle in Zurich and came to his Anabaptist convictions while poring over the text of Erasmus's New Testament. The only Anabaptist leader with university credentials was Balthasar Hubmaier, who was made a doctor of theology (Ingolstadt, 1512) in the same year as Luther. His reflections on the Bible are found in his numerous

[45]*The New Scofield Reference Bible* (New York: Oxford University Press, 1967), vi.
[46]George H. Williams, *The Radical Reformation*, 3rd ed. (Kirksville, MO: Sixteenth Century Journal Publishers, 1992), 1247.

writings, which include the first catechism of the Reformation (1526), a two-part treatise on the freedom of the will and a major work *(On the Sword)* setting forth positive attitudes toward the role of government and the Christian's place in society. Melchior Hoffman was an apocalyptic seer who wrote commentaries on Romans, Revelation, and Daniel 12. He predicted that Christ would return in 1533. More temperate was Pilgram Marpeck, a mining engineer who embraced Anabaptism and traveled widely throughout Switzerland and south Germany, from Strasbourg to Augsburg. His "Admonition of 1542" is the longest published defense of Anabaptist views on baptism and the Lord's Supper. He also wrote many letters that functioned as theological tracts for the congregations he had founded dealing with topics such as the fruits of repentance, the lowliness of Christ, and the unity of the church. Menno Simons, a former Catholic priest, became the most outstanding leader of the Dutch Anabaptist movement. His masterpiece was the *Foundation of Christian Doctrine* published in 1540. His other writings include *Meditation on the Twenty-fifth Psalm* (1537); *A Personal Exegesis of Psalm Twenty-five* modeled on the style of Augustine's *Confessions; Confession of the Triune God* (1550), directed against Adam Pastor, a former disciple of Menno who came to doubt the divinity of Christ; *Meditations and Prayers for Mealtime* (1557); and the *Cross of the Saints* (1554), an exhortation to faithfulness in the face of persecution. Like many other Anabaptists, Menno emphasized the centrality of discipleship *(Nachfolge)* as a deliberate repudiation of the old life and a radical commitment to follow Jesus as Lord.

Reading Scripture with the Reformers

In 1947, Gerhard Ebeling set forth his thesis that the history of the Christian church is the history of the interpretation of Scripture. Since that time, the place of the Bible in the story of the church has been investigated from many angles. A better understanding of the history of exegesis has been aided by new critical editions and scholarly discussions of the primary sources. The *Cambridge History of the Bible*, published in three volumes (1963–1970), remains a standard reference work in the field. The ACCS built on, and itself contributed to, the recovery of patristic biblical wisdom of both East and West. Beryl Smalley's *The Study of the Bible in the Middle Ages* (1940) and Henri de Lubac's *Medieval Exegesis: The Four Senses of Scripture* (1959) are essential reading for understanding the monastic and scholastic settings of commentary work between Augustine and Luther. The Reformation took place during what has been called "le grand siècle de la Bible."[47] Aided by the tools of Renaissance humanism and the dynamic impetus of Reformation theology (including permutations and reactions against it), the sixteenth century produced an unprecedented number of commentaries on every book in the Bible. Drawing from this vast storehouse of exegetical treasures, the RCS allows us to read Scripture along with the reformers. In doing so, it serves as a practical homiletic and devotional guide to some of the greatest masters of biblical interpretation in the history of the church.

The RCS gladly acknowledges its affinity with and dependence on recent scholarly investigations of Reformation-era exegesis. Between 1976 and 1990, three international colloquia on the

[47]J-R. Aarmogathe, ed., *Bible de tous les temps*, 8 vols.; vol. 6, *Le grand siècle de la Bible* (Paris: Beauchesne, 1989).

history of biblical exegesis in the sixteenth century took place in Geneva and in Durham, North Carolina.[48] Among those participating in these three gatherings were a number of scholars who have produced groundbreaking works in the study of biblical interpretation in the Reformation. These include Elsie McKee, Irena Backus, Kenneth Hagen, Scott H. Hendrix, Richard A. Muller, Guy Bedouelle, Gerald Hobbs, John B. Payne, Bernard Roussel, Pierre Fraenkel, and David C. Steinmetz (1936–2015). Among other scholars whose works are indispensible for the study of this field are Heinrich Bornkamm, Jaroslav Pelikan, Heiko A. Oberman, James S. Preus, T. H. L. Parker, David F. Wright, Tony Lane, John L. Thompson, Frank A. James, and Timothy J. Wengert.[49] Among these scholars no one has had a greater influence on the study of Reformation exegesis than David C. Steinmetz. A student of Oberman, he emphasized the importance of understanding the Reformation in medieval perspective. In addition to important studies on Luther and Staupitz, he pioneered the method of comparative exegesis showing both continuity and discontinuity between major Reformation figures and the preceding exegetical traditions (see his *Luther in Context* and *Calvin in Context*). From his base at Duke University, he spawned what might be called a Steinmetz school, a cadre of students and scholars whose work on the Bible in the Reformation era continues to shape the field. Steinmetz served on the RCS Board of Editorial Advisors, and a number of our volume editors pursued doctoral studies under his supervision.

In 1980, Steinmetz published "The Superiority of Pre-critical Exegesis," a seminal essay that not only placed Reformation exegesis in the context of the preceding fifteen centuries of the church's study of the Bible but also challenged certain assumptions underlying the hegemony of historical-critical exegesis of the post-Enlightenment academy.[50] Steinmetz helps us to approach the reformers and other precritical interpreters of the Bible on their own terms as faithful witnesses to the church's apostolic tradition. For them, a specific book or pericope had to be understood within the scope of the consensus of the canon. Thus the reformers, no less than the Fathers and the schoolmen, interpreted the hymn of the Johannine prologue about the preexistent Christ in consonance with the creation narrative of Genesis 1. In the same way, Psalm 22, Isaiah 53, and Daniel 7 are seen as part of an overarching storyline that finds ultimate fulfillment in Jesus Christ. Reading the Bible with the resources of the new learning, the reformers challenged the exegetical conclusions of their medieval predecessors at many points. However, unlike Alexander Campbell in the nineteenth century, their aim was not to "open the New Testament as if mortal man had never seen

[48]Olivier Fatio and Pierre Fraenkel, eds., *Histoire de l'exégèse au XVIe siècle: texts du colloque international tenu à Genève en 1976* (Geneva: Droz, 1978); David C. Steinmetz, ed., *The Bible in the Sixteenth Century* [Second International Colloquy on the History of Biblical Exegesis in the Sixteenth Century] (Durham: Duke University Press, 1990); Irena Backus and Francis M. Higman, eds., *Théorie et pratique de l'exégèse. Actes du troisième colloque international sur l'histoire de l'exégèse biblique au XVIe siècle, Genève, 31 août–2 septembre 1988* (Geneva: Droz, 1990); see also Guy Bedouelle and Bernard Roussel, eds., *Bible de tous les temps*, 8 vols.; vol. 5, *Le temps des Réformes et la Bible* (Paris: Beauchesne, 1989).

[49]For bibliographical references and evaluation of these and other contributors to the scholarly study of Reformation-era exegesis, see Richard A. Muller, "Biblical Interpretation in the Era of the Reformation: The View From the Middle Ages," in *Biblical Interpretation in the Era of the Reformation: Essays Presented to David C. Steinmetz in Honor of His Sixtieth Birthday*, ed. Richard A. Muller and John L. Thompson (Grand Rapids: Eerdmans, 1996), 3-22.

[50]David C. Steinmetz, "The Superiority of Pre-Critical Exegesis," *Theology Today* 37 (1980): 27-38.

it before."[51] Rather, they wanted to do their biblical work as part of an interpretive conversation within the family of the people of God. In the reformers' emphatic turn to the literal sense, which prompted their many blasts against the unrestrained use of allegory, their work was an extension of a similar impulse made by Thomas Aquinas and Nicholas of Lyra.

This is not to discount the radically new insights gained by the reformers in their dynamic engagement with the text of Scripture; nor should we dismiss in a reactionary way the light shed on the meaning of the Bible by the scholarly accomplishments of the past two centuries. However, it is to acknowledge that the church's exegetical tradition is an indispensible aid for the proper interpretation of Scripture. And this means, as Richard Muller has said, that "while it is often appropriate to recognize that traditionary readings of the text are erroneous on the grounds offered by the historical-critical method, we ought also to recognize that the conclusions offered by historical-critical exegesis may themselves be quite erroneous on the grounds provided by the exegesis of the patristic, medieval, and reformation periods."[52] The RCS wishes to commend the exegetical work of the Reformation era as a program of retrieval for the sake of renewal—spiritual réssourcement for believers committed to the life of faith today.

George Herbert was an English pastor and poet who reaped the benefits of the renewal of biblical studies in the age of the Reformation. He referred to the Scriptures as a book of infinite sweetness, "a mass of strange delights," a book with secrets to make the life of anyone good. In describing the various means pastors require to be fully furnished in the work of their calling, Herbert provided a rationale for the history of exegesis and for the Reformation Commentary on Scripture:

> The fourth means are commenters and Fathers, who have handled the places controverted, which the parson by no means refuseth. As he doth not so study others as to neglect the grace of God in himself and what the Holy Spirit teacheth him, so doth he assure himself that God in all ages hath had his servants to whom he hath revealed his Truth, as well as to him; and that as one country doth not bear all things that there may be a commerce, so neither hath God opened or will open all to one, that there may be a traffic in knowledge between the servants of God for the planting both of love and humility. Wherefore he hath one comment[ary] at least upon every book of Scripture, and ploughing with this, and his own meditations, he enters into the secrets of God treasured in the holy Scripture.[53]

Timothy George
General Editor

[51]Alexander Campbell, *Memoirs of Alexander Campbell*, ed. Robert Richardson (Cincinnati: Standard Publishing Company, 1872), 97.
[52]Richard A. Muller and John L. Thompson, "The Significance of Precritical Exegesis: Retrospect and Prospect," in *Biblical Interpretation in the Era of the Reformation: Essays Presented to David C. Steinmetz in Honor of His Sixtieth Birthday*, ed. Richard A. Muller and John L. Thompson (Grand Rapids: Eerdmans, 1996), 342.
[53]George Herbert, *The Complete English Poems* (London: Penguin, 1991), 205.

INTRODUCTION TO HEBREWS AND JAMES

A Controversial Epistle: Hebrews in Reformation Commentary

The epistle to the Hebrews occupies an important place in the history of Reformation biblical interpretation.[1] Some scholars have argued that Luther's lectures on Hebrews (1517/1518) contributed directly to the emergence of his mature Reformation theology. Earlier in his career Luther had treated faith as a kind of humility that the Christian was both able and obliged to produce in response to the accusing Word in order to merit grace; in his *Lectures on Hebrews* the Wittenberg professor treats faith as trust in the promises of the Word.[2] Luther instructs his students in these lectures to despair of their self-made penitence and purification from sin, because their forgiveness does not depend on these: it is Christ's purification for sins (Heb 1:3) that produces their penitence, and the same purification has already forgiven them before they begin to repent.[3] For Luther, faith is now a "clinging to the Word," that is, a deep trust that causes the heart to soften toward God and ultimately unites it with Christ, causing the believer to become like the Savior. As Luther explains,

> For this clinging is the very faith in the Word. Indeed, it is that tie of betrothal about which Hosea 2:20 says: "I will betroth you to Me in faithfulness," according to the well-known statement in 1 Corinthians 6:17: "He who clings to God is one spirit with him." . . . It follows as a corollary that faith in Christ is every virtue and that unbelief is every vice. . . . For through faith a man becomes like the Word of God, but the Word of God is the Son of God.[4]

Luther makes the gift of faith the defining mark of the Christian:[5] "For if you ask a Christian what the work is by which he becomes worthy of the name 'Christian,' he will be able to give absolutely no other answer than that it is the hearing of the Word of God, that is, faith. Therefore the ears alone are the organs of a Christian man, for he is justified and declared to be a Christian,

---

[1]For a helpful overview of the interpretation of Hebrews in the Reformation period, see Craig R. Koester, *Hebrews: A New Translation with Introduction and Commentary*, Anchor Bible 36 (New York: Doubleday: 2001), 33-40.

[2]Ernst Bizer, *Fides ex Auditu: Eine Untersuchung über die Entdeckung der Gerechtigkeit Gottes durch Martin Luther*, 3rd ed. (Neukirchen-Vluyn: Neukirchener Verlag, 1966), 165. On Luther's concept of faith in the *Lectures on Hebrews*, see Kenneth Hagen, *A Theology of Testament in the Young Luther: The Lectures on Hebrews* (Leiden: Brill, 1974), 71-90.

[3]WA 57,3:101.19-22; LW 29:112-13.

[4]WA 57,3:151.9-15; LW 29:155.

[5]On faith as a divine gift in the *Hebräervorlesung*, see WA 57,3:233.12; LW 29:235.

not because of the works of any member but because of faith."[6] As Luther reached the end of his lectures on Hebrews (summer 1518), he could declare that Abraham, the man of faith (Heb 11:8), "gave a supreme example of an evangelical life, because he left everything and followed the Lord. Preferring the Word of God to all else and loving it above all else, he was a stranger of his own accord and was subjected every hour to dangers of life and death."[7] Abraham clung to the Word by faith and willingly endured the suffering that both proved this faith and followed from it. He was the ideal Christian for Luther as the monk-professor became caught up in the indulgence controversy (fall 1517 to fall 1518).[8]

Not all scholars agree with this argument about the centrality of the *Lectures on Hebrews* in the development of Luther's Reformation theology; many would say that Luther's evangelical understanding of faith may be found in his earlier works as well.[9] Nevertheless, for some time now, Reformation scholars have paid close attention to the way Luther and a whole host of reformers treated Hebrews in their sermons, lectures, and commentaries. Kenneth Hagen, who has done the most work on this topic, has concluded that "among the epistles, the one to the Hebrews was the most controversial" in the eyes of the reformers.[10]

The pages that follow provide warrant for Hagen's claim. It will be helpful to provide the reader with a general orientation to the central theological and exegetical issues that appear in the reformers' comments on Hebrews. Authorship is foremost among them. The reformers were well aware of debates since the early church about the authorship and apostolicity of the epistle to the Hebrews. They express different opinions on these important matters, some claiming Pauline authorship, others denying it and either leaving the question of authorship open or suggesting an alternative, such as Apollos. The early arguments of Cajetan and Erasmus against Pauline authorship, which Luther and Calvin shared, appears to have set the scene for ongoing debate among reformers. Still, many accepted the traditional position: Zwingli argues for Pauline authorship, as do a number of Reformed theologians. Unlike debates about the authorship of James (see below), disagreements about the authorship of Hebrews did not lead to more thoroughgoing questioning of its canonical status—although a few Lutherans attempted to relegate Hebrews to a kind of apocryphal status within the New Testament.[11]

Christology is a major theme in Hebrews. The reformers comment at length on the relevant passages as they seek to explain how the Son is related to the Father and Holy Spirit, as well as to the created order, including angels. The reformers affirm Nicene and Chalcedonian orthodoxy; however, they disagree vigorously concerning the nature of Christ's presence in the holy bread and

[6]WA 57,3:222.5-9; LW 29:224.

[7]WA 57,3:236.4-7; LW 29: 238. Luther had also referred to Abraham's faith in *Die sieben Bußpsalmen*; see WA 1:171.33; LW 14 152.

[8]This paragraph draws on Ronald K. Rittgers, *The Reformation of Suffering: Pastoral Theology and Lay Piety in Late Medieval and Early Modern Germany* (New York: Oxford University Press, 2012), 102-4.

[9]See Berndt Hamm, *The Early Luther: Stages in a Reformation Reorientation*, trans. Martin J. Lohrmann (Grand Rapids: Eerdmans, 2014).

[10]See especially Kenneth Hagen, *Hebrews Commenting from Erasmus to Bèze, 1516–1598* (Tübingen: Mohr Siebeck, 1981; repr., Eugene, OR: Wipf and Stock, 2011), 97.

[11]See Koester, *Hebrews*, 35-36.

wine. Christ's session at the right hand of the Father (1:3, 13) especially provoked these christological debates. Following Luther, Lutheran commentators insist on a figurative session of Christ along with the ability of his human nature to participate in the ubiquity of his divine nature, thus making it possible for Christ to be present in, with, and under the auspices of bread and wine. Reformed theologians argue against the Lutheran view of Christ's session, especially what it assumed about the relationship between Christ's humanity and divinity, and thus insist on Christ's spiritual presence in the Lord's Supper, depicting Lutherans as perpetuating the traditional "superstitious" view of the sacrament.[12]

The reformers were especially impressed with another aspect of Christology in Hebrews, especially in their comments on Hebrews 2:5-18: the veiled nature of Christ's glory. The reformers saw in this hiddenness a summons to faith in the hidden God. The reformers also reflect on the nature of Christ's suffering, especially the suffering of his soul, but they consistently move from considerations of Christology to pastoral concerns, finding in Christ's incarnation and humiliation consolation for the suffering and persecuted (Protestant) Christian. The reformers make a great deal of the "fellowship of suffering" that they see between Christ and Christians in Hebrews and offer it as a source of solace to their contemporaries.

The reformers also tackle the thorny christological issue of how Christ, the God-man, may be said to have learned obedience through what he suffered (Heb 5:8). Most emphasize that Christ learned by experience what he already knew in theory about obedience, especially in the midst of suffering, and that by suffering to the point of death he showed Christians what true obedience to God entails. But pastoral concerns again predominate as the reformers see in Christ's suffering a source of consolation for the afflicted Christian. Edward Dering says that this passage contains a "salve against the wounds of sorrow,"[13] for Christians can know that Christ is present with them in their afflictions, and that their prayers for help and comfort will be heard because of Christ's obedience in their stead.

That Hebrews ostensibly teaches that salvation can be lost through serious postbaptismal sin (2:1-4; 6:4-12; 10:19-39) sits rather awkwardly with most versions of justification by faith. Theologically speaking, this was the most challenging aspect of Hebrews for the reformers. The magisterial Protestants were trying to deliver their contemporaries from a theology of salvation that, in their eyes, provided no certainty of forgiveness because it was based on the dubious foundation of human good works rather than on the sure foundation of God's word and character. In the eyes of the reformers, this teaching had caused untold anxiety in human consciences, as Christians wondered whether they had ever done enough to appease the divine Judge. Justification by faith rested on the conviction that salvation was God's good work from beginning to end, and that this gift could in no way be earned but only received by faith, itself a gift. Salvation was certain because it rested

[12]See, for example, "Eucharist," *OER* 2:71-81; Lee Palmer Wandel, *The Eucharist in the Reformation: Incarnation and Liturgy* (Cambridge: Cambridge University Press, 2006); and Amy Nelson Burnett, *Karlstadt and the Origins of the Eucharistic Controversy: A Study in the Circulation of Ideas* (Oxford: Oxford University Press, 2011).

[13]Dering, *27 Lectures on Hebrews*, Z5v*.

on God's character and action, not in any way on human effort. Thus, an uncertain salvation—a salvation that could be lost through human failure—was diametrically opposed to the theological and pastoral designs of the reformers. But they also wished to be true to Scripture, including its difficult passages, for they insisted that unlike "popish" theology, theirs was based on the Word of God. For the most part, the reformers interpret the "harsh" or "rigorist" passages on loss of salvation in Hebrews as being either hyperbolic or as applying to the reprobate and indolent rather than to the elect, although some do allow for the possibility of a complete fall from grace among believers, apparently owing to the strength of indwelling sin, the world, and the devil. In other words, on the whole, the reformers see in such passages a dire warning to keep believers in the narrow way of salvation, or they see these passages as applying to those in whom the seed of salvation had never taken firm root.

The reformers also take up a related issue: the nature of the sin that could (theoretically) cause a Christian to fall from saving grace. They entertain various possibilities, typically concluding that nothing short of direct, persistent, and intentional blasphemy of God would qualify as the "unforgiveable sin." But defining categories of sin was not the reformers' primary concern when handling such "troubling" passages in Hebrews. Time and again they seek to dissuade the anxious Christian conscience from worrying about losing grace. The Protestant reformers seek to console Christians—through the pastors who read their commentaries on Hebrews—that normal, everyday sins are not in view in Hebrews, and that God is eager to forgive these and even more serious sins to those who are penitent. The verses that seem to threaten loss of salvation for serious sin are taken to apply to those who willfully, persistently, and maliciously reject Christ and his gospel, not to the Christian who sincerely struggles with sin. Given that many Protestants faced persecution for their Protestant faith, the reformers also urged their readers to take heart from the example of persecuted Christians in the past who remained steadfast in faith.

Hebrews has a great deal to say about the relationship between Christ and the Old Testament, especially between Christ and the Levitical system of sacrifices for sin. The reformers saw in this comparison a warrant for distinguishing their evangelical Christianity from the Catholic Christianity that most of them opposed so deeply. They identified "popish" religion with the religion of the Old Testament sacrificial system and thus saw in Hebrews a strong argument in favor of their creed. They regularly depict Catholic Christianity as a religion of external ritual only and evangelical Christianity as a religion of true, inward faith. In this context they also reject the Catholic priesthood, especially the connection that traditionalists sought to make between the priesthood of Melchizedek, Christ, and the Catholic clergy. Owing to the emphasis in Hebrews on the one-time and unique nature of Christ's sacrifice for sin, the reformers similarly refuted Catholic claims for the necessity of a Christian priesthood to offer ongoing sacrifices for sin in the Mass. The only sacrifice in the Lord's Supper was the sacrifice of praise and thanksgiving for Christ's one-time and all-sufficient sacrifice for sin on the cross. This in turn meant that the Christian clergy was no longer a priesthood but a company of pastors whose primary responsibility was the proclamation of the Word. Especially in their comments on Hebrews 2:1-4, the reformers nearly deify

Protestant preachers. Even as they restrict miracles and the like to the apostolic age, they refer to the ministry and effect of the Word with quasi-prophetic language. As William Jones put it, "The preacher is a man as you are, but God speaks by him, and if you despise him, you despise God who speaks in him."[14]

As the reformers address the way Hebrews seeks to relate Christ and the Old Testament, they also reveal something important about their own approach to Scripture. In comparison to medieval exegetes, who regularly looked for a fourfold sense in Scripture that included allegorical or spiritual interpretation, Protestant reformers are typically viewed as wooden literalists who stuck to the historical and literal meaning of the biblical text. While Protestants did eschew what they saw as the fanciful exegesis of the Middle Ages, they could engage in their own version of spiritual interpretation, which becomes quite clear in the comments on Hebrews 1, where they follow the christological reading of the Psalms. Beyond this, they offer elaborate interpretations of the furniture and various utensils of the tabernacle in their comments on Hebrews 9:1-10. Lucas Osiander explains, "And the lampstand with the seven lamps signified the ministers of the church, shining with the word of truth and an innocent life, and showing the way to the heavenly Father by means of the guide Christ, who is the true light. The table designated the ministry of the Word, by which the bread of life is offered, Christ having been revealed and offered to the world by the work of the twelve apostles."[15] Heinrich Bullinger similarly asserts, "For more regarding the table, read Exodus 25. Now, it can be seen as a type of the ministers of the word, who should be above reproach, imbued with sound faith, portable, that is, accommodating, who adjust to the capacity of the hearers, not by flattery, but with holy cunning, so that they might win very many to Christ. Others have understood the table as referring to Scripture."[16] Thus early modern commentators had their own version of spiritual exegesis.[17]

Protestant Christianity placed a premium on faith in the Christian life. One was justified by faith and one lived from faith. Thus the reformers comment at length on the treatment of faith in Hebrews 11:1-40. They offer differing interpretations of the word *hypostasis*, "substance" or "conviction" (Heb 11:1). Many conclude that faith makes future realities present in the heart and mind of the believer by trusting in the faithfulness of God, who promises such realities to those who believe. The reformers also treat faith as a kind of wisdom that defies the learning and wisdom of this world. Faith is an inward matter, it is essential for true religion, and it entails radical trust in God. Luther provides what has become a famous statement about faith: "And this is the glory of faith, namely, not to know where you are going, what you are doing, what you are suffering, and, after taking everything captive—perception and understanding, strength and will—to follow the bare voice of God and to be led and driven rather than to drive."[18] The reformers also note that faith requires one to be a sojourner in this world, headed for another heavenly country; additionally, they assert

[14]Jones, *A Commentary upon the Epistles of St Paul*, 54*.
[15]Osiander, *Epistola ad Hebraeos*, 56.
[16]Bullinger, *In Pauli ad Hebraeos Epistolam*, 87v-88r.
[17]For a similar discussion, see RCS OT 7:xlvi-lii, and RCS NT 9a:liv-lvi.
[18]Luther, *Lectures on Hebrews*, LW 29:238 (WA 57:235.24-236.7).

that faith is a virtue or a divine gift that women can possess in equal measure as men. Perhaps most important, faith sees Christ hidden in the manifold sufferings and crosses of the Christian life, bearing these afflictions with and for the Christian, owing to his complete identification with human weakness in the incarnation (Heb 4:15-16; 12:3-14).

An Epistle of Straw? James in Reformation Commentary

Owing to Luther's dismissive comment about James as an "epistle of straw," by which he meant that it was unfit to be placed on the foundation of salvation in Christ in the building up of the kingdom,[19] this epistle suffered no little disdain in the Reformation, at least among Luther's followers.[20] Veit Dietrich, a Lutheran reformer in Nuremberg who knew Luther well, writes in his *Summaria vber das newe Testament* that he has not included James because it "is not only worthy of censure in some places, because it extols works so highly against faith, but it is also throughout a patchwork teaching comprised of many pieces that do not fit together."[21] Other Lutheran reformers, such as Erasmus Sarcerius, took a more optimistic view of James, and it appears to have suffered little reproach among Reformed and Anabaptist Christians. The latter found in it numerous warrants for lambasting magisterial Protestants and their alleged accommodations with the world.

The crucial related issues, of course, are authorship and whether James's doctrine—especially its doctrine of justification—is truly apostolic, at least in Protestant eyes. The reformers argue for various possibilities as to authorship, and this leads to differing conclusions about its apostolicity and canonicity. Generally speaking, Lutherans (following Luther) are skeptical about its apostolic origins, as is Erasmus, while the Reformed and Anabaptists accept and defend its authenticity and authority. The central concern of most reformers is to try to account for the emphasis on justification by works in James and the assertion of justification by faith in the Pauline corpus—James says Abraham was justified by works while Paul says that he was justified by faith.

In James 2:14-26 the magisterial Protestant reformers explore a number of ways of reconciling James and Paul, most of which seek to demonstrate that the faith that justifies is a lively and active faith that necessarily issues forth in good works. As Richard Turnbull puts it, "For outward profession without holy conversation is hypocrisy, and pretended religion without true sanctification is double iniquity."[22] Reformed Protestants and some Lutherans also insist that Paul and James are not opposed in their teaching about justification; rather, they deal with two different

[19]Luther, "Preface to the New Testament," WADB 6:12.29-34 (LW 35:362). The editors of the LW note that Luther had 1 Cor 3:12 in mind when he referred to James as an epistle of straw. Luther may also have been reacting to Andreas Bodenstein von Karlstadt's high praise for James. See LW 35:362 n. 11. Luther also cast doubt on the apostolicity of James in *The Babylonian Captivity of the Church*. See LW 36:118 (cited in LW 35:362 n. 12.)

[20]For considerations of the interpretation of James in the Reformation period, see Jennifer Powell McNutt, "James, 'The Book of Straw,' in Reformational Biblical Exegesis: A Comparison of Luther and the Radicals," in *Reconsidering the Relationship Between Biblical and Systematic Theology in the New Testament*, ed. Benjamin E. Reynolds, Brian Lugioyo, and Kevin J. Vanhoozer (Tübingen: Mohr Siebeck, 2014), 157-76; and Luke Timothy Johnson, *The Letter of James: A New Translation with Introduction and Commentary*, Anchor Bible 37a (New York: Doubleday, 1995), 140-43.

[21]Dietrich, *Summaria vber das newe Testament*, Rrr3v.

[22]Turnbull, *An exposition upon the canonical Epistle of Saint James*, 126r-v, 127v*.

kinds of justification, one before God and the other before human beings, because they were addressing two different problems: legalism and works righteousness versus lax Christianity. Behind this effort to reconcile James and Paul was another concern that dogged magisterial Protestants throughout the Reformation era, namely, the need to refute Catholic and Anabaptist claims that they taught an easy salvation that required mere belief without amendment of life and service to neighbor. Anabaptists in particular used the emphasis on works in James to criticize Lutherans and Reformed Christians, who in their eyes had compromised the true faith by making alliances with temporal rulers and failing to walk the way of the cross and persecution. However, Lutheran and Reformed theologians countered that they indeed taught the necessity of good works in the Christian life, flowing from justifying faith.

In their comments on James, Lutheran and Reformed exegetes sought to avoid another criticism from Catholics and Anabaptists: that they made God responsible for sin and evil. Their insistence on monergism and human bondage to sin could potentially leave magisterial reformers open to this charge. Especially in their comments on James 1:13-18, the reformers assert that the sovereign God is not the author of sin or evil, for God is good and only good flows from him; human beings are responsible for the entry of sin into the world. In the same section, the reformers tackle the issue of concupiscence (or lust), which in Catholic theology was not considered a sin itself but the result of sin. The reformers uniformly attack this position, insisting that the desire to sin is itself sin, part of their larger effort to emphasize the utter depravity of fallen humankind and the utter sovereignty of God.

James contains harsh criticisms of the rich and the way they oppress and persecute the poor (Jas 2:1-13). Such assertions proved challenging for many of the magisterial reformers, who sought to fulfill Christ's commands to aid the poor while also appealing to the protection and patronage of ruling elites. Most reformers believed that God had ordained human beings to their various stations in life and that the distinction among ranks in society was necessary in order to avoid chaos and anarchy. In the spiritual realm there might be equality, but not in the temporal sphere. Thus, in their comments on James, the magisterial reformers seek to make distinctions between the good rich, who use their wealth to support God's work in the world, and the evil rich, who trust in themselves and seek to oppose God's purposes. The strong statements of God's preference for the poor also posed a potential threat to the Protestant theology of justification, which taught that faith alone brought one into favor with God. The reformers seek to solve this apparent conundrum by stressing that the elect poor are in view in this section of James. Still, the reformers have sharp words about the rich and readily acknowledge that wealth is as much an impediment to salvation in their own day as in the past.

As in Hebrews, so too in James, Protestant reformers level many criticisms against Catholic Christianity. This is especially apparent in their comments on James 5:7-12, which they insist provides no support for either the sacrament of unction or the sacrament of penance. (The Catholic

Cajetan agreed with respect to unction.)[23] On the whole, they confine miracles of healing to the apostolic age, interpreting them as a sign that confirmed the authenticity of the gospel, although they allow that God may still choose to heal through natural means, which are also viewed as a divine gift. They argue against the persistence of the gift of healing based on empirical observation: according to James, the prayers of the elders will effect healing every time; because such prayers in their own day were not producing such healing, the reformers reasoned that the gift must have long since ceased.

Despite the fact that James placed many reformers on their heels, so to speak, because of its strong emphasis on works in the Christian life, they genuinely appreciate the epistle's call to a rigorous Christianity that entails much suffering and persecution, but also much consolation. James inspired, challenged, and guided them, even as it troubled (some of) them.

A Note on the Sources

In keeping with the purposes of the RCS, every effort has been made to gather sources for this volume from a variety of reformers across the confessional spectrum. Many more sources could have been used, but the ones presented here should provide a sufficiently diverse collection of voices from the Reformation period. The sources reflect confessional, geographical, and linguistic diversity as well as a considerable diversity of genres: sermons—some standalone, others from postils—lectures, commentaries, along with excerpts from theological treatises and works of devotion.

A number of sources are here translated into English for the first time. The reader will also notice that some authors predominate while others appear less frequently, the latter serving primarily to provide counterpoint and alternative perspectives. For Hebrews the most frequently cited authors are Johannes Bugenhagen, Heinrich Bullinger, Johannes Oecolampadius,[24] Lucas Osiander, Cardinal Cajetan, and Huldrych Zwingli; for James, Andreas Althamer, Lucas Osiander, Desiderius Erasmus, John Mayer, and Richard Turnbull. Luther and Calvin are present throughout,[25] although, in keeping with the design of the RCS, neither is allowed center stage.

Precritical Exegesis and the Life of Faith

Finally, all of the sources exemplify the close connection between theology and the Christian life that is so typical of "precritical" Christian exegesis. They are all, at root, pastoral or devotional sources that seek to nurture Christian faith and life; not one of them engages in interpretation of the biblical text for purely "scholarly" reasons. In this sense, the sources are completely in step with the spirit of the RCS project, which, in the words of the late David Steinmetz, seeks to extol "the superiority of pre-critical exegesis," or at least its enduring value.[26]

[23]See Johnson, *James*, 141.

[24]For a recent treatment of Oecolampadius's work on Hebrews, see Jeff Fisher, *A Christoscopic Reading of Scripture: Johannes Oecolampadius on Hebrews* (Göttingen: Vandenhoeck & Ruprecht, 2016).

[25]For recent works on Luther's treatment of Hebrews and James, see Jason D. Lane, "Luther's Criticism of James as a Key to His Biblical Hermeneutic," in *Auslegung und Hermeneutik der Bibel in der Reformationszeit*, ed. Christine Christ-von Wedel and Sven Grosse (Berlin: de Gruyter, 2017), 111-24; and Sarah Stützinger, "Die Auslegung des Hebräerbriefs bei Luther und lutherischen Theologen des sechzehnten Jahrhunderts am Beispiel von Hebr 9," in Christ-von Wedel and Grosse, *Auslegung und Hermeneutik*, 125-46.

[26]David C. Steinmetz, "The Superiority of Pre-critical Exegesis," *Theology Today* 37, no. 1 (1980): 27-38.

In that spirit, Reformed exegete and theologian Johannes Oecolampadius encouraged readers to find in the words of the epistle to the Hebrews comfort and confidence in Jesus Christ, who understands our sufferings:

> We have no reason to fear. For surely a very different priest meets us than one by whom we could be despised. And how could he loath sinners, when he came into the world to save sinners? He is like us in every respect, he has been thoroughly tried by evils (albeit without any sin). Therefore, how could he not sympathize with our weaknesses, when to prompt us to faith in him he freely chose to be tempted and afflicted in every way? He is indeed God, but still he was not ashamed to experience our misfortunes in his own flesh, so that he might entirely persuade us that he is moved with feeling for our weaknesses, and so that he might provide free access to himself for all.[27]

Ronald K. Rittgers

[27]Oecolampadius, *In Epistolam ad Hebraeos Explanationes*, 48v-49r; citing 1 Tim 1:15; Heb 2:11.

COMMENTARY ON HEBREWS

Overview: The reformers were well aware of debates since the ancient period about the authorship and apostolicity of the epistle to the Hebrews. In their introductory observations they voice their varying opinions on these important matters, some claiming Pauline authorship, others denying it and either leaving the question of authorship open or suggesting an alternative, such as Apollos. The reformers also discuss the structure, genre, argument, occasion, and audience of the book.

Prolegomena: Introduction to Hebrews

The Mixed Genre of the Epistle. Heinrich Bullinger: The style is indeed plain, serious, clear, understandable, and distinctive, but the genre of the discourse is mixed. For one may recognize the middle part of the letter as the didactic genre; for the apostle teaches, as by a laudatory antithesis, that the shadows of the old institutions, including the priesthood and the sacrificial system, have been abolished completely, but that Christ is the true priest and the eternal sacrifice. But the beginning and end of the letter can be classified under the deliberative genre, for in both parts he urges similar things: at the beginning, not to reject Christ, and at the end, to believe Christ and persist in the truth with patience. Commentary on Hebrews.[1]

The Argument of Hebrews. John Calvin: Not only various opinions were formerly entertained as to the author of this epistle, but it was only at a late period that it was received by the Latin churches. They suspected that it favored Novatus in denying pardon to the fallen.[†] But that this was a groundless opinion will be shown by various passages. I, indeed, without hesitation, class it among the apostolical writings; nor do I doubt that it has been through the craft of Satan that any have been led to dispute its authority. There is, indeed, no book in the Holy Scriptures that speaks so clearly of the priesthood of Christ, so highly exalts the virtue and dignity of that only true sacrifice which he offered by his death, so abundantly treats of the use of ceremonies as well as of their abrogation, and, in a word, so fully explains that Christ is the end of the law. Let us not therefore suffer the church of God nor ourselves to be deprived of so great a benefit, but firmly defend the possession of it.

Moreover, as to its author, we need not be very solicitous. Some think the author to have been Paul, others Luke, others Barnabas, and others Clement, as Jerome relates; yet Eusebius,[‡] in the sixth book of his *Church History*, mentions only Luke and Clement. I well know that in the time of Chrysostom[§] it was everywhere classed by the Greeks among the Pauline epistles; but the Latins thought otherwise, even those who were nearest to the times of the apostles.

I indeed can adduce no reason to show that Paul was its author; for they who say that he designedly suppressed his name because it was hateful to the Jews bring nothing to the purpose. Why, then, did he mention the name of Timothy, as by this he betrayed himself? But the manner of teaching, and the style, sufficiently show that Paul was not the author; and the writer himself confesses in the second chapter that he was one of the disciples of

[1]Bullinger, *In Pauli ad Hebraeos Epistolam*, 7r.

the apostles, which is wholly different from the way in which Paul spoke of himself. Besides, what is said of the practice of catechizing in the sixth chapter does not well suit the time or age of Paul. There are other things we shall notice in their proper places. Commentaries on the Epistle of Paul the Apostle to the Hebrews.[2]

The Outline of the Epistle. Gasparo Contarini: The apostle [Paul] wrote this epistle from Italy to those who had believed, who were Hebrews, because they were depending on the law and were erring by being devoted to the observances of the law, as if faith in Christ does not justify believing human beings, but is a shadow of the old law. For that reason he first establishes the dignity of Christ, then treats the divine nature, and next the human nature that Christ assumed. In the first place the apostle compares and prefers him to angels, then to Moses, and finally to the Levitical priests. At last he ends in faith, which he defines … declaring all saints to be pure who have been justified by faith and through faith. Scholia in the Epistles of the Divine Paul, the Epistle to the Hebrews.[3]

The Design of the Writer. John Calvin: The object at the beginning is not to show to the Jews that Jesus, the son of Mary, was the Christ, the Redeemer promised to them, for he wrote to those who had already made a profession of Christ; that point, then, is taken as granted. But the design of the writer was to prove what the office of Christ is. And it hence appears evident, that by his coming an end was put to ceremonies. It is necessary to draw this distinction; for as it would have been a superfluous labor for the apostle to prove to those who were already convinced that he was the Christ who had appeared, so it was necessary for him to show what he was, for they did not as yet clearly understand the end, the effect, and the advantages of his coming; but being taken up with a false view of the law, they laid hold on the shadow instead of the substance. Our business with the papists is similar in the present day; for they confess with us that Christ is the Son of God, the Redeemer who had been promised to the world: but when we come to the reality, we find that they rob him of more than one-half of his power. Commentaries on the Epistle of Paul the Apostle to the Hebrews.[4]

Why This Epistle Was Written. Edward Dering: For this cause, the apostle having compassion on his weak brothers, who believed in Christ (but were also thus addicted to the law), he writes to them this epistle, by all means persuading them never to join together our Savior Christ with the ceremonies of the law, whose glory is perfect in himself alone.… He created alone, and he will redeem alone; he made alone, and he will save alone. To be set in comparison with him, all the gold, silver, precious stones, and all the ornaments of the temple, they are but "beggarly elements." Nothing else in earth, nothing under earth, nothing in heaven, nor in the heaven of heavens, no virtue, no power, no strength, no name else that is named, in which, or by which, we can be saved, but only the name of Jesus Christ. And for this cause this epistle was written. Wherein it shall be good for us to mark how from the beginning Satan strove to obscure and darken the glory of Christ: and how he held still the same purpose unchangeably, even to our days.… So now in these our last times (in which the devil strives as at the first) we see how many say unto us, "The church, the church, the pope, the pope, the fathers, the fathers," and many thousands are led with the sound of words; yet in these words is no wisdom, for they only

[2]CTS 40:xxvi-xxvii. †Novatus, or Novatian, was a Roman presbyter who joined a rigorist party that denied concessions to those who had lapsed during the Decian persecution (AD 249–250). He was consecrated rival bishop of Rome and suffered martyrdom in 257–258. Novatianist views were eventually deemed heretical. ‡Jerome, *Ad Dardanum* 129.3 (PL 30:1103); Eusebius, *Ecclesiastical History* 6.14.2-3 and 6.20.3 (NPNF 1:643, 669). §Chrysostom, *Homilies on the Epistle to the Hebrews* (NPNF 14:363-64).
[3]Contarini, *Opera*, 515.

[4]CTS 40:xxviii.

renew the old deceit, in which the devil first troubled the Church of God. . . . And for my part, who wrote this epistle, I cannot tell, nor I see no cause why I should seek it. For if the Spirit of God had left it out, can I think it the better, if I should add it? 27 Lectures or Readings on the Epistle to the Hebrews.[5]

The Primary Concern of the Epistle. Veit Dietrich: This epistle to the Hebrews or Jews is concerned to emphasize in the first place that the Jews should accept the gospel and recognize and regard Christ as the true Messiah, who is the true high priest and who offered the true sacrifice for sin on the cross, his own body, and thus fulfilled everything in the Old Testament that is signified by the priesthood, the temple, and the sacrificial system. Summary of the Epistle to the Hebrews.[6]

Paul Is Not the Author. Desiderius Erasmus: As for the so-called epistle to the Hebrews, not only can it be gathered from many indications that it is not Paul's, but it is written in a rhetorical style unlike the apostle's, and therefore does not present nearly so much difficulty. Paraphrases on James.[7]

The Audience: All Christian People. William Jones: To them [i.e., Hebrews] was this epistle written, and in them to us who are English men, and to all Christian people in the world: that which I say to you, says Christ, I say to all, watch: So that which Saint Paul writes to the Hebrews, he writes to us all: therefore let us all with reverence attend to it. A Commentary upon the Epistles of St. Paul.[8]

A Marvelously Fine Non-Pauline Epistle. Martin Luther: Up to this point we have had [to do with] the true and certain chief books of the New Testament. The four that follow [i.e., Hebrews, James, Jude, and Revelation] have from ancient times had a different reputation. In the first place, the fact that Hebrews is not an epistle of St. Paul, or of any other apostle, is proved by what it says in chapter 2, that through those who had themselves heard it from the Lord this doctrine has come to us and remained among us. It is thereby made clear that he is speaking about the apostles, perhaps long after them. For St. Paul, in Galatians 1, testifies powerfully that he had his gospel from no man, neither through men, but from God himself.

Again, there is a hard knot in the fact that in chapters 6 and 10 it flatly denies and forbids to sinners any repentance after baptism; and in chapter 12 it says that Esau sought repentance and did not find it. This [seems, as it stands, to be] contrary to all the Gospels and to St. Paul's epistles; and although one might venture an interpretation of it, the words are so clear that I do not know whether that would be sufficient. My opinion is that this is an epistle put together of many pieces, which does not deal systematically with any one subject.

However that may be, it is still a marvelously fine epistle. It discusses Christ's priesthood masterfully and profoundly on the basis of the Scriptures and extensively interprets the Old Testament in a fine way. Thus it is plain that this is the work of an able and learned man; as a disciple of the apostles he had learned much from them and was greatly experienced in faith and practiced in the Scriptures. And although, as he himself testifies in chapter 6, he does not lay the foundation of faith—that is the work of the apostles—nevertheless he does build well on it with gold, silver, precious stones, as St. Paul says in 1 Corinthians 3. Therefore we should not be deterred if wood, straw, or hay are perhaps mixed with them, but accept this fine teaching with all honor, though, to be sure, we cannot put it on the same level with the apostolic epistles.

[5]Dering, *Lectures on Hebrews*, Av, A2r-v*; citing Gal 4:9 (ESV: "worthless elementary principles").
[6]Dietrich, *Summaria vber die Epistel an die Ebreer*, Ooo ii r [663].
[7]CWE 44:132 (the comment comes from Erasmus's work on James, even though the comment is on Hebrews). Erasmus reverses himself in his *Paraphrases on the Epistle to the Hebrews*, CWE 44:214.
[8]Jones, *A Commentary upon the Epistles of St Paul*, 51*; citing Mk 13:37.

Who wrote it is not known, and will probably not be known for a while; it makes no difference. We should be satisfied with the doctrine that he bases so constantly on the Scriptures. For he discloses a firm grasp of the reading of the Scriptures and of the proper way of dealing with them. Preface to the Epistle to the Hebrews.[9]

Despite Luther's Reproaches, This Epistle Undeniably Establishes Faith in Christ. Johannes Oecolampadius: Paul urges the Hebrews, who hitherto had heard the Law and the Prophets, that they now hear Christ with faith, from which they must not fall away on account of any of the tempests of this age which pursue the godly; rather, by patience and holiness they should produce the good fruit of faith. Luther, in his preface, speaks thus: "It seems to me that this epistle is composed of many things, and that it does not discuss the same thing in an orderly fashion." He also adds that it does not lay the foundation of faith.[†] But if this argument of ours will stand, as it does stand very firmly, then we will vindicate the epistle from both of these reproaches. For how does it not lay the foundation of faith, when by so many arguments it drives at this one thing, namely, that Christ must be heard, and that with faith, which it praises so much? And everywhere it tacitly refers to that which we read in Deuteronomy 18 and Acts 7. Moses says, "The Lord your God will raise up for you a prophet like me from your people, from my brothers—to him *you shall listen*—just as you desired of the Lord your God at Horeb, when the assembly was gathered, and you said, 'Let me not hear any more the voice of the Lord my God, and let me not see any more this great fire.' And the Lord said to me, 'They have spoken everything well. I will raise up for them a prophet like you from among their brothers. I will put my words in his mouth, and he will speak to them the words which I will command him.'" It also refers to that which was said by the Father in Matthew 17, "This is my beloved Son, with whom I am well pleased; listen to him." Moreover, he introduces a particular discourse, which he sets out regarding the priesthood of Christ, for the sake of this most important purpose: that he may confirm our faith. Therefore, it indubitably and successfully discusses this, and so much so that whoever attends to this end will bear witness that a marvelous light has been granted to him to understand this epistle. Explanations of the Argument of Hebrews.[10]

The Holy Spirit as the Fountain of the Epistle's Doctrine. William Jones: Since the gospel of Christ has been published to the world, this has been received as Paul's epistle. So that though the matter is not weighty, it seems most probable to be Saint Paul's. Whosoever was the pipe to convey it to us, the Holy Spirit, as appears by the heavenly doctrine contained in it, was the fountain from whence it was derived: therefore let it be reverently embraced by all. A Commentary upon the Epistles of St. Paul.[11]

A Refined Author. Martin Luther: It is a trustworthy opinion that it [i.e., this powerful and lofty epistle] is not St. Paul's, because he uses a more refined speech than is St. Paul's custom in other places. Some think he is St. Luke, some St. Apollos . . . he is whoever he may be. Christmas Postil.[12]

The Epistle Was Written in an Apostolic Spirit. Lucas Osiander: That it is not of the apostle Paul (beyond that the diction is not Pauline) even can be gathered from the second chapter of this epistle, where the author confesses openly that he was a disciple of the apostles, which

[9]Luther, "Preface to the Epistle to the Hebrews," LW 35: 394-95 (WADB 7:344.1-33); citing Heb 2:3; Gal 1:1; Heb 6:4-6; 10:26-27; 12:17; 6:1; 1 Cor 3:12.

[10]Oecolampadius, *In Epistolam ad Hebraeos Explanationes*, 3v-4v; citing Deut 18:15-18; Acts 7:37; Mt 17:5. [†]WADB 7:344-45; LW 35:395.

[11]Jones, *A Commentary upon the Epistles of St Paul*, 50*.

[12]Luther, *Weihnachtspostille* 1522, WA 10.1.1:143.13-20. In a 1537 sermon on 1 Cor 1:12 Luther said Apollos wrote Hebrews. WA 45:389.34-35.

Paul expressly denies concerning his own person in the epistle that he wrote to the Galatians. But it was certainly written in an apostolic spirit, for there were, along with Paul and the twelve disciples, many excellent men in those times who were illumined by the Spirit of God and excellently practiced in sacred letters. EPISTLE TO THE HEBREWS.[13]

PAUL CALLS THE JEWS TO COME TO CHRIST. HULDRYCH ZWINGLI: When all the ceremonies and observances of the Mosaic law were gradually rendered entirely obsolete by the preaching of the gospel, the Jews, who clung to the Mosaic law, even those who had been initiated from Moses into Christ, not only bore this with discomfort, but also devised unbridled and ubiquitous trouble and disputation about these things. Therefore Paul wrote this epistle because of these things, and to refute and clear away an excessive love of the ceremonies from the souls of those who were wavering. In it he teaches that all these things were a symbol and type of Christ; and that Christ is the end and consummation of these things; and thus that we today have another temple, that is, heaven, and other purifications, another priest and sacrifice, that is, Christ. He shows that he is the true Son of God, and that he existed as God himself from eternity. He warns them earnestly not to reject him, but to receive him, and he shows clearly how much danger and trouble they have incurred by despising him. He explains that everything in the Old Testament was a type and symbol of the New, as we said above. In this way Christ has made atonement for the sins of the world by the single sacrifice of his death, and by continually sanctifying and perfecting those who draw near to him, he leads them into the heavenly tabernacle. There is also much regarding faith in Christ and encouragement to endurance, and he does this by a multitude of suitable examples. In the final chapter, as is his habit, he adds exhortations to good behavior and very earnest reminders. ARGUMENT OF THE EXPOSITION OF HEBREWS.[14]

PAUL'S ADDRESS TO WAVERING JEWISH CHRISTIANS. THE ENGLISH ANNOTATIONS: The apostle Paul, observing that the Hebrews (at least a great and considerable part of them) were ready to fall from the faith of Christ into their former Judaism, by reason of those cruel persecutions that they suffered, hence took occasion to write this epistle to them; wherein he labors to conform them in that faith which they had received, and to stir them up to stand steadfast in it; and that by diverse arguments: as first, from the excellency of Christ's nature, person, and offices; but chiefly his priestly office above that of Aaron. Second, from the danger of apostasy. Third, from the excellency and great power of faith. Fourth, from the gracious effects and fruits of affliction. And then concludes the epistle with exhortations to diverse Christian duties, both general and particular.

There is some controversy about the author of the epistle. Some ascribing it to Barnabas, others to Clement of Rome, others to Luke, but generally it is received that St. Paul was the author thereof. And it is observed that all the Greek copies, save one, bear this inscription. And generally, by a Hebrew, we are to understand the whole posterity of Abraham, by Isaac, who was the first (we read of) who was styled a Hebrew. . . . In this place, we are to understand hereby those of the Hebrews, who having received the gospel continued in Judea before their dispersion. ANNOTATIONS ON HEBREWS.[15]

THE STRUCTURE OF HEBREWS. JOHANNES OECOLAMPADIUS: [The author] also accomplishes his task with very becoming order, even as, by means of numerous reasons and testimonies of Scripture, which he explains beautifully, from the start he sets forth the worthiness and accessibility of Christ our instructor and teacher, who speaks to us. He shows that he is equal to God the Father, loftier and worthier than the highest and worthiest creatures, namely, the angels and Moses, through whom humans were instructed at one time. He also frightens us with threats if we should scorn to hear

[13]Osiander, *Epistola ad Hebraeos*, 1-2; citing Heb 2:3.
[14]Zwingli, *In Epistolam Beati Pauli ad Hebraeos Expositio*, 564.
[15]Downame, ed., *Annotations*, MMMiv*; citing Gen 14:13.

so great an apostle and teacher, but he invites and attracts us with the kindness and mercy of the very best priest, who is so well disposed toward us. And with remarkable sobriety he continues on this theme all the way to chapter 10. Then he skillfully teaches our role, that is, the role of students, so that we may not be unworthy of such a teacher and lose faith. So he commends patience, peace, charity toward strangers, prisoners, and the poor, chastity, obedience, discernment, and prayer, so that we may thus be made complete in every good work. And what could be clearer or more orderly? But this will melt away further as it is explained in detail. EXPLANATIONS OF THE ARGUMENT OF HEBREWS.[16]

[16]Oecolampadius, *In Epistolam ad Hebraeos Explanationes*, 4v.

1:1-4 God Has Spoken Through His Son

Long ago, at many times and in many ways, God spoke to our fathers by the prophets, ²but in these last days he has spoken to us by his Son, whom he appointed the heir of all things, through whom also he created the world. ³He is the radiance of the glory of God and the exact imprint of his nature, and he upholds the universe by the word of his power. After making purification for sins, he sat down at the right hand of the Majesty on high, ⁴having become as much superior to angels as the name he has inherited is more excellent than theirs.

Overview: The epistle to the Hebrews opens with a strong assertion of the supremacy of Christ over the whole created order, demonstrating this supremacy by the Son's unique relationship with the Father and his central role in creating and sustaining all things. He alone has made purification for sins, and he alone sits at the right hand of Father, which makes him superior to the angels in every way. The reformers find many of the defining themes of their theology confirmed in this passage, the most central of which is the centrality of the Word and the way it provides reliable access to the divine will. They continue to discuss the authorship of the epistle, but beyond this, they display a deep commitment to trinitarian theology, engaging in extended reflections on the relationship of the Son to the Father and to the Holy Spirit, drawing on Nicene and Chalcedonian categories and language along the way. All reformers affirm the fully human and fully divine natures of Christ, but, as in the early church, some emphasize the union of the natures while others stress their distinction. The reformers speak at length about forgiveness being found only in Christ through faith, seeking to distinguish their theology from the errors they find in late medieval theology. They also clearly demonstrate their christological exegesis of the Old Testament, especially the Psalms, which was so characteristic of many reformers.[1]

Distinction Between Law and Gospel. Veit Dietrich: The person who wrote this epistle addresses the matter directly right away, making a distinction between the law and the gospel. He says that the Jewish people received the law on Mt. Sinai albeit through an angel. By way of contrast, Jesus Christ, the Son of God himself, brought and revealed the gospel. Summary of the Epistle to the Hebrews, Preface to Chapter 1.[2]

1:1 *God Previously Spoke Through the Prophets*

No Other Religion Is Supported by So Many Diverse Testimonies. Heinrich Bullinger: It says that God spoke to the fathers on many occasions; that is, at various times he would repeatedly send some prophets, and then others. For there is no nation that has had more true and divinely inspired seers than the Jews. Hence the prophet also says, "He declares his words to Jacob, his statues and judgments to Israel. He has not dealt thus with any other nation, and they do not know his judgments." Hence it follows that there is no other religion in existence that is supported by firmer foundations and demonstrated by more certain testimonies than Christianity. Commentary on Hebrews 1:1.[3]

Hebrews Cannot Be the Sole Basis of Any Doctrine. Cardinal Cajetan: The attentive reader may note that Jerome was not

[1]See Herman Selderhuis, ed., *Psalms 1–72*, RCS (Downers Grove, IL: IVP Academic, 2015).

[2]Dietrich, *Summaria vber die Epistel an die Ebreer*, Ooo ii r-v [663-64].

[3]Bullinger, *In Pauli ad Hebraeos Epistolam*, 8r-v [35-36]; citing Ps 147:19-20.

entirely certain regarding the author of this epistle. And since we have taken Jerome as our guide so that we may not go astray in identifying the canonical books (for we hold as canonical those he passed down as canonical, and those he separated from the canonical we hold as outside the canon); therefore, as the author of this epistle is in doubt, the epistle itself is also rendered in doubt, because if it is not by Paul, it is not clear that it is canonical. For this reason, if anything in matters of faith should happen to be in doubt, it cannot be determined on the basis of the authority of this epistle alone. COMMENTS ON HEBREWS 1:1.[4]

NOW GOD HAS SPOKEN IN ONE WAY. EDWARD DERING: Out of this verse first let us note and consider well, touching this doctrine that we are taught by Christ: the certainty of it, which is first in the Author, who is God himself, even the same God of our fathers, who so many times and ways, spoke ever by his prophets. Even he in assured truth also spoke by his Son, thus giving the authority of the word of Christ to God the Father, that it might be confessed true, and to take away all vain quarrelling of contentious humanity, who under pretense of the name of God would easily have disputed against our Savior Christ, and said: We know God is true, and he spoke to Moses, he spoke to the prophets; but this man speaks of himself, and we will not hear him. . . . Now, as our Savior Christ is our certain teacher of undoubted truth; so how far this truth is taught by him appears also in the words "at many times and in many ways, God spoke to our fathers by the prophets." Of all these we must set apart our Savior Christ, that God spoke by him, not many times, revealing his will by measure, now some, then more; but once he sent him, filled with all treasure of wisdom and understanding. And before God spoke many ways, either by angels, or by the cloud, or between the Cherubim . . . or by visions, or by dreams. But now he has spoken one way, even by Christ made our brother, with the voice of a man, in the midst of the congregation, plain and evident in all people's hearing, and all variety shall cease forevermore. Likewise before, God spoke by many prophets; now he does not so, but has sent his Son alone in the stead of all, that all his people hear him. Likewise those times they are old and past; but the times of Christ's teaching does not pass away but is forever. 27 LECTURES OR READINGS ON THE EPISTLE TO THE HEBREWS 1:1.[5]

SCRIPTURE IS DIVINE SPEECH. NIELS HEMMINGSEN: Therefore, it is first worthy of note that he says God has always spoken to the church and establishes that God himself is the author of sacred Scripture, that he might lead us more by it into the admiration and veneration of Scripture, and that we should certainly establish that it is divine speech, which has been written, handed own, and commended to us by means of the prophets, evangelists, and apostles. COMMENTARY ON THE APOSTOLIC EPISTLE TO THE HEBREWS 1:1.[6]

THE MIRACLE OF THE GOSPEL. EDWARD DERING: Now let us see the difference here spoken of, between our Savior Christ and all other prophets. What we may learn of them was revealed at diverse times, but that which Christ teaches is revealed but once. . . . The second difference is that the doctrine of Christ is taught after one sort. For though first were miracles and now none, first apostles, now none, these were but means to confirm the preaching, the word alone was the power of salvation, which is the same as it was then. And because it is but one, therefore it is perfect. For if any had before been absolute in himself, no others should have come after him. But it did not please God to give the glory to all those manner of revelations, but he reserved it to the preaching of the gospel, which he has made his own power to save all that believe, and he has given it so great grace that it works more mightily than all miracles, and pierces deeper into the human heart than any

[4]Cajetan, *In Epistolam ad Hebraeos Commentarii*, 156v-157r.

[5]Dering, *Lectures on Hebrews*, A4r-A4v*.

[6]Hemmingsen, *Commentarius in epistolam apostolicam ad Hebraeos*, 831 [855].

other means of persuasion, yes, even if one should rise from the dead to speak to us. 27 Lectures or Readings on the Epistle to the Hebrews 1:1.[7]

The Minister as God's Mouthpiece. William Jones: Therefore God has wonderfully honored us in the time of the gospel, above those in the time of the law. If a king should speak to us by one of his privy council, it is much: but if he speaks to us by his son and heir apparent to the crown, it is a greater dignity. The prophets were of God's council, as the preachers are in this day. The Jews were honored that God would speak to them and by them. But to us he has spoken by his only Son, therefore our honor is the greater. We are set in a high chair of dignity above them. . . . In this the Old and New Testament are equal; God is the author of them both. God spoke by the prophets then, and he speaks now by his ministers. . . . When we teach, God teaches; when we exhort, God exhorts; when we reprove sin, God reproves sin. It makes no matter who the person is who speaks, so long as he is the lawful minister of Christ; God speaks by the man when the man speaks God's word. . . . Oh that this were imprinted in the hearts of all that come to church! The preacher is a man as you are, but God speaks by him, and if you despise him, you despise God who speaks in him. A Commentary upon the Epistles of St. Paul, Heb 1:1.[8]

The Necessity of Divine Revelation. Lucas Osiander: For the keenness of human genius is able to discover neither the essence of God nor his will, unless God reveals it through his Word. Epistle to the Hebrews 1:1.[9]

Paul Followed the Way of Humility When He Wrote Hebrews. Gasparo Contarini: Certain people doubt whether this epistle is of Paul, having supported themselves with several arguments, among which is this, that in the beginning no mention is made of his name, as is his custom in all of his other epistles. We follow the authority of the church, which recognizes this epistle and reads [it] as an epistle of Paul. . . . Paul was an apostle to the gentiles, not to the circumcision, as is clear in the epistle to the Galatians. For this reason when writing to the Hebrews, to whom he was not sent, he has followed the way of humility. He says that God has spoken in the prophets, rather than through the prophets, and in the Son rather than through the Son, while nevertheless both are proper forms of speech, so that he was showing that God had thus spoken through the prophets, so that he was nevertheless in them. Wherefore it was necessary to regard their words as words of God rather than as words of the prophets, for thus speaks a king through his own orator, so that he might be in him himself. Scholia in the Epistles of the Divine Paul, the Epistle to the Hebrews 1:1-2.[10]

God Speaks Through Christ in the Heart. Dirk Philips: God does not now, at the present time, speak with us through an external voice from heaven, nor through visions and dreams as happened in the Old Testament, but he speaks with us through his Son, Jesus Christ, and Christ speaks with us through his Word. Whenever Christ now grants and impresses his living Word in someone's heart and thereby calls, that person is without any doubt called of the Lord through his Word. But whereby one shall know that anyone is thus called of God through the living Word and through the Spirit of Christ, we have said above, namely, that he speaks God's Word truly, bears fruit, and seeks the honor of Christ and the salvation of souls with wholehearted zeal. The Enchiridion.[11]

1:2 *Christ Is God's Ultimate Revelation*

Christ's Divine and Human Sonship. Johannes Bugenhagen: With regard to his divinity, Christ is the Son of God by nature; with

[7]Dering, *27 Lectures on Hebrews*, A5v, A6r-v*.
[8]Jones, *A Commentary upon the Epistles of St Paul*, 54*.
[9]Osiander, *Epistola ad Hebraeos*, 4.
[10]Contarini, *Opera*, 515; citing Gal 1:16.
[11]CRR 6:217-18*; citing Jn 6:63; Is 55:10-11; Jn 3:34.

regard to his humanity, he is the Son of God by adoption. This adoption was completed in his resurrection, just as it will be completed for us, as it says in Romans 8. Consequently, in the same chapter he is called the firstborn of many brothers, and in Colossians 1 and Revelation 1 he is called the firstborn from the dead. For this reason also, when Paul talks about Christ's resurrection in Acts 13, he cites the Scripture, "Today I have begotten you." This is something he never said of the angels, although we are accustomed to interpret it as referring to Christ's divinity, concerning which see Dr. Martin's postil.† Certainly the phrase that follows, "whom he appointed the heir of all things," pertains to Christ's humanity, just as later on he makes evident from the Psalm, "You have put all things under his feet." The final chapter of Matthew says the same thing: "All authority has been given to me." Hence it follows that all who are in Christ are heirs of all things through him, heirs of God and fellow heirs with Christ. For in the next chapter he makes us, rather than the angels, brothers of Christ, while at the end this chapter they are called our servants. This is an incalculable honor for us, if only we believe, for thus "our faith glorifies Christ."‡

On the other hand, who does not see that when it says, "through whom also he created the world," it pertains to his divinity? This is what you find in Genesis 1, John 1, Colossians 1, and elsewhere. Hence, on the other hand, it follows that no one can be lost who is under the reign of Christ, for he as God almighty has established all things. From the aforesaid it is not necessary to suppose two sons, for in Christ God and man are one person, but still two natures. Thus in Scripture it is needful to discern carefully what pertains to Christ's divinity and what to his humanity. COMMENTARY ON THE PAULINE EPISTLES HEB 1:2.[12]

CHRIST IS THE FULLEST EXPRESSION OF GOD'S WILL. MATTHIAS FLACIUS ILLYRICUS: In the Word through the Son is proclaimed most fully the revelation that is the will of God concerning the salvation through Christ that is to be obtained. For the apostle wants to say to all here that it was produced in this ultimate disclosure to us, which was made most fully through the Son from the bosom of the Father according to his counsel for our salvation. This is why we constantly reject all revelations that differ from this Word, whether from the papists, and those spiritual ones, or from Muhammad, and last, from whatever other fanatical deeds. GLOSS ON HEBREWS 1:2.[13]

THE PERSONHOOD OF THE WORD. PHILIPP MELANCHTHON: That in John's account "Word" indicates a person is shown first from the account itself, for later John says of Christ, "He was in the world, and the world was made through him." For it is obvious that the world was not made through the human nature of Christ; therefore, it is necessary that in the Christ who was born of a virgin there also be and remain a second nature, also Creator with the Father. Similar passages elsewhere also show the same thing, that in Christ there are two natures. . . . These passages clearly testify that the divine nature, co-Creator with the Father, is and remains in Christ. Therefore "Word" does not mean a design or thought outside Christ, nor does it mean a passing word, but rather the nature, Creator with the Father, that remains in Christ. Therefore, the Word is a person. LOCI PRAECIPUI THEOLOGICI.[14]

AN ECONOMIC APPOINTMENT. THE ENGLISH ANNOTATIONS: [The Son] is ordained Possessor, Lord, and Dispenser, which is not to be understood of that essential dominion or lordship which he had in common with the Father and the Holy Ghost, being God equal with them; but of that economical, dispensed, or delegated dominion or

[12]Bugenhagen, *Annotationes in epistolas Pauli recognitae* (1525) [311-12] 139r-v; citing Rom 8:23, 29; Col 1:18; Rev 1:5; Acts 13:33; Rom 1:4; Ps 2:7; Mt 28:18; Heb 2:5-9; Gen 1:3; Jn 1:3; Col 1:16. †See Luther, *Weihnachtspostille* 1522, WA 10.1.1:166.1-167.19. ‡Hilary of Poitiers, *Tractatus Super Psalmos* 136.8 (PL 9:366).

[13]Flacius, *Glossa Compendaria*, 1109.

[14]Melanchthon, *Loci Praecipui Theologici*, 23*; citing Jn 1:10; Col 1:16-17; Heb 1:2.

lordship, whereunto he was foreordained before the foundations of the world, being appointed the mediator of the new testament, and wherein he was actually constituted and placed, after that he had finished the work of humanity's redemption. Annotations on Hebrews 1:2.[15]

Christ Is the Father's Heir Not as His Successor, but as His Equal. Heinrich Bullinger: Now, the little word "heir" plays on human categories, not that the human attains to the divine, or that these things can properly refer to it; but he adjusts his discourse to be like human categories, so that in some degree we may understand the indescribable mysteries of God. For those who succeed by inheritance to the riches of their father are absolute lords of all of it. Though their father had been their lord, now they are equal to the father in terms of possession and lordship. So also the Son of God is called the heir of all the Father possesses, which is to say, the Father has placed all things under the Son. These two statements—"Christ is the heir of all things," and "All things have been placed under the Son"—have the same force. For in the gospel he also says, "Everything the Father has is mine." But among human beings "the son's augmentation is the parent's termination";[†] with them there is an earlier and a later. But between God the Father and the Son you find nothing of the kind. For although the persons are distinct, nevertheless they share one sovereignty, equal kingship, equal power and glory. With the Father and the Son there is no earlier, no later, no greater, no lesser; for just as the Father gives life to whom he wishes, so also the Son gives life to whom he wishes. Therefore, the Father does not withdraw, nor does the Son advance more, as one does with a human inheritance, but there is full equality on both sides. Commentary on Hebrews 1:2.[16]

The Title "Son of God" Reveals the Two Natures of Christ. Cardinal Cajetan: "By the Son." He has not spoken to us through the prophets, but through the Son, who for so many years preached and did miracles in Galilee and Judea. The last days are appropriately described as reserved for the Son, inasmuch they were all prophets because of him. "Whom he appointed the heir of all things." The name of "Son" is really a special name of the Messiah according to the divine nature, but among the Hebrews, who did not penetrate the mystery of the Trinity, the name "Son of God" was recognized as a special title of the Messiah. Hence the high priests of the Jews accused Christ of making himself the Son of God. Therefore Paul first introduces the name "Son of God," which they recognized was a special title of the Messiah, by saying of God, "He has spoken to us in his Son." Then he adds the qualifications of this Son. The first of these is, "Whom he appointed the heir of all things." This properly refers to the Son in regard to his humanity, although it is because of his divine sonship. For being appointed an heir is an attribute of a man, but being appointed the heir of all things is an attribute of a man, but not of a mere man, but of a man who is the Son of God. For truly because of this it is fitting for him to be the Son of God, because this very man has been appointed the heir of all things. Therefore, the natural right of his sonship by this subsistence procures for the man the right to inherit all things without any exception whatsoever. So Paul is subtly showing that there are two natures in the Son of God. And, so that he may explain more clearly the divine nature of the Son, he adds, "Through whom he also made the worlds." It is necessary that he through whom God made the worlds—not just some of them and not others, but all without any exception whatsoever—is God himself. For if he were a creature, the world itself would not have been made through him. Therefore, from the fact that God made the worlds through the Son, it is clear that the Son is above the worlds, and therefore eternal. Comments on Hebrews 1:2.[17]

[15]Downame, ed., *Annotations*, MMMiv*; citing Ps 89:27; Mt 28:18; Lk 24:26; Jn 5:27; Acts 2:36; Rom 14:9; Eph 1:20; Phil 2:9,10; Rev 4:11.

[16]Bullinger, *In Pauli ad Hebraeos Epistolam*, 9r-v [37-38]; citing Ps 8:6; Jn 16:15; 5:21. [†]It has not been possible to locate the origin of this quotation.

[17]Cajetan, *In Epistolam ad Hebraeos Commentarii*, 157r; citing Jn 19:6-7.

Universal Heirs Through Union with Christ. John Calvin: And when he speaks of "these last days" he intimates that there is no longer any reason to expect any new revelation; for it was not a word in part that Christ brought, but the final conclusion. . . . But the word "heir" is ascribed to Christ as manifested in the flesh; for being made man, he put on our nature, and as such received this heirship, and that for this purpose, that he might restore to us what we had lost in Adam. For God had at the beginning constituted man, as his Son, the heir of all good things; but through sin the first man became alienated from God, and deprived himself and his posterity of all good things, as well as of the favor of God. We hence only then begin to enjoy by right the good things of God, when Christ, the universal heir, admits us into a union with himself; for he is an heir that he may endow us with his riches. But the apostle now adorns him with this title, that we may know that without him we are destitute of all good things. Commentaries on the Epistle of Paul the Apostle to the Hebrews 1:2.[18]

Christ First as Heir and Then as Agent of Creation. Martin Luther: He describes the same Christ as the Son of Man and the Son of God. For the words "He was appointed the Heir of all things" are properly applicable to him because of his humanity, but the words "the worlds were made through him" apply to him because of him divinity. . . . One should also note that he mentions the humanity of Christ before he mentions his divinity, in order that in this way he may establish the well-known rule that one learns to know God in faith. For the humanity is that ladder of ours, mentioned in Gen. 28:12, by which we ascend to the knowledge of God. . . . Therefore he who wants to ascend advantageously to the love and knowledge of God should abandon the human metaphysical rules concerning knowledge of the divinity and apply himself first to the humanity of Christ. For it is exceedingly godless temerity that, where God has humiliated himself in order to become recognizable, humans seek for themselves another way by following the counsels of their own natural capacity. Lectures on Hebrews 1:2.[19]

The Author Launches Straight into His Case. Johannes Oecolampadius: What a sublime beginning! For by what other opening could he have more aroused and inflamed the hearts of his hearers to listen than by thundering forth right out of the gate that God, who spoke to the fathers, now also speaks to us, and this by a more exalted means, not through ministers and angels, but through the Son himself, and in the last time, so that no one could expect any other teacher besides this one? If in the prophets "Thus says the Lord" is not an improper beginning, neither does this author begin absurdly with, "God has spoken to us through the Son." Thus he straightaway argues his case effectively, so that Christ may be heard as the Son of God. But he reasons by this kind of syllogism: "Since God spoke formerly through various kinds of speech and in various ways, and now in a far superior way he speaks through the Son, consequently, one ought to pay attention more earnestly." Here you have the first part of the syllogism, and then after a long transitional passage regarding the worthiness of the Son, you find at the beginning of the second chapter the second part of the syllogism, that is, the inference, so that you may see how beautifully it hangs together. Christ similarly said, in a parable in Matthew 21, that the father of the family, the Lord of vineyard, sent servants to the farmers, who beat some of them, killed others, stoned others, but last he sent to them his own son, saying, "They will respect my son." For this is the final refuge and remedy: for the Son to be sent. Explanations of Hebrews 1:1-2.[20]

Muhammad and the Pope Confuse Law and Gospel. Lucas Osiander: Therefore after the revelation of the gospel another doctrine is not to be expected. For God used the works of Moses

[18]CTS 40:33, 34*.

[19]LW 29:110, 111 (WA 57:98.12-14, 99.1-10).

[20]Oecolampadius, *In Epistolam ad Hebraeos Explanationes*, 5r-v; citing Mt 21:33-41.

in promulgating the law; truly Christ was the preacher of the gospel. But Muhammad, who brought a third kind of doctrine (a certain kind of confusion having been mutilated from the law and the gospel), was . . . a prophet to whom the Roman Antichrist is not much dissimilar, who corrupts the teaching of the law and the gospel, and fills the church with human opinions and traditions. . . . And whatsoever the Father gave to the Son in time must be referred to the humanity of Christ. Therefore we have the richest and most powerful brother, Jesus Christ, the Lord of heaven and earth; therefore in all adversities let us place our total faith in him. Epistle to the Hebrews 1:2.[21]

God's Inaudible Word Speaks in Various Ways. Johannes Oecolampadius: It is God's nature to speak invisibly and without the sound of a voice, within the minds of the saints, to inspire them with his will and right understanding, or to reveal things to come, as with the holy prophets. Thus the psalmist, "Let me hear what God may say in me" (Psalm 85), and Job 4, "To me a hidden word was spoken, and as if in secret my ear caught the words of a whisper." It is one way with the eternal word of God, and another with temporal speech, which should not be attributed to God in a simplistic fashion. For when God said, "Let there be light," and there was light (Genesis 1), he commanded by his own authority and will that it should come forth and begin in time, because he possessed in himself from eternity his own purpose and idea, and when it was to begin. Thus the psalmist should be interpreted, "He spoke, and they came to be; he commanded, and they were created" (Psalm 33). But the present discourse is not about these things. But there are many kinds and many ways of God's speaking. Sometimes he spoke through subjected creatures, as to Moses, when he appeared in a bush and in fire, and to Abram and Jacob, to whom he was manifested in angels. Second, he spoke in dreams, as to Jacob and the prophet Zechariah. Finally, he spoke without an appearance, neither through a visible creature nor through a dream, but by merely by invisibly touching the hearts of the saints with a secret inspiration, so that they were presented as speaking. Thence the prophets, when inspired, would suddenly say, "Thus says the Lord." So he spoke and appeared in manifold ways. Hosea 12, "I multiplied visions, and by the hands of the prophets I imitated." And in Jeremiah, "Rising early at dawn, I sent their prophets" (Jeremiah 7). Likewise he sends the laborers into the vineyard, some at the first hour, others at the third, others at the sixth, and others at the ninth (Matthew 20). There were indeed also various visions in nearly every one of the prophets. And when these occurred of old, those who heard the prophets had to integrate them. But now in the last days, when there is no expectation of any other teacher, it is far more important to listen to the Son of God. The days of the coming and preaching of Christ are called the last days and the twilight. First John 2: "Children, it is the last hour." And Galatians 4, "When the fullness of time had come." Isaiah 2: "It will come to pass in the last days that the mountain of the house of the Lord will be established as the highest of the mountains and will be elevated above the hills, and all the nations shall flow to it." Explanations of Hebrews 1:1-2.[22]

1:3-4 *The Son Upholds the Universe*

We Own All Things Through Christ the Heir. Edward Dering: By "heir of all things," meaning, how in the person of a mediator [God] has restored all things, as in the person of the Son, he was the wisdom of God to make all things. And therefore he is called the heir, because he restored

[21]Osiander, *Epistola ad Hebraeos*, 5.

[22]Oecolampadius, *In Epistolam ad Hebraeos Explanationes*, 5v-6r; citing Ps 85:8 (Oecolampadius's editors refer to this as Psalm 84[:9], in keeping with Latin chapter divisions. Oecolampadius quotes the version based on the Septuagint, which includes the words "in me"); Job 4:12; Gen 1:3; Ps 33:9 (in keeping with Latin chapter divisions, Oecolampadius's editors refer to this as Psalm 32[:9]); Ex 3:2; Gen 18; 19:1; 32:24-30; Hos 12:4; Gen 28:10-17; 31:9-13; Zech 1:8; 4:1; Hos 12:10; Jer 7:25; Mt 20:1-5; 1 Jn 2:18; Gal 4:4; Is 2:2.

not the world, but by redeeming it and purchasing for himself, according as God the Father had given it to be a recompense for his work, in which respect it is said that God appointed him "heir of all things." ... First, that he is the brightness of his Father's glory, which title is absolutely given him as essential to the Son of God, not only before us, but even before his Father; that as all the properties of the Godhead have their being in the person of the Father, so the brightness and beauty of them is in the person of the Son, and so this name was proper to him before the world was made, noting, that eternally he was of the Father. ... "After making purification for sins," put in here as a parenthesis, because it shows the way Christ purchased that excellent dignity to sit down "at the right hand of the Majesty on high." ... In that he says, "After making purification for sins," expressly he warrants his Godhead, for what creature could have done so excellent a work? ... Now a little further we will examine the words and apply them more particularly to our instruction. In that it is said first, God made him "heir of all things." ... We must learn that of ourselves we have nothing, but being engrafted into him, we are owners of all things. In my own right, I am naked and void of all, I have not meat to feed my hungry body, nor drink to comfort my faint and thirsty spirit. ... For the earth is the Lord Jesus Christ's and all that is in it. I may have from man my warrant here in earth that my house is mine, and my land is mine, and he is a thief and a robber who takes it from me. But all the men in the world cannot give me my possession before the living God, but only his Son Christ, who is "heir" of all. I am a thief and a robber, if before God I claim any other right to it.
27 Lectures or Readings on the Epistle to the Hebrews 1: 2-3.[23]

In Christ We Perceive the Father. Johannes Bugenhagen: "The radiance of the glory of God" marks the Son as a different person from the Father within the godhead. While God is glory, the Son is the radiance of his glory, or rather the glory of the glory of the Father. He is like the Father in every way, not of a different substance, but the very same substance and nature, as indicated by the addition, "the exact image"—not in appearance, but in his substance. Therefore Christ is the omnipotence of the Father, the wisdom of the Father, the righteousness of the Father, and so on. Of course, he was begotten from the Father, but nevertheless he is divine by nature, like the Father and with the Father truly one God, as indicated by what follows: "and he governs"—or better, "and he upholds"—"all things by the word of his power"—that is, by himself. For he is the Word, by whom all things exist and are preserved and directed, just as he says, "My Father is working until now, and I also am working." What good would it be for all things to be established by him, unless they were also preserved and governed by him? In Christ, therefore, all divinity is present, with all the glory of God himself. In Christ we perceive the Father, because he is the radiance, glory, and image of the substance of the Father. But we perceive him through his word, provided that his Spirit has taught us; for in the face of Christ we see the glory of God, not in the face of Moses, as it says in the letter to the Corinthians. Commentary on the Pauline Epistles, Heb 1:3.[24]

A Truly Profitable Philosophy. John Calvin: It ought also to be observed that frivolous speculations are not here taught, but an important doctrine of faith. We ought therefore to apply these high titles given to Christ for our own benefit, for they bear a relation to us. When, therefore, you hear that the Son is the brightness of the Father's glory, think thus within yourself, that the glory of the Father is invisible until it shines forth in Christ, and that he is called the impress of his substance, because the majesty of the Father is hidden until it shows itself impressed as it were on his image. They who overlook this connection and carry their

[23]Dering, *Lectures on Hebrews*, A8v, B1r-v, B2r-v*; citing Ps 24:1; 1 Cor 10:26.

[24]Bugenhagen, *Annotationes in epistolas Pauli recognitae* (1525) 139v-140r [312-13]; citing Jn 5:17; 2 Cor 3:7–4:6.

philosophy higher weary themselves to no purpose, for they do not understand the design of the apostle. For it was not his object to show what likeness the Father bears to the Son; but, as I have said, his purpose was really to build up our faith, so that we may learn that God is made known to us in no other way than in Christ: for as to the essence of God, so immense is the brightness that it dazzles our eyes, except it shines on us in Christ. It hence follows that we are blind as to the light of God until in Christ it beams on us. It is indeed a profitable philosophy to learn Christ by real understanding of faith and experience. Commentaries on the Epistle of Paul the Apostle to the Hebrews 1:3.[25]

Christ Both Preserves and Governs the World by Virtue of His Divinity. Cardinal Cajetan: "And he upholds all things by the word of his strength (or power)." If it is read as "upholding" or "bearing," it signifies his preservation of all things by the metaphor of supporting all things. But if (as some believe) it is read as "doing," it signifies his administration of all things. Either meaning fits with the subsequent words, namely, "by the word of his power." For he both preserves all things by the same word of his power by which "he spoke and they were created," and likewise he governs all things by the word of his power, by which he commands and does whatever he pleases. And this qualification also refers to the divine nature of the Son. For both preserving and governing the universe belong to him by reason of his divine nature. Because of this it also says, "by his own power," not another's, the same power belongs to the Son and to God. Comments on Hebrews 1:3.[26]

Christ Purged Our Sins Himself. William Jones: Not of his own, for he knew no sin: but ours, that are bred, born, and brought up in sin: of all our sins he left not one unpurged.

Not by ourselves, nor by angels. Here the sly and nice distinction of the Jesuits is taken away, which they invented of late to make us believe that by the doctrine of merits they derogate nothing from the glory of Christ. Indeed they say that we may make satisfaction for sin and merit heaven: yet it is not we that do it, but Christ by us: not our works simply in themselves, but as dyed in the blood of Christ. Our merits are Christ's merits, and therefore they may deserve heaven. Yes, but Christ has purged our sins by himself, not by ourselves: he has done it by his own blood immediately, not mediately by our works dyed in his blood. Therefore that is a mere delusion to mock the world withal. . . . If Christ had not purged us from sin, we would have fried in hell forever. A Commentary upon the Epistles of St. Paul, Heb 1:3.[27]

God's Tender, Motherly Upholding of All Things. Martin Luther: This participle, "upholding," has special emphasis and is a Hebrew idiom with which neither the Greek nor the Latin expression is sufficiently in agreement. For the apostle employs a Hebraism. What we call "to preserve" the Hebrews state more suitably with "to uphold," which expresses a certain tender and, so to speak, motherly care for things that he created and that should be cherished. Lectures on Hebrews 1:3.[28]

A Kenotic Pattern of Redemption. Johannes Oecolampadius: [This is added] because he said that the world was made through Christ the Son, so that we will not think of the Son as assisting instrumentally, but naturally, just as an artisan constructs and builds by means of his own innate wisdom. By the language of "the splendor of his glory and the exact imprint," he declares that the nature of the Son is coeternal with and inseparable from the Father. And we will find in this passage or conclusion the reason why

[25]CTS 40:35-36.

[26]Cajetan, *In Epistolam ad Hebraeos Commentarii*, 157v; citing Ps 148:5; 115:3 [113:11].

[27]Jones, *A Commentary upon the Epistles of St Paul*, 60-61*.

[28]LW 29:112 (WA 57:101.4-14). Luther goes on to reference Deut 32:11; Is 46:3-4; and Num 11:12.

Christ has been established as the heir of all things. And almost the very same things are affirmed here as in the letter to the Philippians (Philippians 2); for he says there, "When he was in the form of God," which he here expresses as, "When he was the splendor of his glory, the exact imprint of his (i.e. God's) substance, who upholds all things by the word of his power." And he says to the Philippians, "He did not count equality with God a thing to be grasped, but emptied himself by taking the form of a servant, being made in the likeness of men. And being found in the likeness as a man, he humbled himself by becoming obedient to the point of death, even death on a cross," which here he expresses as, "Since through him purification was made for our sins," which could not have happened to us except by that amazing humiliation and salvific death. Then he says there, "Therefore God has exalted him and has given to him the name that is above every name, so that at the name of Jesus every knee should bow." The same thing is said here with different words, "He sat down at the right hand of majesty in the highest." . . . Behold here is the manner of our redemption. For it was necessary for the Christ to suffer, and so to enter into his glory. Explanations of Hebrews 1:3.[29]

Divine Purification and Our Purification. Martin Luther: With this brief word he makes useless absolutely all the righteousness and deeds of penitence of human beings. But he praises the exceedingly great mercy of God, namely, that "he made purification for sins," not through us but through himself, not for the sins of others, but for our sins. Therefore we should despair of our penitence, of our purification from sins; for before we repent, our sins have already been forgiven. Indeed, first his very purification, on the contrary, also produces penitence in us, just as his righteousness produces our righteousness. Lectures on Hebrews 1:3.[30]

The Son Is the Permanent Reflection of the Father. Johannes Oecolampadius: *Charactēr*, that is, an exact portrait, or imprinted figure. In a mirror the image of a man does appear, but not the imprint, so that an imprint is more than an image that is found in wax or any other thing, for an imprint is a permanent image. But you should know that, where we read "of his substance," *hypostasis* appears in Greek, which they translate sometimes as "substance," but sometimes as "subsistence." But it possesses a certain distinction from "essence." But what he means to say here is, "Whatever glory is found in God, rather, even whatever is in the substance of God, this is totally and completely reflected in the Son." Thus we cannot detach from the Son anything that belongs by nature to the Father, so that you may come to acquaintance with the Father only through the Son. Explanations of Hebrews 1:3.[31]

Equal to the Father in Authority, but Still Human. Johannes Oecolampadius: To sit at the right hand of God is to be endowed with good things equally with God and to be the heir of all things, by which exaltation the human nature in Christ is marvelously ennobled, but not glorified with so much better gifts that it ceases to be human. For it does not follow, because God is everywhere and beyond every place, that it should also be affirmed regarding the body of Christ that it is either everywhere, or beyond every place. Nevertheless, the most glorious gifts must be attributed to it. Further, when he depicts him sitting, it displays peace and rest, and his authority as judge. And when he says, "at the right hand of the majesty of God," again he shows that the Son is equal to God the Father, and above the angels, just as he writes to the Ephesians: "He stationed him at his right hand in the heavenly places, above all rule and authority and power and dominion, and every name that is named, not only in this age. . . ." Here it is clear what "to station at the right hand" means, from the obedience of the angels. Explanations of Hebrews 1:3.[32]

---

[29]Oecolampadius, *In Epistolam ad Hebraeos Explanationes*, 8v-9v. Eph 1:4-7; Phil 2:6-10; Col 1:14-16; Lk 24:26.
[30]LW 29:112 (WA 57:101.16-22).
[31]Oecolampadius, *In Epistolam ad Hebraeos Explanationes*, 11v.
[32]Oecolampadius, *In Epistolam ad Hebraeos Explanationes*, 12v-13r; Eph 1:21.

We Must Look to the Son to Know the Father Rightly. Lucas Osiander: The Son of God is called the splendor of the glory of the Father, because the Son is "light from light, true God from true God." For truly just as the splendor from the body of the sun goes forth, so the Son of God is the splendor of the Father, to whom belong goodness and majesty and in whom the clemency and majesty of the Father are most clearly perceived. And for this reason the imprint of the Father's substance is called these very things. For the Son is the truest image of the Father: but he is not the vanishing, painted, or fictitious image but the substantial image, "of the same substance with the Father." And so since we have wanted to know the Father rightly, we are contemplating the Son (whose nature is described to us in sacred letters). And we shall see the immense goodness, wisdom, and power of the Father in the only-begotten Son as a living expression [of the Father]. And it is said with respect to the Word that he carries all things by his strength, that is, by the power of his Word, because Christ is not only the Creator of the universe, he truly also sustains and conserves all things. Epistle to the Hebrews 1:3.[33]

Christ's Natures Are Distinct, but Not Separated. Huldrych Zwingli: "After making purification through himself."† By contrast with the preceding verses, we judge that this should be referred to the human nature of Christ. For only the flesh of Christ, which was taken on by the Word and united to him by an indissoluble communion, died on the cross, was sacrificed for our sins as an acceptable offering, and made satisfaction for divine justice. He had taken it on for this very reason, so that he might be made a sweet-smelling sacrifice for the sins of the whole world. For the Godhead could not die and make atonement for sin in any other respect besides the flesh of the Word. Therefore Christ is true God, and at the same time true man; here Paul says that he performed true purification in himself, that is, through his flesh. By these statements we do not separate the natures of Christ, but we show the distinct quality of each nature in Christ. For even though the natures in Christ cannot be separated without blasphemy, still it is necessary to distinguish the distinct quality and operation of each nature. I wish to set out this antidote here at the start, so that in what follows no one may fabricate accusations against me when I attribute to either nature its properties, or make the critique that I have a wrong view of Christ as true God and man.

"He sat down at the right hand." That is, after he had made atonement for the sins of the world through his death, he was raised up to heaven and the ether and now sits "at the right hand of majesty," that is, the peaceful and glorious throne of blessings, from which he will not come again except to judge the world on the final day of judgment. But in the meantime he is with us by his divine power and influence, by which (as we said above) he rules and preserves all things. Therefore we should not dream or imagine that there is anything substantial or fleshly about his presence in the supper of believers. Exposition of Hebrews 1:3.[34]

Against a "Fanatical" Interpretation of Christ's Session. Martin Luther: In the first place, we take up the article that Christ sits at the right hand of God, which the fanatics† maintain makes it impossible for Christ's body also to be in the supper. Now if we ask how they interpret God's "right hand" where Christ sits, I suppose they will dream up for us, as one does for the children, an imaginary heaven in which a golden throne stands, and Christ sits beside the Father in a cowl and golden crown, the way artists paint it. For if they did not have such childish, fleshly ideas of the right hand of God, they surely would not allow the idea of Christ's bodily presence in the supper to vex them so or castigate

[33]Osiander, *Epistola ad Hebraeos*, 6. The references to the Nicene Creed are obvious throughout.

[34]Zwingli, *In Epistolam Beati Pauli ad Hebraeos Expositio*, 565; citing Eph 5:2; Mt 28:20. †The reading "through himself" reflects a textual variant in the Greek text of this verse that was accepted by Erasmus but is rejected by most modern editions.

themselves so with the saying of Augustine (whom in other respects they do not believe at all, or anyone else) "Christ must be bodily in one place, but his truth is everywhere."†

From these childish ideas it must follow further that they also bind God himself to one place in heaven, on the same golden throne, since apart from Christ there is no God, and where Christ is there is the Godhead in all its fullness. . . . We ask them further: Where is the Scripture that limits the right hand of God in this fashion to one place? . . . Why do you not ponder and learn first whether it is or is not Scripture that God's right hand is a specific place, because the Scripture speaks quite abundantly of the right hand of God? But you erect such a great, a risky fanaticism on your empty dream and then boast that you produce much Scripture. . . . Thus, since it pleases you that Christ is in heaven and not in the supper, you let St. Augustine's saying persuade you so easily to affirm that God's right hand is a place in heaven. . . . The Scriptures teach us, however, that the right hand of God is not a specific place in which a body must or may be, such as on a golden throne, but is the almighty power of God, which at one and the same time can be nowhere and yet must be everywhere. It cannot be at one place, I say. For if it were at some specific place, it would have to be there in a circumscribed and determinate manner, as everything that is at one place must be at that place determinately and measurably, so that it cannot meanwhile be at any one place. But the power of God cannot be so determined and measured, for it is uncircumscribed and immeasurable, beyond and above all that is or may be. THAT THESE WORDS OF CHRIST, "THIS IS MY BODY," ETC., STILL STAND FIRM AGAINST THE FANATICS, HEB 1:3.[35]

[35]Luther, Martin. *Das diese wort Christi (Das ist mein leib etc.) noch fest stehen widder der Schwarmgeister/That These Words of Christ, "This Is My Body," etc., Still Stand Firm Against the Fanatics* (1527), LW 37:55-57 (WA 23:131.7-20, 131.28-29, 133.5-9. 133.11-14, 133.19-33). †Luther has Reformed Protestants in mind here, especially Oecolampadius. LW note: "Gospel of John, Tractate 30, 1. PNF 1, 7, 186." 56 n. 893.

THE SESSION OF CHRIST. JOHN CALVIN: "The right hand" is by a similitude applied to God, though he is not confined to any place, and has not a right side nor left. The session of Christ then means nothing else but the kingdom given to him by the Father, and that authority which Paul mentions, when he says that in his name every knee should bow (Phil. 2. 10). Hence to sit at the right hand of the Father is nothing else than to govern in the place of the Father, as deputies of princes are wont to do to whom a full power over all things is granted. COMMENTARIES ON THE EPISTLE OF PAUL THE APOSTLE TO THE HEBREWS 1:3.[36]

CALVIN LIMITS CHRIST'S SESSION. MATTHIAS FLACIUS ILLYRICUS: The present case concerning the presence and absence of Christ can hence be explained: for it is clearly indicated here that his ascension in that highest place is not a certain local transmigration into the crystal heaven from outside the total frame of the world, but is particularly from that so great emptiness in which he had been cast down on account of our sin, or rather had voluntarily humbled himself, a translation into the highest dignity, glory, and majesty, which certainly confirms the following verse. Truly, Calvin conveniently limits the session at the right hand, to which I applied this passage, on account of those removing, and, as it were, tearing off Christ, the head of the church, from his own body, and enclosing it in what place in utopia outside the whole world I do not know; for actually he had to possess the glorious majesty of his Father within the frame of this world, or he would not have been able to exercise it. This matter is especially spoken about abundantly afterward by the apostle himself in chapters 8 and 9, where he expounds in what manner Christ ascended into heaven. GLOSS ON HEBREWS 1:3.[37]

[36]CTS 40:39.

[37]Flacius, *Glossa Compendaria*, 1111.

CHRIST IS EQUAL TO THE FATHER, FOR HE SHARES IN HIS NAME. JOHANNES OECOLAMPADIUS: Here you learn that he is Lord of Hosts, a name by which God is called. The name of Christ is more splendid, because he is not only Lord of the angels but also equal with the Father, and is the Son, sitting with him at his right hand. And if he were not the Son, equal with the Father, he would by no means have the highest name, and the name that is above every name. For a king is allowed to place anyone in command over the entire host, but he still does not confer upon him his own honor, which is the highest. But the son of the king, at whose name the knee must bow no less than at the king's, is partaker of the highest name. Therefore the Arians are to be pitied, who along with the Jews call Christ the commander of angels and saints, rather than the Son of God and God. EXPLANATIONS OF HEBREWS 1:4.[38]

[38]Oecolampadius, *In Epistolam ad Hebraeos Explanationes*, 13r-v.

1:5-14 CHRIST IS HIGHER THAN THE ANGELS

5For to which of the angels did God ever say,

"You are my Son,
today I have begotten you"?

Or again,

"I will be to him a father,
and he shall be to me a son"?

6And again, when he brings the firstborn into the
world, he says,

"Let all God's angels worship him."

7Of the angels he says,

"He makes his angels winds,
and his ministers a flame of fire."

8But of the Son he says,

"Your throne, O God, is forever and ever,
the scepter of uprightness is the scepter of your kingdom.
9You have loved righteousness and hated wickedness;
therefore God, your God, has anointed you
with the oil of gladness beyond your companions."

10And,

"You, Lord, laid the foundation of the earth in the beginning,
and the heavens are the work of your hands;
11they will perish, but you remain;
they will all wear out like a garment,
12like a robe you will roll them up,
like a garment they will be changed.[a]
But you are the same,
and your years will have no end."

13And to which of the angels has he ever said,

"Sit at my right hand
until I make your enemies a footstool for your feet"?

14Are they not all ministering spirits sent out to
serve for the sake of those who are to inherit
salvation?

a Some manuscripts omit *like a garment*

Overview: On full display in this section is the common early modern Protestant hermeneutic of reading the Old Testament, especially the Psalms, through christological lenses. Specifically, the reformers interpret the psalms cited in this passage as declaring Christ's eternal generation, incarnation, and victorious exaltation at the right hand of God. Among the exegetical insights of note is the observation of Christ as the "Solomon" who would erect the spiritual temple, the church, in ultimate fulfillment of God's promise to David.

1:5 *The Son's Eternal Generation*

The Firstborn Son Calls Out to the Father. Veit Dietrich: The little word "today," because it is spoken by God, means an eternal day that has no beginning. His Son is also eternal and has no beginning, otherwise he could not be the exact image of the divine essence. Thus the words in Psalm 89 are also clear: "He," David (that is, Christ, who was promised to David), "will call out, 'You are my father, my God and lord who helps me,' and I will make him the firstborn son, etc." Summary of the Epistle to the Hebrews 1:5.[1]

The Eternal Generation of the Son Separates Him from All Creatures. Cardinal Cajetan: "For to which of the angels

[1]Dietrich, *Summaria vber die Epistel an die Ebreer*, Ooo ii v-Ooo ii v-iii r [664-65]; citing Ps 89:26-27.

did he ever say." He is discussing the clause that he set forth last, "As he has inherited a name better than theirs." And first he discusses it with regard to the name of "Son." "You are my Son, today I have begotten you." This decree is taken from Psalm 2, in which the prophet presents God speaking to the Messiah and saying two things. One of them is, "You are my Son," which God also said regarding others. For concerning the people of Israel he also said, "Israel is my firstborn son" (Exodus 4). But the whole established by these two statements ("You are my Son, today I have begotten you") is nontransferrable. For the timing and completeness of this begetting, which are indicated by "today" and "I have begotten," demonstrate the eternity of this begetting. For eternity is always today, nor does it have a yesterday or tomorrow. And, so that you may not go astray by supposing that a begetting that is always present is incomplete, he says in the past tense, "I have begotten," so that, by saying, "I have begotten," you may understand that the begetting is complete, and by saying, "Today," you may understand that it is so perfect that it is always a present begetting, so that he is always being begotten and has been begotten. Hence, to give the reason why "You are my Son," he says, "Today I have begotten you. Therefore you are my Son, because I, God, have begotten you on an eternal timescale." This cannot be transferred to any other created being, for no other created being has its extent measured by eternity. COMMENTS ON HEBREWS 1:5.[2]

CHRIST'S TWO BIRTHS. MARTIN LUTHER: One may understand the words "today I have begotten thee" to refer to both births of Christ. St. Augustine understands it as referring to the divine birth.[†] Therefore he explains that "today" means "in eternity." So does the first book of the Master of the *Sentences*.[‡] But it is not improper to understand it as referring to the human birth, because, in the first place, the divine birth is described nowhere else in Scripture as occurring in time or with the word "today." . . . Second, because the Hebrew idiom expresses a definite and, so to speak, a special time with the word "today," as their articles usually do among the Greeks. . . . Third, it agrees with Isaiah 8:2-3. LECTURES ON HEBREWS 1:5.[3]

CHRIST IS THE TRUE AND SPIRITUAL SOLOMON. JOHANNES OECOLAMPADIUS: This quotation is taken from 2 Samuel 7 and 1 Chronicles 28:6. But, again, the Judaizers are offended, as if the saying did not pertain to Christ, but rather to Solomon, because before this it clearly says, "Solomon your son will build for me my house and my courts; I have chosen him to be my son." But Scripture must be examined more thoroughly. Thence it should be understood that just as Christ is called "David" in Scripture, so he is also called "Solomon." In Jeremiah 30 we read that Christ is called David. There it says, "They will serve the Lord their God and David their king, whom I will raise up for them." It does not say, "I have raised up," but "I will raise up." Likewise in Hosea 3 and Ezekiel 34, "I will raise up a shepherd." So he is also called "Solomon" in the Song of Songs. Therefore Christ is also more accurately, truly, and perfectly the peacemaker, who has made peace with all things. Besides, just as a carnal Solomon was promised to David, who would construct a temporary temple, so a spiritual king Solomon, Christ, was promised to David, who has constructed a spiritual temple and house, which was to be a perpetual temple, like the reign of Christ. And David was indeed certain regarding the promises of God. But he was capable of making a mistake without risk regarding the person and the beginning, just as Eve regarding Cain and Abraham regarding Isaac are thought to have made mistakes in another way, while they clearly still believed that God is entirely truthful. But straightaway God revealed that the promises were not fulfilled in

[2]Cajetan, *In Epistolam ad Hebraeos Commentarii*, 157v-158r; citing Ps 2:7; Ex 4:22.

[3]LW 29:113 (WA 57:102.5-103.1). [†]LW note (113 n. 5): "Augustine, Ennarationes in Psalmos, II, 6, Corpus Christianorum, Series Latina, XXXVIII, 5." [‡]LW note (113 n. 6): "Peter Lombard, Sententiae, Book I, Dist. 2, ch. 6, Patrologia, Series Latina, CXCII, 528."

Solomon, or in Cain and Isaac. For perpetual peace was promised to Solomon, but in 1 Kings 12 we read that at the end of the reign of Solomon enemies were sent up against him and Israel rebelled. Likewise, Solomon's temple and his kingdom were desecrated by the Chaldeans, Greeks, and Romans, so that there was not left one stone on another that was not thrown down, as Christ testified in Matthew 24. But the church and kingdom of Christ remain forever. Thus in the times of Solomon, when he was transformed from the wisest man into an idolater, straightaway the believers recognized that they must await another, in whom the promise of God would be fulfilled, who would be greater than Solomon, as Christ says (Luke 11). Therefore, this saying, "He will be to me a Son," rightly and more correctly applies to Christ rather than to Solomon. Finally, since the Jews confess that Christ is to proceed from the seed of David, let them produce today anyone from David's clan—but they cannot. For even when Domitian was emperor, that line had utterly died out or been forgotten.[†] Explanations of Hebrews 1:5.[4]

Solomon and Christ. Martin Luther: We do not deny that word for word this text (2 Sam 7:14) can be understood as referring both to Solomon and to Christ. Nevertheless, as one can gather from the text itself, then from the prophets, who repeat the same text so often and proclaim it with the greatest diligence, especially in the Psalms, it can be abundantly shown that it has been stated as well as understood concerning Christ alone. For he says to David (2 Sam 7:11-12): "Moreover, the Lord declares to you that the Lord will make you a house. And when your days are fulfilled and you lie down with your fathers, I will raise up your son after you, who shall come forth from your body, and I will establish his kingdom." This is proclaimed in Psalm 132:11: "One of the sons of your body I will set on your throne." It is clear, however, that before the days of David were fulfilled, his son Solomon was raised up and went forth from his body, yes, was established in the kingdom. Therefore Christ is understood here—Christ, who is "the fruit of the womb" of David, that is, of the Virgin Mary, who was born from the seed of David. . . . Therefore is proper for us, along with David and the other prophets, to understand this promise as referring to Christ. Lectures on Hebrews 1:5.[5]

God's Prayer to David Speaks of Christ. Matthias Flacius Illyricus: Even though another testimony from the prayer of God to David seems to be speaking typologically of Solomon, it is nevertheless, to be sure, particularly an antitype that pertains to Christ himself, the one who finally most worthily established the Father's heavenly temple. For Scripture says many things concerning types, which assemble either more or also merely one antitype, or rather to prefigure the person of a thing. Wherefore in the same place it is added that God never removes his compassion from him.

The fifth argument is an indication that the title of the great name is suitable to Christ alone, and to absolutely no creature. This testimony is brought forth by Psalm 110, which speaks most certainly about Christ. Except that the Lord himself indeed interprets this sentence about his divinity. Gloss on Hebrews 1:5.[6]

For God, All Days Are Present. Huldrych Zwingli: "You are my Son, today I have begotten you." It is as if he were to say, "From these passages of Scripture those who worship in the clearer light of faith can easily infer and understand who Christ is and in what way he surpasses not only the prophets but also the angels." The statement "Today I have begotten" does not detract at all from

[4]Oecolampadius, *In Epistolam ad Hebraeos Explanationes*, 15v-16v; citing 2 Sam 7:14; Jer 30:9; Hos 3:5; Ezek 34:23-24; Col 1:20; 2 Sam 7:10-11; 1 Kings 11:14, 23, 26; Mt 24:2; Lk 11:31. [†]Perhaps this is a reference to Domitian's intended extermination of the Davidic dynasty recorded in Eusebius, *Ecclesiastical History* 3.19-20 (PG 20:251-55; NPNF2 1:148-149). But even if this purge actually was begun, it is clear in Eusebius's account that it was incomplete.

[5]LW 29:114 (WA 57:103.10-104.6).

[6]Flacius, *Glossa Compendaria*, 1112.

Christ's eternality. For since all things are present and visible to God, the highest and infinite Good, no time so befits and accords with him as the present. For this reason when he speaks of himself, he uses no other tense than the present, as is evident in Exodus 3, "He said, 'I am who I am.'" So also in this passage, the psalmist speaks in the present tense of Christ, who is eternal just like the Father. Exposition of Hebrews 1:5.[7]

1:6-7 *The Son Worshiped and Served by the Angels*

Christ as God Is Worthy of Worship. Veit Dietrich: The apostle inserts these words from Psalm 97: "Worship Him all you gods and angels." Now Scripture clearly says, "You should worship God the Lord and serve him only." If one should worship Christ, as this psalm testifies, then it certainly follows that he is God. Summary of the Epistle to the Hebrews 1:6.[8]

Christ Coeternal with the Father. Veit Dietrich: These words appear in Psalm 45: "God, your throne endures from eternity to eternity." That is also a strong witness that Christ is God, because nothing is eternal except God, as Psalm 107 also says, "Your years will not end." Summary of the Epistle to the Hebrews 1:6.[9]

1:8 *The Son Rules with God*

The Staff of the Word. Martin Luther: Therefore although others interpret this staff to mean inflexible power,[†] as it seems to be, actually, however, it is nothing else than the same gospel, namely, the gospel itself or the Word of God. For Christ rules the church with no other power than the Word, as it is written (Ps 33:6): "By the Word of the Lord the heavens were made." Lectures on Hebrews 1:8.[10]

Only Faith Sees God's Throne. Martin Luther: But everything that is said in this verse is so inconsistent with all understanding that those who want to grasp the truth of these things have need of an exceedingly robust faith. For if considered according to the outward appearance, nothing is more unlike a throne and the throne of God than the people of Christ, since it does not seem to be a kingdom but a place of exile, or to be living but to be constantly dying, or to be in glory but to be in disgrace, or to dwell in wealth but to dwell in extreme poverty, as everyone who wants to share in this kingdom is compelled to experience in himself. The ornaments of Christians are poverty, tribulations, afflictions. This is the way God's throne, which is man, should be adorned. Lectures on Hebrews 1:8.[11]

The Scepter Is the Preached Word of God. Edward Dering: The scepter is the word of his mouth, that is, the preaching of the gospel, not decrees, nor decretals, nor human traditions, nor unwritten verities; by none of all these have we received the spirit of God, but only by hearing faith preached: it therefore alone is the scepter. . . . Now, why is this called the scepter of righteousness? It is because (says the prophet [i.e., the psalmist]) it kills the ungodly; the apostle immediately adds the same exposition, "You have loved righteousness and hated wickedness": therefore it is called a scepter of righteousness, because it makes the faithful righteous and destroys the sinners from the face of the earth. In this sense Saint Peter calls it "the seed of regeneration," because by it we are begotten anew into the image of God, which is in righteousness. So that here we know whether we are of the kingdom of Christ, even by the scepter by which we are ruled. If the knowledge of the gospel of Christ has reformed us into a

[7]Zwingli, *In Epistolam Beati Pauli ad Hebraeos Expositio*, 566; citing Ex 3:14.

[8]Dietrich, *Summaria vber die Epistel an die Ebreer*, O oo iii r [665]; citing Ps 97:7; Deut 6:14; Lk 4:8.

[9]Dietrich, *Summaria vber die Epistel an die Ebreer*, O oo iii r [665]; citing Ps 45:8; 107:1.

[10]LW 29:118 (WA 57:108.5-109.2). [†]LW note (118 n. 19): "A reference to the *Glossa interlinearis* on Heb 1:8."

[11]LW 29:117-118 (WA 57:107.15-108.3).

new image, to be holy as our Savior Christ is holy, that by his spirit the world is crucified to us, and we to the world, then we have our enfranchisement in this kingdom: if not, though we dwell in the midst of the sanctuary, yet we would be strangers to the law that came out of Mount Zion. And though we were baptized with all the water in the sea, or as the prophet says,† though we wash ourselves with lye and take much soap, yet our iniquities are marked before the Lord, except we feel the forgiveness of our sins in the righteousness and holiness of this kingdom of Christ. . . . Are not God's children his saints? Are they not brought to him with the scepter of righteousness? Does he not keep them with the seal of his Holy Spirit? If I see no good works in my hands, if I never know that the preaching of the gospel killed concupiscence in me, and made me hunger and thirst after righteousness, if I do not feel the Spirit of God to sanctify more and more my heart and all my affections, how can I say I am the child of GOD?" 27 Lectures or Readings on the Epistle to the Hebrews 1:8-9.[12]

1:9-12 *The Son Anointed*

The Father Anointed the Son with the Holy Spirit. Heinrich Bullinger: Now, "Oil" metaphorically signifies the powers of the Holy Spirit, as Isaiah 61 makes clear. But the fruits of the Holy Spirit are righteousness, courage, vigor, readiness for action, perseverance, truth, gladness, and exultation. But, as the Baptist says, the Father has given "the Spirit without measure" to the Son. Even beyond the kings and prophets who partook of the Spirit and foreshadowed Christ, God anointed the Son, for which reason Daniel calls him the Holy of the Holy Ones. You will observe next that there is a repetition to declare the distinction between the persons and unity of the Godhead. For we heard just now that this our anointed king is called God; but at the start of the quotation we saw that the one who anoints God is also said to be God. So the Father is God, and the Son is God, and these two are one, namely, the one living, true, and eternal God. Commentary on Hebrews 1:9.[13]

Christ Alone Loves Righteousness. Martin Luther: This text aptly follows the expression "a staff of guidance," for the staff itself brings about this love of righteousness and this hatred of lawlessness. Therefore this verse fits no one but Christ, because no one but Christ alone loves righteousness; all others love money, pleasure, or honor, or, if they despise these, at least love glory. Or if they are the best of all, they love themselves more than they love righteousness. . . . Therefore since love of himself remains, it is utterly impossible for humankind to love, speak, or do righteousness, even though they can feign all this. The result is that the virtues of all the philosophers, yes, of all people, be they jurists or theologians, are virtues in outward appearance but vices in reality.

Yet one must know that this righteousness means the righteousness of God, not the righteousness of humanity. For the righteousness of humanity always remains incomplete, since it renders to everyone what is theirs,† namely, in money, possessions, honors, etc., but does not give to others their own things and at least covets the things of others for itself. Then, what is worse, it never renders glory to God. The righteousness of God, however, renders and gives itself and everything it has to God and to people. Therefore it is the nature of Christ alone to love righteousness and to hate lawlessness, but it is the nature of humanity to love lawlessness and to hate righteousness. It is the nature of a Christian person, however, to begin to hate lawlessness and to love righteousness. And they do not love it except through Christ, that is, because Christ, who loves righteousness, completes our incipient love with his love. Lectures on Hebrews 1:9.[14]

[12]Dering, 27 *Lectures on Hebrews*, D4r, D4v-D5r*; citing 1 Pet 1:23; Jer. 2:22. †Here "prophet" refers to Jeremiah.

[13]Bullinger, *In Pauli ad Hebraeos Epistolam*, 18v-19r [56-57]; citing Is 61:1; Jn 3:34; Dan 9:24.

[14]LW 29:119-120 (WA 57:110.1-27). † LW note (119 n. 20): "One definition of *justitia* in the first section of Book I of the *Institutes* of Justinian."

God Has Anointed Christ by Exalting Him as the Victor. Johannes Oecolampadius: For because you are so splendid, O Christ, so energetic, so truthful, so gentle, and full of grace, it is no wonder that God has anointed you, that is, has judged you to be of higher worthiness by exalting you and giving you the name that is above ever name. Certainly, we say that with Mary we anoint Christ by believing in him, because our faith is the most fragrant oil in the sight of God. But God anoints him by elevating him to the highest majesty, when he delights him with the oil of gladness as the victor. For the psalmist depicts before our eyes a happy and sweet-smelling king, for it is the oil of gladness. Matthew 6:† "When you fast, anoint your face with oil," for he is blessed and glad, and we are also refreshed and revived with the aroma of his happiness—the pleasing aroma of the name of Christ, which in the Song of Songs is compared to outpoured perfume. And as in this very psalm, his garments drip with myrrh and cassia to embrace us. For as we recognize that we have been redeemed by him as the Son of God, we are so immersed in his goodness and the fragrance of his mercy that with amazing sweetness of heart we follow the one who is delightful far beyond all creatures and yield ourselves to him with complete trust. For none of the angels or the saints, who are Christ's companions and partners, possesses such a name, so as to merit like Christ such a seat and such an anointing. From this also comes the name of "Christ." Others say that Christ was anointed by the Holy Spirit, who gives joy to the heart, or the grace of the Spirit, but our explanation is simpler. Explanations of Hebrews 1:9.[15]

God the Son Anointed by God the Father and God the Holy Spirit. Lucas Osiander: Even the mystery of the Trinity must be noted in this verse. God the Father anoints the Son: God the Son is anointed by the Father. And he is anointed with the oil of gladness, that is, God the Holy Spirit, conferring his own gifts abundantly and without measure on the Son of Man: who by another reason is the eternal God. But in the first place it must be observed that the apostle to the Hebrews here adduces the prophecy concerning Christ so that he might commend the divinity of Christ, and might remove him (according to his divine nature) from the number of creatures. Epistle to the Hebrews 1:9.[16]

The Messiah Is Uniquely Related to God the Father. Cardinal Cajetan: "Therefore God, your God, has anointed you with the oil of gladness beyond your participants." There can be two meanings here. The one is, "To the end that you may love righteousness and hate wickedness, God has anointed you." Thus this statement would be about the anointing of grace that he had from the very beginning of his conception. The other meaning is, "Because you have loved righteousness and have hated wickedness, God has anointed you." In this case, this statement would be about the anointing of glory that Christ has earned by loving righteousness and hating wickedness. He makes reference to the custom of the Hebrews in which kings were anointed, from which the name "Messiah" ("Christ" in Greek), is derived. He "was anointed with gladness"—either of grace or of glory—"beyond your participants"—beyond all created beings that he made partakers of you. For not only humans but also the angels are participants in the Messiah. Note also in this connection that in the very same context the Messiah is called "God" and "anointed by God," thus indicating the absolutely unique mode in which God is the God of the Messiah, a man. For he is "his God" as a particular person of the Trinity,† which is not the way God is the God of anyone else. Comments on Hebrews 1:9.[17]

---

[15]Oecolampadius, *In Epistolam ad Hebraeos Explanationes*, 19r-v; citing Mt 6:17; Song 1:3; Ps 45:8. †Oecolampadius mistakenly cites this as Matthew 5.

[16]Osiander, *Epistola ad Hebraeos*, 9.

[17]Cajetan, *In Epistolam ad Hebraeos Commentarii*, 158r. †Latin *personaliter*, a technical term indicating internal relationships among the persons of the Trinity, as opposed to *essentialiter*, which denotes the entire Godhead in relation to his creation. Richard A. Muller, *Dictionary of Latin and Greek Theological Terms* (Grand Rapids: Baker, 1985), 106.

1:13-14 *The Son Seated at God's Right Hand*

THE RIGHT HAND OF GOD. MARTIN LUTHER: Many interpret the phrase "at the right hand of God" to mean "preferable blessings."† Although we do not disapprove of this, it seems that with these words dominion that is universal and completely on a par with God's dominion is expressed, as the apostle says in 1 Corinthians 15:27, which is taken from Psalm 8:6: "He has put all things in subjection under his feet." Certainly, "he is excepted who put all things under him." Therefore the meaning seems to be this: "Sit at my right hand," that is, "Reign over as many as I myself reign over and as widely as I myself reign, except that thou should be subject to me alone." Then a beautiful admonition to mildness is commended when He says: *Till I make*, not "till thou make," in order that we may learn to leave vengeance to God; for even Christ, Lord of all, left it to God, as Deuteronomy 32:35 states: "Vengeance is mine." Therefore, it belongs to no one else. LECTURES ON HEBREWS 1:13.[18]

THE GLORIOUS SESSION OF THE SON. VEIT DIETRICH: The most glorious witness comes from Psalm 110, where God says, "Sit at my right hand." The Lord Christ himself employs this witness against the Jews in Matthew 22. To sit at God's right hand means to have the same authority as God, that is, to rule and govern over all things. SUMMARY OF THE EPISTLE TO THE HEBREWS 1:13.[19]

A CONFESSION REGARDING ANGELS. EDWARD DERING: Now follows in the last verse this definition of angels, whereof we spoke before, in which we learn, and so confess, that they are ministering spirits sent out for our safety and defense. Whosoever hereafter will dispute with us about angels, with one word we will answer them and cut off all curiosity: this we know, and it is all we can know, and whosoever knows more, they know nothing but the vanity of their own mind. Angels are spirits that serve the Lord for his church's safety. 27 LECTURES OR READINGS ON THE EPISTLE TO THE HEBREWS 1:13-14.[20]

A SIMPLE DEFINITION OF ANGELS. HEINRICH BULLINGER: But see, O Christian reader, with how much simplicity, lucidity, and purity the Scripture discusses the angels, surely to far more benefit than the schools of the Sophists have done thus far. While they have invented many doubtful doctrines concerning the angels, they have written innumerable vain and superstitious ones. But what need is there of so much talk? Angels are created beings, spiritual in their substance, ministers, and, as the prophet says, flames of fire. Or, as the Greeks have defined it, *angelos estin zōon logikon, hymnologikon athanaton*. Reuchlin, a man of incomparable learning, has translated this definition as, "An angel is a being that is living, rational, hymn-singing, and immortal." COMMENTARY ON HEBREWS 1:14.[21]

ANGELS PRAISE GOD AND SERVE HIS PEOPLE. DIRK PHILIPS: The congregation of God was first begun in heaven with the angels, who were created by God as spirits and flaming fire, that they should stand before the throne of God, praising and serving God. They should also be ministers and fellow servants of believers. For although they are such noble and high creatures of God, nevertheless they are at the same time serving spirits, just as the apostle said, sent out from God to serve those who are the ones who shall inherit the salvation of God. For they guard the children of God. They encamp around the camp of the God-fearing. They go before Israel. They led Lot out of Sodom. In sum, they minister to the saints and the chosen people of God. They keep them in all their ways and see evermore the face of the Father in heaven. And thus the congregation of God was first begun with the angels in heaven. THE ENCHIRIDION.[22]

---

[18]LW 29:120-21 (WA 57:111.10-19). †LW note (120 n. 21): "Lyra, *Postilla super Psalterium, ad* Ps. 110:1."

[19]Dietrich, *Summaria vber die Epistel an die Ebreer*, O oo iii r-v [665-66]; citing Ps 110:1; Mt 22:44.

[20]Dering, *Lectures on Hebrews*, E8r*.

[21]Bullinger, *In Pauli ad Hebraeos Epistolam*, 20r [59].

[22]CRR 6:351-52*; citing Ps 104:4; Heb 1:7; Rev 22:9; Ps 34:7; Ex 14:19; Gen 19:16; Ps 20:6; Mt 18:10.

JESUS GREATER THAN THE ANGELS. VEIT DIETRICH: The sum of this chapter is that Jesus Christ is more than all angels. Because the gospel is revealed through Jesus Christ everyone should accept such a sermon through faith. SUMMARY OF THE EPISTLE TO THE HEBREWS.[23]

[23]Dietrich, *Summaria vber die Epistel an die Ebreer*, O oo iii v [666].

2:1-4 Warning Against Drifting Away from Salvation

Therefore we must pay much closer attention to what we have heard, lest we drift away from it. ²For since the message declared by angels proved to be reliable, and every transgression or disobedience received a just retribution, ³how shall we escape if we neglect such a great salvation? It was declared at first by the Lord, and it was attested to us by those who heard, ⁴while God also bore witness by signs and wonders and various miracles and by gifts of the Holy Spirit distributed according to his will.

Overview: This section of the epistle presented certain doctrinal challenges to the reformers, not least of which was its teaching that salvation could apparently be lost. The reformers wrestled with this teaching here and continued to do so as they encountered it in other parts of Hebrews. In their comments on this passage, the reformers also came to various conclusions about Pauline authorship (in light of 2:3), and uniformly asserted that the miracles of the apostolic age were confined to that age, having served the purpose of an initial confirmation of the truth of the gospel. Along the way the reformers also emphasized the centrality of the ministry of the word in a truly evangelical church along with the indispensible role of the preacher in this ministry.

God Will Punish the Despisers of His Word. Erasmus Sarcerius: Is it certain that God will punish the despisers of the divine Word? Yes. If God punished those who disobeyed the word of the law, which was given through angels, how much less will he let those go unpunished who despise the word of the gospel and who do not obey it. Summaries and Brief Content, Heb 2:1-4.[1]

2:1 *Heed Sound Doctrine*

We Must Guard Against the Gospel Leaking Away. Cardinal Cajetan: "Therefore we must pay much closer attention to what we have heard." "Therefore" refers to the greatness of the Son beyond the angels, which was proclaimed by the entire previous chapter. For the Christ's superiority to the angels was proclaimed, from which he deduces that we should pay attention to the teaching of the gospel far more than we should pay attention to the teaching of the Old Testament. This gospel teaching comes from the Lord himself, but the other was given through angels. He argues for this by adding the danger: "Lest we flow through." That is, lest we leak out entirely, like cracked vessels that leak because they finally "flow through" and retain no water. He employs this metaphor so that we may guard what we have heard, lest it flow through after we have heard it and we be left empty. Comments on Hebrews 2:1.[2]

We Must Not Be Leaky Tubes. Edward Dering: After this, the apostle adds his reason to persuade us to this special carefulness above all other people, to hearken to the voice of Christ; and that is, of the peril that ensues, "lest" (he says) "we run out" [i.e., "lest we drift away"]. The apostle uses a metaphor, taken of old tubes, which run out at the joints, and can hold no liquor. In such a phrase of speech one says of himself: "I am full of crevasses or little holes, and I flow out on this side and on that," meaning thereby that every vain thing he heard, he would blab it out. So we, if we take into us the sweet wine of the word of Christ, as into old

[1] Sarcerius, *Summarien vnd kurtzer Jnhalt*, 4:HH1v [SB 927].

[2] Cajetan, *In Epistolam ad Hebraeos Commentarii*, 158v.

bottles and broken vessels, that it run out again, we become then altogether unprofitable, all goodness falls away, and we are as water poured upon the ground. This metaphor the women of Tekoa used with David when describing an utter desolation of the people. 27 Lectures or Readings on the Epistle to the Hebrews 2:1.[3]

We Must Suck Sweet Doctrines from the Word. William Jones: It is not enough to hear sermons every week, which is good and commendable, but we must give diligent attention to the things that we hear, especially now in the time of the gospel when God speaks by his own Son. . . . We must not only hear the preacher but also attend to the things that he says. An infant does not only take the breast into his mouth, but he sucks at it, and that with greediness. So we must not only lie at the breast of the Word, but we must suck sweet doctrines and heavenly instructions from it. . . . It is said of the people that they hung on Christ, watching the words that came from his mouth, ready to receive them before they came: so with all care and diligence we must hang on the preacher, mark his words, and be ready to receive them into our ears and hearts, even before they are delivered, so eager should we be of the Word. A Commentary upon the Epistles of St. Paul, Heb 2:1.[4]

Salvation from the Swift Stream of Damnation. Lucas Osiander: And the similitude has been adduced of a human being who has fallen into a swift stream and is snatched away by the strength of the stream [and who] soon is about to perish. . . . Helpers go before to the bank in the lower part of the stream, and they stretch out helping hands to that one, but he himself, as he flows by, does not give heed to them, and so perishes in the stream. Thus the Lord by the ministry of the gospel longs to help sinners who are in danger with respect to their eternal salvation. But many neglect the gracious offer and by their own guilt flow past the gate of salvation, where they would have been able to be extracted and kept if they had wanted. Therefore let us embrace with great gratitude the salvation that has been offered, lest we also, whether through errors or pleasures and the cares of this sunken world, flow past and fall away from the heavenly inheritance. Epistle to the Hebrews 2:1.[5]

The Meaning of *Pararuomen*. William Jones: Lest we run by or run over: lest we be like sieves and vessels full of holes, out of which water runs out immediately, as soon as it is poured in, as Terrence said, "I am full of cracks, and also I flow here and there,"[†] lest we run by, as water does by a way, and stays not. So lest we pass by the celestial doctrine propounded to us, and regard it not, we must dwell upon the things which we hear by serious meditation, and not flow like water from thing to another.

We must let the Word slip at no time though we have never such weighty business: One thing is necessary. This one necessary thing is to be preferred before all others: Never let a sermon slip from you without some profit. A Commentary upon the Epistles of St. Paul, Heb 2:1.[6]

2:2-4 *Do Not Neglect the Word of Salvation*

The Gospel of Christ Is Salvation—Whoever Neglects It Is Lost. Johannes Oecolampadius: You may understand these words as referring to the law, which the Lord gave through Moses. For the law was put in place through angels by the hand of a mediator, as we read in the letter to the Galatians 3[†] and Acts 7. But it is evident that all who transgress the law were punished; how much more will those who neglect the gospel of Christ be punished? And observe how he contrasts the gospel to the law. For the law

[3]Dering, *Lectures on Hebrews*, F5 v-F6 r*. Mt 9:17, Mk 2:2; 2 Sam 14:14.
[4]Jones, *A Commentary upon the Epistles of St Paul*, 78*.

[5]Osiander, *Epistola ad Hebraeos*, 11-12.
[6]Jones, *A Commentary upon the Epistle of St. Paul*, 79.* [†]Terrence, *Eunuch*, 1.105.

was given through angels, the gospel through the Son. The law is called a "message," but the gospel is called "salvation," because the gospel is the word of salvation. Howbeit, in Acts the law is also called the "living word," just as in Deuteronomy 5, "Do what the Lord commands you, that you may live," and Leviticus 18, "Keep my laws and judgments; a person who does them will live eternally." There, and in similar passages, it speaks of the righteousness of faith, for without faith it is not fulfilled. Again, the gospel of Christ is the power of God for salvation to all who believe, so that here it is rightly called "salvation," and when someone neglects the Word of God, that person neglects salvation.

Others understand "the message of angels" to refer to all the words of the angels, which are not made void, but always achieve their purpose. Consequently they are not to be despised, as the angel promised Sarah a son in Genesis 18 and predicted that Sodom would perish in chapter 19, and so it came about. How much more, then is the message of Christ truthful! And whoever does not believe Christ will not escape punishment, according to this statement from Deuteronomy 18: "Whoever refuses to hear his words that he will have spoken in my name, I myself will step forth as the avenger." But note the emphasis of the words, for he says, "If we neglect"—*amelēsantes*—that is, if we should have transgressed in the smallest way, we will be punished heavily, just like those who did not believe the words of the angels. And what offense is smaller than to be neglectful? Who then will absolve himself? Therefore, there is need for great zeal among Christians. Anyone who has not fulfilled the law has an escape with Christ the mediator; but how will anyone restore himself who neglects Christ and the word of faith? Whom else will he invoke as mediator? Explanations of Hebrews 2:2-3.[7]

Christ as the Veiled Lawgiver. John Calvin: Here also another question arises: Was not the law also given by Christ? If so, the argument of the apostle seems not to be well grounded. To this I reply that in this comparison regard is had to a veiled revelation on one side, and to that which is manifest on the other. Now, as Christ in bringing the law showed himself but obscurely or darkly, and as it were under coverings, it is nothing strange that the law should be said to have been brought by angels without any mention being made of his name; for in that transaction he never appeared openly; but in the promulgation of the gospel his glory was so conspicuous that he may justly be deemed its author. Commentaries on the Epistle of Paul the Apostle to the Hebrews 2:2.[8]

Paul Has Written in a Spirit of Humility. Gasparo Contarini: From this place certain ones suspect that this epistle is not from Paul but of someone who came after him. Truly I have thought that Paul, because of his humility of spirit, mingled himself with others, as if he were one of the Hebrews to whom he was writing. For he so strives to avoid being seen as arrogant. Scholia in the Epistles of the Divine Paul, the Epistle to the Hebrews 2:3.[9]

Proof That Paul Is Not the Author. John Calvin: Moreover, this passage indicates that this epistle was not written by Paul; for he did not usually speak so humbly of himself as to confess that he was one of the apostles' disciples, nor did he thus speak from ambition, but because wicked men under a pretense of this kind attempted to detract from the authority of his doctrine. It then appears evident that it was not Paul who wrote that he had the gospel by hearing and not by revelation. Commentaries on the Epistle of Paul the Apostle to the Hebrews 2:3.[10]

Paul's Description of Himself Matches the Order of 1 Corinthians 15. Heinrich Bullinger: No favor should be shown to those

[7]Oecolampadius, *In Epistolam ad Hebraeos Explanationes*, 23r-24r; citing Gal 3:19; Acts 7:53; Rom 1:16; Acts 7:38; Deut 5:33; Lev 18:5; Is 55:11; Gen 18:9-15; 19:13; Deut 18:19. †Oecolampadius incorrectly cites this as Galatians 2.

[8]CTS 40:52*.

[9]Contarini, *Opera*, 516.

[10]CTS 40:54.

who conclude that the author of this letter himself testifies that he had learned the gospel from the apostles, whereas the apostle Paul denies this in Galatians. From this it would follow that this letter was not written by any apostle, let alone by Paul, but by one of the associates of the apostles. But we desire to know where the author of this letter gives this testimony? They respond, "He does so in 2:3, which says, 'It began to be declared at first by the Lord himself, and by those who heard him it was confirmed to us.' You hear," they say, "'from those who heard.'" But the wretches do not see that the phrase "from those," on which they rely so stupidly, is not the mark of succession from another, but rather of chronology. Thus the meaning is, "In the beginning, the business of the gospel was preached by the Lord himself, then by those apostles who had kept company with him, but finally and after them the exercise of the gospel was conferred upon me," so that, I maintain, this observes the same order that is observed in 1 Corinthians 15:5-8, where we read that the Lord appeared first to Peter, then to the twelve apostles, next after them to more than five hundred brothers, "but last of all," says Paul, "as to one untimely born, he appeared also to me." Commentary on Hebrews 2:3.[11]

Paul's Authorship Is Not Disproved. Johannes Oecolampadius: From this passage some have adopted the conjecture that this epistle was not by Paul, because Paul everywhere says that he received the gospel from Christ. But here he says that it was confirmed to him by those who heard. But note the word "confirmation," and that Paul does not speak of himself alone, but also of others who believed later. For earlier Stephen and Peter and others had become renowned for miracles. We cannot deny that Ananias laid his hands on Paul, saying, "Brother Saul, the Lord Jesus has sent me so that you may regain your sight and be filled with the Holy Spirit." Theophylact also dissolves this objection in this way: "Why elsewhere does he say that he did not receive from men? Because there it was essential and necessary, as he was insisting, that he maintain that he was not a disciple of men, but his preaching was jeopardized on account of those who were denying that Paul had heard the Lord. But in this letter there was no need for such boasting."† Hence, these conjectures prove nothing. Explanations of Hebrews 2:3-4.[12]

The Saving Proclamation of Christ. Huldrych Zwingli: "If we neglect such a great salvation." He appropriately adds the word "salvation," for it contains the emphasis that the preaching of Christ does not promise us only the earth and earthly things but also salvation, that is, the annihilation of death, the absolution of sin, release from the tyranny of the devil, and eternal life. Now he recounts the evidences concerning those by whom the true preaching of Christ was imparted, saying, "which was declared first by the Lord himself." This is the first evidence that produces faith. It demonstrates that the word of Christ and the preaching of him is true, and it is adduced from the person of Christ. For he declares that it was proclaimed first by our Lord Christ Jesus himself, who was not only the preacher and herald of eternal salvation but also its author. "Attested to us by those. . . ." That is, by the apostles, who were present from the beginning and saw and heard, as it is written. And thus it is manifest that the second evidence which produces faith in the words and preaching of Christ is derived from the persons of the apostles. "While God bore witness." The third is drawn from God himself. For he teaches that God also bore witness that the preaching of Christ is true, and that he confirmed it with signs, miracles, and portents, just as the Holy Spirit apportioned to each person. For there are varieties of activities, but it is the same God who empowers them all in everyone. What is written at the end of the final chapter of Mark

[11]Bullinger, *In Pauli ad Hebraeos Epistolam*, 4v-5r [28-29].

[12]Oecolampadius, *In Epistolam ad Hebraeos Explanationes*, 24v-25r; citing Gal 1:1, 11-12; Acts 9:17. †Theophylact, *Expositio in Epistolam ad Hebraeos* (PG 125:205-6).

contributes to this point. So in a few words in this passage Paul discloses the use and goal of signs, namely, to bear witness to the energy and power of God. Exposition of Hebrews 2:3-4.[13]

The Authority of the Gospel and of Signs. Heinrich Bullinger: All these testimonies are added to the gospel, lest anyone find it lacking in trustworthiness, or majesty, or authority. For if one ought to have confidence in any religion that was started by an instructed founder or disseminated by great and praiseworthy teachers or confirmed by amazing portents, surely we should embrace the teaching of Christianity first of all. For it does not have as its founder an angel, a philosopher, a prophet, or a man who is great in some other way, but the Son of God himself. As teachers, it has no commonplace, inconsistent, contentious, or fickle Sophists, but divinely inspired prophets and apostles filled with the Spirit of God, who proved what they taught not only by their blameless lives but also by their blood. Not only that, but to their heavenly teaching they added such signs and portents (as God worked through them) as no other religion in the world has possessed or seen. Consequently, it will turn out disastrously for us if by our unbelief we neglect both a salvation and a teaching that are so very holy, unique, certain, established, and so very undeniable.

Furthermore, note in this statement by the apostle that the signs are added to the teaching, and not the teaching accommodated to the signs. For signs in themselves prove nothing, especially if they are contrary to Scripture. For thus the Lord says in Deuteronomy 13: "If a prophet arises and predicts a sign or a wonder, and what he has said comes about, but he says to you, 'Come, and let us follow other gods,' you shall not listen to the prophet, for the Lord your God is testing you." You may find more arguments of this kind in Augustine's *Against the Letter of Petilian the Donatist,* [book 2,] chapter 16.[†] Commentary on Hebrews 2:4.[14]

Miracles Confirmed the Gospel and Then Ceased. Niels Hemmingsen: He posits the distributions of the Holy Spirit by which the Holy Spirit not only attested the gospel on the day of Pentecost but also oftentimes in the apostolic church by the prayers of the apostles and the imposition of hands on people. These miracles ought to be signs of the truth of God for us, the use of which endures perpetually in the church, whose only legitimate and true use is the attesting of the heavenly doctrine.

And although today miracles of this kind do not occur, nevertheless it is necessary to look back perpetually to those miracles of old that did occur, and which now ought to cease, having confirmed the gospel of Christ through the world. Commentary on the Apostolic Epistle to the Hebrews 2:4.[15]

These Miracles Marked the Ministry of Paul and Barnabas. Cardinal Cajetan: "While God bore witness by signs and wonders and various marvels (that is, miracles) and endowments of the Holy Spirit according to his will." The author of this letter indicates four kinds of evidences that the apostles employed. The first is "signs," which seems to refer to public miracles of healing. Then comes "wonders," or greater miracles such as raising the dead and similar things. The third is "various powers" for casting out demons and in regard to inanimate objects, such as fire or water or other things like that. And, finally, there are "endowments of the Holy Spirit" in the form of the gift of tongues, the gift of prophecy, etc. Now, when it says "according to his will," it is attached to "God bore witness." If you read the letters of Paul, you will see that he often says regarding himself that through him God produced signs and wonders and various powers and so on. From this it follows that Paul was numbered among those whom the author of this letter had in mind, who confirmed the truth of

[13]Zwingli, *In Epistolam Pauli ad Hebraeos,* 566-567; citing Jn 15:27; 1 Jn 1:1; 1 Cor 12:6, 11.

[14]Bullinger, *In Pauli ad Hebraeos Epistolam,* 24r-v [67-68]; citing Deut 13:1-3. †PL 43:270.

[15]Hemmingsen, *Commentarius in epistolam apostolicam ad Hebraeos,* 840 [864].

the gospel to the author of this letter. Hence it is also clear that the author of this letter was not Barnabas, but one of those who followed later. COMMENTS ON HEBREWS 2:4.[16]

NO GAPING AFTER MIRACLES. WILLIAM JONES: The gospel at the beginning was adorned with many miracles.

1. Because it seemed strange to the world, a new doctrine.
2. Because it seemed repugnant to the law of Moses instituted by God.
3. Because it could not be proved and confirmed by natural reasons.

But now since the famous miracles of Christ's resurrection, ascension into heaven, of the sending of the Holy Spirit, of the spreading of the gospel over all the world, we must not still curiously gape after miracles: that is reproved, Matthew 12:39, John 4:48, and Luke 23:8. To the law and the testimony, Isaiah 8:20, the people must resort. A COMMENTARY UPON THE EPISTLES OF ST. PAUL, HEB 2:4.[17]

[16]Cajetan, *In Epistolam ad Hebraeos*, 158v; citing Rom 15:19; 2 Cor 12:12.

[17]Jones, *A Commentary upon the Epistles of St Paul*, 85*.

CLEAR DOCTRINE OBVIATES THE NEED FOR MIRACLES. EDWARD DERING: Signs were when doctrine was more obscure: now it is so clear, the signs are gone. . . . And Christ once showed loving signs, to make his people put their trust in him, but now he has spoken in our hearts: "Come ye blessed of my Father into everlasting life," a voice that goes deeper into the soul and spirit than the hearing of all the miracles, by which Israel was led into the land of Canaan. And we shall do injury to our Savior Christ if now we will ask that to these words he should add miracles. For if we bring faith to that which is spoken, it will fill our hearts with all fullness, and will sell the sight of all the miracles in the world, to buy but one grain of a constant faith in Christ, wherein whosoever shall stumble, let them accuse themselves if God give them over to their own blindness, that because they had no love to believe the truth, therefore they should be led with lies and deceitful things. Thus much I thought to speak of miracles, that we might be wise to know them as they be, and from henceforth forever put our only trust in the word of our Savior Christ, which only in the world is the power of God to save all that do believe." 27 LECTURES OR READINGS ON THE EPISTLE TO THE HEBREWS 2:4.[18]

[18]Dering, *Lectures on Hebrews*, G5r (G3r)*; citing Mt 25:34.

2:5-18 CHRIST HAD TO BE MADE LIKE HIS BROTHERS AND SISTERS

*5For it was not to angels that God subjected the world
to come, of which we are speaking. 6It has been
testified somewhere,*

> *"What is man, that you are mindful of him,*
> *or the son of man, that you care for him?*
> *7You made him for a little while lower than the angels;*
> *you have crowned him with glory and honor,[a]*
> *8putting everything in subjection under his feet."*

*Now in putting everything in subjection to him, he
left nothing outside his control. At present, we do not
yet see everything in subjection to him. 9But we see
him who for a little while was made lower than the
angels, namely Jesus, crowned with glory and honor
because of the suffering of death, so that by the grace
of God he might taste death for everyone.*

*10For it was fitting that he, for whom and by whom
all things exist, in bringing many sons to glory, should
make the founder of their salvation perfect through
suffering. 11For he who sanctifies and those who are
sanctified all have one source.[b] That is why he is not
ashamed to call them brothers,[c] 12saying,*

> *"I will tell of your name to my brothers;*
> *in the midst of the congregation I will sing your praise."*

13And again,

> *"I will put my trust in him."*

And again,

> *"Behold, I and the children God has given me."*

*14Since therefore the children share in flesh and blood,
he himself likewise partook of the same things, that
through death he might destroy the one who has the
power of death, that is, the devil, 15and deliver all those
who through fear of death were subject to lifelong
slavery. 16For surely it is not angels that he helps, but he
helps the offspring of Abraham. 17Therefore he had to
be made like his brothers in every respect, so that he
might become a merciful and faithful high priest in the
service of God, to make propitiation for the sins of the
people. 18For because he himself has suffered when
tempted, he is able to help those who are being tempted.*

a Some manuscripts insert *and set him over the works of your hands* **b** Greek *all are of one* **c** Or *brothers and sisters*. In New Testament usage, depending on the context, the plural Greek word *adelphoi* (translated "brothers") may refer either to *brothers* or to *brothers and sisters*; also verse 12

OVERVIEW: In this passage the reformers make much of the hidden nature of Christ's glory, seeing in this hiddenness a summons to faith. They wrestle with Hebrews 2:5-8, seeking to determine whether the reference in the Old Testament quotations is to a human being or to Christ or to both. The reformers thus try to establish the proper relationship between historical and christological exegesis of the Old Testament. They also discuss in what sense Christ was made lower than the angels (Heb 2:9), in some cases moving from considerations of Christology to pastoral concerns, finding in Christ's incarnation and humiliation consolation for the suffering Christian. The reformers make much of the fellowship of suffering that exists between Christ and Christians in this passage, again seeking to encourage steadfastness in the midst of tribulations. Finally, they reflect at length on the nature and extent of Christ's suffering.

2:5-9 *Christ Humiliated and Exalted*

THE CHURCH IS THE WORLD TO COME. THE ENGLISH ANNOTATIONS: The apostle, following the tradition of the Septuagint, calls the church under the gospel, especially after Christ's resurrection and ascension, when he had entered his eternal kingdom and priesthood, the world to come: first, in relation to the church before and under the law, second, because of the restoration of all things by Christ begun already and shall be finished hereafter at the general day of resurrection, which is called the time of restitution of all things. Annotations on Hebrews 2:5.[1]

Christ's Office. Erasmus Sarcerius: Does one now see that Christ is such a lord? No. And this is because of the cross, in which the elevation of Christ is hidden until it will at last be revealed according to the form and manner as Paul describes in 1 Corinthians 15. . . . Christ's office is to make Adam's children holy; the office of Adam's children is to allow Christ to make them holy. Summaries and Brief Content, Heb 2:5-18.[2]

The Kingdom of Christ Is Spiritual. Johannes Bugenhagen: "The world that is to come" refers to the kingdom of Christ, which was predicted to come about, a kingdom far worthier than all the kingdoms of the world, just as Isaiah calls Christ "the Father of the Age to Come."† And although the kingdom of Christ is spiritual, all created things are subject in the Spirit to Christ and to those who are in Christ, for all things serve us for our benefit, including sheep, oxen, fish—even death, sin and hell. But "we do not see everything in subjection" because the things which pertain to the spiritual kingdom of Christ cannot be seen by the flesh. These depend upon faith and hope. Watch; you will see it when the Father places all Christ's enemies under his feet. Commentary on the Pauline Epistles, Heb 2:5-8.[3]

The Psalms Foretell the Humility and Exaltation of Christ's Humanity. Huldrych Zwingli: "For it was not to the angels." This seems to be the second part of the chapter, in which he employs quotations of Scripture like a shield to fortify the preeminence of Christ, which surpasses the angels. He began to discuss this matter a little earlier in chapter 1; straightaway he adds in what respect he may be regarded as lower. We should understand what he discusses here especially with reference to his human nature.

"What is man that. . . ." Although these things were said about the shared humanity of all mortals, that is, about all humans, still the apostle appropriately applies it to the humanity of Christ. For indeed many psalms are applied to Christ through *anagogē*, as is especially the case here. But by *eratēman*† and the passionate vehemence of his discourse the Holy Spirit insists on the humiliation of Christ, while, on the other hand, he immediately and without delay magnifies him when he declares that he has been crowned with glory and honor and that all things are subjected beneath his feet. "He left nothing out of his control." Now, as we have said, he exalts Christ and shows that he is greater than the angels as he explains this psalm. It is as if he were to say, "If by the subjection of all things God left nothing out that he did not subjugate to Christ, it follows that the angels have also been subjected beneath his feet; and thus it is clear that he is superior to the angels." "We do not yet see." Someone might say, "How can it be that they say that that all things have been subjected to him, when many resist him, most notably the ungodly, who defame the word of Christ by the complete filthiness of their lives and their stubborn hearts?" "But we do see him who for a little while. . . ." He replies that the prediction of the prophet has been fulfilled partly, but that it will partly be fulfilled in the age to come. In addition, he shows how he was lower than the angels when it says, "Because of the suffering of death." For angels are not subject to death or pain. But he shows that he is superior to them when he explains the words of the prophet when he says, "Crowned with glory and honor." No

[1]Downame, ed., *Annotations*, MMM2r*; citing Is 9:6; 2 Cor 5:17; Acts 3:21; Eph 1:10.

[2]Sarcerius, *Summarien vnd kurtzer Jnhalt*, 4:HH2r.

[3]Bugenhagen, *Annotationes in epistolas Pauli recognitae* (1525) 141v [316]. †Is 9:6. This translation reflects the Latin *patrem futuri saeculi*. The usual English rendering of the original Hebrew is "everlasting Father."

one can fail to see that this has been fulfilled, for after the resurrection he departed from the dead into the heavenly places. To this pertains what he says in Ephesians 1, "And he seated him at his right hand in the heavenly places, far above all rule." Exposition of Hebrews 2:5-9.[4]

Humiliation and Exaltation of Christ Prophesied. The English Annotations: The words in the literal sense are to be understood, both in the misery and baseness, as also the prerogative and dignity of humankind in general, especially of the faithful, but in the mystical or prophetical sense, they are to be understood of the humiliation and exaltation of the man Christ Jesus, in whom they are most exactly and exquisitely fulfilled. Annotations on Hebrews 2:6.[5]

Christ's Dignity Is the Christian's Dignity. Edward Dering: In all these words we learn the exceeding honor unto which God has raised his Son Christ: to be crowned with glory and honor is to have the excellence of all dignity given unto him, as the words following in the apostle do plainly expound it, where he says, "In that he put all things in subjection under him, he left nothing not subject unto him." And in this, according to the prophet, we must see our own dignity also as we are Christ's. For this honor is not the natural person's, as all the miseries of our life can testify; but it is him who sees himself to be Christ's who can say as Saint Paul says, "I live not now, but Christ lives in me." Over such a one the providence of God watches, the angels pitch their tents about him, and he sees great security in all his ways. 27 Lectures or Readings on the Epistle to the Hebrews 2:7-8.[6]

God the Father Forsook Christ for a Short Time. Martin Luther: Many have worked hard to expound this verse. A great number of teachers . . . seem to understand it as referring to humankind alone. But we state briefly that though it is possible to understand this verse in an improper sense as referring to man . . . yet in the proper sense this verse can be understood only as referring to Christ. Otherwise it is necessary to force the words that precede and those that follow into that meaning by means of extraordinary twistings and turnings. Therefore those who think that this verse refers to the dignity of human nature, which is very close to that of the angels, follow an improper understanding, which is the death of true understanding. Others understand this verse as referring to Christ, namely, that he is lower than the angels, not according to his soul but according to his body, which is capable of suffering.[†] But even this interpretation is inadequate, since he was not only made lower than the angels. Indeed, he himself says in Psalm 22:6: "I am a worm, and no man." . . . Speaking without rashness, therefore, it seems that this verse says nothing about the dignity of our nature but is an explanation of the preceding verse, namely, of that wonderful memory and visitation of God, who is most mindful when he forgets and who visits most when he abandons. For he exalted Christ above all things when he cast him down below all things. For his very passion was a "Passover," that is, a passing over to the highest glory. The reason for this lack of knowledge is the translation of this verb "You made lower." For the Hebrew word . . . in this place means "to fail," "to be wanting," etc. Therefore the meaning is this: You made him to be forsaken and deserted by God or the angels, and not for a long time but for a little while, yes, less than a little while, that is, for a very short time, namely, for three days, because you delivered him over into the hands of sinners. . . . One concludes, therefore, that the verse "You made him for a little while lower than the angels, you have crowned him with glory and honor" has the same meaning as Isaiah 54:7-8: "For a brief moment I forsook you, but with great compassion I will gather you. And in a moment of indignation I hid my face a little while from you,

[4]Zwingli, *In Epistolam ad Hebraeos*, 567; citing Eph 1:20-21. [†]The meaning of this Greek word is obscure; it may mean something like "eloquence."
[5]Downame, ed., *Annotations*, MMM2r*; citing Ps 8:4.
[6]Dering, *Lectures on Hebrews*, H3v *; citing Gal 2:20.

but with everlasting mercy I have had compassion on you." Lectures on Hebrews 2:7.[7]

The Lord's Absolute Sovereignty. Edward Dering: He calls it here the "taste of death" to have indeed the sense and feeling of the pains, not diminishing the passions as a thing lightly touched, but warranting the bitterness and all the sorrow of it, even to the bottom of the grave, and death to be tasted and felt indeed. . . . Thus you have seen Christ, even when he was lowest, highly exalted; that you have no good cause to reason against your dignity, though your eye sees not, even in this time, all things subject unto you. But see further into our Savior Christ, and you shall see more of your own honor. . . . It follows in the apostle, "for whom are all things, and by whom are all things." This is a singular reason why we should be obedient and ask no account of all the doings of the Lord: Is man afflicted? Why should he not be so? The Lord has done it, and for the Lord we were made. Are the reprobate ordained to destruction? Why should they not? The Lord so ordained it, and for the Lord they were made. Are the elect freely saved? Why should they not? The Lord has saved them, and for the Lord they were made. Yes, but the reason of these things I do not see. Yes (O man) who are you who takes up a contrary part to dispute against God? . . . That which follows in the latter end of the verse, "to consecrate him by afflictions," or "to make him perfect by afflictions," the meaning is that Christ in his death accomplished a full redemption and so was prepared to receive an inheritance of glory, not attributing this work only to his death, as though all his life had been impertinent, for in all his life, Christ was made our redemption. 27 Lectures or Readings on the Epistle to the Hebrews 2:8-10.[8]

In What Way Was Christ Less Than the Angels? Heinrich Bullinger: Now he shows from the same prophetic quotation that Christ was indeed a little lower than the angels, but he also tells in what way or how he was lower, such that it in no way detracts from the glory of Christ. For anyone can see that the cross and death, which certainly do not befall the angels, were lower. But he prevents this as by the parenthesis, "nevertheless he was crowned with glory and honor"; that is, after death it was declared by the resurrection that he was the Son of God; and, indeed, that the very death of Christ was not the punishment or penalty for sin, but the demonstration of divine grace. For that is what it means when it says, "So that by the grace of God he might taste death for everyone." From this it is now clear that the glory of Christ was not clouded at all by the cross and death, so that even if he appears to be lower in this regard, actually the glory of the one who suffered is greater than if he had not suffered. But nor am I unaware that in the Hebrew Scriptures it reads, "You have made him a little lower than God"; but this reading does not differ at all from Paul in its meaning. For indeed, Christ himself testified that the Father was greater than him, which Athanasius, the greatest defender of the divinity of Christ, does not conceal; he said, "The Son is the equal of the Father in divinity, but less than the Father with regard to his humanity."† Commentary on Hebrews 2:9.[9]

A Corrupted Text. Martin Luther: This text has been corrupted either by a translator or by a scribe, since not one iota makes it mean that Christ was made a little lower than the angels. In fact, in the Greek text the words are identical with those used above (v. 7). . . . Therefore the text can be understood to have been arranged as follows: "But him who was made lower than the angels for less than a short time." . . . Here the Holy Spirit consoles us, in order that in the time of suffering we may have patience and hope; for tribulation lasts for a little while, but the consolation is eternal,

[7]LW 29:125-28* (WA 57:116.8-117.10, 118.13-119.14). †LW note (126 n. 9): "Thomas Aquinas, *Super epistolam S. Pauli apostoli ad Hebraeos expositio*, Chapter 2, Lection 2, *In omnes S. Pauli apostoli epistolas commentaria* (2 vols.; Turin, 1929), II, 314."
[8]Dering, *Lectures on Hebrews*, H6 v, H7 r, I3 r, I4 r*.

[9]Bullinger, *In Pauli ad Hebraeos Epistolam*, 26r-v [71-72]; citing Rom 1:4; Jn 14:28. †The (Pseudo-)Athanasian Creed (Schaff 2:69).

as stated in 1 Peter 5:10: "And after you have suffered a little while, the God of all grace . . . will himself perfect, etc." Lectures on Hebrews 2:9.[10]

Christ Was Humbled for a Little While Not by Necessity, but by Grace. Cardinal Cajetan: "But we do see him who was made for a little while lower than the angels, namely, Jesus." He explains one clause, "He was made lower than the angels." Thus he says, concerning the identity of the person, "We see Jesus." So, regarding the statement that he was made for a little while lower than the angels, he adds, "Because of the suffering of death." And, by way of including another clause, he adds, "Crowned with glory and honor." The author explains here that being made less than the angels is what merited the crowning with glory and honor. "So that by the grace of God he might taste death for everyone." He means that he was not compelled by necessity to be made less than the angels, and he explains that it was not by necessity but by the grace of God (for "grace" is in the ablative case†) that he tasted death for all. For this grace is made evident when he says that it was "for all." And it says "tasted" because he was dead for only a short time; for on the third day he rose. Comments on Hebrews 2:9.[11]

2:10-13 *Christ's Humiliation Exalts Us as God's Children*

Through Christ's Suffering We Surpass the Angels. Johannes Bugenhagen: This is just what Christ himself said: "It was necessary for the Christ to suffer and rise again and enter into his glory." This was not only because Scripture had predicted it but also because otherwise he could not have become like us, whom Scripture calls our brothers, so that we surpass the angels. From this it follows in turn that the teachings which were passed down through the angels have been abolished, and so far is it from the case that the angels are preferred to Christ or the prophets, that even mortals who are in Christ have glory above the angels. Commentary on the Pauline Epistles, Heb 2:10.[12]

The Reason for the Incarnation. Heinrich Bullinger: Since he has the opportunity, now he openly asserts the true flesh of Christ and discusses the reasons for his incarnation. He does this, first, so that we may see that the glory of Christ was so little dimmed by the incarnation, that it was actually displayed more clearly to the whole world. Second, so that now he may show that Christ was true man, whom he proved in the previous chapter to be true God. But the first reason for the incarnation and death of Christ is the appointment, purpose, and righteousness of God, whom here, because of his indescribable majesty, he involves in a circumlocution; he, I say, is the one for whom and by whom all things exist, that is, who is the life and being of all things. Therefore he says, "Thus it had been established by God," or rather, "the righteousness of God demanded it, and so it was fitting for God to bring back our wretched dying race from exile to an eternal habitation by no other means than through the death of Christ." For it was right for those who were impure and imperfect first to be purified and perfected through the one who was pure and able to perfect or make atonement. The flesh, or rather the entire human person, had been ruined; so it had to be restored by flesh and a human person. Humanity merited death; so by death they must be redeemed. In short, all flesh had become corrupt; accordingly, it was right for the Son of God to descend and be made flesh from the virgin by the Holy Spirit. For how could he have died, when he did not possess flesh? And this is the chief reason for the incarnation of the Lord, regarding which the apostle himself has much to say in what follows. Commentary on Hebrews 2:10.[13]

[10]LW 29:129 (WA 57: 121.15-122.5).

[11]Cajetan, *In Epistolam ad Hebraeos*, 159r. †Since he is commenting on the text of the Vulgate, Cajetan uses the terminology of Latin grammar, which (unlike Greek) has an ablative form distinct from the dative.

[12]Bugenhagen, *Annotationes in epistolas Pauli recognitae* (1525) 141v-142r [316-17]; citing Lk 24:26.

[13]Bullinger, *In Pauli ad Hebraeos Epistolam*, 26v-27r [72-73]; citing Gen 6:11-12.

How Was Disgrace Fitting? Johannes Bugenhagen: "It was fitting for him" refers to God the Father. "For whom all things exist" means, "who established all things by his own goodness alone," because without him they would not exist. This should be understood as referring to God, Father, Son, and Holy Spirit; for what is said here about Christ is intended with regard to his humanity. "It was fitting for him," I say, "that he would lead to glory many sons," that is, believers. This is to say, for a long time to come and afterward, all the way to the end of the world, in accord with predestination, he would lead them, but through disgrace meted out by the world, and no other way. How, I ask you, was this fitting for him? It was fitting because in no other way would he have glorified Christ, their founder and leader. Commentary on the Pauline Epistles, Heb 2:10.[14]

The Conforming of the Head to the Members in Suffering. John Calvin: It is not yet clear what he intends by saying that it became Christ to be thus consecrated. But this depends on the ordinary way that God adopts in dealing with his own people; for his will is to exercise them with various trials, so that they may spend their whole life under the cross. It was hence necessary that Christ, as the first-begotten, should by the cross be inaugurated into his supremacy, since that is the common lot and condition of all. This is the conforming of the head with the members, of which Paul speaks in Romans 8:29. Commentaries on the Epistle of Paul the Apostle to the Hebrews 2:10.[15]

Christ Is the Perfect Example. Martin Luther: Therefore since he [i.e., God the Father] has determined to draw his sons through Christ, the text says correctly that "it was fitting that he should make the most perfect through suffering," that is, that he should make him the most perfect and the complete example through which to inspire and draw his sons. For God does not compel people to salvation by force and fear, but by this pleasing spectacle of his mercy and love he moves and draws through love all whom he will save. . . . Thus here—"It was fitting to make perfect through sufferings"—[the preposition "through" signifies] "by means of," so that the sense is that it was fitting for God to make Christ the perfect author of salvation and, in order to accomplish this, to make use of sufferings. The reason is that without sufferings the perfection of the example would have been lacking—the example by which he would move and draw us even to the point of loving death and suffering. Lectures on Hebrews 2:10.[16]

Christ Is the One "Through Whom" All Things Exist. Johannes Oecolampadius: It seems to me that those who explain this passage have not examined everything properly so as to ascertain the real meaning. For it is agreed by very few regarding *autō*, "him," which is written here. Some understand this to mean the Father, others the Trinity, others the Word, but the following words *di' hon kai di' hou*, "for whom and through whom," make it clear to everyone that these explanations are not nearly consistent enough. For in the ordinary manner of Scripture, these words do not fit the Father, but the Son, as is easily observable from Ephesians, Colossians, and nearly all the writings of the apostle. But we will follow the thread of the following discourse more certainly. For my part, I understand this simply as referring to Christ, who, it must be acknowledged, was not from eternity a man, but was Christ, through whom all things are, and as was said earlier, "through whom he established the world," in whom we were chosen before the foundations of the world were laid, through whom at last things in heaven and on earth are being restored. But nor does it escape me that in 1 Corinthians 1

[14]Bugenhagen, *Annotationes in epistolas Pauli recognitae* (1525) 142r [317].
[15]CTS 40:63*.
[16]LW 29:132-33 (WA 57: 125.8-126.5).

di' hou is also said of the Father, where it says, "through whom you were called into the fellowship of his Son." But this is by the cooperation of the Son and the Holy Spirit, and I do not know that there is any other place in the apostolic writings where the same form of speech appears that is not properly to be applied simply to the Son. Surely we would speak far more properly if we were to say that all things are "from the Father," rather than "for" or "through" the Father. For "through" indicates the means through which we act, and thus it frequently prompts our recollection of Christ the mediator, as the only one by whom all our salvation and redemption is assured. At the same time, you know that the Son is coequal with the Father in everything, and is the same as him. Cyril denies that *autō* refers to the Son, certainly because he did not want to seem to give an opportunity to the Nestorians, who propose two Sons of God or two Christs and teach that the founder of the salvation of those who were to be saved was perfected by the Word. But if you interpret it so that, instead, so to speak, he sanctified the founder of salvation through those sufferings, their mockery will collapse. EXPLANATIONS OF HEBREWS 2:10-11.[17]

CHRIST IS OUR BROTHER BECAUSE HE PARTAKES OF OUR HUMANITY. JOHANNES OECOLAMPADIUS: Next, some understand the phrase "All are from one source," as "are from God," but how can this prove the true humanity of Christ? For the Jews never denied this, so that it does not counter them at all; but to assert that Christ was true man, this was offensive to them. You should simply read "from one" as "one man," but not from the same sinful nature of which we wretched mortals are born. For it was necessary that the one who wished to cleanse others from their sins should be holy and without blemish. But because we are all "from one," it surely follows that Christ is our brother and has borne our flesh. He says "all" and not "each," because it provides more elucidation of that which he intends to demonstrate. And it is a very effective argument against the Valentinian heretics, who irreverently dare to blaspheme that the body of Christ fell from heaven and received nothing from the Virgin Mary.† EXPLANATIONS OF HEBREWS 2:10-11.[18]

CHRIST'S HUMANITY RESTS ON AS FIRM A SCRIPTURAL FOUNDATION AS HIS DIVINITY. HEINRICH BULLINGER: Because he was descended from one father along with us, he does not blush to call us brothers and sisters. But the text confirms this by very clear passages of Scripture, so that the doctrine of the humanity of Christ may not rely on lesser or weaker testimonies of Scripture than his divinity, which he confirmed vigorously enough in chapter 1. The first testimony, then, is taken from Psalm 22, which was written about David. But he acted as a type of Christ, who calls us mortals his brothers and sisters and has lavishly announced the glory of God throughout the world by the proclamation of the gospel. Then the second testimony comes from Psalm 18,† which is allegorically applied to Christ for the same reason. But here is how it applies to the present issue: if Christ had been pure God alone, and not also true man, he would not have said, "I will put my trust in him." For who in his right mind would say that God trusts in God? But Christ does trust in God; therefore, he can be right to trust according to his humanity. And so it is necessary that Christ is human. Finally, the author borrows the third

[17]Oecolampadius, *In Epistolam ad Hebraeos Explanationes*, 28v-29r; citing Eph 1:5; 2:18; Col 1:16, 20; 1 Cor 1:9; 8:6; Heb 1:2; Rom 11:36.

[18]Oecolampadius, *In Epistolam ad Hebraeos Explanationes*, 30r. Valentinus was a second-century Gnostic theologian who founded the Valentinian sect. This sect held that Christ was a spiritual "aeon" who had emanated from the "Primal Ground of Being." This aeon united with the man Jesus at some point in order to save human beings by providing them with knowledge (*gnōsis*) of their spiritual origins and destiny, the "pleroma" or spiritual world. The Valentinians denied the incarnation, positing a strict separation between Jesus the man and Christ the spiritual being. †Irenaeus, *Against Heresies* 1.7.2 (PG 7:513-514; ANF 1:325).

testimony from Isaiah 8, employing once again the same analogical method. Commentary on Hebrews 2:11-13.[19]

Ministers of the Word Are Christ's Brothers. William Jones: In respect of the ministry, the preachers of the Word are Christ's brethren; for he was a minister and a preacher of the gospel as we are, although in gifts and graces he excelled us all as the sun does the stars. But more nearly and properly, the faithful are his brethren, being made the sons of God by faith in Christ Jesus. Commentary upon the Epistles of St. Paul, Heb 2:12.[20]

2:14-15 *Christ's Incarnation Frees Us from Slavery*

Christ Purifies Humans Because He Is Our Brother in Real Human Flesh. Huldrych Zwingli: "He who sanctifies." Now he seems to rehearse the reason why the Word was made flesh. He says that he took on a human body so that, as a human, he might purify humans. For Christ is a human, born (albeit in a different way) from one and the same father, Adam or "Man," from whom we also are humans, for whom he died as an acceptable sacrifice. You see here that this attribute of the humanity of Christ—namely, that it sanctifies and makes us clean—should not be understood with reference only to his humanity in isolation, but to the whole Christ, just as we said above. "That is why he is not ashamed to call them brothers, saying . . . ." It is as if he were saying, "Because it is established that Christ comes from one and the same parent as us, and because he partakes equally in the flesh and sanctifies us, it follows that we are bound up in brotherhood with him." So he shows the fruit of Christ's incarnation and coming to us. It was that he was made man and came to us so that by making us his brothers he might set us free as fellows heirs in the kingdom of the Father. He did this so that it might be impossible for him to forget his brothers or to be ashamed to call us his brothers.

"They partake. . . ." That is, they really are flesh and blood and real humans. For this is a circumlocution, as if he were to say, "Christ himself also became a human so that he might partake of these things." And thus he gives the reason why he chose to take on human nature rather than the nature of the angels—so that he might be made like his brothers (that is, like us) in everything and might produce confidence and unhampered hope in his promised favor. Those who today invent for Christ I know not what kind of heavenly, spiritual, and deified flesh from heaven, and who dream and rave about such kinds of vain and frivolous things regarding a substantial and corporeal presence of Christ in the supper of believers, should investigate this passage. Exposition of Hebrews 2:11-14.[21]

Christ, Our Brother. Martin Luther: Here the apostle distinguishes the brotherhood between us and the angels from that between Christ and us. He praises the abundance of God's love, namely, that he made Christ our brother not only according to the spirit but also according to the flesh, so that at the same time the very same Christ is higher than the angels, like us, and nearer to us than the angels. Lectures on Hebrews 2:14.[22]

Christ Defeats the Devil with the Devil's Own Weapon. Martin Luther: God's proper work† . . . is "life, peace, and joy," and the other fruits of the Spirit in Galatians 5:22. Yet in this the Lord "exalted his holy One" (Ps 4:3) and is "wonderful among all his saints" (Ps 68:35) that he destroyed the devil, not by a work of God but by a work of the devil himself. For this is the most glorious kind of victory, namely, to pierce the adversary with his own weapon and to slay him with his own sword. . . . For in this way God promotes and completes his work by means of an

[19]Bullinger, *In Pauli ad Hebraeos Epistolam*, [74] 27v; citing Ps 22:22; 18:2; Is 8:18. †Bullinger, employing standard sixteenth-century chapter numbers, cites this text as Ps 17.
[20]Jones, *A Commentary on the Epistles of Saint Paul*, 103.

[21]Zwingli, *In Epistolam ad Hebraeos*, 567-568; citing Rom 8:17.
[22]LW 29:134 (WA 57:126.24-127.2).

alien deed, and by his wonderful wisdom he compels the devil to work through death nothing else than life, so that in this way, while he acts most of all against the work of God, he acts for the work of God and against his own work with his own deed. For thus he worked death in Christ, but Christ completely swallowed up death in himself through the immortality of his divinity and rose again in glory.... Therefore just as in "the Author of salvation," in "the holy of holies," in Christ, our Head, death and all the works of the devil have been destroyed, so it will have to happen in each of his members. For just as Christ was at once mortal and an immortal person, he was indeed subject to death by reason of his humanity; but because his whole person could not be slain, it happened that death failed, and the devil succumbed in slaying him; and thus death was swallowed up in life.[†] In this way the curse was swallowed up and conquered in the blessing, sorrow, and joy, and the other evils in the highest good. Thus now, too, it pleases our most gracious God to destroy death and the works of the devil in us through Christ. We Christians should learn, in order that we may die joyfully. For just as it is impossible for Christ, the Victor over death, to die again (cf. Rom 6:9), so it is impossible for one who believes in him to die; as Christ says in John.... For just as Christ, by reason of his union with immortal divinity, overcame death by dying, so the Christian, by reason of their union with the immortal Christ—which comes about through faith in him—also overcomes death by dying. And in this way God destroys the devil through the devil himself and accomplishes his own work by means of an alien work. This is what the world does not grasp.... Corollary: He who fears death or is unwilling to die is not a Christian to a sufficient degree; for those who fear death still lack faith in the resurrection, since they love this life more than they love the life to come.... He who does not die willingly should not be called a Christian.... For God makes death, judgment, and hell manifest in order to show the power of faith in Christ, so that a Christian may overcome these through faith.... For that contempt for death and the gratitude for it, proclaimed by the apostle [i.e., Paul] and for the saints, is the goal and perfection toward which the whole life of Christians should strive, even though very few are so perfect.... He [i.e., Christ] left death, but he left it conquered. LECTURES ON HEBREWS 2:14.[23]

CLING TO GOD THROUGH CHRIST. JACOBUS ARMINIUS: It is not sufficient for us only to approach to God; it is likewise good for us to cleave to him. To confirm this act of cleaving and to give it perpetuity, it ought to depend on a communion of nature. But with God we have no such communion. Christ, however, possesses it, and we are made possessors of it with Christ, "who partook of our flesh and blood." Being constituted our head, he imparts unto us his spirit, that we (being constituted its members, and cleaving to him as "flesh of his flesh and bone of his bone") may be one with him, and through him with the Father, and with both may become "one Spirit." THE OBJECT OF THEOLOGY.[24]

THROUGH CHRIST WE ARE NOW DELIVERED FROM THE FEAR OF DEATH. JOHANNES OECOLAMPADIUS: Those who are wholly terrified of death love themselves too much and in a way fight against God. They pursue good works less than a pleasant mindset, and tremble at the bare mention of death, so dear to them is this light. And surely this is no surprise. For those who are ignorant of the life to come cannot bear up in this life with less than all their souls, whenever it is laden with misfortunes. In addition, if this present life were not sweetened for the godly by hope of the life to come and of the resurrection, by the kindness of the Savior, how could it be anything but immeasurably bitter? What wonder is it, then, that those destitute of the hope of

[23]LW 29:135, 136, 137-38, 139, 140 (WA 57:128.7-19, 129.6-130.1, 131.5-9. 132.1-3 and 24-26, 133.16); citing Jn 11:25-26. [†]LW note (135 n. 30): "On the distinction between the 'alien' and the 'proper' work of God, based on Is. 28:21, cf. *Luther's Works*, 13, p. 79, note 9." [‡]LW note (136 n. 33): "An allusion to the third stanza of the Easter sequence of Wipo, 'Victimae paschali laudes.'"
[24]Arminius, *Works*, 1:74*.

the resurrection are subject to lifelong slavery to the fear of death? But through his own death Christ has destroyed this fear, and has emerged the victor over all, and that not for himself, but for us.

Those who lived before the coming of Christ were seized with great dread of death, of which the behavior of Abraham affords an example in Genesis 12 and 20, where he was not ashamed to expose Sarah to be violated in order to deliver himself from the risk of death. For at that time the tyranny of death had not yet been undone, nor was its sting blunted. It was also possible to hold this outlook because of the carnal promises and threats given to the Jews in the law. But we who believe that Christ has come in the flesh, has risen again in victory over death, and is now seated in the heavenly places—we make fast our hope such that we may say with the apostle that neither death, nor life, nor angels nor any other creature can separate us from the love of God, which is in Christ; indeed, we desire to depart and be with Christ (Rom 8; Phil 1). Explanations of Hebrews 2:14-15.[25]

Christ Had a Real Human Body and He Truly Suffered. Edward Dering: Here (dearly beloved) we must not only reject the foul and rotten thoughts of such heretics, as have denied the humanity of our Savior Christ, but many other vain fancies of men, who grant indeed a natural body to our Savior Christ, but they give it such qualities, as no body in the world has ever had.

Some say, it may be everywhere, whom God will teach better in his good time. Others say, it may be made with five words spoken with one breath, *Hoc est enim corpus meum*—for this is my body; a foolish people, and of no understanding. And yet they are more vain than this; they think it may be made of a piece of bread, without form or figure, and into bread they think it may return again, if the wicked eat it, if it begin to digest in the good person's stomach. Is this to make him like unto us, sin only excepted? No (dearly beloved) it is to be drunk or else to be mad, in dallying with the body of Christ, we cannot tell how. . . .[†]

If he has overcome death and the power of it, both in our body and soul, then Christ has suffered the pain of it both body and soul, that we might rise again from the bands of death and live with him forever. For this is true, by death he has overcome death, and he has broken the force of it, no, further, he has felt the sting of it in himself. Therefore, this let us hold, and let us so believe: Christ, body and soul, was made a Sacrifice for our sins. . . . That which made Christ to tremble would have crushed his apostles in pieces; and that which made him to sweat blood so plentifully would have made them sink into the bottom of hell. And that which made him cry would have held both humans and angels under everlasting woe and lamentation. If then our Savior Christ were, as the prophet says, like water poured out, and all his bones out of joint; if his heart was like wax, molten in the midst of his bowels; if his strength were dried up like a potsherd, and his tongue cleaved unto his jaws; if he were brought with his sorrows into the dust of death; fie upon the blasphemous speeches and cursed words that say he suffered nothing but bodily pain. I would those which are papists among us, and in their simplicity are deceived with the error of many, I would (I say) they knew the wickedness of this one point of their doctrine, that they say the soul of Christ suffered nothing but only for the body's sake, as our souls suffer when our bodies are weak, or are sick, or die.[†] . . . Do they not know what the Scripture says? "He bore our sins in his body, he submitted himself unto death of them, and by the wounds of his stripes we are healed." Do our sins deserve only a bodily death? Or did they not deserve the second death, which is the wrath of God, holding body and soul in an everlasting fire? . . . Let them pray, and let us pray for them, that if it be the will of God, they may soon be converted, and know the unspeakable love of our Savior Christ, who was accursed for our sakes, and suffered for us, not only the torments of his body, but the anguish of his soul, and the wrath of his father, which wounded his flesh and spirit unto death. . . .

[25]Oecolampadius, *In Epistolam ad Hebraeos Explanationes*, 34r-v; citing Gen 12:12-13; 1 Cor 15:55-57; Rom 8:38-39; Phil 1:23.

So this is our blessing, not that we shall not die, but that we shall not be held in death, and not that we shall not fear, but that we shall not be overcome with fear. . . .

Thus it is now accomplished that here is spoken that Christ has set us free from the bondage of the fear of death: which (dearly beloved) if we will learn and know, assuredly it will work great increase of grace, it will change our minds more than we are aware of, and when we are wise-hearted to see indeed, no doubt we shall be as bold as Paul, and say unfeignedly, we desire to be dissolved, and be with Christ. . . .

These words, "he had to be made like his brothers in every respect," which are repeated again in 4:15, we are to mark them well, that we see how expressly still the apostle urges, that Christ is a very natural man, altogether as we are, except sin. Christ has like nature, the same flesh, like affections, the same soul, like properties of body, the same hunger, thirst, and other desires. And as he is now, so shall be our bodies glorified as his is; nor is his more infinite or in many places than ours shall be: and thus it was necessary it should be, that he might be a faithful high priest, to reconcile us, even us, body and soul, unto God his Father. 27 Lectures or Readings on the Epistle to the Hebrews 2:14-17.[26]

Death and the Devil Defeated, but They Still Exist. Martin Luther: Therefore when Christ took away the fear of death, he set us free from slavery to sin and by this same act destroyed him to whom we were subject only through the fear of death. Yet he did not destroy him in such a way that he did not exist; but just as we are freed from the law by the Spirit, not so that the law does not exist, but so that the law is not feared, so we are also freed from the devil, not so that he does not exist, but so that he is not feared, and from death, not so that it does not exist, but so that it is not feared, etc. I conclude, therefore, that for a Christian there is nothing more to fear either in this life or in the life to come, since for him both death and all evils have been changed into a blessing and a gain. Lectures on Hebrews 2:15.[27]

Bondage to Sin and Freedom in Christ. Jacobus Arminius: Liberty, generally, is a state according to which everyone is at their own disposal, and not bound to another person. Bondage or slavery is opposed to it, according to which a person is not their own master, but subject to another, either to do what they command, to omit what they forbid, or to endure what they inflict. Christian liberty is so called chiefly from Christ the author, who procured it; it has received this appellation also from its subjects, because it belongs to Christians, that is, to believers in Christ. But it presupposes servitude, because Christ was not necessary for any, except for "those who, through dear of death, were all their lifetime subject to bondage." Christian liberty is that state of fullness of grace and truth in which believers are placed by God through Christ, and are sealed by the Holy Spirit. It consists partly of a deliverance from both real and economic bondage to sin and the law, and partly of adoption into the right of the sons of God, and of the mission of the Son and Spirit into their hearts. Its end is the praise of the glorious grace of God in Christ, and the eternal salvation of believers. Disputation on Christian Liberty.[28]

2:16-18 *Christ, Our High Priest*

God Takes Hold of Christians by His Mercy and Grace. Martin Luther: Chrysostom notes the emphasis on the verb "to take hold of."† For the apostle did not say that he received, but that "he took hold of," namely, from the figure of persons pursuing and doing everything to seize and

[26]Dering, *Lectures on Hebrews*, K6v-K7, Lr-v, L3r-v, L4r-v*; citing Ps 22:14-15; 1 Pet 2:23-24; Phil 1:23. †Dering is here referencing both Lutheran and Catholic views of the Eucharist. Lutherans taught that Christ's human body shared in the properties of his divinity, one of which was ubiquity. ‡Here Dering may have in mind Aquinas's teaching that Christ suffered in the lower parts of his soul but not in the higher parts. See *Summa Theologica*, III, 41, Q. 46, art. 7.

[27]LW 29:141 (WA 57:135.6-14).

[28]Arminius, *Works*, 1:601-2*.

take hold of those who are fleeing. For when human nature fled far away, he pursued, and took hold of it. He showed that he did this only out of mercy and grace and because of the care he has for us. This is what Chrysostom says. And this is clear in the Gospel from the parables of the lost sheep (Mt 18:13) and the lost coin (Lk 15:8), which he sought and found, certainly not because of what they did, but out of compassion. Lectures on Hebrews 2:16.[29]

It Was Appropriate for Christ to be Made Like His Brothers. Desiderius Erasmus: It was appropriate, therefore, that in all things he be make like those whom he wanted to be his brothers. He did this to instill in them a greater confidence that they would obtain forgiveness, because he who, to expiate the sins of the whole people, had undertaken the office of high priest to intercede with God and to reconcile the entire race of mortals to him, would by this sign seem likely thereafter to be merciful and faithful to his own. Not only did he share the same nature as they, but it was also his lot to be tried and tested by the countless sufferings of this world, so that he might more readily seem likely to aid those who were being harassed by the evils of this world. Paraphrases on the Epistle to the Hebrews 2:16-18.[30]

The True Humanity of Christ Necessitates a Finite Body. Heinrich Bullinger: By this additional comment, he finally shows clearly that Christ put on true humanity; for he is the one who "has been made like us in every way," except our sin. And in consequence, just as he has flesh that is capable of sensation, he has a soul capable of thought. I declare that he does not have a soul bereft of perception and thought,† as Apollinaris maintained, nor flesh deprived of soul, whose place was taken by his divine nature,‡ as Eunomius supposed, but as a real man he has a soul with its thinking and flesh with its sensations, through which he underwent real sensations in his suffering, and sorrows beyond the suffering of the flesh, in accordance with the prophecy of Isaiah. As another consequence, the body of Christ must be finite, limited, and stationed in a particular place. For we also are limited to a particular place. Further, we read that he was aggrieved, he thirsted, he was hungry, he wept, he grew weary, he was flushed with joy, he was troubled by anger and indignation, he was overcome by weakness (which we understand as distress, not sin), and at last he was tempted and became subject to death. Furthermore, we also see that he never dismissed or took off the humanity that he put on continually, not even through his resurrection. His body was clearly glorified, but that does not mean that it was annihilated; the accidents were changed, but the same substance remained, "For this perishable must put on the imperishable," from which it follows that even the glorified body also remains limited. For God alone is infinite. But the flesh of Christ was not transformed into God, because when something is transformed into something else, that is the end of the original thing.§ Therefore it is finite and confined to a particular place. For if after the resurrection the body had become infinite, then it would not be a body at all, and there would not be any resurrection of our flesh at all.

Therefore, those who both deny the real flesh of Christ and overthrow the resurrection of our own flesh by that "bodily presence in the bread" of theirs should see what they are playing around with. For if the real and natural body of Christ is really and naturally everywhere, so that it must be unlimited, if it is always and simultaneously bodily or substantially in every piece of sacramental bread on the globe, then the real body of Christ is no longer a real body. For, to make use of Augustine's words to Dardanus, "If you take away extension in space from bodies, they will be nowhere; and because they are nowhere, they will not exist. If you take away the body itself from its attributes, it will not be where they are; and therefore it is necessary that the attributes will not exist."◊ But the body of Christ is a real body, and hence it is limited to a particular place. Therefore, it is not diffused by

[29]LW 29:141-142 (WA 57:135.16-23). †LW note (141 n. 45): "Chrysostom, *Homiliae*, V, 1, cols. 45-46 (271)." In the Vulgate the verb is *aprehendit* (to take hold of).
[30]CWE 44:220.

nature among all the individual pieces of sacramental bread. On the other hand, if the glorified body of Christ is not contained in any particular place, but like God diffuses itself through everything, then our own bodies will also be everywhere, since the resurrection of our bodies ought to be just like what Christ's resurrection was. Furthermore, if our bodies will be everywhere, they will no longer be bodies at all; and thus neither was the body of Christ actually a body. But if that is true, then the article of our faith in which we "believe in the resurrection of the flesh" collapses. But our flesh will rise again, just as Christ rose again. Indeed the angel speaks of these things: "He has risen, he is not here, behold the place where they laid him." Even Christ himself spoke of this to his disciples: "See my hands and my feet, that it is I myself. Touch me and see, for a spirit does not have flesh and bones, as you see that I have." Therefore, it is certain that even the glorified body of Christ is in a particular place, and that it is therefore a real body, and that, in consequence, the resurrection of our flesh will also be a real resurrection, and therefore they hold a completely false position who say that the glorified body of Christ is contained in the sacrament of the altar. All the while, in reality the presence that is found in the supper of Christ is not substantial, natural, or local, but rather spiritual or sacramental. For faith sees things absent in space as present in the mind. COMMENTARY ON HEBREWS 2:17.[31]

CHRIST AS THE MODEL PRIEST. MARTIN LUTHER: The apostle commends the two things in Christ that should shine forth in every priest according to the example of Christ; namely, he should be merciful to the people and faithful to God for the people. For through mercy he should empty himself and make all the evils of those who are under him his own, and should feel them in no other way than if he himself were in them. But through faithfulness he should share with them all his own good things. For thus, as Philippians 2:6-7 says, Christ "emptied himself of the form of God and took the form of a servant"; that is, he considered the things that were ours, not those that were his. For his things were righteousness, wisdom, salvation, glory, peace, joy, etc.; ours were sin, foolishness, perdition, dishonor, the cross, sorrow, etc. Therefore he took these things of ours and acted as if he did not know his own. Therefore in the law in Exodus 28:38 it is stated that "Aaron shall bear the iniquities of the things the Children of Israel brought as offerings." And Numbers 18:1 states: "The Lord said to Aaron: 'You and your sons and your father's house with you shall bear iniquity in connection with the sanctuary; and you and your sons with you shall bear iniquity in connection with your priesthood.'" LECTURES ON HEBREWS 2:17.[32]

CHRIST FULLY ENTERED INTO HUMAN EXPERIENCE. JOHANNES OECOLAMPADIUS: Because he has assumed the nature of the seed of Abraham, not of angels, hence it is that he is our true brother, like us in every respect. He was born, he was swaddled in strips of cloth, he was laid in a manger, he was fed, he was circumcised, he was taken up in [Simeon's] arms, he matured, he grew strong in the Spirit, he increased in wisdom and stature, he was hungry, he was thirsty, he wept, he became tired, he was pleased, he was moved by anger and indignation, he was troubled, he was saddened, he was

[31]Bullinger, *In Pauli ad Hebraeos Epistolam*, 30r-31r [79-81]; citing Is 53:3-4, 11; Mk 16:6; Lk 24:39; 1 Cor 15:53. †Apollinaris (d. 390) was a bishop of Laodicea in Syria. Although a staunch opponent of Arianism, his emphasis on the divinity of Christ led him to deny that Jesus had a fully human mind, thus affirming a version of docetism and denying the full humanity of Jesus. His view was opposed by, among others, Gregory of Nazianzus, who argued that Christ must have become fully human in order to redeem humanity. ‡Eunomius (d. 394) was a radical Arian theologian (an Anomoean) who opposed the "same essence" (*homoousios*) Christology of the Council of Nicaea. According to him, the Father generated the Son but not from within the divine nature; the Son then created the Holy Spirit. §Bullinger is here arguing against the Lutheran doctrine of ubiquity with respect to the Lord's Supper. ◊Augustine, *Epistolae* 187.6.18 (PL 33:838).

[32]LW 29:142 (WA 57:136.1-16). For a similar use of Phil 2:6-7 in the works of Luther, see *Sermo de duplici iustitia/Two Kinds of Righteousness* (1519) (LW 31: 297, 301; WA 2:145.3-6, 147.34-148.6) and *Tractatus de libertate christiana/The Freedom of the Christian* (1520) (WA 7:64.65-65.25; LW 31:365-66).

tempted. At length he was tempted by every weakness, along with us; he even underwent death for us of his own accord, and an ignominious death at that. Now, is this not what it means to resemble his brothers in every way? Clearly it is, but with one exception, that he did not yield to the devil and committed no sin. From this it should be clear to any believer that temptations, sorrows, and consternation at death truly extended to the soul of Christ as well, as the Evangelists copiously testified. For he intended to suffer for us absolutely perfectly and to experience everything pertaining to our weakness, so that we might know with absolute certainty that he is our brother. (Of course, in us the fear and dread of death is sin, but not in Christ.) EXPLANATIONS OF HEBREWS 2:17.[33]

THOSE WHO RELY ON OTHER INTERCESSORS DEMONSTRATE THEIR UNBELIEF. HEINRICH BULLINGER: These things should be pondered carefully by those who, against the mystery and power of the incarnation of the Lord, promote the intercession of the saints. For what is the reason that you call on the saints? "I am a sinner," you say, "I would not dare to draw near to Christ, even if he has now become more approachable." But since you do not dare to draw near, you do not have faith, nor do you understand why God took on human nature. But it was for this that he took it on: so that he might be an intercessor who is merciful to the concerns of sinners. So since you are unwilling to approach mercy itself, but you instead go to creatures, it is evident that you do not believe in this divine mercy, and consequently Christ's incarnation does not benefit you at all. For it benefits only those who truly believe. COMMENTARY ON HEBREWS 2:18.[34]

CHRIST LEARNED OF OUR AFFLICTIONS THROUGH HIS HOLY HUMANITY. LUCAS OSIANDER: But also we perceive another consolation . . . [namely] that the Son of God was made man. Because he also tasted human miseries (nevertheless without sin), therefore he has compassion on us in our trials. . . . Christ learned in his own most holy humanity, by experience itself, how many and how great the afflictions and miseries are to which the human race is subjected. And thus he has mercy on us and takes away or mitigates our calamities at the right time. EPISTLE TO THE HEBREWS 2:18.[35]

[33]Oecolampadius, *In Epistolam ad Hebraeos Explanationes*, 35v-36r; citing Lk 2:7, 21, 28, 40; 1:80; 2:52; 4:2; Jn 19:28; Lk 19:41; Jn 11:35; 4:6; 11:15; Mk 3:5; Jn 11:33; Mk 1:13; 9:24.

[34]Bullinger, *In Pauli ad Hebraeos Epistolam*, 32r [83].

[35]Osiander, *Epistola ad Hebraeos*, 18.

3:1-6 Christ's Glory Far Exceeds the Glory of Moses

Therefore, holy brothers,[a] you who share in a heavenly calling, consider Jesus, the apostle and high priest of our confession, [2]who was faithful to him who appointed him, just as Moses also was faithful in all God's[b] house. [3]For Jesus has been counted worthy of more glory than Moses—as much more glory as the builder of a house has more honor than the house itself. [4](For every house is built by someone, but the builder of all things is God.) [5]Now Moses was faithful in all God's house as a servant, to testify to the things that were to be spoken later, [6]but Christ is faithful over God's house as a son. And we are his house, if indeed we hold fast our confidence and our boasting in our hope.[c]

a Or *brothers and sisters;* also verse 12 **b** Greek *his;* also verses 5, 6 **c** Some manuscripts insert *firm to the end*

Overview: The reformers see in this passage important theological statements regarding the nature of the true church, namely, that it is composed of true believers who have been called to follow Christ and who are themselves habitations of Christ. The reformers reflect at length on the nature of this divine indwelling, making of it an essential mark of the Christian, even as they stress the importance of perseverance in faith to the end. They also continue to advocate a high Christology that stresses the full divinity of Christ.

3:1-4 *Jesus Is Worthy of More Glory*

Preach Christ Peacefully. Martin Luther: Softly and gently the apostle draws them to Christ by calling them "holy" and, as it were, flattering them. Here he teaches us that we should not preach Christ with fury or with a tempest or words. Indeed, Christ can be preached in no other way than peacefully and calmly. For roaring talk pertains to the law, as has been pictured in Exodus 20:18, where the hearers were terrified by the sound of the trumpet, the darkness of the mountain, and the fire of lightning. Likewise in 1 Kings 19:11-13, where, after the wind, after the earthquake, and after the fire, there came "a still small voice," and there the Lord was. Therefore the law should be revealed with thunderbolts to those who are foolish and stiff-necked, but the gospel should be presented gently to those who are terrified and humbled. Therefore Isaiah 42:1, 3, says about Christ: "Behold, My Servant. . . . A bruised reed he will not break, and a dimly burning wick he will not quench"; that is, he will prefer to console the timid and the afflicted. Lectures on Hebrews 3:1.[1]

Christ Is Greater Than Both Moses and Aaron. Cardinal Cajetan: "Therefore, holy brothers, partakers in a heavenly calling." After he set Jesus above the angels, now he means to set him above Moses and Aaron, so that the New Testament surpasses the Old in every respect. "Therefore"—on the basis of this so great worthiness and grace of Christ—"holy"—that is, pure—"brothers, partakers in a heavenly calling" as much with regard to the end (because you have been called to a heavenly country) as with regard to the beginning (because you have been called by the one who descended from heaven). "Consider Jesus, the apostle and high priest of our confession." He calls him "apostle" from the sphere of Moses, but "high priest" from the sphere of Aaron. Moreover, he is called "the apostle and high priest of our confession" because, as God's ambassador, he brought to us the confession of faith, and, as high priest, he earned

[1]LW 29:143* (WA 57:136.19-137.2).

the confession of our faith when he offered himself for us. COMMENTS ON HEBREWS 3:1.[2]

CHRIST, THE HEAVENLY LEGATE. LUCAS OSIANDER: The apostle calls Christians saints because they have been sanctified and cleansed by the blood of Christ and they are being sanctified by the Holy Spirit, so that they might lead a holy and blameless life, as much as is possible in this weakness of the flesh. And we ought to remember that we have been called to a heavenly inheritance, not to the fulfilling of worldly desires or to unfit pleasures. And that divine calling, by which we have been called to eternal life through the ministry, never fails us, unless we repudiate Christ or through unbelief we fall away again from him. And, if Christ Jesus is the apostle or legate whom the Father has sent to us, it is certainly fitting to believe on him, for he reveals the will of the heavenly Father to us. Thus he says, "God so loved the world. . . ." He even gives us his own body and blood to eat and drink in the sacred meal, saying, "Take, eat. . . ." Therefore let us believe in this heavenly legate. And because the same is our high priest, who expiated our sins by his very own blood, let us confess him intrepidly before the world, so that also he might confess us before the Father. EPISTLE TO THE HEBREWS 3:1.[3]

BROTHERS (AND SISTERS) OF CHRIST. JOHANNES OECOLAMPADIUS: He showed above that Christ is our brother, when he said, "I will tell of your name to my brothers." Here he did not choose to say "my" brothers, but "holy brothers who share in a heavenly calling," so that he might make them look not to himself, but to Christ the Savior. And surely for this reason he addresses them with such grand titles, so that he might stir up their memory of the worthiness of God and of the salvation Christ has obtained for them. It is as if he were saying, "You who are brothers of Christ, saints—that is, sanctified and cleansed by his blood—who share in a heavenly calling—that is, called into the heavenly community—consider, I implore you, what a high dignity you possess, which you have received in Christ. Fix your mind's eye on him, and surely there will be no danger that you will either drift away or encounter a stumbling block in the word of the cross, much less put anyone ahead of Christ. . . ."

Incidentally, here you may observe what a "Christian" is, namely, a brother of Christ, a saint, and a partaker in the heavenly calling. Therefore, we should remind ourselves by that title to be that about which we are hearing, and we should live worthily of Christ our Savior, who has united us to himself by his own blood. EXPLANATIONS OF HEBREWS 3:1-2.[4]

CHRIST CREATED ALL THINGS. HEINRICH BULLINGER: The apostle demonstrates that, just as Christ is greater than the angels, so he is also greater than Moses. He accomplishes this by means of a certain allegorical figure, whereby he also hints in passing at the divinity of Christ. For by "house" he means the world, by "building" he means creation, and by "builder" he means God the Creator. For then one concludes thus: the builder is greater than the house itself; but Christ is the builder; therefore, Christ is greater than the house itself. But this argument would probably carry no weight, unless you understand "builder" here (as we have pointed out) to refer to God the Creator. For Paul says, "For every house is constructed by someone, but the one who created all things is God." But all things were created through Christ; therefore Christ is God, and hence he is also greater than Moses. COMMENTARY ON HEBREWS 3:3.[5]

3:5-6 *Under Christ, We Are God's House*

CHRIST HIMSELF IS IN US. JACQUES LEFÈVRE D'ÉTAPLES: We are the house of Christ, and he himself is in us as in his own house, if in the Lord of the house we will have placed our faith and hope,

[2]Cajetan, *In Epistolam ad Hebraeos Commentarii*, 159v; citing Heb 11:16.

[3]Osiander, *Epistola ad Hebraeos*, 18-19; citing Jn 3:16; Mt 26:26-29; Mk 14:22-25; Lk 22:17-20; 1 Cor 11:23-25; Mt 10:32; Lk 12:8.

[4]Oecolampadius, *In Epistolam ad Hebraeos Explanationes*, 37r, v.

[5]Bullinger, *In Pauli ad Hebraeos Epistolam*, 34r-v [87-88].

and in him alone we glory, rather than in any other who may be part of his house. EPISTLE TO THE HEBREWS 3:5-6.[6]

THE HOUSE OF GOD. JOHANNES OECOLAMPADIUS: "We are his house." He explains what he means by "house." He says, "We are the house of which we have been speaking, that is, if we truly believe, for God dwells in us by his grace." Again, it is exceedingly common in the Scriptures for believers to be called the temple of God, the house of God, the dwelling place of the Holy Spirit, as is shown in 1 Corinthians 3 and 6, as well as 2 Corinthians 6 and elsewhere. In addition, to prevent anyone from boasting about this house, he admonishes them to perseverance and endurance. For, as the Savior said, "The one who endures to the end will be saved." It is not enough to begin well; you must also continue perseveringly in that which you have well begun if you want to have an expectation of any reward. *Parrhēsia* means boldness or confidence in speaking; this shows that we must boldly, openly, and fearlessly confess the truth. For he says, "Whoever confesses me before this adulterous generation. . . ." EXPLANATIONS OF HEBREWS 3:5-6.[7]

THE NATURE OF THE CHURCH OF CHRIST. HEINRICH BULLINGER: From this we learn that the church, which is God's house, is the totality and assembly of the saints, that is, of believers; because as the church relies on God with complete faith, so it is born from the same faith through the word of truth. By faith, likewise, it stands firm and overcomes the world, so that it was not without cause that the apostle said, "I have written these things so that you may know how you ought to behave in the house of God, which is the church of the living God, the pillar and base of the truth, whom Christ loved, and gave himself up for her, that he might sanctify her, having cleansed her by the washing of water with the word, so that he might wed to himself a glorious church without spot or wrinkle or any such thing, but that she might be holy and blameless." The head, shepherd, bridegroom, life, strength, and health of this house, the church, is Christ Jesus. In this house Moses, the prophets, and the apostles are servants. The Word of God is its rule of life, light, law, and curriculum. This house is the single fold of the sheep of Christ, of which Christ is the door, who said, "If anyone enters by me, that person will be saved and will go in and out and find pasture." Therefore, outside this true church of Christ there is no salvation, no faith, no truth, no true religion. For the pontifical church in which the pope[†] is the head, lawgiver, judge, the prow, and stern—in short, everything in one—is a demonic and schismatic church, torn away from the true head, Christ, from the truth of the Scriptures, and from the unity of faith, founded on its own laws, decrees, ceremonies, and human follies, as others have plentifully demonstrated. COMMENTARY ON HEBREWS 3:6.[8]

CHRISTIANS ARE A TABERNACLE OF GOD'S GLORY. EDWARD DERING: Another purpose of this speech is for their better instruction in the truth of the gospel of Christ: that they should not, as their fathers did, hold their faith toward GOD with respect of the temple, then commonly called the house of God; nor with any religion of all the ceremonies used in it; for all these things had an end. God was now gone out of the sanctuary and dwelt no more between the cherubim, but had made himself a new tabernacle to dwell in, which was the body of man: which tabernacle alone we must have care of, to keep it pure from the concupiscence of the flesh, and to keep it holy from the vain inventions of our heart, and then the Lord should be always with us, as with the people whom he had chosen, to make them an habitation for himself, and

[6]Lefèvre d'Étaples, *Epistola ad Hebraeos*, 234r [515].
[7]Oecolampadius, *In Epistolam ad Hebraeos Explanationes*, 39v; citing Eph 2:22; 1 Cor 3:9, 16-17; 6:19; 2 Cor 6:16; Mt 24:13; Mk 8:38; Mt 10:32.
[8]Bullinger, *In Pauli ad Hebraeos Epistolam*, [90-91] 35v-36r; citing 1 Jn 5:4; 1 Tim 3:15; Eph 5:25-27; 2:19-20; Jn 10:9, 16. [†]Latin *pontifex*, which is translated "high priest" when referring to Christ or the high priests of Israel, is also employed as a title of the pope, as reflected in the translation here.

a tabernacle of his glory. 27 Lectures or Readings on the Epistle to the Hebrews 3:6.[9]

The House of Suffering. Martin Luther: The apostle says this here because he had called us the house that Christ "builds" (Heb 3:4, 6). The construction, however, is nothing else than tension, pressure, and in every way the cross and the sufferings that are in Christ. Therefore he wants us to know that if we are to be built and constructed, we need firm confidence and the glory of hope in him, lest we fail and suffer worse destruction while the building takes place. Lectures on Hebrews 3:6.[10]

The Church of God Is Found in the Human Heart. Edward Dering: It follows now, "If we hold fast the confidence and rejoicing of our hope unto the end." These words he adds to teach them manifestly to know themselves, whether they are this house or not. For if they are, they do hold and shall hold the rejoicing of their hope constantly and faithfully unto the end. These words, dearly beloved, let us mark them well, and learn them every jot and tittle with a wise heart, for they contain a blessed instruction and most necessary for our time. There is not this day any other thing that holds back a great number from the gospel of Christ, but only the ignorance of this one sentence. For what say all our adversaries against us, but only this: shall we leave the Catholic Church to believe a few who are newly sprung up? Shall we leave the church and follow Luther or Zwingli? The church has believed as we believe, the church has taught as we teach, and in the church we abide. Thus the church mimics the world, and as Paul says, the hearts of many that are not evil are seduced, so that though they have nothing to blame in us, yet they dare not come unto us, lest they should forsake the brotherhood in the church of Christ. This general plague is easily cured and all the evil of it is soon remedied if we can but hold our peace and hear the apostle speak for us all. The very same question is here handled: the Jews were now afraid to receive Christ, because they thought him a new teacher. They had Moses, the temple, the ceremonies, things full of excellent glory, and they were sure the church was here and these things were in the church. To leave them all suddenly and cleave to Christ alone would mean to leave the church and follow new doctrine. The apostle, to stop this offense, sets down first this plain doctrine without question or controversy, that the church of God, or (to use his own word) the house of God, is not any building of wood or stones, not any city or any material temple, but humankind is the house of God. Here first we learn one necessary lesson: if you want to know the house of God, that is, his church, look not at Jerusalem, nor at Mount Zion, for neither the city nor the temple in it are now the house in which God dwells. . . . This therefore learn for a truth: the church of God is not in any material temple, nor it is known by any city or country. . . . But to find the church of God, seek in the heart of humanity; for the apostles have all spoken plainly, "we are his house." . . . In every nation and in every country, the ones that fear God and work righteousness, they are the church, and the house in which God dwells. 27 Lectures or Readings on the Epistle to the Hebrews 3:6.[11]

Believers Are Dwelling Places of Christ. Lucas Osiander: Truly that house in which Christ dwells is the church itself; he did not merely create it but also built it and caused it to be born anew through the ministry of the gospel. Moreover, we are all dwelling places of Christ who believe in him. It is necessary that we constantly persevere in true fidelity to him and in the hope of eternal life. Epistle to the Hebrews 3:6.[12]

[9]Dering, *Lectures on Hebrews*, N5r *.
[10]LW 29:146-147 (WA 57: 141.2-6).
[11]Dering, *Lectures on Hebrews*, N5 v-N6 r *; citing Rom 16:18.
[12]Osiander, *Epistola ad Hebraeos*, 20.

3:7-19 A WARNING AGAINST HARD-HEARTEDNESS

7 Therefore, as the Holy Spirit says,

"Today, if you hear his voice,
8 do not harden your hearts as in the rebellion,
on the day of testing in the wilderness,
9 where your fathers put me to the test
and saw my works for forty years.
10 Therefore I was provoked with that generation,
and said, 'They always go astray in their heart;
they have not known my ways.'
11 As I swore in my wrath,
'They shall not enter my rest.'"

12 Take care, brothers, lest there be in any of you an
evil, unbelieving heart, leading you to fall away from
the living God. 13 But exhort one another every day, as
long as it is called "today," that none of you may be
hardened by the deceitfulness of sin. 14 For we have
come to share in Christ, if indeed we hold our original
confidence firm to the end. 15 As it is said,

"Today, if you hear his voice,
do not harden your hearts as in the rebellion."

16 For who were those who heard and yet rebelled?
Was it not all those who left Egypt led by Moses?
17 And with whom was he provoked for forty years?
Was it not with those who sinned, whose bodies fell in
the wilderness? 18 And to whom did he swear that they
would not enter his rest, but to those who were
disobedient? 19 So we see that they were unable to enter
because of unbelief.

OVERVIEW: In commenting on this passage the reformers stress the necessity of true faith in the Christian life, even as they readily acknowledge how difficult having faith can be, especially because of the requirement that it persevere to the end. The reformers are like-minded in interpreting the "today" of this passage as the time of the preaching of the gospel. They are especially impressed with the fact that the author of the epistle to the Hebrews attributes the opening citation from Psalm 95 not to David but to the Holy Spirit, seeing in this attribution apostolic confirmation of the divine inspiration of the Word. The reformers also comment at length on the deep sinfulness of the human heart, which causes the heart to harden in its unbelief toward God and his Word.

3:7-13 *Unbelief Leads to Falling Away*

THE GREATEST THING REQUIRED BY GOD. MARTIN LUTHER: One should note that this is the one, and the greatest, thing God requires of the Jews, yes, of all people, namely, that they hear his voice. . . . And rightly so, because without faith it is impossible for God to be with us (cf. Heb 11:6) or to work, since he does everything through his Word alone. Thus no one is able to cooperate with him unless he adheres to the Word. This takes place through faith, just as a tool does not cooperate with a worker unless it has been taken hold of with their hand. Therefore, it is perverse in the extreme for one to hasten to works before God works in us, that is, before we believe.

But human nature recoils violently from this hearing, because it must be reduced to nothing and to sheer darkness. . . . Thus when a potter fashions a vessel out of clay, it is impossible to preserve the previous form of the clay and at the same time to fashion a vessel, since the previous form resists, and lacks the form of a vessel, and, in general, as the philosophers say: "The evolvement of one thing is the destruction of another, and motion is from opposite to opposite."† And in this way nature with its own light is disposed toward the light of grace, just as darkness is disposed toward light and formlessness toward form. . . . Consequently, it is impossible for the natural state, the wisdom, prudence, purpose, or good intention of that man with whom and in whom God works to remain as it is or to move forward. For all these are the raw material and the unformed clay, as it were, which gives place to the direct opposite when God has begun to work. . . . Therefore faith in Christ is an exceedingly arduous thing, because it is a rapture and a removal from everything one experiences within and without to the things one experiences neither within nor without, namely, to the invisible, most high, and incomprehensible God. Lectures on Hebrews 3:7.[1]

"Today" Is the Time in Which the Gospel Is Preached. Edward Dering: "Therefore, as the Holy Spirit says": and let us learn, even as the Hebrews ought to have learned, with reverence to hear and to obey the word, for it is not the word of humans but of God, nor spoken by humans, but by the Holy Spirit. . . . I must acknowledge, this his word alone is my wisdom, and my understanding before all people: his word is my warrant, of all pure, holy, and blameless religion. . . . Now, touching the words that he says, "today": he means all the time in which the gospel is preached, teaching us hereby, that so long as the word is preached, so long salvation is offered. . . . And this (I beseech you) once again to remember, that when the gospel is preached unto us, then it is "today." Take away this word preached, which is the power of God to your salvation, and what time are you in? Surely you are in the night in which no one can work; for this is the day, when his voice is heard. 27 Lectures or Readings on the Epistle to the Hebrews 3:7.[2]

Ignoring Christ Carries Grave Consequences. Johannes Oecolampadius: Anyone who wants to understand the author correctly should connect all these words back to the purpose, and that is that we must listen to Christ. Recall in your memory here the beginning of the second chapter, "Therefore we must pay attention all the more intently to the things which have been said to us so that we do not drift away at any time." Now he proceeds with the same argument, explaining the extreme danger for those who do not hear by means of the example of their ancestors. He quotes this passage from Psalm 95.† Here *dio* does not seem to indicate an inference, but merely acts as a conjunction. But here he significantly wrote, "The Holy Spirit," not David, whose words these were, evidently so that they would not imagine this to be the opinion of a human, whose words are sometimes despised without consequence, but the word of God, and so of the Holy Spirit, which God will never permit anyone to despise unpunished. Explanations of Hebrews 3:7-11.[3]

Exclusion Through Unbelief. Lucas Osiander: And as the Israelites were excluded from the land of Canaan through unbelief and impiety, so the unbelieving and impious so-called Christians shall be excluded from eternal happiness, which was adumbrated through the land of Canaan. Epistle to the Hebrews 3:11.[4]

The Word Alone Purifies the Heart. Martin Luther: The whole emphasis of this statement is on the word "heart." For he does not say: "Take care, lest there be in any of you a grasping hand, a deceitful eye, a lustful ear." For above all one must take care that the heart is good, pure, and holy, as Psalm 51:10 states: "Create in me a clean heart, O God, and renew a right spirit within me." It is as if he were saying that cleanness of the works of the body is nothing unless there first is cleanness of the heart. But this uncleanness of the heart is so deep that no human being is sufficiently aware of it, much less can purge it away by his own strength, as Jeremiah 17:9-10 says: "The

[1]LW 29:148-149 (WA 57:142.18-19, 143.1-22, 144.10-12). †See Gregorius Reisch, *Margarita philosphica nova* (1508) 8.33: *De generatione et corruptione*, 149 n. 10.
[2]Dering, *Lectures on Hebrews*, O4r, O5v, O6r *; citing Rom 1:16.
[3]Oecolampadius, *In Epistolam ad Hebraeos Explanationes*, 40r; citing Ps 95:7-11. †In keeping with Latin chapter divisions, Oecolampadius refers to this as Psalm 94.
[4]Osiander, *Epistola ad Hebraeos*, 22.

heart of man is deceitful and inscrutable. Who will search it out? I the Lord search out the heart and the reins." Therefore the heart becomes pure and good only through faith in Christ, as we read in Acts 15:9: "He made no distinction between us and them, but purified their hearts by faith." For faith in the Word purifies, because just as the Word of God is completely pure and good, so it makes the one who adheres to it pure and good like itself. Whatever it has and is able to do it shares with him who adheres to it and believes it. . . . He who believes in the Word of God is righteous, wise, true, good, etc. Thus, on the contrary, he who is separated from the Word of God or departs from it will necessarily remain in wickedness, in uncleanness, and in everything that is opposed to the Word of God. . . . This is what the apostle means here when he speaks of "falling away from the living God." For one falls away from the living God when one falls away from his Word, which is alive and gives life to all things, yes, is God himself. Therefore they die. He who does not believe is dead. But falling away comes about through unbelief. And thus it is clear what an "evil heart" of unbelief is. It is a heart in which nothing is good, but everything is evil, because it departs from everything that is good. LECTURES ON HEBREWS 3:12.[5]

THE MAIN POINT OF HEBREWS IS A WARNING AGAINST UNBELIEF. HEINRICH BULLINGER: This is the main point and goal of everything that he has already said in the Hebrew manner, and everything that follows is directed toward it. "For this reason," he says, "I have brought out from the prophet this wretched example of more things, so that each one among you may take good care not to be unbelieving in the business of God. For unbelief causes us to fall away from the true, living, and eternal God." This is not as evident from this example of the fathers as from the fall of Adam, our original ancestor. For when he believed the seductions of the serpent more than the words of God, he fell away from God and his promise and became the source of our ruin. Thus we ourselves will unquestionably perish if we contend against the gospel that has been announced through Christ. What then shall we do? It says, "But exhort one another every day." Indeed, he says the same thing that he said above, but since his expression has been modified by the passage [from the Psalms] that he has cited, he states that it will be most beneficial if during this brief and feeble life (or what still remains of it) we exhort one another with all diligence to believe God and his Word. Otherwise, someone might eventually be hardened by the sin of unbelief, so that in the end he can do nothing for his whole life but live without hope. COMMENTARY ON HEBREWS 3:12-13.[6]

FAITH IN CHRIST IS EVERY VIRTUE. MARTIN LUTHER: One should note that here "hardening" means absolutely every thing that makes it difficult to believe. . . . The metaphor is taken from wax, which, when it is hard, does not take the figure of the seal but, when it is soft, is easily shaped into everything. Thus the human heart stands at a place where four roads intersect. For when it clings to God, its nature melts through the Word, softens toward God, and hardens toward the creature. But when it clings to the creature, it hardens toward God and softens toward the creature. For continually the human heart is now hard, now soft with regard to different things. For this clinging is the very faith in the Word. Indeed, it is that tie of betrothal about which Hosea 2:20 says: "I will betroth you to me in faithfulness," according to the well-known statement in 1 Corinthians 6:17:[†] "He who clings to God is one spirit with him." . . . It follows as a corollary that faith in Christ is every virtue and that unbelief is every vice, as is sufficiently clear from what has been said. For through faith a person becomes like the Word of God, but the Word is the Son of God. LECTURES ON HEBREWS 3:13.[7]

[5]LW 29:152-53* (WA 57:147.10-21, 148.1-17).

[6]Bullinger, *In Pauli ad Hebraeos Epistolam*, 37r-v [93-94].

[7]LW 29:155 (WA 57:151.1-15). [†]LW note (155 n. 18): "The original has '1 Cor. 7.'"

3:14-19 *Admonition to Persevere*

Faith Without Perseverance Is Not Faith. Heinrich Bullinger: But since there are many among the godly (for it seems that these words are an aside to those who were more godly) who still boasted too little in the knowledge of Christ, or who were not even continuing after having begun the journey, and sometimes even falling away in the middle of the route, he says, "It is not enough to have begun well, unless we bring the life thus begun to completion, mature and steadfast with constancy." For perseverance in faith is especially necessary, and without it faith is not faith, but rather empty opinion. Commentary on Hebrews 3:14.[8]

We Must Not Withdraw Our Hearts from God. Edward Dering: The words following, "to fall away from the living God," show both what it is to be unfaithful and what work it has in us. For to doubt when the Lord has spoken, or to mistrust what he has promised, is to fall away from him. And when we begin to waver in heart and call into question whether his word shall be performed or not, we lay ourselves open to the assaults of sin, and soon fall away from the living God to our own vanity. And this general rule, that infidelity makes us fall from God, we must particularly apply to all the works of our life, that we are not hardened (as the apostle says) with the deceit of sin. If I fall into danger and mistrust God's providence, and seek worldly means and unlawful help of humans for my deliverance, the prophet Jeremiah curses this infidelity and says, "we withdraw our hearts from the Lord." 27 Lectures or Readings on the Epistle to the Hebrews 3:12-14.[9]

Faithlessness Is the Primary Sin. John Calvin: He indicates that God has never been angry with his people without just cause, as Paul also reminds us. Whatever punishments we read of as inflicted in the ancient people, we shall find the same number of the most grievous sins that provoked the vengeance of God; yet we must always return to this point, that faithlessness is the chief of all the evils. Although he recounts this toward the end, he understands it to be the first cause of their being cursed. Certainly from the very moment of their first unbelief, they never stopped committing one sin after another, and so continually brought new scourges on themselves. Those same people who through their distrust rejected the possession of the land that was offered to them continued in their stubbornness, sometimes by covetousness, sometimes by complaining, sometimes by prostitution, sometimes by defiling themselves with pagan superstitions, so that their wickedness became more clearly attested. That unbelief, therefore, which they had shown from the beginning, prevented them from enjoying the blessing of God, because their contempt for his word was always inciting them to sin. Just as at first by their unbelief they earned God's deprivation of their promised rest, so whatever sins they later committed came from the same source. Commentary on Hebrews 3:17.[10]

---

[8]Bullinger, *In Pauli ad Hebraeos Epistolam,* 37v [94].

[9]Dering, *Lectures on Hebrews,* P6r-v *; citing Jer 17:5.

[10]CNTC 12:43*; citing 1 Cor 10:5-6.

4:1-13 ENTERING GOD'S REST

Therefore, while the promise of entering his rest still
stands, let us fear lest any of you should seem to have
failed to reach it. 2 *For good news came to us just as to*
them, but the message they heard did not benefit them,
because they were not united by faith with those who
listened.[a] 3 *For we who have believed enter that rest, as*
he has said,

> *"As I swore in my wrath,*
> *'They shall not enter my rest,'"*

although his works were finished from the foundation
of the world. 4 *For he has somewhere spoken of the*
seventh day in this way: "And God rested on the
seventh day from all his works." 5 *And again in this*
passage he said,

> *"They shall not enter my rest."*

6 *Since therefore it remains for some to enter it, and*
those who formerly received the good news failed to
enter because of disobedience, 7 *again he appoints a*
certain day, "Today," saying through David so long
afterward, in the words already quoted,

> *"Today, if you hear his voice,*
> *do not harden your hearts."*

8 *For if Joshua had given them rest, God*[b] *would not*
have spoken of another day later on. 9 *So then, there*
remains a Sabbath rest for the people of God, 10 *for*
whoever has entered God's rest has also rested from
his works as God did from his.

11 *Let us therefore strive to enter that rest, so that no*
one may fall by the same sort of disobedience. 12 *For the*
word of God is living and active, sharper than any
two-edged sword, piercing to the division of soul and
of spirit, of joints and of marrow, and discerning the
thoughts and intentions of the heart. 13 *And no creature*
is hidden from his sight, but all are naked and exposed
to the eyes of him to whom we must give account.

a Some manuscripts *it did not meet with faith in the hearers* **b** Greek *he*

Overview: The commentators reflect at length on the theme of rest in this passage, frequently interpreting it as cessation from good works in favor of reliance on divine grace for salvation, but they also offer other interpretations. The reformers also wrestle with the intended audience of this passage, the elect or the reprobate, which is part of their larger wrestling with the question raised by the epistle to the Hebrews as to whether salvation can be lost or not. Finally, the reformers have a great deal to say about the concluding verses of the passage, commenting at length on the identity and properties of the Word of God.

4:1-2 *True Faith Necessary to Enter God's Rest*

Hearing and Obeying. Erasmus Sarcerius: Through what means does such rest come? That one hears and obeys God's voice and word and does not harden one's heart against them. . . . What prevents this rest? Unbelief. What fosters it? Belief in God's Word. Summaries and Brief Content, Heb 2:1-4.[1]

Believers Have a Perpetual Sabbath. Johannes Bugenhagen: This chapter is connected to what precedes it. He takes the opportunity to show from the Psalm that there is a sabbath for believers other than the one associated with the seventh day. The one was observed externally every week even by the ungodly; the other the godly alone recognized even from the beginning of the world. Into this sabbath unbelievers have never come, for they cannot enter. For where people seem best, they try to be justified by their own works, which is

[1] Sarcerius, *Summarien vnd kurtzer Jnhalt,* 4:HH3r [930].

diametrically opposed to the sabbath of God. When the godly, on the other hand, enter into this sabbath, they rest from all their own works, just as God rested from all his work. Thus they now allow the word by which they have been established afresh and made new creatures to work effectively in them in accordance with all his will, not their own, just as God permits his word, by which he established all things, continually to impart strength and potency into those same created things. This is what it means to rest and nevertheless to be always at work, just as Christ says: "My Father is working until now, and I also am working." Therefore, those who truly believe—which is to say, those who cling to God alone and put absolutely no trust in any object in this world, nor in any righteousness or human merit—these have this sabbath, which is sanctified by God, which is continually observed and is eternal. Commentary on the Pauline Epistles, Heb 4:1.[2]

Faithful Teachers Will Teach Themselves. Robert Cleaver: Those who faithfully instruct others will also instruct themselves with their own precepts. The neglect of this is greatly condemned by the apostle Paul, who speaks to the Jews in this manner, "you then who teach others, do you not teach yourself? While you preach against stealing, do you steal? etc." In this place he shows that it is a fearful and inexcusable sin for one to take on himself to be an informer of others, and in the meantime to be utterly untaught himself with respect to any working and saving instruction. Neither was this holy apostle ready to censure the omission of this duty in others, but he was careful to practice it himself. For in 2 Corinthians 7:1, where he says, "Since we have these promises, beloved, let us cleanse ourselves from every defilement of body and spirit, bringing holiness to completion in the fear of God," we see that makes himself one of the number. First Sermon on Chapter 4 of Hebrews.[3]

[2]Bugenhagen, *Annotationes in epistolas Pauli recognitae* (1525) 143v-144r [320-21]; citing Jn 5:17; Is 58:11, 13; 66:23. In the Vulgate, which Bugenhagen quotes following this selection, Is 58:11 begins, "And the Lord your God will give you rest continually."

[3]Cleaver, *Four Sermons*, 2-3; citing Rom 2:21, 7:15; 2 Cor 7:1.

Hearing Does No Good Unless We Believe. Heinrich Bullinger: He removes another misunderstanding. He says, "But the promise did not benefit them, because they did not believe God or his messages." Indeed they rejected Moses himself and murmured against God himself. In the same way it will not benefit any of you to hear the gospel, unless you also inscribe what you hear on a believing heart. For St. James also says, "Be doers of the word, and not hearers only." The apostle also taught in 1 Corinthians that the fathers were baptized and fed on the sacred mysteries, but that they were not acquitted on that account, for most of them were overthrown by the wrath of God in the wilderness. Therefore it will do us no good to have been initiated into the sacred mysteries, unless by true faith we also cling to God with all our might. Commentary on Hebrews 4:2.[4]

The Union of Faith, the Word, and the Heart. Martin Luther: That uniting or combination of the Word and the hearts is reciprocal. For these three—faith, the Word, and the heart—become one. Faith is the glue or the bond. The Word is on one side; the heart is on the other side. But through faith they become one spirit, just as man and wife become "one flesh" (Gen 2:24). Therefore it is true that the heart is combined with the Word through faith and that the Word is combined with the heart through the same faith. Lectures on Hebrews 4:2.[5]

The Blessed Drink of the Blessed Tavern. Edward Dering: Now, touching these words of the apostle, that he says, "Let us fear lest any of you should have failed to reach it," we must not take them as though the apostle taught that the elect should fear, as though they might fall from their hope or that their election were not sure, for you have heard before how he said, "if indeed we hold our original confidence firm to the end."

[4]Bullinger, *In Pauli ad Hebraeos Epistolam*, 40r [99]; citing Jas 1:22; 1 Cor 10:1-5.

[5]LW 29:160 (WA 57:156.19-157.4).

But here we must consider to whom the apostle is speaking, that is, to such as are far off from a true faith, who have shown no great regard to the voice of the Lord Jesus, which are yet in many temptations of sin, doubtful to be carried away with the deceits of it. . . . So when we are bid to fear, it is as when we are bid to watch, to be sober, to stand with our loins girded, to have before us the ways of God with reverence and obedience; it forbids presumptuous and vain boasting of salvation, when the glorious and fearful name "the Lord thy God" is not regarded by you. . . . This fear is a fear of falling into sin lest we should offend so merciful a father; it is not a fear of falling from his grace, lest he should take his mercy from us.

As those that love to sit at the tavern do mingle their drink with spices or their wine with sugar, so we in that most blessed tavern, in which the Word of God is offered us to drink, we must mingle it with the sweet spice of faith, and it is a cup of eternal life unto us; otherwise, if we be unfaithful, we have lost our blessing and are fallen from the hope of life. 27 Lectures or Readings on the Epistle to the Hebrews 4:1-2.[6]

4:3-10 *Sabbath Rest for the People of God*

Three Kinds of Rest. Johannes Bugenhagen: What is said here regarding "rest" cannot be understood as referring to the sabbath of the seventh day, because certainly no one can be unaware that this was said with reference to the Promised Land. Furthermore, who does not see that it is neither concerning the sabbath of the seventh day nor concerning the Promised Land that David warns us so that we may not harden our hearts to the voice of the Lord, as they had, lest we also fail like them to enter into the rest of God. For when David was writing, they were already in that Promised Land. As I say, you see here three kinds of rest: rest from labors on the seventh day; rest from enemies in the Promised Land; and rest in the kingdom of heaven. This is real rest that really belongs to believers and is perfected in the final resurrection. In the meantime, this flesh mourns and is compelled into combat, just as of old the nations that remained in the Promised Land trained that people for battle. Commentary on the Pauline Epistles, Heb 4:3.[7]

Scripture Speaks of Three Distinct Rests or Sabbaths. Johannes Oecolampadius: This sentence seems to be incomplete, but the meaning is clear enough. For it means that there is another rest for us besides that which may be obtained from the Promised Land, surely the rest that God indicated when he created everything, which he ordained to be related about himself: "And the Lord rested. . . ." But there is a threefold sabbath or rest. There is a sabbath recorded by Moses when God rested from all his works on the seventh day, but he rested in the sense that he created nothing new. Yet we know from our Savior in John 5 that the Father is working until now, and so also is the Son. One cannot interpret the prophet as referring here to this sabbath. Another rest, according to the narrative, is that which the people had in the desert, for they did not labor, although they were wandering around awaiting the Promised Land. There is still a third rest besides these, and it is concerning this that the prophet is speaking here, who was already in the land of Canaan or of promise when he wrote these things. Chrysostom also explains this with almost the same interpretation.† Explanations of Hebrews 4:3-5.[8]

The True and Perfect Rest. Edward Dering: This scripture, which now I have read to you, I must confess, to me it seems yet somewhat obscure, neither has God so revealed it to me, that I dare boldly pronounce, "this is what it means." But . . . according to that which God has given me, so I will

[6]Dering, *Lectures on Hebrews*, R3r-v, R3v-R4r, R7v*; citing Heb 3:14.

[7]Bugenhagen, *Annotationes in epistolas Pauli recognitae* (1525) 144r [321]; citing Ps 95:7-11; Judg 3:2.

[8]Oecolampadius, *In Epistolam ad Hebraeos Explanationes*, 45r; citing Jn 5:17; Ex 20:11; 16:30. †John Chrysostom, "Homily 6," in *Homilae XXXIV in epistolam ad Hebraeos* (PG 63:53-54; NPNF 14:393).

show you what I think most likely, and so much the more boldly I will show you my opinion, because by the grace of God, I will speak nothing but what is agreeable to all that the apostle before has most plainly taught us. . . . Now, touching this work whereof we have heard so much, that is, the rest of God, we must mark how the Scripture uses it, sometimes for the truth, which is ever one, sometimes for the figures, which have been diverse. The true and perfect rest is that which is now begun in us, the resting from our own works, that is, our dying to sin, and the crucifying of the old person, that we may give over our bodies to the Lord to be servants of righteousness, and that only his Spirit may reign in us, that as Paul says, it be not now we that live, but that it be Christ that lives in us. This rest shall be made perfect in the resurrection of the just, when we shall be joined unto Christ our head, and God shall be unto us, all in all. 27 Lectures or Readings on the Epistle to the Hebrews 4: 3-10.[9]

An Evangelical Sabbath Rest. Desiderius Erasmus: Therefore, there remains some other sabbath rest for the people of God; there remains another rest, not in Palestine, but in the homeland of heaven, to which we are hastening under the leadership of Jesus Christ. But we shall not reach it if we do not celebrate in purity here an evangelical sabbath rest by abstaining from the words of this world. Paraphrases on the Epistle to the Hebrews 4:4-13.[10]

The Gravest Sin. Lucas Osiander: For those who have persisted in that unbelief not only have not entered into the land of Canaan, they have even truly been excluded from that eternal rest. . . . This is the exhortation of the Holy Spirit, most gravely warning, lest we harden our hearts to the voice of our pastor Jesus Christ. For this sin is graver than all others that have been committed against the Decalogue. Epistle to the Hebrews 4:6-7.[11]

Listen to Christ. Johannes Oecolampadius: This is the conclusion of the matters that have been discussed to this point, namely, that this sabbath or rest belongs to the people of God, by which name here he means all believers, whether they are from Jews or from Gentiles. For these are truly those who share in this rest, if they listen to Christ. Moreover, he admonishes beautifully when he says, "Let us strive." He is saying, "Not only should we not despise, but we must also make every effort, press on, or—although others oppose us—let us hurry to enter into that rest." But such striving consists in this: that we listen to Christ, as the one with whom alone the Father is well-pleased, unless we wish to perish in dreadful imitation of the unbelief of the fathers. "The servant who knew his master's will and did not get ready or act according to his will be beaten with many blows" (Lk 12). Cain was a murderer, but he was avenged sevenfold; Lamech thereafter decreed an even weightier vengeance on one who injured him (Gen 4). You will come to the same conclusions regarding the flood and the destruction of Jerusalem. For as sin increases, so does the penalty, as in the instance of the first temple. Let us remind ourselves of this so that we may be on the highest alert against unbelief, the ruin of our souls. For, granted that in this life one may be free from punishment, in the next we will not escape the penalty, and a very severe one at that. For these things were written for our instruction. Explanations of Hebrews 4:9-11.[12]

A Higher Rest. Gasparo Contarini: Some say that our works are to be understood as labors and troubles, from which they shall rest, who shall rest in the rest of God. But I think there was a higher sense in Paul, namely, that he shows, what Dionysius says,† namely, that our happiness, which is our union with God and absorption by God, is higher than whatever work or operation of ours; whence that rest consists in the cessation

[9]Dering, *Lectures on Hebrews*, Sr-v, S5r-v*; citing Gal 2:20.
[10]CWE 44:223.
[11]Osiander, *Epistola ad Hebraeos*, 26.
[12]Oecolampadius, *In Epistolam ad Hebraeos Explanationes*, 46r-v; citing Mt 17:5; Lk 12:47; Gen 4:15, 23-24; 1 Cor 10:11.

of all our works; because it transcends and surpasses them. SCHOLIA IN THE EPISTLES OF THE DIVINE PAUL, THE EPISTLE TO THE HEBREWS 4:10.[13]

ETERNAL REST AND TEMPORAL LABORS. LUCAS OSIANDER: And this sabbath begins in this life in us when we rest from works of the old Adam and by faith and in the hope of eternal life we rejoice in the Lord. . . . And since we are looking for eternal and most blessed rest, the labors and troubles that we sustain in our vocation in these lands do not irk us, for all things will be most abundantly compensated to us. EPISTLE TO THE HEBREWS 4:10.[14]

EVEN THE SAINTS FEAR DAMNATION AT TIMES. JOHANNES BUGENHAGEN: "For the word is living. . . ." The purpose of the preceding discourse is to prevent us from following the Israelites' unbelieving example and perishing as they did. People are accustomed to quote these words everywhere in connection with the grace of the Word of God, but actually they are very frightening, just as those who were not able to enter into the promised rest found by experience. See Numbers 14, where it says, "The people mourned greatly," which is the penalty felt by those condemned for eternity by the word of God's judgment. The saints also feel at times that they have been abandoned and live in fear of the judgments of God. This is the source of such cries in the Psalms as "There is no soundness in my flesh before your wrath" or "All my bones are troubled." Here the defeated conscience feels that it is under the judgment of the Word of God and eternal condemnation, and as long as the soul has no instruction and everything is full of despair, it is inevitable for the bones to tremble and the body to pine and all the powers of both body and soul to grow weak and divided among themselves. For indeed it is terrifying to fall into the hands of the living God. But our devoted Father does not abandon his own in such a fearful hell. This, in contrast, is the source of those cries of thanksgiving for deliverance, such as "All my enemies shall be ashamed and greatly troubled" and "You have saved me from those who go down into the pit." COMMENTARY ON THE PAULINE EPISTLES, HEB 4:10.[15]

4:11-13 *Strive to Enter God's Sabbath Rest*

THIS CALL COMES FROM JESUS. CARDINAL CAJETAN: "Therefore let us hurry to enter into that rest, so that no one may fall into that very (that is, 'into the same') sort of unbelief." If we do not hurry, if we do not strive so as to enter into that rest, our carelessness creates the danger that someone might fall into the same sort of unbelief, that is, that someone might fall into an unbelief like the unbelief of the ancients, which was why they did not enter into the promised rest. "For the speech of God is living." That which is stated in John, "In the beginning was the Word," is here referred to as "the declaration of God," for it is the same sort of expression. Therefore, when this text speaks of "the declaration of God," it is intended to refer to the Son of God. And he provides the reason why we should strive so as to enter into that rest so that we may not fall into unbelief and the punishment of unbelievers, which is drawn from the standing of the author, who is the Son of God, the Declaration of God, the Word of God. For assuredly he is the author of salvation and eternal rest. And it says concerning him, first, that he is "living." And truly he is alive with divine, intellectual, eternal life. . . . "And effective" for everything he chooses to achieve, for rewarding and punishing, for the rest he has offered and the penalties he has threatened. "And more penetrating than any two-edged sword," which is called "two-edged" because it is sharp everywhere. He

[13]Contarini, *Opera*, 517 (519). †The theme of mystical absorption into the divine may be found throughout Dionysius the Areopagite's *Mystical Theology*.
[14]Osiander, *Epistola ad Hebraeos*, 27.
[15]Bugenhagen, *Annotationes in epistolas Pauli recognitae* (1525) 144r-v [321-22]; citing Num 14:39; Ps 38:3; Ps 6:2; Heb 10:31; Ps 6:10; 30:3.

declares that his power exceeds all penetration by the metaphor of a penetrating sword sharpened on one side and on the other. And he truly is more penetrating, because he penetrates into everything by his divine action. Comments on Hebrews 4:11-12.[16]

The Hammer of the Word. John Calvin: What he says here of the efficacy or power of the word, he says it that they might know that it could not be despised with impunity, as though he had said, "Whenever the Lord addresses us by his word, he deals seriously with us, in order that he may touch all our inmost thoughts and feelings; and so there is no part of our soul that ought not to be roused." . . . It indeed appears evident that the word of God is not equally efficacious in all. For in the elect it exerts its own power, when humbled by a true knowledge of themselves they flee to the grace of Christ; and this is never the case except when it penetrates into the innermost heart. For hypocrisy must be sifted, which has marvelous and extremely winding recesses in the human heart; and then we must not be slightly pricked or torn, but be thoroughly wounded, that being prostrate under a sense of eternal death, we may be taught to die to ourselves. In short, we shall never be renewed in the whole mind, which Paul requires (Eph 4:23) until our old person be slain by the edge of the spiritual sword. . . . Nothing of this kind is found in the reprobate. . . . In short, as the word of God is a hammer, so they have a heart like the anvil, so that its hardness repels its strokes, however powerful they may be. . . . Hence it appears that this its character is to be confined to the faithful only, as they alone are thus searched to the quick. Commentaries on the Epistle of Paul the Apostle to the Hebrews 4:12.[17]

The Distinction Between Soul and Spirit. Balthasar Hubmaier: The human being is a corporal and rational creature, created by God as body, spirit, and soul, Genesis 2:7. These three elements are found essentially and in varying ways in every human being, as the Scripture thoroughly proves. When the Lord God made the human being out of the dust from the earth, he blew a living breath into his face and thus the human being became a living soul, Genesis 2:7. Here Moses points to three things with distinct names. First, the flesh or the body is made out of the earth, which clod of earth or lump of clay, *ʿāpār* and *ʾereṣ* in the Hebrew, is translated in German as "dust," "ashes," or "mud taken from the earth." Second, notice the living breath, *nəšāmâ* in the Hebrew, translated as "blowing on," "breathing on," "blowing upon," or "spirit." Third, the soul, call *nēpēš*, is expressed separately; it is that which makes the body alive. Saint Paul mentioned these three essential substances quite clearly also with special and distinctive Greek names in writing to the Thessalonians: *pneuma*, *psychē*, and *sōma*; in Latin: *spiritus, anima, corpus*; in German: *Geist, Seel, Leib*. He said . . . 1 Thessalonians 5:23. Likewise, we read in Hebrews the distinction between the soul and the spirit thus . . . Hebrews 4:12. Freedom of the Will, Heb 4:12.[18]

The Blows of the Spirit's Sword. William Jones: This sword of the Spirit is sharper than any two-edged sword, and will either open the sores of your souls, that they may be healed, or it will wound you to death everlasting: therefore despise it not, but as God commands you in his Word, so study to enter into this rest. . . . But what manner of Word is this that is so lively and mighty in operation? Not the word that God speaks immediately with his own mouth from heaven, as he thundered at the giving of the law: but the word that he speaks by the mouth of his ambassadors. Romans 10:8; 1 Corinthians 1:21; 1 Peter 1:25. Though a weak person handles this sword, yet because the Spirit of God strikes with it, it will give a sound blow. . . . A strange thing! There has been wonderful plenty of

[16]Cajetan, *In Epistolam ad Hebraeos Commentarii*, 160v; citing Jn 1:1.
[17]CTS 40:100-101*.

[18]CRR 5:429-30.

preaching in this land, yet small profiting by it, and why? Because we have not the reverent estimation of the word of God that we ought to have: we think too basely of it, we imagine it not to be of half the power it is. A Commentary upon the Epistles of St. Paul, Heb 4:12.[19]

The Holy Efficacy of the Word. Lucas Osiander: The reference here is to the threats of the word of God by which the evangelical ministers threaten eternal damnation to those who have contempt for the word. These threats abide in the souls of human beings and effectually upset the mind and all the powers of the soul, and penetrate into the conscience, as no sharp, double-edged sword is able to penetrate the human body and part the joints of the body. And so such contemptors of the gospel, where they feel the judgment of God . . . in their consciences, are quickly carried into desperation; they even sometimes do violence to themselves with their own hands. Of this efficacy of the divine word one sees some examples in our times, in human desperations among those who have blasphemed and persecuted the gospel teaching that they knew to be true in their hearts. And while sometimes even the pious and the elect fall into such grave temptations, so that they come close to desperation, the Lord keeps them marvelously, lest their faith (which still lies hidden asleep in the heart) fails. And the Lord raises them up again, consoles, and restores them in his own time. The ancients called this kind of testing a "suspension of grace." Epistle to the Hebrews 4:12.[20]

The Living Word of God. Edward Dering: It is said first, "the word of God is living," which property may be attributed to the word of God in diverse respects. First in respect of us, because it quickens us into a spiritual life, and without it we are in darkness and in the shadow of death; therefore it is a living word, and the "seed of our new birth." Another cause why the word is called living is in respect of itself, because it is eternal and ever abides according the nature of the living God, whose word it is. . . . Another cause yet there is why the word of God is called living, and this cause most agreeable to this place; that is, because it enters with power into every part of us, so that, as our life is dispersed into every part, and we feel it, both in grief and pleasure, even so, the virtue of the word of God pierces into every member, to bruise (as the prophet says) the very bones, or to fill them with marrow and fatness. This sense is plain and agreeable to all the words following. 27 Lectures or Readings on the Epistle to the Hebrews 4:12.[21]

The Word of God Here Is the Sentence Pronounced by God Himself. Johannes Oecolampadius: Some apply these verses to the word of God that we proclaim, as Augustine also does somewhere, but that is not very accurate.† For we know that we speak a dead word and letter; thus you should rightly interpret it as referring to the word of divine warning and of the overwhelmingly powerful wrath of God. But the apostle intends to append this to what he has already said for the sake of confirmation, so that no one will think that it is a light matter to provoke the wrath of God upon themselves, or that without penalty they can fall away from the one who is the fountain of life. This is done by those who do not listen to his voice and shrink from receiving Christ with true faith. This word of God is the sentence of God, as one might say. Someone may perhaps disregard the word of a human, with its threats and wrath, as that which has less power, and thus is less to be feared. But with the word and sentence of God it is very different, for it is more living and powerful that can be expressed, of which the overthrow of the fathers was example enough. Therefore, it will not do to disregard it, for it is a very fearful thing to fall into the hands of the living God.

"And sharper. . . ." These things are appended, as the preceding paragraph explains. He says that the

[19]Jones, *A Commentary upon the Epistles of St Paul*, 179, 183-84*.
[20]Osiander, *Epistola ad Hebraeos*, 27-28.
[21]Dering, *Lectures on Hebrews*, T3r, T3v, T4r*; citing Lk 1:79; 1 Pet 1:23; Ps 51:8.

word is piercingly sharp, which nothing at all can withstand. He calls the sword *distomon*, for it is the custom of Scripture to call the edge of the sword the *stoma*, or mouth, as in Isaiah 3, Luke 21, Revelation 1. "And from his mouth came out a two-edged sword," that is, a sword sharpened on both edges. But, speaking fittingly, the gospel cannot be called a sword, inasmuch as it teaches promises and the forgiveness of sins. But the sentence of God, that is aptly called a sword, for it is wholly unavoidable. And, because knowing this is of no small importance to godliness, by such an amplification he intended to set the power of the word almost before their very eyes, so that by examining it they could escape in time from the judgment of God.

"Piercing all the way to. . . ." By "soul" he means that part of our nature in which the affections have dominion, and by "spirit" the mind, or "a fragment of the divine breath," as someone says;‡ by "joints and marrow" he means the body. He is indicating that though another sword may not penetrate the inner organs and cut them off from the interlaced bones and joints, this one pierces right through the joints and bones, and even the most hidden marrow, so that there is nothing that is not accessible and penetrable to it. Clearly it distinguishes between godly and ungodly thoughts, between upright and distorted intentions of the heart in such a way that nothing could do it better.

"And there is no creature. . . ." He speaks about the word or sentence of God and about God himself without distinguishing between the two. This should be taken in reference to God, from whom nothing can hide. Many things can indeed be concealed from humans, but nothing at all from God, to whose eyes all things are manifest, naked and stretched out face-upward. *Trachēlizō* is to peel, remove the skin, and bend back. (See other works on the subject.) Hypocrites and the ungodly appear open indeed, but God is the one who lays bare and opens up their inner workings and at last exposes all things to the eyes. For nothing can be painted over forever. We should take note of this and strive after wholehearted godliness; otherwise we will be cut in pieces, and our portion will be assigned with the ungodly. EXPLANATIONS OF HEBREWS 4:12-13.[22]

THIS WARNING CONCLUDES THE OPENING DISCOURSE. HEINRICH BULLINGER: With these words we have completed the first part of this letter, in which Paul urged the Hebrews to receive Christ, who is greater than the angels and Moses, inasmuch as he is the Son of God. Hence it is impossible safely to treat this matter with contempt, when the fathers' contempt for the word of God that was preached through Moses was punished as they wandered and died wretchedly in the wilderness. For the word of God truly is alive and more penetrating than a double-edged sword, so that it is able to punish enemies just as swiftly, and indeed it was discharged to punish the Israelites without restraint. COMMENTARY ON HEBREWS 4:12-13.[23]

CHRIST IS THE PENETRATING WORD. DESIDERIUS ERASMUS: The threat made by the Word of God, Christ Jesus,† must not be ignored. For he is alive and active and more penetrating than any two-edged sword. He cuts not only into the parts of the body, but also into the emotions deep within the mind where he can sever the soul from the spirit, can sever all the joints and marrow of the mind; he discerns the hidden thoughts and intentions of our heart. So far is any human thought from deceiving him that no creature exists anywhere at all either in heaven or under the earth that is hidden to his eyes. All things are naked and laid open for scrutiny to the eyes of him to whom we must give an account of our life. Just as God was not deceived in the past by the murmuring of

22Oecolampadius, *In Epistolam ad Hebraeos Explanationes*, 46v-47v; citing Is 3:25 (?); Lk 21:24; Rev 1:16; Heb 10:31; Mt 24:51. †Augustine, *City of God* 20.21 (PL 41:692; NPNF 2:441). ‡This phrase is drawn from Horace, *Satire* 2.2.79. Oecolampadius's text as printed is garbled by the misprint *auris* (ear) instead of *aurae* (breath, wind).

23Bullinger, *In Pauli ad Hebraeos Epistolam*, 45r [109].

the Hebrews and had no need of any other sword to destroy them than his divine command, so Christ will not be deceived now by the person who professes to live according to the gospel but is secretly in love with what belongs to the world and does not hasten in all sincerity toward the promised rest. Paraphrases on the Epistle to the Hebrews 4:12-13.[24]

[24]CWE 44:223-24.†The CWE editors note that Chrysostom also interpreted the Word as Jesus Christ in this passage. See John Chrysostom, *Homiliae in epistulam ad Hebraeos* 7 (PG 63:60; NPNF 398a).

4:14–5:10 Jesus, the Great High Priest Who Has Suffered

[14]Since then we have a great high priest who has passed through the heavens, Jesus, the Son of God, let us hold fast our confession. [15]For we do not have a high priest who is unable to sympathize with our weaknesses, but one who in every respect has been tempted as we are, yet without sin. [16]Let us then with confidence draw near to the throne of grace, that we may receive mercy and find grace to help in time of need.

5 For every high priest chosen from among men is appointed to act on behalf of men in relation to God, to offer gifts and sacrifices for sins. [2]He can deal gently with the ignorant and wayward, since he himself is beset with weakness. [3]Because of this he is obligated to offer sacrifice for his own sins just as he does for those of the people. [4]And no one takes this honor for himself, but only when called by God, just as Aaron was.

[5]So also Christ did not exalt himself to be made a high priest, but was appointed by him who said to him,

> *"You are my Son,*
> *today I have begotten you";*

[6]as he says also in another place,

> *"You are a priest forever,*
> *after the order of Melchizedek."*

[7]In the days of his flesh, Jesus[a] offered up prayers and supplications, with loud cries and tears, to him who was able to save him from death, and he was heard because of his reverence. [8]Although he was a son, he learned obedience through what he suffered. [9]And being made perfect, he became the source of eternal salvation to all who obey him, [10]being designated by God a high priest after the order of Melchizedek.

a Greek *he*

Overview: In this passage the pastoral concerns and exegetical talents of the reformers come together. Having commented at length on the divinity and majesty of Christ in the epistle to the Hebrews, they now turn to emphasize his mercy, grace, and understanding for sinners as a divinely chosen high priest who has suffered in the flesh. The reformers wrestle with what it might mean for Christ to have learned obedience through what he suffered (Heb 5:8), and they also begin to reflect on the comparison between Christ and Melchizedek. Prior to this, they draw important lessons from Christ's priesthood for the proper role and function of the evangelical ministry, emphasizing especially the importance of the external call to this office.

4:14-16 *Jesus, the High Priest Who Sympathizes*

Christ's Majesty and Mercy. Johannes Bugenhagen: Because he had begun to discuss the high priesthood of Christ, but in the meantime (since he had the opportunity) he interpreted the words of the Psalm, "Today if you hear his voice," he returns, saying, "Therefore, since we have. . . ." Consequently, we should mark the next chapter as starting with this verse. To begin with, he pursues this theme to prevent us from fleeing from Christ in the consciousness of our own weakness and sins, because he has been described above in such terms of worthiness and excellence. For he also has been tested, and made lower than the angels for a little time, as it says above, so that he might become a merciful and faithful high priest. Accordingly, the exclusion of Christ gives us confidence to approach [the throne of grace], now that we know that he was excluded for us. On the other hand, his power gives us confidence to persevere, because certainly no one can take us out of his hands. Commentary on the Pauline Epistles, Heb 4:14.[25]

[25]Bugenhagen, *Annotationes in epistolas Pauli recognitae* (1525) 145r [323]; citing Heb 2:17-18; Jn 10:28.

THE MEDIATOR MUST PARTAKE OF BOTH NATURES. HEINRICH BULLINGER: He says this because, since it is should be sufficiently evident from the preceding discourse that Jesus Christ is true God and man, clearly it is also evident that he alone should be the true mediator and high priest with God for the human race, the one who made atonement for all the sins of the world by the sacrifice of his own body. And it rightly befalls that he who is our high priest should also be our mediator, precisely for this reason, because they both pertain to the same function. But it was required that this mediator between God and humanity be a participant in both natures; hence this doctrine that the apostle revisits with so much attention: that our high priest is the Son of God, true God, and that in everything he has been made like men, true man. For also St. John Chrysostom, in homily 7 of his expositions of the first letter of Paul to Timothy, says, "Now a mediator ought to be joined in fellowship with both of those for whom he is a mediator. So indeed it is the distinctive quality of a mediator to become a participant in both parties for whom he would be the mediator. . . . For just as the middle of any place is in contact with both sides, so also it was required that the middle of the two natures should connect and combine both natures. Therefore, just as he was made man, so also he was God. Indeed a mere man would never have become a complete mediator, for this kind of mediator had to converse with God. Likewise, one who was only God could not have been the mediator, for those whom he would have approached as a mediator could not have received him."† What Augustine wrote about the mediator in *The City of God*, book 9, chapter 15, harmonizes in every way with Chrysostom's explanation.‡ Therefore our high priest was true God and man, and he passed through the heavens, by which the author alludes to the role of the priests and the tabernacles. For Christ has not entered into a tabernacle built by humans, but into heaven itself, so that now he might appear for us in the sight of God. COMMENTARY ON HEBREWS 4:14-15.[1]

A HIGH PRIEST WITH SINNERS. JOHANNES OECOLAMPADIUS: "For we do not have a high priest. . . ." This is the reason for his statement that we must hold on to the confession, and by it he also answers an unspoken question. For someone might say, "Great priests are entirely disdainful; they readily despise those who are lower than them, and not only do they distance themselves from interaction with the masses, but they also deeply loath it. So what friendship can I hope for from them, since I am a sinner from the crowd? Truly, I feel my confidence that they will intercede for me slipping away; how often does my sin and unworthiness steal upon my soul?!" Therefore he says, "We have no reason to fear. For surely a very different priest meets us than one by whom we could be despised. And how could he loathe sinners, when he came into the world to save sinners? He is like us in every respect; he has been thoroughly tried by evils (albeit without any sin). Therefore, how could he not sympathize with our weaknesses, when to prompt us to faith in him he freely chose to be tempted and afflicted in every way? He is indeed God, but still he was not ashamed to experience our misfortunes in his own flesh, so that he might entirely persuade us that he is moved with feeling for our weaknesses, and so that he might provide free access to himself for all." EXPLANATIONS OF HEBREWS 4:14-15.[2]

CHRIST IS NOT ONLY ABLE BUT ALSO READY TO HELP US. HULDRYCH ZWINGLI: "For we do not have a high priest who is unable to sympathize with our weaknesses, but one who has been tested in every way, as we are, but without sin." Someone might say, "Our high priest ascended into the heavens; he now enjoys and delights in glory; he is not mindful of us, nor is he troubled with feeling for our feebleness." To this sort of unspoken objection Paul responds, "Not at all! For we do not have a high priest who is unable," etc.

[1]Bullinger, *In Pauli ad Hebraeos Epistolam*, 45v-46v [110-12]; citing 1 Tim 2:5; Heb 9:24. †PG 62:536-37; NPNF 13:430. ‡Bullinger's Latin translation appears independent of that found in PG. [2]Oecolampadius, *In Epistolam ad Hebraeos Explanationes*, 43v-49r; citing 1 Tim 1:15; Heb 2:11.

"Let us therefore draw near with confidence to the throne of grace, so that we may encounter mercy and find grace. . . ." He says, "To the throne," from which we may be confident that our high priest is powerful and able to fulfill the request with which we come to him. But he calls it the seat of grace, lest, terrified by his greatness, we should shrink back and despair of help. And thus he finely sets Christ in opposition to the severity of the law that was given on the mountain. By this Christ is revealed as entirely ready to help, and that not just once, but as often as the case may require. EXPOSITION OF HEBREWS 4:15-16.[3]

ALWAYS SEEK THE MEDIATOR IN PRAYER. PHILIPP MELANCHTHON: We have repeatedly said that in every prayer we must first ask for the remission of sins, and faith regarding our reconciliation must shine forth always in all of our petitions. Always we should begin by looking to our mediator and ask and believe that for his sake we are received by God and heard by him, and understand that this high priest intercedes for us. In this confidence we should draw near to God, as is often said. . . . Therefore, though in our prayer our unworthiness always troubles us and frightens us away from God so that with terrified minds we flee from him, at the same time Christ commands us to seek reconciliation. And he would not command us to seek unless it was going to be given. Therefore the attentive mind should diligently think about the remission of sins and Christ the Mediator. LOCI PRAECIPUI THEOLOGICI.[4]

THE TWOFOLD THRONE OF GOD. NIELS HEMMINGSEN: Furthermore there is a twofold throne of God. One of glory, from which we flee on account of the majesty of the judge, for our sin repels us from this throne. The other is a throne of grace, to which we accede by faith through our high priest, so that we might receive mercy and find grace in opportune help, that is, that we might obtain the things necessary for salvation, of our calling in this time. For as long as we dwell in this mortal life, it is the opportune time. For in it, by the voice of the ministers of the gospel, we are called to the throne of the grace of Christ, so that having been freed from our miseries, we might find a propitious Father in Christ. COMMENTARY ON THE APOSTOLIC EPISTLE TO THE HEBREWS 4:16.[5]

CHRIST ALONE IS THE THRONE OF GRACE. JOHANNES OECOLAMPADIUS: Because Christ is such an exceptional priest like this who has obtained such exceptional benefits for us, it would surely be an utterly shameful deed if we were to fail to draw near to him with the utmost confidence, and with the same freedom with which one speaks with one's dearest friend, without any uneasiness, pouring out before him whatever may be found in our soul. But to prevent anyone from shrinking back, when he hears of "the throne," as if he intended to indicate a terrifying seat of judgment, he adds "of grace." This clearly refers to the mercy seat, which is Christ alone, and so he is also "the throne of grace." And he is appropriately called the throne of grace, for the Father has determined that however many he saves, he saves them all in the name of Christ. Look here, you who lead the way to any other throne than this one, or who go there yourselves! Christ clearly says, "Come to me, all you who are weary and heavy laden, and I will revive you" (Matthew 11), and "I am the door; if anyone enters through me, he will be saved" (John 10), and again, "I am the way, and the truth, and the life; no one comes to the Father except through me" (John 14). Farewell, then, to the promoters of the saints, for they are the blind leading the blind. EXPLANATIONS OF HEBREWS 4:16.[6]

5:1-3 *Limitations of the Levitical High Priest*

UNPACKING CHRIST'S PRIESTHOOD. THE ENGLISH ANNOTATIONS: At this chapter the apostle

[3]Zwingli, *In Epistolam ad Hebraeos*, 570.
[4]Melanchthon, *Loci Praecipui Theologici*, 392-93*; citing Rom 5:1.
[5]Hemmingsen, *Commentarius in ad Hebraeos*, 853 [877].
[6]Oecolampadius, *In Epistolam ad Hebraeos Explanationes*, 49v; citing Rom 3:25; Mt 11:28; Jn 10:9; 14:6; Mt 15:14.

makes a further declaration of Christ's priesthood, comparing it to and preferring it before the legal priesthood. Our apostle, having shown that Christ was a great and merciful high priest, first shows what was required in the high priest for his qualifications to his office, and then shows how both of these were fulfilled in Christ. ANNOTATIONS ON HEBREWS 5.[7]

CHRIST AND THE PRIESTS OF THE OLD LAW. JOHANNES BUGENHAGEN: The role of the priest according to the old law was to mediate between God and humanity, which he did by teaching and prayer. Furthermore, sacrifice is also connected with prayer, but this mediation was conducted through carnal symbols all the way up to the high priesthood of Christ. For the priests in those days were anointed with carnal oil; they taught, to be sure, but they did not give the Spirit, by whom all things are understood and preserved. They prayed, but they were not heard for their own sakes. They would offer sacrifices for sins, but they did not offer themselves, because they were sinners. Granted, though the carnal high priests would offer carnal sacrifices, still they were chosen by God for this. These sacrifices were not done according to their own innovations, but according to the direction of God, just as we see in the law of Moses. Nevertheless, these men were not only weak, but also mortal, so that their priesthood expired with their life.

Jesus, on the other hand, after being anointed with the Holy Spirit by God the Father, was consecrated with an oath as Priest and High Priest forever. He is the one who by his own word gives the Spirit in the hearts of believers, who for the sake of his own dignity was heard by the Father when he offered himself as a sacrifice just once on the cross, by whom we are sanctified, who has no need to pray for sins of his own. For us, however, he stands before the Father through his own blood, which was offered just once, having entered into the holy of holies, a worthy sacrifice to God as a pleasing aroma, just as the law says.

See, therefore, that nothing is said here about those who today are called pontiffs[†] and priests. Rather, this passage shows that the carnal priesthood according to the law was a symbol of the eternal priesthood, which has been fulfilled in Christ, just as the carnal kingship has been fulfilled in Christ, so that both have become spiritual, and are now no longer external and visible. But the fact that the priesthood of Christ was not going to be according to the law was displayed in the priesthood of Melchizedek, concerning which the Holy Spirit spoke through David: "The Lord has sworn and will not change his mind, 'You are a priest forever after the order of Melchizedek.'" Much more is said of this later in the book.[‡]

We have no greater consolation than we find in the priesthood of Christ. He is Priest and King. As priest he reconciles us to God; as king he restores us to safety and preserves us. As priest he justifies, as king he saves, and so on. COMMENTARY ON THE PAULINE EPISTLES, HEB 5:1.[8]

THE HIGH PRIEST AS SIN-BEARER FOR EACH BELIEVER. MARTIN LUTHER: This discourse gives the emphasis to that phrase "on behalf of men." It is as if he were saying: "Let us approach the throne of grace with confidence and without fear, because we have Jesus Christ as our High Priest." If we have a high priest, he is certainly for us and not against us, since "every high priest," even "one appointed and chosen from among men is appointed for men," as Exodus 28:38 states: "And Aaron shall take upon himself any guilt incurred in the holy offering which the people of Israel hallow." This definitely prefigured that Christ, the High Priest, would bear the sins of all who bring offerings, that is, who believe. . . . Therefore all priests should imitate this priest and know that they are not priests for themselves but for others, in order that they may bear the iniquities of others. . . . One should note that it is not enough for a Christian to believe that Christ was appointed to act on behalf of human beings unless he believes

[7]Downame, ed., *Annotations*, MMM3R*.

[8]Bugenhagen, *Annotationes in epistolas Pauli recognitae* (1525) 145r-146r [323-25]. [†]*Pontifex*, which is translated "high priest" when it refers to Christ or figures in the Old Testament, is also employed as a title of the pope, or pontiff. [‡]Heb 7:11-28, which is alluded to frequently throughout this selection.

that he, too, is one of them. For both the demons and the godless know that Christ is a priest for humans, but they do not believe this way about themselves. Lectures on Hebrews 5:1.[9]

Different Priesthoods. Johannes Oecolampadius: "For every high priest. . . ." This is the first passage that the champions of the Mass use to prove that it is a sacrifice and offering for the living and the dead, as if even today a sacrifice must be offered according to the pattern of the law. And this is why: they dare to say that the words "every priest" pertains to every age, and so even to our time. These wretched people do not comprehend that the apostle is using a comparison drawn from the Mosaic law, and that only for the purpose of showing that the role of a priest in time past was to present himself as gentle and kindly to those who had been caught in ignorant and sinful violations. Now, since it is certain that only Levites were chosen, it is clear that this comparison does not pertain to all priests indiscriminately (since it is different from the priests of our age), but only to those who were from the Jewish race. In 1 Corinthians 9 we read, "Those who serve at the altar share in the sacrifices of the altar"; but it is not right to infer from this that today there should also be this kind of priests, who "offer gifts and sacrifices."

For it is not unusual for Scripture to draw frequent comparisons even from unlawful things. Thus Christ proposes comparisons to usurers, an unjust judge, the sons of this light, and other things; but still he never commends usury in general, injustice in judgment, and the shrewdness of the sons of this age. We must bear in mind this common saying: "Every comparison wobbles,"† so that we should pay attention to that in it which serves the discourse that is provided and discard the inconsistent elements. Explanations of Hebrews 5:1-3.[10]

[9]LW 29:168, 169, 171 (WA 57:165.15-23, 166.26-167.2, 169.10-13).

[10]Oecolampadius, *In Epistolam ad Hebraeos Explanationes*, 51r-v; citing 1 Cor 9:13; Mt 25:27; Lk 18:1-8; 16:8. †On the origin of this adage, see Carol Clark, "Montaigne and the Imagery of Political Discourse in Sixteenth-Century France," *French Studies* 24, no. 4 (1970): 338.

5:4-10 *A Priest After the Order of Melchizedek*

Ministers in the New Covenant. Lucas Osiander: And although today in the new covenant there are no such ministers in the church who should sacrifice as in the old, nevertheless it is pleasing to God that the ministers are human beings, not angels, so that, mindful of human infirmities, they might conduct themselves commodiously toward sinners and bring them back into the way and not cast off the penitent. Neither should anyone betake to themselves to sit in the ecclesial ministry, but they should take up that function through a legitimate vocation. Epistle to the Hebrews 5:4.[11]

No One Should Seek Priestly Office out of Ambition. Johannes Oecolampadius: Heed this, you who wish to live a godly life. For currying favor for the sake of ambition or for any kind of official status is not void of offense. See how this passage fits together with that found in 1 Timothy 3, "If anyone aspires to the office of bishop, he desires a noble task." It is not the place of a Christian to look out for their own interests, but to desire to benefit others; this truly is exactly the role of a Christian. Now, there is no better way by which you can benefit others than performing the office of a bishop, seeing as it confers the highest usefulness to humanity; therefore it is honorable to aspire to it, but only for someone who perceives himself to be sufficient for the task. For people like this more capably look out for the work and the interests of Christ than for recognition, success, and their own interests. To desire the episcopal office is to undertake the examination and care of everyone, not himself; but he will never achieve this unless he is endowed with great love. We must so desire to benefit our neighbors that all ambition and pride is banished, so that we do not run without having been called. For the priesthood is such an important office that it is necessary that a person be called by God, just as Aaron was called.

[11]Osiander, *Epistola ad Hebraeos*, 31.

In Numbers 17, when Aaron's staff blossomed, it was as a clear proof that Aaron had been selected by God as a priest. Obviously the apostles of the Anabaptists, who assume apostleship because they are called by themselves, failed to consider this passage. For they cannot provide any reason sufficiently compatible with Scripture for their behavior, to which they must be incited by their hollow wisdom and inquisitiveness. But in olden times priests were ordained from the tribe of Levi and the family of Aaron, which we read endured until the time of Herod and Hyrcanus. If you wish to know about the settlement by which the priesthood ceased among the Hebrews, and all the worst people were promoted to that dignity by Herod, you may consult Josephus, *Antiquities* book 20.† Explanations of Hebrews 5:4-6.[12]

Christ, the Eternal Priest. Lucas Osiander: And Christ is called "a priest into eternity" or an "eternal priest" not because he was intending to suffer perpetually for sins, but because the strength of his passion and sacrifice remains perpetually. Neither is it necessary that he as another high priest should succeed those in the Old Testament who succeeded another, for their sacrifices were only adumbrating the true expiation of sins, and they themselves were mortals. But Christ also to this day intercedes for penitent sinners (while they live) at the right hand of the Father, Romans 8. And he is a priest according the order of Melchizedek because there are many similarities between Melchizedek and Christ. Melchizedek was simultaneously a king and a priest: Christ is also a king and a priest. Melchizedek was the king of Salem, and although Salem is the name of a place, nevertheless that name signifies peace, so that the king of Salem is the same as the king of peace: the same is most rightly said concerning Christ, certainly of the one who is called the Prince of Peace, Isaiah 9. Melchizedek blessed Abraham, and Christ blesses us and abolished the curse, Galatians 4. Melchizedek's father and mother are nowhere named in Scripture; Christ according to his human nature did not have a father, according to the divine nature he did not have a mother. Epistle to the Hebrews 5:6.[13]

Christ, the True High Priest. Heinrich Bullinger: This latter section corresponds to the verses above in this way: priests were chosen from among men, so that, as men, they could sympathize with men. But they were chosen for this reason: so that they might manage those affairs which must be managed for human beings because of their transgressions—that is, so that they might intercede for the unintentional sins of the people and offer sacrifices for human transgressions. Now to that previous section this one is added: Christ Jesus also was born from men, took on our weakness, so that as a man he could sympathize with men, although inasmuch as he did not offer for his own sins (because he had none), he is different from—or rather, greater than—the Mosaic priests. For Christ interceded for the people and offered the sacrifice of his own body for us. From this it follows that Christ is a true priest. Or, more briefly, arrange the sequence in this way: the role of a priest is to intercede and make offerings; Christ interceded and made an offering; therefore he is a priest. The argument is based on a correspondence in function.

Now we will touch on the remainder of the import of this verse. First, the word order is somewhat obscure. Thus the text can be rendered this way: "While he was active among human beings here on earth," for this is what he means by the expression "the days of his flesh," "he offered prayers and supplications with strong cries and tears to him who was able to save him from death, as a result of which he was heard because of his reverence." But in these expressions you may see a remarkable emphasis and reiteration. For *deēsis* is prayer in which we ask to be delivered from evil;

[12]Oecolampadius *In Epistolam ad Hebraeos Explanationes*, 52v-53r; citing 1 Tim 3:1; Num 17:8; Phil 2:4. †Josephus, *Antiquitates Iudaeorum* 20.247-251 (LCL 456:132-33).

[13]Osiander, *Epistola ad Hebraeos*, 31-32; citing Rom 8:34; Is 9:6; Gal 4:4-5.

but *biketēria* is more earnest prayer in which we also stretch out our hands. So by these verbal displays the author tries to communicate that Christ's affections were great and his prayers for us were full of passion. To this we would also relate the statement that he offered such prayers "with loud cries and tears"; that is, he performed the offering with the utmost torments of body and the greatest feeling, thus in every respect in a the highest and most faithful way. Perhaps you may ask, where did the apostles relate this about Christ? I can exhibit no other passage than the seventeenth chapter of John, and that which he cried out when he was nailed to the cross: "Father, forgive them, for they do not know what they are doing." For even though this was said particularly about those who crucified Christ, still it can be applied generally to the entire human race; for the things he did on the cross were generally directed. But setting these things aside, let us hold on to the fact that by these most emphatic statements the apostle desired to communicate that Christ endured and performed the role of a priest completely perfectly and with the greatest feeling.

Further, it seems especially worthy of our notice that it says Christ prayed (for this is said according to his humanity), and that he prayed to the one who was able to save him from death. For from this we learn to whom we also should offer our vows, prayers, and entreaties—namely to the One wise, powerful, true, and eternal God. For he alone is omniscient, he alone is omnipotent, he alone is the source of all good, he alone is immortal and provides life and breath to all, and he alone does not share his glory with another. Therefore, those who offer their prayers, vows, and soul's intentions either to creatures, or even to the souls of the blessed, are insane. For these have nothing (if they have anything) other than what they have received by grace from the Highest Good, nor have they received from God the power to be gods themselves—omniscient, omnipotent, infinite, hearing and seeing us wherever we may be. See, meanwhile, what the one to whom we offer our prayers should possess and must be able to provide. Hence in the Gospel the Lord said with so much emphasis, "Whatever you ask of the Father *in my name*, he will give it to you."

There follows, "And he was heard because of his reverence." In this case *kai* (and) is again an indicator of inference or summary. Thus it means that then he was heard for the sake of his reverence (*apo tēs eulabeias*) by his very reverence; that is, either he was heard by the very God whom he revered, or he was heard because of his singular holiness and conscientiousness. For *eulabeia* signifies not only reverence but also godliness. Notwithstanding, if he was heard, then we have been redeemed and saved; then the world, sin, the devil, and whatever could destroy us are all ruined. Commentary on Hebrews 5:7.[14]

Hell Lacks the Praise of God. Martin Luther: Why the apostle says, "in the days," in the plural, can seem strange, even though he seems to be speaking about that one day, namely, the day on which Christ offered himself on the cross. For he was offered only once and on one day. It can be said that he takes the part for the whole, according to the Hebrew custom, that is, that "days" are taken collectively for the whole time of his life, during a part of which he offered himself. For this is a very common way of speaking in the Scriptures, as is clear in book of Kings. . . . One should also note that this text elucidates beautifully the mystery of the old sacrifices. For against the gifts and sacrifices that "the priests chosen from among men" offered, Paul here sets the "prayers and supplications" that Christ, who was mystically prefigured through them, offered. Therefore calves, goats, and the other sacrifices—in addition to the fact that they signify tropologically the mortification of the flesh and the members on earth, as it taught in Romans 12:1 and Colossians 3:5—also prefigured offerings of prayers and praises.[†] For Christ made the justification of the new law so easy that we can accomplish with the mouth what they could

[14]Bullinger, *In Pauli ad Hebraeos Epistolam*, 52r-53v [123-26]; citing Heb 9:7; Lk 23:34; Is 42:8; 48:11; Jn 16:23.

scarcely obtain with everything they had, even with their physical goods. Therefore Hosea 14:2 says: "Take away all iniquity, and receive the good; and we will render the calves of our lips." The apostle comes close to this explanation below in Hebrews 13:15 when he says: "Through him, then, let us continually offer up a sacrifice of praise to God, that is, the fruit of lips that acknowledge his name." . . . Nevertheless, this "sacrifice of praise" does not mean that praise with which even a godless person blesses God, as the well-known words in Psalm 48:18 state. . . . On the contrary, it means praise in the midst of sufferings, as the well-known words in Isaiah 48:19 prove. . . . Hence hell is hell not because punishment is there, but because praise of God is not there. . . . Thus heaven is heaven not because joy is there, but because praise of God is there. Lectures on Hebrews 5:7.[15]

Christ Did Not Have an Iron Heart. John Calvin: The second thing he mentions respecting Christ is, that he, as it became him, sought a remedy that he might be delivered from evils; and he said this that no one might think that Christ had an iron heart that felt nothing; for we ought always to consider why a thing is said. Had Christ been touched by no sorrow, no consolation could arise to us from his sufferings; but when we hear that he also endured the bitterest agonies of mind, the likeness becomes then evident to us. Commentaries on the Epistle of Paul the Apostle to the Hebrews 5:7.[16]

Christ's Obedience. Gasparo Contarini: He did not learn an obedience that he did not already know and to which he had no inclination. But he learned by experience and the acting out of obedience: whence his obedience justified many; just as Adam's disobedience constituted many as sinners. For "he was made obedient to the point of death." Scholia in the Epistles of the Divine Paul, the Epistle to the Hebrews 5:8.[17]

Christ Learned the Extent to Which God Must Be Obeyed. John Calvin: The proximate end of Christ's sufferings was thus to habituate himself to obedience; not that he was driven to this by force, or that he had need of being thus exercised, as the case is with oxen or horses when their ferocity is to be tamed, for he was abundantly willing to render to his Father the obedience he owed. But this was done from a regard to our benefit, that he might exhibit to us an instance and an example of subjection even unto death itself. It may at the same time be truly said that Christ by his death learned fully what it was to obey God, since he was then led in a special manner to deny himself; for renouncing his own will, he so far gave himself up to his Father that of his own accord and willingly he underwent that death which he greatly dreaded. The meaning then is that Christ was by his sufferings taught how far God ought to be submitted to and obeyed. Commentaries on the Epistle of Paul the Apostle to the Hebrews 5:8.[18]

Christ Learned by Experience What It Meant to Obey. William Jones: Although he was a Son, "equal with his Father," Philippians 2:6, by his sufferings he learned what obedience meant. As Cajetan has put it, *experimento didicit*:[†] he felt by experience what it was to obey. A Commentary upon the Epistles of St. Paul, Heb 5:8.[19]

Through Suffering, Christ Achieved Perfection in Experience. Cardinal Cajetan: "He learned obedience through the

[15]LW 29:174-77 (WA 57:172.18-24, 174.4-176.1). [†]In the *Quadriga*, the tropological sense was the moral meaning of a biblical passage.
[16]CTS 40:121.

[17]Contarini, *Opera*, 520; citing Phil 2:8. Cf. Cajetan, "In Epistolam ad Hebraeos Commentarii," in *In omnes D. Pauli et aliorum apostolorum epistolas commentarii . . .: tomus quintus*, 339.
[18]CTS 40:123-24.
[19]Jones, *A Commentary upon the Epistles of St Paul*, 200*. [†]Cajetan, *In Epistolam ad Hebraeos Commentarii*, in *In omnes D. Pauli et aliorum apostolorum epistolas commentarii . . .: tomus quintus*, 339.

things that he suffered." Although he was the Son of God (knowing all things and displaying all power), nevertheless he learned by experience. By suffering, he learned obedience. For he was made obedient unto death. "And, having been made completed, he became the source of eternal salvation for all who obey him." Not only did he obey by suffering, but he was also completed (that is, perfected) through suffering. For through suffering he attained to perfection (not of capacity, but of action), and thereby to perfection of immortality. And by doing so he became the source of eternal salvation for all who obey him, by offering himself for the eternal salvation of those who obey him. Comments on Hebrews 5:8-9.[20]

A Salve Against the Wounds of Sorrow. Edward Dering: Dearly beloved, we whom it has pleased God to keep in heaviness through many temptations therefore have here a salve against the wounds of sorrow. Our afflictions teach us how far we can obey the Lord. If in all grief of body I can say with patience, "I have held my peace, O Lord, because you have done the same," then I know that in all sorrows of flesh I have glorified God and my heart rejoices. If my mind is full of anguish and sorrow, so that all hope is faint within me; if I can still say to my soul, "I will wait patiently for the Lord's leisure," then I know assuredly that God has made me obedient, and he will hear my prayer, so that this experience has bred in me the hope that shall never be confounded. 27 Lectures or Readings on the Epistle to the Hebrews 5:7-9.[21]

Christ Alone Was Heard Because of His Own Worthiness. Johannes Oecolampadius: *Eulabēs* is an august person, who is welcome no matter what he does and is accepted freely; hence *eulabeia*, which means not so much authority as the dignity and worthiness by which someone is admitted into the presence of another; in other words, he is received because of his dutiful conduct. Christ knew that he was always heard, as he himself testifies in John 11. But in obedience to the Father he chose to receive this humiliation to himself, clearly as an example for us. But of none of the saints do we read that they were heard because of their own personal dignity and worthiness, except in the case of Christ, the one and only savior. Saints and believers are indeed heard, provided they ask the Father in the name of Christ, whose worthiness and merit alone he regards. This is why the church concludes its prayers, "Through our Lord Jesus Christ." Explanations of Hebrews 5:7-10.[22]

Christ's Priesthood Provides Complete Salvation. Heinrich Bullinger: These words are a recapitulation, in which the author returns to explain the way in which Christ "was heard"; that is, he explains what is the goal and fruit of the sacrifice and priesthood of Christ: eternal life, forgiveness of sins, and perfection. Later on he harps on this theme. For it is not enough if we merely believe that Jesus is a priest; for we must also believe that Jesus is a priest for us. So he rightly revisits this topic again, because earlier he instructed them more than once that the fruit of Christ's priesthood—or rather, of his entire work—is eternal life. For his sacrifice is so complete that there is nothing left to be desired from it; so rich and abundant that there is no race of people which it does not absolve and redeem, if only they believe. For, as the Baptist said, "Whoever believes in the Son has eternal life; whoever does not believe in the Son will not see life, but the wrath of God remains on him." For since Christ was *teleōtheis*, which is translated "perfected," his sacrifice and atonement for us are *teletē*, perfection itself, as well as the *aitios*—the cause, energy, and originator of eternal salvation. For Christ himself was made for us wisdom from God, righteousness, sanctification, and redemption. Nor is there any

[20]Cajetan, *In Epistolam ad Hebraeos Commentarii*, 161r; citing Phil 2:8.
[21]Dering, *Lectures on Hebrews*, Z5v*.
[22]Oecolampadius, *In Epistolam ad Hebraeos Explanationes*, 54v; citing Jn 11:32.

other salvation in any other person, but he is the priest of all who believe in all ages, having been established by God after the order of Melchizedek. Commentary on Hebrews 5:9-10.[23]

Christ Consecrated to His Priesthood Through Suffering. John Calvin: Here is the ultimate or the remoter end, as they call it, why it was necessary for Christ to suffer: it was that he might thus become initiated into his priesthood, as though the apostle had said that the enduring of the cross and death were to Christ a solemn kind of consecration, by which he intimates that all his sufferings had a regard to our salvation. It hence follows that they are so far from being prejudicial to his dignity that they are on the contrary his glory; for if salvation is highly esteemed by us, how honorably ought we to think of its cause or author? For he speaks not here of Christ only as an example, but he ascends higher, even that he by his obedience has blotted out our transgressions.

Sanctified suits the passage better than "made perfect" . . . but as he speaks here of the priesthood, he fitly and suitably mentions sanctification. . . . It hence appears that this is to be properly applied to his human nature, in which he performed the office of a priest, and in which he also suffered. Commentaries on the Epistle of Paul the Apostle to the Hebrews 5:9.[24]

[23]Bullinger, *In Pauli ad Hebraeos Epistolam*, 54r [127]; citing Jn 3:36; 1 Cor 1:30.

[24]CTS 40:124-25*.

5:11–6:3 PRESSING ON TO MATURITY IN CHRIST

[11]About this we have much to say, and it is hard to explain, since you have become dull of hearing. [12]For though by this time you ought to be teachers, you need someone to teach you again the basic principles of the oracles of God. You need milk, not solid food, [13]for everyone who lives on milk is unskilled in the word of righteousness, since he is a child. [14]But solid food is for the mature, for those who have their powers of discernment trained by constant practice to distinguish good from evil.

6 Therefore let us leave the elementary doctrine of Christ and go on to maturity, not laying again a foundation of repentance from dead works and of faith toward God, [2]and of instruction about washings,[a] the laying on of hands, the resurrection of the dead, and eternal judgment. [3]And this we will do if God permits.

a Or *baptisms* (that is, cleansing rites)

OVERVIEW: The reformers take the author's exhortations to spiritual growth in this section to relate in the first place to Scripture and its proper role in the growing Christian's life. The sluggishness or lack of zeal addressed here have nothing to do with alleged obfuscations in Scripture; rather, they have everything to do with human sin, for Scripture is clear to those who truly follow Christ. The reformers also seek to define what the writer meant by "elementary doctrine of Christ" (Heb 6:1). For the most part they interpret it as basic catechetical instruction of the kind one receives when one is a child; the point is to grow beyond such introductory instruction to become a mature Christian. But some reformers also see in these verses an exhortation to move beyond a merely external piety to true inward faith.

5:11-14 *Rebuke for Doctrinal Immaturity*

NEGLECT OF THE SCRIPTURES. MARTIN LUTHER: This is better expressed in Greek with the words "since you have become sluggish," so that it is properly in accord with what follows. For because of the time they ought to have been teachers if they had been watchful and eager in the understanding of the Scriptures. Now, however, they have been sluggish and have not worked that land of promise flowing with milk and honey, that is, Holy Scripture. LECTURES ON HEBREWS 5:11.[1]

THE AUTHOR MUST PAUSE TO MOTIVATE HIS READERS. JOHANNES OECOLAMPADIUS: When more difficult topics arise, it is the custom of public speakers to shake the sleepiness and stupefaction from their hearers by some more passionate exhortation. Here the apostle also follows this method when he is about to commend the excellence of the eternal priesthood of Christ. He has introduced the mystery concerning Melchizedek, but to impress it more readily on their minds as the means by which our confidence before God is immensely confirmed, he first intends to reprove their sluggishness in many ways. Meanwhile, however, he is capturing their goodwill and getting them to pay attention. Indeed, it was very appropriate to tax the Jews with their sluggishness and ignorance. For because of the multitude of ceremonies that weighed down on them, they almost always crawled along on the ground without ever lifting their mind's eyes to the heavens. And because they legalistically held on tight to the husk of the letter, they neglected the kernel of the Spirit and became scarcely fit to receive mysteries. The same thing happens today; those who immoderately esteem ceremonies are little able to penetrate to the

[1]LW 29:179 (WA 57:178.14-18).

meaning of the Scriptures. And how many lines of text, by dwelling only on the story of Melchizedek, would be able to explain to us so great a mystery? Explanations of Hebrews 5:11.[2]

Difficulties Arise from Our Own Laziness. Heinrich Bullinger: The author declared that this matter of the priesthood of Christ is not difficult in itself, but that it is received by a sluggish mind. This shows that all difficulty arises, not from the Scriptures themselves, but from our own sloth, which he explains with even clearer words in 2 Corinthians 4. Consequently he rebukes their laziness and magnifies it by passage of time, as if he were to say, "If anyone were to notice the time at which you first heard the sacred teachings, they would expect you to be teaching others by now, so ignoble is it that you who have been students for so many years have learned nothing else than to be the students of others, and even elementary schoolchildren." Commentary on Hebrews 5:11-12.[3]

Baptism May Precede Knowledge. Johannes Oecolampadius: Here he makes use of the image of elementary schoolchildren. But the "basic elements" were Jewish ceremonies and certain external instructions and education, by which infants and people who have not yet surpassed childish notions are trained, as when I say to someone, "Do you want to be a Christian? You must be baptized," and I do not immediately tell them what a Christian is, what faith is, and what baptism is. Or when I say, "Do you want to pray? Bow your knees, fold your hands," all the while remaining silent on what prayer is, or how one should pray. And likewise with other things. Even so, you should recognize that you would still not really be a Christian because of these things; but nevertheless these are the basic elements for godliness. I have said this because this passage contradicts the error of the Anabaptists, because it can speak of the symbol of baptism before pure and solid teaching in godliness. First come childish things and milk, then the word of righteousness and solid food are offered. Spiritual things also have their gradations. Do you think so many thousands of Jews could have been baptized and instantly taught the word of righteousness? I do not believe it. For such precise knowledge of God is not immediately called for upon baptism. Explanations of Hebrews 5:12.[4]

Rise Up to the Hidden Meaning of Scripture. Desiderius Erasmus: Many years have passed since you first confessed Christ, and in view of this length of time you ought to be teachers of others. Instead you still need us to teach you the first rudiments of divine Scripture, that is, the things commonly taught those who are being reborn to the gospel through baptism in the way that children are taught their ABCs. At this point in time you should be hardy and robust students of evangelical philosophy; however, instead of being ready for the solid food of higher learning, like tender infants you still need the milk of elementary instruction. You still cling to and creep along, as it were, in the literal meaning of divine Scripture; you do not yet rise to the higher meaning hidden within it. But such a person whose condition is such that they still need to be nourished with milk is unformed and not yet strong enough to be instructed in evangelical righteousness, which is not found in the literal meaning but in allegories. Paraphrases on the Epistle to the Hebrews 5:11-14.[5]

6:1-3 *Advance Beyond Basic Principles of Doctrine*

Those Who Rely on External Works Are Not Christians. Johannes Bugenhagen: Therefore, let us leave those first basic lessons with which children are initiated into Christ, now that

[2]Oecolampadius, *In Epistolam ad Hebraeos Explanationes*, 55r-v.
[3]Bullinger, *In Pauli ad Hebraeos Epistolam*, 55r-v; citing 2 Cor 4:3-4 [129-30].
[4]Oecolampadius, *In Epistolam ad Hebraeos Explanationes*, 56v.
[5]CWE 44:226.

we have heard and understood them, so that we may learn higher things that are appropriate for adults in the faith of Christ, as it says in Ephesians 4, if God allows.

The basic lessons include teaching and relying only on external sacraments, along with certain optional observances, according to the ceremony observed by the apostles. The laying on of hands was among these, but without it the Holy Spirit could be given, and often was given, and always is given to believers. They also include teaching that you should say, "I believe in God the Father Almighty," and so on. Likewise, teaching that you should abstain from fornication, slander, and the like. Likewise, teaching that you should say the Lord's Prayer. Such things, or only these things, the papists† teach us when they are at their best. But since they do not know of the perfection of faith, and how rich it is in God, neither can they teach it. For this reason, the people go astray along with them, as long as they never truly come to their senses, and always remain stuck in the same mud, for all that once a year they contrive for themselves penitence from dead works. Therefore they go astray and are not Christians, until God takes pity on them and reveals the way of salvation through the gospel, so that they may learn not to cling childishly and uselessly to external works, but to hope for salvation in God alone through Jesus Christ. Such people should be challenged to better things, just as you see in this passage. For in regard to those who truly learned Christ and afterward blasphemed his grace, which is a terrible sacrilege, we will hear a different judgment. Commentary on the Pauline Epistles, Heb 6:1.[6]

Build on the Foundation of Christ. Huldrych Zwingli: "Laying a foundation of repentance." He draws a telling and very apt metaphor from building. For things are built harmfully and wastefully when, after the foundation has been laid at great expense, one builds nothing more; or when, once the frame of a house has been erected, one does not put on the gables or the roof. It is as if he were saying, "A foundation was laid among you, which is Christ; it only still remains for us to attain to completion of the manifold virtues." Exposition of Hebrews 6:1.[7]

The Complexity of the Laying on of Hands. Heinrich Bullinger: The fourth subject is "laying on of hands," which encompasses all at once the entire duty of the prophet, which is the greatest of all duties in the church. It encompasses calling, commission, and the authority to teach. For the hands of the elders were laid on those to whose faith were committed the care of the church and the ministry of the word of God. For the apostle writes to Timothy, "Do not neglect the gift which is in you, which was given you by prophecy, and which was confirmed when the elders laid their hands on you" (1 Timothy 4). And if only this kind of laying on of hands, a most holy and most beneficial ceremony, would be restored to us again. There can be no doubt that many schisms and stumbling blocks would be removed by this, and there would be a check on the shameless impudence of those who force their way into the office of teaching on their own initiative without having been called. These are the most presumptuous of people, children of the factious Korah and Abiram, who by their arrogance have reached such a point that they believe that whatever they want is permissible. Indeed, from this source proceeds the material for the wrangling of heresies and factions for all of us in the church. But nor would I doubt that under the rubric of the laying on of hands the apostle includes at the same time within the church other necessary ceremonies, assemblies, prayers, feasts, fast days, indeed, the very sacraments of the church. These (namely, baptism and the Eucharist) are most wholesome, honorable, and sacred in meaning and mysterious significance. For it is reasonable that we should understand the ceremonies and sacred rites

[6]Bugenhagen, *Annotationes in epistolas Pauli recognitae* (1525) 146v [326]; citing Eph 4:13-14. †The subject of this sentence is not stated; "papists" is supplied, as fitting the context.

[7]Zwingli, *In Epistolam Beati Pauli ad Hebraeos Expositio*, 571.

of the church of Christ, once we have been converted to God, and that we should learn all the grace and fullness there is in Christ, the unity, truth and righteousness, the beauty and order that are lavished on the church itself, which he guides with the word, guards with the Spirit, seals in baptism, and rouses by the holy memorial of the Eucharist. Others, by a kind of substitution, understand the laying on of hands as the gifts of the Holy Spirit described in 1 Corinthians 12; I would make no objection against them on this score. Commentary on Hebrews 6:1-2.[8]

The Elementary Doctrines of Christ. Martin Luther: For these matters that the apostle adduces, namely, to believe in God, to believe in Christ, to believe in the Holy Spirit, to believe in one baptism, to believe in the remission of sins, to believe in eternal life, are the things communicated to those who are to be catechized and baptized. Therefore they are also called the rudiments of faith in which those who are still uninformed are instructed, as is clear in the Apostles' Creed. . . . He calls "maturity," as Chrysostom says, "the completely good life."[†] But what that life is St. James explains when he says in James 1:4: "Patience has a perfect work." Therefore Christ also said that this good ground will bear fruit in patience (cf. Luke 8:15). And here the apostle immediately says below (v. 11): "We desire each one of you to show the same earnestness in realizing the full assurance of hope." For through tribulations patience divests the soul of the figure and all visible things and transfers it into the hope of the things that are invisible, as Romans 5:4-5 states: "Experience works hope, but hope does not put to shame." Lectures on Hebrews 6:1-2.[9]

This List Represents the Apostolic Catechism. Heinrich Bullinger: From these words it is clear what the author meant in chapter 5 by "basic principles" and "nourishment from milk," namely, those essential subjects of Christian doctrine that he here enumerates for the most part and calls "foundations," that is, the beginnings. For the foundations are the first parts to be established in the whole building. So we learn from this list what should be the entryway into the faith, that is, into the religion of Christ, and how the Christian religion can and should rightly be introduced among us. And it is no wonder if we learn first the more general and especially necessary things, namely, what Scripture is, what is its authority, what are truth, piety, God, faith, Christ, sin, grace, and righteousness. But why should we enumerate such things, when the apostle himself has counted them far more ably? Others have reduced these things to this sequence, because candidates for the name of Christian were instructed first regarding repentance and faith in God, and then (I mean in the case of adults) they were baptized, and after baptism they were taught about receiving the Holy Spirit, and likewise about the resurrection and judgment. So we will ponder each one of these in turn. Commentary on Hebrews 6:1-2.[10]

The Signs of Evangelical and Christian Repentance. Thomas Walkington: What are the special afflictions whereby repentance appears to be truly wrought? Those seven mentioned [in] 2 Corinthians 7:11. First, a true sorrow for sin, as it is the offence of a most gracious God, called godly sorrow. Second, a clearing of ourselves from all suspicion of sin by avoiding all appearances of evil, or by humble confession of our faults. Third, a holy indignation and anger for all evils past. Fourth, a fear lest such things by our corruption should break forth again. Fifth, a great and ardent desire to prevent them. Sixth, a zeal against all evil in ourselves and others, and of doing all good we can in our general and special callings. Seventh, a godly revenge and punishment by bridling our lusts and refraining not only from things forbidden but even from some

---

[8]Bullinger, *In Pauli ad Hebraeos Epistolam*, 58v-59r [136-37]; citing 1 Tim 4:14.

[9]LW 29:180-81 (WA 57:179.20-25, 180.19-181.6) [†]LW note (181 n. 3): "Chrysostom, *Homiliae*, IX, col. 78 (300)."

[10]Bullinger, *In Pauli ad Hebraeos Epistolam*, 57r [133].

things that are indifferent, and be under our liberty if either they are an offence to others, or occasion of sin to ourselves. Exposition of Hebrews 6:1-2.[11]

Let Us Not Always Be Beginners. Edward Dering: In the following words he shows by particular points what is this beginning beyond which we must go so that we may be perfect. He lists four points: repentance from dead works, faith toward God, the resurrection of the body, and eternal judgment. These principles were learned and confessed by Christians' children on the day of their confirmation and by Gentiles that came to the faith of Christ on the day of their baptism. In this meaning, some think he calls these forenamed points the doctrine of baptism and laying on of hands, meaning thereby that seeing this confession and knowledge is in us when first we are received into the fellowship of the church to be partakers of their mysteries, how ought we to grow into greater knowledge and wisdom, when now for many years we have been members of the church and daily taught all the counsels of God? Or it may be that the apostle here recites the manner of catechizing used then in churches for the instruction of children, in which they were taught especially these six principles of religion, what they are, and how they should learn them; that is, repentance, faith, baptism, laying on of hands, the resurrection, and eternal judgment. These things being first learned by them and presented to them in books (such as our catechisms), the apostle may seem to speak thus: "Let us not always be beginners. When we were yet children, we learned this. Since we have been hearing the word preached for so long a time, and religion has thus been more perfectly taught us, how shall we be blameless if we learn no more?" The meaning of the apostle in such words is to give us no time of rest when we should think we were wise enough so that we need learn no more. But as long as God continues our life, so long we should continue our efforts still to know more of his unsearchable wisdom and goodness. … It is milk to know these things in the simplicity of the words: it is strong meat to be able to distribute them into every part and apply it to ourselves in our life. 27 Lectures or Readings on the Epistle to the Hebrews 6:1-2.[12]

Baptism Prepares Us for More Advanced Matters. Johannes Oecolampadius: In former times, those who were getting baptized were first admonished to repent, and then a confession of faith would be required of them, after which they were washed and received the laying on of hands along with an affirmation of the resurrection and eternal judgment. For, as we said a little earlier, simpler people and those who had not yet attained to complete understanding were not excluded from these ceremonies anymore than the infant children of believers. And although the statements, "I renounce," "I believe," "I receive the laying on of hands," and other similar phrases are heard in baptism, yet more is promised in it than the initiate can actually fulfill, for they declare a perfect and new life, which is prefigured by baptism, whereby Christ is put on and sins are washed away. He says *baptismōn* in the plural in accordance with the custom of the Hebrews, for whom there were many baptisms; for us there is one, just as there is one God and one faith. But it could be the case that he spoke of "baptisms" in the plural because children were typically immersed three times, as if he were saying, "I am not talking about the baptisms and affairs of children, or such matters as are typically received at first by those who are baptized. I am teaching you far more advanced things." Baptism contains in itself the death of Christ, and the apostle clearly states that he knew nothing except Christ and him crucified. But although wondrous mysteries are hidden in baptism, nevertheless he declares that he gave them childish things and milk. But no one should conclude that such things are to be condemned for these reasons; rather, by such training he should advance to higher things. Explanations of Hebrews 6:1-2.[13]

[11]Walkington, *Exposition of the First Two Verses of the Sixth Chapter of Hebrews*, 13-14*; citing 1 Cor 8:13; Rom 14.

[12]Dering, *Lectures on Hebrews*, Bb5r-v*.

[13]Oecolampadius, *In Epistolam ad Hebraeos Explanationes*, 58v-59r.

"Baptisms" Refers to the Purifying Results of Faith in Christ. Heinrich Bullinger: In the third place, the author lists "teachings about baptisms."† Some understand this as referring to the initial teaching, because baptism is the beginning of the Christian life; thus the meaning would be that this describes that faith in God which initiates the candidates, not that which gradually produces righteous abundance. Others differ from each other; thus some of them join "teachings" to what follows, so that it reads, "teachings about the laying on of hands," while the rest connect it to what precedes, so that it reads, "teachings about baptisms," as if water baptism followed faith, but a fuller teaching about perfection followed baptism. No one can deny that this would be true for adults, but the reader may judge whether this is really what is being said in this passage. Surely, since in the church of God there is no more than one baptism, while at the same time the apostle uses a plural when he says *baptismōn didachēs*, "teachings about baptisms," it would seem that he is speaking not about the sacrament of baptism or the catechism, but about the tradition of baptisms, that is, of various kinds of purifications. For *baptizō* means to immerse or bathe; but because washing or bathing cleanses things, it came about that "baptism" can be taken to mean "cleansing" by association. Consequently, he attaches the teaching about various kinds of purification to faith on that account, because faith itself looks to God only for this reason, so that we may believe not only that our sins are washed away by the blood of Christ but also that all other kinds of things that need cleansing have been abolished through Christ's single purification. For in chapter 9 we will hear plainly that the apostle meant "baptisms" in precisely this way and described such things as a carnal justification, "imposed until the time of reformation." But in that passage the interpreter should translate it more clearly as "washings." Here, however, it must refer to the forgiveness of sins, redemption, and everything that follows through Christ. Commentary on Hebrews 6:1-2.[14]

Eph 4:5; 1 Cor 2:2; 3:1-2.

Laying on of Hands Refers to Confirmation. The English Annotations: Which is usually called confirmation, which stood, first, in examining those who had been baptized, what progress they had made in the doctrine of Christianity. Second, in praying for them, that God would continue them in the faith and give them more grace, strengthening them by his Holy Spirit. Now when the chief pastor or pastors of the church prayed for them, they laid their hands on them, whence the apostolic constitution was called the laying on of hands, so Augustine, and so most of the fathers, with one consent. Or, understand thereby a ceremony used in the ordination of ministers. Annotations on Hebrews 6:2.[15]

[14]Bullinger, *In Pauli ad Hebraeos Epistolam*, 58r-v [135-36]; citing Heb 9:10. †Bullinger's text at this point reads *baptismata doctrinae* (baptisms of teaching) rather than *baptismatum doctrinae*, which is preserved elsewhere in this paragraph and is almost certainly intended here.

[15]Downame, ed., *Annotations*, MMM3v-MMM4r*; citing Augustine, *De fide et operibus* 11.

6:4-20 Christ, the Anchor of Our Soul

[4]For it is impossible, in the case of those who have once
been enlightened, who have tasted the heavenly gift,
and have shared in the Holy Spirit, [5]and have tasted
the goodness of the word of God and the powers of the
age to come, [6]and then have fallen away, to restore
them again to repentance, since they are crucifying once
again the Son of God to their own harm and holding
him up to contempt. [7]For land that has drunk the rain
that often falls on it, and produces a crop useful to those
for whose sake it is cultivated, receives a blessing from
God. [8]But if it bears thorns and thistles, it is worthless
and near to being cursed, and its end is to be burned.

[9]Though we speak in this way, yet in your case,
beloved, we feel sure of better things—things that
belong to salvation. [10]For God is not unjust so as to
overlook your work and the love that you have
shown for his name in serving the saints, as you still
do. [11]And we desire each one of you to show the same
earnestness to have the full assurance of hope until
the end, [12]so that you may not be sluggish, but
imitators of those who through faith and patience
inherit the promises.

[13]For when God made a promise to Abraham,
since he had no one greater by whom to swear, he
swore by himself, [14]saying, "Surely I will bless you and
multiply you." [15]And thus Abraham,[a] having
patiently waited, obtained the promise. [16]For people
swear by something greater than themselves, and in
all their disputes an oath is final for confirmation.
[17]So when God desired to show more convincingly to
the heirs of the promise the unchangeable character of
his purpose, he guaranteed it with an oath, [18]so that
by two unchangeable things, in which it is impossible
for God to lie, we who have fled for refuge might have
strong encouragement to hold fast to the hope set
before us. [19]We have this as a sure and steadfast
anchor of the soul, a hope that enters into the inner
place behind the curtain, [20]where Jesus has gone as a
forerunner on our behalf, having become a high priest
forever after the order of Melchizedek.

a Greek *he*

Overview: The reformers wrestle mightily with this section of the epistle, which appears to teach that salvation can be lost through grievous sin, a position that is at odds with most versions of justification by faith. For the most part, the reformers interpret this passage as being either hyperbolic or as applying to the reprobate and indolent rather than to the elect, although some do allow for the possibility of a complete fall from grace among believers. The reformers also seek to define what the unforgiveable sin in question might be. But the clear emphasis of the reformers' comments on this section is to console those who worry that they have committed this heinous sin and have therefore forfeited eternal life. To such troubled souls the reformers offer the epistle's numerous promises of divine grace and mercy for those who are penitent. In the last section of this passage the reformers focus primarily on the image of the anchor of the soul (Heb 6:19), stressing the assurance of the believer's eternal inheritance in Christ and urging their readers to remain focused on the certainties of heaven in the midst of the uncertainties and temptations of life in this world. Faith in the anchor, Christ, and trust in the Father's utter trustworthiness are also key themes in the reformers' comments.

6:4-6 *Impossible to Repent After Falling Away*

The Sin Against the Holy Spirit. Lucas Osiander: The apostle is not speaking here about just any kind of sin that is committed, even sin against conscience; rather, he is speaking about the sin against the Holy Spirit, which John calls the sin unto death, and for which according to John we should not even pray. Epistle to the Hebrews 6:4.[1]

Excommunicate False Believers. Dirk Philips: Those who . . . receive this grace in vain do not keep it, never produce any fruit by it, walk according to the flesh, cannot enter into the heavenly Jerusalem, but shall have their part outside in the lake of fire, which is the second death.

This will happen to all false Christians who have fallen away from the truth (which they have once known and received). In this occasion Jesus Christ has commanded his church and given her power to separate from herself all false brothers who break from it by disobedience, to testify that they shall have no part with Christ and all his saints, since they keep persevering in iniquity. For he who wishes to reach life eternal with Christ must love him with true faith, cleave to him, suffer and die with him, i.e., to be with him one spirit, and to be one body with his church, persevering therein perpetually. Evangelical Excommunication.[2]

The True Christian Can Never Fall Away from Faith. Edward Dering: For our part it does not matter at all what this great and heinous sin should be of which the apostle says one can never repent of it. Whatever it is, it is none of ours. This sin is the sin of those who have despised knowledge; but we are desirous to learn more. This sin is of the condemners of the cross of Christ; but the delight of our life is in it. This sin is of those that have made the world their God; but God, whom we serve, has had mercy on us, so that we account all the world as but dung, to the end that we may win Christ. Therefore, whatever this sin may be, God himself bears us witness, it is none of the sin that we have committed. And wherever they dwell who are under this condemnation, their tents and tabernacles are not near us. . . . I do not say this out of my own head, but by good warrant of the apostle himself, and by the word of the Holy Spirit, for after this heavy threatening, does not the apostle say to them immediately, and does he not say it to us this day, that because we have loved God's saints and have rejoiced to glorify his name, our state is faster knit unto salvation, and these heavy things shall never come near to us? . . . And thus far of the purpose of the apostle has been to confirm that though we should fall through many infirmities, yet we can never fall away. 27 Lectures or Readings on the Epistle to the Hebrews 6:4-6.[3]

No Repentance After Falling Away. Dirk Philips: Those who have now tasted the sweetness of the divine Word and the power of the coming world, and have received the Holy Spirit, and again turn away therefrom and sin willfully, according to the known and accepted truth, despise Christ and his word out of pride—these may not, according to the word of the apostle, be renewed through repentance. For they have themselves crucified the Son of God and made mockery with it. Yes, they trample the Son of God with their feet and regard the blood of the testament through which they are sanctified as impure, and outrage the Spirit of grace. Therefore also no sacrifice is left for their sins, but a strong and fearful fire is prepared for them that shall consume the adversary, that is, those who set themselves against Christ and his Word. The Enchiridion.[4]

Departure from Faith and True Betrothal. Melchior Hoffman: This is furthermore a sin† of which Saint Paul writes, namely, those who have once been enlightened and have received the taste of the wisdom of God, and who have delivered themselves up and given themselves over to the Lord Christ and who then fall away again and, after having confessed the truth, have

[1]Osiander, *Epistola ad Hebraeos*, 37-38; citing 1 Jn 5:16. Osiander goes on to cite Francesco Spiera (1498–1548) and Adam Neuser (c. 1530–1576) as examples of apostates. Spiera renounced his Protestant faith at the hands of the Inquisition at Venice; Neuser renounced the doctrine of the Trinity and may have converted to Islam.
[2]CRR 6:596*; citing Rev 21:8; 22:15; Heb 10:26; Jn 3:16; 5:24; 11:26; 15:21; 15:5; 1 Cor 6:17; 12:13.
[3]Dering, *Lectures on Hebrews*, Cc1r-Cc2r*; citing Phil 3:8.
[4]CRR 6:169*; citing Heb 10:29, 27-28; 12:29.

departed from the faith and the true betrothal. It is impossible to restore these broken ones. In this sense also Christ Jesus speaks: Where Satan has been driven out and the house cleaned and swept and where also there is emptiness and vacancy and dead belief, where the Spirit is unfruitful in godly works and fruits, where the tree decks itself out in words and leaves without power and deed—here the spirit of Satan with seven spirits more wicked than himself takes possession of that empty vessel for his use according to his lust and will, and the last [state] thereby becomes worse than the first. THE ORDINANCE OF GOD, HEB 6:4-6.[5]

THE UNFORGIVEABLE SIN. EDWARD DERING: This then is the sin against the Holy Spirit; it is a continual apostasy and a general falling from God. It is to sin against your own conscience, so that you despise the graces of God that he has given to you for the setting forth of his praise, and to turn them to the contempt of his majesty and glory. Now, a word or two to show this sin by examples. . . . Our first example is Satan himself and the angels that fell with him . . . [as a second example] Cain slew his brother Abel . . . [and as a third example] the scribes and Pharisees. . . . Our Savior Christ calls this great, willful, malicious working against the Son of God, of people utterly fallen away from the living God, the sin against the Holy Spirit. To these (I think) we may add Julius the emperor, who for his most willful renouncing of the Lord Jesus, is called to this day the *Apostata*. . . .† This sin is a mocking and scoffing at the Son of God; it is not a weeping and mourning, lest you should fall into it. 27 LECTURES OR READINGS ON THE EPISTLE TO THE HEBREWS 6:4-6.[6]

A TWOFOLD FALLING AWAY. NIELS HEMMINGSEN: It is impossible to renew the lapsed to repentance,† but the apostle is the kind of person who understands what sort of people the lapsed are. With respect to sin, what he here asserts may be understood as a periphrasis. There is a twofold falling away, or fall, namely, particular and universal. The particular falling away is to transgress in particular ways against the precepts of the Decalogue, including what has happened from infirmity or ignorance or even from the will or malice. This kind includes many errors in life, namely, ignorance, murder, theft, adultery, and other things against the commandments of God. . . . But although these sins . . . are deserving of eternal death, nevertheless God's favor is not denied to those who are penitent. As for instance the many witnesses and illustrious examples in Scripture display, such as Manasseh, David, the Magdalene,‡ Paul, and others. Therefore the present place [in the text] cannot be understood as concerning particular lapses.

The universal lapse is not simply to transgress against one or many or even all the commandments of the Decalogue; rather, it is when one who has known Christ and his gospel renounces it utterly. Such a person not only does not believe in Christ any longer but also condemns him, is full of anger against him, mocks him, and becomes a tyrant against him, as the Pharisees and Julian the Apostate did. COMMENTARY ON THE APOSTOLIC EPISTLE TO THE HEBREWS 6:4-6.[7]

THE REPROBATE TASTE GRACE AND FALL AWAY. JOHN CALVIN: This passage has given occasion to many to repudiate this epistle, especially as the Novatians armed themselves with it to deny pardon to the fallen.† Hence those of the Western church, in particular, refused the authority of this epistle, because the sect of Novatus annoyed them; and they were not sufficiently conversant in the truth so

[5]LCC 25:199-200; citing Mt 12:43-45. †The sins in question here are those that lead to death (1 Jn 5:16). The larger context makes it clear that for Hoffman these are sins of various kinds of blasphemy, including the blasphemous assertion that God desires for human beings to sin and is himself the cause of it within us.

[6]Dering, *27 Lectures on Hebrews*, Cc7v-Cc8r *; citing Mt 12:30-32; Mk 3:28-30; Lk 12:8-10. †Emperor Julian (r. AD 355–360), dubbed "the Apostate" by his Christian critics, sought to restore traditional Roman religious practices that had been abolished by the Christian emperors who preceded him.

[7]Hemmingsen, *Commentarius in epistolam apostolicam ad Hebraeos*, 859 [883]; citing 2 Chron 33:13; Ps 51; Lk 8:1-3; Gal 1:11-16. †Hemmingsen may have Mk 3:28-30 in mind here. ‡Hemmingsen may be referring here to the medieval view of Mary Magdalene as a repentant prostitute, which is not attested in the canonical Gospels.

as to be equal to refute it by argument. But when the design of the apostle is understood, it then appears evident that there is nothing here which countenances so delirious an error. . . . Since the Lord gives the hope of mercy to all without exception, it is wholly unreasonable that any one for any cause whatever should be precluded.

The knot of the question is in the words "fall away." Whoever then understands their meaning can easily extricate themselves from every difficulty. But it must be noticed that there is a twofold falling away, one particular, and the other general. The one who has in anything, or in any way offended, has fallen away from their state as a Christian; therefore all sins are so many fallings. But the apostle speaks not here of theft, or perjury, or murder, or drunkenness, or adultery; but he refers to a total defection or falling away from the gospel, when a sinner offends not God in some one thing, but entirely renounces his grace. . . .

If anyone asks why the apostle makes mention here of such apostasy while he is addressing believers, who were far off from a perfidy so heinous, to this I answer that the danger was pointed out by him in time, that they might be on their guard. . . .

But here arises a new question: How can it be that one who has once made such progress should afterward fall away? For God, it may be said, calls none effectually but the elect, and Paul testifies that they are really his sons who are led by his Spirit (Rom 8:14); and he teaches us that it is a sure pledge of adoption when Christ makes us partakers of his Spirit. The elect are also beyond the danger of finally falling away; for the Father who gave them to be preserved by Christ his Son is greater than all, and Christ promises to watch over them all so that none may perish. To all this I answer that God indeed favors none but the elect alone with the Spirit of regeneration, and that by this they are distinguished from the reprobate; for they are renewed after his image and receive the earnest of the Spirit in hope of the future inheritance, and by the same Spirit the gospel is sealed in their hearts. But I cannot admit that all this is any reason why they should not grant the reprobate also some taste of his grace, why he should not irradiate their minds with some sparks of his light, why he should not give them some perception of his goodness, and in some sort engrave his word on their hearts. Otherwise where would be the temporary faith mentioned by Mark 4:17? There is therefore some knowledge even in the reprobate, which afterward vanishes away, either because it did not strike roots sufficiently deep, or because it withers, being choked up.

And by this bridle the Lord keeps us in fear and humility; and we certainly see how prone human nature is otherwise to security and foolish confidence. Commentaries on the Epistle of Paul the Apostle to the Hebrews 6:4-6.[8]

Rebaptism Is a Mockery of the Cross. Johannes Oecolampadius: Many have been troubled by this passage, and hence they have dared to cast out this epistle as if it were not really confirmed, because the apostle here denies repentance. Hence the Novatianists[†] cited this passage in support of their views, saying that, for the baptized, if they fall again into sin, there no longer remains any pardon. And now the Anabaptists jabber in a similar way. But all these things should be expounded in relation to the sacrament of baptism, since it is not permitted to repeat it. Ambrose, in opposition to the Novatianists themselves, cites these words of the apostle in *On Repentance*, book 2, chapter 2, "That baptism may not be repeated," which no one will regret perusing.[‡] Nowhere does Paul deny pardon for penitents. This is demonstrated by the single example (along with many other evidences of the same thing) of the Corinthian fornicator, whom he most emphatically commanded to be received into the church once he had repented. Certainly, seven times in a day the righteous person falls, and rises again. Others understand this passage as referring to the sin against the Holy Spirit, but I

[8]CTS 40:137-38. [†]Novatian (d. c. 258), a presbyter in the Roman church, and his followers formed rival churches to protest the lenient policies adopted by orthodox churches toward Christians who lapsed during times of persecution.

do not see how this could agree with the argument thus far. Therefore, we will more straightforwardly interpret it along with Ambrose as referring to the sacrament of baptism, for that is regularly called by exalted names. Dionysius calls it the *mystērion phōtismatos*, that is, "the sacrament of enlightenment."[§] And thus we take "those who have been enlightened" as "those who have been baptized," although it is not absolutely certain that those who have been baptized have also been enlightened by the Holy Spirit. We heard earlier that they had not yet attained to the more hidden mysteries. Because baptism was called "enlightenment," ancient writers chose to depict it by means of blazing lights that they bore in procession. Similarly, it is called "tasting of the heavenly gift," which some have represented by the figure of salt, others by that of honey. Likewise "partaking of the Holy Spirit," which they chose to depict by chrism or oil. (But just as I do not endorse such ceremonies, neither do I disapprove of them very much, if they are performed reverently. Scripture certainly does not teach anywhere that they must be employed; therefore, they may be omitted without any lack of reverence.) See with how many *paraphrastikōs*, that is, "paraphrastic," words he chose to point out to us those who have been baptized, and nothing else besides. For thus he heaps up the blessings of God that are given to believers in baptism.

"If they have fallen away." He is saying that there is no need for them to be restored in repentance, or, what is the same thing, to be rebaptized. And this is not my interpretation alone, but especially of others of the Fathers who surely studied this passage more diligently. "How then," you may ask, "do these words produce that point?" Very well indeed, for it all hangs neatly together. He means to say, "Must I deal with you as I would with children? Must I continually propound childish things to you? We may indeed impart teaching to all the world, but the sacrament we do not grant to just anyone." Why is this?

"Crucifying and holding up to contempt." Baptism signifies the death and cross of Christ. Romans 6: "Have not all of us who were baptized into Christ Jesus been baptized into his death? We were buried therefore with him by baptism into death," etc. And Colossians 2, "Having been buried with him through baptism," etc. By all this he means to say nothing else than that baptism is a symbol of the death (or cross) and burial of Christ. Such things are also said here from the same perspective. Indeed, this is the habit of Scripture, namely, to speak of the sacraments with the utmost reverence. But because baptism is called the death or cross of Christ, so when someone is rebaptized, he says of it that he is crucifying again the Son of God. That is, he does not indicate or believe that [Christ] was crucified for him, and so to this extent he is crucifying him again in himself. But "we know that Christ does not die again, for death no longer has dominion over him" (Romans 6). Explanations of Hebrews 6:4-6.[9]

Paul Uses Hyperbole to Prevent Us from Deserting Christ. Huldrych Zwingli: "For it cannot be the case that those who have once been enlightened, and have tasted. . . ." He gives the reason why he does not wish to repeat the fundamentals of Christian teaching, which he had already recounted word for word, and by which they had been established at the beginning of their conversion. Afterward he shows how dangerous it would be (as we declared in the introduction) to forsake the knowledge of Christ; not that it could be possible for a believer and lover of true godliness to depart from the faith. For if one did fall away, it would show that it was a counterfeit and hypocritical faith. But when it says that such people cannot be restored again through repentance, the passage is only made clearer, and is only obscure to the unrepentant. For it does not refuse or deny pardon and forgiveness of sins to those who amend their ways, but it shows that amendment of life is hard

[9]Oecolampadius, *In Epistolam ad Hebraeos Explanationes*, 59v-60v; citing 1 Cor 5:1-5; 2 Cor 2:5-8; Prov 24:16; Lk 17:4; Mt 12:31-32; Rom 6:3-4; Col 2:12; Rom 6:9. [†]Novatian (d. c. 258), a presbyter in the Roman church, and his followers formed rival churches to protest the lenient policies adopted by orthodox churches toward Christians who lapsed during times of persecution. [‡]PL 16:497-99; NPNF^2 10:345-46. [§]Pseudo-Dionysius the Areopagite, *Ecclesiastical Hierarchy* 3 (PG 3:425-26).

for corrupt or hopeless people, or rather, for those who shrink from nothing without regard to right and wrong, and whose life is so abandoned that they neither fear God nor respect humans. For how can someone pursue innocence while blaspheming and denying the Prince of innocence? But in Scripture it is one thing to change one's life, or to be renewed through repentance, and another to obtain remission of sins from God; nevertheless, the one never or rarely occurs without the other. Thus he adds:

"Impossible." The Novatianists[†] went astray as a result of this word. He explains himself clearly enough in that which goes along with it.

"If they fall away, since they are crucifying once again the Son of God to their own harm and holding him up to contempt." It is as if he were saying, "It is difficult, and scarcely possible, for those who have embraced the faith of Christ and have lived a life worthy of God, if they fall away—thus throwing away all the fundamentals of the faith to which they have attained (like Judas the traitor, or those whom Paul mentions elsewhere) and being quick and even eager either to fall away again or to bestow contempt on the Son of God—to amend their ways and be restored to a life of integrity and innocence." . . . And although we may learn that it is impossible for such people to return to the way, nevertheless we may sometimes marvel that they do return. And thus we rightly consider that these statements are made hyperbolically, just it says in Matthew 18 that Christ made the statement regarding the power to bind and to loose being given to the church. Thus by this exaggeration Paul intends not only to divert us from sins but also to deter us from falling back into our original blindness or wickedness. Here we must show what sin is, and what it is to oppose or depart from the truth, and what is the difference between a believer who sins and an ungodly sinner. Exposition of Hebrews 6:4-6.[10]

[10]Zwingli, "*In Epistolam Beati Pauli ad Hebraeos Expositio*," 571-572; citing Lk 18:2; Mt 26:24; 1 Tim 1:19-20; Mt 18:18. [†]For Novation, see previous footnote.

On Not Contending Against the Gospel. Johannes Bugenhagen: John, in his epistle, asserts that there are two kinds of sin, one not unto death, the other unto death. For the former he desires prayer to be made, if a brother should sin, but not for the latter. Concerning the former he also says, "My little children, I am writing these things to you so that you may not sin. But if anyone does sin, we have an advocate with the Father, Jesus Christ the righteous. He is the propitiation for our sins, and not only for our sins, but also for the sins of the whole world." Does not John there say the same thing as this author of ours, except that he calls Christ the Advocate, while here he is the High Priest, whereas Paul in a word speaks of the Mediator? In Mark 3, Christ calls the sin unto death blasphemy against the Holy Spirit, which will not be forgiven. This statement about that sin, as well as the statements made here, must be understood, and therefore we will see in the author's words, if we have previously indicated, just what that sin is. It happens when the truth which God has revealed is evident, so that you are overcome within your very being in your heart and conscience, because it is the way things really are, and it cannot be otherwise. And nevertheless you dare to speak impiously, and contend to the contrary that this is not true, it is not from God, it is perverse, it is from the devil. By this horrible blasphemy you show no reverence for the sword of the Lord who testifies to the contrary, as though it were lawful for someone like you to fight deliberately against God without fear of punishment. You can see this in Mark 3, where in violation of conscience they attributed the manifest work of God to Beelzebub. This is why after Christ's statement, "Whoever blasphemes against the Holy Spirit will not be forgiven in eternity," the Evangelist adds, "because they were saying, 'He has an unclean spirit.'" But if Christ said this regarding others who were ungodly and refused to receive the truth, but fought against something so manifest that they could not deny it, why do we accuse this our author because he condemns those who were illuminated not only in external words or external miracles but also inwardly in the heart, who had tasted the heavenly gift, received the Holy Spirit, and tasted the goodness of the word of God, and the influences and power of the kingdom of God, and nevertheless fall away from all these things and blaspheme against the grace that had been made evident by so much testimony from the Spirit? Commentary on the Pauline Epistles, Heb 6:4-6.[11]

Repentance Is from God. John Calvin: In short, the apostle warns us, that repentance is not at the will of human beings, but that it is given by God to those only who have not wholly fallen away from the faith. It is a warning very necessary to us, lest by often delaying until tomorrow we should alienate ourselves more and more from God. Commentaries on the Epistle of Paul the Apostle to the Hebrews 6:6.[12]

Repetition of Baptism Dishonors the Cross of Christ. Cardinal Cajetan: If he had said that it is impossible for them to be restored to repentance without any further comment, it would be a difficult statement; or rather, if it were not an authoritative statement, it would be regarded as heretical. But because this epistle has achieved authority, it may be explained by the gloss that this does not refer to just any restoration, but to the restoration of baptism. But because it expressly adds, "recrucifying in themselves the Son of God," it restricts consideration to not just any kind of repentance, but to repentance by crucifying in oneself the Son of God. Therefore, the meaning is that it is impossible for those who have once been baptized to be restored again to repentance by crucifying again the Son of God in themselves. For surely "crucifying again" clarifies the mode of restoration. It is just as if he had said that it is impossible to be restored again to repentance through baptism, for he called a repeated baptism, "crucifying again in themselves the Son of God." He carefully and skillfully shows the reason why restoration through baptism cannot be repeated: because it would be to crucify again the Son of God, not in the actual individual flesh of the Son of God, but in the persons of those who would be baptized again. For we are baptized into the death of Christ and buried with him through baptism, and we emerge from baptism into newness of life, being raised together with Christ; and therefore to repeat baptism is to crucify again the immortal Christ, not in his own person (so to say) but in the person of the one who is rebaptized. Moreover, because the sign should be similar to what it signifies, therefore, just as Christ died once and rose, never to die again, so I must be crucified once and am allowed to rise once with him into new life. The additional comment, "holding him up as a spectacle," or, "defaming," or (by way of paraphrase), "making him an example of dishonor," refers to the same thing. Or rather, it explains that this kind of "recrucifixion" aims at the public dishonor of the Son of God, as if someone were to crucify the Son of God repeatedly. Comments on Hebrews 6:6.[13]

The Author Seems to Affirm the Possibility of Repentance. Johannes Bugenhagen: Every day we continually appeal to the mercy of God, not only because of our temptations, but also because of our sins, for the Lord commands us to do so. Therefore, we will not deny such Christian repentance, which Scripture proclaims in all its statements and examples, even if an angel from heaven were to proclaim to us a different gospel. Therefore, you should not attend to this author, if you cannot understand him in any other way than that he denies repentance. For you have the divine word, to which every human word must give way.† But it is amazing that, while this author, whoever he was, very diligently proves everything from the holy Scriptures, this statement, in which he seems to deny pardon to those who have fallen after their first conversion to Christ, is the only one he does not prove. But whence could he prove it? For then there would be complete contradictions in the Scriptures, unless you

[11]Bugenhagen, *Annotationes in epistolas Pauli recognitae* (1525) 147v-148r [328-29]; citing 1 Jn 5:16-17; 2:1; Mk 3:29, 22-30.
[12]CTS 40:139.

[13]Cajetan, *In Epistolam ad Hebraeos Commentarii*, 162r; citing Rom 6:3-4; Col 2:12; Rom 6:9; Gal 2:20.

understand this as referring to the sin against the Holy Spirit, as we will maintain. But this very section, concerning the priesthood of Christ, which draws very worthily here from the Scriptures, shows clearly that the author does not deny repentance and forgiveness of those sins into which human frailty falls, as long as one still stands on Christ, the foundation. Otherwise, after initial forgiveness this priesthood of Christ will be idle. And the author himself says, "Let us draw near with confidence to the throne of grace." Likewise in Hebrews 7, "Consequently he is able to save forever as he comes to God through himself, for he always lives to make intercession for us." Again, in Hebrews 9, "that he might appear now in the presence of God for us." And in Hebrews 12, "every heavy burden, and the sin which clings so closely." It is certain that such things are not addressed to those who were not yet converted. For he is writing to Christians who have been converted to Christ from Judaism, as is clearly stated in Hebrews 3,‡ "Holy brothers, partakers of the heavenly calling," to say nothing of other statements. Since he does not deny pardon, as is clear from Scripture and from elsewhere here in this epistle, as we have demonstrated above, we must explain why he seems to deny it, with no Scriptures added, and so renders us uncertain of his intention, from clearer Scriptures (and, if we can, even from the words of the author himself), just as should be done in any passage of Scripture that is more obscure. COMMENTARY ON THE PAULINE EPISTLES, HEB 6:4-6.[14]

THE DIFFERENCE BETWEEN A PARTIAL FALL AND A TOTAL FALL. WILLIAM JONES: The elect fall but only in part, either in their understanding or their will. Those who commit this sin fall wholly in their understanding and will too; they obscure the light that they have received, choke the good motions that were in them, and with their whole will, might, and mien run against the truth they professed. . . . A person may fall on their knees, yet not on the whole body; so a person may fall from one fundamental point, though not from the whole body of the heavenly calling, as many heretics do. But these fall from the whole. A COMMENTARY UPON THE EPISTLES OF ST. PAUL, HEB 6:6.[15]

UNBELIEF AND WORKS RIGHTEOUSNESS CANNOT BE FORGIVEN. MARTIN LUTHER: Some think that these words are spoken by the apostle about those who in any way have fallen into sin.† And in order to counteract the error of the Novatianist‡ they are compelled to distort the word "impossible."§ and to declare that it was used instead of the word "difficult."◊ But because it is dangerous to twist clear words of Scripture into a different meaning, one should not readily permit this, lest in the end the authority of all Scripture vacillate, except where the context demands it. . . . Furthermore, in this way they still neither escape nor refute the Novatian error, since it is no less difficult for God to justify any godless person again, and it is impossible for humanity to rise from any sin. Therefore, the truth must be asserted, and heresy must be refuted, and not till then should one, so far as possible, harmonize the text. But that repentance remains for those who have fallen is clear. . . . Indeed, if there were no repentance, the entire epistle to the Galatians would amount to nothing, since it is not the so-called actual sins that are censured in this epistle but the greatest sin, namely, the sin of unbelief, because of which they had fallen away from Christ to the law. Thus we read in the Old Testament that the very saintly David fell three times and rose again just as often. In like manner the brothers of Joseph, although they were fratricides, were restored through repentance. And lest the heretics reason captiously that their opinions are in accord with the New Testament, behold. Peter, along with all the apostles, fell from faith; and they all fled. Yet they were restored. Therefore, one must

[14]Bugenhagen, *Annotationes in epistolas Pauli recognitae* (1525) [327-328] 147r-v; citing Mt 6:12; Heb 4:16; 7:25; 9:24; 12:1; 3:1. †Following Luther, Bugenhagen denied the Pauline authorship of Hebrews, which called its canonical status into question. Here he is at least willing to consider the possibility that Hebrews could be classed as "human" in distinction from the "divine" word of genuine apostolic Scripture. ‡Bugenhagen, apparently citing from memory, incorrect identifies this verse as coming from chapter 2.

[15]Jones, *A Commentary upon the Epistles of St Paul*, 216*.

understand that in this passage the apostle is speaking about the falling of faith into unbelief, namely, because of their opinion that they can be saved without Christ by their own righteousness, which is altogether impossible. For this reason he says at the beginning (Heb 6:1) that he will omit the words about faith and the elementary doctrines of Christ. This means that it is "impossible" for him to be restored who at one time began with Christ and, after backsliding, seeks someone else. And that this is his meaning he seems to point out clearly enough below, in Hebrews 10:26, where he says, "If we sin deliberately . . . there no longer remains a sacrifice for sins." Accordingly, it was the need of the primitive church that compelled the apostle to speak so severely against those who had fallen. Here there was danger not only with regard to the changing of morals after faith had taken root but more so with regard to the newly planted faith itself. The apostle also shows this concern abundantly enough in the rest of his epistles. Lectures on Hebrews 6:6.[16]

6:7-8 *Fruit and Thorns*

You Cannot Mock God and Suppose You Can Repent Later. Johannes Bugenhagen: This is what he says in Hebrews 10, "sinning deliberately after the truth has been made evident." He calls turning away from Christ sinning, just as he calls unbelief sin, if you rightly consider chapters 3 and 4. Christ also says in John 16, "The Holy Spirit will convict the world concerning sin, because it does not believe in me." But he adds "deliberately," lest he make it seem that people are guilty of this sin if it happens to them by chance, as God allots, as it happened to Peter. Rather, he intends those who among the godly confess that they know these things are the truth, but among the ungodly blaspheme and live a filthy life with the others in violation of conscience. Thus, while they are attentive to their own interests, they willfully mock both God and humans, in the hope that they can repent when they want to, as they wrongly suppose. This is what it means to "crucify afresh the Son of God and hold him up to contempt," as it says here. For, as it says in Isaiah 55, the land is blessed by God, which always drinks in the rain of the word of God as it comes from heaven and grows from faith to faith, bearing the fruit of faith with the confession. But the land that mocks the work both of those who tend it and of God who sends the rain, bearing nothing except insults and a confession of blasphemy, is rejected; that is, it is next door to the terrible decree that it must be burned. Commentary on the Pauline Epistles, Heb. 6:4-7.[17]

God Accepts the Fallen but Not the Indolent. Veit Dietrich: Before he introduces such teaching he exhorts the Jews again very strongly that they should be on their guard that they do not fall away again from the gospel that they heard from Christ, for if that were to happen it would be a sign that the word has produced no fruit in them and God would punish them horribly.

It is the same as when after the rain that frequently comes and is fruitful in itself the ground remains unfit and is therefore under the curse because it produces nothing but thistles and thorns.

One should not interpret this saying to mean that God does not want to accept the fallen again in grace, which is thoroughly opposed to the gospel; rather, it has this meaning: those who have heard the gospel for a long time and neither improve themselves by drawing on it nor receive it, but rage against it more and more as time passes, here there is cause to worry that God will not endure this and will see to it in his good time that the well-deserved punishment occurs. Summary of the Epistle to the Hebrews 6:4-8.[18]

[16]LW 29:181-83 (WA 57:181.9-182.24); citing 2 Cor 12:21-22; 1 Cor 5:5; 1 Tim 3:5; 2 Tim 2:25; Tit 1:7; 3:10. †LW note (181 n. 5): "Cf. Lyra, *Postilla, ad* Heb 6:6." ‡Vulgate, Heb 6:4: *impossibile*. §Vulgate: *difficule*. ◊Novatian (d. c. 258), a presbyter in the Roman church, and his followers formed rival churches to protest the lenient policies adopted by orthodox churches toward Christians who lapsed during times of persecution.

[17]Bugenhagen, *Annotationes in epistolas Pauli recognitae* (1525) 148r-v [329-30]; citing Heb 10:26; Jn 16:8-9; Mt 26:34, 69-75; Is 55:10-11.

[18]Dietrich, *Summaria vber die Epistel an die Ebreer*, P pp iii r-P pp iii v [673-74].

6:9-12 *God Does Not Overlook the Christian's Faithfulness*

BECAUSE GOD IS TRUE, LET US STRIVE TO SHOW MERCY. HEINRICH BULLINGER: This is the reason why he expects their salvation; the meaning is clear, except that God's "justice" in this verse should be taken to means God's "truth." Thus, on the basis of God's truthfulness, he urges them to press on. For that salvation will be certain if they press on. But he also adds something in the way of praise. Again, praise can do more than anything in persuading someone. For nature has so shaped the souls of mortals that, when the heart is cast down, it can hardly exist at all unless it is stirred up with praises. Thus he praises their good words, especially their love, because God desires mercy, not sacrifice. For *diakonein*, which others have translated as "to minister," means to attend to and provide for those who are in need according to one's capacity. Besides, what we share with a needy person in the name of the Lord, we share with God himself, who says in the Gospel, "What you did to one of the least of these of mine, you did to me." So we also should strive to please God with similar acts of love, but to reject those foolish ceremonies that are not sacred rites but heathen absurdities, and direct all the zeal and promptitude of our souls for the benefit of the needy. For he will talk with us about mercy when he comes to judge the living and the dead† (Matthew 25). Mercy is what he demanded of our forebears in Isaiah 58; so let us strive after mercy. COMMENTARY ON HEBREWS 6:10.[19]

GOD'S JUSTICE DEMANDS HE RESPECTS HUMAN FREEDOM. JACOBUS ARMINIUS: It is certain that God can, by the act of his own absolute power, prevent all things whatever, which can be done by the creature, and it is equally certain that he is not absolutely under obligation to anyone to hinder them from evil. But he cannot, in his justice, do all that he can in his absolute power. He cannot, in his justice (or righteousness), forget the "work and labor of love" of the pious. The absolute power of God is limited by the decree of God, by which he determined to do anything in a particular direction. And though God is not absolutely under obligation to anyone, he can yet obligate himself by his own act, for instance, by a promise, or by requiring some act from humankind. He is obligated to perform what he promises, for he owes to himself the immutability of his own truth, whether he has promised absolutely or conditionally. By requiring an act, he places himself under obligation to give ability and the strength without which that act cannot be performed; otherwise, he would reap what he had not sown. It is plain, from these positions, that God, since he conceded the freedom of the will, and the use of that freedom, ought not, and indeed could not, prevent the fall in any mode that would infringe on the use of that freedom; and, further, that he was not obligated to prevent it in any other way than by the bestowment of the ability that should be necessary and sufficient to the avoidance of the fall. EXAMINATION OF THE TREATISE OF PERKINS ON PREDESTINATION.[20]

THE BELIEVER HANGS BETWEEN HEAVEN AND EARTH. MARTIN LUTHER: How beautifully he combines the two, faith and patience! For faith causes the heart to cling fast to celestial things and to be carried away and to dwell in things that are invisible. For patience is necessary in order that by it the heart may be sustained not only in its contempt for the visible things that attract but also in its endurance of those that rage. For this is how it happens that the believer hangs between heaven and earth, and, as Psalm 68:13 says, "sleeps among the sheepfolds," that is, that in Christ he is suspended in the air and crucified. LECTURES ON HEBREWS 6:12.[21]

---

[19]Bullinger, *In Pauli ad Hebraeos Epistolam*, [144-145] 62v-63r; citing Hos 6:6; Mt 25:40, 31-46. †*Iudicare vivos et mortuos* occurs in both the Nicene and the Apostles' Creeds.

[20]Arminius, *Works*, 3:300-301*.

[21]LW 29:185 (WA 57:185.2-8).

6:13-20 *The Steadfast Anchor of the Soul*

The Anchor Is Made Fast in Heaven. Desiderius Erasmus: We have not placed our happiness in the goods of this life, but have found refuge in the belief that in the age to come we shall take possession of the hope placed before us. Meanwhile in the tempests of the world we hold on to this hope as an anchor of the soul, both sure and steadfast, because it has been made fast for us not in transitory things but in heaven; that is, it stretches all the way to those things that are behind the veil where change does not exist, but all is eternal and secure. This is that inner part of the temple which Jesus Christ, our forerunner and revealer of the way, has entered to intercede for us with the Father, having become . . . high priest forever according to the order of Melchizedek. Paraphrases on the Epistle to the Hebrews 6:14-20.[22]

God's Oath Gives Us Certainty. Heinrich Bullinger: On the basis of human custom, *kat' exēgēsin*[†] of the ceremony of oath-taking that has been introduced, he shows why God swore an oath, and how reliable his truth is. But the human ceremony of oath-taking is described by Moses in Exodus 22 in these words: "If someone gives to his neighbor a donkey or an ox or any beast for safekeeping, and it dies or is damaged or stolen without anyone seeing it, there shall be an oath by the Lord between the two of them that he has not put his hand to his neighbor's property. And its owner shall accept the oath, and he shall not be required to make restitution." From these words it is clearly settled how an oath breaks off a dispute and is the end of all debate. For once the oath has been taken, the defendant is acquitted, and the plaintiff is so bound by the oath that he has accepted that he is compelled to lay aside the accusation and assent to the oath. In this way, when God wished to demonstrate to the human race the certainty of these things, about which human feebleness is accustomed to dispute, he presented his oath, so that in this way he might assist our weakness. For since we have been bound by the oath, we see plainly that the purposes of God are unchangeable, inasmuch as they have been confirmed by oath and promise; so let us not hesitate, but let us hold to the firm encouragement that we will certainly attain to the things that he has promised and confirmed with an oath. He swore that we will enter into his rest, but we must believe and offer receptive ears to his word; likewise, he swore that Christ will be the eternal priest of believers after the order of Melchizedek, and hence we will certainly reach salvation and delight in Christ, the one and only priest. For now by a very smooth and natural transition he returns to the subject from which he had turned aside a little earlier, which we will certainly show in what follows, if we recall the previous discourse. Commentary on Hebrews 6:16-18.[23]

Our Anchor Is Secure and Steadfast Because It Enters into the Heavens. Cardinal Cajetan: He compares hope to an anchor that holds a ship in place, explaining that hope is like an anchor that has three qualifications. First, that it is "secure" from adversaries. Second, that it is "steadfast," having in itself a basis for steadfastness. And, finally, that it "enters in," that it penetrates to the inner places behind the veil. For an anchor is secure and steadfast when it penetrates to the inner places within the depths. Likewise, hope penetrates into the heavens, unto the coming bliss of the saints. He calls this "the inner places behind the veil," that is, the holy of holies, the innermost part of the temple, which was separated by a veil from the rest of the temple. "Where a forerunner, Jesus, has entered for us, having become a high priest forever according to the order of Melchizedek." Access was granted only to the high priest to the inner places behind the veil, namely, to the inner places of the heavens, where a forerunner, Jesus, has entered for us (both

[22]CWE 44:229.

[23]Bullinger, *In Pauli ad Hebraeos Epistolam*, 64r-65r [147-49]; citing Ex 22:10-13. [†]That is, "as an explanation."

because he entered before us and because he entered to prepare a place for us there), having become the true high priest, not for a time, but eternally, according to the order of Melchizedek. Comments on Hebrews 6:18-20.[24]

Christ, Our Sure Anchor. Lucas Osiander: Just as an anchor holds a ship fast in the dangers of navigation, lest by the violence of the winds throwing it this way and that way it drives against and perishes in the sand banks or another dangerous place, so Christ, who is our hope, keeps us, lest we perish among the thousand temptations and afflictions by which we are thrown about. Our anchor, Christ, is safe and firm, so that it is neither shattered nor pulled out by the strength of spiritual tempests. Thus through faith in Christ not only are we certain that God embraces us with fatherly benevolence, truly we, the ones who are safe because of this most firm and safe anchor, also ought to be certain that to the end of life we shall be kept for eternal happiness. Epistle to the Hebrews 6:19.[25]

Christ Is Our Anchor and Hope in Heaven. Heinrich Bullinger: Here it should be noted that by "hope" the author means the thing for which we hope. The object of faith is God himself, his truth, Jesus Christ, whom, by a deeply beautiful analogy, he calls "a safe and steadfast anchor for the soul." For by his protection we live in safety, and resting on the solid rock we stand firm against all ills. For Erasmus in *Chiliades* says, "The Greeks used 'anchor' proverbially to mean 'refuge,' and anything on which we lean and in which we put our trust. This metaphor is derived from ships, which are steadied by anchors and so are at rest and protected from the waves."† Moreover, Paul represents this anchor as extending into and fastening on to heaven itself (which is what is depicted by "the inner place"). This means that our hope is fixed on the heavenly places, for Christ has been received into heaven; he is our way, truth, life, and priest, through whom all who confess that he is the priest ordained by God after the order of Melchizedek are saved. Commentary on Hebrews 6:18-20.[26]

Perpetually Anchored in Heaven. Huldrych Zwingli: "Which we have as an anchor." By means of a metaphor taken from the anchor used by sailors he teaches that our hope is like the bent iron prong that grabs onto the projecting rocks to keep a ship in one place. For hope is the anchor to which we flee in this world and in the stormy waves of this life. In these tribulations, faith, that is, trust in God, is a holy anchor for us and our refuge. This is the same thing that Paul says in Romans 8, "For in hope we were saved."

"Which enters into the inner place within the curtain." That is, this anchor, which is hope, leads us within the curtain and the holy of holies, that is, heaven, where our forerunner, Christ Jesus, the chief priest, has entered. This teaches that, if we have once entered into heaven with our forerunner, we are established there perpetually. This is the same thing that Christ says: "Where I am, there my servant will also be." And thus he beautifully explains the symbol of the chief priest in the Old Testament, and of the articles that were within the curtain. Exposition of Hebrews 6:19-20.[27]

[24]Cajetan, *In Epistolam ad Hebraeos Commentarii*, 162v; citing Jn 14:2.
[25]Osiander, *Epistola ad Hebraeos*, 43-44.
[26]Bullinger, *In Pauli ad Hebraeos Epistolam*, 66r-v [151-52]; citing Acts 3:21; Jn 14:6. †Erasmus, *Adagia* 1.3.43 (*Erasmi Roterodami Proverbiorum Chiliades* [Basel: Froben, 1518], 92; cf. CWE 32:273).
[27]Zwingli, *In Epistolam Beati Pauli ad Hebraeos Expositio*, 573; citing Rom 8:24; Jn 12:26.

7:1-28 CHRIST IS THE PERFECT ETERNAL PRIEST

For this Melchizedek, king of Salem, priest of the Most High God, met Abraham returning from the slaughter of the kings and blessed him, 2and to him Abraham apportioned a tenth part of everything. He is first, by translation of his name, king of righteousness, and then he is also king of Salem, that is, king of peace. 3He is without father or mother or genealogy, having neither beginning of days nor end of life, but resembling the Son of God he continues a priest forever.

4See how great this man was to whom Abraham the patriarch gave a tenth of the spoils! 5And those descendants of Levi who receive the priestly office have a commandment in the law to take tithes from the people, that is, from their brothers,[a] *though these also are descended from Abraham. 6But this man who does not have his descent from them received tithes from Abraham and blessed him who had the promises. 7It is beyond dispute that the inferior is blessed by the superior. 8In the one case tithes are received by mortal men, but in the other case, by one of whom it is testified that he lives. 9One might even say that Levi himself, who receives tithes, paid tithes through Abraham, 10for he was still in the loins of his ancestor when Melchizedek met him.*

11Now if perfection had been attainable through the Levitical priesthood (for under it the people received the law), what further need would there have been for another priest to arise after the order of Melchizedek, rather than one named after the order of Aaron? 12For when there is a change in the priesthood, there is necessarily a change in the law as well. 13For the one of whom these things are spoken belonged to another tribe, from which no one has ever served at the altar. 14For it is evident that our Lord was descended from Judah, and in connection with that tribe Moses said nothing about priests.

15This becomes even more evident when another priest arises in the likeness of Melchizedek, 16who has become a priest, not on the basis of a legal requirement concerning bodily descent, but by the power of an indestructible life. 17For it is witnessed of him,

> *"You are a priest forever,*
> *after the order of Melchizedek."*

18For on the one hand, a former commandment is set aside because of its weakness and uselessness 19(for the law made nothing perfect); but on the other hand, a better hope is introduced, through which we draw near to God.

20And it was not without an oath. For those who formerly became priests were made such without an oath, 21but this one was made a priest with an oath by the one who said to him:

> *"The Lord has sworn*
> *and will not change his mind,*
> *'You are a priest forever.'"*

22This makes Jesus the guarantor of a better covenant.

23The former priests were many in number, because they were prevented by death from continuing in office, 24but he holds his priesthood permanently, because he continues forever. 25Consequently, he is able to save to the uttermost[b] *those who draw near to God through him, since he always lives to make intercession for them.*

26For it was indeed fitting that we should have such a high priest, holy, innocent, unstained, separated from sinners, and exalted above the heavens. 27He has no need, like those high priests, to offer sacrifices daily, first for his own sins and then for those of the people, since he did this once for all when he offered up himself. 28For the law appoints men in their weakness as high priests, but the word of the oath, which came later than the law, appoints a Son who has been made perfect forever.

a Or *brothers and sisters* **b** That is, completely; or *at all times*

Overview: In this section, the reformers comment on the relationship of the priesthood of Christ with the Levitical priesthood, on one hand, and the priesthood of Melchizedek, on the other. In their commentary, they continue to castigate a number of traditional Roman Catholic beliefs and practices, including the sacrificial nature of the Mass, the legitimacy of the Roman priesthood, the existence of purgatory, the intercession of the saints, and the status of the pope as vicar of Christ. The reformers believe that each of these is refuted in this section of the epistle, which in their view stresses the unique, eternal, and permanent nature of Christ's priesthood, entailing that it cannot be transferred to a human being. The reformers also maintain that Christ's priesthood brought with it a new evangelical law of the Spirit that cancels the Old Testament ceremonial law and its Roman counterpart. Finally, throughout there is an emphasis on the full, complete, and unitary nature of Christ's sacrifice for sin, which negates the need for any further sacrifices or meritorious works.

As the reformers explore the connections between Christ and Melchizedek in this passage, they stress several essentials to the reforming movement. For example, they insist that there is no warrant in these verses for the traditional Catholic position that priests sacrifice Christ in the Mass, they emphasize that Christ alone is the true King of Righteousness, and that human beings only become righteous by placing their faith in this King, who is himself their righteousness. Beyond this, the reformers underscore the eternal high priest and king, who alone brings true peace to humans through his death and resurrection.

7:1-4 *Melchizedek the King*

This Passage Provides No Warrant for the Sacrifice of the Mass. Lucas Osiander: But the papists are foolish, who affirm against the text of Scripture that Melchizedek offered bread and wine to God, and from this they want to deduce that in the sacrifice of the Mass the body and blood of Christ must be offered under the species of bread and wine. Further, that it pertains to the benediction that Abraham received from Melchizedek is addressed more fully a little later in this same chapter. Epistle to the Hebrews 7:1.[1]

Melchizedek's Lost Heritage Brings Conformity to Christ. The English Annotations: So described, because neither his father, mother, descent, birth, or death are registered, in whose omission he was made a type both of the eternity of Christ's person and of his priesthood. Not that our savior Christ was without father and so forth, for these we find recorded, but because that which was chiefly intended by the description of Melchizedek, most absolutely and perfectly agrees unto Christ, and that was the eternity of his person and of his priesthood. Annotations on Hebrews 7:3.[2]

Melchizedek as a Type of Christ. John Calvin: The apostle wants to express something more emphatic than the mere fact that the family of Melchizedek was obscure or unknown. I am unimpressed by the objection that the reality does not correspond with the figure in that Christ has a father in heaven and a mother on earth. The apostle quickly shows his meaning in adding the single phrase "without genealogy." By this he exempts Melchizedek himself from the general law of descent by birth, and by this he shows that he was eternal, and that his recent birth among humankind is not to be looked for. It is certain that he was begotten by parents, but the apostle is not discussing them here as an individual man, but rather setting him forth as the type of Christ. Therefore he allows himself to see in him nothing but what Scripture teaches. In dealing with everything that has to do with Christ we must scrupulously observe that we do not accept anything that is not in the Word of God. Now, since the Holy Spirit in introducing this king as the most outstanding of his time makes no

[1]Osiander, *Epistola ad Hebraeos*, 45.
[2]Downame, ed., *Annotations*, MMM4r*.

mention of his origin, nor later does he make any mention of his death, does this not have the force of ascribing to him eternity? What was foreshadowed in Melchizedek was shown in reality in Christ. We ought therefore be content with this moderate knowledge that in showing us Melchizedek as one who was never born and never died, Scripture is setting forth as in a picture the truth that for Christ there is neither beginning nor end.

From this we learn how much reverence and restraint is called for in dealing with the spiritual mysteries of God. What he cannot find written anywhere in Scripture the apostle not only freely ignores but wishes us also to ignore. Surely it is not legitimate for us to assume anything about Christ from our own senses. Melchizedek is not thought of here (as the phrase goes) in his private capacity, but as a sacred type of Christ. It must not be thought to be an omission either by accident or by lack of thought that he is given no family connection, and that there is no word of his death. The truth is that the Spirit has done this purposely so as to elevate him for us above the common herd of humanity. It does not seem a likely conjecture of those who accept Melchizedek as Shem, the son of Noah. If we try to refer to some definite and known man, then this third likeness between Melchizedek and Christ will not hold good. Commentary on Hebrews 7:3.[3]

Christ Fulfills All That Was Foreshadowed in Melchizedek. Johannes Oecolampadius: All these things that happened of old as a symbol in Melchizedek are most excellently appropriate for Christ our Lord. For he is indeed the Lord and our righteous king. And he truly is the King of Jerusalem (which was formerly called Salem), that is, of the church and all the elect. He is also the "king of peace," as it says in Psalm 76:† "His abode has been established in peace, and his dwelling place in Zion." For he alone possesses absolute righteousness, by which he justifies us who believe in his name and pardons our sins. For believers are indeed righteous, if you take into account God's regard for them; but if you inspect the work of a person, you will see that even the holiest people are not free from sin. Therefore, there will be no other "king of righteousness" except Christ alone, who by his own righteousness is abundantly sufficient to appease the Father and obtain sanctification for all who cling to him. Moreover, he is called the "king of peace," and especially, "a peacemaker."‡ For he has conciliated the Father, who was angry with us because his image had been disfigured in us, and made peace through the blood of his cross with the things that are in heaven and the things that are on the earth. For he is our one and only peace (Col 1:20; Eph 2:14). Thus he is superbly depicted by Melchizedek. For this reason also our Lord Jesus Christ is called Solomon, the peacemaker, for that king was a symbol of him. Again, because he was remarkable for such righteousness and gifts beyond all his companions, he is rightly called a priest of the Most High, for the Most High gave him his approval and was pleased that all fullness should dwell in him.

"Who met Abraham." The righteousness of Melchizedek is revealed in two ways, namely, in faith and the work of love. The latter is seen in that he fed Abraham's troops (for in Hebrew idiom, every kind of victuals with which people are fed goes by the name of "bread"), while the former appears in that he praised the Lord, who had delivered Abraham's enemies into his hand. If someone seeks an allegory, it is that Christ, the Living Bread, feeds and strengthens his people who are victorious over this world. But an allegory should not be introduced at random, but rather on the basis of a well-prepared foundation from the literal meaning of the New Testament. In John 6 and 10 you may read how Christ feeds those who believe in him, for he gives to them all of himself, so that we may see how affectionately he is transmitted to those who belong to him. Perhaps it seems surprising to someone that this Melchizedek received a tithe of everything from Abraham, who was by far the most illustrious person, as it is said.

[3]CNTC 12:89-90*.

Surely by the revelation of the Spirit he did homage in this man to Christ, the highest priest, whom he also saw in his heart. For it is written, "Abraham rejoiced that he would see my day; he saw it and was glad" (John 8). EXPLANATIONS OF HEBREWS 7:1-2.[4]

CHRIST HIMSELF IS OUR RIGHTEOUSNESS. LUCAS OSIANDER: For Christ, whom Melchizedek was representing, justifies through faith all who believe in him, Acts 13, and, indeed, Christ himself, by reason of his own most holy and perfect merit, is our righteousness, 1 Corinthians 1. . . . For Christ, being represented by Melchizedek, made peace between God and human beings, and he gives peace in the consciences of those whom he justifies by faith. For those justified by faith have peace in relation to God, Romans 8. EPISTLE TO THE HEBREWS 7:2.[5]

CHRIST IS THE REAL KING OF RIGHTEOUSNESS AND PEACE. HEINRICH BULLINGER: Now he explains individually whatever contributes to the present business, but first of all he unpacks the attributes, namely, the subject's name, ancestry, place, and condition, each of which we will ponder in turn. First, the etymology of Melchizedek is "king of righteousness." For *mlk* means "king," and *ṣdq* means "righteousness." Further, the holy Gospel informs us about Christ that he is the gentle and righteous king of the holy people of God who justifies those who are in him by faith. For [it tells us] that this Jesus "was made for us wisdom from God, and sanctification, righteousness, and redemption." Thus Christ is the real Melchizedek, the righteousness of the whole world, whom the Canaanite king Melchizedek formerly depicted as a type. But then we hear that Melchizedek was king of Salem, that is, "king of peace," for *šlôm* means "peace." Moreover, the apostle wrote in Ephesians 2, "Christ is our peace, who has made the two one . . . so that he might reconcile Jews and Gentiles to God in one body, through the cross." And in Colossians 1: "It pleased the Father that all fullness should dwell in Christ and reconcile all things to himself through him, whether on earth or in heaven, making peace by the blood of his cross through him." So Christ is the true "Melchizedek king of Salem," the true peace of the soul and true joy of the conscience. . . . But what is the point of all this? That we may understand what is the order of Melchizedek, namely, an arrangement in which there is only and always one priest. For now there follows plainly, "He *remains* a priest *forever*."[†] Thus Christ, who is our righteousness and peace, true God and man, is the eternal priest promised in the Prophets and the Law, after whom believers expect no other priest, because he is eternal and has no successor. For hence it very clearly says *menei*, "he remains a priest," and not "he is a priest," for the former is clearer. For if he remains, he has no need for either a vicar or a successor. Much will be said about this in what follows. But from these things it is clearly manifest what is the order (*taxis*), manner, ground, nature, and establishment of the priesthood of Melchizedek, in accordance with which we believe Christ holds the office of priest. And since these things are so clear and sure, and the church of God recognizes no other order than that of Melchizedek, it is no wonder if someone wonders by what order priests are established in the papistical church, who sacrifice the sacred body of Christ daily for sins? Perhaps according to the order of Baal, Ahab, and Jezebel! COMMENTARY ON HEBREWS 7:2-3.[6]

CHRIST IS AN ETERNAL HIGH PRIEST. LUCAS OSIANDER: Thus Christ on earth, according to his human nature, did not have a father. In heaven,

[4]Oecolampadius, *In Epistolam ad Hebraeos Explanationes*, 68r-69r; citing Ps 76:2; 45:7; Heb 1:9; Col 1:19; Gen 14:20; Jn 8:56. [†]In keeping with Latin chapter divisions, Oecolampadius refers to this as Psalm 75. The rendering "in peace" reflects the reading of the LXX, whereas the MT points the same word as "in Salem." [‡]This is probably a reference to 1 Chron 22:9; whereas most English translations read, "His name shall be Solomon," the Vulgate has "He shall be called the peacemaker" (*pacificus vocabitur*).

[5]Osiander, *Epistola ad Hebraeos*, 45; citing Acts 13:39; 1 Cor 1:30; Rom 8:1.

[6]Bullinger, *In Pauli ad Hebraeos Epistolam*, 67v-68r, 69r-v; citing 1 Cor 1:30; Eph 2:14, 16; Col 1:19-20. [†]Emphasis original.

according to his divine nature, he did not have a mother. And according to [his] divinity he has neither beginning nor end. But also according to [his] humanity he is an eternal Priest, because he does not die anymore, neither does death have dominion over him, Romans 6. Epistle to the Hebrews 7:3.[7]

Apparent and Real Immortality. Cardinal Cajetan: The statement here about Melchizedek being "without father or mother" should be understood applying to Melchizedek only formally. For he appears in Scripture with such a reputation—without recorded father, without recorded mother, without recorded genealogy, without beginning of days (for it is not recorded when he was born), and without end of life, because neither is it recorded how long he lived. And therefore he is likened to the Son of God, who is the king of righteousness and king of peace, without father (insofar as he is human) and without mother (insofar as he is God), without genealogy, since he had no grandfathers or great-grandfathers insofar as he is God. Nor does he have beginning of days or end, since he is eternal. And he truly remains a priest forever positively. But Melchizedek remains a priest forever negatively, because he is described as a priest, but the end of his priestly office is not described. Therefore, he is a complete symbol of the Son of God. Comments on Hebrews 7:3.[8]

7:5-10 *Melchizedek Received Tithes from Abraham*

We Owe Christ Not a Tenth, but Everything. Johannes Oecolampadius: Everything that is stated here promotes the worthiness of Christ. For he is the true Melchizedek and priest forever, who blesses those who believe in him with every spiritual blessing in the heavenly places and makes the work of God grow in them more and more day by day, until at last they attain to maturity. We, in turn, owe him not only a sixth, eighth, or tenth part of what we possess, but our very selves, as much as we are. (For the number ten, like the number seven, is held to be absolutely complete and perfect.) Hence the Savior says, "If anyone comes to me and does not hate his father and mother and wife and children and brothers and sisters, yes, and even his own life, he cannot be my disciple" (Luke 14). For whoever puts anything before Christ is not worthy of him. Romans 12 relates to this. Explanations of Hebrews 7:5-7.[9]

Christ Is Greater Than All the Patriarchs. Lucas Osiander: Therefore Christ, being represented through Melchizedek, is greater than all the patriarchs, for through this our high priest we obtain true blessing, that is, the favor and eternal happiness of God, which not the Levitical priests but Christ alone is able to give. Epistle to the Hebrews 7:7.[10]

7:11 *The Priesthood of Melchizedek Is Perfect*

Jesus Is the One Priest Who Sanctifies by the Spirit. Johannes Bugenhagen: He declares the imperfection of the Levitical priesthood, in place of which it was necessary to establish an eternal priesthood in the Son of God, which, according to the law, could not be a priesthood at all. For Christ is from Judah, not from Levi, and no one from Judah could be a priest according to the law. And besides, the priest to come was described as eternal, which is a kind of priest that the law was not able to ordain. And from this it follows, that if the carnal priesthood has been annulled, then the carnal law has also been annulled through the newly accepted priesthood. If the carnal and temporary priesthood has been exchanged for a spiritual and eternal one, then the carnal and temporary law has also been exchanged for a spiritual and eternal law.

[7]Osiander, *Epistola ad Hebraeos*, 46; citing Rom 6:9.
[8]Cajetan, *In Epistolam ad Hebraeos Commentarii*, 163r.
[9]Oecolampadius, *In Epistolam ad Hebraeos Explanationes*, 71v*; citing Eph 1:3; 4:13; 2 Cor 4:16; Mt 10:37-38; Lk 14:26; Rom 12:1.
[10]Osiander, *Epistola ad Hebraeos*, 47.

The old priesthood and the old law themselves declared their imperfection, because it was necessary for new priests to replace the previous ones again and again when they died, and to repeat the works of the law again and again, and to reiterate the yearly—even daily—sacrifices. For the law brought no one to perfection; otherwise they would have stopped offering sacrifices, just as it says below in Hebrews 10. Therefore the Lord God truly established that priesthood, but not with an oath, because actually it would eventually be abolished along with everything that pertains to it. But God established the priesthood of Christ with an oath, because it is eternal and cannot be changed at all. The former priests would sanctify the people symbolically and repeatedly with carnal sacrifices. The latter by a single offering performed just once on the cross, truly and eternally sanctified his people, that is, those who believe. When, I ask you, have priests who were sinners and mortals themselves produced perfect people? But Jesus, who is both free from sin and immortal, as the high priest before God sanctifies us just once from all sin and gives us the Spirit, who is the law of life in our hearts forever. Before, the law compelled and condemned so much that it was intolerable; now the Spirit of Christ in those who believe performs the requirements of the law willingly, not under compulsion. Indeed, so far is the spiritual person from objecting to the law that all things in him that are contrary to the law of God are burdensome, though they still feel them because of their unrenewed flesh. Though these things are still sins in the sight of God, nevertheless they are not counted against them because of the Spirit, who resists and convicts and because of our priest who intercedes continually. Only those who have the Spirit of God understand this annulment of the law, just as Paul says, "Where the Spirit of the Lord is, there is liberty." All the rest are still under the law and condemnation, regarding which see the relevant passages in Philippians.†

Priest, law, sacrifices, temple, altar, consecration, and anointing all become spiritual in Christ and are no longer external. For the priesthood of Christ is in the heavens before the Father, not on the earth, as described below in Hebrews 8, just as his kingdom is not of this world. Commentary on the Pauline Epistles, Heb 7:11.[11]

The Impermanence of the Old Priesthood. Heinrich Bullinger: If the Aaronic priesthood had been ordained by God with the intention that nothing in it would be changed, but that on its own it would be sufficient for salvation, as the Hebrews were trying to maintain, then there would have been no need to promise any other, non-Aaronic priest. But another was promised by the prophet, who would be established not after the order of Aaron, but of Melchizedek. Therefore, the Aaronic priesthood was not what the Hebrews want it to appear it to be, but imperfect and destined to be abolished along with its one law. The verses that follow are subordinate to these conclusions. Commentary on Hebrews 7:11.[12]

Only Christ's Priesthood Truly Expiates Sin. Lucas Osiander: Therefore the Levitical priesthood does not truly expiate sins, but it only represented that future expiation that Christ, the promised priest according the order of Melchizedek, was intending to make. Thus the Lord's Supper is not a sacrifice of expiation, but rather it reminds us of that past sacrifice of Christ, having been offered on the cross, through which the human race has been reconciled with God. Epistle to the Hebrews 7:11.[13]

7:12-19 *Change of Priesthood Means Change of Law*

The Perfect Spiritual Priest Fulfilled the Law. Johannes Oecolampadius: He demonstrates what he has already asserted,

[11]Bugenhagen, *Annotationes in epistolas Pauli recognitae* (1525), 151r-152r; citing 2 Cor 3:17; Jn 18:36; Heb 10:2; Heb 8:1-4. †Perhaps Phil 1:28 or Phil 3:18-19 is intended. Neither law nor condemnation feature prominently in Philippians.
[12]Bullinger, *In Pauli ad Hebraeos Epistolam*, 71v-72r [162-63].
[13]Osiander, *Epistola ad Hebraeos*, 48.

namely, that the Aaronic priesthood is imperfect. In the works of God, that which is more perfect follows after that which is less perfect. Therefore, David rightly foretold a more perfect priesthood while the Aaronic priesthood was still thriving. For if the Aaronic order had been perfect, it surely would have been suitable for Christ, but it was not. Therefore, it was transferred, as something less perfect, and with it the law, which you must understand as the law of tithes and ceremonies. For it does not appear that this should be taken as referring to the entire law, as we have said, which is not at all nullified, anymore than the priesthood, which is transferred from mortal priests to an immortal priest, Christ. This is why Christ says, "I have not come to abolish the law, but to fulfill it." And just as an artist who fleshes out and paints in color the lines that they had drawn earlier is not rightly described as undoing the picture, but rather as completing it, so Christ perfected and fulfilled the things that were weak under the law, and did not entirely nullify them. For a single religion and the same worship of God was present in all ages, and shall be forever. We no longer observe the Jewish sabbath, but one that is spiritual, internal, and continual; nor is the flesh of the foreskin circumcised, but the very heart. Again, we do not offer sheep and cattle, but we do offer ourselves as a living sacrifice to God. So it is in regard to other things as well. This declaration by the apostle hilariously mocks those who patch together decrees, saying that the priesthood has been transferred to Peter, whereas it can never by be transferred from Christ to any man, for he retains it forever, as we have said. To be sure, the elect are called "a royal priesthood," but by way of participation, not by independent fulfillment of the office. They also say, "Where there is a law, there it is necessary that a priest and sacrifices also be provided." We acknowledge this, but the priesthood and the sacrifices must be just like the law, namely, spiritual and invisible. Moreover, take note here that the argument on the basis of law draws no support from ceremonies. For these have been transferred and redirected to the Spirit through Christ, as we have heard. Explanations of Hebrews 7:12.[14]

The Law Has Changed. Huldrych Zwingli: "When there is a change of priesthood, there is necessarily a change of law as well." This is an argument from necessity based on the consequences. It is as if Paul were to say, "If the priesthood is replaced, it necessarily follows that the law—that is, the covenant, ordinance, and appointed ceremonies of the Levitical priesthood, and everything else pertaining to its exercise—must also be nullified because of its imperfection." For if another priest must come about and appear, even more must another priesthood, or rather much more another law and covenant must be instituted. For there cannot be a priest without a law, without a covenant, without an ordinance. . . . And therefore it refers not to the whole law, but to the Levitical law, and the ceremonial law of the outward priesthood. Therefore, as was just said, we take "the law" in this passage to mean the covenant, appointment, and ceremonies of the Levitical priesthood. We take the new covenant of Christ (referred to below) in the same way. Exposition of Hebrews 7:12.[15]

Christ Alone Mediates as Priest. John Calvin: Since Christ is set up as priest, and is also invested with the power of a lawgiver in order to be the servant and interpreter of the New Testament, the word law is applied, somewhat inappropriately, to the gospel. This impropriety, however, is not really absurd, but rather by its very antithesis adds grace to the argument. . . .

The depravity of the pope was utterly impudent in inserting in his decretals that he was now endowed with this same power that Aaron once had in that the law with the priesthood has been transferred to him. We see what the apostle is

[14]Oecolampadius, *In Epistolam ad Hebraeos Explanationes*, 74r-75r; citing Mt 5:17; Heb 4:9; Gen 17:10-27; Rom 2:28-29; Phil 3:3; Rom 12:1; Mt 9:16; 1 Pet 2:9.

[15]Zwingli, *In Epistolam Beati Pauli ad Hebraeos Expositio*, 574.

saying. He maintains that the ceremonies have ceased from the time that Christ came forth with the command to proclaim the new covenant. It is nonsense to conclude from that that anything has passed to the ministers of Christ. It is the person of Christ alone that is contrasted with Moses and Aaron. On what pretext will Antichrist arrogate to himself any such right? I do not argue here simply for the sake of refuting such gross impertinence, but it is worthwhile indicating to readers this sacrilegious impudence so that they can see how unconcerned this good servant of the servants of Christ is about the honor of his master, and how horribly he violates the Scriptures in order to give pretence to his tyranny. COMMENTARY ON HEBREWS 7:12.[16]

CHRIST THE PERFECT HIGH PRIEST. DESIDERIUS ERASMUS: The old law would purify the flesh by washings and various lustrations. The new law purifies souls by a more efficacious victim. Just as Aaron does not remain forever, so the order of his priesthood was not eternal; and just as Melchizedek was said to remain forever, so the order of his priesthood will have no end. The mystic psalms† show that these elements truly fit Christ when it says, "You are a priest forever according the order of Melchizedek." The temporary priesthood gives way to the everlasting, and the mortal high priest to the immortal. As the more imperfect priesthood yields to the more perfect, so the imperfect law gives place to the more perfect law of the gospel through which the Mosaic ordinances of the Old Testament are in effect repealed because they lacked sufficient power and did not provide the usefulness that they ought to have provided. God wanted us to be made perfect, but the law brought nothing to perfection and was not given for this purpose. PARAPHRASES ON THE EPISTLE TO THE HEBREWS 7:12-19.[17]

THE PENALTY OF THE LAW HAS BEEN REVOKED—NOT THE LAW ITSELF. HEINRICH BULLINGER: This passage requires us to say a few things regarding the revocation of the law. Hence, because others discuss this with intricate argumentation with the help of rhetorical categories† we will explain it very clearly and succinctly. Surely, it is by a kind of substitution that it is said that the law has been revoked. For if you take "law" to mean the will of God, inasmuch as there obviously is no other law than the perpetual will of God, who, I ask you, would say that the will of God has been revoked, so that it should not be performed or proclaimed? But when in the law of God there are some external and symbolic elements adapted to the occasion and audience, it comes about that the law may be said to be revoked, when actually the only part that has been revoked is that in which symbolic things are expressed. For it is proper that, as a shadow gives way to a body, the weaker should give way to the superior. For this reason, it is more true for us to say that part of the law has been transformed than to say that it has been revoked. On the contrary, when we say that the law of commandments itself has been revoked, we do not, as many believe, mean that the commandments of godliness and innocence have been revoked. Rather, we mean that the hatred of the law within our hearts has been revoked. For when we are given the Spirit of liberty with Christ's help, it comes about that now we do willingly and with joy what we previously vilified with the utmost hatred through the weakness of the flesh. This is how the law is said to be revoked, that is, the hatred of the law that was in the flesh before it drank of the Spirit. But who here is so dull that they do not understand metonymy?‡ For by association, the law itself stands in place of that which was prompted and revealed by the law. But sin and condemnation are revealed through the law; so it has been taken over by sin and condemnation. So it is in this sense that we say we have been set free from the law, when through the cross of Christ we believe that our sins (which we recognize as sins at the instigation of the law) have

[16]CNTC 12:96-97*.
[17]CWE 44: 231; citing Ps 110:4. †Erasmus refers to psalms that contain prophecies concerning Christ as "mystic psalms."

been revoked. Thus Paul says, "For what the law could not do, in that it was weakened by the flesh, God has done," and so on; for Romans 8 is an important passage of Paul's. Further, when the law is elsewhere substituted for the punishment that God ordains to be meted out for evil deeds, Christians are said to be freed from the law, because they are righteous in another way—by faith, they do wrong to no one, and they do not come within the scope of such laws. Thus Paul said that "the law is not laid down for the righteous." Likewise, on occasion "law" stands in for Scripture itself. But who here would claim that the entire Scripture has been revoked? Further, who does not know that many things in the Old Testament, especially the promises about Christ, have been fulfilled in Christ? Since many do not see this, or do not wish to see it, it comes about that some pass on ungodly teachings, while others discuss an otherwise straightforward business as convoluted,[§] so that they themselves almost stand in need of other interpreters who could explain what they have discussed. Commentary on Hebrews 7:14.[18]

The Holy Spirit Enables Christ's Eternal Priesthood. The English Annotations: That is, of God, or the anointing of the Holy Ghost, which was to continue on him and to qualify and enable him to be an everlasting priest, who should always live to make intercession for us, and communicate unto us the merit and power of his sacrifice, which he once offered for us unto everlasting life. Annotations on Hebrews 7:16.[19]

[18]Bullinger, *In Pauli ad Hebraeos Epistolam*, 72v-73v [164-66]; citing 2 Cor 3:17; 1 Cor 12:13; Rom 8:3; 1 Tim 1:9. [†]*Figurarum et schematum beneficio*. As the rest of the paragraph makes clear, Bullinger does not mean that his own explanation will make use of figurative language, but that he will employ the categories of classical rhetoric to identify and explain the figurative expressions of the text. [‡]Metonymy is a figure of speech characterized by substituting for a word or phrase denoting an object, action, or institution a word or phrase denoting a property associated with that object, action, or institution. [§]I take *intricate* here to be the ablative of an otherwise unattested adjectival form (*intricatis*) derived from *intrico*.

[19]Downame, ed., *Annotations*, MMM4v*; citing Rom 6:9; Rev 1:8.

The Law Apart from Faith and the Spirit. Johannes Oecolampadius: With these words he explains why in the preceding remark he called the law "carnal,"[†] not because it almost entirely deals with carnal matters, but because it does not bring a person to perfection. For those who knew only the law were not made complete by the law that ignores faith and the Spirit, but those who possessed both at the same time are those who were perfected, such as Abraham, David, and others who fulfilled the law, not by compulsion, but with a willing spirit. The external law can save no one. But the law produces wrath as long as it brings the knowledge of sin, as it says in Romans, however holy and useful it is in itself. But because it cannot supply what is needed rightly to complete what it demands (for that is the role of the Spirit of Christ), the result is that the more it presses, the more human virtue is wounded and accused, and the more evil becomes pleasing to us. And thus that which ought to be a remedy is turned into venom by our depraved nature.

A little earlier, he said that the law was to be "changed," but here "rejected" or "nullified," which must be taken with sound understanding, for that which belongs to godliness and the Spirit remains one and the same in all ages. As for works of the law without the Spirit and faith, these are precisely what have always been the greatest abomination to God, which appears in many passages of the prophets. . . . Do you see the rejection here? But only of external ceremonies, which the Jews performed without faith and the Spirit, all the way until they were carried into exile. A body, no matter how well-formed, is a corpse if it is devoid of spirit; so every work, no matter how seemly in appearance, is dead if the life-giving Spirit does not come. Explanations of Hebrews 7:18.[20]

[20]Oecolampadius, *In Epistolam ad Hebraeos Explanationes*, 76v-77r; citing Rom 4:15; 3:20; Is 1:11-14; Hos 6:6; Mic 6:6-8; Ps 40:6; 51:16. [†]This is a literal rendering of the adjective usually rendered in English translations by a phrase such as "concerning bodily descent" (ESV) or "of physical requirement" (NASB).

THE LAW CANNOT JUSTIFY OR SAVE. CARDINAL CAJETAN: "There is a setting aside of the former commandment because of its weakness and uselessness, for the law brought nothing to perfection." He began his argument by saying, "If perfection had come through the Levitical priesthood (for under it the law was given), what need would there have been for another priesthood and another law?" (Hebrews 7:11). Now he gives the reason why it was necessary for another law to arise—namely, because the law with its priesthood did not bring anything to perfection. The meaning, then, is that when the Scripture prophesied a new priest forever after the order of Melchizedek, it set aside the former commandment of the law of Moses. Not that it was evil, but that it was weak and useless. "Weak," because it could not justify, because it did not convey the forgiveness of sins. "Useless," because it did not lead to eternal happiness. Thus he gives both reasons and says, "For the law brought nothing to perfection"; that is, it brought nothing to perfect righteousness in this life, and it brought nothing to a perfect country directly after this life. "But a better hope is introduced." This is done by prophesying, "You are a priest forever, after the order of Melchizedek," inasmuch as this "hope" is not for an earthly promise but for an eternal country (for this hope is introduced through the priesthood of Christ), or rather, it is the "better hope" of the resurrection of the dead, which we have received simply through the priesthood of Christ. "Through which we draw near to God." In contrast to "useless," he spoke of "a better hope." Now, in contrast to "weak," he says, "Through which we draw near to God." For justifying hope makes us close to God according to the Spirit in this life, and this is the same as the hope of a better, good country—that is, a heavenly one. COMMENTS ON HEBREWS 7:18-19.[21]

7:20-22 *Jesus Guarantees a Better Covenant*

GOD'S OATH MAKES CHRIST'S PRIESTHOOD IMMUTABLE. HEINRICH BULLINGER: This is the first contrast, the essence of which is that Christ has been ordained by an oath, and thus into an irrevocable priesthood. This is demonstrated by the prophetic testimony, "You are a priest forever." But the Levites were established as priests without an oath, as though they were shortly to be changed. From this it follows that the Levitical priesthood is mutable, weak, and useless in this regard, whereas the priesthood of Christ is perpetual, perfect, and the only necessary priesthood in the world. But with great spirit he extends this argument, and by an exclamation he adds the final touch, "To this extent Jesus has become the guarantor of a better covenant." By this he meant, the salvation that relies on the priesthood of Christ, not that of the Levites, is the most reliable by far, inasmuch as it has been established by a stronger and more reliable ordination. For "covenant" was written in place of "ordination," and "guarantor" in place of "priest," although I do not doubt that it alludes to human covenants. Further, the statement of the prophet is majestic: "The Lord has sworn and will not change his mind," since for God to alter his decree would be for him to change his mind. Therefore God has bound himself by an oath that the priesthood of his own Son would absolutely not be changed. COMMENTARY ON HEBREWS 7:20-22.[22]

THE DIVINE TESTATOR DIES IN CHRIST. MARTIN LUTHER: One should note that where it is recorded in the Holy Scripture that God makes a will, there it is pointed out somewhat obscurely that at one time or other God will die and arrange the inheritance, as below in Hebrews 9:6: "Where there is a testament, the death of the testator must intervene." This has been fulfilled in Christ. Hence the words "testament," "inheritance," "part," "portion," "cup," etc. occur so frequently in Scripture. All this points to the death of Christ and to faith in his resurrection. LECTURES ON HEBREWS 7:22[23]

[21]Cajetan, *In Epistolam ad Hebraeos Commentarii*, 163v; citing Heb 11:14, 16.

[22]Bullinger, *In Pauli ad Hebraeos Epistolam*, 75r-v [169-70].
[23]LW 29:194-95 (WA 57:193.18-24).

7:23-25 *Christ's Priesthood Continues Forever*

Christ Has No Successors. Heinrich Bullinger: The second contrast is, "The former priests were many in number." And reasonably so, because mortals would need successors. But Christ is a single and unique priest, and reasonably so, for since he is eternal and immortal, he has no need whatsoever for successors. From this it follows that the Levitical priesthood is weak and useless, but that the priesthood of Christ is single and perpetual. The priests of the Roman pontiff,† who surpass in number not only the Jewish priests, but even the sands of Libya, should ponder this. They should also ponder that which follows, "He holds the priesthood permanently, because he remains forever." For if he remains a priest in perpetuity, he has no vicars or successors. For vicars are vicars of those who are absent, and successors are successors of those who are gone. But Christ remains a priest in perpetuity, he has not gone away, nor has he resigned his priesthood to us; so whose office are you filling, O you deceitful men? What can be added that would be clearer? *Aparabaton echei tēn hierōsynēn*, that is, "Immovably (if I may express myself thus) he holds the priesthood." Or, as others have translated it, "He holds a perpetual priesthood." But call "perpetual" that which is untainted, entire, and never interrupted. For *aparabaton* is compounded from *bateō*, which means "I go," the preposition *para*, and the negative particle *a*. For he means that kind of priesthood that certainly cannot pass in succession to anyone else. Hence Erasmus also says in the *Paraphrases*, "But this priest of ours stands alone on behalf of all, nor does he perform his office through a successor, but because he remains forever he holds a perpetual priesthood."‡ And John Chrysostom says, "Therefore, he who saves does not die, because he always lives and has no successor."§ And why does he have no successor? Because, Paul says, "He is completely able to safeguard all who believe." *Eis to panteles* means completely and without failure, and to such an extent that nothing more could be desired. For he always lives, and he lives for this purpose (look how he constantly adds what is clearer and more evident), so that he might intercede for us, *eis to entynchanein hyper autōn*, that is, so that he might conciliate, intervene, and take our cause on himself. What, I ask you, could be said that would be clearer, more pleasant, or holier? So what need is there for your priestly performance, O you utterly shameless Romanists? Of whom, pray tell, are you the successors? Or do you not yet understand that Christ has no successor, that his priesthood is truly perpetual, so much so that one man (yes, one and one alone!) personally intercedes for us all (yes, personally!) now and always? For he is the only pontiff† of his church. He is the only mediator and intercessor, not for just one particular sin, but for the whole multitude of sins; nor merely for one period or for just some people, but for all humanity and for the whole world. For he always lives (yes, always lives!), and *tous proserchomenous*, which is an unrestricted kind of expression, may be explained as pertaining to each and every one of those who approach by faith. But such believers approach God, not the saints, and they do so through Christ's intercession, not that of the saints. "For you," says Isaiah to God, "are our Father, though Abraham does not know us and Israel is unacquainted with us; but you, O Lord, are our Father, our Redeemer, and your name is from eternity" (Isaiah 63). So where is the intercession of the saints now? Where is the papistical priesthood? Yes, where is that most ungodly teaching in which the sophists were relating to us that Christ offered himself only for some sins and for some people? For here we learn that Christ holds a perpetual priesthood, saves completely, and always lives. And if he saves completely, then what cleansing is left for the fire of purgatory? Commentary on Hebrews 7:23-25.[24]

[24]Bullinger, *In Pauli ad Hebraeos Epistolam*, 76r-77r [171-73]; citing Is 63:16. †Latin *pontifex*, which is usually translated "high priest" when referring to Christ or the high priests of Israel, is also employed as a title of the pope, as reflected in the translation here. ‡EOO 7.6:66. §Chrysostom, "Homily 13," in *Homilae XXXIV in epistolam ad Hebraeos* (PG 63:105-106; NPNF 14:429).

Our Prayers Are Always Heard Because of Christ Our Mediator. Lucas Osiander: Our high priest Christ is fully able to help us, because he always lives. For as often as we approach God through the faithfulness of this Mediator and ask for either remission of sins or something else, we are always heard. Because this our high priest lives into eternity, he always intercedes for us in the presence of the Father, Romans 8. And the Father is not able to reject the prayers of this heavenly One. Epistle to the Hebrews 7:25.[25]

Christ Being Our Benefit. John Calvin: What is the nature and extent of the pledge of his love toward us? The fact that Christ lives for us and not for himself, and that he was received into eternal bliss to reign in heaven—this happened, says the apostle, for our sakes. Thus the life and the kingdom and the glory of Christ aim at our salvation as their target, and Christ has nothing that is not to be put to our benefit, because he was given to us by the Father on this condition, that everything he was should be ours. At the same time he shows us by what he does that Christ performs the office of Priest, it belongs to a priest to intercede, in order that the people may find favor with God. Christ is continually doing this because he rose from the dead for this purpose. He justifies his rightful name of priest by his continual task of intercession. Commentary on Hebrews 7:25.[26]

7:26-28 *Christ's Sacrifice Once and for All*

On Earth, Christ Drew Near to Sinners. Johannes Oecolampadius: "Separated from sinners." For the priests of the law it was the rule that they should not dwell together with sinners, nor mix with the profane, for from familiarity with the wicked we easily soak up some of their fault, since by nature we all tend toward depravity. But it is different with Christ, who neither committed sin nor was inclined toward it. But the issue does not rest with separation of bodies, but of souls, which can exist even in the midst of sinners. For Isaiah (6) laments that he dwells in the midst of a people of unclean lips, Ezekiel (2) was among scorpions, and so it was with the other prophets, but all the while they were clean in themselves, and acceptable to God. Thus Christ himself so feasted with tax collectors and sinners, for whom especially he had come as Savior, that he heard from the Pharisees, "The friend of tax collectors and sinners." But while in his soul he was completely estranged from them, inasmuch as they were sinners, nevertheless, inasmuch as they were curable, he was the closest of all. For he was not enticed by their sins, nor could the most holy one be tainted by contact with them, much less could he appear to approve of sinners by dining with them. As for us, however long we may live in this world, we will dwell among the wicked; therefore, let us imitate the example of Christ, and nothing will harm us. For no one is contaminated by associating with the wicked in external things, but in internal things, namely, sins; otherwise, for those who would shun the wicked, it would have been necessary to depart from this world.

Meanwhile, however, we assert that no one has ever been as separated from sinners or from sin as Christ was. He did draw near to them, but as a physician draws near to the sick. Now, however, since his ascension into the heavens, he is completely separated from sinners; and we also will be separated some day, when the judge of the world will separate the goats and the sheep. Explanations of Hebrews 7:26.[27]

For the Christian, Death Is Life. Marguerite of Navarre: Death is no other thing to a Christian but a liberty from mortal bounds. And death, which is fearful to the wicked, is pleasant and agreeable to those who are good. Then is death through your death destroyed. Therefore, my God, if I were rightly taught, I should call death life, end

[25]Osiander, *Epistola ad Hebraeos*, 50-51; citing Rom 8:34.
[26]CNTC 12:101*.
[27]Oecolampadius, *In Epistolam ad Hebraeos Explanationes*, 80v-81r; citing Is 6:5; Ezek 2:6; Mt 9:10-13; 11:19; 1 Cor 5:10; Mt 25:32.

of labor, and beginning of everlasting joy. For I know that long life does let me from your sight. O death, come and break this obstacle of life, or else, love, do now a miracle. Since I cannot yet see my spouse, transform me with him both body and soul, and then shall I the better tarry for the coming of death. Let me die that I may live with him: for there is none that can help me unless it be you only. Mirror of a Sin Sick Soul.[28]

Do Not Claim to Repeat Christ's Offering in the Mass. Heinrich Bullinger: This verse is also connected to the foregoing description and contrast. For it says that the Levites made sacrifices daily, whereas Christ did so not daily, but only just once. The Levites, moreover, offered first for their own personal sins and then for the sins of others and of the people as a whole. But since Christ had no sin, he did not offer for his own sins, but only for ours; and he did not offer cattle or the blood of beasts, but the whole burnt offering of his own completely pure body. From which it is again apparent that the Levitical law was revoked for no other reason than because of its weakness and uselessness, whereas the priesthood of Christ is single and perpetual. So, since we hear so clearly from the apostle that daily sacrifices are rejected, along with the kind of priesthood that makes sacrifices both for their own sins and for the people's, the kind that has need to be purified by something else, and since the papistical priesthood is precisely this kind of order, it follows from the same logic that the papistical priesthood, just like the Jewish priesthood, has been abolished by the single priesthood of Christ. So tell me, O pontiffs,† what do you have to say in reply to these little tiny words of Paul? For Paul says, "He did this *just once*, when he offered up *himself*." You hear that Christ was offered just once, yes, just once, and only once. You hear that the sacrifice was made not by anyone other than Christ himself. With what audacity do you assume for yourselves as your own special prerogative a power that not even the angels possess? For in the gospel the Lord himself says even more clearly, "I lay down my life that I may take it up again. No one takes it from me, but I lay it down of my own accord. I have power to lay it down and to take it up again; this charge I have received from my Father." You wretches, how do you dare to repeat what cannot be repeated, nor needs to be repeated? What are you claiming for yourselves, which cannot be true for any mortal? Commentary on Hebrews 7:27.[29]

Our High Priest Is Not Only a Man but Also God. Huldrych Zwingli: "For it was indeed fitting that we should have such a high priest." Having made his argument from necessity, or from the excellence of the Christian priesthood, Paul now gathers together all the earlier *antitheses* and shows that we are in need of this kind of high priest and chief priest, who would be holy, innocent, and so forth. All of these things were lacking in the priests of the old covenant, whom Christ, the true priest, has surpassed.

"Exalted above the heavens." Now he also commends our high priest on the basis of his exalted position. But he explains his statement that he is "separated from sinners," by the additional statement that he is "exalted above the heavens." For to the very degree that our high priest was separated and distant from sinners, to that same degree he was higher and more excellent than the firmament. Thus, by this series of stronger and stronger statements, he declares not only that Christ is a holy, pure, and sinless man but that he is also God and the true Son of God, and as much higher than the very heavens as he who, as Lord of heaven and earth, has authority over all things in every place. Exposition of Hebrews 7:26.[30]

[28]Marguerite of Navarre, *Mirror of a Sin Sick Soul*, 32r-33r*.

[29]Bullinger, *In Pauli ad Hebraeos Epistolam*, 78r-v. citing Jn 10:17-18.
†Latin *pontifex*, which is usually translated "high priest" when referring to Christ or the high priests of Israel, is also employed as a title of the pope, as reflected in the translation here.
[30]Zwingli, *In Epistolam Beati Pauli ad Hebraeos Expositio*, 575.

8:1-13 CHRIST, THE HIGH PRIEST OF THE NEW COVENANT

Now the point in what we are saying is this: we have
such a high priest, one who is seated at the right
hand of the throne of the Majesty in heaven, 2 a
minister in the holy places, in the true tent[a] that the
Lord set up, not man. 3 For every high priest is
appointed to offer gifts and sacrifices; thus it is
necessary for this priest also to have something to
offer. 4 Now if he were on earth, he would not be a
priest at all, since there are priests who offer gifts
according to the law. 5 They serve a copy and shadow
of the heavenly things. For when Moses was about
to erect the tent, he was instructed by God, saying,
"See that you make everything according to the
pattern that was shown you on the mountain." 6 But
as it is, Christ[b] has obtained a ministry that is as
much more excellent than the old as the covenant he
mediates is better, since it is enacted on better
promises. 7 For if that first covenant had been
faultless, there would have been no occasion to look
for a second.

8 For he finds fault with them when he says:[c]

> *"Behold, the days are coming, declares the Lord,*
> *when I will establish a new covenant with the house of Israel*
> *and with the house of Judah,*
> *9 not like the covenant that I made with their fathers*
> *on the day when I took them by the hand to bring them out of the land of Egypt.*
> *For they did not continue in my covenant,*
> *and so I showed no concern for them, declares the Lord.*
> *10 For this is the covenant that I will make with the house of Israel*
> *after those days, declares the Lord:*
> *I will put my laws into their minds,*
> *and write them on their hearts,*
> *and I will be their God,*
> *and they shall be my people.*
> *11 And they shall not teach, each one his neighbor*
> *and each one his brother, saying, 'Know the Lord,'*
> *for they shall all know me,*
> *from the least of them to the greatest.*
> *12 For I will be merciful toward their iniquities,*
> *and I will remember their sins no more."*

13 In speaking of a new covenant, he makes the first
one obsolete. And what is becoming obsolete and
growing old is ready to vanish away.

a Or *tabernacle*; also verse 5 **b** Greek *he* **c** Some manuscripts *For finding fault with it he says to them*

OVERVIEW: The reformers strive in this section to emphasize the spiritual, inward, invisible, and eternal nature of Christ's priestly ministry over against the bodily, external, visible, and temporal nature of the ministry of the Levitical priesthood. There is continuing discussion of Christ's session at the right hand of the Father and also ongoing criticism of papal religion, which is depicted as a Levitical religion that is out of step with New Testament Christianity. This criticism is particularly focused on the perceived similarities between the Levitical priesthood and the Catholic priesthood, especially the latter's alleged claims to offer Christ as a sacrifice for sin over and over again in the Mass. The reformers emphasize that Christ alone is the only true Christian priest, and that his sacrifice of himself for sin was a one-time event that is eternally valid and efficacious. They also stress against the "enthusiasts" (i.e., the Spiritualists), who claimed to receive direct divine revelation in their hearts via the Holy Spirit, that the external ministry of the Word was still vital and necessary. Finally, the reformers seek to explain the relationship between the old and the new covenants, some stressing continuity, and others discontinuity.

8:1-3 *As High Priest, Christ Ministers Before God*

God Rules His Spiritual Kingdom Through Christ, the Priest and King. Johannes Bugenhagen: Over against the symbol of the priest of the law, on the basis of the preceding discourse he presents Christ as the reigning high priest and minister within the holy of holies and the tabernacles not made with hands, a high priest who has an eternal sacrifice, which he offered just once, as we shall see in what follows. God does not now dwell in temples made with hands, but through Christ, the priest and king, he superintends over the kingdom of heaven as well as on the earth, an invisible kingdom, an eternal kingdom, which he rules invisibly by the Spirit, not by the elementary principles of this world. These are the tabernacles of God, the tabernacles of confidence and security, the eternal tabernacles, which are often sung about in the Psalms and the Prophets. Commentary on the Pauline Epistles, Heb 8:1.[1]

Christ's Priesthood Is Spiritual. John Calvin: That readers might know the subject he handles, he reminds them that his object is to prove that Christ's priesthood, by which that of the law had been abolished, is spiritual.

He has already shown that Christ is a high priest; he now contends that his priesthood is celestial. It hence follows, that by his coming the priesthood established by Moses under the law was made void, for it was earthly. and as Christ suffered in the humble condition of his flesh, and having taken the form of a servant, made himself of no reputation in the world (Philippians 2:7); the apostle reminds us of his ascension, by which was removed not only the reproach of the cross but also of that abject and mean condition that he had assumed together with our flesh; for it is by the power of the Spirit that gloriously appeared in the resurrection and the ascension of Christ that the dignity of his priesthood is to be estimated. Commentaries on the Epistle of Paul the Apostle to the Hebrews 8:1.[2]

Christ's Heavenly Session. Lucas Osiander: It is to be observed that apostle does not define the session of Christ at the right hand of God in terms of a certain place in the heavens, but in terms of the heavenly majesty in which Christ reigns and all the things he governs by his will. Epistle to the Hebrews 8:1.[3]

Christ Continues to Serve and Uphold His Church. Johannes Oecolampadius: "Minister of the holies." Where there is the greatest authority, it is proper that there also be the greatest humility and modesty. And the greater the worthiness, so much greater should be the readiness to serve all. This is what our high priest is like. But Christ may be said to serve us in two ways. On the one hand, he served as a servant; this happened just once, at the appointed time, when he died for us. For he came not to be served for his own sake, but to serve others (Matthew 20). On the other hand, he serves as Lord, when now he imparts to us his Spirit and lavishes gifts and the merit of his blood for the establishment of his church. And so he still performs his ministry and completes the salvation of those who will be saved.

There are those who relate the genitive *hagiōn* to the holy places. I take it as referring to the saints themselves, for that is simpler, and the subsequent statements that have been added as an explanation seem to require it. Besides, it is customary for

[1]Bugenhagen, *Annotationes in epistolas Pauli recognitae* (1525) 152r-v; citing Heb 7:11-28; 9:25-10:14; Acts 17:24; Col 2:8; Ps 27:5-6; Is 4:6; 32:18.

[2]CTS 40:178-79.

[3]Osiander, *Epistola ad Hebraeos*, 52.

Scripture to refer to the saints as the tabernacle, the temple, the city, the house, the church, because God dwells in their hearts and displays his glory in them. He calls it "true" and "which the Lord pitched, not man," to distinguish it from the Mosaic tabernacle, in which God exhibited his presence after a fashion; but it was a type or shadow of the true tabernacle.

It should also be noted here that he says, "God pitched it." For he alludes to the earthly tabernacle, which used to be pitched with stakes. Before the foundation of the world, from eternity all the elect were predestined to life and written with the blood of Christ in the book of life. But this pitching or establishment of the church and tabernacle of the saints is certain; therefore, the gates of hell will not prevail against it, nor the floods and winds, for it has Christ as its foundation, not Peter, Paul, or any human. Thus the audacity of the Roman pontiffs is exposed, who say that they are the head and foundation of the church. EXPLANATIONS OF HEBREWS 8:1-2.[4]

JESUS MINISTERS BY PRESENTING US TO GOD. CARDINAL CAJETAN: "A minister of the holies and of the true tabernacle, which God determined, not humans." It is unclear whether the gender of "holies" is masculine or neuter. It could truly be either form. For Jesus is a high priest, the minister of "the holies," that is, of holy things, of spiritual graces and of heavenly glory. For both of these are holy things, and Jesus bestows them ministerially as a man. On the other hand, he is also the minister of holy people in that he ministers by presenting them to God with the gifts of grace here and with the gifts of glory there. This interpretation fits better with "minister," because "minister" signifies a relation to God, as when one ministers by presenting pure persons to God. But in the first interpretation, it would refer to the ministry of bestowing grace and glory on humankind.[†] But the ministry of a high priest is primarily in relation to God. He is also called "minister of the tabernacle" in reference to the high priest of the law, who was a minister of the tabernacle as the place in which he performed his ministry. But he was a minister of the symbolic tabernacle, whereas Jesus is the minister of "the true tabernacle," which is the church both militant and triumphant. Thus Jesus is the minister of elect persons in two ways: first, as objects which he offers to God, and second, as the tabernacle in which he performs his ministry. For Jesus dwells in the hearts of the elect, for which reason the church is called his tabernacle. And it is the true tabernacle, not the symbolic one, for it the one which God determined, not humans. For God is the one who determines the elect, and there is no one who can construct this kind of tabernacle, in contrast to the material tabernacle, which Moses made and in which Aaron performed his ministry. COMMENTS ON HEBREWS 8:2.[5]

CHRIST'S BODY, THE TRUE TABERNACLE. THE ENGLISH ANNOTATIONS: That is, of his own body or human nature, whereof the corporal tabernacle was a type; hence Saint John says "that the word tabernacled with us," speaking of his being in our flesh, or his taking on himself our human nature. ANNOTATIONS ON HEBREWS 8:2.[6]

8:4-5 *Levitical Priesthood Is a Shadow of the Heavenly One*

ONLY CHRIST, THE HEAVENLY PRIEST, CAN OFFER A TRUE SACRIFICE. HEINRICH BULLINGER: Now the author restates the arguments he has made regarding his second point, namely, that

[4]Oecolampadius *In Epistolam ad Hebraeos Explanationes*, 83v-84r; citing Mt 20:28; Rev 13:6; 1 Cor 3:16-17; 2 Cor 6:16; Eph 2:21; Mt 5:14; Heb 12:22; Rev 21:10; Heb 3:6; 1 Pet 2:5; Eph 3:17; Acts 13:48; Phil 4:3; Rev 13:8; 21:27; Mt 16:18; 7:25; 1 Cor 3:11.

[5]Cajetan, *In Epistolam ad Hebraeos Commentarii*, 164r. [†]The Latin verb *ministro* can mean both "serve/minister" and "give/present/bestow." To indicate this lexical range for the English reader, the participles *ministrando* and *ministrans* are here translated by the phrase "ministers by presenting," and the noun *ministerium* is translated "ministry of bestowing."

[6]Downame, ed., *Annotations*, MMM4v*; citing Jn 1:14; Heb 7:27; 9:14; Jn 2:19; Col 2:9.

Christ was not made a priest after the order of Aaron, but after the order of Melchizedek, not by the fleshly law, but by a perpetual and heavenly order. For the ideas that the Levites were ordained into a fleshly order, but Christ into a heavenly one, so that he holds a single and unchangeable priesthood, are all treated more extensively in chapter 7. Then as a new element he attaches to these things a testimony of Moses, selected from Exodus 25. By this he even more firmly achieves his point that those things that pertained to the old Levitical order were merely shadowy and derivative. *Hypodeigma* means the mold and model that provides the pattern according to which something is made. . . . Now, then, observe with me the import and distinctness of this declaration and testimony. It says, "The model of the true things is in the heavens, in the likeness of which these Levitical things on earth were copied." So the truth itself is in heaven, and the shadow on earth. Therefore, that which is in the heavens is older, but that which is on the earth is recent. Hence those who served as priests were not true priests, but mere shadows of the heavenly priesthood. Therefore, as the true and eternal priest, Christ ascended into heaven, so that he might truly serve as the true, unique, and perpetual priest. From this it is as clear as can be that the universal priesthood of making offerings for sin has been translated into the heavens. For he who was offered just once always appears in the sight of God. He is not offered anymore, but by a single sacrifice he has absolved and purified all who are sanctified for all time. You utterly senseless sacrificial lackeys of the Roman prelate! Why do you fight for your earthly order of making offerings? How can you not see that by your teaching, or rather by your incoherent incantations, the entire Aaronic or Jewish priesthood has been introduced into the church of Christ? Why don't you give God the glory and abandon your profane, Jewish, and earthly priesthood to take hold of the One by whom those who believe will never be put to shame? Commentary on Hebrews 8:4-5.[7]

Moses Foresaw the Church. Johannes Oecolampadius: "See that you make. . . ." You may say, "What, then, was this pattern?" The church of God, and the elect who have been written in the book of life. Moses first saw this type on the mountain, so that everything that would afterward come about in the church might be signified in the tabernacle. This pattern, which he saw in the Spirit, existed only as a mental image, namely, that Christ would come and erect the tabernacle and the church on which he would pour out his Spirit. All the believers of the Old Testament in some measure perceived this heavenly and perfect tabernacle, but Christ alone dwells in it. Would a Jew say here that a simple pattern had been depicted and presented, which God desired Moses to imitate? This is nothing, for something higher was to be considered, something that the eyes of the Spirit, not of the flesh, could perceive.

But take note that, where there is a form, there is also something that conforms; where there is a pattern, there is also something corresponding to it. The Aaronic priesthood was established in accordance with the pattern or shape of another priesthood. Therefore, it is no wonder if Moses in the Spirit saw another priesthood belonging to Christ and also the true tabernacle beyond the external one. Explanations of Hebrews 8:4-5.[8]

Christ Was Not an Earthly Priest. The English Annotations: Reasons are given why Christ could not be a priest on earth. First, because earthly priests were ordained by the law to offer only earthly and carnal sacrifices, but there were no such sacrifices required of that priest according to the order of Melchizedek. Second, the legal priesthood and the sacrifices administered by it were shadows of heavenly things, viz., of the priesthood of Christ and his heavenly sacrifice, whence it evidently follows that his priesthood was to be a heavenly priesthood, and

[7]Bullinger, *In Pauli ad Hebraeos Epistolam*, 80r-81r; citing Ex 25:40; Is 28:16; Rom 9:33; 10:11; 1 Pet 2:6.

[8]Oecolampadius, *In Epistolam ad Hebraeos Explanationes*, 85r; citing Ps 69:28; Phil 4:3; Rev 21:27; 13:6; Is 16:5; Rom 5:5; Is 44:3; Joel 2:28.

his sacrifice to be a heavenly sacrifice. Annotations on Hebrews 8:4-5.[9]

Christ Has Freed Us from the Law and Its Shadows. Catherine Parr: For they [the Jews] lived under shadows and figures, and were bound to the law. And Christ (we being his greatest enemies) has delivered us fro[m] the bondage of the law, and has fulfilled all that was figured in their law, and also in their prophecies, shedding his own precious blood to make us the children of his Father, and his brethren, and has made us free, getting us a godly liberty. I mean not license to sin as many be glad to interpret the same. The Lamentation of a Sinner.[10]

8:6-7 *Christ's Ministry Is More Excellent*

Only Christ's Sacrifice Saves. Huldrych Zwingli: "Which has been ordained with better promises." This means that this testament and law of the priesthood of Christ was superior to the law of the Levites. For by the offering and sacrifice of Christ we have been saved, which was not accomplished by the Levitical sacrifices. And thus he shows that the law of Christ is superior and possesses superior things. Accordingly, as he cites a passage from Jeremiah, he adapts it to his own purpose. It is as if he were saying, "From Jeremiah also it is established that God had predicted that this old covenant, that is, this Levitical ritual of making sacrifices, would be abolished and a new one established in its place. For God would give his own Son, who, by offering himself just once as an acceptable sacrifice, would appease the wrath of the heavenly Father. And this would be not only for the Jews but also for all the nations." Exposition of Hebrews 8:6.[11]

The New Covenant Is Far Superior to the Old. Lucas Osiander: For the old covenant promised possession of the land of Canaan under the condition of the observance of the law. Truly the new covenant promises remission of sins and eternal life (imperfectly represented through the land of Canaan), without the condition of the fulfillment of the law, to all who are penitent and who believe in Christ. Therefore Christ as a mediator sanctions a covenant that is far superior to Moses. . . . And that one [i.e., the old covenant] has ceased, not because of the covenant itself, but because of human beings, who were not able to keep it on their own. And thus the old covenant has been made void because it depended on the condition of observing the law, and this condition has been rejected because it was not able to make satisfaction for sin. Epistle to the Hebrews 8:6-7.[12]

8:8-13 *The New Covenant Makes the Old Obsolete*

There Is Only One Covenant. Heinrich Bullinger: This covenant is unchangeable, single, and eternal. For there is one single church of the saints, including both us and the saints of old; there is one God, and only one true religion in all ages. From where, then, do we get the names "old covenant" and "new covenant"? When they are called "old" and "new," are they not being described as two things? But if there are two, how can there be only one? In substance, it is as single as can be, but there were two modes of expression. For examine, and you shall find that what was expressed to those of old is really the very same thing that was expressed to us—namely, that there is one God, that he alone is to be worshiped, and that he is to be worshiped in spirit, blamelessness, and faith. Likewise, that there is only one righteousness and redemption of the world, and only one true priest and sacrifice, Jesus Christ, the Son of God and of man. Also, that we should hope that God will preserve our souls and raise our bodies. And this is undeniably the religion and faith of Adam, Noah, Abraham, Moses, Samuel, David, and all the prophets, as well as of Stephen, John the Baptist,

[9]Downame, ed., *Annotations*, MMM4v*; citing Ps 40:6.
[10]Catherine Parr, *The Lamentation of a Sinner*, n.p.
[11]Zwingli, *In Epistolam Beati Pauli ad Hebraeos Expositio*, 576.
[12]Osiander, *Epistola ad Hebraeos*, 53-54.

Peter, James, Paul, Athanasius, and Augustine, even as it will be the faith of all the elect of God until the end of the world. Therefore, as far as the substance of the faith and the covenant are concerned, the very same thing is expressed in both; so it follows that there is only one covenant. Commentary on Hebrews 8:8-9.[13]

The Author Is Concerned About Meaning, Not Specific Words. Johannes Oecolampadius: The author of this epistle, as we also explained earlier, uses quotations according to the Septuagint rather than according to the Hebrew original, which does not have *synteles̄ō*, "I will complete," or "I will perfect," but *bryt*, "I will inaugurate" a new covenant. In this we see that the apostles and ancient writers were not overly scrupulous about reckoning up words, as long as the meaning is rendered rightly. We also learn not to be overly concerned about this, as long as we do not stray from the genuine meaning of Scripture, which one may approach and draw up from the well if one can. I say this so that no one will be regarded as a deceiver when they stray from a minor word; otherwise, we will end up maintaining that the translators of the Septuagint were deceivers. Explanations of Hebrews 8:8-9.[14]

Christ's Sacrifice Is the Center of the Gospel. Heinrich Bullinger: He treats the sacrifice of Christ in almost the same order of exposition as he used in his treatment of Christ's priesthood. For first he teaches that Christ is the only true sacrifice for the sins of the whole world, far greater and more excellent than the offerings of the Aaronic system. From this he demonstrates that the Aaronic offerings were ineffectual and a mere shadow, so that they have been abolished by the offering of Christ, who is the only and eternal sacrifice for all who believe. This is the main point of everything that follows until the middle section of chapter 10. But in these things the thrust and object of the gospel is mentioned and discussed with such clarity and precision that nothing plainer and more evangelical could be said. Nor is there anything as necessary for a Christian individual to understand, or anything passed down by the prophets and apostles more diligently, repeatedly, and seriously than the fact that the Son of God was made a sacrifice for our sins. For why did Moses write out his account of the sacrifices and offerings at such length? Because by these things he prefigured the sacrifice of Christ—why else? Isaiah, for example, cried out, "All we like sheep have gone astray, but the Lord has laid on him all our iniquities so that they may be propitiated." And John the Baptist said, "This is the lamb of God, who takes away the sin of the world." Nay, Christ himself says, "And as Moses lifted up the serpent in the wilderness, so must the Son of Man be lifted up, that everyone who believes in him may not perish, but have eternal life." Paul also said, "Christ loved us and gave himself up for us as an offering and sacrifice to God to be a fragrant aroma." But if righteousness were earned by our works or by our sacrifices, ceremonies, and rituals, then obviously Christ was offered in vain. But that offering cannot be vain, because it was performed by the Son of God; consequently, the unique sacrifice of the Son of God is the salvation of all believers and of all ages. Therefore, this is surely the sacred center and thrust of the gospel, which Paul clearly discusses so very worthily and extensively here to the end that he might draw the Hebrews away from the shadowy sacrifices and bind them to the single sacrifice of Christ. Commentary on Hebrews 8:9-10.[15]

External Versus Internal Teaching. Martin Luther: The grace of the New Testament consists in this, that what is spoken and written there teaches the things that are of the Spirit, and the words of grace are spoken according to the well-known statement in Psalm 45:2: "Grace is poured upon your lips." Not so Moses, who

[13]Bullinger, *In Pauli ad Hebraeos Epistolam*, 82v-83r.
[14]Oecolampadius, *In Epistolam ad Hebraeos Explanationes*, 86v.
[15]Bullinger, *In Pauli ad Hebraeos Epistolam*, 85r-v; citing Is 53:6; Jn 1:29; 3:14-16; Eph 5:2; Gal 2:21.

stammers and is not eloquent, and, as he says, in Exodus 4:10: "I am slow of speech and of tongue." Hence the apostle has the courage to say that "the Law works wrath" (Rom 4:15) and is a "law of sin" (Rom 7:25; 8:2), and that Moses is a servant of sin, so that one could say: "Wrath is poured upon your lips." Therefore it happens in the New Testament that while the Word of life, grace, and salvation is proclaimed externally, the Holy Spirit teaches internally at the same time.[†] Therefore Isaiah says (Is. 54:13): "All your sons shall be taught by the Lord." And in Jeremiah we read: "I will give my laws. . . . And they shall all know me" (cf. Jer 31:33-34). Hence Christ refers to these two prophets when he says in John 6:45: "It is written in the prophets: 'They shall all be taught by God.'" . . . Accordingly, this is how Scripture must be understood when it says that the laws are written in the minds and in the hearts. For by "mind" and "heart" (for this is how we are speaking now) it means intellectual and feeling. For to be in the mind means to be understood; to be in the heart means that it is taught; to say that it is in the ear means that it is heard; to say that it is in the eyes means that it is seen. Therefore, it is not enough for the law to be in the soul formally;[‡] that is, the law must be written in the heart out of love for the law. Lectures on Hebrews 8:10.[16]

The New Covenant Is Not New in Substance, but in Degree and Mode. Johannes Oecolampadius: Formerly the laws were inscribed on tablets of stone, and now on tablets of flesh. That is, God inscribes them on their heart and inmost parts, and by his Spirit he makes it so that all their thoughts and actions incline to his will. Paul has a similar kind of statement in 2 Corinthians 3, "You are our letter . . . , written by us not with ink, but with the Spirit of the living God, not on tablets of stone, but on the tablets of flesh of the heart." And thus you see that putting the law into the mind and writing the law on the heart is nothing else than giving the Holy Spirit, who rules, changes, and renews hearts, so that now we like the divine things, which we formerly detested. When we receive this Spirit, an eternal covenant is established between us and God. You may ask here, "Were not those who were godly before the coming of Christ, such as Abel, Noah, Abraham, and others, also in this covenant? And if that is so, how can this be called 'new'?" I answer that they certainty were, inasmuch as they were pleasing to God, which could not have been the case had they not partaken of this Spirit, and in such a way that they were treated as sons of God. Nevertheless, at that time this covenant had not yet been revealed, nor had the fullness of time come. Clearly Christ himself bore testimony to Abraham that he saw the day of Christ and was glad. Next, therefore, it is not called "new" because it is really a new or different covenant in substance from the former, which is obviously always the same, but because it was inaugurated in a new mode and manner. For of old he chose for himself and accepted the one people of the Hebrews, but now all the peoples of the earth—that is, some people from all nations. Again, he gave to those whom he accepted a paltry portion of the Spirit, and so bound it up with many ceremonies; but now he gives the Spirit in superabundance, and attaches to it very few ceremonies. This is the difference between us and those who believed before Christ. Such matters are explained by us at greater length in our commentary on Jeremiah, which you may consult if you wish.

"And they shall not teach, each one." Clearly all those who are accepted in this covenant will know God, for they have an anointing within to teach them, so that, regarding what pertains to salvation, they have no need for anyone to summon them. Nevertheless, regarding what produces perfection, they will never neglect the word of teaching and exhortation. Indeed, they are called *theodidaktoi* by Christ himself (John 6). On the basis of this passage

[16]LW 29:197-98 (WA 57:195.22-196.19). [†]LW translates the Latin *foris . . . intus* as "outside" and "inside"; I have opted for "externally" and "internally," which expresses better the strong emphasis in Luther's theology on the importance of the external Word as the necessary means of divine revelation, which is then applied to the heart by the Holy Spirit. [‡]LW note (198 n. 4): "That is, it must present in actuality; for an analogous use of *formaliter*, see, for example, Thomas Aquinas, *Summa Theologica*, I-1, Q. 89, art. 5."

some have been taken in by the amazing craft of Satan so as to abolish the ministry of the word from church, but it clear enough to the godly how terribly they have fallen. For the discussion is not concerned with an unfettered skill of explaining the Scriptures, but with the knowledge of the fear of God, which the Spirit was to impart into the hearts of the godly when the new covenant was to come into effect. EXPLANATIONS OF HEBREWS 8:10-12.[17]

[17]Oecolampadius, *In Epistolam ad Hebraeos Explanationes*, 88r-89r; citing 2 Cor 3:2-3; Col 3:15; Gal 4:4; Jn 8:56; 1 Jn 2:27; Jn 6:45.

9:1-10 The Earthly Tabernacle

Now even the first covenant had regulations for worship and an earthly place of holiness. [2]For a tent[a] was prepared, the first section, in which were the lampstand and the table and the bread of the Presence.[b] It is called the Holy Place. [3]Behind the second curtain was a second section[c] called the Most Holy Place, [4]having the golden altar of incense and the ark of the covenant covered on all sides with gold, in which was a golden urn holding the manna, and Aaron's staff that budded, and the tablets of the covenant. [5]Above it were the cherubim of glory overshadowing the mercy seat. Of these things we cannot now speak in detail.

[6]These preparations having thus been made, the priests go regularly into the first section, performing their ritual duties, [7]but into the second only the high priest goes, and he but once a year, and not without taking blood, which he offers for himself and for the unintentional sins of the people. [8]By this the Holy Spirit indicates that the way into the holy places is not yet opened as long as the first section is still standing [9](which is symbolic for the present age).[d] According to this arrangement, gifts and sacrifices are offered that cannot perfect the conscience of the worshiper, [10]but deal only with food and drink and various washings, regulations for the body imposed until the time of reformation.

a Or *tabernacle*; also verses 11, 21 **b** Greek *the presentation of the loaves* **c** Greek *tent*; also verses 6, 8 **d** Or *which is symbolic for the age then present*

Overview: In this section, the reformers treat Old Testament tabernacle worship as merely external worship that did nothing to justify the sinner, even though they concede that it was commanded by God. They see this worship as prefiguring New Testament worship, which they characterize as inward and spiritual, and therefore as more mature. While most reformers were eager to stress the "plain sense" of Scripture against the allegorical and allegedly fanciful interpretations of ancient and medieval exegetes, in this section we see examples of Reformation spiritual exegesis, as the reformers seek to find spiritual meaning in the objects of Old Testament tabernacle worship.

9:1-7 *Sacred Furnishings and Priestly Practices*

The Old Ceremonies Merely External. Heinrich Bullinger: This is clearly a transitional formula. For the greatest distinction of a discourse is if it is closely bound together, and is not, as Caligula said of Seneca's writings, "sand without lime."[†] Thus Paul connects his discourse, as if he were saying, "And having thus far discussed the new covenant, now we will return to the old to show what sort of ceremonies it had." To be sure, he does not say that these things were "justifications" in reality;[‡] rather, he adds the limitation *to te hagion kosmikon*, as if he were to say, "To be sure, I am speaking of the way in which external cleansing is effected." For the Jewish rituals justified no one in reality, but were all worldly. We call something "worldly" when it is external and elementary, as was indicated in the fifth chapter of this epistle. John Chrysostom, holding to another interpretation, says, "He calls the holy place 'worldly,' because all were allowed to enter it, and in the same tabernacle there was displayed the place where the priests stood, where the Jews, where the proselytes, Gentiles, and Nazirites. Since then it was accessible even to the Gentiles, he calls it 'worldly.'"[§] Commentary on Hebrews 9:1.[1]

[1]Bullinger, *In Pauli ad Hebraeos Epistolam*, 86r; citing Heb 5:11-14. [†]Suetonius, *Caligula* 53.2 (LCL 31:494). Mortar is a compound of sand and lime; without lime, the sand crumbles. Bullinger probably learned this phrase from Erasmus's *Adagia* 2.3.57. *Erasmi Roterodami Proverbiorum Chiliades* (Basel: Froben, 1518), 335; cf. CWE 33:166. [‡]Bullinger's comments here spring from the Latin

Spiritual Interpretation of the Lampstand and the Table. Lucas Osiander: The lampstand with the seven lamps signified the ministers of the church, shining with the word of truth and an innocent life, and showing the way to the heavenly Father by means of the guide Christ, who is the true light. The table designated the ministry of the Word, by which the bread of life is offered, Christ having been revealed and offered to the world by the work of the twelve apostles. Epistle to the Hebrews 9:2.[2]

Symbols of Spiritual Things. Johannes Bugenhagen: The tabernacle, in which God dwelt among humans (as is said in the law, and later by Solomon, and still later by Jeremiah) is actually the hearts of men and women, as Paul says, "The temple of God is holy, which you are." But two tabernacles were originally built, or two parts of the one tabernacle. The first section lay open and exposed to human view, into which the priests would enter every day, symbolizing the old law, the old priest, and that people, when the worship of God was performed by means of the elements of this world and visible things, though in accordance with God's Word it symbolized things to come. Thus the things that were visible then signified the invisible things: the light of the lamp signified the word of God; the table, holy Scripture; the bread, the nourishment of the word; the golden altar of incense, the prayers and petitions of the saints; the manna in a golden jar, the word of God in a perfect and excellent heart; Aaron's staff, God's choice of a person for the office of teaching, which is followed by freshness of mind, leaves of eloquence, and the sweetest fruit in both teacher and hearers. It should not be difficult to interpret these things in this way from the Scriptures. Commentary on the Pauline Epistles, Heb 9:1-5.[3]

The Divided Tabernacle Represents the Old and New Priesthood. Heinrich Bullinger: These verses constitute a *topographia*, or description of the place in which the people of old presented their offerings, and at the same time an explanation of the form taken by the religion of the old covenant. He begins with a discussion of these things because in the course of the argument there has often been reference to the tabernacle, to the entrance of the priests into the holy place, and to the entrance of the chief high priest into the holy of holies; so, to keep the reader from being hindered, he decided to sketch the place with a few of the holy objects. Next, it did not say that there were two tabernacles for the people of old, though that could appear to be the case for those who are insufficiently attentive. For it was a single unit, although divided into two parts by a veil, in approximately the same way in which our temples are divided into the choir on the one hand and the church or congregational area on the other. So here, imagine the choir as the holy of holies and the church as the holy places. Hence it is necessary for Paul's words, "After the second veil was a tabernacle . . . ," to be a *synchysin*, that is, a confusion, in which the proper order of the words has been disturbed, but which can be restored as, "After the veil there was a second tabernacle," that is, the second part of the tabernacle. For if you apply "second" to the veil instead of the tabernacle, then there would have to be two veils and three tabernacles, which is false; though I am well aware that almost the same conception is to be found in Josephus.† Or perhaps the apostle was thinking of that veil that hung at the entrance of the tabernacle separating the holy place from the court of the tabernacle. You may read of this in Exodus 26: "You shall also make a screen for the entrance of the tabernacle." Now, those places were neither sacred nor profane in themselves, but their use made them either sacred or profane. The symbolic priesthood and sacrifices were holy; hence the place in which that holy enterprise was conducted was called "the holy place." But far holier is the intercession and sacrifice of Christ; hence the place in which the depiction of the most

text's use of *iustificationes* as a literal translation of *dikaiōmata*.

§Chrysostom, "Homily 15," in *Homilae XXXIV in epistolam ad Hebraeos* (PG 63:117; NPNF 14:438).

2Osiander, *Epistola ad Hebraeos*, 56.

3Bugenhagen, *Annotationes in epistolas Pauli recognitae* (1525), 153v; citing Ex 25:8; 1 Kings 8:13; Jer 7:12(?); 1 Cor 3:17; Col 2:8.

sacred sacrifice of Christ was executed came to be called "the holy of holies." For Christ is, as Daniel says, the Holy of the holy ones, that is, the holiest one of all. For this common use of repetition in Hebrew is now very well known. But there was a single tabernacle, because there is only one church belonging both to the people of old and to us, while at the same time it was in two parts, that is, divided into a twofold people and ritual. The part that is called "the holy place" in which offerings were presented every day, represents the form of the old church. But the inner part, in which there was only the ark without any altar, and which was called "the holy of holies," represents the appearance of the new church. Next, because both parts had their own furnishings, it was made with remarkable mystery. We will explain them *kat' allēgorian* in a cursory fashion with what little ability we have. COMMENTARY ON HEBREWS 9:2-5.[4]

THE GOLD-PLATED ARK SYMBOLIZES THE GLORY-CROWNED CHURCH. JOHANNES BUGENHAGEN: The second section was withdrawn in shadows from human sight, and no one entered it except the chief high priest only once a year, when expiation was made for the sins of all the people, as described in Leviticus 16. This symbolized the priesthood of Christ, through whom alone we have been given access to the Father and have been purified from our sins by his blood, which he offered just once, so that the things which formerly were hidden from the sight of the people have now been revealed through the gospel, just as Christ said, "Many kings and prophets desired to see and to hear what you do." This is the kingdom of heaven, when one has no justification in the flesh and one does not serve God by the elementary principles of this world, but rather worships God in Spirit and in truth. Consequently, in this section everything was hidden in symbols that were represented in the outer section by invisible things. For here there was the ark of God, that is, his habitation, in which the tablets of the law (which at the time were not allowed to be seen according to the flesh with the eyes) were kept. This signified the law of God written in the hidden recesses of the heart, in accordance with prophecy of Jeremiah quoted above, no longer as letter, but as Spirit. And note here also that it was announced beforehand, and when the former tablets were made by Moses after they were read the second time, after they were sufficiently presented as letter, they were kept in the ark, where the Lord dwells, to signify the spiritual law of God hidden in our hearts by the Spirit of Christ. This ark is the church of the living God. It is not made of solid gold, lest anyone should become arrogant, but is gilded with divine splendor and the shining riches of God inside and out. It is honored by the golden crown of the kingly dignity and eternal priesthood of Christ, and it is made of imperishable timbers,[†] for, since it is enlivened by the Spirit of Christ, it can never see corruption. But the mercy seat that covers the ark is made of purest gold, for Romans 3 and Hebrews 4 tell us that the mercy seat signifies Christ, by whom we may be reconciled to God. COMMENTARY ON THE PAULINE EPISTLES, HEB 9:3-5.[5]

THE LAMPSTAND REPRESENTS TRUE DOCTRINE. HEINRICH BULLINGER: Regarding the lampstand, see Exodus 25, and bear in mind what the prophet said: "Your word is a lamp to my feet and a light to my path." But the lampstand consisted of purest gold, because true doctrine should be pure and unmixed and should shine so as to disperse all shadows of error. It had seven branches, or lamps. Now the seventh number, as is shown in Macrobius's *Commentary on the Dream of Scipio*, is the number of perfection.[†] So true

[4]Bullinger, *In Pauli ad Hebraeos Epistolam*, 86v-87v [192-94]; citing Ex 26:36; Dan 9:24. [†]Josephus, *Jewish Antiquities* 3.122 (LCL 242:372-73).

[5]Bugenhagen, *Annotationes in epistolas Pauli recognitae* (1525) 153v-154r [340-41]; citing Lk 10:24; Col 2:8; Jn 4:24; 2 Cor 3:3-6; Ex 24:12; 25:16; Rom 3:25; Heb 4:16. [†]Ex 25:10. The wood of the ark being imperishable may be found in Augustine (*Tract.* 6.19), Thomas Aquinas (*super Heb.* 31), and Thomas à Kempis (*Imitatio* 4.1.5).

doctrine is entirely perfect and complete, so that it has no need for any additional precepts or instructions. Commentary on Hebrews 9:2-5.[6]

The Bread and the Table Represent the Word of God and Its Ministers. Heinrich Bullinger: For more regarding the table, read Exodus 25. Now, it can be seen as a type of the ministers of the word, who should be above reproach, imbued with sound faith, portable, that is, accommodating, who adjust to the capacity of the hearers, not by flattery, but with holy cunning, so that they might win very many to Christ. Others have understood the table as referring to Scripture.

Upon the table were set the loaves of presentation (Leviticus 24), which other passages have called the "bread of the presence," surely because they were repeatedly displayed in the sight and presence of human beings. Coelius, however, in his *Lectionum Antiquarum*, book 5, chapter 35, puts forth another fabrication derived from that eminent babbler of the Hebrews, Rabbi Solomon, which I will leave to the judgment of the diligent reader.[†] Clearly the loaves prefigured the word of God for those people who "live not by bread alone, but by every word which proceeds from the mouth of God." These loaves were unleavened; so that Christ later warned his disciples, "Be on your guard against the leaven of the Pharisees," which was hypocrisy and human tradition. So the word of God is pure and holy and must not be tainted with our passions. On these loaves was placed the most rarified incense as an aroma of pleasing fragrance to God. But the word of God, when it is combined with faith in a devout heart, produces a clear conscience; then from a clear conscience prayers are poured out to God that are pure and wholly acceptable to God. For the rest, the fact that they were placed on the purest table and eaten only by the priests symbolizes the fact that all minds that would become partakers of heavenly wisdom must obviously be pure and holy. For the Lord did not wish us to throw holy things to the dogs. Consequently, Aquinas was in error when, deceived by a perverse allegorical reading of this passage, he incorrectly sang, "Which priests alone should bring, For whom it is meet and fit that they should eat of it, and in their turn to others give,"[‡] because he did not pay attention either to the analogy of faith[§] or to the correspondence of the subject to its type. For the apostle expresses a different view in 1 Corinthians 11. Commentary on Hebrews 9:2-5.[7]

The Ark Represents the Church of God. Heinrich Bullinger: Regarding the ark, read Exodus 25. It is called "the ark of the covenant" on account of the tablets of the covenant that were placed inside it; indeed, the tablets themselves were similarly called "the covenant," as we noted above in chapter 8 in connection with the biblical divisions. And the first tablets were smashed, but the second ones were preserved. For the spiritual law, which comes later, is immutable and everlasting. This was placed in the ark, that is, in the hearts of believers, or rather in the universal church of God. For the ark was a sacrament of the divine presence, a symbol of the church of God, which is never free from sins as long as it lives, but yet has been cleansed of them. In this ark the manna had been placed after the tablets, which God in Exodus 16 commanded to be kept *eis mnēmosynon*. So Paul in this passage says that it was placed in a golden urn,

[6]Bullinger, *In Pauli ad Hebraeos Epistolam*, 87v; citing Ex 25:31-40; Ps 119:105. [†]Macrobius, *Commentary on the Dream of Scipio* 6.5.75. *Opera* (Leipzig: B. G. Teubner, 1868), 485, 501. An English translation is available as *Commentary on the Dream of Scipio*, trans. W. H. Stahl (New York: Columbia University Press, 1952), 100, 115.

[7]Bullinger, *In Pauli ad Hebraeos Epistolam*, 87v-88r; citing Ex 25:23-30; Lev 24:5-9; 1 Cor 9:19; Mt 4:4; Deut 8:3; Lk 12:1; Mt 16:11-12; 7:6; 1 Cor 11:18-22, 33-34. [†]Lodovico Ricchieri (Caelius Rhodiginus), *Lectionum Antiquarum Libri XVI* (Basel: Froben, 1517), 240. "Rabbi Solomon" here is probably Rashi (Shlomo Yitzhaki, or Salomon Isaacides). [‡]"Sacris Solemniis," trans. J. M. Neale in *Breviary Offices: From Lauds to Compline Inclusive*, 2nd ed. (London: Palmer, 1880), 194. [§]"The analogy of faith" refers to the clear teaching of Scripture as a whole, which provides a controlling limit on the interpretation of any particular passage. Though Aquinas's hymn does not itself appeal to the exclusive right of the Aaronic priests to the bread of the presence in support of its doctrine (i.e., that the clergy should communicate separately from the laity), others likely did make such an allegorical argument. Bullinger's point is that such a reading is illegitimate because it contradicts the clear literal sense of 1 Cor 11.

because the heavenly nourishment of the truth of God is protected in a devout and good heart. In this same ark there was the rod of Aaron, which is described in Numbers 17. It signified the office of teaching, the unconquerable scepter of the truth, the calling and election that is followed by fresh mental growth both in the teacher and in the hearer, the leaves and most delicious and sweet fruits of righteousness.

But what shall we say to that which is written in 2 Chronicles 5, "There was nothing in the ark except the two tablets of the covenant"? Some reply that in the time of the kings there was indeed nothing in the ark except for the tablets alone, while the other things were placed inside it in later times. Others say that the exclusive particle *plēn*, which occurs in the Septuagint version, is not found in the Hebrew texts. But it can also be understood as a synecdoche, whereby we list the most important things and supply the rest. For the "ark of the covenant" takes its name from the tablets of the covenant, so that they are listed in preference to all others. Commentary on Hebrews 9:2-5.[8]

The Cherubim Represent Divine Glory. Heinrich Bullinger: Above the ark were the cherubim of glory. Now, "cherubim," if we believe Josephus, were living beings with a winged form that no human being can behold, but which Moses said he saw depicted as the throne of God.[†] Certainly, if you examine the derivation of the word, "cherubim" means "an abundance of knowledge." But if you consider the method of Scripture, mention is usually made of them when God appears to be present. For this reason, Paul does not simply call them "cherubim," but "cherubim of glory," as if you were to call them the attendants, heralds, and *hyperaspistai* or shield-bearers of the glorious God. These overshadow the mercy seat, that is, the divine majesty preserves the humanity that Christ took on. For the humanity of Christ, which Paul, the author of Romans, depicts by means of the mercy seat, is purely derived from the undefiled virgin, the pledge of grace and the price of redemption, yes indeed! And he is the *dvyr*, that is, the oracle or *lalērion*, the meeting place through which God has spoken to the world. Further, this mercy seat, that it might be placed under the cherubim, was covering the ark, for Christ is the head and shelter of the church insofar as he is God and man. Commentary on Hebrews 9:2-5.[9]

The Divided Tabernacle Foreshadows the Church Militant and Triumphant. Johannes Oecolampadius: Since we have lighted on this passage, let us see in a few words what these shadows mean in themselves. We do also have an explanation of these things in Josephus,[†] but one that is entirely fashioned in a Jewish manner, which you may see for yourselves if you like. The tabernacle is the people of God, which is divided into two, so that some are experiencing eternal happiness and are within the veil, while others are not yet, and are still outside the veil. The latter perceive in a mirror dimly, but the former face-to-face. The tabernacle was one, and thus the people is one, one church triumphant and militant. But we have said earlier that the people are called the tabernacle and dwelling place of God, for he dwells in it; but they will be called that more perfectly when they have been saved and disburdened of the flesh. Before we proceed further and penetrate to perfect knowledge, the intervening veil must be removed, which is our flesh. For while it encompasses us, we will never clearly see God as he is. Those who are outside the veil walk in darkness as long as they are in this world, which is why they need a lamp to keep them from stumbling; this is the word of God, by which we perceive what pleases God and what does not. Next, the table is preachers of the word, from whom we receive the food of life. Then within the holy of holies are the desires of godly people, where the knowledge of God is perfected. In that place are not merely the bread of

[8]Bullinger, *In Pauli ad Hebraeos Epistolam*, 88v-89r; citing Ex 25:10-22; Ex 16:33; 2 Chron 5:10.

[9]Bullinger, *In Pauli ad Hebraeos Epistolam*, 89r-v; citing Rom 3:25. [†]Josephus, *Jewish Antiquities* 3.137 (LCL 242:380-81).

the presence, but also heavenly food—manna—and whatever can strengthen the human heart. Here also appears angelic excellence and Christ, our mercy seat. These are what the apostle has said beforehand regarding the tabernacle, so that he might secure the way to the subsequent discourse, in which he sets before our eyes in many ways the infinitely worthy priestly office of Christ and shows how he discharges it. Explanations of Hebrews 9:2-5.[10]

Spiritual Interpretation of the Tabernacle. Lucas Osiander: The structure, which is called the holy of holies, was denoting Christ, who is the most holy temple of the Trinity, John 2, in whom all the fullness of deity dwells bodily, Colossians 2. The golden censor was designating the most efficacious prayers of Christ for the salvation of the church. The ark of the covenant, having been made of wood and having been covered with a layer of gold, was denoting Christ as human and God in one person. The manna is Christ, the bread of heaven, John 6. The rod of Aaron, which flowered (Num 17), was prefiguring the kingdom of Jesus Christ, our priest and king, which sometimes seems to dry up, but soon again blossoms unexpectedly. The tablets of the testament or Decalogue in the ark were signifying that in Christ we have the perfect fulfillment of the law, which is imputed for righteousness to all who believe in Christ, Romans 5. The two cherubim above the mercy seat, mutually looking at each other and averting their faces from the mercy seat, were designating the two testaments, the old and the new, which are mutually interpreted by each other. For the old, insofar as it represents Christ in the priesthood, points to the new by means of figures: truly the figures of the old testament become clear in the new. And the two testaments look to that one mediator Christ, who is the propitiation, not only for our sins, but even for the whole world, John 2. The cherubim that were covering the mercy seat and the ark were denoting that the ministry of the gospel is under the protection of the angels. Epistle to the Hebrews 9:3-5.[11]

The Two Parts of the Tabernacle Are Law and Gospel. Dirk Philips: The figures of the Old Testament must be well observed and understood, not according to human tradition, but just as they came forth from God through the Holy Spirit, were spoken and given, thus they must also be revealed, taught, and interpreted to Christians through the same Spirit. Therefore, we also do not think to write something new or strange about the tabernacle of Moses, but the apostolic interpretation is the foundation on which we build. Also we interpret some things a little more broadly than the apostle did. Nevertheless, there is one foundation. But the present necessity and the misunderstanding of some brethren move and cause us to clarify these things more broadly. Even then, the apostle is our master teacher in these matters, and his interpretation we wish actually to follow just as it came out of the Holy Spirit, and thereby we wish simply to remain.

In the first place, then, we wish to note the words of the apostle to the Hebrews, with which he has revealed and written the correct understanding of the tabernacle.

As it was then ordained, so the priests did the service of God in the first tabernacle. But into the second tabernacle, the high priest went alone once a year, not without blood, which he offered for himself and for the people in their ignorance. Thereby the Holy Spirit indicated that the way to the holy place had not yet been revealed, so long as the first tabernacle still remained standing, as a parable of the time that was then present, in which gifts and sacrifices were offered, which could not make the consciences of those who offered them perfect. For it was no more than food or drink, and manifold washings, and justifications of the flesh, which at the that time were instituted for improvement.

[10]Oecolampadius, *In Epistolam ad Hebraeos Explanationes*, 92v-93r; citing 1 Cor 13:12; Rev 13:6; Eph 2:22; Heb 10:20; Rom 3:25. †Josephus, *Jewish Antiquities* 3.179-87 (LCL 242:402-7).

[11]Osiander, *Epistola ad Hebraeos*, 57-58.

These words give us a clear understanding of the tabernacle; therefore, they must also be well observed. In the first place, then, the apostle speaks of two tabernacles, that is, of the holy place and the holy of holies. Of the courtyard he says nothing in particular, except that it was an entrance to the tabernacle. He names the first tabernacle a parable of the time that was then present, in order to indicate to us with the two tabernacles two times (that is, the time of the law and the time of the gospel). For just as the tabernacle of Moses was built at God's command, one tabernacle and one holy place, even though it was divided into two parts, and each had its own wash basins, sacrifices or offerings, and its own glory, thus also the law and gospel are one Word and one truth of God. Nevertheless, they are also divided, namely, the law has the shadow of coming good things, but the gospel has the being of these things themselves. The law has many figures and ceremonies, which are all fulfilled in Christ, but the gospel has the clear steadfast truth that abides in eternity. The law is the letter that kills, but the gospel is the spirit that makes alive.

Therefore the gospel and the law are divided so far as the figures, shadows, and letter of the law are concerned or involved, which are all removed through the gospel. But it is because of this that one observes the spirit of the law (for the law is also spiritual, as Paul says). So we discover that the meaning, content, and actual understanding of the law accords with the gospel in every way and corresponds with it, yes, is one truth. For just as there is not more than one God, so also there is not more than one truth: for God himself is the truth. But the letter (in which the truth is hidden) will indeed come to an end. Thus that literal command of the Lord about the circumcision of the flesh has come to an end. Nevertheless, that command of the spiritual circumcision of the heart remains. Yes, thus have all the figures of the law (which are too long to relate here) come to an end so far as the letter is concerned. Nevertheless, the genuine and essential significance of these same figures remains and harmonizes with the gospel.

Thus the apostle correctly and with all insight compares and indicates that the tabernacle of the Lord (which was divided into two parts and was nevertheless one tabernacle) with the law and the gospel of the two testaments are one in spirit and truth and belong to each other. Therefore Paul also said that the believing Israelites and we have one spirit of faith. Also thus have the apostles, yes, the Lord Jesus Christ himself, frequently and many times established the truth of the gospel with sayings and testimonies of the Law and the Prophets, thereby letting us know that the truth of the gospel is included in the Law and the Prophets.

In the second place, the apostle says that the priests went into the first tabernacle, for they had to sacrifice to the Lord daily, which indicates the imperfection of the law, as the apostle says in the same letter that the law has not brought us to perfection, but it is an introduction to a better hope through which we draw near to God. But into the holy of holies, says the apostle, the high priest went alone once a year and offered there a sacrifice. This signifies to us that Jesus Christ has made a sacrifice (wherewith we are reconciled to God), and that sacrifice shall not happen anymore, for it endures eternally, and is sufficient for the sins of the entire world. And that is prefigured through the fact that the high priest yearly offered a single sacrifice in the holy of holies and that no one of the priests, of the Levites, or of the whole people of Israel might go into the holy of holies in order to offer the yearly sacrifice and reconcile the Lord, other than the high priest alone, who was ordained by God to do so. Thus no one was able to reconcile us to God other than Jesus Christ alone, the true high priest, anointed by God the Father with the Holy Spirit and ordained according to the order of Melchizedek.

In the third place, so says the apostle, the priests went daily into the holy place and there sacrificed to the Lord, but the high priest went into the holy of holies once a year, but not without blood, which he offered for himself and for the people in their ignorance. With this the Holy Spirit signified that the way to the holy place was not yet revealed so long as the first tabernacle still stood. This signified to us not only the one sacrifice of Christ, which is spoken of above, but also that as long as the law of Moses was in power and ran in its true course, then the gospel of grace in Jesus Christ was indeed promised, but had not yet appeared or been revealed in glory.

But when this was revealed, then the law of Moses, according to the letter, had to cease and come to an end in Christ. Yes, as Jesus Christ, the true High Priest came, he went into the holy of holies and offered there his own flesh and blood as a sweet-smelling offering to God the Father for the sin of the whole world, with which sacrifice he has opened a new and living way to the holy of holies (that is, to the hiddenness and fellowship of the divine and heavenly goods, yes, to heaven itself) for all those who believed in him. For just as he through death destroyed death, and through sin (that is, through his sacrifice for sin) condemned sin, thus he has through that veil, that is, through his flesh, taken away the veil before the holy of holies. And this is clearly to be observed through the fact that the veil before the holy of holies was rent in the death of Christ Jesus. This is a sure sign that through the Lord Jesus Christ the veil that hung before the face of Moses (because the children of Israel could not bear the glory of his face) is removed and his death is the portal and entrance into eternal life, to the kingdom of heaven, and that the most costly and glorious gifts of God are given and revealed to us, and that we have free access to God who now speaks to us from the throne of grace, that is, through Jesus Christ, who has reconciled us with God through his flesh and blood, which he has sacrificed in the holy of holies as the only true and most holy sacrifice. And all who believe in Christ have come to faith in his name in the Holy Spirit. The Enchiridion.[12]

[12]CRR 6:267-70*; citing 2 Pet 1:20; Heb 10:1; Col 2:16; 2 Cor 3:7-8; Jn 6:63; Rom 7:14; 2:29; Col 2:11; 2 Cor 4:13; Heb 7:18; Ex 30:10; Heb 9:7; Ps 110:4; Heb 5:9-10; 7:17; Eph 5:2; Heb 7:26; 9:14; Rom 5:10; 8:3; 2 Cor 5:21; Mt 27:51; Mk 15:38; Lk 23:44-45; 1 Pet 1:18-19; Heb 10:19; 12:22-24.

9:8-10 *The Levitical Sacrifices Were Not Perfect*

Christ Alone Cleanses the Soul, Not External Sacrifices. Heinrich Bullinger: These things are set against and correspond to the first section [i.e., Heb 9:1-7], in which the author showed what the first and outermost tabernacle signified, namely, the Levitical sacrifice, which was utterly vain and useless. This was confirmed by almost as many arguments as the number of words employed on the subject. For if the holy of holies, that is, heaven itself, would not become freely approachable when they entered it, even when they performed sacrifices with the utmost exertion, clearly it follows that the Levitical sacrifices did not equip one to enter heaven, and hence they are useless. He soon adds this idea with the slightly obscure words, "These things cannot perfect the conscience of the worshiper." This statement has the following force: "The Levitical sacrifices could not pacify the consciences of those for whom they were offered." This is because, just as all the other components of the Levitical system rely on and consist merely in external things, the same is especially true of the fleshly sacrifices. But sin is not a stain on the body, but on the soul, so that the Levitical (that is, fleshly) sacrifices do not cleanse the conscience of sins, and thus they are useless, or rather, they are a merely external righteousness. For Paul in Romans 4 also employs the label of "flesh" to refer to eternal realities when he says, "What then shall we say that our Father Abraham merited" (for *eurēkenai* means not only "to find," but also "to obtain" and "to merit"), "according to the flesh?" that is, by merits and work, or external righteousness. But read Leviticus 11 and Numbers 19 for an indication of the variety of foods, drinks, and washings or baptisms. Again, when it says that all things were imposed until the time of reformation, who is so senseless as not to perceive that the things that were to be reformed were weak and useless, whereas the things that were to replace them for the purpose of reformation are more perfect? Further, Christ is the reformation and consummation of the law. Therefore, Christ is the true and eternal whole burnt offering of believers; he is enough for the believing soul, since he alone uniquely and perfectly possesses everything that the soul can desire. This is what the second section of this passage speaks of. Commentary on Hebrews 9:8-10.[13]

The Distinction Between the Old Law and the New Law. Martin Luther: From this text, as has also been stated above, one has a clear statement of the proper distinction between the old and the new law; for then the sins, righteousness, sacrifices, sacred rites, promises, doctrines, and priests were all carnal and did not sanctify "according to the conscience" but according to the body. Now, however, our sins, righteousnesses, sacrifices, sacred rites, promises, and doctrines, and our Priest are all spiritual and sanctify according to the conscience. Yet both were commanded by God, but the former were "imposed"—as he states here—"until the time of reformation." Lectures on Hebrews 9:9.[14]

[13]Bullinger, *In Pauli ad Hebraeos Epistolam*, 90r-91r; citing Heb 7:18; Rom 10:4; 4:1.
[14]LW 29:206-7 (WA 57:205.18-25).

The Regulations of the Law Were Not Bad, but Imperfect. Cardinal Cajetan: The reason why they could not give this kind of perfection follows: ". . . but deal only with foods and drinks and various washings and regulations"—that is, justifications of the flesh—"imposed until the time of reformation." . . . He provides the reason why gifts and sacrifices could not make one perfect, because they were imposed only through foods and drinks and external things like those. But someone might object, "Why, then, were they imposed?" To answer this unspoken question, he adds that they were not imposed without qualification, but "until the time of reformation," until the time when all things would be reformed—not only evil things but also imperfect things. For these things were to be reformed not as evil things, but as imperfect things. For they were imposed as belonging to childhood, so that by these imperfect things they would gradually be led to the perfect. Comments on Hebrews 9:9-10.[15]

[15]Cajetan, *In Epistolam ad Hebraeos Commentarii*, 165r-v; citing Gal 3:24-25; 4:1-7.

9:11-28 Christ Is the Mediator of a New Covenant

11 But when Christ appeared as a high priest of the
good things that have come,[a] then through the greater
and more perfect tent (not made with hands, that is,
not of this creation) 12 he entered once for all into the
holy places, not by means of the blood of goats and
calves but by means of his own blood, thus securing
an eternal redemption. 13 For if the blood of goats and
bulls, and the sprinkling of defiled persons with the
ashes of a heifer, sanctify[b] for the purification of the
flesh, 14 how much more will the blood of Christ, who
through the eternal Spirit offered himself without
blemish to God, purify our[c] conscience from dead
works to serve the living God.

15 Therefore he is the mediator of a new covenant, so
that those who are called may receive the promised
eternal inheritance, since a death has occurred that
redeems them from the transgressions committed under
the first covenant.[d] 16 For where a will is involved, the
death of the one who made it must be established. 17 For
a will takes effect only at death, since it is not in force as
long as the one who made it is alive. 18 Therefore not
even the first covenant was inaugurated without blood.
19 For when every commandment of the law had been
declared by Moses to all the people, he took the blood of
calves and goats, with water and scarlet wool and
hyssop, and sprinkled both the book itself and all the
people, 20 saying, "This is the blood of the covenant that
God commanded for you." 21 And in the same way he
sprinkled with the blood both the tent and all the vessels
used in worship. 22 Indeed, under the law almost
everything is purified with blood, and without the
shedding of blood there is no forgiveness of sins.

23 Thus it was necessary for the copies of the heavenly
things to be purified with these rites, but the heavenly
things themselves with better sacrifices than these. 24 For
Christ has entered, not into holy places made with hands,
which are copies of the true things, but into heaven itself,
now to appear in the presence of God on our behalf.
25 Nor was it to offer himself repeatedly, as the high priest
enters the holy places every year with blood not his own,
26 for then he would have had to suffer repeatedly since
the foundation of the world. But as it is, he has appeared
once for all at the end of the ages to put away sin by the
sacrifice of himself. 27 And just as it is appointed for man
to die once, and after that comes judgment, 28 so Christ,
having been offered once to bear the sins of many, will
appear a second time, not to deal with sin but to save
those who are eagerly waiting for him.

a Some manuscripts *good things to come* **b** Or *For if the sprinkling of defiled persons with the blood of goats and bulls and with the ashes of a heifer sanctifies*
c Some manuscripts *your* **d** The Greek word means both *covenant* and *will*; also verses 16, 17

Overview: The reformers set out in this section to show how and why Christ and the new covenant in his blood exceed and fulfill the old covenant. As in the previous section, the reformers stress that the new covenant is inward, spiritual, and eternal, whereas the old covenant was external, fleshly, and temporal. The commentators emphasize that the new covenant provides what the old covenant never did or could: true and lasting purification from sin, which they assert is entirely a gift of grace and not the result of good works, even as good works are to flow from this grace. They also spend a good deal of time focusing on the one-time, all-sufficient nature of Christ's sacrifice for sin, expanding at length on how this completely undermines and refutes the medieval Catholic teaching of the Mass as an ongoing sacrifice for sin.

9:11-12 *Christ Entered the Heavenly Tabernacle*

The High Priest and His Temple. Johann Spangenberg: How does this epistle describe Christ the high priest? It says that Christ came so that he might be a high priest of future good things through a greater and more perfect tabernacle, etc., as if it wanted to say, "Aaron and his descendants entered into [the tabernacle] in bodily adornment, in gold and diamonds. They performed their priesthood by means of external ceremonies and achieved for the people an external purification. But Christ, the Son of God, went into [the tabernacle] in spiritual adornment, not in gold and diamonds, but in godly love, patience, and obedience. He performed his priesthood and sacrifice on the cross and achieved for those who believe in him an internal, spiritual, and eternal purification and forgiveness of all sin."

How does this epistle describe the tabernacle and temple of Christ the High Priest? . . . The tabernacle and temple of Christ is spiritual, and everything that is in it is also spiritual. God perpetually builds these tabernacles from simple living stones that he hews and polishes through many assaults, crosses, and suffering. He lays them in his building according to his pleasure, high or low, each according to his calling, and sprinkles them with his costly blood. He anoints them with the oil of the Holy Spirit and illumines them with his divine grace; he blesses them both bodily and spiritually. EPISTLE FOR THE FIFTH SUNDAY IN LENT, HEB 9:11[1]

IN EVERY ASPECT, CHRIST SURPASSES THE PRIESTS OF THE OLD COVENANT. HULDRYCH ZWINGLI: "But when Christ appeared as the high priest." This is the application of the analogy, or the antithesis. It is as if he were to say, "Now that the ceremonies of the old covenant have been surveyed, there must be a discussion of our high priest." This is obviously not an inappropriate antithesis, but a suitable one, as we have already said, which we will explain phrase by phrase.

"Of the good things that were to come." He first contrasts the temporal high priesthood (which was manifested in transitory and corporeal matters) with the eternal. For by the blessed eternal high priesthood of Christ we attain to eternal life.

"Through the greater and more perfect tent." We should carefully ponder all these things by comparing their correspondences, since they correspond to one another with a very skillful contrast. Thus the old high priest entered into a tent made with hands, but Christ into one pitched without hands. The former high priest entered into the holy of holies, but ours into heaven. The one went with the blood of another, the other with his own blood. The Mosaic high priest offered frequently; Christ offered just once. Otherwise his offering, like that of the high priests of the old covenant, would not have been completed or finished. Finally, the priest of the law brought outward purification, while Christ our priest obtained an endless redemption. EXPOSITION OF HEBREWS 9:11.[2]

CHRIST'S OFFERING ENDURES FOREVER. HEINRICH BULLINGER: These verses correspond to the second section [i.e., Heb 9:1-7]. In them he explains what the holy of holies prefigured, namely, the people of the new covenant and the most holy sacrifice of Christ, which solely and alone is enough to atone for all the sins of the world. All this is made clearer by the contrast that follows, in which Christ is compared to the chief high priest, so that we may see that he is far greater. For he says that, when the chief high priest traversed the holy place, he was entering a tabernacle made with human hands. Therefore, it was necessary for Christ to enter a tabernacle, since he was a high priest. Therefore, Christ did enter into a tabernacle, but into one that was greater. For the Aaronic high priest entered a merely earthly tabernacle to offer sacrifices, but Christ ascended into heaven itself. For he was the high priest of the good things that were to come; that is, he was the real high priest, through whom we have obtained the blessing for which all the holy fathers waited with expectation, not some temporal good, but the one that is eternal and unfading, which in the glory to come will belong to all of us. Again, when the chief high priest entered into the inner tabernacle, he would not enter without blood;

[1]Spangenberg, *Postilla Teütsch*, 4:168v-169r-v; citing 1 Pet 2:5.

[2]Zwingli, *In Epistolam Beati Pauli ad Hebraeos Expositio*, 577.

therefore, it was necessary for Christ also to enter his tabernacle with blood. So Christ shed blood, but far better blood. For the Aaronic high priest carried in the blood of animals, whereas Christ brought his own, human, holy blood. Moreover, the high priest entered into the holy of holies alone and only once to offer for his own sins and for those of the people. Thus it was necessary that Christ also make an offering for sins on his own. And he did make an offering, but much more perfectly. For the Aaronic high priest would repeat that single act of offering once every year, and would offer for his own sins as well as those of the people. But Christ poured out his blood to God only once, without any repetition—yes, just once—not for his own sins (for he had none), but for the sins of the world. And the fact that he poured out such blood just once was the reason why, by his single offering before God, he achieved an *ever-enduring* atonement for all those who have believed, believe now, and will believe. Therefore, by the single sacrifice of the body of Christ not only the Jewish sacrifices have come to an end, but all other sacrifices for sins on earth, for the single sacrifice of Christ is enough for the whole world. Therefore, this sacrifice alone is presented to all the earth to be adored with true faith. Therefore, that person is anathema who has established another sacrifice, or has multiplied that which is unique, or has said that Christ has not blotted out all the sins of the world. That person is anathema who seeks any atonement for sins other than that which was accomplished by the unique blood of Christ, which was shed just once. Commentary on Hebrews 9:11-12.[3]

Our Redemption Is the Fruit of Christ's Suffering. Johannes Oecolampadius: "Discovering an eternal redemption." With these words he discloses the fruit of Christ's suffering, and what he achieved by his blood is comprehended in a single statement, namely, that he obtained a redemption, and one that lasts forever. *Lytrōsis* means not only propitiation or redemption but also the price of redemption from slavery and punishment. We were deserving of ultimate slavery and death, [but] Christ gave the payment of his own blood to redeem us, and thus brought us to eternal freedom. Take note that it says, "Discovering." We do not give credit to our own merits or diligence for things we have found, for they come our way entirely by accident. So this redemption was not discovered by our good works—which are nothing—but by divine mercy. For before we existed, he foreknew that he would redeem us. But he redeemed the elect in such a way that he takes away not only their guilt but also all penalty. Explanations of Hebrews 9:11-12.[4]

Christ Sacrificed Himself Once for Sin. Johannes Bugenhagen: It says "just once," because this redemption is eternal. Previously, atonement was temporary, so that it was repeated every year. But it was performed only once a year to symbolize the atonement accomplished by Christ, which was performed just once. The repetition showed the imperfection. But since the sacrifice of Christ pardoned everything and was completed at once, it cannot be repeated. Otherwise, the one charged with atoning from the first sin of the world all the way to the last sin of the world would have needed to die repeatedly from the foundation of the world, as it says below. Those who want to sacrifice Christ daily in the sacrament of the altar should beware. In the sacrament he did not charge us with performing a sacrifice—that is, the slaughter of Christ—but with commemorating the sacrifice that was offered just once by Christ himself, as often as we ourselves eat and drink his body and blood, not as often as we pass this off on others, as we stupidly mistake today. Nevertheless the teaching of Christ regarding this sacrament is clear in this regard. Why do we expose to mockery what Christ instituted? Commentary on the Pauline Epistles, Heb 9:12.[5]

[3]Bullinger, *In Pauli ad Hebraeos Epistolam*, 92r-v [203-4].

[4]Oecolampadius, *In Epistolam ad Hebraeos Explanationes*, 96v-97r.

[5]Bugenhagen, *Annotationes in epistolas Pauli recognitae* (1525), 155r-v [343-44]. Heb 9:25-26; 1 Cor 11:23-26.

Christ Has Earned Eternal Redemption for Us. Lucas Osiander: If therefore Christ having entered into the holy of holies once earned eternal redemption, why do the priests offer Christ so often in the Mass (as a sacrifice of propitiation)? And, if Christ achieved eternal redemption for us, why are we disturbed on account of sins we have committed if we believe in this priest and redeemer? Epistle to the Hebrews 9:12.[6]

Against Private Masses. Johann Spangenberg: Why do the papistical Christians sacrifice daily in their private Masses? What they do is wrong and they sin greatly, because as often as they sacrifice Christ in their Masses for the dead and sacrificial Masses they do no other than crucify and kill Christ anew, for sacrificing means slaughtering and strangling. That which one should sacrifice must give blood. The Christian church henceforth knows no other sacrifice than that we should sacrifice ourselves to God as a living and pleasing sacrifice, as Saint Paul shows in Romans 12. Epistle for the Fifth Sunday in Lent, Heb 9:12.[7]

9:13-22 *Redemption Through Christ's Blood*

Nothing but the Blood of the Son of God Can Purify the Soul. Heinrich Bullinger: The author confirms the preceding statements by means of a comparative argument. In effect, he says, "If this unbelievable thing was believable for you, namely, that your sins were purged by the blood of animals—though I must believe that such cleansing was nothing but an external ceremony of purification and a symbol of the truth (see how the apostle anticipates everything!)—how much more realistic is that which is entirely believable, that the sins of believers have been expunged by the blameless death of Christ and the holy outpouring of his blood?" For he was true God, and offered himself without blemish to God. St. Chrysostom says, "For if the blood of animals is able to purify the flesh, much rather shall the blood of Christ wash away the defilement of the soul. For, that you may not suppose that it is some great thing when you hear 'sanctifies,' he immediately shows the difference between each of these cleansings."[†] As for the blood of bulls and goats, read Leviticus 9 and 16. Regarding the ashes of the heifer, read Numbers 19.

The statement that Christ was offered "through the eternal Spirit" should not be interpreted as if he only suffered spiritually, and not also in reality. For Peter says, "Christ suffered in the flesh," "He died according to the flesh, but was made alive in the Spirit." So by "the eternal Spirit" he intends to indicate the true deity in Christ by a periphrastic reference and to express this matter without intermingling of the two natures. So these things can be expressed as follows: Christ offered himself without blemish to God, and did so through the eternal Spirit. That is, because he offered himself without blemish to God, his offering endures through the eternal Spirit, that is, through his deity, by which it was accomplished that the humanity of Christ could not be corrupted by any defilements. Hence the angel expressively said to the virgin, "That holy thing which shall be born from you shall be called the Son of God." (John Chrysostom seems to hold a different interpretation, for he says that Christ offered himself "not through fire, or any other things," but through the eternal Spirit.[‡]) And the blood in itself, since it is an eternal and human thing, would not have cleansed the stains upon the soul unless the one who did the cleansing and shed the blood was also the Son of God. Hence John says, "And the blood of Jesus Christ the Son of God cleanses us from all sin." So Paul says in this passage, "The blood of Christ, who through the eternal Spirit offered himself without blemish to God, will purify our conscience." This is a supremely delightful truth, for he contrasts this with his earlier statements in which we have heard that sacrifices were continually offered in the old covenant, but that such daily sacrifices could not perfect the conscience of the worshipers. But now we hear that the blood of Christ, which was

[6]Osiander, *Epistola ad Hebraeos*, 60.
[7]Spangenberg, *Postilla Teütsch*, 4:172v-173r; citing Rom 12:1.

poured out just once, washes away the sins and purifies the consciences of believers from dead works, that is, from those sins that would ruin and damn the soul apart from faith, as we heard in chapter 6. "But how," you may ask, "does it cleanse sins? So that thereafter we may sin freely, since we have learned that all the sins of the world have been expunged by the blood of Christ?" The apostle replies, "By no means! For it purifies so that we may spend what remains of this momentary span of life blamelessly." He discusses this at greater length in Romans 6 and 13, as does Peter in 1 Peter 4. Therefore, the sanctification of every person, and the entire ground of the purging and purification of offenses, does not consist in indulgences, absolutions, our own reparations, or in the fire of purgatory, but in the blood of Christ alone. The blood of Christ is the death and redemption of Christ. But the fire of purgatory, indulgences, and the certificates of the Roman prelate are not the blood of Christ; therefore they do not purify, but are mere contrivances by which they swipe the riches of the careless—or rather, of the superstitiously careful—and make them their own. COMMENTARY ON HEBREWS 9:13-14.[8]

THE TRUE CLEANSING POWER OF THE BLOOD OF CHRIST. JOHANNES OECOLAMPADIUS: Someone might say, "How can we be purified by the alien blood of Christ? We are the ones who have sinned; should we not also be the ones to make satisfaction?" So say unbelievers. He responds with an argument from the lesser to the greater: if the blood of bulls and goats could do something in the way of purification, much more could the blood of Christ. It is as if he were saying, "If, by divine ordination, those who had been defiled under the law by a discharge or contact with the dead could be purified by the blood of bulls and goats or sprinkled water with the ashes of a heifer, how much more, by the same ordination of God, can the blood of Christ, which was ordained for this purpose from eternity, cleanse our hearts and souls from all sins!" The whole argument depends on the ordination and mercy of God; albeit it is not at all evident to this flesh. Blood does not literally cleanse a person, but rather contaminates more, for it is not its nature to be able to wash something away after the fashion of pure water, nor can water mixed with ashes. But because God had ordained it thus, they were treated as means of cleansing, and they were no longer barred from the temple as though unclean.

"For the purification of the flesh." That is, it contributed a certain external purity, so that they were not considered unclean. In other respects, just as it could not cleanse inwardly, so neither could it defile a person, as the Lord also attested, who said, "It is not what goes into the mouth that defiles a person." Thus all external things in themselves neither defile nor purify the inner person. But do take note that, in appearance and in the flesh, the Jews were purified. If the symbol could do this, the symbolized reality itself can do much more. Moreover, you know that through all the sacrifices of the people of old the sacrifice of Christ was indicated; if you consider him, it will be entirely obvious who would cleanse and sanctify. Animals without reason that had not sinned were sacrificed; thus the innocent blood of Christ was sacrificed for us and has cleansed and sanctified us from all sins and defilements. EXPLANATIONS OF HEBREWS 9:13-14.[9]

THE PURITY OF THE OLD TESTAMENT AND THE NEW TESTAMENT. MARTIN LUTHER: He gives a beautiful description of the difference between the purity of the New Testament and that of the Old Testament, and he deduces it by pointing out the contrasts. For the purity of the Old Testament lay in the flesh, in clothing or vessels; the new purity lies in the conscience, in the heart or mind. The impurity of the Old Testament is contracted by

[8]Bullinger, *In Pauli ad Hebraeos Epistolam*, 93r-94r [205-7]; citing 1 Pet 3:18; 4:1; Lk 1:35; 1 Jn 1:7; Heb 7:27; 9:9; Heb 6:4-8; Rom 13:11-14; 1 Pet 4:1-3. †Chrysostom, "Homily 15," in *Homilae XXXIV in epistolam ad Hebraeos* (PG 63:119-120; NPNF 14:440). ‡Ibid. (PG 63:120; NPNF 14:440).

[9]Oecolampadius, *In Epistolam ad Hebraeos Explanationes*, 97v-98r; citing Mt 15:11.

touching a dead or an unclean person, that of the New Testament by dead works or sins. The purity of the Old Testament tended to serve creatures or desires, that of the New Testament to serve the living God. Lectures on Hebrews 9:14.[10]

True Peace for the Conscience. Lucas Osiander: For no human merits are able to restore tranquility to our conscience but only the sacrifice of Christ, apprehended by faith. And the apostle calls sins dead works, as they are perpetrated by spiritually dead human beings, and they lead to eternal death. Truly he calls the Holy Spirit the eternal Spirit, because the Holy Spirit is from eternity. And the apostle teaches that we have been cleansed from our sins so that we might henceforth live for God and serve him, who also lives in eternity and bestows eternal life to all his true worshipers, according to John 14, "I live and you shall live." Epistle to the Hebrews 9:14.[11]

Christ's Blood Is the Ultimate Sign. Dirk Philips: It is true that the miracles and signs of wonder are witnesses of the gospel and the divine Word and that they confirm and strengthen the same. The miracles also move people toward faith but with the understanding that not the teaching which is already accepted and established must therewith be confirmed, but every new doctrine that is from God. Therefore these signs are not necessary now at the present time, just as they were necessary at the time of Christ and his apostles. The reason: Since Christ is the end of the law and a mediator of the New Testament, therefore his teaching had to be confirmed with strong signs and wonderful works, just as the Old Testament was confirmed with signs and miracles. But now that the teaching of Christ has once been established, and no other teaching is taught or may be taught, yes, cursed is the one who preaches another gospel than that which Christ and his apostles have preached to us.

Thus the signs are not a necessity. For the law was after all not established more than once with signs and with the blood of calves and goats. And as it was for a period of time obscured and hides and was again found and came to the light of day, even so it was not confirmed by signs a second time. So also the pious Josiah, as he heard the book of the law read desired no sign but indeed allowed himself to be satisfied with the words and carried out all things according to it, and also kept the Passover. The same no king in Israel had done before him.

Because the gospel has now been confirmed with such glorious miracles (the like of which had never taken place) and in addition was empowered with the innocent death and precious blood of the spotless Lamb, Jesus Christ, and was for a long time obscured, but now through the grace of God has again come to light, so all devout Christians must allow themselves to be satisfied therewith. So that whoever requires a sign beyond must hear "an evil and adulterous nature seeks for a sign," etc. The Enchiridion.[12]

9:23-28 *Christ's Sacrifice Put Away Sin*

Christ Is the Final Priest and Sacrifice for Sin. Desiderius Erasmus: He [Christ] transferred to himself not only the sins of those who had placed their hope of salvation in him many years before but also the sins of those who would believe his gospel for many generations afterward. Therefore, the world has no reason to wait for another priest or another victim for the expiation for sin. Paraphrases on the Epistle to the Hebrews 9:23-28.[13]

The Sin of the "Papists." Erasmus Sarcerius: Therefore it is now clear and obvious how terribly the papists sin in that they offer and crucify Christ daily in their masses for

[10]LW 29:208 (WA 57:207.9-14).
[11]Osiander, *Epistola ad Hebraeos*, 60; citing Jn 14:19.
[12]CRR 6:223-24*; citing Rom 10:4; Heb 7:11; Gal 3:20; Heb 12:24; Gal 1:9; Ex 19:16; 24:6; 2 Kings 22:8; 23:21-23; Mt 12:39.
[13]CWE 44:238.

sin and despise and blaspheme his one-time sacrifice for all sins. Summaries and Brief Content, Heb 9:23-28.[14]

The Law's Use of Blood Was Modeled on an Eternal Reality. Heinrich Bullinger: He calls the model "the thing itself," not the symbol or shadow. For in chapter 8 we heard that the Mosaic hallows were copied from a heavenly model and vision, and that therefore the heavenly hallows are more real, while the Mosaic ones were merely shadowy. So now the apostle restates the matter as follows: since everything symbolic had been purified with blood, this rite could not have been derived from any other source than from the heavenly model. For this reason, it is necessary for the truth itself to be cleansed by the shedding of blood. But there is this particular difference. For inasmuch as the true hallows are better and more venerable than the shadowy ones, it was necessary for the real ones to be cleansed with better sacrifices and purer and nobler blood. And from this he derives his explanation of Christ, the sole and eternal sacrifice. Commentary on Hebrews 9:23.[15]

Which Heavenly Things Were Purified? The English Annotations: Some understand thereby Christ himself, and those spiritual blessings that the faithful obtain through faith in him. For Christ himself was consecrated, or made perfect through sufferings. Others understand thereby the church under the gospel, and those spiritual graces whereof the members are made partakers therein. The church under the gospel being called the heavenly Jerusalem, and those graces being called spiritual blessings in heavenly places. Others understand thereof heaven itself, whereinto Christ entered. Annotations on Hebrews 9:23.[16]

Christ Never Ceases to Appear Before the Father. Johannes Oecolampadius: At last he proceeds to demonstrate that Christ is more highly exalted than those who were under the old law, and he approaches this point almost in a new way. The "holy places made with hands" means the tabernacle of Moses or the holy places of the temple of Solomon. Christ did not enter these, as the copies of the true things, but he entered into heaven itself, so that he might appear in the presence of God; that is, he performs the duty of a priest for us and reconciles us to the Father. Yet we know that all things are visible to God, and that the Son would never have not appeared in the presence of the Father as entirely present. But by such modes of speech allowances are made for our weakness, since we grasp heavenly things with great difficulty. The worthiness of Christ is such that it prevails with the Father sufficiently for all our sins, for he sacrificed himself for us, even before the foundation of the world, although not in such a way that the price of redemption had yet been paid the way it is completely today. Hence it is obvious that the re-presentation of the Son in the irreverent Mass is laughable, as if he had now given up appearing in the presence of God or were to give up his worthiness. If they were to say that it is a memorial with the Father rather than a re-presentation, it would be tolerable. But let us dismiss them for the present and pray that the Lord would condescend to open their eyes at last to the glory of this name and cast out the clouds of error from the minds of all. Explanations of Hebrews 9:24.[17]

Christ Is Not Offered in the Mass. Heinrich Bullinger: This is a return to the same subject, for here he continues the proof that he has begun. Christ has not died more than once, therefore he has not been offered more than once, and therefore by a single offering he has made atonement for all the sins of the entire world, and

[14]Sarcerius, *Summarien vnd kurtzer Jnhalt*, 4:JJ1r.
[15]Bullinger, *In Pauli ad Hebraeos Epistolam*, 96r [211]; citing Heb 8:5.
[16]Downame, ed., *Annotations*, NNN1v*; citing Heb 2:10; 12:22; Eph 1:3.
[17]Oecolampadius, *In Epistolam ad Hebraeos Explanationes*, 101r-v; citing Eph 2:16-17; Heb 4:13; Rev 13:8.

hence the sacrifice of Christ is an exclusively single and perpetual sacrifice. But it is amazing how much individual emphasis is given to these things. For first it says, "Now, however," that is, not from the commencement of the world, but "at the end of the world he was offered just once." And then he does not say, "to overthrow sin" but "for the overthrow of sins," that is, for the removal not of just one sin, but of everything that can be classified as sin. Third, it says that this offering was not made by another, but by the Son of God himself. For no one among mortals can offer the Son of God. For in chapter 7 we heard, "It was fitting that we should have such a high priest." Therefore, what Erasmus has written on this present passage is so very appropriate and elegant that I add it almost by necessity. He says, "Christ was of such a kind that it was sufficient for him to offer himself just once and to abolish the sins of all ages until the end of the world by the sprinkling of his own blood just once. And this was done not from the beginning of the world, but with the end impending, when it was manifest to all that everything was infected with sins, and that there was no remedy except from God, so that it might be evident how effective that high priest must be who would atone for such a vast heap of sins by a single sacrifice. Then the available and easy remedy was abandoned, so that the same sacrifice might make satisfaction through the countless years for all who would not render themselves unworthy of it. For he bore in himself the sins not only of those who had put their hope of salvation in him many years before but also of those who would believe in his gospel many ages later."†

But I would be surprised if the hapless Mass-mongers have anything to present in favor of the sacrifice of the Mass in opposition to these extremely clear statements by Paul. For although John in Revelation 13 calls Christ "the Lamb who was slain from the beginning of the world," he not only does not contradict Paul's statements here, but he agrees exactly. For John intended to indicate that all the sins of the saints from the commencement of the world have been purged by the single death and sacrifice of Christ. But though they say that Christ is offered mystically and spiritually, everyone now recognizes that this fabrication rests on mere verbal juggling. We, however, present two things in opposition to the sacrifice of the Mass on the basis of this passage of Paul's. First, "Christ does not die again; death no longer has dominion over him" (Romans 6). Therefore he is not sacrificed again by anyone. This conclusion is proved by Paul's own words in the present passage. Second, in the case of any sacrifice that is fit to atone for sins, it is necessary for blood to be shed and death to take place. This is proved by Paul's words: "Without the shedding of blood there is no forgiveness," and, "Wherever there is a testament, the death of the testator must take place." But in the Mass no blood is shed, nor does Christ die. It is proved by the authority of Paul in Romans 6 and Hebrews 9 that the blood that was once shed is not shed again, but is sufficient to blot out all the sins of the world. Thus the Mass is not a sacrifice for sin. Commentary on Hebrews 9:26.[18]

Like All People, Christ Died Just Once. Huldrych Zwingli: "And just as it is appointed for all men to die once." Now he adds the reason and proof of why Christ, having been offered just once, was made a finished sacrifice. It was because he could not be offered repeatedly, because, after the manner of human beings, he died just once and received his judgment; that is, as we say in German, "He received his judgment just like all people who die." For here we do not take this to mean the universal judgment, but particular, that is, either life or death. Not that there was any need for Christ to be put in the balance after death, since he was free from the guilt of offenses, and to him the Father was to give all judgment. Indeed, the prince of this world did not have anything in him. Accordingly, we call "judgment" what Christ received after death, when, exalted to the right

[18]Bullinger, *In Pauli ad Hebraeos Epistolam*, 97v-98v; citing Heb 7:26; Rev 13:8; citing Rom 6:9; Heb 9:22; 9:16. †EOO 7.6:74; CWE 44:238.

hand of God in the glory of the resurrection, he was "declared to be the Son of God" to the world. Exposition of Hebrews 9:27.[19]

There is No Room for Purgatory Between Death and Judgment. Johannes Oecolampadius: Here the apostle uses the language of dying and offering or sacrificing interchangeably. It should be noted, however, against those who construct a purgatory after this age, that here it reads, "It is appointed for all men to die once, and after that the judgment." (It makes no difference whether you take this in reference to a general or an individual judgment.) Consequently, you can see that after death no further place of penitence will be left, and nothing but judgment remains. If you believe in Christ, you have already passed from death to life. If you do not believe, you will not see life, and the wrath of God will remain on you forever (John 3 and 5). Explanations of Hebrews 9:27-28.[20]

[19]Zwingli, *In Epistolam Beati Pauli ad Hebraeos Expositio*, 578; citing Jn 5:22; 14:30; Rom 1:4.

[20]Oecolampadius, *In Epistolam ad Hebraeos Explanationes*, 103v-104r; citing John 3:36; 5:24.

10:1-18 CHRIST, THE FULL AND SUFFICIENT OFFERING FOR SIN

For since the law has but a shadow of the good things to come instead of the true form of these realities, it can never, by the same sacrifices that are continually offered every year, make perfect those who draw near. [2]Otherwise, would they not have ceased to be offered, since the worshipers, having once been cleansed, would no longer have any consciousness of sins? [3]But in these sacrifices there is a reminder of sins every year. [4]For it is impossible for the blood of bulls and goats to take away sins.

[5]Consequently, when Christ[a] came into the world, he said,

"Sacrifices and offerings you have not desired,
but a body have you prepared for me;
[6]in burnt offerings and sin offerings
you have taken no pleasure.
[7]Then I said, 'Behold, I have come to do your will, O God,
as it is written of me in the scroll of the book.'"

[8]When he said above, "You have neither desired nor taken pleasure in sacrifices and offerings and burnt offerings and sin offerings" (these are offered according to the law), [9]then he added, "Behold, I have come to do your will." He does away with the first in order to establish the second. [10]And by that will we have been sanctified through the offering of the body of Jesus Christ once for all.

[11]And every priest stands daily at his service, offering repeatedly the same sacrifices, which can never take away sins. [12]But when Christ[b] had offered for all time a single sacrifice for sins, he sat down at the right hand of God, [13]waiting from that time until his enemies should be made a footstool for his feet. [14]For by a single offering he has perfected for all time those who are being sanctified.

[15]And the Holy Spirit also bears witness to us; for after saying,

[16]"This is the covenant that I will make with them
after those days, declares the Lord:
I will put my laws on their hearts,
and write them on their minds,"

[17]then he adds,

"I will remember their sins and their lawless deeds no more."

[18]Where there is forgiveness of these, there is no longer any offering for sin.

a Greek *he* **b** Greek *this one*

OVERVIEW: The reformers find plenty of material in this section to continue their assault on the Catholic Mass, including Masses for the dead, insisting that Christ's sacrifice for sin occurred once and that it provides forgiveness for all sin to those who place their faith in Christ. This critique leads naturally to statements about the doctrine of the Lord's Supper and in what manner it should be understood as a sacrifice. Bullinger's extended comment on the Lord's Supper captures this theme; he argues that it is a sacrifice of praise and thanksgiving for Christ's one-time sacrifice, not a repeated sacrifice of Christ himself. Our commentators also seek to deal with the divine promises of forgiveness that were attached to the Old Testament sacrifices, which makes it difficult for the reformers to dismiss them as mere external religion. Additionally, the reformers stress the freedom of conscience one receives from the sacrifice of Christ, which unburdens the conscience from its feelings of guilt. Finally, the reformers also provide diverse commentary on how the word "body" (Heb 10:5) should be understood.

10:1-4 *Sacrifices Could Not Take Away Sin*

Two Types of Sacrifice. Philipp Melanchthon: There are two kinds of sacrifices that are very similar to one another, and there are no others. There is the propitiatory sacrifice, that is, a work which merits for some the remission of guilt and eternal punishment, or a work that reconciles God and placates the wrath of God on behalf of some people and is a means of satisfaction for sin and eternal punishment. The second kind of sacrifice is the eucharistic sacrifice, which does not merit the remission of sins or reconciliation, but comes from those who have been reconciled, so that we give thanks to God for the remission of sins we have received and for his other benefits, or we return thanks by means of our obedience. This distinction can be clearly shown from the epistle to the Hebrews, which teaches that there was one propitiatory sacrifice made in the world. Therefore, there remain all the other works in which those who have been reconciled must demonstrate their obedience. Loci Praecupui Theologici.[1]

The Eyes of the Community Versus the Sight of God. Huldrych Zwingli: "Good things to come." Someone may say, "How were such sacrifices mere shadows, since God attached to these offerings promises of the forgiveness of sins, as is plain from the first through the eighth chapters of Leviticus?" We may reply that, when these offerings were made, sins were indeed forgiven in the sight of the church, but not in the sight of God. For the church would judge one who made an offering to be cleansed, when perhaps he still appeared defiled in the sight of God; this is affirmed by many statements of the prophets. This is the same thing that Paul said above in chapter 9, "for the sanctification, cleanliness, and purification of the flesh," and, "which cannot cleanse the conscience." And this is now made clearer as he expands on this theme. Exposition of Hebrews 10:1.[2]

The Law Is to the Gospel as a Shadow Is to an Image. Cardinal Cajetan: "For as the law has a shadow of the good things to some, not the true image of the realities, it can never, by the same sacrifices that are offered endlessly once a year, make perfect those who draw near." Take note of what he says regarding the law. For he does not say that the sacrifices had a shadow, but that the law had a shadow. So the law of Moses is described as having "a shadow of the good things to come" in the heavenly country, not "the true image of the realities." He does not say that it did not have the realities themselves, but that it did not have "the very image" of the realities, so that we may understand the difference between the old law and the new. The former has a shadow of the good things of the heavenly country, while the latter is the true image of those things. For a shadow very imperfectly represents that of which it is the shadow, but an image closely represents that of which it is the image, because it resembles it, so that we can learn many things about a person through a true image of that person that we cannot learn from a shadow. For the law, by promising good things in the Promised Land, promised a kind of shadow of the good things of the heavenly country; but the new law in its words promised the heavenly country itself, and in its substance (which is the grace of the Spirit poured out through love in our hearts) it is the likeness of the heavenly life. Comments on Hebrews 10:1.[3]

A Draft or an Unclear Image? The English Annotations: Some are of the opinion that here Saint Paul alludes to the custom of painters, who first make a rude draft, and then out of it a perfect and lively picture. These make the sense this: that the old covenant contained only dark resemblances and types of heavenly things, no lively representations of them, this being reserved for the time of the gospel, wherein Christ and all spiritual blessings in him are clearly and plainly

[1]Melanchthon, *Loci Praecipui Theologici*, 280*.
[2]Zwingli, *In Epistolam Beati Pauli ad Hebraeos Expositio*, 578; citing Lev 1:4; 4:20, 26, 31, 35; 5:6, 10, 13, 16, 18; 6:7; Is 1:11-16; Jer 6:20; 7:20-21; Amos 5:21-24; Heb 9:13, 9.
[3]Cajetan, *In Epistolam ad Hebraeos Commentarii*, 166r-v; citing Heb 11:14-16; Rom 5:5.

manifested. Others are of the opinion that Saint Paul alludes unto the shadow of a body, and these make this the sense of the words: that the old covenant had only types, wherein Christ and heavenly things through him were darkly represented, not the substance and truth of the things themselves. This is the more probable opinion. Annotations on Hebrews 10:1.[4]

Christ's Single Sacrifice Has Done What Repeated Masses Can Never Do. Heinrich Bullinger: But here I address you Mass-mongers, yes, I address you who would peddle the Mass as a sacrifice that washes away the sins of the living and the dead. Yes, I address myself to you. Tell us, by a properly executed Mass do you wash away the sins of those for whom it is offered, or do you not wash them away? If you do not wash them away, your Mass is ineffective and useless, and your sacrifice is a fraud. But if you do wash them away, why, I ask you, do you offer it for the dead, not only twice, but yearly, like the Jews, or rather hundreds and hundreds of times? Why do you celebrate with numerous offerings on the day of their passing, and again in a week, a month, and then every year on the anniversary? "But," they say, "We sin daily; therefore we sacrifice daily." This is their objection with regard to the living; for with regard to the dead that have nothing else to say. Nevertheless even to this contrived objection regarding the living the apostle replies that the sacrifice of Christ is single, and single in such a way that it was offered only once, it cannot be repeated, nor does it need to be. For all by itself it is always sufficient to pardon every last sin that we may commit in the course of this life. Commentary on Hebrews 10:1-2.[5]

When We Look to Christ, We Are Free from the Consciousness of Sin. Johannes Bugenhagen: So, do Christians no longer have any consciousness of sins? Yes, that is the case; but blessed is the person who understands! "Since we have been justified by faith, we have peace," says Paul, who always combines grace and peace in his letters. It is important to know that our merits and righteous works do not save us, but when will we know at last that our sins do not condemn us? This is what Christian freedom should be and is—freedom of the conscience, which cannot possibly be experienced by those who conclude inwardly on the basis of this declaration that now they can sin freely. They would not draw such an inference from this statement, thus insulting Christ the liberator, if they had even a speck of faith; rather, they would be overcome with wonder at the great generosity and love of this kind Father to his children, namely, those who believe. Christians are not unaware, if they look at themselves, that they are sinners and condemned, for they do not have in themselves a righteousness of their own; but by faith they look on Christ, who for us became righteousness from God, and wisdom, sanctification, satisfaction, and so forth. Here all sins vanish, even from a person's conscience, if only there is a proper faith, which cannot judge the righteousness of Christ to be incomplete. Here all things are possible for the one who believes. There is therefore now no condemnation for those who are in Christ Jesus, who do not walk according to the flesh, who always entreat by faith and say, "Father, forgive us our debts." But attempts at justification by works can never imitate this freedom, as we said on another occasion. Here we do the will of God as we believe in the one whom he sent after the sacrifices of the law had been rejected (as he shows below on the basis of Psalm 40.† By that will alone we are sanctified through the satisfaction of the body of Christ, which was offered just once, and we are sanctified forever, so that we may have no consciousness of sin as long as that offering is ours. But it is ours as long as we believe that it is complete for the sins of the whole world from the very beginning. This is what it says in Jeremiah 31: "I will remember their sins and lawless deeds no more." Furthermore, as the author concludes, "where there is forgiveness of sins, there is no longer

[4]Downame, ed., *Annotations*, NNN1v*; citing Col 2:17.
[5]Bullinger, *In Pauli ad Hebraeos Epistolam*, 100r-v [218-20].

any offering for sin." Where, then, is that papistical offering to give satisfaction? Everything that follows after "Therefore brothers, since we have," looks to this and declares that we are priests and high priests in Christ. Commentary on the Pauline Epistles, Heb 10:2.[6]

The Church's Sacraments Point to Redemption. Johannes Oecolampadius: It is certain that the blood of bulls and goats does not wash away sin, but rather they are a reminder of sins. For in the sacrifices they testified that because of their sin they merited death and the shedding of blood, and that they could not be released from these without the shedding of blood. But as long as those who were about to sacrifice poured out the blood, they indicated that they were sinners and needed a true sacrifice. Now someone may ask, "So, do our sacraments, which are also a reminder, have nothing better to offer than the ceremonies of the ancients?" Paul replies here that the ceremonies of the old law held an accusation of sin, and not pure thanksgiving, as we have in the Eucharist. The reason is that, at that time, Christ had not yet suffered or made satisfaction for sins. Our ceremonies are as much superior to those of old as it is greater to testify that you have been freed from sins than to confess that you are still a sinner, in need of purification and awaiting salvation. For as often as we gather together and consume the bread of the Lord and drink his blood, we announce and proclaim the Lord's death until he comes, and we give thanks that we have now been redeemed from slavery to sin, with which they accused themselves by their own sacrifices. We do not memorialize so much sin as the redemption from sin achieved by Christ our Lord. Explanations of Hebrews 10:2-4.[7]

10:5-7 *God Takes No Pleasure in Burnt Offerings*

It Is Important to Distinguish Between Christ's Humanity And Divinity. Dirk Philips: Anthonius has asked me to answer a little to your letter and make a small confession about the deity and incarnation of the Lord Jesus Christ. And that is my confession about the deity and incarnation, that Jesus Christ is true God and human being, God born out of God the eternal Father and became a pure, unspotted human being in time, conceived by the Holy Ghost and born out of Mary, the virgin, a son of the Most High.

Furthermore, his humanity has come out of the Word and not out of a human seed, after the birth out of God, which has happened from eternity. Thus he is God and God's Son, the only, unique, and firstborn Son of God. After his birth further, which happened in time, he is also a holy human being, son of God and of human beings.

Therefore one must speak differently about the deity and humanity of Jesus Christ so that one not confess and hold the deity for humanity nor the humanity for deity. For John writes that in the very beginning was the Word, and the Word was with God, and God was that Word. And that Word has become flesh and has at the same time remained the Word of life, God and God's Word, wisdom, truth, and eternal life.

Since now Christ has become that flesh and had a beginning (certainly out of the Word) so may it not be held for God himself. For God has neither beginning nor end, and Scripture names Christ the first and the last, that is to be understood as from his eternal deity.

Likewise, since Christ speaks to the Father, "You have prepared a body for me," so the body of Christ may not be held for God, but in the body dwells the entire fullness of deity bodily, and that God was in Christ and reconciled the world with himself, etc.

In this manner the Scripture teaches us to confess Christ Jesus and to distinguish in our

[6]Bugenhagen, *Annotationes in epistolas Pauli recognitae* (1525) 156r-v [345-46]; citing Rom 5:1; 1 Cor 1:30; Mk 9:22; Rom 8:1, 4; Mt 6:12; Jn 6:29; Ps 40:6-8; Jer 31:34; Heb 10:19. †Bugenhagen cites Ps 39[:7-9], following the chapter divisions of the Vulgate.

[7]Oecolampadius, *In Epistolam ad Hebraeos Explanationes*, 105v-106r; citing 1 Cor 11:26.

speaking between the eternal deity and holy humanity of Jesus Christ. Undated Letter.[8]

Open Ears Prepare for Service. The English Annotations: Hebrew, "mine ear hast thou opened"; or "digged open." It is a proverbial manner of speech, whereby there is implied the qualifying or fitting a person to obedience in service, the ear, or opening of the ear, being an emblem or symbol, or a metaphorical sign of obedience. Now Saint Paul, following the translation of the Septuagint, and being directed by the Spirit of God, expounds this of God's sanctifying and fitting a body unto Christ, wherein he was obedient even unto the shameful death of the cross. Annotations on Hebrews 10:5.[9]

The Obedience of Christ. Heinrich Bullinger: By a prophetic testimony the apostle now confirms what he has maintained thus far, namely, that by the sacrifice of Christ all the offerings of the people of old have been abolished, whereas the sacrifice of Christ is single and perpetual. He derives this testimony from Psalm 40[†] and represents Christ as saying it upon entering the world. But it should be recognized that in the original Hebrew it does not say, "A body you have prepared for me," but "You have pierced my ears." But although the words are thus in disagreement, still the meaning is the same. For the apostle uses the word "body" so that he may set it up in contrast to the shadow, that is, as the thing itself that was foreshadowed by the symbol. But the prophet here employs the word "ears" so that, as they are the instrument of faith and obedience, by association he puts down "ears" to signify obedience itself. But the obedience of Christ is the actual body, that is, the actual thing itself, which the symbols depicted. So Christ refused to serve the shadow, but rendered up his own actual body through obedience to death on the cross. It should also be recognized that "the head of the book"[‡] signifies the main point and purpose of the law. But the main point and purpose of the law is to submit to God and to be conformed to his will. Commentary on Hebrews 10:5-7.[10]

Christ Received the Body of a Servant. Johannes Oecolampadius: "A body you have prepared for me." That is, "You have given me a body prepared to serve you." Surely, when Christ became incarnate, he put on the body of a servant, becoming obedient to the Father even unto death, and that on a cross. This sacrifice of self-giving was most acceptable to the Father, for he far prefers obedience to any kind of sacrifices, as it says in Hosea 6. Moreover, the Hebrew wording, "My ears you have pierced," seems to be an allusion to the custom that was observed on the basis of the law, when a servant who was liberated by the Year of Jubilee would cast himself back into perpetual servitude, and his ears would be nailed down by his master as a sign of the utmost submission and complete servitude. But howsoever that may be, it is readily apparent to anyone that here there is no change in the meaning. It does not escape me that there are those who explain it otherwise, and oppose "body" to "shadow," but their explanation seems to me more forced and violent than that understood by one that is concerned with simplicity. And our exposition seems to be confirmed by that which follows: "Then I said, 'Behold, I have come; in the scroll of the book.'" Explanations of Hebrews 10:5-7.[11]

Christ's Heavenly Flesh. Dirk Philips: But if the body of Christ had been made by Mary (as the world thinks and says with such want of understanding regarding it), then there would be no difference between the body of Christ and that

[8]CRR 6:633*; citing John 1:1.

[9]Downame, ed., *Annotations*, NNN2r*; citing Is 50:5; Job 33:16.

[10]Bullinger, *In Pauli ad Hebraeos Epistolam*, 101r-v [221-22]; citing Rom 5:19; Ps 40:6-8. [†]Bullinger, employing standard sixteenth-century chapter numbers, cites this text as Ps 39[:7-9]. [‡]The Latin and Greek words (*capitulum* and *kephalis*) used to translate the original Hebrew word for "scroll" (*mglh*), are both diminutive forms of the words for "head" (*caput* and *kephalē*).

[11]Oecolampadius, *In Epistolam ad Hebraeos Explanationes*, 106v-107r; citing Phil 2:7-8; Hos 6:6.

of Adam, because like as Christ was conceived of the Holy Spirit in Mary, so also Adam was made by God and had no other Father than God. What difference would there be, then, between the body of Christ and the body of Adam if the body of Christ had been made of the earth, the same as the body of Adam? . . . Far from it! God, the heavenly Father, prepared for Jesus Christ, his only begotten Son, a body, but not of corrupt human seed, rather of his incorruptible seed, with which he caused Mary, the pure virgin, to conceive through the power of his Holy Spirit. . . . Therefore Christ everywhere testifies that he came down from heaven, but he speaks of his origin especially in John 6:51. . . . Now, if Christ is the bread of heaven, and if the bread of heaven, moreover, is the flesh of Christ, it is impossible for the flesh of Christ to be formed of the seed of Mary; for neither the seed of Mary nor that of any earthly creature can by any means to be the true living bread that came down from heaven, to be so called. On the Incarnation, Heb 10:5.[12]

Christ's Willing Self-Sacrifice. Lucas Osiander: The Son of God is speaking in these words in this sentence: "Heavenly Father, the Levitical sacrifices are not pleasing to you in this way, that on account of them you might pardon sins to the human race. And thus I myself decided that I wanted to come into the world and to fulfill the law, and to satisfy your will and justice by my most bitter passion, for this was first predicted concerning me in the writings of the prophets." (Christ is chiefly having to be sought in sacred Scripture: this is the goal of the whole of sacred Scripture. And the one who does not know Christ from it, this one profits nothing in the reading of the Bible.) Epistle to the Hebrews 10:7.[13]

[12]LCC 25:238-39 n. 10*; citing Lk 1:35. Philips here propounds the doctrine of the celestial flesh of Christ, which he borrowed from Melchior Hoffman. This doctrine held that the incarnate Christ possessed heavenly glorified flesh during his earthly ministry, which enabled him to be sinless and to draw human beings to a truly spiritual existence. The doctrine was popular among some early Anabaptists.

[13]Osiander, *Epistola ad Hebraeos*, 66.

10:8-18 *Sanctified Through Christ's Offering of Himself*

The Sacrifice of Praise and Thanksgiving Continues in the Church. Heinrich Bullinger: "So," you may ask, "have all sacrifices been so abolished that the Christian Church has nothing to offer up to God?" I would reply that there are two kinds of sacrifices, one for the forgiveness of sin, but the other the sacrifices of praise, righteousness, and thanksgiving. But there is no longer any further sacrifice for the forgiveness of sins that is offered any longer in the church. For the single offering of Christ is the one sacrifice for all sins, and having been offered just once, it is always sufficient. Thus far the apostle has been discussing this offering. . . . From this, however, it is obvious what we should think about the Lord's Supper—not what the pontiffs think, that in it the priest offers the real and natural body of Christ to atone for the sins of the living and the dead. For this is more than three octaves out of tune with the truth and power of the death and offering of Christ. But we should think about the Lord's Supper as we were commanded to think by Christ, who said, "Do this in remembrance of me." Thus the supper is the holy and believing commemoration of the death and sacrifice of Christ, which was offered for us just once on the cross, in which we take the signs he commanded us to take, and we give thanks because he redeemed those who were sold under sin. Additionally, along with the commemoration the name itself is also communicated, because we really possess that which is commemorated. And the supper is a commemoration of the sacrifice of Christ that was accomplished just once, on the cross; consequently, among all the ancients the name of "sacrifice" was applied to the supper, and thus the supper itself was called "the sacrifice of Christians," not in itself, but by communication of the name. And there is another reason why the ancients called the supper or Eucharist a "sacrifice." For since thanksgiving and praise are the sacrifice of Christians, and the Eucharist is nothing other than a thanksgiving (if you consider its derivation), consequently, the ancients call the Eucharist a "sacrifice." They did not use that name because flesh and blood are offered (as the pontiffs would have it), but because fellowship, harmony, charity, unity, prayer, praise, and thanksgiving are the true sacrifice of Christians. And we may call all the ancient writers as witnesses to this fact, especially Irenaeus, *Against Heresies* book 4, chapters 32, 33, and 34.[†] Then see Tertullian *Against the Jews* and *Against Marcion* 3 and 4, where on the basis of the verse from Malachi, "From the rising of the sun to its going down a pure sacrifice will be offered to my name," he very clearly says, "such as the ascription of glory, and blessing, and praise, and hymns," and, "simple prayer from a pure conscience."[‡] I also call as a witness the Letters of St. Cyprian Caecilianus, book 2, letter 3, as well as book 4, letter 5 by the same author.[§] He makes mention of sacrifices for the dead in such a way that it is clearly established that those sacrifices are nothing else than praises of the deceased and thanksgivings to God for the blessings they delivered. We may also invoke the testimony of Augustine in Letter 23 to Boniface and in *The City of God* Book 10, chapters 4-6.[◊] The pontiffs here have no cause to plume themselves. . . .

Therefore, those of us among the Swiss who have said goodbye to the papistical Mass have set up something better and more divine, closer to Christ's ordinance and more reflective of the apostolic tradition, namely, the Lord's actual ordinance, in place of the abolished Mass. . . . So I declare that the holy sacrifice of the Lord never ceases in the churches of us who are in Zurich, Bern, Basel, St. Gallen, Schaffhausen, Biel, Mulhouse, and many other places—that is, the perpetual sacrifice of Christ, its commemoration, praise, and thanksgiving. For those who accuse us of impiety and of profaning the sacraments and all other sacred things are shamelessly telling lies. For we have abolished the profanation of sacred things—the Mass—and have set up in its place the sacred Lord's Supper. For we firmly believe that no one can ordain a ceremony that is better or more pleasing to God than the one that Christ, the Son of God, has ordained. Then the apostles passed it on as if with their very hands to the church of God, and the church preserved it uncorrupted for more than five hundred years after the time of the apostles. But why must our rite render an account, and why must it please Scholasticus, Gregory the Great, Adrian, and the other prelates of the Roman Church? For we are not the disciples of men, but of Jesus Christ the Son of God, after whom we are named Christians. Commentary on Hebrews 10:15-18.[14]

The Holy Spirit Confirms God's Covenant in Our Hearts. Johannes Oecolampadius: He says that "the Holy Spirit also testifies and confirms in our hearts" what these things are. I do not take *martyrei* here for the witness born by the Scriptures or words, as elsewhere it is not infrequently used, but rather for a kind of hidden power and conviction of the mind regarding everything that pertains to salvation. For the hearts of the godly have been sealed with this Spirit, so that they may be sure that God is their truthful, kindly, and most affectionate Father. He is the one who bears absolutely certain testimony to the covenant that God has made with us; whoever feels nothing of this in themselves must be found very weak in faith. For those who are uncertain of the salvation imparted by the merit of the blood of Christ do not have in themselves the Holy Spirit as the pledge of an eternal inheritance, just as they do not feel in themselves his internal

[14]Bullinger, *In Pauli ad Hebraeos Epistolam*, 103r-107r [225-33]; citing Lk 22:19; 1 Cor 11:24-25; Rom 7:14. [†]PG 7:1070-86; ANF 1:505-12. In point of fact, chapters 32–34 have little bearing on this question; Bullinger is probably thinking of *Against Heresies* 4.17-18 (PG 7:1019-29; ANF 1:484-86). [‡]Tertullian, *Against the Jews* 5 (PL 2:647; ANF 3:156-57), and *Against Marcion* 3.22, 4.1 (PL 2:381-82, 391; ANF 3:341, 346). [§]*Beatissimi Cecilii Cypriani carthaginensium praesuli . . . opera* (Paris: Robert Fortuné, 1512), 25v-29r, 61r-62r. This corresponds to Letters 63 and 34 in PL (4:383-401, 329-33), or 62 and 33 in ANF (5:358-64, 312-14). [◊]Augustine, *City of God* 10.4-6 (PL 41:281-84; NPNF 2:182-84). The relevant letter to Boniface is listed as *Letter* 98 (paragraph 9) in later editions of Augustine's epistles (PL 33:359-64; NPNF 406-10); Bullinger's numbering is consistent with sixteenth-century editions, such as *Liber Epistolarum beati Augustini episcopi Hipponensis ecclesiae* (Paris: Johannes Parvus & Jodocus Badius, 1515), 24v-25r.

testimony, nor are they led by him as sons of God. Explanations of Hebrews 10:15-18.[15]

Do Not Devalue Christ's Sacrifice. Marie Dentière: It was not enough for the wickedness of human beings to attribute and bestow the honor that belongs to Jesus Christ on those visible things that were ordained by God, but also on things ordained and invented by human beings, without the authority of Scripture, such as pilgrimages and money given for indulgences and pardons, and a full lot of other evil idolatries that human beings have discovered, created, and invented through their good intentions, or rather, to pillage and rob the poor people, going against the holy Word of God. It has reached the point where the earth is filled with idolatries, and if God did not intervene, it would not be within human power to extirpate and tear them out.

But I pray you, who could sufficiently tell, write, and express the great blasphemy and injury that we do to our Lord, to his very holy death, and to his precious blood that he shed for us, when instead of the voluntary sacrifice that he made and offered once for us, we come again daily to offer a visible thing, without soul, for our redemption? That offering, once made, alters, even destroys, the pure and holy teaching of Jesus Christ, when, as if swollen and proud in their spirits, they come to invent and contrive such ceremonies and repetitions of sacrifices. It is as if Jesus Christ had not been sufficient to redeem us, and they had to make another redemption, contrary to holy Scripture. They turned the people into idolaters, who adore the bread and the wine as their own God, when God does not abide in these things made by human hands. Nor does God wish to be served or adored in things made by human industry or artifice. But you, wiser than God, will make a beautiful image of him out of wood, half of which you will use to cook your stew and warm your flesh and from the other half you will make a God to adore and serve, asking his aid and help. From a little wheat you will make bread, one part you will give to the poor as God commands, from the other, you will make a God to adore, eat, and devour, which is forbidden. Oh what a servant, eating his master! What service do you do him, what adoration, yet this practice is highly praised, defended, and upheld. Certainly not by Scripture, right, or reason, because they want none of it. But it is enough for our masters that they be maintained by force of tyrannies. Epistle to Marguerite de Navarre.[16]

[15]Oecolampadius, *In Epistolam ad Hebraeos Explanationes*, 108v-109r; citing 1 Jn 5:6; 1 Cor 1:22; 5:5; Eph 1:13-14; 4:30; Rom 8:14.

[16]Dentière, *Epistle to Marguerite de Navarre*, 59-60.

10:19-39 HOLDING FAST TO THE CONFESSION OF HOPE

[19]Therefore, brothers,[a] since we have confidence to enter the holy places by the blood of Jesus, [20]by the new and living way that he opened for us through the curtain, that is, through his flesh, [21]and since we have a great priest over the house of God, [22]let us draw near with a true heart in full assurance of faith, with our hearts sprinkled clean from an evil conscience and our bodies washed with pure water. [23]Let us hold fast the confession of our hope without wavering, for he who promised is faithful. [24]And let us consider how to stir up one another to love and good works, [25]not neglecting to meet together, as is the habit of some, but encouraging one another, and all the more as you see the Day drawing near.

[26]For if we go on sinning deliberately after receiving the knowledge of the truth, there no longer remains a sacrifice for sins, [27]but a fearful expectation of judgment, and a fury of fire that will consume the adversaries. [28]Anyone who has set aside the law of Moses dies without mercy on the evidence of two or three witnesses. [29]How much worse punishment, do you think, will be deserved by the one who has trampled underfoot the Son of God, and has profaned the blood of the covenant by which he was sanctified, and has outraged the Spirit of grace? [30]For we know him who said, "Vengeance is mine; I will repay." And again, "The Lord will judge his people." [31]It is a fearful thing to fall into the hands of the living God.

[32]But recall the former days when, after you were enlightened, you endured a hard struggle with sufferings, [33]sometimes being publicly exposed to reproach and affliction, and sometimes being partners with those so treated. [34]For you had compassion on those in prison, and you joyfully accepted the plundering of your property, since you knew that you yourselves had a better possession and an abiding one. [35]Therefore do not throw away your confidence, which has a great reward. [36]For you have need of endurance, so that when you have done the will of God you may receive what is promised. [37]For,

"Yet a little while,
and the coming one will come and will not delay;
[38]but my righteous one shall live by faith,
and if he shrinks back,
my soul has no pleasure in him."

[39]But we are not of those who shrink back and are destroyed, but of those who have faith and preserve their souls.

a Or *brothers and sisters*

OVERVIEW: The reformers stress in this section that one must enter the way opened to heaven by Christ through faith, not works. They sternly exhort and also tenderly invite readers to this faith, emphasizing that the faithfulness of God is the source of the Christian's confidence. The differing Protestant views on baptism are represented in the reformers' comments on this section, and they continue to define their view of the Lord's Supper over against the medieval Catholic view. The reformers comment at length on the thorny issue of forgiveness for serious postbaptismal sin and, on the whole, adopt a pastoral approach that seeks to assure earnest Christians that the verses in question (Heb 10:26-27) do not apply to them as they struggle with daily sin, even serious sin, provided they are penitent. Rather, the verses apply to those who willfully, persistently, and maliciously reject Christ and his gospel. The reformers also urge Protestants under threat to take heart from the example of persecuted Christians in the past, who remained steadfast in faith.

10:19-25 *The Full Assurance of Faith*

Christ, Our Ferryman. Martin Luther: But the apostle challenges us with a twofold exhortation to enter this new life. For it is an arduous and exceedingly hard thing, especially for those who are inexperienced, to put everything, even life, on Christ. Therefore, he first sets forth the example of Christ, our leader, who fights in the forefront. Although under no compulsion, yet for the purpose of buoying up our confidence he crossed over first of all, and he smoothes the exceedingly rough road. Then the apostle points out that Christ not only gave an example by crossing over, but that he also holds out his hand to those who follow. Therefore, he says that we "have confidence to enter," for he himself opened this way for us and at the same time is for us the priest who sympathizes with our weaknesses and is able to help those who are tempted. For this reason, we have no excuse for delaying, since he certainly cannot do more for us than he is doing. For while others can teach and exhort us to cross over, this Christ alone is not only the companion but also the one who leads the way, not only the leader but also the helper, yes, the ferryman, as we read in Deuteronomy 32:11: "As an eagle incites its nestlings forth by hovering over its brood, so he spread his wings to receive them and bore them up on his pinions." For he who relies on Christ through faith is carried on the shoulders of Christ,† and he will cross over successfully with the bride, of whom it is written that "she comes up through the desert learning on her beloved." Lectures on Hebrews 10:19.[1]

Heaven Is Obtained Through Christ Alone. Heinrich Bullinger: This is a long transition; for only a little after these words, in the next verse the sentence is concluded. Its meaning is transparent, for Paul meant, "Therefore—since a way has been opened to the heavens through Christ, who for us was made by God a mediator, priest, and sacrifice—come, let us believe in Christ, so that through him we may have the right to enter the heavens." This is the main point of everything,† but Paul recounts and expatiates on its amazing abundance by enumerating each aspect separately. Further, when he says that we have the freedom, resources, and capacity to enter into the holy places, he is obviously looking back at the statement that we heard in chapter 9, "As long as the first tabernacle was still standing, the way was not yet open into the holy places." Therefore, he intends to set the verse before us over against that previous statement. For by the death, sacrifice, and blood of Christ that former tabernacle has been overthrown, and therefore the way to the holy places has been opened. Hence it is called "new" and "living"—"new" relative to the former way, because many had hitherto believed that a way stood open to the heavens through the sacrifices, ceremonies, and eternal rites; and "living" because we believe that now the entrance to life really has been laid open through Christ, the Son of the Living God. For in the Gospel as well the Lord said, "I am the way, the truth, and the life; no one comes to the Father except through me." But if this really is the straight, true, and certain way to the heavens, then it follows automatically that the kingdom of God cannot be obtained through monastic vows or sacrifices or any other means. For if the entrance is laid open by anything else, then clearly Christ died in vain, or he is not the only way. For the rest, the flesh of Christ is deservedly called "the curtain," for when the flesh of Christ was received into heaven, then the heavenly things became visible. Thence in the Gospel as well he said, "It is to your advantage that I go away." And Paul says, "Even though we regarded Christ according to the flesh, now we regard him thus no longer." Commentary on Hebrews 10:19-21.[2]

[1]LW 29:225-26* (WA 57:223.24-224.15); citing Heb 4:15; Heb 2:18; Song 8:5. †Luther makes use of the Christophorus legend elsewhere. See *Sermon vom Leiden und Kreuz/Sermon at Coburg on Cross and Suffering* (1530), LW 51:201-2 (WA 32:32.18-34.28).

[2]Bullinger, *In Pauli ad Hebraeos Epistolam*, 108r-v [235-36]; citing Heb 9:8; 1 Cor 1:30; Jn 14:6; 16:7; 2 Cor 5:16. †*Haec omnium summa est.* It is not entirely clear whether Bullinger is identifying this as the main point of this lengthy sentence (Heb 10:19-22) or of the entire book of Hebrews. The latter seems more likely.

Access to God Through Christ's Torn Body. Johannes Oecolampadius: To enter into the holy places is to have free access to heaven, and even to God himself. But whence comes this? From our works? Not at all, but through the blood of Jesus our Savior. "The holy of holies" signifies divinity to us, of which we are made partakers by the merit of Christ alone, because the Father loves the Son, and has given all things into his hand. He chose to give him up for us all, whereby he sufficiently made known to us his love for us, and thus he drew us to himself. And to whom better could we draw near than to him whom we can know best, who wishes us well and bestows unutterable benefits upon us? But you may ask, "By what way should we travel to know divine things?" That which Christ has inaugurated for us. Today there is another way of drawing near to God than that of old in the time of the law, when the countenance of the Lord was terrifying and they heard thunders and lightnings, so that the people of Israel were not able to bear the voice of the Lord. The law of faith and perfection (which we also discussed above, in chapter 9) had not yet been revealed while the first tabernacle was still standing; but now by the blood of Christ it has been opened. This is that sweetest way. But it is called "new," because it had been known to few, and "living," because it leads to true life, which the blood of bulls could never do.

"Through the curtain." He explains what he means by "curtain," namely, the flesh of Christ. But at the same time he hints at something higher, that the body of Christ is the veil by which, while it had not yet been torn, that is, had not yet suffered, it was not permitted to enter and go into the holy places. But once Christ had died, a way to the experience of divinity was opened, for then the Spirit revealed to the elect such mysteries, which had previously been concealed. Explanations of Hebrews 10:19-23.[3]

God Is Completely Faithful. Desiderius Erasmus: It only remains for us to persevere in that which we have once begun and, without wavering at any point, to hold fast to the hope of immortal life, which we professed at baptism. We are to rely on one thing and one thing alone, that God, who made the promise, is completely faithful and, even if he wanted to deceive, cannot. We have only one condition to fulfill, to continue in our faith. Paraphrases on the Epistle to the Hebrews 10:19-25.[4]

Confident Faith in Christ Provides True Spiritual Cleansing. Heinrich Bullinger: With these words the transition is completed; but the idiom of the discourse is entirely metaphorical. For we come to God with our soul, not our feet. But the soul must be sincere, not all counterfeited. For God hates nothing as much as hypocrisy; for, because God is true, he loves truth. He wrote "full assurance of faith" in place of assured and confident faith, by which the hearts and consciences of human beings are purified. This is not accomplished by various washings, with which the Hebrews washed themselves every day, but by faith, as Peter also proposed in Acts 15. All the same, Paul does adorn his discourse with images such that he seems to attribute purification to external things; but he actually attributes nothing to them. For he intends to penetrate past the external things to the internal realities and to speak of the one faith by means of a kind of hendiadys, as if he were discussing various kinds of washings. Nevertheless, he intends to say nothing but this: if anyone makes much of the Jewish rites of purification and absolutely refuses to leave them behind, they should understand that human hearts are purified by faith, not by these elementary principles. Therefore, if anyone has faith, that person necessarily has true purification. So let us henceforth hold on to the unwavering confession of our hope—that is, the firm and immovable confession, which does not sway from side to side—the confession of our

[3]Oecolampadius, *In Epistolam ad Hebraeos Explanationes*, 110r-v; citing 2 Pet 1:4; Jn 3:35; Rom 8:32; Ex 19:16; Deut 5:23-27; Heb 9:8; 1 Pet 2:25.

[4]CWE 44:241.

hope, I say—that is, that true religion which comes from Christ, who is our hope, the baptism of believers, and our expiation (1 Peter 3). Commentary on Hebrews 10:22-23.[5]

True Christian Baptism. Balthasar Hubmaier: In this passage of Scripture, Christian soul, ponder the beautiful and divine order, how Scripture tells all the different steps in such an orderly way. Therefore he would be a wicked person who would want to turn this order around and put the cart before the horse. O God, forgive us our blindness and our wickedness! Dear, friendly reader, this passage and John 5:24 move me to call outward baptism a public confession or witness. For I do not like to deal with new, sophisticated, and invented words. There is no need to invite strangers to the church feast; one finds friends enough.

From all these passages of Scripture it clearly follows that all those who baptize the previously instructed in the Word of God and believers baptize correctly and in the Christian way. But those who introduce additionally a different baptism without prior teaching are false and deceitful masters who rob us of the true baptism and show us a hoop before an inn in which there is no wine. He who has ears, let him hear. But him who is dissolute, may our Lord God cleanse. Amen. On the Christian Baptism of Believers, Heb 10: 22-23.[6]

The "Sprinkling" Described Is Spiritual. Balthasar Hubmaier: This Paul writes to the brethren of the New Testament who were not bound by the washings of the old law. Here one can obviously see, smell, taste, and grasp that all those who want to go to God through the blood of Christ have to go with a true heart, in a full faith, sprinkled in their hearts from an evil conscience. And this must, must, must be accompanied by the washing of the body with pure water. If you believe this, then you believe the Word of God. If you do not believe this, then tear and scratch these words out. What are they in the Book for, if they are not true? Alas, dear paedobaptist, do not tear them out. I beseech you for peace. The words of God cannot be torn apart; they remain for eternity. On the Christian Baptism of Believers.[7]

True Christian Love. Martin Luther: The church of this time has been gathered from the diverse believers of the world, and very many who are weak, impotent, imperfect, and sinful have been intermingled. . . . But human nature is constituted in such a way that it prefers to deal with those who are good and perfect to dealing with those who are imperfect and difficult—because of this sin it comes about that those who are weaker cause those who are more perfect to be haughty, to despise, to judge, etc., while, on the other hand, those who are more perfect cause those who are weaker to envy and disparage—for this reason the apostles strove with all their might to counter this evil, lest schisms and heresies arise in the church. These, of course, are prevented by mutual love. Furthermore, the love that is shown equals or betters is (as one sees everywhere) either no love at all, or it is not Christian, as Matthew 5:43-47 states. . . . This, therefore, is the Christian love that is shown to those who are contemptible and unworthy of love; this, in fact, is the kindness that is bestowed on those who are evil and ungrateful. For this is what Christ and God did for us; and we, too, are commanded to love as he did. In the same place we read: "You, therefore, must be perfect, as your Father is perfect" (Mt 5:48). Lectures on Hebrews 10:24.[8]

Hold Fast the Unity of the Church. Gasparo Contarini: The greatest duty of the Christian is to hold fast the unity of the church, not to be separated from the unity because of any temptations or vexations. Paul advises this in this

[5]Bullinger, *In Pauli ad Hebraeos Epistolam*, 108v-109r [236-37]; citing Acts 15:9; Heb 6:1; 1 Pet 3:21.
[6]CRR 5:135.
[7]CRR 5:123-24.
[8]LW 29:226-27 (WA 57:224.18-225.6).

place. SCHOLIA IN THE EPISTLES OF THE DIVINE PAUL, THE EPISTLE TO THE HEBREWS 10:25.[9]

CHRISTIANS MUST MEET REGULARLY. LEUPOLD SCHARNSCHLAGER: Because manifold deceptions are everywhere making inroads, it is necessary for the called, committed, and obligated members of Christ's body, wherever they may be in the world or in distress, insofar as it is possible, should not neglect the assembly. Wherever and however they may, according to the place and the persecutions, they should gather together for the sake of their love for Christ, be their number small or great, 2, 3, 4, 6, 10, 15, 20, more or less. Such meetings should take place with wisdom, modesty, reason, discipline, friendliness, and quiet demeanor, especially since we see the day of the Lord drawing near. CONGREGATIONAL ORDER.[10]

THE PROPER PARTS OF AN ASSEMBLY. THE ENGLISH ANNOTATIONS: That is, the public congregation of the faithful, wherein the Word of God is taught, the sacraments administered, and common prayer and thanksgiving made, unto which God has promised a blessing. ANNOTATIONS ON HEBREWS 10:25.[11]

10:26-29 *Judgment Awaits Those Who Deliberately Sin*

IF YOU BLASPHEME AND DENY CHRIST, YOU HAVE NOTHING BUT JUDGMENT. JOHANNES BUGENHAGEN: I ask you to look carefully at the wording . . . so that you may understand clearly what the author intended to say. It says, "For if we sin deliberately after receiving the knowledge of the truth, there no longer remains a sacrifice for sins." For with the ungodly you have blasphemed and denied Christ the Priest, and his sacrifice, by which he sanctifies forever, and you have done it deliberately. Therefore, you no longer have a sacrifice wherewith you may be reconciled to God, because there is no sacrifice apart from this one. But if you are in Christ, no matter how great a sinner you are, you now have a sacrifice, and you cannot be other than pleasing to God for the sake of Christ, with whom he is well-pleased, for the sake of this High Priest, who always stands for us before the Father, so that he may intercede for us. It says, "There no longer remains a sacrifice, but a fearful expectation"; because you have deliberately denied and blasphemed the Savior, you can have nothing but judgment. It also says, "A fire that will consume the adversaries," that is, the adversaries of Christ and of God. Take this description of the people of whom he speaks as referring, surely, to those who blaspheme the gospel and Christian truth, not to those sinners who are indeed in Christ, for what person is there on the earth who does not sin? Yes, and what follows is evident enough in his statement that he "has trampled underfoot the Son of God, and treated as profane the blood of the covenant," by which our High Priest has entered into the holy places, "by which formerly he had been sanctified," that is, set apart unto God, "and has outraged the Spirit of grace?" That is, he has blasphemed against the Holy Spirit, which is frightening. As for those who are deliberately bold in violation of conscience, whoever they may be, in the hope that they intend to make satisfaction through some kind of works, which is a total and utter delusion in the sight of God—they should look and beware. But since I should not overlook how easily the delicate and weak consciences of some people are injured and driven to despair, I assert that whoever returns to God from the heart has the certain testimony that never, as God preserves him, will he be liable to this sentence, even when he may seem to have fallen away. For those who actually do fall away can never recover. For they are blinded, either by open wickedness or feigned righteousness, just as we see the Jews perish. COMMENTARY ON THE PAULINE EPISTLES, HEB 6:4-6/10:26.[12]

[9]Contarini, *Opera*, 526.
[10]CRR 12:406*.
[11]Downame, ed., *Annotations*, NNN2r*; citing Mt 18:20; Ps 27:4; 122:1.
[12]Bugenhagen, *Annotationes in epistolas Pauli recognitae* (1525), 148v-149r; citing Eccles 7:20. Rom 2:12.

A Sinner Cannot Be Baptized More Than Once. Cardinal Cajetan: "For if we go on sinning deliberately after receiving the knowledge of the truth, there no longer remains a sacrifice for sins." Just as previously he said that it is impossible for those who have once been baptized "to be restored to again to repentance, as they are crucifying again" (etc.), so now he says that if we sin after receiving knowledge of the truth, there no longer remains a sacrifice for sin, because Christ cannot be crucified again. The same idea lies beneath both statements; he refers to rebaptism under the label "crucifying again" there and under the label "sacrifice for sins" here. For those who are sinning before baptism, there remains a sacrifice for sins that is transmitted in baptism; but for those who are sinning after baptism, there remains no sacrifice for sins, because it cannot be transmitted to them through baptism. Comments on Hebrews 10:26.[13]

Do Not Spurn the Plain Truth of Christ. Huldrych Zwingli: "For if we go on sinning deliberately." Both the immediately preceding statements and the thrust of the epistle make it clear that this is not said with reference to any and every kind of sin. For there is no sin, no matter what kind of deliberation or brashness were involved in its commission, that would not encounter grace and mercy in the sight of God, if only the transgressor were to repent. Therefore, this is said with reference to the sin against the Holy Spirit, which is nothing else than brazenly and abominably despising, spurning, rejecting, and opposing the truth when it is fully understood. Here Paul means sinning after the knowledge of the truth has been received, because earlier he spoke of not holding on to the confession of hope, forsaking Christ and his congregation, and not believing in Christ; for these things he says that there remains no sacrifice for sins, and no other atonement. For Christ, having been offered just once, sanctifies forever those who believe. Therefore, whoever spurns the unique offering of Christ and seeks another satisfaction and sacrifice deserves no mercy. For how could anyone obtain mercy from Christ that he does not ask of him, or not believe in? Good God, how many multitudes of people do they deceive with their papistical satisfactions? Exposition of Hebrews 10:26.[14]

Despisers of the Gospel. Desiderius Erasmus: Do you think that if someone has despised the law of the gospel he will go scot-free? The more merciful and the more beneficial it is, the more severe will be the penalties paid by the one who willfully and knowingly makes a mockery of it. Paraphrases on the Epistle to the Hebrews 10:26-27.[15]

You Shall Not Obtain Another Means to Salvation. Heinrich Bullinger: And now with these words, with which he here begins, he warns the deserters and turncoats of the church to withdraw from such treachery and to continue in faith and duty. But he derives his argument from the penalties and enlarges on them in every way. But in the meantime, we must understand that the people who "sin deliberately" are not those who sin as a result of any weakness, or who succumb to the desires of the flesh; rather, they are those who suppress the truth with a lie with deliberate malice. For although they know very well that there can be no other sacrifice for sins in the whole world other than the single sacrifice of Christ, they not only do not entrust themselves to that single sacrifice but also spurn it all the more and thus continue to live irreverently in contempt of God. For there is no other sacrifice for sin apart from this one. But they have despised this single sacrifice; they will certainly not obtain another. For Peter, when the Lord asked him whether he wished to go away with the others, replied, "Lord, to whom shall we go? You have the words of eternal life, and we have

[13]Cajetan, *In Epistolam ad Hebraeos Commentarii*, 167r; citing Heb 6:4-6.

[14]Zwingli, *In Epistolam Beati Pauli ad Hebraeos Expositio*, 580; citing Heb 2:11; 7:25; 10:10, 14.

[15]CWE 44:242.

believed and have come to know that you are the Christ, the Son of the Living God." Therefore, for such despisers, there remains nothing else than the fearful expectation of judgment, that is, of vengeance and condemnation, which is fire and furious and unceasing wrath on the irreverent. This is treated in the prophets and, by Paul, in 2 Thessalonians 1. Commentary on Hebrews 10:26-27.[16]

Vengeance for the Fallen, Grace for the Penitent. John Calvin: He shows how severe a vengeance of God awaits all those who fall away from the grace of Christ; for being without that one true salvation, they are now as it were given up to an inevitable destruction. With this testimony Novatus† and his sect formerly armed themselves, in order to take away the hope of pardon from all indiscriminately who had fallen after baptism. They who were not able to refute his calumny chose rather to deny the authority of this epistle than to subscribe to so great an absurdity. But the true meaning of the passage, unaided by any help from any other part, is quite sufficient of itself to expose the effrontery of Novatus.

Those who sin, mentioned by the apostle, are not those who offend in any way, but those who forsake the church, and wholly alienate themselves from Christ. For he speaks not here of this or of that sin, but he condemns by name those who willfully renounced fellowship with the church. . . . But as to sinners who fall in any other way, Christ offers himself daily to them, so that they are to seek no other sacrifice for expiating their sins. He denies, then, that any sacrifice remains for them who renounce the death of Christ, which is not done by any offense except by a total renunciation of the faith. Commentaries on the Epistle of Paul the Apostle to the Hebrews 10:26.[17]

[16]Bullinger, *In Pauli ad Hebraeos Epistolam*, 110r [239]; citing Jn 6:68-69; Mt 16:16; 2 Thess 1:6-9.

[17]CTS 40:243-44*. †Novatus, or Novatian, was a Roman presbyter who joined a rigorist party that denied concessions to those who had lapsed during the Decian persecution (AD 249–250). He was consecrated rival bishop of Rome and suffered martyrdom in 257–258. Novatianist views were eventually deemed heretical.

Outside the Church There Is No Sacrifice for Sin. Niels Hemmingsen: The other reason why faith must hold fast to the mediator, and why one must not separate from the church, is that outside the church there is no sacrifice for sins, but only the wrath of God can be expected toward the insolent and the deserters of the gospel. For here the apostle is not speaking about just any kind of lapse or about voluntary sin, but only about those who, having known this Priest, repudiate Christ and exclude themselves from the church and from the priesthood of Christ, renouncing all the benefits of Christ. Here the Donatists† and Novatianists err dangerously, who understand this place to refer to any kind of sin, against the mind of the apostle, and against infinite testimonies and examples of Scripture. And, that I may touch on just one, the apostle Paul by no means would have received the incestuous person into the church if this place is to be understood concerning just any kind of lapse. Therefore, according to the context of the apostle, this place should be applied to a certain species of lapse, and to the renunciation of the recognized truth, by which many envious Hebrews at that time died. For they wanted to renounce Christ rather than to endure the Gentiles as sharers in the gospel. But those who remain in the church, although they often fall, whether knowingly or unknowingly, nevertheless, when they repent, they are most certainly received in grace. For this decree of God stands immoveable: "I do not wish the death of the sinner, but that he might turn and live," and Christ commands that the saints should pray daily for the remission of sins, that when they sin, they sprinkle their consciences perpetually with the blood of the efficacious victim Jesus Christ. For that one victim is valid perpetually for expiating the sins of all people who are fleeing to grace, that is, for the converting of them to God through faith in Jesus Christ. For grace abounds over sin. This admonition of the apostle produces terror in the impious who defect impiously from the church, and it admonishes the pious, so that they might live in the fear of God, lest having been assailed by their own numerous lapses they open themselves to defection from the church. Commentary on the Apostolic Epistle to the Hebrews 10:26.[18]

Blasphemers Must Be Rooted Out from the Congregation. Melchior Hoffman: Of all such intentional sins [e.g., blasphemy] against the high Holy Spirit of God, the Lord Jesus Christ says that neither now nor in the next world nor in all eternity can they ever attain forgiveness. Saint Paul also says the same in Hebrews, namely, that no more sacrifice remains over for such sins but rather fearful revenge and ordeal of fiery indignation. In this manner God also speaks through Moses that one shall, without any mercy, root out from the congregation all such willful sinners against the Spirit of God and shall accept for them no further sacrifices, for they will forever have no forgiveness. The Ordinance of God, Heb 10:26-27.[19]

No Sacrifice for Presumptuous Sins. William Jones: He does not simply say, "if we sin," for then it would go badly for all of us, because "we all stumble in many ways." Neither does he say, "if we sin contrary to our knowledge," or "if we sin because of weakness and infirmity," as the dearest children of God may do. David sinned against his knowledge when he committed adultery and murder. So did Peter, when he denied Christ. But, "If we do on sinning deliberately," yielding ourselves voluntarily to Satan, maliciously opposing ourselves to Christ and his gospel, and rending ourselves from the society of his church and members, suffocating and choking the knowledge of the Lord Jesus revealed to us. . . . There is a sacrifice for idolatry, for common swearing, for profanity, for theft, treason, adultery, murder; these are horrible sins, and the Lord preserve us from them, yet these may be washed away in the blood of Christ, sacrificed on the cross for us. But there is no sacrifice for these sinners. "Lord keep me," says David, "from presumptuous sins." But much more let us pray, "Lord keep us from this sin of sins, the sin against the Holy Spirit," and undoubtedly he will keep all those who belong to him from it, for "those who are born of God cannot sin unto death." A Commentary upon the Epistles of St. Paul, Heb 10:26-27.[20]

The Apostle Does Not Deny Postconversion Repentance. Johannes Oecolampadius: Many people have taken so much offense at this statement by the apostle that they therefore hold the entire epistle suspect, supposing that it denies repentance to those who have once come to know Christ and the truth if they fall into sin. But this is not at all what the apostle had in mind, if only we examine it honestly. But this, in brief, is what he means to say: henceforth, Christ will not come again to save, but to judge. By these words he spurs into action the reluctant and the idle. But he does not at all say, "No opportunity for repentance is left once the truth is known," but, "No other sacrifice for sins is left"; take note of this! For no one else after Christ may be expected as redeemer and savior. And thus this statement superbly agrees with the foregoing context. Those who sinned under Moses were expecting Christ, the Savior who would come in humility. We, after he has already come, expect nothing of the kind, but a strict Judge. Therefore, we must be mindful of our salvation and serve him faithfully, as servants expecting their master to return from the wedding feast. But we will make it evident by an example that he does not deny repentance. A master gave a talent to his servant, commanding him to invest it faithfully, for when he returned he would render an account. But he negligently performed his master's command, and

[18]Hemmingsen, *Commentarius in epistolam apostolicam ad Hebraeos*, 886; citing 1 Cor 5:1-5; Ezek 18:23; Mt 6:12; Lk 11:4; Rom 5:20. †Donatus (died c. 355) was the leader of a schismatic Christian group that denied the sacramental power and authority of Catholic church leaders such as Felix of Aptunga, who had betrayed the faith during persecution, but later returned to his ecclesiastical office. The Donatists were opposed in their views by Augustine, who appealed to the need for church unity and pointed out the sinfulness of all Christians and the need for God's grace.
[19]LCC 25:199*; citing Mk 3:29; Num 25:8.

[20]Jones, *A Commentary upon the Epistles of St Paul*, 416, 419*; citing Jas 3:2; Ps 51:1-19; Lk 22:54-62; Ps 19:13; 1 Jn 3:9.

thus he heard, "If you persist in being negligent, surely the master will not come to entrust another talent, but to exact punishment as a judge." By these words do I deny the use of the talent, so that he could not deposit it to earn interest, because I said that it was to be expected that his master would be exacting? Not at all! Rather, I have spurred him on to attention and a worthy use of the talent. You may perceive the same thing in this passage. EXPLANATIONS OF HEBREWS 10:26-27.[21]

CARING FOR DISTRESSED CHRISTIAN SOULS. LUCAS OSIANDER: The apostle does not here address sins that are committed against conscience, which are perpetrated by the elect. For he knew that David had committed the sin of adultery; he also knew that he had committed the sin of murder—David polluted Bathsheba by adultery and killed her innocent husband by the sword of the Ammonites. Nonetheless, when he was truly penitent, he pursued mercy. Peter denied Christ and nevertheless was received in grace. Therefore the apostle is addressing in this place not all lapses against conscience, nor the denial of the truth by the simple; he is addressing the kind of apostasy that is voluntary and that makes from confessors of the gospel enemies and blasphemers against the true religion. . . . These things are not being said so that we may coddle sins that people commit against conscience, but so that we may cure the perturbations of Christians, who falsely imagine to themselves that they have committed the irredeemable sin against the Holy Spirit, and the their souls are wasting away in distress, while they are actually very far from such wickedness. EPISTLE TO THE HEBREWS 10:26-27.[22]

10:30-31 *Judgment Is a Fearful Thing*

PUBLIC AND PRIVATE VENGEANCE. PHILIPP MELANCHTHON: Vengeance is twofold. One kind has been ordained, that is, public vengeance, which takes place through the ruler according to a definite order, under certain laws. Neither the gospel nor the law of God forbids this kind of vengeance; indeed, it has already been said repeatedly that it has been divinely instituted and approved by God and is supported by him. This vengeance is part of the civil order or a part of the function of the rulers, as Paul so correctly calls the ruler the avenger. Just as there is no doubt that in the gospel the office of ruler is approved, so also it is clear that this vengeance which he carries out according to the law is likewise approved. . . . God as the righteous judge is angry with sin and he punished either without human help, as when he destroyed Sodom and the Egyptians in the Red Sea, or he punishes the guilty according to the regular system of punishments that he has given to rulers, as when robbers feel the full force of the severity of civil rulers, or when Cyrus punishes the lustfulness of the Ionians, or Augustus punishes Anthony, who was corrupted by all kinds of lusts and who started a civil war without just cause. . . .

The second kind of vengeance is one that deviates from the divine order, which for the sake of explanation I call private revenge. This is when, in the heat of anger or hatred in our fury, we take up arms without the directives of the laws and serve our own hurt feelings, refusing to endure in other people what God has ordained we should, as when Joab killed Abner in his own personal hatred of him. LOCI PRAECIPUI THEOLOGICI.[23]

NO DELIVERANCE AFTER THE FINAL SENTENCE. JOHANNES OECOLAMPADIUS: "It is a fearful thing to fall . . . ," because there is no one who can deliver out of his hand. Once sentence has been passed, no other redemption remains. With human judges, someone may perhaps be able to bring something about through an influential connection, entreaties, bribes, or some other means, but with God, the incorruptible and perfectly impartial judge, it is very different. And if the righteous are terrified when they consider this judgment, what shall we

[21]Oecolampadius, *In Epistolam ad Hebraeos Explanationes*, 113r-v; citing Lk 12:36.

[22]Osiander, *Epistola ad Hebraeos*, 70; citing 2 Sam 11:1–12:23; Ps 51:1-19; Lk 22:54-62.

[23]Melanchthon, *Loci Praecipui Theologici*, 418-19*.

say concerning the ungodly? This is the first topic of the exhortation. You may ask here how the apostle can say, "It is a fearful thing to fall into the hands of the living God," when David says, "It is better to fall into the hands of the Lord, for his mercy is great, than into the hands of humans, since they do not know how to have mercy" (2 Samuel 24†)? I reply that the apostle is considering the life to come, in which, as the sentence has already been passed, there is no forgiveness of sins; David, however, considers the present life, in which forgiveness comes readily to everyone who repents from the heart, although the Lord may punish them in the meantime. But this is a more effective remedy for sins than to assess penalties for trespasses. Explanations of Hebrews 10:30-31.[24]

10:32-39 *Do Not Shrink Back*

On Divine Enlightenment, Endurance, and Not Shrinking Back. Johann Spangenberg: What is the enlightenment from God? It is nothing other than that the person, when they accept God's Word in faith, through which full understanding comes to them, knows what they have in God and what they should expect and receive from him. It is where the Holy Spirit through his divine working takes away all human darkness, ignites faith, and illumines the heart, so that we come to know God the Father and his Son Jesus Christ, how he is and how he is minded toward us. Such knowledge is truly called eternal life (John 17).

Where does one receive such enlightenment? Through faith, through the frequent hearing of the divine Word in many ways, and through prayer. . . .

Who is the light that enlightens us? It is alone Jesus Christ, God's only Son, who himself says so in John 8. . . .

What is endurance? Endurance is a very glorious gift of God, namely, that one in the perseverance of faith and in true hope endures the adversities of this world and all trials, whether spiritual or bodily, and thus awaits the gracious redemption of God, and is patiently deprived of those things they cannot have. . . .

What is the source of such shrinking back? It comes from unbelief and impatience. One believes that that one cannot trust our Lord God in the time of need. One seeks means and ways to help oneself and creates one's own counsel and protection. When a situation entails suffering, as when one expects the disfavor of great lords or the loss of goods and other dangers, one behaves rashly and gives in some here and yields some there, so that one gives unbelief free rein. The clever reason—"Frau Hulda"†—and worldly wisdom are also present—she is certainly a well-trained, agile master. Others do not want to wait a while with God the Lord and help bear the cross. They murmur and become unwilling and in the end do whatever one desires from them so that they may be free of the cross. Epistle for the Feast of All Martyrs.[25]

Long-Suffering Believers Called to Endure. Heinrich Bullinger: Up to this point, the author has threatened the treacherous despisers with penalties and punishments, but he has also called to faith those who were pondering, as they stood at the crossroads, whether to join the camp of Christ or of Moses, that is, whether to accept Christ as the single sacrifice or to continue to cling to the Levitical sacrifices. But now with a direct address he turns to the believers who had devoted themselves entirely to Christ the Lord, and for a long interval he leaves behind all the others to focus on the events that took place when they were being immensely tormented by the ungodly. He exhorts these believers to continue in the faith with patience. And so he exhorts them on the basis of past events, as Virgil's Aeneas encouraged his suffering companions,

[24]Oecolampadius, *In Epistolam ad Hebraeos Explanationes*, 116v-117r; citing Deut 32:39; Is 43:13; 1 Pet 4:18; 2 Sam 24:14. †In keeping with the Latin identification of Samuel–Kings as 1–4 Kings, Oecolampadius cites this as 2 *Reg.* 28 (2 Sam 24).

[25]Spangenberg, *Postilla Teütsch*, 6:95v-96r, 96v, 97v, 103r; citing Jn 17:3; Jn 8:12. †Frau Hulda was a synonym for natural reason as opposed to divine revelation in the Reformation period.

O comrades, since we indeed have all known
hard trials before this—
Ye men trained by worse pains, even these
God will bring to a swift end.†

Thus Paul, likewise, declares that the little difficulty that now remains should be swallowed as well, since thus far they had overcome so many and such great tests. He records the first category of these, and (with Hebraic verbosity) says, "You sustained a hard struggle of sufferings," which is to say, "You endured many hardships." But then he describes these hardships as divided, since indeed (as he says), "At times you endured some painful things in your own persons; namely, you were buried in reproaches and insults and afflicted with various troubles, so that you became a public spectacle to all." They were made a spectacle when they were led out into the theater and the forum as criminals to be struck on the head; thus they were made the laughingstock and butt of the mob. But, "At other times you were afflicted by perceiving the trouble of others. For you were partners with those who are afflicted for the sake of Christ." But it is frequently the case that the godly suffer more grievously from perceiving the trouble of others than from sorrow at their own personal misfortunes. Commentary on Hebrews 10:32-33.[26]

Persecuted Believers Should Heed These Words. Heinrich Bullinger: "And you joyfully accepted the plundering of your property, since you knew that in heaven you had a better possession and an abiding one." By these words he explains the first part [of verse 33], from which we hear that the Hebrews experienced not only insults but also oppressive acts; for now he explains what those acts were, namely, the "plundering of their property." To this, for their consolation, he also adds, "Since you knew that you had a better and more lasting treasure in the heavenlies." Christ also speaks of this in Matthew 6. Therefore, a person suffers no injury who loses the temporal to gain the eternal. As an illustration of most of these things, they experienced the same things that this same apostle wrote regarding this same persecution to the Thessalonians in these words: "You, brothers, became imitators of the churches of God in Christ Jesus that are in Judea. For you suffered the same things from your own compatriots as they did from the Jews, who, as they killed both the Lord Jesus and their own prophets, so they also persecuted us, and displease God and oppose all humanity" (1 Thessalonians 2). I most zealously commend all these things to you, beloved, who throughout Germany and France have been oppressed by tyranny, heaped with abuse, and finally banished from your ancestral homes, because you suffer so much accusation because you rely on the unique priesthood and sacrifice of Christ and deny the Mass, idols, the worship of the saints, and papistical religion. To you I say that I want these Pauline declarations to be highly commended. To you I repeat the same thing that Paul said to his Hebrew readers, "Therefore do not throw away your confidence, which has a great reward." For by these words the message is completed, and the purpose of his discussion of affliction is explained, namely, that they should stand firm in faith and by faith continue to break down all remaining opposition, seeing as they have plunged into such a host of evils. But they must continue in *parrhēsia*, that is, freedom in believing, speaking, and acting. For Christian faith is a certain kind of *parrhēsia* that is completely happy, active, and free. He adds the inducement, "For this has a great reward." For in Matthew 5 Christ himself says, "Blessed are you when all people persecute you and say all kinds of evil against you falsely on my account. Rejoice and be glad, for great is your reward in heaven." And in Mark 8, "Whoever loses his life for my sake and the gospel's will save it." You will find similar statements in Mark 10 and John 12 and 16. Commentary on Hebrews 10:34-35.[27]

[26]Bullinger, *In Pauli ad Hebraeos Epistolam*, 111v-112r. †Homer, *Aeneid* 1.198-99 (LCL 63:274).

[27]Bullinger, *In Pauli ad Hebraeos Epistolam*, 112r-113r; citing 1 Jn 5:4; Mt 6:19-21; 1 Thess 2:14-15; Mt 5:11-12; Mk 8:35; Mk 10:29-31; Jn 12:25-26; Jn 16:20-22, 33.

We Partake of Christ by Faith, Not by the External Symbol of the Bread. Huldrych Zwingli: "But the righteous one shall live by faith." After engaging in lengthy discussion of the priesthood of Christ, in which he demonstrated that he is the complete and finished sacrifice, now he shows how we may become partakers of the merit and offering of Christ by the covenant or mediator. He does this by means of the oracle of the prophet Habakkuk, in which he declares that the righteous shall live by faith. This passage stands in opposition to those who offer the essential flesh of Christ under the bread and proclaim that it is eaten for the forgiveness of sins, and who, no less than the Jews, attribute to the external symbols the communication of grace. Exposition of Hebrews 10:38.[28]

[28]Zwingli, *In Epistolam Beati Pauli ad Hebraeos Expositio*, 580.

11:1-40 Faith Seeking the Promised Homeland

Now faith is the assurance of things hoped for, the conviction of things not seen. [2]For by it the people of old received their commendation. [3]By faith we understand that the universe was created by the word of God, so that what is seen was not made out of things that are visible.

[4]By faith Abel offered to God a more acceptable sacrifice than Cain, through which he was commended as righteous, God commending him by accepting his gifts. And through his faith, though he died, he still speaks. [5]By faith Enoch was taken up so that he should not see death, and he was not found, because God had taken him. Now before he was taken he was commended as having pleased God. [6]And without faith it is impossible to please him, for whoever would draw near to God must believe that he exists and that he rewards those who seek him. [7]By faith Noah, being warned by God concerning events as yet unseen, in reverent fear constructed an ark for the saving of his household. By this he condemned the world and became an heir of the righteousness that comes by faith.

[8]By faith Abraham obeyed when he was called to go out to a place that he was to receive as an inheritance. And he went out, not knowing where he was going. [9]By faith he went to live in the land of promise, as in a foreign land, living in tents with Isaac and Jacob, heirs with him of the same promise. [10]For he was looking forward to the city that has foundations, whose designer and builder is God. [11]By faith Sarah herself received power to conceive, even when she was past the age, since she considered him faithful who had promised. [12]Therefore from one man, and him as good as dead, were born descendants as many as the stars of heaven and as many as the innumerable grains of sand by the seashore.

[13]These all died in faith, not having received the things promised, but having seen them and greeted them from afar, and having acknowledged that they were strangers and exiles on the earth. [14]For people who speak thus make it clear that they are seeking a homeland. [15]If they had been thinking of that land from which they had gone out, they would have had opportunity to return. [16]But as it is, they desire a better country, that is, a heavenly one. Therefore God is not ashamed to be called their God, for he has prepared for them a city.

[17]By faith Abraham, when he was tested, offered up Isaac, and he who had received the promises was in the act of offering up his only son, [18]of whom it was said, "Through Isaac shall your offspring be named." [19]He considered that God was able even to raise him from the dead, from which, figuratively speaking, he did receive him back. [20]By faith Isaac invoked future blessings on Jacob and Esau. [21]By faith Jacob, when dying, blessed each of the sons of Joseph, bowing in worship over the head of his staff. [22]By faith Joseph, at the end of his life, made mention of the exodus of the Israelites and gave directions concerning his bones.

[23]By faith Moses, when he was born, was hidden for three months by his parents, because they saw that the child was beautiful, and they were not afraid of the king's edict. [24]By faith Moses, when he was grown up, refused to be called the son of Pharaoh's daughter, [25]choosing rather to be mistreated with the people of God than to enjoy the fleeting pleasures of sin. [26]He considered the reproach of Christ greater wealth than the treasures of Egypt, for he was looking to the reward. [27]By faith he left Egypt, not being afraid of the anger of the king, for he endured as seeing him who is invisible. [28]By faith he kept the Passover and sprinkled the blood, so that the Destroyer of the firstborn might not touch them.

[29]By faith the people crossed the Red Sea as on dry land, but the Egyptians, when they attempted to do the same, were drowned. [30]By faith the walls of Jericho fell down after they had been encircled for seven days. [31]By faith Rahab the prostitute did not perish with those who were disobedient, because she had given a friendly welcome to the spies.

[32]*And what more shall I say? For time would fail me to tell of Gideon, Barak, Samson, Jephthah, of David and Samuel and the prophets—* [33]*who through faith conquered kingdoms, enforced justice, obtained promises, stopped the mouths of lions,* [34]*quenched the power of fire, escaped the edge of the sword, were made strong out of weakness, became mighty in war, put foreign armies to flight.* [35]*Women received back their dead by resurrection. Some were tortured, refusing to accept release, so that they might rise again to a better life.* [36]*Others suffered mocking and flogging, and even chains and imprisonment.* [37]*They were stoned, they were sawn in two,*[a] *they were killed with the sword. They went about in skins of sheep and goats, destitute, afflicted, mistreated—* [38]*of whom the world was not worthy—wandering about in deserts and mountains, and in dens and caves of the earth.*

[39]*And all these, though commended through their faith, did not receive what was promised,* [40]*since God had provided something better for us, that apart from us they should not be made perfect.*

a Some manuscripts add *they were tempted*

OVERVIEW: Owing to the centrality of faith, especially justification by faith, in most forms of Protestant Christianity, the reformers have a great deal to say about the treatment of faith in this chapter. They begin by entertaining different definitions of faith, which largely turn on differing interpretations of the word *hypostasis*, or "substance" or "conviction." Many conclude that faith makes future realities present in the heart and mind of the believer by trusting in the faithfulness of God, who promises such realities to those who believe. The reformers also treat faith as a kind of wisdom that defies the learning and wisdom of this world. Faith is an inward matter—it is of the heart—and it is essential for true religion. In this section the reformers also note that faith requires one to be a sojourner in this world, headed for another heavenly country; additionally, they assert that faith is a virtue or a divine gift that women can possess in equal measure to men.

BY FAITH WE ACQUIRE LIFE. JACQUES LEFÈVRE D'ÉTAPLES: We live in God by faith and we acquire life; but through unbelief we die to God and we lose life. Therefore the divine apostle here lifts up faith for praise, first defining faith in a certain manner. EPISTLE TO THE HEBREWS 11.[1]

FAITH AND DOUBT CANNOT COEXIST. ERASMUS SARCERIUS: In this description the first thing to see is that faith cannot coexist with doubt, and that it has to do with things that are future and that which one with one's reason and human wisdom cannot grasp. SUMMARIES AND BRIEF CONTENT, HEBREWS 11.[2]

11:1-3 *Faith Is Assurance and Conviction*

FAITH AS "SUBSTANCE" IS FIRM AND CONFIDENT KNOWLEDGE. HEINRICH BULLINGER: It says, "Faith is the substance of things hoped for." What could be more briefly stated than this? What could be more penetrating and precise? For it is the essential definition, consisting (if anyone should happen to want it) of the general category and the distinguishing characteristic. For "substance" is the general category, "things hoped for" is the distinguishing characteristic. But that which follows immediately, "the demonstration of things not seen," is added by way of explanation, namely, that "substance" means "demonstration," and "things hoped for" are "unseen things." Regarding these things, we recommend that the reader consider them one by one. It says, "Faith is the *hypostasis*," that is, the substance. For *hypostasis* is reality, certitude, and that on which we safely rest and by

[1]Lefèvre d'Étaples, *Epistola ad Hebraeos*, 253r.

[2]Sarcerius, *Summarien vnd kurtzer Jnhalt*, 4:JJ2v.

which we are unfailingly supported. There are those who explain it as "expectation." Certainly, we Swiss would say, "Faith is a sure, certain, constant, and real trust." For now by way of explanation there follows, "Faith is the demonstration," for *elenchos* is "demonstration." This is not the sort of demonstration that Fabius defined, "Demonstration is the thing that is adduced to prove something else."† Rather, demonstration is a clear indication, proof, and certain knowledge so that we no longer have any doubts of the nature of what we have come to know, inasmuch as we have been so convinced by truth itself that nothing remains to hold us back, "a real knowledge and a thorough grasp" [Swiss German]. For *elenchein* is to convict, and thus to bring a certain case into the open, so that nothing remains for the accused that will provide them with any defense. For thus Christ himself used this word, when he said of the Holy Spirit in the Gospel, *elenxei ton kosmon*, which the Latin version renders, "He will demonstrate to the world"; that is, he will bring it out into the light and win his case against it. And in John 8 Christ says concerning himself, *tis ex hymōn elenchei me peri hamartias*, "Which one of you convicts me of sin or error?" And Paul in Titus 1 says, "An overseer must be educated so as to be able *tous antilegontas elenchein*," that is, "to convict those who contradict." Therefore the translator of Chrysostom very accurately rendered as "conviction" what we have as "demonstration." And Chrysostom himself aptly says, "O what a marvelous word he uses when he says, 'The conviction of things not seen.' For conviction inheres in things that are very plain. Therefore, faith is seeing things that are not apparent; it brings other things to the same certainty that is produced by things which appear openly."‡ So faith is not some common kind of knowledge, whereby we give credence to explanation and argumentation, and thus believe. Rather, it is a kind of substantive confidence and knowledge, that is, knowledge that is firm, sure, convinced, and undoubting, on which we rest and are safely supported, and which gives life and salvation. But we exclude from these conditions all credulity and mere opinion, so that here there may be nothing except what is most constant, most certain, and divine, by the power of which we will live and be preserved. Commentary on Hebrews 11:1.[3]

Faith Convinces and Sustains Us. Cardinal Cajetan: "The substance of things hoped for, the demonstration of things not seen." That is, faith is the act of sustaining those things that are hoped for. For *hypostasis* means "that which sustains." Nor does this statement lack evidence, because everything we hope for in the next life is sustained in us by faith. The statement about "the demonstration of things not seen" shows that faith has a broader meaning as "demonstration" than as "substance." For the category of "things not seen" includes both things that are hoped for and things that are not hoped for. For no one hopes for the punishments of hell and eternal torments, and they are nevertheless numbered among those things that are not seen in the present state. Thus, insofar as faith is our act of sustaining, it is directed to things for which we hope; but insofar as it is a demonstration (that is, a kind of argument), it does not provide evidence as a conclusive argument does, but it is defined by the things that are not seen as long as they are believed, as long as faith is directed to them. Comments on Hebrews 11:1.[4]

Faith Is Given by and Directed to God Alone. Heinrich Bullinger: It follows that this is the true meaning of this definition: faith is the most constant mental certainty, which rests on those things to which all our hope is directed, namely, the most certain knowledge of unseen and eternal things, that is, the expectation of salvation and the recognition of our truly blessed God and Savior, who is the inexhaustible fountain of all good. For such faith is not from flesh and

[3]Bullinger, *In Pauli ad Hebraeos Epistolam*, 114v-115v; citing Jn 16:8; 8:46; Tit 1:9. †Quintilian, *Institutio Oratoria* 5.14.1 (LCL 500). ‡Chrysostom, "Homily 21," in *Homilae XXXIV in epistolam ad Hebraeos* (PG 63:151; NPNF 462-63). The Latin translation to which Bullinger refers is different in several respects from that of PG.
[4]Cajetan, *In Epistolam ad Hebraeos Commentarii*, 168r.

blood, but from God alone, who through his Holy Spirit and the Word of the divine Scripture transforms and illuminates our minds. As a result of having been transformed by such a divine metamorphosis we are entirely different people, we depend entirely now on this one God, we seek everything from this one place, we revere this one person, and we despise everything else in comparison with him. In short, faith works in such a way that way we may structure all that we are in accordance with the will of a God who is so holy, righteous, and good, and may not fall away from him in any way. For Paul says, "In all things we overcome through him who loved us. For I am convinced that neither death nor life, nor principalities nor powers, nor things present nor things to come, nor anything else in all creation will be able to separate us from the love of God which is in Christ Jesus our Lord." Therefore this is true faith in God exercised by holy people, of which he is now about to produce many examples. But he prefaces these examples with some further remarks. Commentary on Hebrews 11:1.[5]

Faith Provides Its Own Evidence. Samuel Bird: Faith also in respect of the certainty of it is called an evidence, or a demonstration, a lively representing of a thing before our eyes; yet, because it is not present but to come, therefore is it called the evidence of things that are not seen. The joy that a Christian has in looking for it is such as is the joy of the one who has a thing in possession; yet faith is called the evidence of things that are not seen. "Evidence" and "not seen" seems to be contrary, yet these words notably describe the nature of faith. As for example we die, yet faith notably sets before our eyes eternal life; the contemptible worms feed on our bodies, yet we look for a glorious resurrection. Sin dwells in us, yet we doubt not but for Christ's sake we will be accounted as just; we are in many miseries, yet we look for unspeakable happiness: not but that faith has to do in stirring against forces, as the examples in this chapter testify, but because the thing that faith does rise up until the end is the evidence that is here spoken of; therefore, it is so called. The Lectures on the Eleventh Chapter of Hebrews.[6]

An Incomplete Definition of Faith. John Calvin: Whoever made this the beginning of the eleventh chapter has unwisely disjointed the context, for the object of the apostle was to prove what he had already said—that there is need of patience. He had quoted the testimony of Habakkuk, who says that the just lives by faith; he now shows what remained to be proved—that faith can be no more separated from patience than from itself. The order then of what he says is this: "We shall not reach the goal of salvation unless we have patience, for the prophet declares that the just lives by faith; but faith directs us to things far off that we do not as yet enjoy; it then necessarily includes patience." . . . It is hence also evident that they are greatly mistaken who think that an exact definition of faith is given here; for the apostle does not speak here of the whole of what faith is, but selects that part of it which was suitable to his purpose, that it always has patience connected with it. Commentaries on the Epistle of Paul the Apostle to the Hebrews 11:1.[7]

Faith Cannot Be Separated from Patience. Niels Hemmingsen: It is the nature of faith to demonstrate the necessity of patience. Faith is necessary for all Christians. Faith awaits things hoped for patiently and persuades itself with certainty of that which will happen but does not yet appear. Therefore, patience cannot be separated from faith. And thus the devout ought to await the good promises patiently. Commentary on the Apostolic Epistle to the Hebrews 11:1.[8]

[5]Bullinger, *In Pauli ad Hebraeos Epistolam*, 117r-v [253-54]; citing Mt 16:17; Rom 8:37-39.

[6]Bird, *Lectures on Hebrews 11*, 4-5*.

[7]CTS 40:260-61*; citing Hab 2:4.

[8]Hemmingsen, *Commentarius in epistolam apostolicam ad Hebraeos*, 890.

THE EAGLE EYE OF FAITH. WILLIAM JONES: Faith is an excellent eye. The eye of the eagle is very sharp and piercing: she [i.e., the eye] can see from heaven to earth, she can espy her prey from far off: she and her bird can look on the sun, but the eye of faith is far more piercing that sees Christ, the Sun of righteousness; and by it we look into the sanctuary of heaven and behold what is there. A COMMENTARY UPON THE EPISTLES OF ST. PAUL, HEB 11:1.[9]

FAITH AS CLINGING TO THE WORD. MARTIN LUTHER: In the third place, let us follow the very common use of this noun "substance," which in the Scriptures nearly always means "possession," namely, property, as in the preceding chapter (10:34).... First John 3:17 says: "He who has this world's substance." With this word he—in agreement, as it were, with this passage—certainly distinguishes the "substance of this world" from the substance that is not of this world but of the other world. Therefore since faith is nothing else than a clinging to the Word of God, as is stated in Romans 1:17, it follows that the possession of the Word of God, that is, of the everlasting goods, is at the same time also the taking away (at least so far as affection and clinging are concerned) of all present goods.... Therefore, the apostle, as a wise and faithful agent of his Lord, properly calls the Hebrews, who founded their substance on this world, back to "a better substance, which is the gaining of the soul" (cf. Heb 10:34, 39), yes, of all goods, in order that in this way he may divest them of their affection for temporal things and transfer them to heavenly things. LECTURES ON HEBREWS 11:1.[10]

THE THINGS WE HOPE FOR. JOHANNES OECOLAMPADIUS: Here the apostle defines faith so that no one may suppose that he attributes too much to faith in the preceding passage. He says, "Faith is the *hypostasis* of things hoped for," that is, the substance, basis, prop, or foundation on which things hoped for rest. But things that are hoped for are the forgiveness of sins, rebirth to a new a life, and whatever falls into the category of heavenly benefits. Such things dwell after a fashion in the human soul, as in their own dwelling, and stand firm by the Spirit of God, and are a sort of taste and experience of those things that are hoped for and, though they are not seen, are still held to be completely certain. *Elenchos* means argument, evidence, and demonstration; it amounts to the same statement as the preceding. EXPLANATIONS OF HEBREWS 11:1.[11]

FAITH IS CERTAIN OF WHAT IT DOES NOT YET SEE. LUCAS OSIANDER: Faith is a most certain trust that we are going to obtain the good heavenly promises that we are awaiting in hope. Indeed, faith even extends to the corporeal benefits that have been promised by God. Faith stands with certainty, even concerning those things that are not yet appearing, as if it already had them in hand. (Therefore that saying of the comedy has no place among Christians: "My hands are eyewitnesses, they believe what they see.")† Christ says, "Blessed are those who believe and are not seeing" (John 20). Certainly also the statement of the priests who command us to doubt whether we are in grace before God and whether we are going to persevere in it and obtain eternal salvation must be rejected. For the nearer one comes to doubt, the more one departs from faith. EPISTLE TO THE HEBREWS 11:1.[12]

THE PRACTICE OF FAITH. WILLIAM PERKINS: Concerning faith, two points are necessary to be known by every Christian: the doctrine and the practice of it. The whole doctrine of faith (being grounded and gathered out of the Word of God) is comprised in the creed, commonly called the Apostles' Creed, which has already been expounded. It follows next after doctrine to lay down also the practice of faith, for which purpose we have chosen this eleventh chapter of the epistle to the Hebrews

[9]Jones, *A Commentary upon the Epistles of St Paul*, 437*.
[10]LW 29:230-31 (WA 57:228.11-229.4).

[11]Oecolampadius, *In Epistolam ad Hebraeos Explanationes*, 122r.
[12]Osiander, *Epistola ad Hebraeos*, 74; citing Jn 20:29. †Plauto, *Asinaria*, line 201.

as being a portion of Scripture wherein the said practice is most excellently and at large set down.

This chapter depends on the former in this way: we may read in the former chapter that many Jews having received the faith, and given their names to Christ, did afterward fall away; therefore, toward the end of the chapter there is added a notable exhortation tending to persuade the Hebrews to persevere in faith to the end, as also to suffer patiently whatever shall befall them in the profession of it. . . .

Now, in this chapter he continues the same exhortation, and the whole chapter (as I take it) is nothing else in substance but one reason to urge the audience to perseverance in faith; and the reason is drawn from the excellency of faith, for this chapter sets down in diverse ways what an excellent gift of God faith is. [The author's] whole purpose therefore is clearly nothing else but to urge them to persevere and continue in that faith, proved at large to be so excellent a thing. . . .

Second, it is said that this faith is the "ground" or "substance," for the word signifies both. The meaning is: things hoped for as yet are not and so have no being or substance. Now faith that believes the promises and applies them, that faith gives to those things which yet are not (after a sort) a substance or subsistence in the heart of the believer, so that that thing which never had nor yet had a being in itself, by this faith it has a being in the heart of the believer. This I take to be the true meaning [of "substance"]. . . .

There are other things [in addition to the promises of the Old Testament regarding the incarnation of Christ and the spreading of the gospel to Jews and Gentiles alike] that we hope for as well as they, which are to come, and not seen by either of us. There are six things:

1. Justification, consisting in the remission of sins.
2. Sanctification in this life.
3. The perfection and accomplishment of our sanctification after this life.
4. The resurrection of the body and reuniting it with the soul.
5. Glorification of body and soul.
6. Life everlasting and glory with God in heaven.

These they did not see with the eye of the body and neither do we. Yet they hoped for them, and so do we. These things had no being in themselves to them, neither have they as yet to us. But this true saving faith gave to them, gives to us, and will give to every believer, while the world lasts, such a certain assurance of them that they seem present to us, and we seem presently to enjoy them. We cannot enjoy any of them fully, but saving faith has this power to give them all a present being in our hearts and us such a real possession of them as greatly delights a Christian soul, insomuch as the feeling of the sweetness of this glory, though it is yet to come, overwhelms the feeling of a worldly misery, though it is present. A CLOVD OF FAITHFULL WITNESSES, HEB 11:1.[13]

FAITH IS A LIVING, UNDENIABLE, AND FEARLESS CONFIDENCE GIVEN BY GOD. HULDRYCH ZWINGLI: "Now faith is the substance of those things that are hoped for. . . ." Paul here calls faith the *hypostasin*, the substance or subsistence—that is, a living, certain, unshaken, undeniable, and fearless confidence—of those things that are hoped for continually and are not seen. Since this faith is not learned apart from the instructing Spirit and is obtained through this guide, it is not established by human capacity, as Christ replied to Peter, "Blood and flesh have not revealed this to you." Therefore, "faith" in this passage is not an opinion, a decision, or some sort of feeble human notion, but a firm, certain, and undeniable confidence on which a human being rests in the sight of God, and which has been divinely imparted to the human mind. EXPOSITION OF HEBREWS 11:1.[14]

WRESTLING WITH GOD BY FAITH. WILLIAM PERKINS: If it pleases the Lord thus to deal with us, so that we feel nothing else but his wrath

[13]Perkins, *Workes*, 3:1a, 2a-b*.

[14]Zwingli, *In Epistolam Beati Pauli ad Hebraeos Expositio*, 581; citing Mt 16:17.

wrestling with our consciences, and neither can we think otherwise by present feeling but that God has forsaken us, what should we do in this pitiful case? Should we despair, as reason would bid us? No, but we should take this course: call to mind God's merciful promises and his ancient former love, and cast yourself on that love, even though you cannot feel it. When you have most cause to despair, then labor against it. When you have no reason to believe, then believe with all your power. For remember the power and prerogative of your faith: it believes not things that are, and manifestly appear, so much as such things that are not, and have no being. So then, when God's favor seems to be lost and have no being to you, then is God's favor a fit object for your faith, which believes those things that are not. . . . When God pulls back his favor and fights against you with his wrath, do as Jacob did in Genesis 32:27-29 and wrestle with God, even though you have but one little spark of faith, fight with that little faith, lay hold of God by it, and let him not go until he had blessed you. . . . A Clovd of Faithfull Witnesses, Heb 11:1.[15]

Faith Is Not a Vulgar Credulity. Desiderius Erasmus: Nothing makes the godly more attractive to God than to have a sure confidence about him. For to have doubts about God's words is evidence of a mind that holds only the best thought about him, since the things of which he speaks are nowhere apparent to the human senses and cannot be proved by human arguments. There are things that the mind conceives of only through hope, since they do not exist anywhere in any physical way. Most people believe that such conceptions are insubstantial and no different from dreams. They think it foolish to believe something to be true that cannot be shown to the eyes. And yet this faith through which the righteous person will save their life when others perish is not some vulgar credulity; it is the solid and firm foundation of those things that can be apprehended neither by the senses nor by human-made arguments. Firm hope makes them so present to the mind that they appear to be held in the hands right before the eyes. Hope does not persuade through human-made proofs but through a sure confidence in God their source that those things that cannot be seen in themselves are absolutely sure. Paraphrases on the Epistle to the Hebrews 11:1-2.[16]

A Christian Is Approved by Faith. William Perkins: For what were they "approved"? The text says, "by faith," not because faith is an action of a sanctified mind, and a good grace of God, for so are humility, love, fear of God (all which are graces of the sanctifying spirit, as faith is); but because it is a worthy instrument in the heart of the believer that apprehends and applies to the soul that righteousness of Christ by which he is justified, thus it is the hand and instrument of their justification, by it (it is said) they were approved. A Clovd of Faithfull Witnesses, Heb 11:1-2.[17]

Faith Is True Religion and True Wisdom. Heinrich Bullinger: Now he will produce examples [of faith], but first he prefaces them with some further remarks. First, "For by it the people of old received their commendation." This is the main point of the whole chapter. He says that by this faith the holy people of old were pleasing to God. For "received commendation" is substituted for "pleased God." Therefore, by faith they served God, by faith they were justified before God, and thus true religion consists in faith.

Second, "By faith we understand that the universe was established by the word of God, and that which is now seen was made from things which are not visible." With great labor indeed (as is evident in Plutarch's *On the Opinions of the Philosophers*, Aristotle's *On Heaven and the World*, as well as in Pliny and Coelius)† the philosophers have investigated the principles of reality, as to whether the world is finite or infinite, and whether

[15]Perkins, *Workes*, 3:4a*.

[16]CWE 44: 244-45.

[17]Perkins, *Workes*, 3:5b*.

it is one or many. But such is the power and worth of faith that it alone perfectly imparts what those who had in every other respect been instructed in all wisdom were not able to comprehend, namely, that one God is the author of all these things, who by his own unutterable word in power and might created from nothing the universe that we now see, as well as the unseen realm of angels and spirits. For faith regards God as so splendid that these things that Moses related regarding the creation of the world are but small matters to him. From this it is clear that faith is true wisdom. Now the examples follow, which we will merely glance over in passing. Commentary on Hebrews 11:2-3.[18]

11:4 *Abel's Faith Still Speaks*

The Primacy of Faith. Martin Luther: Here the apostle determines clearly that the importance of the sacrifices and the entire value of the merit did not lie in the worthiness or the greatness of the work, but that faith is the cause; for God weighs the spirits and looks at the heart. Psalm 7:15 states that he "loves the righteous and searches the hearts." . . . Therefore it is clear these words of the apostle have the same meaning that is recorded in Genesis 4:4: "God had regard for Abel"—namely, first because of his faith, not because of his work, for this follows—"and for his offerings." Accordingly, this is the crossroad where the truly righteous and the hypocrites separate. For those who are truly righteous press forward to works through faith and grace; the hypocrites, with perverse zeal, press forward to grace through works, that is, to what is impossible. Lectures on Hebrews 11:4.[19]

Abel Was Justified Not by External Offerings but by Faith. Heinrich Bullinger: From this example we learn that the worship of God does not consist in external things, sacrifices, offerings, or ceremonies, but in genuine and sincere faith. For if you look at the external aspects, Cain no less than Abel offered a sacrifice to God. But Cain did not have faith; therefore that which he offered was unacceptable to God. For whatever is not from faith is sin. Therefore, true religion consists in faith. By faith Abel was justified, and not by sacrifice. For "by faith," says the apostle, "he received the testimony that he was righteous." For works do not justify; faith alone justifies. But that which really belongs to faith is sometimes credited by association to works, nevertheless faith alone is righteousness, although faith without works is dead. For here also we see that God gave testimony regarding Abel's offerings. Commentary on Hebrews 11:4.[20]

Faith Is Life in God. Martin Luther: By means of a remarkable example God proves that he cares for those who are oppressed, since after the death of Abel he himself speaks for him. Even though in this way he points somewhat obscurely that the soul is immortal and that there is eternal life, yet he does so with power. Thus a righteous man lives, acts, and speaks more truly and better when he no longer lives, acts, and speaks in himself, but when he lives, acts, and speaks in God. For that Abel lives in God he shows by reason of the fact that he also speaks in God. Thus "though he is dead, he still speaks," so that he who, when he was alive, could not teach his one brother through his faith and example, now that he is dead, that is, lives far more vigorously, teaches the whole world. So great a thing is faith, that is, life in God. For this reason, it is altogether fitting to sing (Ps. 112:6): "The righteous shall be in everlasting memory" (that is, in the memory of eternity). Thus Chrysostom says: "How does he who is dead still live? For the

[18]Bullinger, *In Pauli ad Hebraeos Epistolam*, 117v-118r. †[Pseudo-] Plutarch, *De Placitis Philosophorum*, in *Plutarchi Chaeronensis Moralia*, ed. G. Bernardakis (Leipzig: B. G. Teubner, 1893), 5.264-372; an English translation is available in *The Complete Works of Plutarch* (New York: Crowell, 1909), 6:49-128. Aristotle, *De Caelo et Mundo* (LCL 338); Pliny the Elder, *Natural History* (LCL 330, 352, 353, 370, 371, 392, 418, 394, 419); Lodovico Ricchieri (Caelius Rhodiginus), *Lectionum Antiquarum Libri XVI* (Basel: Froben, 1517).

[19]LW 29:232 (WA 57:229.25-230.1, 230.16-21).

[20]Bullinger, *In Pauli ad Hebraeos Epistolam*, 118r; citing Rom 14:23; Jas 2:26.

fact that he is in the mouths of all shows that he is alive. For if he had a thousand tongues when alive, he would never be held in such great admiration as he is now held when he is dead."† But by this we are all exhorted, not only that death should not be feared, but that it should even be desired as what for Abel and every righteous person is a door and a crossing over from humanity to divinity, from the world to the Father, from wretchedness to glory. For in this way God has shown from the very beginning of the world and of Scripture what great blessings he can make out of a few evils. For Abel had to be slain in order that the glory of life might be shown in his death and that this consolation of life might be greater in Abel than the perturbation of the death that was brought in had been in Adam. Lectures on Hebrews 11:4.[21]

Cain and Abel as Examples of Faith and Unbelief. Johannes Oecolampadius: In Cain and Abel, two kinds of people are depicted before our eyes. The first kind, depicted in Cain, are the hypocrites; the second, depicted in Abel, are the righteous. And thus the Holy Spirit intended to illustrate by this type the fact that the pure person must persevere as much in evil circumstances as in good.

"Through which he was commended. . . ." It is recorded that both of them made offerings to God, but with dissimilar souls. Abel was believing, Cain unbelieving; and because he was unbelieving, it is recorded that, however attentive and dedicated he was, whatever kind of thing he offered was far inferior to that of his brother Abel, who made offerings "of the firstborn of his sheep and of their fat portions." For this reason, also God "had no regard for Cain." But because he was not motivated by reverence for God, he envied his neighbor and brother and seized and killed him.

Now, let no one imagine that God had regard for Abel and his gifts because they were better chosen and more valuable. Not at all! For he cares nothing for external things, but because he offered these things by faith and did it with the greatest dedication of heart, God bore witness concerning him, and he was reckoned as righteous. But from the behavior of the two it is sufficiently obvious what attitude possessed each of them. Where there is faith, there is love; where there is no faith, there is no love either, but only envy, cruelty, and all the worst things. You have an instance in Cain, who, when he observed that his brother was approved by God while he himself was rejected, did not examine the reason; rather, in the envy and malice of his mind he did not blush to commit fratricide. "And through this, though he is dead, he still speaks." Because God accepted Abel's sacrifice, and he had an offering that was acceptable (that is, which was by faith), Cain, not believing God, began to envy his brother. And because he could not injure God whom he hated, he attacked his servant (as all the ungodly are accustomed to do) and killed him after calling him out into the middle of a field. By this it declares Abel's amazing mildness and obedience, who desired to comply so that he might not give even the smallest occasion for his brother to be angry with him, since he was the older brother to whom providentially belonged, by the right of the firstborn, the authority to command. But "through this," that is, through faith, "though he is dead, he still speaks." If he speaks, it follows that he also lives. By this the apostle sets before our eyes the efficacy and victory of faith. His memory is renowned, and he speaks to us today and does not cease especially to exhort us to faith and endurance. Explanations of Hebrews 11:4.[22]

11:5 *Enoch Pleased God with His Faith*

Enoch and the Hope of Redemption in Christ. Martin Luther: Therefore whatever is stated about them [Enoch and Elijah] outside the Scriptures must be the opinions or notions of people who do not know [why they were taken up], and it is better to have no knowledge of these

[21]LW 29: 233-34 (WA 57:231.13-232.8). †LW note (234 n. 14): "Chrysostom, *Homiliae*, XXII, 2, col. 156 (374)."

[22]Oecolampadius, *In Epistolam ad Hebraeos Explanationes*, 124r-v; citing Gen 4:3-5, 8.

opinions and notions than to be troubled in vain by idle curiosity. But God wanted his taking up to be recorded in the Holy Scriptures for our sakes, namely, "in order that the human soul," says Chrysostom, "might get the hope that death would be destroyed and the tyranny of the devil would be condemned."† For all this took place in order that in the beginning faith concerning the Savior's future redemption might be nourished and sustained, and that the human race might not see itself completely deserted and despair of redemption. For the elect never lacked consolation. Nor did they lack tribulation. Thus although in Abel the human race saw death, yet in him it saw a better life. Although in Enoch it saw no death, yet in him it saw life. Lectures on Hebrews 11:5.[23]

Enoch Was Not Taken Alive to Paradise. Johannes Oecolampadius: In the second place, Enoch is praised, who, according to what we read in the letter of Jude, was the seventh from Adam. The number seven, as you know, is very mysterious. But he has this praise from Scripture, which no one had before him. For Abel, the first righteous person, was slaughtered in the bloom of life. Those who take legends to heart say that he still lives and will return with Elijah before the last day of judgment. But no one will have persuaded me easily. I know that, in the Vulgate, Ecclesiasticus 44 reads, "Enoch pleased God, and he was taken away into paradise to give wisdom to the nations," but this is at variance from the reading of the Greeks, who say, *enōch enēreskēsen kyriō, kai metethē hypodeigma metanoias tais geneais*, "Enoch pleased the Lord, and he was taken away as an example of repentance to the nations." And Genesis 5, according to the Septuagint, *kai euēreskēsen enōch tō theō, kai ouch heurisketo, hoti metethēken auton ho theos*, "And Enoch pleased God, and he was not found, because God took him away." But it is not demonstrated by these words that he did not die; because, if he was of the offspring of Adam, it is necessary that he was mortal. And surely this is realistic and accords with the analogy of faith. For Christ alone is the firstborn from the dead, and he has opened paradise to those who believe. And—what convinces me more—in the time when Christ had not paid the price of redemption, the sword and flaming brand that roved about prohibited entry to paradise. If he had already been taken into paradise, how was the honor of Christ kept intact? Because, if you propose a miracle here, it is necessary that he still be due to undergo death and change.

But if one observes the practice of the apostle, he will not be surprised that he could write that [Enoch] did not see death. For just as we know he previously did regarding Melchizedek, he intended to affirm nothing beyond the testimony of Scripture, and because it did not explicitly record that he died, he did not presume to affirm it. But, still, he is not denying that he died anymore than with Melchizedek. But surely the Scripture keeps silence to show us that hope of eternal life and immortality comes to us by faith. Among the Hebrews I find some who relate that he was hastened to death even when he had not yet reached the same number of years to which his ancestors had attained (that is, seven hundred years and more), but was taken away, that is, was withdrawn from the sight of humankind. So say Rabbi Shlomo† and Abenezra.‡

Saint Chrysostom notes that we should not be contentious on this point, and I will not do so with anyone, for people can be ignorant of these things without impairment of godliness. Explanations of Hebrews 11:5.[24]

11:6 *Faith Is Needed to Draw Near to God*

The Chief Principle of Faith. Heinrich Bullinger: This is another proof that Enoch was

[23]LW 29:234-35 (WA 57:232.10-25). †LW note (234 n. 15): "Chrysostom, *Homiliae*, XXII, 2, col. 157 (375)."

[24]Oecolampadius, *In Epistolam ad Hebraeos Explanationes*, 125r-v. Jude 14; Eccles 44:16; Gen 5:24; Rom 12:6; Col 1:18; Rev 3:7. †Shlomo Yitzchaki, *"Rashi" on the Pentateuch: Genesis*, trans. J. H. Lowe (London: Hebrew Compendium, 1928), 93. ‡Abraham ben Meir ibn Ezra, *Ibn Ezra's Commentary on the Pentateuch: Genesis (Bereshit)*, trans. H. N. Strickman and A. M. Silver (New York: Menorah, 1988), 91.

translated on no other ground other than by faith. The reasoning may be explained as follows: "The one who draws near to God must believe. But Enoch drew near to God; therefore, Enoch believed." But in passing he touches on the chief principle of faith, on which the devout mind rests, namely, "that God exists and is the rewarder." For the first question regarding anything is whether it exists; and the next is what or of what sort it is. But in this connection Diagoras of Melos, Theodorus of Cyrene, and Eumeros of Tegea held that there are no gods at all,† but the prophet also said, "The fool has said in his heart, 'There is no God.'" But in contrast, real truth and faith is convinced, nay, rather it knows for certain that there is a God, and not only that, but also that he is the rewarder of those who seek him. The apostle says "the rewarder"—generous, omniscient, good, omnipotent, and the highest good. For one who chooses to be the rewarder of all those who seek him must necessarily be like this. Therefore, true faith not only believes that God exists but also believes that this God is their own God who intends to do good to the believer and who is that horn of plenty in which he possesses in abundance whatever he desires. And this was the shining faith and religion not only of Enoch but also of all the people of old. COMMENTARY ON HEBREWS 11:6.[25]

WE MUST BELIEVE THAT GOD IS GOOD. DESIDERIUS ERASMUS: Whoever wants to be acceptable to God must believe, first, that God exists, is omnipotent, and wills only what is best; second, that God oversees human affairs and that through his agency the godly, who neglect the visible goods of this world and seek the invisible God, are not cheated of their rewards, however much they may suffer in this life, while the ungodly on the other hand will not fail to receive their due punishment even if they seem to sail along with fair winds in this world. PARAPHRASES ON THE EPISTLE TO THE HEBREWS 11:6.[26]

FAITH FROM NATURE AND FAITH FROM GRACE. MARTIN LUTHER: "To believe that God exists" seems to many to be so easy that they have ascribed this belief both to poets and to philosophers, so the apostle also asserts in Romans 1:20. In fact, there are those who think that this is self-evident. But such human faith† is just like any other thought, art, wisdom, dream, etc., of humankind. For as soon as a trial assails, all those things immediately topple down. Then neither reason nor counsel nor faith has the upper hand. . . . For this reason the apostle James calls this faith "dead" (2:17), and others call it "acquired" faith.‡ But in humankind there is nothing that is not vanity and a lie. In the second place, such faith believes nothing about itself but believes only about others. For even if it believes that God exists and rewards those who seek him, yet it does not believe that God exists and rewards it itself. . . . For this reason another faith is needed, namely, the faith by which we believe that we are numbered among those for whom God exists and is a rewarder. But this faith does not come from nature; it comes from grace. For nature is terrified and flees from the face of God, since it believes that he is not God but is a tyrant, a torturer, and a judge . . . and let us give a simile applicable to the two kinds of faith. Just as a candle exposed to the wind loses not only its rays but all light, while the sun shining from above can be disturbed by no power of the winds either in its rays or in itself, so the first kind of faith is extinguished, the second kind never. LECTURES ON HEBREWS 11:6.[27]

---

[25]Bullinger, *In Pauli ad Hebraeos Epistolam*, 119r-v [257-58]; citing Ps 14:1; 53:1. †[Pseudo-]Plutarch, *De Placitis Philosophorum* 1.7, in *Plutarchi Chaeronensis Moralia*, ed. G. Bernardakis (Leipzig: B. G. Teubner, 1893), 5:281; *The Complete Works of Plutarch* (New York: Crowell, 1909), 6:61. Cicero also names Diagoras and Theodorus as notable atheists in *De Natura Deorum* 1.1, 3.37 (LCL 268:4, 374). For more on Eumeros, see F. W. J. Shelling, *Historical-Critical Introduction to the Philosophy of Mythology*, trans. M. Richey and M. Zisselsberger (Albany: State University of New York Press, 2007), 23.

[26]CWE 44:245.

[27]LW 29:235 (WA 57:232.7-233.19). †LW note (235 n. 16): "*Fides humana* was a faith based on reasoning, persuasion, or some other human ground, rather than on the converting work of the Holy Spirit, which was *fides divina*." ‡LW note (235 n. 17): "Luther is referring to the notion in Franciscan theology of a *fides [naturaliter] aquisita*, such as that of the demons (cf. James 2:19)."

With the Increase of Revelation, More Must Be Believed. Cardinal Cajetan: Believing in these two things has been necessary in every time from the beginning of the world. But believing in other things in particular (such as that God is both three and one, and the mystery of the incarnation, and other things like these) has not been necessary in every time. But to the extent that God revealed them progressively, the content of faith increased, and with it the extent of things that must be believed by necessity. Comments on Hebrews 11:6.[28]

11:7 *Noah Built the Ark from Faith*

By Acting in Faith, Noah Warned and Judged the Worldly. Johannes Oecolampadius: "By this he condemned the world." By "world" he means not the vast structure we inhabit, but worldly people, those who have been entirely abandoned to the world and rejected everything to do with heaven. To these people the word of God is entirely an object of contempt. He judged this world and forewarned it to beware of impending disaster by his construction of the ark, and when it did not come to its senses, it received the just sentence of condemnation. Others say that he did not pass judgment but condemned them by comparison, as it is recorded of the Queen of the South in Matthew, but the former interpretation seems to fit better. Explanations of Hebrews 11:7.[29]

11:8-10 *Abraham Lived by Faith*

The Glory of Faith. Martin Luther: [Abraham] went out with no knowledge of where he was going, with nothing for him to follow except the Word of God concerning things that were nowhere to be seen. For just as for us the place where Enoch and Elijah are is situated in darkness, in gloom, in ignorance, and in the invisible things of God, so to Abraham this place to which he was called was completely hidden. And this is the glory of faith, namely, not to know where you are going, what you are doing, what you are suffering, and, after taking everything captive—perception and understanding, strength and will—to follow the bare voice of God and to be led and driven rather than to drive. And thus it is clear that with this obedience of faith Abraham gave a supreme example of an evangelical life, because he left everything, and loving it above everything, he was a stranger of his own accord and was subjected every hour to danger of life and death. Lectures on Hebrews 11:8.[30]

Abraham's Example. Heinrich Bullinger: By these things he at last really and truly sets before our eyes the reason why faith is such constant reality and patient expectation. For it should not be regarded as such a great deed that when Abraham was called by the magnificent promises of God, he abandoned his ancestral habitation. But it was a hard and rare deed that, when he arrived at the place that he had anticipated, he discovered nothing solid or firm, from which a certain dissatisfaction could have sprouted. But nothing like this can be found in Abraham, that holy man of God. For he does not resist God, he does not grumble, he does not despise the promise because he was compelled to live in tents in the Promised Land, to clash repeatedly with the resident Philistines, and to be occupied with nothing but hardships. But he turns his godly soul away from earthly things, and fixes all hope on the eternal and invisible things, looking to the heavens, for he had learned that a courageous person must despise earthly things as unstable and inconstant. There is more on this subject a little further on. Commentary on Hebrews 11:9-10.[31]

The Patriarchs Looked Forward to the City Built on Christ. Johannes Oecolampadius: It is a remarkable act of virtue to despise riches

---

[28]Cajetan, *In Epistolam ad Hebraeos Commentarii*, 168v.
[29]Oecolampadius, *In Epistolam ad Hebraeos Explanationes*, 127v; citing Mt 12:42.
[30]LW 29:238 (WA 57:235.24-236.7).
[31]Bullinger, *In Pauli ad Hebraeos Epistolam*, 120v [260].

when surrounded by riches, to have all things and possess nothing, to be able to abound and to endure want. The land of Canaan was promised to him by God; nevertheless, he was never puffed up in his heart because of this but always regarded himself as a sojourner. As evidence of this, we do not read that he erected a city, but that he dwelt in tents, from which it is deduced that he always intended to depart. Isaac and Jacob did likewise, living in the same kind of simplicity, even though they knew that the land was promised to them; nevertheless, they also chose to live in tents, because they were looking forward to a better city, whose foundations are in the holy mountains, the heavenly Jerusalem, which is promised to Abraham, Isaac, Jacob, and all who believe. And thus with these words the apostle has an allegory in mind. Since they were looking forward to this city, they acknowledged that they were sojourners on this earth, and thus they chose not to yield themselves in their souls to any of the allurements and delights of this world. But it is well said that it "has foundations." For it is built on the solid rock of Christ. This appears to be an allusion to Isaiah 28. Explanations of Hebrews 11:9-10.[32]

11:11-12 *By Faith Sarah Was Able to Bear Isaac*

Sarah's Example. Lucas Osiander: And even if it seems that there is a great distance between justifying faith and the faith that receives bodily goods from God, nevertheless it is one and the same faith among the sons of God that obtains both spiritual and bodily goods from God. Therefore they are awaiting bodily goods from God, because they believe that they have a merciful heavenly Father on account of the Mediator Christ. And Sarah teaches by example that divine strength is easily able to make it so that those who are by nature sterile may become fecund. Epistle to the Hebrews 11:11.[33]

A Woman's Faith is as Commendable as a Man's. Johannes Oecolampadius: After he has commended to us the preeminence of Abraham's faith, he also intends to recall Sarah his wife, who also excelled in the same faith, and thus by means of an argument from gender he continues to urge us to faith. Clearly, it was her glory that she was the wife of such a patriarch, whom he also called his sister among his enemies, which she actually was. Since she was endowed with conjugal faith, she did not hesitate at all to follow him to an unknown country. And because she believed the promise, to that same degree she received power to conceive, not at all concerned by her spent body and haggish old age. It is true that she laughed when it was first announced to her that she would be a mother, for it seemed so absurd, even impossible, to announce the birth of a child from a woman of such advanced age. But when she was rebutted by the angel, straightaway she had faith in his words. Take note that the apostle does not say *autē* ("Sarah herself") without cause, for it carries with it an emphasis on commending the faith of a member of the weaker sex, whom he presents to us as no less commendable than Abraham himself. So we find that in Christ and in God there is neither male nor female, neither slave nor free, etc. Where he chooses, he is able to work by his own Spirit. Therefore, the female sex is not to be despised; although it is a little weaker, nevertheless it can also be a vessel of the Holy Spirit. Explanations of Hebrews 11:11-12.[34]

11:13-16 *The Patriarchs Desired a Heavenly Country*

Awaiting a Heavenly Home. Heinrich Bullinger: As the main point, he draws out the faith of all the patriarchs. He says, "The fathers never really possessed the Promised Land, but just as those who see a thing from afar have only a taste of the thing they have seen, and those who greet a person only begin to be acquainted with them, so they were like

[32]Oecolampadius, *In Epistolam ad Hebraeos Explanationes*, 129r-v; citing 2 Cor 6:10; Phil 4:13; Ps 87:1; Gen 23:4; Mt 7:24-25; Is 28:16.
[33]Osiander, *Epistola ad Hebraeos*, 77-78. John 14:2-3.

[34]Oecolampadius, *In Epistolam ad Hebraeos Explanationes*, 130r-v; citing Gen 12:10-20; 20:1-13; 1 Pet 3:7; Gal 3:28.

sojourners and aliens in the Promised Land. Nevertheless, they did not grumble against the Lord; rather, they stood firm in faith, and they passed away in faith and certain expectation, believing that God had prepared for them a better land." For here the apostle turns from carnal to spiritual things. And because a little earlier he undertook to show that the faith of Abraham (and indeed of all the people of old) was fixed on invisible and heavenly things, not visible and earthly things (for they were looking for another land and another city), now he explains this more fully and clearly, and reasons in this manner. Those who confess that they are sojourners are confessing that they have a different homeland than that in which they are staying. And the patriarchs confessed that they were sojourners; therefore, they hoped for a different homeland than the one in which they lived. Then there follows the confirmation, for how could they have believed that the land in which they were was their homeland, when they said that they were sojourners? Or what person, living in their own home and ancestral soil, says that they are a sojourner? But also, if they had regarded the land from which they had departed as their homeland, clearly there was no lack of opportunities to return. Therefore, since neither Chaldea, from which they had departed, nor Canaan, in which they were living, was the homeland of the patriarchs, it follows that the patriarchs were looking for no earthly homeland, but for a heavenly one, and thus that God provided a place for the fathers, and that they were looking for heaven as their homeland. Therefore God himself received them as sons and citizens, and is called their God. By these things it is established that God is worshiped by faith alone, and that the world is justified by faith. Commentary on Hebrews 11:13-16.[35]

11:17-19 *Abraham Offered Up Isaac by Faith*

The Victory of Abraham's Faith Is Our Example. Johannes Oecolampadius: So Abraham was tested, as we have said; the magnitude of the matter in which he was tested must be considered. For the struggle was extremely ferocious. For on the one side were flesh, feeling, and intellect; on the other the command and promise of God. Intellect said, "How can a father possess hatred toward his own child, and especially when it is his only one? And nature teaches and prompts all parents to love, cherish, and nurture their own children; and when it is not lawful to kill others, much less is it to kill one's own son." And such thoughts no doubt strengthened the temptation. Add to this that this son was all the more beloved, because he was given in extreme old age, and by a miracle. I ask you, would this thing not have shaken the soul of the old man? Who are more naturally disposed to love their children than those who are closest to death? The grief was augmented by the fact that this son was not to be slain immediately, but after being worn out with three days of labor. But faith, which is supported like a wall of bronze on the omnipotence of God, thought, "The one who gave a son to this hundred-year-old dead body, he is also able to raise the dead. And it is God, the greatest and best, who has given the command; therefore, he must be obeyed, not resisted, nor even complained against on the basis of faith in the promise, nor may it be feared that he is at all unfair." In short, intellect was conquered by the word or command of God, by the strength and constancy of faith.

From this we should learn that we also are being tested when two words or commands of God press on us so that we do not know which one we should choose instead of the other. When we are put in such straits, we should focus all the more strongly in that case on what we know and are certain that the divine will would do; and the Spirit will instruct those who are truly intent in prayer as to what is most important to embrace. So it is here. "You shall not kill," and "Offer your son to me." The latter was so clear and evident to Abraham that he could not contradict it in the least. Therefore, he obeyed directly, but not without faith. Then again, discerning eyes are

[35]Bullinger, *In Pauli ad Hebraeos Epistolam*, 121v-122r.

called for here, lest he who often transforms himself into an angel of light should deceive you in your heedlessness by a semblance of godliness, so that, when you imagine that you have conformed yourself precisely to the will of God, you are infinitely distant from it. Thus long ago in the ancient times of the prophets he influenced those who, endeavoring to imitate this example of Abraham, sacrificed and burned their own children to the idol Moloch. This was a foolish imitation, and was clearly impious and the invention of Satan himself. These things happened, and still things not unlike these happen even in our times. Therefore, fear God, and serve him uprightly in fear and trembling, and he will teach you infallibly what he wants you to do, and what he does not. For no lie will proceed from the Spirit, who has said, "The Lord is near to all who call on him in truth." EXPLANATIONS OF HEBREWS 11:17-19.[36]

ADOPT THE COURAGE OF ABRAHAM. KATHARINA SCHÜTZ ZELL: So I beg you, loyal believing women, also to do this: take on the manly, Abraham-like courage while you too are in distress and while you are abused with all kinds of insult and suffering. When you may meet with imprisonment in towers, chains, drowning, banishment, and such things; when your husbands and you yourselves may be killed, meditate then on strong Abraham, the father of us all; struggle after him as a good child should follow his father in faith like the father's. Do you not think that Abraham also suffered when God told him to kill his only son? When he told Abraham to do it himself!—to kill the son in whom also the blessing of human beings was promised. Yes indeed, he was very grieved, for he was also flesh and blood like all of us, but he knew (as the Scripture says) that God could bring his son back to life. LETTER TO THE SUFFERING WOMEN OF KENTZINGEN.[37]

11:20-26 *The Patriarchs and Moses Endured Hardships by Faith*

THE ISRAELITES SUFFERED FOR CHRIST. WILLIAM PERKINS: Further, whereas it is said, "he considered the reproach of Christ," here mark, the rebuke of God's church and people is called "the reproach of Christ." The people of God in Egypt were laden with reproaches and rebukes, and behold, Christ accounts it as his rebuke, and the Holy Spirit calls it this. Wherefore we must learn this, that Christ esteems the reproach and affliction of his church as his own affliction. . . . Again, the afflictions of the Israelites are here said to be their sufferings for Christ, and therefore we must note that though Christ's coming was then far off, yet the Israelites then knew of Christ, for otherwise they could not suffer for him.

This confutes those who hold that every person may be saved by their own religion, whatsoever it may be, if they live civilly and uprightly therein. Their reason is taken from the Jews, who (they say) had only the knowledge of outward ceremonies, and so were saved. But that opinion is here disproved: for the Jews knew Christ, and professed him, or else they would never suffer for him; and therefore they were saved by him, and not by their obedience to outward ceremonies. And this is much of the reason that moved Moses to make such a choice as he did. A CLOVD OF FAITHFULL WITNESSES, HEB 11:26.[38]

11:27-40 *Old Testament Saints Accomplished and Suffered Much by Faith*

THE OLD TESTAMENT SAINTS LIVED BY FAITH. THOMAS CRANMER: How plentiful this faith is of good works, and how it makes the work of one person more acceptable to God than of another, St. Paul teaches at large in the eleventh chapter to the Hebrews, saying, that faith made the oblation of Abel better than the oblation of Cain. This made Noah build the ark. This made Abraham forsake

[36]Oecolampadius, *In Epistolam ad Hebraeos Explanationes*, 133r-134r; citing Jer 15:20; 2 Cor 11:14; Ps 145:18.
[37]Zell, *Church Mother*, 51; citing Rom 4:16; Gen 22:12.

[38]Perkins, *Workes*, 3:145a*.

his country, and all his friends, and to go into a far country, there to dwell among strangers. So did also Isaac and Jacob, depending only of the help and trust that they had in God. And when they came to the country God promised them, they would build no cities, towns, nor houses, but lived like strangers in tents, that might everyday be removed. Their trust was so much in God that they set but little by any worldly thing; for that God had prepared for them better dwelling places in heaven, of his own foundation and building. This faith made Abraham ready at God's commandment to offer his own son and heir Isaac, whom he loved so well, and by whom he was promised to have innumerable issue, among which one should be born, in whom all nations should be blessed; trusting so much in God that though he were slain, yet God was able by his omnipotent power to raise him from death and perform his promise. He mistrusted not the promise of God, although to his reason everything seemed contrary. This faith wrought so in the heart of Moses that he refused to be taken for Pharaoh his daughter's son, and to have great inheritance in Egypt, thinking it were better with the people of God to have affliction and sorrow than with naughty people in sin to live pleasantly for a time. By faith he cared nothing for the threatening of Pharaoh: for his trust was so in God that he passed not of the felicity of this world, but looked for the reward to come in heaven, setting his heart on the invisible God, as if he had seen him ever present before his eyes. By faith the children of Israel passed through the Red Sea. By faith the walls of Jericho fell down without stroke, and many other wonderful miracles have been wrought. In all good people that heretofore have been, faith has brought forth their good works, and obtained the promises of God. Faith has stopped the lions' mouths: faith has quenched the force of fire: faith has escaped the sword's edges: faith has given weak people strength, victory in battle, overthrown the armies of infidels, raised the dead to life: faith has made good people to take adversity in good part: some have been mocked and whipped, bound and cast into prison; some have lost all their goods, and lived in great poverty; some have wandered the mountains, hills, and wilderness; some have been racked, some slain, some stoned, some sawn, some rent in pieces, some [be]headed, some burned without mercy, and would not be delivered because they looked to rise again to a better state. Homily of Faith[39]

God Gives Plentifully to the Faithful as They Patiently Suffer. John Donne: Our parts are two: how plentifully God gives to the faithful . . . , and how patiently the faithful suffer God's corrections. . . . Though they be both large considerations (benefits by faith, patience in the faithful), yet we shall contain ourselves in those particulars which are expressed, or necessarily implied in the text itself. And so in the first place we shall see first the extraordinary consolation in God's extraordinary mercies, in his miraculous deliverances such as this . . . , and second we shall see the examples, to which the apostle refers here, what women had had their dead restored to life again; and then last, in that part, that this affection of joy, in having the dead restored to life again, being put in the weaker sex, in women only, we may argue conveniently from thence that the strength of a true and just joy lies not in that, but that our virility, our holy manhood, our religious strength consists in a faithful assurance that we have already a blessed communion with these saints of God, though they be dead, and we alive; and we shall have hereafter a glorious association with them in the resurrection, though we never receive our dead raised to life again in this world. And in those three considerations, we shall determine the first part. And then, in the other, the patience of the faithful . . . , we shall first look into the examples which the apostle refers to; who they were that were thus tortured: and second, the height and exaltation of their patience . . . , and last, the ground upon which their anchor was cast, what established their patience. Sermon on Hebrews 11:35.[40]

[39]Cranmer, *Cranmer's Selected Writings*, 25-26.
[40]Donne, *Works*, 1:388-89*.

The Saints of Old Endured in Expectation. Huldrych Zwingli: "Others were tortured, refusing to accept release." That is, they refused to deny the God in whom they believed so faithfully, so that, after being released from their afflictions, they might have something better. This was because of the hope of the resurrection to come, that is, of a greater and better life, when not only will the soul enjoy eternal glory, but also the body of our lowliness will finally be conformed to the body of the splendor of Christ, when we will attain to that greater life that we mean by the term "resurrection." This is a *hysteron proteron*. . . .†

"They did not receive what was promised." That is, they did not receive Christ manifested to humanity, nor even eternal life. For none of those people entered straightaway into complete and entire eternal life, but they were kept waiting in the bosom of Abraham for Christ the deliverer. Unless you prefer to take this as referring to the general resurrection of all the dead, when this body of ours will be conformed to Christ.

"Since God had provided something better for us." He gives the reason why God did this deed. He says that it was for our good, because God did not want them to enjoy glory before he had made his one people in Christ from both Jews and Gentiles and had bonded them together in one church, as is shown in Ephesians 2. Therefore, Paul says, these things were done lest, if they would have preceded us in the glory of the resurrection, and, having been perfected, would have obtained incorruption of the body, we might be disgusted with our exile because we bear with the corruption of our bodies. Moreover, if they had been placed before us, the glory of the resurrection of the righteous would not have been the same. Therefore, he saw to it that the glory of the resurrection would not be bestowed on us in accordance with our merit, but in accordance with his divine providence. This is what Christ meant by the parable of the master of the house hiring workers for his vineyard (Matthew 20). Therefore they will wait for the same day and for the universal bodily resurrection, so that they may hear along with us the same declaration of the Son of Man: "Come, you who are blessed by the Father" (Matthew 25). This is an argument from the lesser to the greater. For if the saints of old endured with such perseverance, such confidence in the coming Christ, and such hope in the promised resurrection, which they nevertheless did not obtain immediately, even as they were butchered for the name and glory of the true God, how much more should we persist firm and constant in faith, to whom Christ has now been manifested, and when the glory of the resurrection is imminent in glory? Exposition of Hebrews 11:35-40.[41]

Faith Triumphs Over the Loss of Everything. Heinrich Bullinger: Several of the prophets "suffered mockery and flogging," and were even punished with "chains and imprisonment"—Elijah, Micaiah, and others. Zechariah son of Jehoiada was "stoned," as was Naboth, the most innocent of men. The ancients related that Isaiah died by being "sawn in two" by Manasseh. Both Saul and Jezebel "killed with the sword" many priests and prophets.

By "the skins of sheep and goats" he means garments that were torn, cast off, and barely fit for human use, but rather the clothing of beasts. And he said that they were *hysteroumenous*, "destitute" of every necessary thing, of food and drink, overwhelmed because of the threatening cruelty of tyrants on every side. They were "afflicted" because of their excruciating troubles, the upheavals and terrors of the soul. He adds that they wandered in deserts, that is, as exiles from their countries and homes, they hid like beasts in the forests and dens of beasts. Look, then, how he has enumerated in brief nearly everything unfit for the human race, and by these same things he has shown that not

[41]Zwingli, *In Epistolam Beati Pauli ad Hebraeos Expositio*, 581; citing Eph 2:14-15; Phil 3:21; Mt 20:1-16; 25:34; Lk 16:22.
†Zwingli, like many of the reformers, relished the categories of classical rhetoric popularized by humanists such as Erasmus. *Hysteron proteron* is a rhetorical device in which something that is logically subsequent is stated first (i.e., the torture occurred after the refusal to accept release, but it is stated first for dramatic effect).

only could death not snatch believers away from God, but neither could exile and misery, which are harder than death. So great is the power of faith! Commentary on Hebrews 11:36-38.[42]

If Rahab Can Come to Faith, Why Don't You? Johannes Oecolampadius: Here it may be asked whether Rahab was a harlot. Some Hebrew writers reply that she was not a harlot, but an innkeeper, and thus a respectable lady, because the noun *zwnh*, which is derived from *zwn*, "to feed," denotes an innkeeper, not a prostitute.† But some take it straightforwardly as "prostitute." Either way, it was not inconsistent with the work of the Lord, who for the most part makes his power perfect through the weak and despised things of this world. Although she was not from Israel and led an indecent life, nevertheless she did not hesitate to put her faith in God and to conclude, on the basis of the miracles that abounded around the Israelites, that God was with them, which also benefited her greatly.

By this the apostle surely disturbed the Jews a great deal, as if he were to say, "If the examples of Abraham, Moses, and the patriarchs do not rouse you to firmness of faith, you should at least be motivated by the faith of the most disreputable female, by which she saved her entire household. It would be shameful for you to be outdone by a hired woman, because such a person is entitled to enter the kingdom of heaven before you. But the faith of this woman is commended, not as the faith of a harlot, but as that of one who now repents and knows the God of Israel. Thus you may learn that you also, however great a sinner you may be, are allowed to come to God when you truly repent. This is what the Savior intended to show by his friendship with us sinners, and thus he came into the world to save sinners."

We will make this story useful for ourselves to the extent that we recognize that the whole world, which is symbolized by Jericho, will perish and pass away, from which perishing the only ones who are saved are those who, like Rahab, have been endowed with true faith. Thus sin will not harm those who repent and resolve on a new life. All the rest without exception are perishing. For without faith there is no safety to be found anywhere. Explanations of Hebrews 11:31.[43]

The Promise of the Resurrection. Heinrich Bullinger: This is the conclusion of the preceding section, as if he were saying, "Up to this point we have supplied examples, by which we have been taught to see that all the people of old were commended by faith." For he began this subject with the words, "By faith the people of old earned a testimony," and therefore he concludes his discussion of faith by repeating the same idea. But when he adds that the ancients did not receive the promise, is must be understood that the only completion of all the promises is Jesus Christ and the resurrection of our bodies. Thus by "promise" the apostle does not here mean rest, but rather the coming of Christ and the resurrection of our bodies. For by these the universal church is completely perfected. By this he lends support to the statements that Peter wrote in 1 Peter 4, "For this is why the gospel was preached even to those who are dead, so that though they are judged in the flesh according to humans, nevertheless they will live by the Spirit according to God." Commentary on Hebrews 11:39-40.[44]

God's General and Particular Providence. William Perkins: The word in the original, translated "had provided," properly signifies "had foreseen," wherein is likewise included God's decree and ordination. Now, this we must know, that it is a peculiar prerogative belonging to the true God alone to be able to foresee things to come, and that many thousand

[42]Bullinger, *In Pauli ad Hebraeos Epistolam*, 125v-126r [270-71]; citing 1 Kings 22:24-28; 2 Chron 24:20-22; 1 Kings 21:1-16; 1 Sam 22:6-19; 1 Kings 18:4; 19:10.

[43]Oecolampadius, *In Epistolam ad Hebraeos Explanationes*, 141v-142r*; citing 2 Cor 12:9; 1 Cor 1:27-28; Mt 21:31; 11:19; 1 Tim 1:15; 1 Jn 2:17. †It appears that Oecolampadius mistakenly wrote *hzwn* rather than *zwnh*.

[44]Bullinger, *In Pauli ad Hebraeos Epistolam*, 126r; citing 1 Pet 4:6.

years before; no creature of themselves can do this. And yet it is true that this property to foresee is ascribed to God, not properly, but in regard of our capacity, for if we speak of God properly, God cannot be said to foresee anything, because all things are present to him, whether past or to come. . . . But what did God here provide and foresee for us? Answer: "something better," that is, God in his eternal counsel provided a better estate for his church in the new Testament than he did for believers in the Old.

Hence we learn that as God has his general providence, whereby he governs all things, so also he has his special and particular providence, whereby in all things he provides and brings to pass that which is best for his church. . . . "That apart from us they should not be made perfect," that is, might not be fully glorified. Here is the reason why Christ was not exhibited in their days. Indeed, all true believers before Christ were justified and sanctified, and in soul received to glory before us, but perfected in soul and body both, they must not be before us, but we must all be perfected together. A CLOVD OF FAITHFULL WITNESSES, HEB 11:40.[45]

[45]Perkins, *Workes*, 3:197a, 198b*.

12:1-17 Jesus, the Founder and Perfecter of Our Faith

Therefore, since we are surrounded by so great a cloud of witnesses, let us also lay aside every weight, and sin which clings so closely, and let us run with endurance the race that is set before us, 2 looking to Jesus, the founder and perfecter of our faith, who for the joy that was set before him endured the cross, despising the shame, and is seated at the right hand of the throne of God.

3 Consider him who endured from sinners such hostility against himself, so that you may not grow weary or fainthearted. 4 In your struggle against sin you have not yet resisted to the point of shedding your blood. 5 And have you forgotten the exhortation that addresses you as sons?

> *"My son, do not regard lightly the discipline of*
> *the Lord,*
> *nor be weary when reproved by him.*
> *6 For the Lord disciplines the one he loves,*
> *and chastises every son whom he receives."*

7 It is for discipline that you have to endure. God is treating you as sons. For what son is there whom his father does not discipline? 8 If you are left without discipline, in which all have participated, then you are illegitimate children and not sons. 9 Besides this, we have had earthly fathers who disciplined us and we respected them. Shall we not much more be subject to the Father of spirits and live? 10 For they disciplined us for a short time as it seemed best to them, but he disciplines us for our good, that we may share his holiness. 11 For the moment all discipline seems painful rather than pleasant, but later it yields the peaceful fruit of righteousness to those who have been trained by it.

12 Therefore lift your drooping hands and strengthen your weak knees, 13 and make straight paths for your feet, so that what is lame may not be put out of joint but rather be healed. 14 Strive for peace with everyone, and for the holiness without which no one will see the Lord. 15 See to it that no one fails to obtain the grace of God; that no "root of bitterness" springs up and causes trouble, and by it many become defiled; 16 that no one is sexually immoral or unholy like Esau, who sold his birthright for a single meal. 17 For you know that afterward, when he desired to inherit the blessing, he was rejected, for he found no chance to repent, though he sought it with tears.

Overview: The reformers have much to say about the first two verses of this section. They offer various interpretations of the "cloud of witnesses" (Heb 12:1), some seeing it as an image of protection and covering while others view it as one of encouragement and guidance. There are also different emphases in the reformers' comments on how Christians are to "run with endurance the race that is set before us" (Heb 12:1): some stress the importance of faith while others highlight the centrality of mortification and the rejection of the world. Christ is presented as both the umpire of the spiritual race, who awaits the victor at the finish line, but also as the encouraging coach, who beckons the runners onward. All reformers agree that this race contains much turmoil and suffering and that fixing one's gaze on Christ is the only way to finish well.

Moreover, the pastoral concerns of the reformers are readily evident in their comments on this passage. They urge Christians not to lose heart in the midst of suffering for the gospel, but rather to see such suffering as the gentle discipline of their heavenly Father, who was preparing them for heaven. The reformers all seek to communicate this basic message of steadfastness in the midst of adversity by encouraging believers that God is hidden in such adversity and is finally sovereign over it. The reformers also comment at length on the reference to Esau (Heb 12:16), seeking to make sense of this in light of the immediate context and of the epistle's larger discussion of forgiveness for serious postbaptismal sin.

Do Not Compromise Holiness. Pilgram Marpeck: My dearest ones, for your own improvement read Hebrews chapter 12 diligently. This is the true admonition of Paul that you tolerate nothing unclean among you. For the whole world would have to be judged and destroyed before God would tolerate evil in his congregation. For this we have ample analogies in Exodus. Pay diligent attention, so that the tempter does not catch you through human temptation, since we have been rescued and kept from all powerful errors through the grace of Christ. May the Lord rescue and redeem us, together with you, from all temptations, as he has done until now. Concerning Unity and the Bride of Christ.[1]

12:1 *Faithfully Run the Race*

We Follow Christ by Faith Alone. Johannes Bugenhagen: Since we see that whoever has been saved was saved by faith, we also by faith should lay aside every weight of conscience and of the sin that always fights against us, and we should run with endurance the race that is set before us, not picking out a method or way for ourselves, but only looking to the method, way, and teaching of Christ, our trainer and referee. In other words, just as the saints of old followed (which is discussed above), let us follow him by faith alone, for he is our leader on the track on which we are running, wherever and by whatever course he may lead. And this is the cross, which is the companion of faith, as is described here with great elegance. Here you will not stray at all from Christ our leader, as long as you do not make your own ways, as Isaiah says. For he is the leader of our of faith; that is, the beginning and continuation of all our good. And he is the finisher of all our salvation, so that you may know that "nothing is left for us mortals."† For this reason the author here earnestly warns them not to fall away because of passing afflictions from faith and the Christian life that accompanies faith, so that you can actually see where the entire letter is looking from this one passage. Commentary on the Pauline Epistles, Heb 12:1.[2]

An Exhortation to Patience. Heinrich Bullinger: Now he turns to the subject of patience, from which he departed at the end of chapter 10. He exhorts his readers to this virtue by examples, comparisons, rewards, and penalties. For without patience, which is never present without perseverance of the soul, faith would be nothing at all. But with these words he lays down the essence of the matter and connects what follows with what has gone before. He addresses believers as those sweating it out in a race and contest, since (as Job testifies) the life of humankind on the earth is nothing but a battle. But those who run in a race are accustomed to cast off all hindrances and weights so that they may run it unencumbered. So Paul alludes to this when he exhorts believers to the end that, once they have cast off laziness and the cares of this world and the remaining cravings of this kind implanted in us by nature that draw us away from holy living, they may run with patience in the truth of the gospel, since they see that such a multitude of saints (for he calls great force and abundance "a cloud") have persevered in faith with steadfast patience all the way to the end. Commentary on Hebrews 12:1.[3]

The Great Race. John Calvin: This conclusion is, as it were, an epilogue to the former chapter, by which he shows the end for which he gave a catalog of the saints who excelled in faith under the law, even that every one should be prepared to imitate them; and he calls a large multitude metaphorically a cloud, for he sets what is dense in

[1]CRR 12:113.

[2]Bugenhagen, *Annotationes in epistolas Pauli recognitae* (1525), 157r-v; citing Is 58:13. †I have been unable to identify the source of this reference.

[3]Bullinger, *In Pauli ad Hebraeos Epistolam*, 126r-v; citing Job 7:1.

opposition to that is thinly scattered. . . . Now the metaphor of a race is often to be found in Scripture, but here it means not any kind of race, but a running contest, which is wont to call forth the greatest exertions. The import of what is said then is that we are engaged in a contest, even in a race of the most celebrated, that many witnesses stand around us, that the Son of God is the umpire who invites and exhorts us to secure the prize, and that therefore it would be most disgraceful for us to grow weary or inactive in the midst of our course. And at the same time the holy people whom he mentioned are not only witnesses but also have been associates in the same race, who have beforehand shown the way to us; and yet he preferred calling them witnesses rather than runners, in order to intimate that they are not rivals, seeking to snatch from us the prize, but approvers to applaud and hail our victory; and Christ also not only is the umpire but also extends his hand to us, and supplies us with strength and energy; in short, he prepares and fits us to enter on our course, and by his power leads us on to the end of the race. Commentaries on the Epistle of Paul the Apostle to the Hebrews 12:1.[4]

The Protective Cloud. Gasparo Contarini: Just as the clouds defend us from the heat of the sun, so, just as the clouds, the example of so many excellent people defends us from the heat of temptation, lest we turn aside from faith. Scholia in the Epistles of the Divine Paul, the Epistle to the Hebrews 12:1.[5]

The Cloud of Self-Mortification. Desiderius Erasmus: Therefore, since we are surrounded by so great a crowd and, if I may so speak, a cloud of those who through the endurance of such evils have given testimony even in the Old Testament that they put their faith wholeheartedly in God's promises, let us ourselves, encouraged by their example, be likewise concerned to cast aside the weight and burden of material goods and desires that hold back the care-laden mind in its quest for heaven and to shake off the sin that attaches itself to us from all sides. Paraphrases on the Epistle to the Hebrews 12:1.[6]

A Cloudburst of Holy Witnesses. Wenzeslaus Linck: The apostle exhorts readers to this [bearing of the cross] at the beginning of this chapter because so many holy fathers and patriarchs at the time of the Old and New Testaments lived in faith [and] confessed and witnessed to the same. They also suffered much for it to provide an example for us, and following them we should battle like knights and remain steadfast in the cross and in it testify to our faith. The Latin text has *nubeum testium* etc., that is, as one says, a great cloud. And it is a beautiful similitude or comparison, because just as a cloudburst holds and gives forth a great abundance of water, so we have a great abundance of witnesses who do not fly here and there like fickle persons, who are like waterless clouds, which the wind blows here and there. Rather, they are around us on every side and float above us as a cloud in its heavenly course that protects us from sunstroke with its shadow and the rains of the salutary doctrine with words and examples. The Twelfth Chapter of the Epistle to the Hebrews 12:1.[7]

The Divine Contest. Lucas Osiander: God has set before us a contest of a kind that is usually proposed to those who are running into the stadium, looking for some proposed reward. And so that as victors we might come forth and be crowned, we must run strenuously by means of good works and by means by patiently bearing afflictions, chiefly those that press upon us on account of our confession of Christ. Those who desire to win set aside those things that are onerous and an impediment, thus let us cast aside

[4]CTS 40:310-12*.
[5]Contarini, *Opera*, 528.
[6]CWE 44:252.
[7]Linck, *Das zwoelfft Capitel der Epistel an die Ebreer*, Bv-Bii r; citing Eph 4:14.

all those things that are wont to retard that sacred course of ours. The onerous things are sins, avarice, lust, hatred, pride, etc., but also the inhering depravity—as far as possible, let us drive it out and purge it. And much patience is necessary to us in this contest or course, lest in the middle of the course we fail by ingratitude or the bitterness of affliction. They are not crowned who remain standing in the course and do not run to the goal. Let us proceed full of courage, let us be summoned forth by the examples of all of holy people and martyrs whose constancy in true devotion and endurance in the cross the Lord proposes to us for consideration and imitation. Epistle to the Hebrews 12:1.[8]

The Cloud in the Wilderness Compared to the Cloud of Witnesses. William Perkins: They are compared to a cloud (as I take it) by allusion to the cloud that directed and led the Israelites in the wilderness. . . . Now, as that cloud guided the Israelites from the bondage of Egypt to the land of Canaan, so this company of famous believers directs all the true members of God's church in the New Testament in the right way from the kingdom of darkness to the spiritual Canaan the kingdom of heaven. And this is the true cause why these worthy believers are compared to a cloud. A Clovd of Faithfull Witnesses, Heb 12:1.[9]

12:2-3 *Look to Jesus*

Christ Did Not Turn Back from Opposition—How Can We? Heinrich Bullinger: He exhorts them not only by the examples of the holy fathers, but by the example of Christ, who is the beginning and end of faith (that is, of our religion), the prow and stern—that is, he is everything all by himself. For this is what is intended by *archēgon kai teleiōtēn,* that is, beginning and end, leader and perfecter. He could have kept himself exempt from all troubles, but he chose to suffer death for us; after this, then, who would be reluctant to undergo the worst experiences whatever for the name of Christ and of the truth? Disgrace and the libels of slanderous people did not turn Christ away from his purpose; for that reason, he was also received into glory. Hence if, with our face set firm from the beginning we go forward on our journey, however the world may rage and malign us, we will come at last with Christ into glory. Commentary on Hebrews 12:2.[10]

The Patient Beholding of Christ. Wenzeslaus Linck: No one shall be preserved through patience in their life except through the beholding of Jesus Christ, just as no one could recover from the bites of the fiery serpents except through the beholding of the honorable serpent. The Twelfth Chapter of the Epistle to the Hebrews 12:2.[11]

Let Us Follow Christ Our Captain. Johannes Oecolampadius: He is not content to exhort them to endurance and constancy of faith by the examples of the holy fathers, but he also ventures to summon them by the example of Christ, as the most important of all, if perhaps there were someone who would not be moved by other things. Supposing that there may be someone who is too weak to follow the fathers, still they should not lose heart—we have the mightiest captain of faith in Jesus, who longs to lead us by the hand, and he does this so delightfully because he is our way, our forerunner, and our shepherd, the one most ready to help us. For we fix our eyes on him who goes before us and completes us, for he perfectly suffered and endured both pains and insults all at once. It would certainly be highly inappropriate for a servant to desire to be greater than their master. Likewise, would it not be absolutely disgraceful, while our captain leads us on the march, to stoop to desire to be at home and

[8]Osiander, *Epistola ad Hebraeos,* 87-88.
[9]Perkins, *Workes,* 3:200b*; citing Ex 13:21.
[10]Bullinger, *In Pauli ad Hebraeos Epistolam,* 126v-127r.
[11]Linck, *Das zwoelfft Capitel der Epistel an die Ebreer,* Biv r-Biv v; citing Num 21:4-9.

not to apply ourselves to any campaign, especially one from which we are allowed to hope to benefit so much? Take note of how the expression "captain of faith"† for "captain of those who have faith" (just as, earlier, he used "high priest of the confession" for "high priest of those who confess") is an instance of the concrete substituted for the abstract. Thus you have Christ our Savior to whom especially believers should look and whom they should imitate, then the saints to the degree that they imitated Christ. This is evident from the apostle's words in 1 Corinthians 11, where he says, "Be imitators of me, as I am of Christ." Others interpret "captain of faith" as "giver of faith"; this interpretation is reasonable, but less relevant. Explanations of Hebrews 12:2.[12]

Christ's Suffering as Sacrament and Example. Wenzeslaus Linck: Christ's suffering is a sacrament and an example for us, a sacrament of faith, that is, a certain sign on which we can set our trust, and an example of the life that we should follow and order our lives after. The Twelfth Chapter of the Epistle to the Hebrews 12:3.[13]

12:4-6 *God Disciplines Those He Loves*

Consolation in the Midst of Suffering. Wenzeslaus Linck: In such a case it is consoling when a person thinks about their previous suffering, because they will certainly not want to have it forgotten. It is just as when a person has invested a lot of money in a mine that they do not want to lose. They always put more into it in the hopes of the yield. Just so it makes one steadfast in suffering when they think on previous suffering. They are consoled to suffer more in the future and to remain steadfast in the battle against sin. They regard past suffering as being much too little. . . . But the consideration of the end of eternal salvation consoles much more. The Twelfth Chapter of the Epistle to the Hebrews 12:4.[14]

We Should Delight in the Lord's Fatherly Discipline. Johannes Oecolampadius: He quotes an axiom from Proverbs 3, by which he exhorts us to endure hardship patiently. To undergo many things as sent from God is a sign of the highest love. Those who are greatly disciplined are especially loved by God. This the world does not understand. But he is not speaking about those who suffer as thieves, murderers, and that kind of criminal, but only as followers of the truth. He means discipline in general, whether delivered through prophets or tyrants or sicknesses or poverty or any other means. For God often chooses to give exercise to the faith of his people with such things. Howsoever it may come about, take care not to be discontented and downcast at heart, but rather be pleased. For he says that it is normal for the Lord to discipline or instruct those whom he loves. In Hosea it says as immediate retribution that the Lord, in his hatred of the adulterous Israelites, refused to discipline them, but permitted their worst desires. Surely the Lord disciplines those he disciplines here as the most forbearing Father, and as one who has not yet abandoned his concern for his people. Revelation 3: "Those whom I love, I reprove and chastise." David, Jeremiah, and others gave thanks to God for this chastisement or correction. For this is how we are trained up to salvation. He seems to intend to say the same thing in what follows below. "He chastises every son whom he receives." As long as we are chastised as sons, we are still in the favor of the Father, who, when he sees that we are lazy and too little mindful of our duty, incites us to attention with goads like

[12]Oecolampadius, *In Epistolam ad Hebraeos Explanationes*, 149v-150r; citing Jn 14:6; Heb 6:20; 13:20; 4:16; Jn 13:16; 1 Cor 11:1. †This is *dux fidei*, Erasmus's rendering of *pisteōs archēgon*, which is usually translated "author . . . of our faith" in English. The Greek can bear either meaning.

[13]Linck, *Das zwoelfft Capitel der Epistel an die Ebreer*, Cii r-Cii v. On the use of Christ's suffering as sacrament and example in Luther's writings, see Ronald K. Rittgers, *The Reformation of Suffering: Pastoral Theology and Lay Piety in Late Medieval and Early Modern Germany* (New York: Oxford University Press, 2012), 115.

[14]Linck, *Das zwoelfft Capitel der Epistel an die Ebreer*, Ciii r-C iii v.

these and rouses us so that we press on vigorously in faith and patience. Further, he whose mercy is beyond all telling does not delight in our chastisements, but because we ourselves forget, he chooses to remedy this evil when he disciplines. But he does this for his own so that he need not condemn them with this depraved world, as we read in 1 Corinthians 11:32. Explanations of Hebrews 12:4-6.[15]

We Must Learn to Recognize the Father Under the Cross. Wenzeslaus Linck: Holy Scripture holds before us such consolation, which the apostle here indicates with these friendly words of rebuke when he says, "you have already forgotten this consolation," namely, that God wishes to say to you who battle under the cross, to you as to his children, "Your suffering is not so great as you think; you have not battled in a manly fashion long enough against sin—you have not withstood the point of shedding your blood." [The Apostle says further,] "you have also forgotten the friendly consolation of God for those who suffer, whom he calls his children under the cross." He speaks through Solomon under the cross, "My son." He is so good and merciful toward the afflicted that he sees them as his children. What Christian would not then be consoled under the cross? We call to God always as a father, as Christ calls us to pray, "Our Father, who art in heaven, etc." Therefore, we should learn to recognize such a Father under the cross by the rods [he uses], and we should allow his faithfulness and goodness to console us, holding as certain that he will not leave us without consolation (2 Cor 1). For he himself is the one who discipline us out of love. The cross or suffering is in the first place a discipline through which we are taught and instructed just as students in the liberal studies (*disciplinis liberalibus*), so that we are not like horses and mules, who have no understanding and in whose mouth one must place bridle and bit, when they will not go to God. . . . Only punishment or vexation teaches us to look to the Word.

It is not possible for a person to be a child and friend of God and not have trials, crosses, or afflictions. The Twelfth Chapter of the Epistle to the Hebrews 12:5-6.[16]

The Result of Rebellion. Helena Von Freyberg: I confess and acknowledge my guilt from the bottom of my heart before God and all his saints in heaven and on earth, how I have transgressed and incurred guilt in the matter that has now been revealed to me by God's grace through the goodness of the Holy Spirit through the mercy and goodness of God my Lord and Father. God does not neglect to discipline his wicked, quarrelsome child; unfortunately, I have rebelled against God and as a result I have lost the grace of the Holy Spirit. The fruit of the Spirit—patience, righteousness, gentleness, humility, kindness, true love, faithfulness, peace, self-discipline—can no longer be seen in me, which mocks true faith and the Word of God. Confession.[17]

12:7-15 *God's Discipline Is Evidence of Our Adoption*

God Offers Himself to Us in Our Crosses. Wenzeslaus Linck: From this a Christian should draw consolation in every cross and suffering and strengthen himself when he considers the great benefit that they bring. Therefore, the apostle turns from the external examples of the beloved saints to us ourselves and explains the previous saying of Solomon. In the first place we should be consoled in crosses because God offers himself to us in them as a Father, and when we think that we are abandoned by God, he proves most fully that he cares for us as a good father and holds us as his beloved children. The suffering that

[15]Oecolampadius, *In Epistolam ad Hebraeos Explanationes*, 152r-v; citing Prov 3:11-12; 1 Jn 3:1; 1 Pet 4:15-16; Hos 4:14; Rev 3:19; Ps 25:8; 141:3-5; Jer 10:24; 31:18-19; Ps 119:67, 71, 75; 1 Cor 11:32.

[16]Linck, *Das zwoelfft Capitel der Epistel an die Ebreer*, Ciiii r-Ciiii v and D v; citing Prov 3:11-12; Mt 6:9; Lk 11:2; 2 Cor 1:3-4; Jas 3:3.

[17]CRR 12:508; citing Gal 5:22.

the world sees as evil is a sign of [God's] friendship and of our status as his children. . . . Therefore, God proves through the cross who are his true children. The Twelfth Chapter of the Epistle to the Hebrews 12:7-11.[18]

Spiritual Discipline from a Good Father. Cardinal Cajetan: He employs an argument from experience, and from the lesser to the greater. If we endured our physical fathers when they disciplined us when doing so involves fear, we are far more bound to endure the discipline of our spiritual Father when doing so results in life. The Father of spirit is as much greater than the father of flesh as the fruit of life is greater than the fruit of fear or respect. For God is the "Father of spirit" both because he gives the intellectual soul as a person emerges from the womb, and because he is the bestower of the spiritual grace by which we have eternal life. Comments on Hebrews 12:9-10.[19]

God's Perfect Correction. William Jones: "For they disciplined us for a short time as it seemed best to them," but they were often corrupt and erring in judgment and affection. Sometimes our fathers correct us for things we have not done and leave uncorrected that which deserves correction. Often they correct in anger and fury, doing that which they repent of afterward. But what seems best to God is always good, for he is most wise and knows how to correct: he is not subject to sinful passions and affections, as these fathers are.

They in chastening us often respect their own ease and peace of mind, their own credit and commodity, more than ours. Or if they correct us for our profit, yet it is but for a temporal profit, that we do not run not into outrages in the world, that we may lead a civil, honest life among men and women—that is the mark at which most parents aim. Whereas the Father of spirits disciplines us for our profit, a profit that he himself does not in need from us, not only to make us civil people . . . but "that we may be share his holiness," that we might be holy in soul and body in this life, and citizens of the holy Jerusalem in the life to come. A Commentary upon the Epistles of St. Paul, Heb 12:10.[20]

12:16-17 *Esau Rejected*

The Ungodly Ask for Forgiveness. Johannes Bugenhagen: The repentance and lamentation of Esau is properly understood as the repentance of the ungodly, which in the sight of God is no repentance at all if they only feel sorrow for their painful circumstances and the distress of their soul, into which they perceive they have fallen at present through the judgment of God, while, if they could be released from their distress, they would despise God forever. Esau's story openly teaches this very thing, for after he had wept before his father with great lamentation, he went out and, in pure contempt of his father, took a third wife whom his father had never seen. In the same way Cain desired to escape from the fear into which he had fallen, but he could not ask pardon for his transgression from the heart. Likewise, Saul, when he was confined in a difficult strait, did not ask to be forgiven for having despised God, though he had wanted to escape from the difficulty, and when he saw no other remedy, he cut short his own life with a sword, as Judas did with a noose. Who does not see from this act that Judas felt sorrow at the time because he was inwardly distressed by the judgment of God, though he still could not ask pardon for his sin? These fearful examples ought to terrify those who regard repentance as within their reach as often as they want, as if that faith by which only we may be delivered were a matter of human righteousness, and not rather the work of God. Consider the repentance of Pharaoh, who was often lashed by God but expected that he could ask for deliverance. Likewise, the demons would like to be released, but still they cannot ask pardon for their transgressions. Likewise the foolish

[18]Linck, *Das zwoelfft Capitel der Epistel an die Ebreer*, Diii v, Diiii v.
[19]Cajetan, *In Epistolam ad Hebraeos Commentarii*, 170r.
[20]Jones, *A Commentary upon the Epistles of St Paul*, 555*.

virgins would surely like to enter into the wedding, but they do not ask pardon for their foolishness (that is, their unbelief, just as it says in Ps 14).† In fact, as it is written elsewhere, the plausible hypocrites experience the same thing as the virgins without oil who tried to be sanctified by their own merits. "Lord," they say, "did we not prophesy in your name?" And so forth. Commentary on the Pauline Epistles, Heb 12:16.[21]

Contempt for Holy Things Leads to Eternal Loss. Heinrich Bullinger: Defilement is related to contempt for holy things. For what regard for holy things would there be in someone who holds the conviction that pleasure is the highest of things? Such a person would sell all the preaching of the gospel for less than that for which Esau sold his birthright. For you can find those who say that they would rather have a pint of wine than a gospel sermon. But these people in due time will suffer appropriate punishments. For even Esau purchased eternal penitence with a brief flicker of enjoyment. For when he wanted to obtain the blessing by right of inheritance, he was so rejected that he was left with no hope of its restitution. For of course no one understands this as referring to repentance from sins, but rather to change of fortune. For it was not permissible for Esau to recover his birthright after he had once sold it with such carelessness. Therefore, those who argue from this passage whether repentance is denied to those who have fallen away undergo contortions uselessly. For *metanoia* in Greek is turning around and correcting, or rather changing any matter at all, not only in the sense of repentance that is in use among theologians. But we find no mention of the forgiveness of sins; rather we speak of the right of primogeniture, or how great an evil it is to despise holy things. In any case, by the example of Esau he intends to indicate that all the best things are lost by defilement and contempt for holy matters. Commentary on Hebrews 12:16-17.[22]

Willful Sinners Will Find Themselves in the Same Position as Esau. Johannes Oecolampadius: Those who pursue wealth and pleasure and regard godly religion with indifference are unworthy of the kingdom of heaven. By "sexually immoral," he refers not to someone who has fallen into this degradation once or twice, but who has already contracted the habit of wickedness. Likewise, "unholy" refers to those who are settled in neglect of a life that is pure and according to godliness and in disregard for the mysteries of God. But you must not suppose that the apostle would have made mention of these things if he had not known that they had already sprung up in the church at that time. You may see here that there is nothing blessed in any part of humanity; therefore, be careful how you walk, sympathize with those who have fallen through weakness, but in such a way that you never consent to join in the errors of your brothers.

"Like Esau." The apostle very shrewdly introduces this example with which, by his warning, he could call back or keep on the way brothers who were more neglectful of religion and more devoted to the flesh than befitted their calling. Certainly Esau sold his birthright, which he should have held in the highest honor, for a paltry meal. For what reason? For the sake of his gluttony and the pleasure of the moment. His birthright should not have been so contemptible to him, because it had actually been given by God, and contempt for it could only bring him other troubles. For afterward, when he was brought to repentance too late, he lost the blessing by the righteous judgment of God. See Genesis 25 and 27. Clearly the apostle explains this passage dexterously, and in accordance with the very mind of the Spirit. There are those who slander this passage as one in which repentance is denied, just as the Novatian heretics dared to assert, but they do so contrary to reason.† No chance for repentance will

[21]Bugenhagen, *Annotationes in epistolas Pauli recognitae* (1525), 157v-158r; citing Gen 27:38; 28:6-9; 4:13-14; 1 Sam 28:20; 31:4; Mt 27:3-5; Ex 8:8, 14, 28, 32; Mt 8:28-34; 25:1-13; 7:21-23; Ps 14:1. †Bugenhagen cites Ps 13[:1], following the chapter divisions of the Vulgate.

[22]Bullinger, *In Pauli ad Hebraeos Epistolam*, 130r-v.

be left at the time when the sentence of judgment will have been passed. Surely the damned in hell will weep in vain and be motivated to repent of their sins. And that this is the apostle's meaning will readily appear to be more probable to the careful observer. The blessing that Isaac gave, as it was surely performed at the instigation of the Holy Spirit, took the place of the final sentence, and thus it was necessarily settled and irrevocable. Because if Esau had changed his conduct and had repented truly and from the heart before the blessing was performed, then he would not have been rejected by God. This seems to me to be a faithful explanation of the passage. Others remark here that Esau did not really repent; for he wished the deed had not been done, but he behaved thus more with a view to the penalty, just as Judas did, and all the ungodly are accustomed to do, who more dread the punishment when they lament their crimes than because they hate sin and perceive that they have offended against God. Explanations of Hebrews 12:16-17.[23]

[23]Oecolampadius, *In Epistolam ad Hebraeos Explanationes*, 156r-157r; citing Eph 5:15; Jude 23. †Novatian (d. c. 258), a presbyter in the Roman church, and his followers formed rival churches to protest the lenient policies adopted by orthodox churches toward Christians who lapsed during times of persecution.

12:18-29 The Gift of the Unshakeable Kingdom

[18]For you have not come to what may be touched, a blazing fire and darkness and gloom and a tempest [19]and the sound of a trumpet and a voice whose words made the hearers beg that no further messages be spoken to them. [20]For they could not endure the order that was given, "If even a beast touches the mountain, it shall be stoned." [21]Indeed, so terrifying was the sight that Moses said, "I tremble with fear." [22]But you have come to Mount Zion and to the city of the living God, the heavenly Jerusalem, and to innumerable angels in festal gathering, [23]and to the assembly[a] of the firstborn who are enrolled in heaven, and to God, the judge of all, and to the spirits of the righteous made perfect, [24]and to Jesus, the mediator of a new covenant, and to the sprinkled blood that speaks a better word than the blood of Abel.

[25]See that you do not refuse him who is speaking. For if they did not escape when they refused him who warned them on earth, much less will we escape if we reject him who warns from heaven. [26]At that time his voice shook the earth, but now he has promised, "Yet once more I will shake not only the earth but also the heavens." [27]This phrase, "Yet once more," indicates the removal of things that are shaken—that is, things that have been made—in order that the things that cannot be shaken may remain. [28]Therefore let us be grateful for receiving a kingdom that cannot be shaken, and thus let us offer to God acceptable worship, with reverence and awe, [29]for our God is a consuming fire.

a Or *church*

Overview: In light of the many different themes in this section, the reformers' comments head in several directions. But in general they seek to stress once more how ineffective the Levitical law was in purging sin and how much superior to the law is the blood and sacrifice of Christ, which opens the way to heaven. The reformers urge great zeal in the pursuit of this way and insist that there are no excuses for those who are negligent or lazy in doing so, for which divine punishment will surely follow. Still, the reformers do not emphasize this punishment; rather, they continue to focus on the consolation that comes to the believer through faith in Christ.

12:18-21 *God Unapproachable Under the Law*

The Superiority of the Gospel. The English Annotations: The apostle further presses on the Hebrews the exhortation begun in verse 12, from the excellence of their condition who are under the gospel, or new covenant, above others who were under the law or old covenant. Those ordinances in giving and receiving the law, being so terrible, so that the people could not bear that which was commanded, showed the nature and use of the law, that it was a killing letter, working wrath, contrary to the gospel given on Mount Zion. Annotations on Hebrews 12:18.[1]

The Gospel Brings Clarity and Friendship. John Calvin: He shows the greatness of the grace that is opened to us by the gospels so that we may learn to receive it with reverence, and second he commends to us its sweetness so as to entice us to love and desire it. He emphasizes both of these by comparing law and gospel. The more the kingdom of Christ excels the dispensation of Moses, and the more glorious our calling is than that of the people of old, the baser and more inexcusable is our ingratitude if we do not accept the blessing that is offered to us with proper piety, and humbly receive the majesty of Christ that is here evident. Further,

[1]Downame, ed., *Annotations*, NNN3v*; citing Rom 4:15; 5:18.

since God does not show himself to us as terrible, as he did to the Jews, but invites us to come to him in friendship and fellowship, so we are doubly guilty of ingratitude if we do not accept his gracious invitation with the utmost earnestness. Let us remember therefore that the gospel is here compared with law, and second, that this comparison has two parts, the first that the glory of God shows itself more clearly in the gospel than in the law, and the second, that the calling of God today is in friendship when previously it held nothing but terror. Commentary On Hebrews 12:18.[2]

The Image of Sinai. Heinrich Bullinger: After much and varied discussion, he at last concludes what he has been treating throughout the entire epistle, and by means of a particular image he sets it before our eyes to be considered. He first draws together the arguments he had made regarding the weakness and ineffectiveness of the law, then those regarding the worthiness of the gospel and the finished redemption of Christ, and finally those by which he exhorted the reader in the first and second parts[†] of the epistle to believe in Christ and receive the preaching of the gospel. But here is the image of all this, by which he recalls the second part of the epistle before our eyes: imagine that there are two mountains standing—on the one hand, Sinai, on the other hand, Zion. The law is represented by the first, Christ and the gospel by the second. Here he describes at length the mountain on which the law was given, which comes from chapter 19 of the second book of Moses. But since everything there is terrifying and gloomy, it signifies that as much as the worshipers were not perfected or acquitted by the law, so they were terrified and accused. For peace is granted to the conscience not by the law, but by the gospel. Hence he said, "You have not come to a mountain which is touched . . . but to Mount Zion." Commentary on Hebrews 12:18-21.[3]

Urging to Holiness. Johannes Oecolampadius: He urges them by a stronger argument, namely, by the exalted station of Christ, with whom we have all enlisted, and whose church we are called. If we truly believe in him, it behooves us to remember our calling, righteousness, peace, purity, and to be zealous for holiness. And this corresponds with what we saw earlier. I said above, where we read, "Strive for peace with everyone, and the holiness without which no one will see the Lord," that the apostle had in mind this same passage from Exodus 19; because he is doing enough for his purpose, he takes it upon himself to discuss it. But this argument is frequently found in Paul's writings: that it would befit us to put forth more effort for holiness than those who lived under Moses, because under Christ we walk in greater light. Formerly, when Moses was going to receive the law from the Lord, when the people of Israel approached that cruder mountain, they heard that they must first consecrate themselves for three days, just as we said a little earlier. We have not come to such a mountain, blazing fire, tempest and darkness, and so on, but to Mount Zion, to the city of the living God, just as he will say in a moment; therefore, consider with how much more holiness we are required to show ourselves approved unto God. Explanations of Hebrews 12:18-21.[4]

The Invitation of Christ. Huldrych Zwingli: "For you have not come to a mountain that can be touched. . . ." By means of another argument he warns us not to fall away from the grace of God, namely, by a comparison of the preaching of the law and the teaching of Christ. For he establishes that the voice of Christ stands out as far more gracious and gentle than that of the law. For the law cries out to the students of its teaching, "Cursed is the one who does not remain in everything that is written. . . ." But Christ, the preacher of the gospel, kindly invites and urges, saying, "Come to me, all who labor and are heavy

[2]CNTC 12:199*.

[3]Bullinger, *In Pauli ad Hebraeos Epistolam*, 131r; citing Heb 9:9; Ex 19:23. [†]Bullinger divides Hebrews into three parts: 1:1–4:13; 4:14–10:18; and 10:19–13:25.

[4]Oecolampadius, *In Epistolam ad Hebraeos Explanationes*, 157r-v; citing Ex 19:10-11; 1 Cor 1:26; Eph 4:1; Heb 3:1; 2 Tim 2:15.

laden, and I will give you rest," and, "Whoever believes in me has eternal life." Exposition of Hebrews 12:18-21.[5]

12:22-24 *Through Christ, We Have Entered the City of God*

The Heavenly Jerusalem Replaces the Earthly Mountain. John Calvin: He compares Mount Zion with Mount Sinai, and he calls it the "heavenly Jerusalem," using the word "heavenly" so that the Jews will not stick to that earthly mountain where the law had flourished. When they sought stubbornly to remain under the servile yoke of the law, it was turned to Mount Sinai, as Paul says. He understands the heavenly Jerusalem as that which was to be built throughout the whole world, as the angel in Zechariah stretched his line from the east to the west. Commentary on Hebrews 12:22.[6]

Christ's Sacrifice Opens a Way to Heaven. Heinrich Bullinger: With these words he draws together what he taught more fully in the second part,[†] that by Christ's sacrifice we have been acquitted, and by his death and priesthood a way has been opened into the heavens. And all these things he also treats at greater length and clothes in symbols in his conclusion. So "Mount Zion" is what he calls Christ and the grace of the gospel. For just as the law proceeded from Sinai, so from Zion came life and salvation. This has alluded to Isaiah 2 and Micah 4. But the city of God is the heavenly the Jerusalem, that is, eternal life. In it the chorus of angels rejoices continually. In it one may see the firstborn, that is, those chosen by God, all the holy fathers; these are called "firstborn" in reference to the firstborn children of their fathers, who are the favorites and lords of the property. In it one may see God himself, the judge of all, that is, the master of all, as well as the souls of all the righteous. This matter is by no means commonplace. For Socrates himself, when he was about to die, said, "If death is a passage to those shores that are inhabited by the departed dead, who can be happier than I? For then to me it will be granted to meet the men who have lived righteous and faithful lives. For what value do you place on the privilege of conversing with Orpheus, Musaeus, Homer, and Hesiod? For my part I could feel in my heart the wish to die many times, that I might have the privilege of finding what I am speaking of." Plato wrote these words about Socrates, as found in Tullius's *Tusculan Disputations*, book 1.[‡] But next there comes, by way of interpretation, "You have come to Mount Zion," that is, "To Jesus, the mediator. . . ." For the previous statements are explained by this, because the way into the heavens is opened by the blood of Christ. Meanwhile, he makes mention of "sprinkling," referring to the type, which he discussed in chapter 9. But he says that the blood of Christ says better things than the blood of Abel, because the latter spoke of vengeance, while the former spoke of atonement. This is said by way of personification. Commentary on Hebrews 12:22-24.[7]

The Real Mount Zion. Thomas Adams: Not literally that Mount Zion where Solomon built the temple and David his palace. That local Zion became like Shiloh, first, exceedingly and superlatively loved; afterward, abhorred and forsaken, like the "tabernacle of Shiloh, the tent where he dwelt among humankind." This was threatened to that sacred place as a just punishment of their rebellious profaneness. "Therefore I will do to the house that is called by my name, . . . as I did to Shiloh." It lies in the power of sin to make the most blessed places accursed. God turns "a fruitful land into a salty waste because of the

[5]Zwingli, *In Epistolam Beati Pauli ad Hebraeos Expositio*, 582; citing Deut 27:26; Gal 3:10; Jn 3:36; 11:25-26.
[6]CNTC 12:200*; citing Gal 4; Zech 14:4.

[7]Bullinger, *In Pauli ad Hebraeos Epistolam*, 131v-132r; citing Is 2:2-3; Mic 4:1-2. †Bullinger divides Hebrews into three parts: 1:1–4:13; 4:14–10:18; and 10:19–13:25. ‡Marcus Tullius Cicero, *Tusculan Disputations* 1.41 (LCL 116-119). Bullinger's quotation slightly condenses and rearranges the original, but preserves the main idea.

evil of its inhabitants. . . ." The ruin of a city is not the breach of the walls, but the apostasy of manners. Were the fences stronger than the sevenfold walls of Babylon, the sins within would hurl down the bulwarks without. . . .

This Zion then stands not on earthly foundations; for at the general dissolution, "the earth and the works that are done on it," cities, castles, towns, towers, "will be burned up." If it were built on a sandy foundation, when the rain, the floods, and the winds shall conspire against it, and it would fall, and the fall of it would be great. But Zion is built on Christ: "Behold I am laying in Zion a stone, a cornerstone chosen and precious, and whoever believes in him shall not be put to shame." This is made conspicuous by the antithesis of Mount Zion with the gospel, to Mount Sinai with the law. The Happiness of the Church.[8]

The Clear Voice of Christ's Blood. Wenzeslaus Linck: This is the highest and final consolation, that Christ shed his blood for us for reconciliation, and with this our heart or conscience has been sprinkled and sanctified so that before God we are without blemish and pure, for which we should be thankful. Christ's blood does not only sanctify and purify when it is sprinkled out through the sermon, rather it also speaks and continually cries to God for grace and forgiveness of sins for us, so that we should be grateful for such grace in believing and preaching as Christ makes us pious or righteous. Abel's blood screams revenge against his brother, testifies to his innocence, and praises his name (Ps 11),[†] but Christ's blood has a much clearer and more distinct voice, because it cries out that among all other things it gives the true and proper holiness. The Twelfth Chapter of the Epistle to the Hebrews 12:24.[9]

In Christ, We Are the Firstborn of God. Johannes Oecolampadius: He desires us to attend to our exalted station: if we really are genuine Christians, we have come to a different people, namely, the church of God, which is symbolized to us by Mount Zion. For that is where it had its beginning, and afterward it was extended to the ends of the earth, as is evident in Acts. In Galatians, where he contrasts Mount Zion and the earthly Jerusalem from the heavenly, it is also like this. Our mother is the heavenly Jerusalem, to which belong all those who have been righteous since the foundation of the world, but we will see this in the words of the apostle, who explains things clearly enough. But surely he puts our situation before that of the people of old so that he may inflame and awaken in us a zeal for more godliness. You may see here that this church of God cannot be perceived by human eyes, for the believing dead and those who were then living in the flesh and we who were to come later and even the very angels belong to this church. He calls it "the city of the living God," because God dwells in it and abundantly displays his grace in it, and "the heavenly Jerusalem," because it has no savor of any earthly defilement. He calls it "the assembly of the firstborn," because those who are gathered surpass their other brothers according to the flesh, and are almost their masters. Alternatively, they may be called "firstborn" by way of participation, because Christ, their head, is called the firstborn from the dead, as a result of which they are granted a share in his name. This honor particularly belongs to Christ, and that by nature, while it is ours only by grace. From eternity God predestined and foreknew those who would be saved, and this is recorded in heaven or in the book of life. Surely this is the source of joy for the sons of God, that their names are written in heaven, as Christ said regarding his disciples in Luke 10. Explanations of Hebrews 12:22-24.[10]

[8]Adams, *The Happiness of the Church*, 7-8*; citing Ps 78:60; Jer 7:14; Ps 107:34; 2 Pet 3:10; Mt 7:27; 1 Pet 2:6.

[9]Linck, *Das zwoelfft Capitel der Epistel an die Ebreer*, Jiiii r. †It is not clear whether Linck is here referring to Ps 11 in the Luther Bible, which corresponds to Ps 11 in the ESV, or to Ps 11 in the Vulgate, which corresponds to Ps 12 in the ESV.

[10]Oecolampadius, *In Epistolam ad Hebraeos Explanationes*, 159r-v; citing Acts 1:8; Gal 4:24-26, 28-31; Col 1:18; Rom 8:29; Rev 3:5; 13:8; Lk 10:20.

The Superior Splendor of the Second Abel. Johannes Oecolampadius: "And to the judge of all." It is not without reason that he mentions God the judge. For thus he inflicts care and fear on them so that they would not neglect to adorn their life with true holiness. For God is the judge, and the judge of all, from whom they cannot conceal anything that they have done. He says, "To the spirits of the righteous who have been made perfect," that is, who have set free from the body. For we are still waiting for true perfection, when God will be all in all. We should desire to come to these righteous ones. We said that "testament" is substituted for "covenant" at an earlier point, at which point we explained it as well.[†] In the same way Christ is our mediator, as if he were to say, "If there is nothing else that can move you, at least the most precious blood of Christ shed for us may move you to gratitude to him; if you scorn this blood, what excuse will you have when you pass away?"

"To the sprinkled blood." He alludes to propitiation accomplished through blood, which is discussed above in chapter 9. That was a symbol of the most precious blood of Christ, which cleanses us from all sins and defilements. Let us then take care not to be contaminated from now on. He says that the blood of Christ is far holier than that of Abel, who was killed by his brother and acted as a type of Christ. For Christ was also killed in complete innocence by his brothers the Jews. Surely the second Abel is far more splendid than the first Abel, who was the son of Adam, whereas the other is the Son of God. All murderers live in fear until the last day of their lives; this is the revenge of the blood of Abel until God brings them to judgment. For God does not let murder and the shedding of blood go unpunished. If this is true, how will they escape who daily shed the blood of Christ, as much as they can, and show themselves ungrateful to him in every way? Explanations of Hebrews 12:22-24.[11]

The Congregation of Humans and Angels. Dirk Philips: The congregation of God is a congregation of saints, namely, the angels in heaven and believing born-again people on earth who are renewed according to the image of God. They are joined together in Jesus Christ, just as Paul in his letters certainly declared, principally to the Hebrews. . . . From these words one may clearly understand the crowd of many thousands of angels, the congregation of the firstborn, who are recorded in heaven, and the spirits of the completely righteous, with all the believers who have come in addition, these all with one another are the congregation of God. God reigns over it there as the righteous judge, and Christ is the head of it, and the Holy Spirit dwells there. The Enchiridion.[12]

The Merciful Blood of Christ. Gasparo Contarini: The blood of Abel was crying out for revenge against Cain in the presence of the Lord, and the blood of Christ cries out for mercy and indulgence even toward those through whom it was spilled, namely, Jews and Gentiles. Scholia in the Epistles of the Divine Paul, the Epistle to the Hebrews 12:24.[13]

12:25-29 *Do Not Refuse God's Warning*

We Cannot Excuse Ourselves from the Call of Christ. Johannes Oecolampadius: The apostle cannot forget his purpose. For we have here the aim of the epistle, namely, that the Hebrews, who have hitherto been listeners to the Law and the Prophets, should henceforth listen to Christ, not to their Moses. For if one does not have faith in Christ, one will not be excused from punishment. *Mē paraitēsēsthe*, that is, "Do not offer an excuse by which you may be exempted from listening to Christ." For he not only wants us not to reject the one who is speaking, but not even to make any excuse. "Escape," that is, "escape from punishment."

---

[11]Oecolampadius, *In Epistolam ad Hebraeos Explanationes*, 159v-160r; citing Heb 9:18-22; 1 Cor 15:28; Heb 10:29; 1 Jn 1:7.
[†]Oecolampadius recognizes that the Latin word *testamentum* (corresponding to Greek *diathēkē*), which English translations here render "covenant," is more properly the term for a will or testament. This usage is reflected in Heb 9:15-22.
[12]CRR 6:352; citing Eph 3:6; Col 1:17; Eph 1:22; 1 Cor 3:16; 3:19.
[13]Contarini, *Opera*, 528.

Some understand "the one who spoke on earth" as the angel through whom the law was given, and acted as a symbol of a mediator; others take it as Moses, which meets with my agreement as well. For he asserts his usual argument from the greater to the less: Since those who did not listen to Moses did not escape punishment, far less will they depart unpunished who do not listen to the Son of God, who is now glorified, and persist in their unbelief. To be sure, a far heavier penalty will await them. It says the same thing above, in chapter 2. It so happened that the oracles given by Moses were heard on the earth; now Christ speaks from heaven when he breathes on his ministers with his Spirit and declares his will through humans. Or, when he says, "from heaven," he wants us to fix our eyes on the one who is coming as judge of the living and the dead. This is a very kind warning that we should be careful and cautious, and that we should listen to our one teacher and instructor in heaven, for he calls us to himself and to the very holiest life. Let us not make excuses, as those who were invited to the wedding feast did in the Gospels. Everyone naturally wishes to be exempt and to appear righteous—for example, Adam, Saul, and others. But no excuse avails with God; his authority over us is too great for us suppose that there is any room for excuses. Explanations of Hebrews 12:25.[14]

We Must Listen to the Man from Heaven. Cardinal Cajetan: "See to it that you do not refuse him who is speaking." Having enumerated at length the difference between the things to which the fathers of the Israelites had access when they received the law and the things to which we have access when we accept Christianity, he proceeds in his argument by admonishing us to listen to Jesus, the one who is speaking to us. "For if they did not escape"—doubtless from divine vengeance—"when they refused him who was speaking"—that is, declaring oracles—"to them over the earth." The pronoun "him" refers to Moses, for he declared to the people the divine messages or oracles when the people said, "You speak to us, and let not the Lord speak to us." So the argument is as follows: If the Israelites, who refused to obey Moses who declared to the people the divine oracles while he was upon the earth, did not escape from divine vengeance but wandered in the desert after being punished repeatedly . . . it is far more certain that we will be punished if we turn away from him who delivers messages from heaven. For, in comparison with Moses (who declared the divine oracles over the earth), he places Jesus as declaring the divine oracles from heaven. Jesus is called "from heaven." On the one hand, this is because he is not a mere man, but the man from heaven, in accordance with the word of John the Baptist regarding Jesus, "He who comes from heaven is above all." So Jesus himself says, "I came down from heaven." On the other hand, it is because, when this epistle was written and when these Hebrews came to faith in Christ, Jesus was disclosing the divine oracles from his location in heaven by sending the Holy Spirit and giving gifts such as tongues and prophecy. Comments on Hebrews 12:25-26.[15]

We Must Not Despise the Gospel. Wenzeslaus Linck: From all that is mentioned above the apostle concludes that we should not neglect and certainly not despise the gospel of Christ, rather with all diligence receive, hear, and keep it. And this is the scope and content of the whole epistle, namely, because they previously belonged to the Law and Prophets they should now from this point forward listen to Christ much more and avoid everything that distracts and hinders us from him, so that we may always believe on him firmly.† . . . The apostle provides the reason for all of this at the end, that our God is a consuming fire before whom nothing may stand. God purifies and purges everything most thoroughly of what is opposed to him. He consumes the rust of sin and the old Adam that he did not create, but that was brought

[14]Oecolampadius, *In Epistolam ad Hebraeos Explanationes*, 160r-v; citing Heb 2:1-4; Jn 20:22-23; Mt 23:8; 22:1-14; Lk 14:16-24.

[15]Cajetan, *In Epistolam ad Hebraeos Commentarii*, 171r; citing Ex 20:19; Jn 3:31; 6:38.

about by human evil. He does not permit the godless to survive, and there is nothing that can withstand his wrath. The Twelfth Chapter of the Epistle to the Hebrews 12:25-29.[16]

In Christ, We Have the Eternal and Unshakable. Johannes Oecolampadius: He says, "Look at the mystery in these words: 'Yet once more.'" If they are to be shaken, they are not stable and complete. God, who is the firmest and most immutable, cannot be shaken and displaced. Now, if the law of Moses is as firm and solid as God himself, why does he say that he will yet once more shake not only the earth but also heaven? So the prophet wished to indicate by this quaking the removal of the ceremonies, as things that were not bound to be everlasting and perpetual. How then can it be right for you to glory in these things? Shaking shows that these things are not firm and immovable.

"That is, things that have been made." No created being is actually immutable, because it began to be; not even the angels are really immutable by nature, but only by the grace of God, by which they also hold together. Everything that has been made can be destroyed and shaken. Eternal life, love in God—these are eternal goods that must endure. Mutable things must go first so that immutable things may take their place. It is appropriate to say this about the Levitical priesthood and ceremonies. Others apply these words to the last day, as that on which all things will be changed, which we also confess. Explanations of Hebrews 12:27.[17]

A Concluding Exhortation. Heinrich Bullinger: This is the universal conclusion of the entire subject, as if he had said, "Therefore, O Hebrews, since you are waiting for the kingdom of the Messiah, you may see in the meantime that Christ Jesus is true God and man, who has a perpetual priesthood; well, then, since we have such grace—Christ himself, I say, who is the guarantee of grace—well then, I say, let us receive Christ by faith. We know that he is that king and priest of ours, and that his kingdom is that eternal kingdom. Let us serve him with reverence and devotion, that is, with true faith and abiding patience. To this he adds a splendid exclamation: "For our God is a consuming fire," which is taken from Deuteronomy 4 and Isaiah 33. But these things we have said regarding the kingdom of Christ and the worship of God should be carefully noted by the godly reader.

The verses that preceded in the sequence completed the entire epistle; those that now follow are attached in the place of an appendix. Commentary on Hebrews 12:28-29.[18]

God Is Himself a Consuming Fire. Lucas Osiander: It should be observed that the hope of eternal life and of the heavenly kingdom should not produce dissolute people, but rather should excite to true worship of God and to zeal for good works. It must also be noted that God must be served in true fear and with great reverence, lest we condemn his commandments, because the contempt of his word does not end unavenged. And the statement that God is a consuming fire does not have to be taken in this way, that by this threat our faith or hope is shaken, but so that lethargy and carnal security might be cast out from us. For certain Christians are carelessly transgressing the commandments of God . . . as if there were not an avenger in the world. These are reminded that God is himself a consuming fire, unless they truly have returned to their senses. And the ones who are truly penitent the Lord receives in grace as a most kindly father, and covers and mercifully remits their sins, Luke 15, Psalm 32. Epistle to the Hebrews 12:28-29.[19]

[16]Linck, *Das zwoelfft Capitel der Epistel an die Ebreer*, K r, Kiiii r. †The switch from third-person plural to first-person plural in this sentence is faithful to the original German.

[17]Oecolampadius, *In Epistolam ad Hebraeos Explanationes*, 161v-162r; citing Col 1:16-17.

[18]Bullinger, *In Pauli ad Hebraeos Epistolam*, 132v-133r; citing Deut 4:24; Is 33:14.

[19]Osiander, *Epistola ad Hebraeos*, 96-97; citing Lk 15:11-31; Ps 32:1.

13:1-19 CONCLUDING EXHORTATIONS

Let brotherly love continue. [2]Do not neglect to show hospitality to strangers, for thereby some have entertained angels unawares. [3]Remember those who are in prison, as though in prison with them, and those who are mistreated, since you also are in the body. [4]Let marriage be held in honor among all, and let the marriage bed be undefiled, for God will judge the sexually immoral and adulterous. [5]Keep your life free from love of money, and be content with what you have, for he has said, "I will never leave you nor forsake you." [6]So we can confidently say,

"The Lord is my helper;
I will not fear;
what can man do to me?"

[7]Remember your leaders, those who spoke to you the word of God. Consider the outcome of their way of life, and imitate their faith. [8]Jesus Christ is the same yesterday and today and forever. [9]Do not be led away by diverse and strange teachings, for it is good for the heart to be strengthened by grace, not by foods, which have not benefited those devoted to them. [10]We have an altar from which those who serve the tent[a] have no right to eat. [11]For the bodies of those animals whose blood is brought into the holy places by the high priest as a sacrifice for sin are burned outside the camp. [12]So Jesus also suffered outside the gate in order to sanctify the people through his own blood. [13]Therefore let us go to him outside the camp and bear the reproach he endured. [14]For here we have no lasting city, but we seek the city that is to come. [15]Through him then let us continually offer up a sacrifice of praise to God, that is, the fruit of lips that acknowledge his name. [16]Do not neglect to do good and to share what you have, for such sacrifices are pleasing to God.

[17]Obey your leaders and submit to them, for they are keeping watch over your souls, as those who will have to give an account. Let them do this with joy and not with groaning, for that would be of no advantage to you.

[18]Pray for us, for we are sure that we have a clear conscience, desiring to act honorably in all things. [19]I urge you the more earnestly to do this in order that I may be restored to you the sooner.

a Or *tabernacle*

Overview: As they comment on the various injunctions in this section of the epistle to the Hebrews, the reformers sound a number of the themes they have emphasized throughout, especially the unique and unrepeatable nature of Christ's sacrifice for sin along with the implications of this singular sacrifice for how Christians should think about the clerical ministry and the Lord's Supper. The reformers also stress the importance of neighborly love and gratitude in the Christian life, along with the necessity of taking up one's cross and following Christ through suffering, exclusion, and even death. The reformers also display their high regard for marriage and lament the way they believe it had been denigrated in medieval Christianity.

13:1-3 *Continue Showing Love*

The Future Harvest. Lucas Osiander: This admonition is very necessary, especially in these last times in which, according to the prophecy of Christ, love grows cold in the hearts of many. For many, moved by their own dangers or troubles, or by the injustices of people and the displeasure of offense, have allowed brotherly love to slip away from their souls. Rather let love remain in you and do not tire in doing good, for in due time we, the ones not falling away, shall reap, that is, we shall take possession of eternal rewards as a rich harvest. Epistle to the Hebrews 13:1.[1]

[1]Osiander, *Epistola ad Hebraeos*, 97; citing Mt 24:12; Gal 6:9.

SPECIAL LOVE FOR STRANGERS AND OUTCASTS. JOHANNES OECOLAMPADIUS: A little earlier, he commended two principal virtues, peace and holiness, which he now takes up here. If we ought to have peace with all people, we should have it above all with our brothers and those who share in the same inheritance. For these have the same Father in heaven. You may say, "But is he not the Father of all nations, so that all people are brothers?" Our brotherhood does not derive its name from this, but because in one Spirit we worship God and cry out "Abba, Father!" If anyone really acknowledges God as his Father in heaven, they should also honor him appropriately and not be ashamed of his fellow members of the household of faith when he is thought of as their brother; otherwise he robs this word of its meaning. People speak of "brotherhoods" of monks and indulgence-preachers, which are unworthy of this sacred name, which we should take care not to prostitute. He says, "Let it continue," because it is not enough to do good to one's brother once or twice; they should do continual good. For the true worship of God consists in this. This love of which we are speaking cannot be so sincere among any people as much as among those who profess Christ. You may indeed see some people who begin in a praiseworthy fashion, but because they are not really rooted in Christ, they fall away immediately. Consider this from 1 John 3: "If anyone has the world's goods and sees their brother in need. . . ." Love excludes no one, but it has greater cause toward the members of the household of faith, as those who for the sake of Christ have been forsaken by others, even by their own family according to the flesh. Therefore, he appropriately adds:

"Do not forget to show hospitality." If strangers and exiles come to you, do not be unfeeling toward them; and since you have hitherto excelled in this virtue, I warn you not to forget it. For this should not be thought of as among the meanest virtues; afterward "thereby some have entertained angels unawares." But he does not mean that they should extend hospitality to just anybody, but to strangers, who, as unknown people, have more need of assistance than those who have got themselves some acquaintance with people. Consequently, showing yourself to be hospitable to strangers is evidence of uncommon love, and was honored even among the Gentiles, so that the highest law among them was held to be that of hospitality, namely, that no one might wrong a guest. Homer and the oldest of the poets are witnesses to this. *Philoxenia* possesses more the meaning, "affection and kindness toward guests," rather than a command to undertake a larger expense. You are not required to undertake great expenses. Help as much as you are able, and be welcoming. For if because of insufficient means you are not free to assist as much as someone needs, at least point out the way and show yourself kind. No one in their right mind demands that you do more than you are able.

"For thereby some. . . ." He commends the subject by an example, namely, that the hospitable saints of old received angels hospitably; we read this concerning Abraham and Lot in Genesis 18 and 19. Abraham saw three men tired out from their journey at midday; he entreated and invited them to come into his tent. Lot did the same for two men near evening, not at all supposing that they were angels. By this virtue these men pleased God; and you will certainly please him as well, if you strive not to forget it. When we welcome strangers and the poor, we do not receive angels, but Christ himself, because whatever is done to the poor and the least of his little ones is also done to him. But because they received the angels hospitably, we may learn that we should not be overly selective in welcoming strangers and the poor, although I do not want you to give support to the lazy so that you are less able to assist others who are deserving of it. Christians should take note of this, but especially those who desire to be called leaders of the flock of Christ and who belong to the clergy. EXPLANATIONS OF HEBREWS 13:1-2.[2]

[2]Oecolampadius, *In Epistolam ad Hebraeos Explanationes*, 163r-164r; citing Heb 12:14; Gal 6:10; Acts 17:28-29; Phil 3:3; Eph 4:4; Rom 8:15; 1 Jn 3:17; Jas 1:27; Mt 13:6, 21; Heb 11:13; Mt 25:40; Tit 1:8.

Love and Examples of Deeds of Mercy. Heinrich Bullinger: Love obtains the first place, because (as the apostle testifies) it is the fulfillment of the law. To this he adds in this passage the epithet "brotherly." But since the people of old called Christians "brothers," it came about that brotherly love is called "Christian love," namely, that which conforms to the love of Christ, whereby we love in deed and in truth. Then he added, "Do not neglect hospitality." But by "hospitality," as by a kind of substitution, he embraces all the works of mercy which Christ mentions in Matthew 25. So, to persuade them he adds an example with one particular benefit, namely, that the saints of old received angels with hospitality, as we read of Abraham and Lot in Genesis 18 and 19. Because if someone lacks the opportunity, still they will not lack the will, if they love sincerely. Then he adds, "Remember those who are in prison." For the apostle says elsewhere, "Who is weak, and I am not weak? Who is made to fall, and I am not indignant?" You may read more in 1 Corinthians 12 and chapter 10 of this epistle. Commentary on Hebrews 13:1-3.[3]

13:4 *Honor Marriage*

The Most Blessed Estate. Martin Luther: Although I have previously preached and written often about the married estate and life, nevertheless, in order to honor the wedding,[†] I will now speak a little bit about it, because it is one of the most necessary things that one should preach in Christendom, and it is something that all Christians should understand, because it is also the most common and yet the most noble estate through which all other estates stand and are preserved.... The first thing that one should learn about this estate, as also about all the other estates, is that... the married estate is ordained and established by God. It is certainly the highest art in the married life to learn to regard this estate according to its highest honor, namely, that it is God's institution and has God's word [behind it].... The words, that it is an estate that has been established by God, etc., are quickly learned, but this is the art of which I speak, that one is certain and holds for certain and each one regards one's own marriage and that of others everywhere as created, ordained, sent forth, and, as one says, given as a gift by God. The foolish world and even the intelligent reason do not regard marriage earnestly as such; rather, they are of the opinion that marriage takes place randomly and without cause in the following way: one is allotted this person or that person just as outside marriage two come together.... Therefore, it has come to the point that the married estate is made a charlatanry and everywhere is spoken of so carelessly. Therefore it is not an easy art to know how to distinguish between married life and fornication, so that a husband is certain of this fact and can say, "God gave me this wife so that I should remain with her," and that a wife can say, "God gave me this man and I should share bed and table with him, etc." ... Would that each one were so minded that they could say from their heart, "I am certain that it pleases God that I sit here and live with my spouse, because he himself established and ordained it and through his word tells me this." Such a word consoles married people and gives them a good conscience. However, those who live with one another without being married cannot have such a good conscience, because they do not have God's Word. They live in opposition to this word and are together not in God's but in the devil's name. A Wedding Sermon on Heb 13:4.[4]

13:5-6 *Avoid Greed*

We Are Free to Share Our Possessions with Others. Johannes Oecolampadius: It is not unsuitable for us to connect this to the statements that were made above about relieving

[3]Bullinger, *In Pauli ad Hebraeos Epistolam*, 133v; Rom 13:10; 1 Jn 3:18; 2 Cor 11:29; Mt 25:35-36; Gen 18:1-8; 19:1-3, 6-8; 1 Cor 12:21-26; Heb 10:32-34.

[4]Luther, *Eine Hochzeitpredigt über den Spruch Hebr.* 13, 4, WA 34.1:51.3-8, 53.8-3, 57.29-36. [†]This appears to be a reference to the actual wedding at which Luther preached this sermon.

the poor and taking in strangers, since in this way he could respond to an unspoken objection that an especially stubborn person might throw out: "If I give alms to these and others, I will easily squander everything I have, and who then will feed me? From whom will I receive what I need to sustain my life?" He replies, "It is not the part of us who have set all things aside for Christ to fix our souls on earthly and transient things, for we have been called to far greater things. So then, we should not be so enslaved to what may happen that we shut our heart against a brother who is in need of our kindness out of love for gold and silver; rather, we should be entirely free from the love of money and content with what we have." For nature is content with very little. It reads, "He who feeds the birds of the air and clothes the lilies of the field will abundantly provide for us, his children, along with these." For we are more dear to him than anything else can be. He is "Our Father"; how could he ever refuse daily bread to his children when they ask? Therefore the apostle desires us to be completely free from the love of money, not only so that we refrain from stealing what belongs to others but also that we may be ready to expend what belongs to us for those in need, casting all care and concern for things to come upon God. Thus he cites texts of Scripture to dissuade them all the more from the love of money and to persuade them to be content with little. First he quotes Joshua 1, then from Psalm 118.[†]

"I will never leave you." The Lord said this to Joshua, when he charged him to take up the leadership of his people. But because the Lord purposes not to leave anyone who wholeheartedly entrusts himself into his care, the apostle rightly cites this promise as belonging to all believers in general. For he is near to all who call on him in truth. And we know that whatever is written is written for our instruction. He who did not forsake Joshua will not forsake us who believe in his promise either, for he is both God and helper of all; whoever hopes in him will never be put to shame. *Oud ou mē*. These three negatives in Greek constitute one highly emphatic negative.

"The Lord is my helper." These are the words of David. You may object, "If I help my neighbor with charity, who will take care of me?" The Lord is your helper; cast your concerns on him, and he will take care of you. Do not imagine that the Lord is your helper only in the struggle against the devil, sin, and hell, but also in all difficulties and troubles that can befall a person. A human is a trifle; they can do nothing to the person who has God as their protector. If someone has God for them, who can prevail against them? See what these words have in view! Some people suppose that they are to be employed only in the greatest tribulations, but it would be quite as great a cause of disgrace before God to regard food, drink, or clothing as one's help. Surely no one can rightly hope for eternal salvation from God when they do not trust him for daily bread. Thus, for fending off the love of money, they employ the examples of the saints who readily let go of earthly things, being content with God, the all-sufficient good. Imitate them yourself; because if you do, you need never have any doubts of finding a very present help. EXPLANATIONS OF HEBREWS 13:5-6.[5]

13:7-19 *Sacrifices Pleasing to God*

UPRIGHT TEACHERS AND SOUND TEACHING. HULDRYCH ZWINGLI: "Remember your leaders." He commends to the Hebrews the ministers of the word, namely, those who encountered death for Christ and the glory of God with steadfast endurance, and who bore witness to their sincere faith by their notable and godly deeds. He teaches that these people should be followed, not venerated, nor regarded as occupying the office of intercessors. Hence it is clear that here he does not mean to commend all ministers without distinction, but the blameless and upright, whether living or dead, as the saying goes.

[5]Oecolampadius, *In Epistolam ad Hebraeos Explanationes*, 166r-167r; citing 1 Jn 3:17; Mt 6:25-32; 6:9, 11; 7:9-11; Eph 4:28; 1 Pet 5:7; Ps 145:18; Rom 15:4; Ps 25:3; Rom 8:31; Ps 46:1. [†]In keeping with Latin chapter divisions, Oecolampadius refers to this as Psalm 117[:6].

"Christ yesterday and today." The meaning of this can be taken in two ways. If you consider that it is connected to what goes before, in which he urges them to imitate the faith of their leaders, then he is declaring that the unchanging Christ is always with them forever, just as he was with the believers of old. But if you judge that it is connected to what follows—as it seems to us to be the case—then this is the meaning: "Strange teachings." It is as if he were to say, "Seeing that Christ Jesus is the true and undeniable Son of God yesterday and today (that is, continually), and his teaching is always the same, and among all believers there is the same religion, and his sacrifice is finished and complete, be on your guard lest you be carried away by strange, empty, and foreign teachings." Thus he elegantly warns them to be on their guard against the deceptions of ministers and the pretenses of deceivers. Likewise, Jesus Christ also is not our Lord just at one time, nor did he say this without cause. For just as the church of God is never free from people of this kind, so we see that today it is not free of those who draw away the flock of Christ and lead it about by the nose (as the saying goes) here and there by flatteries at one time and threats at another into errors and strange speculations, just as in the time of Christ and the apostles. Exposition of Hebrews 13:7-8.[6]

The Constancy of Christ. Johannes Oecolampadius: This is another argument to strengthen their confidence in God. For someone might object, "You exhort well, but God was unlimited in his favor toward the apostles and their immediate successors as leaders and standard-bearers; he will not bestow the same degree of favor and grace on me. And because they were so cherished, it is no wonder that they left everything and followed the Lord." This irreverent suggestion of the flesh he throws back with this declaration: "Jesus Christ is the same yesterday and today and forever." This is his meaning: Jesus Christ, who was yesterday—that is, in the bygone time of those people—is also the same today, and will endure forever. His kindness is the same; his hand has not been shortened; the same one who gave food and drink to Elijah and to the people of Israel for forty years in the desert with manna and water from the rock will be able to take care of you as well. Surely, if his kindness were to cease, he would also stop being God. Explanations of Hebrews 13:8.[7]

The Eternity of Jesus. Cardinal Cajetan: "Jesus Christ is the same yesterday and today and forever." This clause can be understood adjectively, as in, "Imitate their faith, namely, that Jesus Christ is the same yesterday and today, and forever." The eternity of Jesus Christ is indicated through three times—past, present, and future. On this statement depends our universal faith that Jesus Christ is believed to be true God and true man. For anyone who believes this is a fool if they do not believe the rest of the Christian faith, that is, what this same Jesus Christ did and taught and commanded. Alternatively, this can be read as the reason for the preceding exhortation, so that by the statement that "Jesus Christ is yesterday, today, and forever," they should understand that, just as he was present for their departed leaders, so he would be for them. Comments on Hebrews 13:8.[8]

Christ and His Gospel Endure Eternally. Lucas Osiander: Christ, the Son of God, who according to his own divinity was before all worlds, who today, even as a human being, lives and reigns at the right hand of God, who is going to conquer and have dominion in all eternity, this Christ will certainly not suffer the light of the gospel to be extinguished, even if all tyrants rave and burst forth. For Christ with his gospel remains; truly tyrants descend to the infernal regions. Epistle to the Hebrews 13:8-9.[9]

[6]Zwingli, *In Epistolam Beati Pauli ad Hebraeos Expositio*, 583-84.

[7]Oecolampadius, *In Epistolam ad Hebraeos Explanationes*, 168r; citing Mt 19:27; 1 Kings 17:3-16; 19:4-8; Ex 16:1–17:16.

[8]Cajetan, *In Epistolam ad Hebraeos Commentarii*, 171v.

[9]Osiander, *Epistola ad Hebraeos*, 100.

THE TRUTH OF CHRIST STANDS AGAINST FALSE TEACHING. HEINRICH BULLINGER: There seems to be a kind of substitution in these words, namely, that a person, Jesus Christ, is substituted for a thing—for salvation, truth, redemption, and the Christian religion. For then the meaning will very clearly be that this religion of Christ always has among all people the effect of the priesthood and sacrifice of Christ. For then there is appropriately added to this, "Do not be led around by diverse and strange teachings." That is, since this is always and consistently the teaching of the truth, it is Christ himself and the very power of Christ for all ages. Therefore, he called it "diverse," because it teaches people to believe first in one thing, then in another. And it is "strange," because since it is drawn from a source other than the single fountain of Christ and of the truth, it is looked for either in the flesh or in philosophy. But see what Paul says in Ephesians 4 and Colossians 2. COMMENTARY ON HEBREWS 13:8-9.[10]

THE KNOWLEDGE OF CHRIST. JOHN CALVIN: Now as he is dealing with the Jews, he teaches them that Christ had ever possessed the same sovereignty that he holds at this day; "The same," he says, "yesterday and today and forever." By these words he intimates that Christ, who was then made known in the world, had reigned from the beginning of the world, and that it is not possible to advance farther when we come to him. "Yesterday" then comprehends the whole time of the Old Testament; and that no one might expect a sudden change after a short time, as the promulgation of the gospel was then but recent, he declares that Christ had been lately revealed for this very end, that the knowledge of him might continue the same forever.

It hence appears that the apostle is not speaking of the eternal existence of Christ, but of that knowledge of him which was possessed by the godly in all ages, and was the perpetual foundation of the church. It is indeed certain that Christ existed before he manifested his power; but the question is, what is the subject of the apostle? Then I say he refers to quality, so to speak, and not to essence; for it is not the question, whether he was from eternity with the Father, but what was the knowledge that men had of him. But the manifestation of Christ as to its external form and appearance was indeed different under the law from what it is now; yet there is no reason why the apostle could not say truly and properly that Christ, as regarded by the faithful, is always the same. COMMENTARIES ON THE EPISTLE OF PAUL THE APOSTLE TO THE HEBREWS 13:8.[11]

CHRIST AS THE ALTAR. HULDRYCH ZWINGLI: "For it is good for the heart to be strengthened by grace." It is as if he were to say, "It is nourishing and useful to rely on grace and faith, not on Jewish observances of external rites, which did not benefit those who were engaged in them," just as was demonstrated earlier in chapter 10. And thus he finds fault not only with the cleansing provided by external Jewish rites but also the deception of those who teach a righteousness from any other source than the merit of Christ. The papistical teaching was no different from this Jewish doctrine, nor is that of those who today attribute justification to anything other than faith. For with good reason Paul said that those who were relying on these things were not benefited. For there is nothing that can cleanse and satisfy the human mind except trust in Christ. Therefore, what you argue regarding the eating of the physical body of Christ is groundless, for "the flesh is of no benefit at all," says the Lord.

"We have an altar from which they have no right to eat." This responds to one who objects, "Not everything is abolished, is it? Where are the offering tables? Where the altars? Where the sacrifices?" Since he previously treated all these things at length, here as an epilogue he again repeats and teaches that Christ is the altar, that is, the offering by which God the Father has been

[10]Bullinger, *In Pauli ad Hebraeos Epistolam*, 134v-135r; citing Eph 4:14-15; Col 2:8.

[11]CTS 40:345*.

made favorable toward us. The metaphor is that Christ is the altar, that is, the offering that was sacrificed on the altar as an acceptable sacrifice.

"Have no right to eat." That is, from this altar and sacrifice, namely, from Christ himself, no one who served the tent—that is, no one except believers and the spiritual—may eat. Nor is anything fleshly eaten here, but all things are spiritual. The contrast is drawn between those who ate from the altars and offerings of the old covenant and the eating of the flesh of Christ, who was offered on the altar of the cross. This is what Christ spoke of in John 6 regarding the spiritual eating of his flesh, as was said a little earlier. Exposition of Hebrews 13:9-11.[12]

God's Sacraments and Promises. Heinrich Bullinger: No one should think that the ancient holy patriarchs and prophets, indeed, the whole believing people of Israel, had the understanding of sacrifice that through such works of theirs they obtained purification from sins, and that the blood of goats and sacrificed flesh of cows had power to forgive sins. For they finally relied on the grace and mercy of God and placed their hope on the promised blessed seed of the Virgin Mary from the line of Adam, Abraham, and David, who would redeem them from all from all their sins through the sacrifice of his body and blood, making them heirs of eternal life. They regarded the external visible sacrifices that they practiced in accordance with God's instructions as sacraments of God's promises. Therefore, when they sacrificed or stood behind the sacrifice they did not looked primarily at the external slaughtering, pouring of out blood, and burning; rather, they looked on the death of the future Messiah with eyes of faith and persistently held it to be certain that they were sinners who deserved eternal death. Yet they also held that the Son of God would become human, suffer death on the cross, and with such a sacrifice make satisfaction for the sin of the whole world. . . . Just as we also in the celebration of the Lord's Supper do not look primarily on the breaking of bread and its distribution along with the drinking of wine, rather with the eyes of faith on the true body and blood of Christ that was poured out for us once for all on the cross, whose sacrament and symbol the Lord's Supper is. The True Sacrifice of Christendom, Hebrews 13:10-16.[13]

Christians Have No Altar Besides Christ. Johannes Bugenhagen: The invisible altar is Christ, who is also the high priest as described above. God does not receive any offering unless it is made on this altar, that is, through Christ, just as Peter says in 1 Peter 2. No prayers are received, and we receive nothing back from God unless we offer on this altar. For he says, "If you ask the Father for anything in my name, he will give it to you." And lest you imagine some other altar here, though the words themselves are perfectly clear, the author himself makes it plain below that he is not talking about the anointed stones, but about an altar other than that of the old law. For he says, "Through him, then, let us offer. . . ." And it is equally clear that he is not talking about the sacrament of the Eucharist either when he speaks of eating from the altar, for Christians have no other altar besides Christ. This altar does not need the sacrament of the body of Christ to be consumed to do it homage, except by those who offer their sacrifice by the testament of Christ. The sacrament is external and is performed by eternal hands in some external place, of which nothing is said as to whether there should be a wooden table or a stone table, unless you say that Christ sinned, because it is believed that he dined at a wooden table, or that it is a sin when the sacrament is given to those who are about to die in their own rooms, and so on. But attend carefully to what he says: "From this altar those who serve the tabernacle have no right to eat." In the law, those who served the altar lived by means of the altar (as Paul also cites in 1 Cor 9, where he similarly urges that it

[12]Zwingli, *In Epistolam Beati Pauli ad Hebraeos Expositio*, 583-84; citing Heb 10:1-4; Jn 6:63.

[13]Bullinger, *Die rechten opffer der Christenheit*, a iii v-a iiii r.

shows that ministers of the word have the right to have their living expenses provided by their hearers). They ate offerings of meat and bread. But from this altar, which is Christ, no one is permitted to eat—indeed, no one is able to eat—who serves the tabernacle of Moses, that is, who considers the worship of God to consist in the external things of this world, who seeks salvation by righteous deeds and works of the law. How much less will they be admitted who seek salvation by works of human tradition; to understand this, see what is written in John 6: "This is the work of God, that you believe in him whom he has sent." This is what the author demonstrates here by means of a very suitable symbol from Numbers 19, which pertains to nothing but this. For when Christ entered into the invisible holy places though his own blood, he chose that his body should be offered in fire to God outside the city as the sweetest whole burnt offering to God, on the one hand, but as a disgrace to the world, on the other. In the same way of old the bodies of the animals that were offered for sin, by whose blood the high priest entered into the holy places, were not burned up with glory on the altar, but in disgrace they were cast away outside the camp and burned up, so that they even rendered those who burned them unclean, because in addition this was a symbol. "Therefore," it says, "let us go out with Jesus, beyond the elements of this world, bearing the disgrace of the world" (while in the meantime the hypocrites and those who are justified according to the elements of the world are glorified), so that with Christ we may die to the world. Commentary on the Pauline Epistles, Hebrews 13:10.[14]

Christ, the Spotless Red Heifer. Heinrich Bullinger: We Christians have neither an external altar nor bodily sacrifice. What sacrifices do we have then? For to be sure everyone and each believer needs a sacrifice for sin. . . . Therefore, our Lord Christ is depicted through the red heifer: no blemish or defect was found on him, as the One conceived by Holy Spirit and born of the pure Virgin Mary. No yoke of sin and disdainful servitude was ever laid on him; no flaw was ever found in his mouth and life. And because he was himself the only high priest, he himself carried his cross from the gate to the place of judgment. There he was also crucified and put to death and offered himself completely and perfectly, as he is, to God his heavenly Father for the purification and forgiveness of the sins of the whole world. And although there was no fire to be found at the place of execution in Jerusalem with which the body of Christ could be immolated on the cross, we have much evidence of a better fire. Christ offered himself to God for us in the fire of ardent and completely perfect love. He was also so heated up and dried out in his body that he cried, "I thirst," so that he showed that he was the true burnt and death offering, which in the law is burned with fire for pardon. Yes, the true water and blood that truly purifies ran out of the wounds of the dead body of our Lord Jesus Christ. The holy apostle and Evangelist John saw this and attested with great earnestness that it was true, namely, that from the torn open side of the dead Christ water and blood truly ran out. In the blood is the life, the payment and the redemption; in the water however is the purification and the renewal or refreshment. Believers have both from the death of Christ. Both of these are prefigured in the blood and water from the red heifer that by the command of God in the law are for purification. In Christ however are the essence and the fulfillment. The True Sacrifice of Christendom, Hebrews 13:10-12.[15]

Christ, the Only Eternal Sacrifice for Sin. Heinrich Bullinger: Therefore, Christ our Lord is the only and eternal priest of believers, the only eternal sacrifice, although without the altar or

[14]Bugenhagen, *Annotationes in epistolas Pauli recognitae* (1525), 158v-159v; citing 1 Pet 2:5; Jn 16:23; 1 Cor 9:13-14; Heb 13:15; Col 2:8; Gal 6:14.

[15]Bullinger, *Die rechten opffer der Christenheit*, a v r -a vi v; citing Num 19:1-10; Jn 19:16-17; Jn 19:28; Jn 19:24.

bodily sacrifice. For although he was once sacrificed bodily on the cross, he will never again be sacrificed on earth. However, the power of his sacrifice, satisfaction, and redemption endures into eternity and is fresh and powerful for all who believe in it. Therefore, all other sacrifices for sin in the law pass away in the death and sacrifice of our Lord Jesus Christ, and the power of the one-time sacrifice of the body and blood of Jesus Christ alone endures into eternity and takes the place of all sacrifices. It alone is also powerful enough to pardon and forgive all the sins of the world, and it therefore requires no help or addition from anyone at all. The memorial and Sacrament of this sacrifice in the holy Christian church is the holy supper of our Lord Jesus Christ.

In this well-founded teaching about the singular sacrifice for sin of our Lord Christ you, beloved, have many reasons for why all the altars and masses have been abolished in our churches. For the sacrifice for sin in the Christian church is not a bodily sacrifice that requires an altar on which it is offered. It is the body and blood of Christ offered one time—it shall not and may not be offered a second, third, or more times.... For in that Christ was once offered, he with this one sacrifice took away all sin and guilt unto the end of the world. The True Sacrifice of Christendom, Hebrews 13:10-12.[16]

The Proper Imitation of Christ's Crucifixion. Desiderius Erasmus: We accept Jesus as our offering and our high priest. He, as though playing on the image of the law, wanted to be crucified outside the gate of the city of Jerusalem to cleanse his people with his own blood. We must imitate his example scrupulously but not superstitiously. We shall do this if we too take up our own cross and follow him in the way he departed from the company of humans like a criminal. Paraphrases on the Epistle to the Hebrews 13:11-13.[17]

Going Out to Christ. Erasmus Sarcerius: To go out to Christ means to go out of the Mosaic and Levitical community, and further not to agree with the fleshly Jewish opinion that one must become righteous and purified through the Mosaic law, ceremonies, and sacrifices. Summaries and Brief Content, Hebrews 13:12-13.[18]

Imitating Christ. Heinrich Bullinger: Because Christ carried his own cross out of the city and abandoned the world, so we should imitate him, leaving the world, willingly bearing our cross, which God places on us, and for his sake and the sake of the truth, willingly suffering shame and abuse. The True Sacrifice of Christendom, Hebrews 13:13.[19]

The Sacrifice of Praise Is an Offering of the Heart. Johannes Oecolampadius: The apostle sets before us three kinds of sacrifices: first, the sacrifice of the body, which must be mortified and brought into submission to the spirit; second, the sacrifice of the soul, which is here called the fruit of the lips, or of praise; third, the sacrifice of doing good for one's neighbor. But take note that the sacrifice of praise does not belong only to lips or mouth, but even more to the heart and soul. For the heart has its own lips, just as it also has knees, feet, and other things. One does not reach God by external feet; likewise, it is not enough to humble yourself before him with external knees, but with those of the mind. Although we cannot always make use of our lips when we are hindered by sickness or some other circumstance, the heart may still not cease to praise God. You know that when Moses prayed he said nothing outwardly, but inwardly with the lips of the mind. You may easily open the lips of the body, but not so those of the mind. For God alone opens them, and he opens them to the praise of his name. Therefore, I say that you should not suppose that the sacrifice of praise, and the fruit of lips that confess the name of

[16]Bullinger, *Die rechten opffer der Christenheit*, a vii r- a vii v.
[17]CWE 44:259.
[18]Sarcerius, *Summarien vnd kurtzer Jnhalt*, 4:JJ v v.
[19]Bullinger, *Die rechten opffer der Christenheit*, b ii r.

the Lord, refers solely to confession by the external lips, but far more to the internal confession, so that where the lips have fallen silent, the spirit continues without ceasing. Indeed, "With the heart one believes and is justified, and with the mouth one confesses and is saved." I know that both are required, but the one is more so than the other. If it is not granted you to declare your faith and you are mute by nature or by accident, the lips of your heart may praise and confess God, and this will suffice for you to be saved. But we do not want any external means to be rejected that can in any way promote the truth of godliness. EXPLANATIONS OF HEBREWS 13:15.[20]

LISTEN TO THE MINISTERS OF THE WORD. JOHANNES OECOLAMPADIUS: The Greek word that is used here, *agrypneō*, strictly means the watchfulness of shepherds in the fields. The apostle now concludes this epistle, after he has fully exhorted them to love and good works, by adding that they should listen to and obey their shepherds, the ministers of the word. It is as if he were saying, "I have taught you enough concerning everything that appears best to bring about your salvation; now, therefore, I wish to add to these things the conclusion, that if it is henceforth needful for you to learn anything by heart, ask the pastors you have who lead you." For with people who are insufficiently instructed in the mystery of godliness, nothing is more useful than for them to turn willing ears to trained and godly people, and to take heed with the highest reverence to that which pertains to salvation. There are some who take this passage as a statement about magistrates, but it is obvious to anyone that this does not fit. Clearly at that time they had few or no magistrates who yielded in obedience to the faith. But I believe that it should be taken entirely with reference to apostles, bishops, shepherds, or teachers, since the apostle also counts himself among their number immediately after this.

"And submit." Suppose someone were to object, "But they are not godly enough, they are covetous and beset with wicked habits; why then should I obey or submit to them?" One should obey all kinds of leaders, as long as they teach according to godliness. For the Lord said, "The scribes and Pharisees sit in the seat of Moses, so observe whatever they command you to observe, but do not consent to act according to their actions, for they say and do not do." An evil life should not cast prejudice on good teaching or bring it into ill repute. If they were relating human dreams, they should not be heard; but because they teach the word of God, you will not be listening to them, but to Christ, if you submit. But it is the role of the magistrate to take care to have the holiest ministers possible. For thus their credibility in the word remains preserved and enters more readily into the hearts of their hearers than if their corrupt life renders the ministry of the word suspect. EXPLANATIONS OF HEBREWS 13:17.[21]

[20]Oecolampadius, *In Epistolam ad Hebraeos Explanationes*, 172r-v; citing Ex 14:15.

[21]Oecolampadius, *In Epistolam ad Hebraeos Explanationes*, 174v-175r; citing 1 Tim 3:16; Mt 23:2.

13:20-25 Final Blessing and Greeting

[20]Now may the God of peace who brought again from the dead our Lord Jesus, the great shepherd of the sheep, by the blood of the eternal covenant, [21]equip you with everything good that you may do his will, working in us[a] that which is pleasing in his sight, through Jesus Christ, to whom be glory forever and ever. Amen.

[22]I appeal to you, brothers,[b] bear with my word of exhortation, for I have written to you briefly. [23]You should know that our brother Timothy has been released, with whom I shall see you if he comes soon. [24]Greet all your leaders and all the saints. Those who come from Italy send you greetings. [25]Grace be with all of you.

a Some manuscripts *you* **b** Or *brothers and sisters*

Overview: In their comments on the final section of the epistle to the Hebrews, the reformers emphasize that the true source of the good works that please God the Father is God himself through the intercessions of Christ. The reformers also urge their clerical readers to imitate the kindly attitude of the author of Hebrews as they interact with their flocks, and finally to understand that Christ himself is the shepherd of the sheep.

13:20-24 *Prayer for God's Spiritual Provision*

Only What Is Done Through Christ Is Acceptable to God. Heinrich Bullinger: This example of a farewell is truly apostolic and full of the mysteries of Christ, as is also the one that he uses in Romans 16. In sum, he invokes soundness and constancy, so that everything that is theirs may be pleasing to God through Christ. For only the things that are done through Christ are acceptable to God, and they are done not through our expectation, but by the will of God. Solely those things that are exclusively from God are truly good works. For, as Paul says to the Philippians, "God is the one who works in us, both that we may will and that we may work for his good purpose." Next, he says, "the God of peace," just like "the God of mercy," that is, the merciful and peaceable God, who has returned to harmony with us, has been reconciled to us, and calms our consciences. This God has appointed Christ as the shepherd of the church, on which subject there is more in John 10. But by his blood Christ obtained eternal redemption; hence his blood is called "the blood of the eternal covenant." Commentary on Hebrews 13:20-21.[1]

Ministers Should Imitate the Apostle's Kindness and Brevity. Lucas Osiander: The ministers of the church ought to observe how kindly and civilly this apostle treats his hearers, and they should imitate such kindness and humanity. But they should also earnestly strive after brevity as much as possible in teaching and exhorting, for long discourses rarely edify much, just as long writings also are either laid aside or rapidly read. Epistle to the Hebrews 13:22.[2]

Only the Great Shepherd Gives True Peace. Johannes Oecolampadius: He very appropriately concludes the epistle with prayers to God. For he is the only one who is able to make us complete in every good work. He means to recommend to them that, in matters which they have trouble understanding, they should ask their teachers, or himself when he has been restored to them. But

[1]Bullinger, *In Pauli ad Hebraeos Epistolam*, 137v; citing Rom 16:25-27; Phil 2:13; Jn 10:1-18.
[2]Osiander, *Epistola ad Hebraeos*, 105.

because he knew that nothing belonged to him and Apollos and Cephas, but all to God, the giver of growth, he prayed that God would condescend to bring them to perfection. "The God of peace" seems to be a saying in the Hebrew fashion. For *šlôm* does not so much mean "peace," as every kind of happiness and success there is, as it says in Psalm 119, "Great peace have those who love your law," and many other passages. He intends to say this: "The God who alone gives growth, success, and happiness in everything and desires life for us, not death, is the one who has brought again that great shepherd from the dead by his powerful hand and can make you complete in every good work," and so on. . . .

Christ is often called a shepherd in Ezekiel and elsewhere, for he pastures and feeds souls unto eternal life, and he is the teacher of eternal salvation, whose voice alone must be heard (John 10). He calls himself the Good Shepherd, and says that he lays down his life for his sheep, that is, for the elect, who are believers. He is here called "great" in distinction from the ministers of the word, who can be called "shepherds" derivatively, because at the proper time they give the household their food; otherwise they are themselves sheep, while Christ alone has preeminence, so that Peter calls him "the chief shepherd." For he says, "And when the chief shepherd appears, you will obtain an unfading crown of glory" (1 Peter 5). Therefore, the apostle prays that God would equip and instruct them for every good work through Jesus, that good, great, and chief shepherd. For we ministers are nothing compared to him. But observe how suitably he arranges everything for his argument and returns again to that by which they may listen to and embrace by faith Christ, the Son of God above all created things and the great shepherd, as the one apart from whom there is no other salvation.

"Make you complete in every good work." See from whom the apostle requests completion and perfection for them in every good work—from God, the Father of mercies—and he does it by the intercession of the blood of our Lord Jesus Christ. This is the best method of preaching and the one most often used by the saints. So let us observe and imitate it. It is as if he were saying, "To be sure, your teachers and shepherds can show us the way to perfection, but they cannot exemplify perfection and completion in every good work. Therefore, we must take refuge in God through prayer that he would condescend to give growth through those who plant and water; and since he grants the willing, so he will not withhold the performing." He deliberately says, "Every good work," so that we may not glory in an empty faith and suppose that we may slacken the reigns on the flesh. True faith is effectual and so active that it pours itself out completely for the benefit of one's neighbors. As for what good works are, we have also said above—namely, those that faith brings forth from itself for the edification of a neighbor, and not those that we ourselves imagine. . . .

Observe here that our works, however good, will never be pleasing to God in themselves unless he condescends to render that which we bring acceptable to himself. He does this through the merit and intercession of the only-begotten, our Lord Jesus Christ, by whose grace God crowns his own works in us.[†] And thus the apostle always sets before our eyes Christ the mediator, the absolutely sure way of salvation, so that as we ponder the Father's love in him, we may show ourselves grateful to him. EXPLANATIONS OF HEBREWS 13:20-21.[3]

13:25 *Commit All to Christ in Steadfast Faith*

LEAVE ALL BUT CHRIST BEHIND. HEINRICH BULLINGER: These thoughts, dear reader, are what we find in that holy and learned epistle of Paul to the Hebrews. For the sake of Christian love we impart them to you, entreating that you ponder each of them with sincere discernment of soul. For by this little labor I have not considered anything except that I might furnish you with some savor of Paul's argument; by tasting it, you may also be able

[3]Oecolampadius, *In Epistolam ad Hebraeos Explanationes*, 176v-178v; citing 1 Cor 3:6-7, 22; Ps 119:165; Ezek 34:23-24; Jn 10:3-5, 16, 27; 1 Pet 5:4; Mic 5:4; Zech 13:7; Jn 10:11, 14; Mt 24:45; Acts 4:12; 2 Cor 1:3; Phil 2:13. [†]Augustine, *De Gratia et Libero Arbitrio* 6.15 (PL 44:890).

to handle the rest of Paul's letters. But I have also intended by these things to set before your eyes the entire glory of Christ, so that you may clearly perceive that Jesus Christ is true God and man, the world's only teacher, priest, mediator, sacrifice, redemption, and only true and eternal life, so that perhaps persuaded by such things, leaving all else behind, you may commit all that you are to him alone with steadfast faith. If I have obtained this from you, I have accomplished what I intended, and I give thanks to God. COMMENTARY ON HEBREWS 13:25.[4]

[4]Bullinger, *In Pauli ad Hebraeos Epistolam*, 138r.

COMMENTARY ON JAMES

Overview: In their introductory comments on the letter of James, the reformers entertain various possibilities as to the author of the epistle, which leads to varying conclusions about its apostolicity and canonicity. Generally speaking, Lutherans (following Luther) are skeptical about its apostolic origins, as is Erasmus, while Reformed Protestants and Anabaptists accept and defend its authenticity and authority. The central concern of all reformers is to try to account for the emphasis on justification by works in James in light of the assertion of justification by faith in the Pauline corpus. Some maintain that the apparent contradiction can be resolved while others are more dubious. All stress that James has important things to say to lax Christians and to believers in the midst of suffering.

Prolegomena: Introduction to James

An Epistle of Straw. Martin Luther: In a word St. John's Gospel and his first epistle, St. Paul's epistles, especially Romans, Galatians, and Ephesians, and St. Peter's first epistle are the books that show you Christ and teach you all that is necessary and salutary for you to know, even if you were never to see or hear any other book or doctrine. Therefore St. James's epistle is really an epistle of straw,[†] compared to these others, for it has nothing of the nature of the gospel about it. Preface to the New Testament.[1]

James Does Not Preach Christ. Martin Luther: Though this epistle of St. James was rejected by the ancients, I praise it and consider it a good book, because it sets up no human doctrines but vigorously promulgates the law of God. However, to state my own opinion about it, though without prejudice to anyone, I do not regard it as the writing of an apostle; and my reasons follow.

In the first place it is flatly against St. Paul and all the rest of Scripture in ascribing justification to works. It says that Abraham was justified by his works when he offered his son Isaac; though in Romans 4 St. Paul teaches to the contrary that Abraham was justified apart from works, by his faith alone, before he had offered his son, and proves it by Moses in Genesis 15. Now although this epistle might be helped and an interpretation devised for this justification by works, it cannot be defended in its application to works of Moses' statement in Genesis 15. For Moses is speaking here only of Abraham's faith, and not of his works, as St. Paul demonstrates in Romans 4. This fault, therefore, proves that this epistle is not the work of any apostle.

In the second place its purpose is to teach Christians, but in all this long teaching it does not once mention the passion, the resurrection, or the Spirit of Christ. He names Christ several times; however, he teaches nothing about him, but only speaks of general faith in God. Now it is the office of a true apostle to preach of the passion and resurrection and office of Christ, and to lay the

[1]Luther, *Vorrede auff das newe Testament/Preface to the New Testament*, WADB 6:12.29-34; LW 35:362. [†]The LW notes that Luther had 1 Cor 3:12 in mind when he referred to James as an epistle of straw. Luther may also have been reacting to Andreas Bodenstein von Karlstadt's high praise for James. See LW 35:362 n. 11. Luther also cast doubt on the apostolicity of James in *The Babylonian Captivity of the Church*. See LW 36:118 (cited in LW 35:362 n. 12).

foundation for faith in him, as Christ himself says in John 15, "You shall bear witness to me." All the genuine sacred books agree in this, that all of them preach and inculcate Christ. And that is the true test by which to judge all books, when we see whether they inculcate Christ. For all the Scriptures show us Christ, Romans 3; and St. Paul will know nothing but Christ, 1 Corinthians 2. Whatever does not teach Christ is not yet apostolic, even though St. Peter or St. Paul does the teaching. Again, whatever preaches Christ would be apostolic, even if Judas, Annas, Pilate, and Herod were doing it.

But this James does nothing more than drive to the law and to its works. Besides, he throws things together so chaotically that it seems to me he must been some good, pious man, who took a few sayings from the disciples of the apostles and thus tossed them off on paper. Or it may perhaps have been written by someone on the basis of his preaching. He calls the law a "law of liberty," though Paul calls it a law of slavery, or wrath, of death, and of sin.

Moreover he cites the sayings of St. Peter . . . and also the saying of St. Paul. . . . And yet, in point of time, St. James was put to death by Herod in Jerusalem, before Peter.† So it seems that [this author] came along after St. Peter and St. Paul.

In a word, he wanted to guard against those who relied on faith without works, but was unequal to the task. He tries to accomplish by harping on the law what the apostles accomplish by stimulating people to love. Therefore I cannot include him among the chief books, though I would not thereby prevent anyone from including or extolling him as he pleases, for there are otherwise many good sayings in him. Preface to the Epistles of St. James and St. Jude.[2]

[2]Luther, *Vorrede auff die Epistel S. Jacobi vnd Judas*, WABD 7:384.3-386.21; LW 35:395-397; citing Jas 2:24, 21; Rom 4:2-22; Gen 15:6; Jas 2:23; Gen 15:6; Jn 15:27; Rom 3:21; 1 Cor 2:2; Jas 1:25; Rom 3:20; Rom 3:20; 4:15; 5:13, 20; 6:15-22; 7:5-13; 8:2; 1 Cor 15:56; Gal 3:23-5:1; Acts 12:2. †LW note (397 n. 53): "Luther overlooks the fact that the James to whom the book is traditionally ascribed is not the brother of John [Mt 4:21] martyred by Herod [Acts 12:2], but the brother of the Lord [Mt 13:55], who became the head of the apostolic church at Jerusalem [Acts 15:13; Gal. 1:19]."

On the Author and Audience. David Dickson: James an apostle, surnamed Alphaeus,† from his office of apostleship did gravely admonish the faithful Hebrews, touching diverse Christian duties whereby he foresaw that the Christian faith would be adorned and their salvation promoted. To this latter end he propounded wisely those virtues that they seemed to have need of and he sharply reproved those vices that they were more prone to, or of which they were guilty. Every chapter has its number of admonitions, as is more especially shown in their explications. All of these admonitions, although written for the use of the catholic church, yet it appears that the apostle would have them read especially by all the dispersed Israelites, and those that were converted to the faith, and that were not. An Exposition of All St. Paul's Epistles.[3]

The Necessity of a Lively Faith. Konrad Pellikan: James the apostle and bishop of Jerusalem, clearly an excellent man, zealous for the glory of God first and foremost, when he saw that there were many boasters of an empty and dead faith in his own time, who certainly believed the gospel and confessed Christ but who still lived according to the flesh and the world, sought to provoke them to true works of living and true faith, without which faith is no more faith than a human being is a body destitute of a soul. It is certainly true that faith justifies and blesses a person, so that one should not deny it when Paul himself irrefutably evinces this in the epistles to the Romans and the Galatians. But this faith is not without its fruits, which are truly observed in the faithful, and without which the dignity and strength of faith is vainly boasted of. Therefore by means of divine prudence the true apostle thus accommodates his speech to both topics, so that he teaches the necessary sacredness of faith and urges by apostolic authority the fruit of faith along with the holy works of the sanctified, and yet he is not silent

[3]Dickson, *An Exposition of All St. Pauls Epistles*, 278*. †See Mt 10:1-3; Mk 3:14-19; Lk 6:13-16; Acts 1:13.

concerning necessity of salvation by faith. . . . [This epistle] has not without cause been called canonical by our great leaders of the church. Comments on the Bible.[4]

There Is No Cause for Rejecting This Epistle. John Calvin: It appears from the writings of Jerome and Eusebius that this epistle was not formerly received by many churches without opposition. There are also at this day some who do not think it entitled to authority. I, however, am inclined to receive it without controversy, because I see no just cause for rejecting it. For what seems in the second chapter to be inconsistent with the doctrine of free justification, we shall easily explain in its own place. Though he seems more sparing in proclaiming the grace of Christ than it behooved an apostle to be, it is not surely required of all to handle the same arguments. . . . Among the Evangelists themselves there is so much difference in setting forth the power of Christ that the other three, compared with John, have hardly sparks of that full brightness that appears so conspicuous in him, and yet we commend them all alike. . . . But as to the author, there is somewhat more reason for doubting.† Commentaries on the Epistle of James.[5]

This Epistle Is Not Worthy of Comment. Veit Dietrich: I have intentionally excluded the epistle of James and the secret revelation of John [from the *Summary of the New Testament*] because the epistle of James is not only worthy of censure in some places, because it extols works so highly against faith, but it is also throughout a patchwork teaching composed of many pieces that do not fit together. Summary of the New Testament.[6]

The Two Purposes of This Epistle. Gasparo Contarini: In this epistle James is chiefly driving at two things: first, he exhorts all to mercy toward the poor and the lowly; second, he restrains the ambition of those who want to become masters and who contend among themselves concerning pride of place. Scholia in the Epistles of St. Paul.[7]

Paul Also Detracts from Faith. Huldrych Zwingli: Those who deny that this epistle is truly apostolic because it says that faith without work is dead will for the same reason carp at the epistle of Paul to the Corinthians, in which the apostle detracts from faith, asserting that apart from love, which is the greatest, it profits nothing. Huldrych Zwingli's Brief and Excellent Exposition of the Epistle of Blessed James.[8]

A Nonapostolic Epistle That Must Be Read with Care. Lucas Osiander: And this epistle, which carried around the name James twelve hundred and more years ago, was not recognized as an apostolic writing, just as Eusebius in his *Ecclesiastical History*, book 2, chapter 23, testifies.† And this is not an injustice, for it only makes mention of the name of Christ in five chapters, nor does it teach anything concerning his benefits (i.e., his passion and merit). Further, it contends that Abraham was justified not by faith alone but even by works, which diametrically contends with the epistle to the Romans, chapter 4, of St. Paul. Further, it calls the church of Christ a synagogue, which is strongly alien to the apostolic custom. Also, certain parts of this epistle seem to be gathered from the writings and sermons of the apostles (but not by the best judgment). And if suitable explanations for these problems are sought, nevertheless they do satisfy to these consciences. Therefore it must be read with great judgment. And nevertheless it has its own use, for it admonishes those who have fallen, who throw off faith, while in the meanwhile they do nothing worthy of

[4]Pellikan, *Commentaria bibliorum*, 7:681. For a similar statement, see Zwingli, *Expositio in Epistolam beati Iacobi* 3r-v.

[5]CTS 42:276-77*. †Calvin says the author could be either the James whom Paul mentions in Gal 2:9, whom Calvin says could be a relative of Christ, or James the son of Alphaeus, but not James the son of Zebedee.

[6]Dietrich, *Summaria vber das newe Testament*, R rr iii v.

[7]Contarini, *Opera*, 529.

[8]Zwingli, *Expositio in Epistolam beati Iacobi*, 3v; citing 1 Cor 13.

the Christian name. There are precepts concerning the preparation of the dying and certain other things in this epistle, which are able to be usefully read and observed. And it is not possible in my judgment to provide a disposition of the chapters in this epistle, because the author deals with various matters in individual chapters and now teaches, now rebukes, now consoles, and thus mixes various things, so that he observes no order. The Epistle . . . to James.[9]

James Addresses Everyone. John Donne: This is one of those seven epistles that Athanasius and Origen called catholic; that is, universal; perchance because they are not directed to any one church, as some others are, but to all the Christian world: and St. Jerome called them canonical; perchance because all rules, all canons of holy conversation are comprised in these epistles: and Epiphanius and Oecumenicus called them circular; perchance because as in a circle, you cannot discern which was the first point, nor in which the compass begun the circle; so neither can we discern in these epistles, whom the Holy Ghost begins withal, whom he means principally, king or subject, priest or people, single or married, husband or wife, father or children, masters or servants; but universally, promiscuously, indifferently, they give all rules, for all actions, to all persons, at all times, and in all places. Sermon on James 2:12.[10]

This Epistle Arms the Saints. Richard Turnbull: Wherefore as all other Scriptures, as inspired from above, are for many causes profitable, as the apostle has taught us (2 Tim 3:16), so this epistle of the blessed apostle, proceeding from the Holy Spirit, the Spirit of truth, is no less profitable. For it contains many excellent exhortations to singular virtues, many grave dissuasions from various vices, many worthy doctrines of heavenly knowledge, and many bitter threats against grievous enormities.

The blessed apostle was motivated by two things to write this epistle: (1) Partly by the horrible hypocrisy that then had entered into the very body and (as it were) the bowels of the church, in so much that many professing the glorious gospel of Jesus Christ and vaunting themselves as members of his body, which is the church, lived in all looseness and licentiousness of their life, without the true fruits of lively faith and unfeigned repentance, against whom he speaks most sharply; (2) Partly by the cruel persecution to which the church was then subject. For then the church was not only driven (as it were) into banishment, and the twelve tribes of Israel dispersed through the wide world, but even of those who professed religion it was molested, so that partly by tyrants without and partly by false brethren within it was afflicted. Wherefore it needed greatly to be comforted. This is what Saint James does immediately after his preface and *exordium*,[†] persuading the saints to patience under the manifold afflictions to which they were then subject. Wherefore the very drift and scope of his epistle is this: partly to arm the saints against their temptations, lest by afflictions they being cast down and should fall from their profession, and partly to call the hypocrites from their vain persuasions, showing that profession of faith is vain and unprofitable without holy conduct and godliness. Wherefore he exhorts all people to the fruits of sanctification and dissuades them from sin and wickedness, lest they through their own iniquities fall into final condemnation. And if we diligently shall consider the manner of our present age, and the vices to which our generation is given, we shall find that the knowledge and consideration thereof serves not a little for our times also. The particular application of things I leave to your discrete and wise judgment, resting contented with that which I have delivered. The Lord increase his graces in our hearts, and prick us daily forward to the advancing of his glory, that we, glorifying him here, may be glorified by him in the kingdom of heaven, to which he brings us who has bought us at such great price, even Jesus Christ the righteous, to

[9]Osiander, *Epistola ad . . . Iacobi*, 107-8. [†]Eusebius, *Ecclesiastical History* 2.23 (NPNF2 1:239).
[10]Donne, *Works*, 5:393-94*.

whom with the Father and the Holy Spirit be praise in the great congregation of the saints, now and forevermore. An Exposition upon the Canonical Epistle of Saint James.[11]

James Writes to Console Suffering Christians. Erasmus Sarcerius: In general James consoles those to whom he writes in the midst of their crosses and trials. He teaches them that they should bear such things with patience. He exhorts them to the following: the hearing of the divine word and how one should accept it; a new life as a worthy fruit of the word they have heard; love and other good works; friendliness; obedience to God; repentance; true holiness; humility; patience; speaking the truth; brotherly reconciliation; and the returning of the erring to the right way.... Further, this epistle teaches about crosses and how to use the same, about help in the midst of crosses and suffering, about patience, about the causes of crosses and all the good that crosses accomplish, about the means of rebirth and their use, about the effects of the divine Word, about true faith, about false faith, about good works, and the causes of the same. Summaries and Brief Content.[12]

This Epistle Is Apostolic and Therefore Canonical. John Mayer: This epistle in order is the first [of the Catholic Epistles], not because James is to be preferred before Peter, who was the first and chief of the apostles, if there were any such; but, as some have well noted, because this epistle is to all Jews in all countries, who were the first people of God, and had the gospel first preached to them, whereas the other of the Catholic Epistles are to the Gentiles who believed in all parts of the world.... This epistle is said to be of the apostle James, and so it is titled by Theodore Beza both in Greek and Latin, and both Eusebius and Jerome testify that this epistle was counted as apostolic in their times. Cyprian also cites it as apostolic, as does Augustine. Pareus also subscribes to this point of view. Yet some think it was written by James, surnamed Justus, or Oblias, that is, the Mute, who according to Epiphanius was called the brother of our Lord, because he was the son of Joseph by a former wife, and he was one of the Seventy sent forth by our Lord, being afterward constituted bishop of Jerusalem. To this Luther subscribes and the Lutherans following him, who do not therefore hold it to be canonical Scripture. But in light of the fact that it has from ancient times been received as canonical and apostolic, not only by the forenamed authors, but also by Origen, Athanasius, Epiphanius, Isidore Hispalensis, Nicephorus, and Damascene, and the very directing of it to all parts after an apostolic manner argues that it was written not by a bishop of any particular place but by an apostle, who was sent to all, I hold it, without doubt, to be the epistle of the apostle James, and consequently canonical, as the epistles of other apostles are. If it be demanded which James wrote it, for there were two of that name, James the son of Zebedee, and brother of John, and James the son of Alphaeus, a kinsman of our Lord, and therefore called his brother also, as James Oblias before spoken of was, I answer with Pareus and others that the consideration of the time when it was written argues that the first of these, James the brother of John, cannot be the author, but James the son of Alphaeus, otherwise called James the Lesser, for the elder James was slain by Herod (Acts 12) before the dispersion of the Jews the second year of Claudius, who afterward cast the Jews and Christians out of the city, and then in the time of their dispersion was this epistle written to them, as appears in superscription. If it be objected that Eusebius and Jerome both do report that it was doubted in ancient times whether it was canonical or not, I answer that they only mentioned such a thing, but they did not doubt it themselves. If it be further objected that he does not call himself an apostle, but the servant of Jesus Christ, I answer that Paul in some of his epistles titles himself likewise, the name of apostle being omitted, and neither John nor Jude refer to themselves as apostles, but only Peter. Last,

[11]Turnbull, *An Exposition upon the Canonical Epistle of Saint James*, B3v-B4v*. †*Exordium* refers to the beginning of anything, especially to the introduction of a written work.
[12]Sarcerius, *Summarien vnd kurtzer Jnhalt*, 4:JJ4r.

if it be objected that here is something delivered contrary to that of Saint Paul, touching justification not by faith alone but by works, and anointing with oil is mentioned, which none of the other apostles speak of, I answer that I have already shown in my comment on Romans 3 that the seeming contradiction between Saint Paul and Saint James is nothing, if they are rightly understood.[†] Regarding the anointing with oil, it shall be considered in the proper place. A COMMENTARIE UPON THE NEW TESTAMENT.[13]

[13]Mayer, *A commentarie vpon the New Testament*, 3:2-4*; citing Eusebius, *Eccl. hist.* 3.25; Jerome, *Letter* 41 *ad Paulina*; Augustine, *Letter* 29 and *Concilium Milevitan*, can. 7; Epiphanius, *Panarion* 3.76; Isidore of Seville, *Etymologies* 6.1; Nicephorus, *Ecclesiastical History* 2.46; John of Damascus, *De fide orthodoxa* 4.11; Suetonius, *Claudius* 25; Eusebius, *Eccl. hist.* 2.22. [†]In his comment on Rom 3:28, Mayer asserts, "This place is misunderstood by those who think that a believer may be saved, though afterwards he lives wickedly and does not live according to the law of God. S. James addresses such, using the same example of Abraham, which follows here, and by comparing S. James with S. Paul, it is clear that S. Paul's intent here is not to give liberty to sin and to neglect the importance of the law for the faithful, but rather to teach that none attain the gift of justification by the merit of any prior works" (*A commentarie vpon the New Testament* 1:31).

AN EPISTLE OF COMMONPLACES. DESIDERIUS ERASMUS: James almost confines himself to commonplaces, for example: For Christ's sake we must bravely endure adversity and therein rely principally on support from God; People become wicked through no fault of nature or of God but by their own fault, whether fortune be cruel or kind. . . . Yet there are certain passages that I had to wrestle with, such as the one that puzzles Augustine,[†] "Whoever shall . . . stumble in one point, he is guilty of all." Again, where he says that faith is of no value without works, while Paul argues on the other side that it happened to Abraham not by works but by faith that he was accounted righteous before God and was called the friend of God. There also seem to be some gaps, so that I have had some trouble in establishing connections. . . . James was the bishop of Jerusalem and in that capacity writes also to the other Jews, who lived scattered among all nations, to instruct and shape their lives through various precepts. PARAPHRASE ON JAMES.[14]

[14]CWE 44:132-33, 135. Jas 2:17, 20; Rom 4:3, 9. [†]See Augustine *Epistle* 167 (NPNF 1:1138-49).

1:1-18 REMAIN STEADFAST IN TRIALS

James, a servant[a] of God and of the Lord Jesus Christ,
To the twelve tribes in the Dispersion:
Greetings.
[2]Count it all joy, my brothers,[b] when you meet
trials of various kinds, [3]for you know that the testing
of your faith produces steadfastness. [4]And let
steadfastness have its full effect, that you may be
perfect and complete, lacking in nothing.
[5]If any of you lacks wisdom, let him ask God, who
gives generously to all without reproach, and it will be
given him. [6]But let him ask in faith, with no doubting,
for the one who doubts is like a wave of the sea that is
driven and tossed by the wind. [7]For that person must
not suppose that he will receive anything from the Lord;
[8]he is a double-minded man, unstable in all his ways.
[9]Let the lowly brother boast in his exaltation,
[10]and the rich in his humiliation, because like a flower
of the grass[c] he will pass away. [11]For the sun rises with
its scorching heat and withers the grass; its flower falls,
and its beauty perishes. So also will the rich man fade
away in the midst of his pursuits.
[12]Blessed is the man who remains steadfast under
trial, for when he has stood the test he will receive the
crown of life, which God has promised to those who love
him. [13]Let no one say when he is tempted, "I am being
tempted by God," for God cannot be tempted with evil,
and he himself tempts no one. [14]But each person is
tempted when he is lured and enticed by his own desire.
[15]Then desire when it has conceived gives birth to sin,
and sin when it is fully grown brings forth death.
[16]Do not be deceived, my beloved brothers. [17]Every
good gift and every perfect gift is from above, coming
down from the Father of lights, with whom there is no
variation or shadow due to change.[d] [18]Of his own will
he brought us forth by the word of truth, that we
should be a kind of firstfruits of his creatures.

a For the contextual rendering of the Greek word *doulos*, see Preface **b** Or *brothers and sisters*. In New Testament usage, depending on the context, the plural Greek word *adelphoi* (translated "brothers") may refer either to *brothers* or to *brothers and sisters*; also verses 16, 19 **c** Or *a wild flower* **d** Some manuscripts *variation due to a shadow of turning*

OVERVIEW: The reformers continue to discuss and debate the authorship and purpose of James in their comments on this first section of the epistle. They also continue to express concerns about its authenticity and canonical status, but they move on to consider the identity of the recipients, and here there is less disagreement. They especially emphasize the central role of suffering in the Christian life, defining suffering not simply as persecution for the sake of the gospel—although they do make much of this form of affliction, as it was immediately relevant to some of their readers—but also including all forms of divinely ordained affliction. They stress that every cross must be borne with patience and faithfulness, and they seek to assure their readers with great pastoral sensitivity that God accomplishes much good through such suffering, for God himself is good. The reformers' opponents maintained that their monergistic soteriology made God responsible for evil, and thus the Protestant commentators felt obliged to refute this claim and stress that God was good and the source of all good, especially salvation; human beings were responsible for sin and evil, along with the devil. There are also interesting discussions of concupiscence—the longing for fleshly desires—in which the reformers stress, in contrast to the Catholic position, that such longing is a sin.

1:1 *The Twelve Tribes That Are Dispersed*

THE RECIPIENTS NEEDED THE GOADS OF EXHORTATIONS. JOHN CALVIN: He then wrote and exhorted all those whom he could not personally address, because they had been scattered far and wide.

But that he speaks not of the grace of Christ and of faith in him, the reason seems to be this, because he addressed those who had already been rightly taught by others, so that they had need, not so much of doctrine as of the goads of exhortations. COMMENTARIES ON THE EPISTLE OF JAMES 1:1.[1]

THE RECIPIENTS ARE BELIEVING JEWS. DAVID DICKSON: Those to whom the epistle is written are Israelites, especially believers, cast out of the Holy Land and dispersed through the regions, but (as to the hope of heaven represented by the Holy Land) gathered to Jesus our Savior. He seriously commands and (as it is allowed to Christians) bids them to rejoice, or greets them with a borrowed salutation from the common use of the heathens, but turned into a Christian sense. AN EXPOSITION OF ALL ST. PAUL'S EPISTLES, JAMES 1:1.[2]

JAMES WRITES TO THOSE IN THE SCATTERED TRIBES OF ISRAEL. JOHN MAYER: The twelve tribes to which he writes, said to be scattered abroad, or in dispersion, are the believers of every tribe [of Israel], now expelled from Jerusalem by Claudius Caesar, as has been already touched. But it is to be understood that ten of the twelve tribes were still in that banishment under Shalmanesar king of Assyria (2 Kings 17), for we read not of the return of any, but of the two and a half tribes in the days of Ezra and Nehemiah, or at any time since, and therefore it is likely that the apostle had respect to that dispersion also, if happily his epistle should come to any of their hands. A COMMENTARY UPON THE NEW TESTAMENT, JAMES 1:1.[3]

A WELL-INTENTIONED BUT UNSATISFYING INSERTION. LUCAS OSIANDER: This is the subscription of the epistle. But these words, "and of the Lord Jesus Christ," seem to have been inserted by some good soul, but one of careful judgment is still not satisfied for great authority to be accorded to this epistle. For in this whole writing nothing concerning the benefits of Christ is said, while nevertheless the principal office of the apostles was that they would teach repentance and remission of sins in the name of Christ. THE EPISTLE . . . TO JAMES 1:1.[4]

THE AUTHOR'S IDENTITY AND PURPOSE. RICHARD TURNBULL: First, touching his name, who he was: he was James, called James the Just, James the Lesser, brother to Jude the apostle, called also the brother of the Lord. Among the apostles there were two of this name, the one was the son of Alphaeus and brother of Jude. This one was also called the brother of the Lord, as Paul calls him when he writes to the Galatians. . . . Not that James was the natural brother of Christ . . . but because he was the son of Mary, the wife of Clopas, sister to the Blessed Virgin, and so his cousin, called his brother after the manner of the Hebrews, who call those brothers and sisters who are of the same kindred, as St. Jerome shows.† According to this manner of speaking Abraham called his nephew Lot, brother, and Jacob did the same with Laban, his uncle, as did Laban with Jacob, his cousin. Thus Matthew speaks in this way when he reports that while Christ was preaching, his mother and brothers came and desired to speak with him. And who these his brothers were, a little after he notes by the confession of the people, who hearing his wonderful wisdom, and seeing the strange miracles that he wrought among the people, as amazed as they were, cried out, "Is not this the carpenter's son? Is not his mother called Mary, and his brothers James and Joses, Simon and Jude? And are not his sisters with us? Where did this man get all these things?" Thus the Hebrews called them brothers who were their kindred; and so was James called the Lord's brother, in that respect only that he was his kinsman and cousin-german, his mother's sister's son.

James the son of Alphaeus, cousin to Christ and one of the twelve apostles, as it appears in the gospel, was the writer of this epistle. For this cause both the Greeks and the Syrians gave him the name of

[1]CTS 42:278*.
[2]Dickson, *An Exposition of All St. Pauls Epistles*, 278*.
[3]Mayer, *A commentarie vpon the New Testament*, 3:5*.
[4]Osiander, *Epistola ad . . . Iacobi*, 109; citing Lk 24:47.

an apostle, affirming that James the apostle wrote this epistle, notwithstanding that fact that there were in former times and are now also some who doubt the authority of this epistle. . . . Another reason [for this doubt] is the following: this writer makes no mention of the merits of Christ as other apostles do, therefore it seems he was not an apostle. For all the apostles were sent to preach Christ and the remission of sins by his death. It is not difficult to answer this concern. . . . His endeavor was in this place to root security and hypocrisy out of the hearts of humans, who with a bare name of faith deceived and flattered themselves, against which fond persuasion and vain ostentation of faith the apostle bonding himself could not so often mention the merits of Christ, as others did. . . . A third reason moves some to doubt: they say this author cites the story of Abraham to prove justification by works, which St. Paul cites in Romans and Galatians to prove justification by faith. . . . This doubt may thus be repelled: these apostles did not speak in the same sense of faith and justification. St. Paul spoke of true faith, St. James of counterfeit faith; St. Paul of justification by faith before God, St. James of being justified before human beings, which is by good works. Therefore they are not contrary. An Exposition upon the Canonical Epistle of Saint James 1:1.[5]

1:2-8 *Asking for Wisdom During Trial*

The Christian's Cross Is a "Pure Relic." Andreas Althamer: Therefore, because St. James writes to the scattered Jews, and above all to the believers among them, he begins immediately to console them in their misery and cross and to exhort them to patience. He does this owing to the fact that the cross comes from God, and that the Lord Jesus has sanctified it through his bitter suffering, so that from now on the suffering of Christians is holy and blessed. It is especially pleasing to God that we are therefore conformed to the image of his Son (Rom 8) and bear the cross with Christ. As the cross was neither a disadvantage nor a hindrance to Christ in his kingdom (for Christ had to suffer in order to enter into his glory, Lk 24:26), so it does not damage those who belong to him and believe, because we also must enter into God's kingdom through much tribulation, Acts 14. If we want to be raised to glory with Christ, then we must suffer with him; if we die with him we will live with him; if we endure, we will rule with him, Romans 8; 2 Timothy 2. Therefore, because the suffering of the saints is blessed, yes, is a pure relic, the holy James exhorts the brothers to regard assaults, persecution, and the holy cross as a something entirely holy and a source of joy and blessing. The Epistle of St. James 1:2-3.[6]

The Lord Uses Different Medicines for Different Spiritual Sicknesses. John Calvin: The Lord then afflicts us in various ways, because ambition, avarice, envy, gluttony, intemperance, excessive love of the world, and the innumerable lusts in which we abound cannot be cured by the same medicine.

When he bids us to count it all joy, it is the same as though he had said that temptations ought to be so deemed as gain, as to be regarded as occasions of joy. He means, in short, that there is nothing in afflictions that ought to disturb our joy. And thus, he not only commands us to bear adversities calmly, and with an even mind, but shows us that this is a reason why the faithful should rejoice when pressed down by them. Commentaries on the Epistle of James 1:2-3.[7]

[5]Turnbull, *An Exposition upon the Canonical Epistle of Saint James*, 1r-3r*; citing Gal 1:19; Mk 15:40; Jude 1; Lk 6:15; Acts 1:13; Mt 4:21; Mt 10:2; Mt 10:3; Mt 27:56; Jude 1; Jn 19:25; Mk 15:40; Jn 19:25; Gen 13:8; 29:15; Mt 12:46; Mt 13:55; Mt 4:21; 10:3; Jude 1; Mt 28:19; 16:15; Lk 24:47. †Jerome, *Against Helvedius: The Perpetual Virginity of Blessed Mary* (NPNF2 6:765-73); cf. *On Illustrious Men* (NPNF2 3:830-31).

[6]Althamer, *Die Epistel S. Jacobs*, Biii v; citing Rom 8:29; Lk 24:26; Acts 14:22; Rom 8:17; 2 Tim 2:11-13. Luther also referred to the Christian's suffering as a relic. See Ronald K. Rittgers, "Embracing the 'True Relic' of Christ: Suffering, Penance, and Private Confession in the Thought of Martin Luther," in *The New History of Penance*, ed. Abigail Firey (Leiden: Brill, 2008), 377-93.

[7]CTS 42:279.

The Necessity of Afflictions in the Christian Life. David Dickson: Joined with an exhortation, there is need of diverse afflictions, and for to stay on you so long as God shall see fit, so that the work of patience may be perfected, and that you who have other endowments may also have the gift of patience, and so the image of Christ may be completed in you, that nothing may be wanting in you, for perfection in holiness: Therefore you ought to count it all joy when you fall into afflictions. An Exposition of All St. Paul's Epistles, James 1:4.[8]

Affliction Is the School of Christ. Richard Turnbull: The holy and blessed martyrs have in like manner counted it exceeding joy when they fell into temptations, wherein they have been by the will of God, above the strength and course of nature, exercised and tried, and have triumphed. Whereas then the wicked shun these as simply evil, the saints embrace them as testimonies of love. Whereas the wicked in their miseries, fret, fume, and foam at the mouth for rage and anger, stamp, stare, murmur, and mutter against God, yes and blaspheme him in extreme desperation, as Saint John in his Revelation testifies, the saints rejoice with joy unspeakable and glorious, as in wholesome documents of their life, corrections of their infirmities, provocations to prayer, invitations to God, repressors of natural corruption, increasers of zeal, and means whereby they are made conformable to the image of the son of God. Whereas the wicked herein faint and fall into despair, and rejoice in other things only, the saints and holy people of God make affliction the greatest matter of their mirth, and to suffer for Christ and his gospel, their soundest joy, remembering the proposition of the apostle here set down.... Second, the word "fall into" is not without significance: it teaches the saints of God that they may neither procure nor hasten their own cross, nor deserve at the hands of the world thus to be afflicted. The papists, who in many places and at sundry times lay heavy crosses on themselves, as beating their own flesh, scourging their own bodies, wearying and wasting themselves with long, tedious, and troublesome pilgrimages, fall not by the will of God into them, but by their own choice.... Third, the circumstances of time may not be lightly passed over: My brothers, count it exceeding joy when you fall, that is, whenever you fall into temptation. This teaches the children of God that once or twice to rejoice under the cross is not enough to perform the perfect duty of a Christian; but whenever, as often as, at whatever time we are assaulted and assailed with temptations, so often to show ourselves patient therein and joyous, because our crown is only given at the end of all our combats. The author to the Hebrews teaches us that we have always need of patience, and that in time and at length we may obtain the promise.... Patience in affliction is the school and nurture-house of Christ and of the Holy Spirit, and the effectual means the Lord our God uses to make us perfect; if we are continually trained in it we shall grow to full measure and perfection of virtue. An Exposition upon the Canonical Epistle of Saint James 1:2-5.[9]

We Must Ask God for Wisdom as We Bear the Cross. Andreas Althamer: Believing and earnest prayer belong to the cross. It appears to me that here the beloved James meant the following: "If you find no patience in your cross and you do not know how you should wisely deal with it and how to withstand the assaults, or you do not know how salutary and necessary the cross and persecution are for you, then flee to prayer, ask God for understanding and wisdom, that he would give you true wisdom and understanding through his Holy Spirit, so that you may know how to conduct yourself in this affliction, that you might live wisely and intelligently, and keep your soul with patience, and also recognize the usefulness of the cross. Because prayer is the only consolation and medicine for all believers. Through prayer one receives and gains all that is good, both spiritual and physical. Through

[8]Dickson, *An Exposition of All St. Pauls Epistles*, 278*.

[9]Turnbull, *An Exposition upon the Canonical Epistle of Saint James*, 12r-13r, 21v*; citing Rev 16:9, 11, 21; Rom 8:29; Heb 10:36.

prayer one drives out all evil and misfortune. If you want to be wise, then seek it from God, because from him alone will you find it. . . . However, wisdom is nothing other than a true knowledge of God, a proper faith, that one knows and understands from the holy and divine Word how one should live and walk before God, how one should conduct oneself with others, what the cross and suffering are, as Paul writes to the Ephesians. The Epistle of St. James 1:5.[10]

God's Divine Generosity. John Calvin: The meaning, then, of "generously" is that God is so inclined and ready to give that he rejects none or haughtily puts them off, being not like the niggardly and grasping, who either sparingly, as with a closed hand, give but little, or give only a part of what they were about to give, or long debate with themselves whether to give or not . . . "without reproach": This is added lest anyone should fear to come too often to God. Those who are the most liberal among humankind, when anyone asks often to be helped, mention their former acts of kindness, and thus excuse themselves for the future. Hence, we are ashamed to weary a mortal, however openhanded they may be, by asking too often. But James reminds us that there is nothing like this in God, for he is ready ever to add new blessings to former ones, without any end or limitation. Commentaries on the Epistle of James 1:5.[11]

Seek Only the True Understanding of Christ Jesus. Melchior Hoffman: Who finds therein a lack, let them pray to God, as the apostle [i.e., James] teaches, and do not hurry or rush them. For to many in this day the Scripture will become a poison and eternal death, which nonetheless is in itself very good, because often it is misused without understanding, and leads the unwary and the willful into damnation and all who are without fear into abiding unbelief and damnation.

For there are many in our time who continuously teach and regard themselves as masters of Scripture, and who nevertheless never really come to the understanding of the truth. Similarly the holy apostle thoroughly warns about such as these who also in that time inflated themselves, and there are now many such all around. Therefore let us—all of us who fear God in truth—earnestly pray to God that we may be saved through Christ Jesus from having to think beyond what is the will, the truth, and the command of the Lord to the end that we hold not to our own opinion and to the leaven of the Pharisees and to the manner of the doctors of Scripture, but rather to regard it and flee from it as eternal death and follow only after the true understanding of Christ Jesus in order thus to be taught by God himself in our hearts and conscience. Thereto may God help us, the gracious, merciful Father, through Christ Jesus, our Savior and eternal Redeemer. Amen. The Ordinance of God, James 1:5.[12]

We Must Seek Wisdom from God. Lucas Osiander: And often Satan or the world present perplexing things to us, so that we do not know what counsels are to be taken or what must be done. In such cases James sends us back to prayers, so that we might seek wisdom and counsel from God. The Epistle . . . to James 1:5.[13]

We Are Unworthy of God's Bounty. Desiderius Erasmus: [God] wants to benefit all and can fulfill whatever he wants. He takes no notice of our merits; he requires us only to have trust in him. It is Pharisaical to say, "Lord, do what I ask because I fast twice a week." One who is truly pious prays, "I am unworthy of your bounty, I am worthy of your wrath, but nevertheless look on your servant because you are naturally good and merciful." Paraphrase on James 1:5-6.[14]

[10]Althamer, *Die Epistel S. Jacobs*, Cii r-Cii v; citing Prov 2:6; Eph 1:16-23.
[11]CTS 42:283*.
[12]LCC 25:203.
[13]Osiander, *Epistola ad . . . Iacobi*, 110.
[14]CWE 44:138.

Prayers Void of Wavering. Richard Turnbull: Seeing then that our wavering prayers are altogether unprofitable, let us neither doubt nor waver in prayer, so that so we may obtain the requests of our hearts with God. And our prayers shall then be void of wavering when (1) we know to whom to pray, this is to God; (2) when we know through whom we must pray, which is Christ, (3) when we know for what we should pray, chiefly for heavenly things and then for the necessities of this life, and (4) when we know to what end to pray, for the advancement of God's glory and the supply of our own needs and of those of our brothers. An Exposition upon the Canonical Epistle of Saint James 1:6-8.[15]

1:9-12 *Remaining Steadfast Under Trial*

True Poverty and True Riches. John Mayer: Here is shown the manner of perfect patience, namely, when a poor dejected person glories not only inwardly and in themselves, but outwardly in respect of others through the hope that they have of future exaltation, for it is promised, that those who humble themselves shall be exalted. That which follows concerning the rich person glorying in their humiliation is expounded by the gloss, as spoken ironically, "Let them rejoice in their humiliation and fall to come, for their pride and love of worldly riches." Or else it may be understood of voluntary humiliation in doing one's duty to the poor through humility.

The apostle, having shown who is fluctuating like the sea in their prayers, now teaches how a person may be stable and steady, viz. if being poor, that is, dejected in a sense of their own spiritual poverty, they persevere in this their humiliation, which indeed will produce all good to them. By the rich he means the proud and supercilious, to whom he ascribes humility, because while he exalts himself, he is in a low and base estate. His meaning is that the rich person should be confounded herein, though he would not use the word, lest he should seem too harsh. . . . I do not think with some that this is an exhortation of the rich to humility, for that is done afterward in chapter 5. But the rich here is the one who is not humbled by reason of their prosperous estate. In willing them to rejoice in their humiliation, he means that the rich should prepare themselves and be ready to suffer for Christ when they should be called to it, and herein seek matters of true joy, that in their mind they should be humbled and ready to bear Christ's cross and to follow him, whenever it should come, and in that they have a fellow-feeling of the miseries of others in their sufferings. And so that they who were for the present in prosperity might be moved to this humiliation, he shows their fleeting estate and condition, even like the flower of the field. The poor here is the poor in spirit, whose exaltation is that theirs is the kingdom of heaven, Matthew 5. The rich made low is the one who suffers the loss of their goods, being made herein like Christ, who being of heavenly glory became poor and abased himself. We are his followers when we show patience in the loss of worldly wealth, rejoicing in this conformity to him. For to be depressed in the world is to be exalted Godward, and to be exalted in the world is to be depressed Godward. For these are contraries, heaven and earth, poverty and riches, eternal and fading, God and the world, exaltation to God, exaltation to the world, depression from the world, depression from God. If you love the world, you lose heaven; if riches, the poverty of Christ; if fading things, eternal; if exaltation to the world, exaltation to God. A Commentary upon the New Testament, James 1:9-10.[16]

The Hot Sun of God's Judgment. Erasmus Sarcerius: The hot sun is God's judgment. Destruction and decay are fruits of such judgment. James further praises the godly who have crosses, suffering, and trials and who bear and suffer them patiently. The reward for this is the crown of life.

[15]Turnbull, *An Exposition upon the Canonical Epistle of Saint James*, 30r*.

[16]Mayer, *A commentarie vpon the New Testament*, 3:6-8*; citing Mt 5:3; Phil 2:5-11.

Does one receive such a crown through merit or through the promise of grace? From the promise. Summaries and Brief Content, James 1:9-12.[17]

Seek Everlasting Goods. Desiderius Erasmus: It is the mark of a pagan to measure happiness by goods like those that, besides depending on fortune's whim and being uncommonly quick to desert us at life's end, bring ruin unless they are held in contempt. It is the Christian's role to follow those pursuits that prepare everlasting goods over which neither fortune nor decay nor death has any jurisdiction. For no one is blessed simply because they are rich. They will be blessed only when they have been stripped of their possessions because of their confession of the gospel and when, having spurned the pleasures of this life that they once enjoyed to the full, they suffer tortures and imprisonments for Christ. They will be blessed when, through their love of Christ, they endure unto death in the midst of evils with their heart unbroken, because they realize in this situation that the greater the number of this world's evils that press him on them, the dearer they are for this reason to God. . . . God has promised it [i.e., the crown of immortal life], not to those who have accumulated the most wealth, or have excelled in physical strength, or have routed the most enemies in battle, but to those who from love of him have spurned the goods of this world and have bravely borne its evils. Paraphrase on James 1:11-12.[18]

Cross-Bearing for the Rich and the Poor. Richard Turnbull: There are two sorts of people, poor and rich: to both the cross and doctrine of patience therein is necessary, so that it is profitable then to all. First to the poor brother, of whom James says, "Let the lowly brother rejoice in his exaltation." The cross and doctrine of afflictions and patience is profitable for the poor brother, for if they be afflicted with poverty, contempt, ignominy, or any other calamity, they must not be pressed down with sorrow, grief, fear, and fainting of heart; but rejoice rather under their cross and calamity, because they by the cross are exalted and called even to the company of Christ and his holy angels in the kingdom of God. For by affliction the poor humbled brothers are thereby exalted, either to the true profession of the cross and gospel of Christ; or to be like Christ and his saints, who have all in this world drunk the cup of affliction; or else to the glorious company of Christ and his holy angels, unto whom the way is persecution and suffering. . . . Now as the cross and afflictions are profitable to the poor brother . . . so also is this doctrine needful and profitable to the rich. Again, he says, "The one that is rich, let him rejoice that he is made low," yea, contemptible to the world, and as it were despised of men, as commonly they are who are under the cross, wherein is taught how those who have all things at their command should behave themselves in wealth, that they wax not proud of their abundance and plenty, neither trust too much to the frailty of their condition, but always to look to the cross that follows them, which if it be laid on them, therein they ought to rejoice also. When God then takes away and removes the flattering and deceitful baits of this world from the rich, and so they become contemptible to others; if they turn their wealth into woe, their mirth into mourning, their plenty into poverty, their abundance into want, their worldly happiness into misery: in this humbling are they exhorted by the apostle to rejoice, for thereby many occasions of many sins are removed, and therefore the rich, by spoil of goods, loss of wealth, decrease of riches, or whatever other way they are tried and are humbled, they must rejoice. Seeing then in the state of this life there are many occasions for impatience both in the poor and those of low degree and also in the rich and plenteous estate of human beings, the only salve of both their sores is in all changes and chances of this life to behave themselves patient under the cross. And thus is the doctrine here delivered profitable for poor and rich. An Exposition upon the Canonical Epistle of Saint James 1:9-12.[19]

---

[17]Sarcerius, *Summarien vnd kurtzer Jnhalt*, 4:KK1r.
[18]CWE 44:140.
[19]Turnbull, *An Exposition upon the Canonical Epistle of Saint James*, 34v-35r, 35v-36r *; citing 1 Cor 4:9-14; Heb 10:33.

God's Love and Election Precede the Elect's Love of God. John Calvin: He adds that it [i.e., the crown of life] is "promised" to those who "love God." By speaking in this way he means not that the love of humans is the cause of obtaining the crown, for God anticipates us by his gratuitous love, but he only intimates that the elect who love him are alone approved by God. He then reminds us that the conquerors of all temptations are those who love God, and that we fail not in courage when we are tried, for no other cause than because the love of the world prevails in us. Commentaries on the Epistle of James 1:12.[20]

1:13-17 *God Is Not the Source of Temptation, but Good*

How God Does and Does Not "Tempt" Christians. John Calvin: Here, no doubt, he speaks of another kind of temptation. It is abundantly evident that the external temptations, hitherto mentioned, are sent to us by God. In this way God tempted Abraham and daily tempts us; that is, he tries us as to what we are by laying before us an occasion by which our hearts are made known. But to draw out what is hidden in our hearts is a far different thing from inwardly alluring our hearts by wicked lusts.... But the whole doctrine of Scripture seems to be inconsistent with this passage; for it teaches us that people are blinded by God, are given up to a reprobate mind, and delivered over to filthy and shameful lusts. To this I answer that probably James was induced to deny that we are tempted by God by this reason, because the ungodly, in order to form an excuse, armed themselves with the testimonies of Scripture. But there are two things to be noticed here: when Scripture ascribes blindness or hardness of heart to God, it does not assign to him the beginning of this blindness, nor does it make him the author of sin, so as to ascribe to him the blame: and on these two things only does James dwell.... The meaning is that those in vain evade who attempt to cast the blame of their vices on God, because every evil proceeds from no other fountain than from the wicked lust of humankind. Commentaries on the Epistle of James 1:13.[21]

Two Kinds of Temptation. Huldrych Zwingli: There are two kinds of temptation.... The first occurs when God examines human beings by means of adversities, so that the helplessness of the pious might become more manifest not only to others but also to the pious themselves, and then so that faith might spring forth. This adversity also reveals and punishes the impiety of the evil, which they either impudently deny or cultivate by their false religion. The other kind of temptation takes place when they are tempted by the suggestions of Satan and the desires of the flesh, and rarely do they not succumb to these temptations. Where others thus fall to eternal death, so that they never rise again, still others after the fall are returned more humble and careful. Huldrych Zwingli's Brief and Excellent Exposition of the Epistle of Blessed James 1:13.[22]

The Seed of Sin. Desiderius Erasmus: A certain propensity to vicious behavior has been implanted in our souls from the vice of our first parents. This propensity is, as it were, the seed of sin. If this seed has been admitted into the soul and taken root, the mind has now, so to speak, conceived sin; and if the vicious desire is not weeded out of the soul, that evil fetus gradually becomes larger and stronger until birth is given to a mortal sin, which in turn begins to reproduce itself when all its parts have reached their full growth. It produces the worst offspring of all, namely, eternal death. Paraphrase on James 1:13-14.[23]

Internal Temptations. John Mayer: Having spoken hitherto of external temptations, now he speaks of internal, that is, evil thoughts suggested to the mind, whereby a person is enticed and drawn to evil. These come not from God, but from our

[20]CTS 42:287*.

[21]CTS 42:288-89*; citing Gen 22:1; Jn 12:40; Rom 1:24-32.

[22]Zwingli, *Expositio in Epistolam beati Iacobi*, 9v.

[23]CWE 44:141.

spiritual enemies. God indeed is said to tempt Abraham, and likewise to tempt the people of Israel (Gen 22; Deut 12), but it is to be understood that there is a twofold temptation, the one of trial, the other of deceit. By the first God tempts, so that humans may be more purified, as the gold being tried in the fire; but not by the other. The devil tempts thus, so that he may deceive us, the flesh that it may allure us, and the world that is may draw us away. . . . The degrees of temptation are here noted: first, there is delight alluring; second, consent conceiving; third, work performing; fourth, custom perfecting. Lust conceives by the devil, who is (as it were) the father, and lust the mother; this conception is by the consent of the will, or by delight. "Brings forth sin," that is, Psalm 7. It is perfected by custom, and then death comes; that is, it becomes guilty of eternal damnation, "for the wages of sin is death" (Rom 6). But why is death assigned only to custom? Does not sin delighted in, or consented to, and acted, bring forth death also? Answer. Yes, doubtless, but it is most properly said thus of custom in sin, because in such there appear no signs of life, and there is little hope of his return, but in such as sometime fall into sin there are signs of life, though more in the consenter, fewer in the actor of sin. A Commentary upon the New Testament, James 1:13-15.[24]

Concupiscence Is Both Cause of Sin and a Sin Itself. John Turnbull: When the apostle here says, "Lust when it has conceived brings forth sin," our adversaries the papists take an occasion to broach this their opinion concerning concupiscence, that it is not sin. This is their argument. Lust brings forth sin, therefore lust is not sin. One thing cannot be both cause and effect, the effect itself, and the cause of itself. Lust therefore cannot be sin, if it brings forth sin, for then it would be the cause of itself, and bring forth itself, which is most improper speech.

To this be it answered that one thing may be cause and effect also, but not cause and effect in the same respect. One thing may be cause of sin, and yet sin: for one sin is often cause of another sin. As idleness, riotousness, and drunkenness, are not only themselves sins, but causes of sin also, even of the sin of uncleanness and fornication, incest and adultery, as Moses records of Lot's incest, of the Sodomical uncleanness, and the Scripture of David's adultery, and many similar examples prove the same. Concupiscence and lust therefore is not only cause of sin, but sin itself, yet not the same sin whereof it is cause. Lust conceives and brings forth sin, that is, an actual sin, a sin done in deed, seen of others, manifestly apparent to the view. Such a sin is not lust . . . lust is a conceived evil, an inward consenting to evil, and therefore sin. Thus lust is not only the cause of actual sin, but sin itself, not only before baptism, but even after also. . . . Again, whatsoever is repugnant to the law of God and his will is sin. Lust and concupiscence is repugnant to the law and will of God; it is sin therefore. An Exposition upon the Canonical Epistle of Saint James 1:14-17.[25]

Concupiscence Is Sin. John Mayer: If it is asked what concupiscence is and whether it is a sin or not, because James seems here to make it but the cause of sin, and how temptation is ascribed only to concupiscence, when as the devil also tempts, and so does the world too, I answer to the first that concupiscence is generally agreed on to be that original inclination to evil, which we draw from the loins of our first parents. To the second, that (St. Paul himself being the teacher, Rom 7), it is sin, and such a sin as is condemned in the tenth commandment, though popish writers mince it and say that it is not truly and properly sin, but the cause of sin, and that by the apostle Paul it is called sin therefore figuratively and improperly. . . . Note again, that humans are drawn to sin by being deceived, like the silly fish or bird, who thinks something is profitable or pleasing that indeed is not so. Wherefore everyone must labor to be wise so that they may judge of things rightly, and this

[24]Mayer, *A commentarie vpon the New Testament*, 3:9-10*; citing Gen 22:1; Deut 12:28(?); 1 Pet 1:7; Ps 7:14; Rom 6:23.

[25]Turnbull, *An Exposition upon the Canonical Epistle of Saint James*, 50v-51r, 52r*; citing Gen 19:33; Ezek 16:49; 2 Sam 11:2.

very consideration should pull us back from sin, that the thing to which we are running is not that which it seems to be. In the green grass of sin, where we think to sleep sweetly for a time, and then to rise again, there lies lurking a fell venomous serpent that will sting us to death; under the sugar of sin there is deadly poison. A Commentary upon the New Testament, James 1:14-15.[26]

The Father of Lights. Johann Spangenberg: "From the Father of lights," etc. It is as if he wanted to say, "If the devil or your flesh wants to tempt you and to move you to ambition, do not submit to such temptations. Give them neither room nor place. No one should raise themselves above the grace and gift that God has given to him. Rather, they should humble themselves and submit themselves to others as our Lord Christ did. And know that all good gifts, both of the body and the soul, have been given by God." . . . He says that all good gifts and all perfect gifts come from above, from the Father of lights, with whom is neither change nor alteration of light and darkness. It is as if he wanted to say, "All that we have and are capable of doing, whether in spiritual or bodily things, we have from God." And this saying is against those who in the matter of justification ascribe something to our power and ability. Although they have for a long time seen and cried out that we can earn this or that with our good works, Scripture opposes them, saying that what we are able to do comes not from ourselves but from God. Therefore Paul says, "What I am I am through the grace of God." . . . If there is a good thought, word, or deed in us, God has worked it in us. He is the source of all good, the Father of all wisdom, the true gift-giver, and the Lord of salvation. And as God is the highest good, so he can do no other than give and distribute good gifts. . . .

Why does he call God a Father of lights? With God there is no darkness, no alteration, no change, rather there is pure light. He is not inconstant, unstable, or rash, but is immutable. Our days are often darkened by clouds and night, but with God there is no shadow nor darkness. Our wisdom is often darkened by error, but with God there is eternal wisdom. Because we know these things we should dutifully attend to them so that we may come out of darkness, lies, and error, and so that we may participate in the divine light, truth, and wisdom. Then we shall be conformed as devout children to our beloved Father. German Postil, James 1:17.[27]

God Is the Fountain of All Good. David Dickson: God is the fountain and author of all good (which is in us, or that which is given to us, either in the state of nature or grace) and of good only, because from him descends all good, and every gift that any ways conduces to our perfection. Therefore we must not say that God is the cause of evil or sin.

God is immutable in his nature, without any variableness, either for worse or better. From all eternity always, so like himself in all things, there is no foundation of changeableness of himself from himself, nor the least shadow of turning or motion in him. Therefore, it is impossible that God should be the author of sin. An Exposition of All St. Paul's Epistles, James 1:17.[28]

New Birth via the Word Through Faith. Johann Spangenberg: Why does he say, "He gave us birth according to his will through the word of truth so that we might be the true firstborn of his creatures"? He wants to show with this statement that our birth was evil, corrupt, sinful, and cursed, but that God called us by grace to the childhood of grace and through the new birth, that is, baptism, he accepted us as newly born children.

How does such a birth take place? God the Father allows the heavenly seed, the divine Word, to be seen and preached through Christ his beloved Son. The one who takes hold of and receives this seed with the ears and a believing heart will become a newly born person and a child of God through the blessed word, as St. Peter says. . . .

[26]Mayer, *A commentarie vpon the New Testament*, 3:11, 14*.

[27]Spangenberg, *Postilla Teütsch*, 5:13r-14v; citing 1 Cor 15:10.

[28]Dickson, *An Exposition of All St. Pauls Epistles*, 279*.

Why has he born us anew? So that we might be the firstborn of his creatures, that is, that we should be a sanctified and distinct people, set apart from all other people, Jews, Turks, heathens, and false Christians. We should be the priests and kings of the Lord Christ alone, yes, God's children and heirs, because Scripture refers to those who inherit the best and have all that belongs to God as the firstborn. Epistle for the Fourth Sunday After Easter.[29]

The Evil in Human Beings Is Due to Human Sin, Not to God. Huldrych Zwingli: Since he had shown that every evil is from us, he now shows through the antithesis that God is the source of every good. Nothing comes from God that is not good. If we detect anything of evil in us, God, the source and origin of all good, should by no means be accused, but all guilt must be ascribed to us, who are sinners by nature. If on the other hand we detect anything of good in us, we know that this is a gift of God. And it seems that this language savors of a Hebraism and exchange of words: "Every good thing is from God" instead of "It is necessary that whatever comes from God or from above is good, for it is not fitting for evil to be ascribed to God." Thence when it says, "from the Father of lights," it is a Hebraism, instead of "author of light," or instead of "the highest light from which flows whatever light there is in heaven and on the earth." Huldrych Zwingli's Brief and Excellent Exposition of the Epistle of Blessed James 1:17.[30]

1:18 *God Birthed Us by His Will Through the Word*

Christians Must Strive to Protect the Divine Gift They Have Been Given. Desiderius Erasmus: Since God, therefore, freely imparted this honor to us, it remains for us in turn to respond vigorously to his munificence. We have been admitted to this felicity without payment. But in the meantime we could lose it through our own fault if we do not strive through godly effort to protect what has been freely given. Our co-option into the fellowship with the Son of God through baptism and our avowal of the teachings of the gospel will be in vain if we do not make the chastity and purity of our behavior match our avowal. Paraphrase on James 1:18.[31]

Christians Must Continue to Fight Against Sin. Martin Luther: We must always be afraid of neglecting to drown this sin further. Therefore we must always pray and work so that grace and the Spirit may increase but the body of sin decrease and be destroyed and our old nature become weak. For God has not yet justified us, that is, he has not made us perfectly righteous or declared our righteousness perfect, but he has made a beginning in order that he might make us perfect. Hence we read in James 1:18: "That we should be a kind of first fruits of his creatures." This is pointed out in the story of the man half dead who was brought to the inn. After his wounds had been bandaged he was not yet cured, but he was on the way to being made whole. Lectures on Romans.[32]

Regeneration Is the Most Eloquent Expression of God's Goodness. Richard Turnbull: In the previous verse he discusses the goodness of God, and here he shows that his goodness especially appears in the work of our regeneration, the instrumental cause of which is the word of God, which he also touches in this verse. So then in this eighteenth verse the apostle gives us, as it were, a taste of that which in general he had spoken of in the previous verse, namely, that God is the fountain of all goodness, which is evident in many things, but especially in the work of our regeneration, the most eloquent testimony of his goodness toward us. Since this is apparent

[29]Spangenberg, *Postilla Teütsch*, 5:14v-15r; citing 1 Pet 1:23.
[30]Zwingli, *Expositio in Epistolam beati Iacobi*, 10v.
[31]CWE 44:143.
[32]LW 25:323.

and manifest, we must needs confess that all good givings and all good gifts come from him, so that we cannot say without blasphemy, nor think without impiety, that God is the author or cause of our evil temptations. And inasmuch as God both first created humankind in perfect innocence and afterward regenerated them to be like the image of his own son in excellent virtue, his great goodness appears to all people, so that it would be incomparable iniquity in any way to make him the cause of our wickedness. An Exposition upon the Canonical Epistle of Saint James 1:18.[33]

[33]Turnbull, *An Exposition upon the Canonical Epistle of Saint James*, 59 r*; citing Gen 1:26; Rom 8:29; Eph 4:24.

1:19-27 Receiving and Enacting the Implanted Word

19Know this, my beloved brothers: let every person be quick to hear, slow to speak, slow to anger; 20for the anger of man does not produce the righteousness of God. 21Therefore put away all filthiness and rampant wickedness and receive with meekness the implanted word, which is able to save your souls.

22But be doers of the word, and not hearers only, deceiving yourselves. 23For if anyone is a hearer of the word and not a doer, he is like a man who looks intently at his natural face in a mirror. 24For he looks at himself and goes away and at once forgets what he was like. 25But the one who looks into the perfect law, the law of liberty, and perseveres, being no hearer who forgets but a doer who acts, he will be blessed in his doing.

26If anyone thinks he is religious and does not bridle his tongue but deceives his heart, this person's religion is worthless. 27Religion that is pure and undefiled before God the Father is this: to visit orphans and widows in their affliction, and to keep oneself unstained from the world.

Overview: In this section of James, the reformers begin by reflecting on who exactly should be slow to speak and quick to listen, Christians in general or preachers in particular. A number of reformers assume the latter interpretation and see in the early verses of this section a stern warning to preachers to be humble and teachable. The reformers also seem to be fascinated by James's reference to "the implanted word," and they comment at length on it, seeking to explain what this word is—most say it is the gospel—and how God makes use of the preacher's words to plant the word in the hearts and minds of Christians. The reformers stress throughout this section the absolute necessity of saving faith being a lively faith that issues forth in numerous good works. They also wrestle with James's reference to the "perfect law of freedom" (Jas 1:25), which on the face of it seems to contradict their view that the law only leads to bondage to sin. Most interpret this law as the gospel. Finally, the reformers reflect on what it means for Christians to "visit" those in need, concluding that, among other things, it entails acting mercifully toward all who are in distress.

Christians Live Out the Philosophy of Christ. Desiderius Erasmus: It must not be enough for you just to have heard the teachings of the gospel as catechumens, to have been baptized and admitted to the mysteries hidden more deeply in the teachings of the gospel, to have learned thoroughly the entire philosophy of Christ and his whole life, and to have accepted the promise of immortality. What Christ taught must be expressed in conduct, what he did must be imitated by us with all our might. Having died to the passions of this world, we must be buried with him; we must come back to a life of innocence with him; we must be taken with him to heaven; in short we must so live on earth that we appear fully worthy of the rewards of heaven. Paraphrase on James 1:19-27.[1]

1:19-21 *Receiving the Implanted Word*

We Should Listen and Watch More Than We Speak. Lucas Osiander: For God gave to us two ears, likewise two eyes, but only one mouth, so that he might signify that there should be more listening and seeing than speaking. Therefore it

[1]CWE 44:144. On the centrality of the "Philosophy of Christ" in Erasmus's conception of Christianity, see the excerpt from his Desiderius Erasmus, *Handbook of the Christian Soldier* in *The Erasmus Reader*, ed. Erika Rummel (Toronto: University of Toronto Press, 1990), 138-54.

follows that we should listen much and speak little. Rash and hasty speech not only is evidence of foolishness but can also often cause tumults. The Epistle . . . to James 1:19.[2]

The Anger That Rejects Instruction by the Word of God. Richard Turnbull: There are many kinds of anger and wrath, and there are reasons for and situations in which people become angry, but the apostle here passes over them as belonging to another discussion. Here the apostle speaks of that wrath and anger that arise from the desire to be contentious, and of being intractable or wayward, which cause us to not allow ourselves to be taught or reproved, not even by the word of God itself. An Exposition upon the Canonical Epistle of Saint James 1:19-20.[3]

A Caution to the Preacher. Johann Spangenberg: Why does he say, "Be quick to listen but slow to speak"? We should be more inclined to listen to God's word than to speak. Why so? Although the one who desires to occupy the teaching office desires a good thing (1 Tim 3), they must be sure that they are suited to it. Because as glorious as the office is when it is carried out appropriately, it can be just as harmful when the one to whom it has been commended has no understanding of Scripture. . . . You must study thoroughly before you teach other people. . . . Prefer to listen rather than to teach, for there is less danger in listening than in teaching.

Why does he say, "Be slow to anger"? He wants to say as much as, "If someone interrupts your poorly developed and formless preaching and chastises you for the same, you should not therefore quickly become angry; rather, you should accept the chastisement in a friendly manner and improve yourself, because wrath accomplishes nothing good." Epistle for the Fourth Sunday After Easter.[4]

[2]Osiander, *Epistola ad . . . Iacobi*, 115.
[3]Turnbull, *An Exposition upon the Canonical Epistle of Saint James*, 67v*.
[4]Spangenberg, *Postilla Teütsch*, 5:15v; citing 1 Tim 3:1.

The Ingrafted Word. Richard Turnbull: This word that we ought to receive with meekness is said to be ingrafted in us, because by God's Spirit moving and inclining our hearts, and by the painful and daily labor of his workers in his heavenly harvest, which are his ministers, it is, as it were, inserted in our hearts where it takes root. For as sprigs and twigs of other trees being engrafted, bound together, wrapped about with clay and moss or some other thing, by long continuance grow and cleave inseparably to the stocks into which they are grafted, so the word of God by the sap of his Spirit, and by the labor of the ministers, being, as it were, ingrafted in our hearts, therein often takes such root in that fruitful ground that it is said to be grafted in us.

And as sprigs or twigs, if either they are set in dry ground of human beings or by them planted on rotten roots and stocks become fruitless and perish and never take root, but dry away and die little by little, so if the word of God is cast in the stony ground of our hearts, or planted on the rotten roots of our carnal affections, it never takes root, but decays, dies, and withers. . . . So if we nourish the word of God in our inward affections, and knit it fast to ourselves by lively faith, if we bind it on our hearts and tie it about our necks, as Solomon and Moses speak, it shall also be engraved and engrafted in us.

Now the reason we should so do so . . . [is] because it is able to save our souls. The word of God is the only medicine for all our inward maladies; it is that sovereign salve that saves our souls; it is the plaster to lay to the wounds of our sins, yes and it has in store a salve for every sore of the mind. Seeing therefore that it brings such great profit with it, we ought with meekness to receive it, which St. James makes known and shows when he says, "receive with meekness the word engrafted in you, which is able to save your souls." An Exposition upon the Canonical Epistle of Saint James 1:21.[5]

[5]Turnbull, *An Exposition upon the Canonical Epistle of Saint James*, 73v-74v*; citing Mt 13:20; Prov 6:21; Deut 6:8; Acts 11:14.

To Save Souls, Prepare the Field of the Heart. Dirk Philips: Because the Word of God is now the seed that is planted by God in the hearts of human beings and desires and must have good soil, therefore it is necessary that the field of the heart be properly cultivated through the grace of the Lord, that all weeds be plucked up or uprooted, so then the field will be made receptive of the divine seed and bring forth fruit, as James says. . . .

To that end, namely, in order to cultivate and prepare the field of the heart, the law of God serves well. Therefore, true preachers must also first and before all things proclaim and preach repentance to the people (even as Christ and the apostles did) and teach them out of the law God's wrath and severe judgment on sin, but out of the gospel rightly to know God the Father in his eternal love and fathomless mercy, Christ Jesus in his grace and merits, through the cooperation of the Holy Spirit in order that the hearts, smitten and broken through the law, may again be comforted and strengthened through the gospel. For this is the nature, character, and power of the divine word, that where it is spoken orderly and through the motivating of the Spirit, flinty hearts are smitten, the cold made fervent and the sorrowful are comforted thereby. The Enchiridion.[6]

1:22-24 *Hearing and Doing the Word*

Mere Historical Faith Is Insufficient. Johann Spangenberg: What does St. Paul do in this epistle? He does not deal with faith or the righteousness of faith but with the righteousness of works. He reproaches those who think they are righteous and saved alone through historical faith. This is when they only confess the articles of the faith concerning the incarnation, the suffering, death, and resurrection of Christ with their mouths and yet no fruit of faith follows. There have always been such people and there still are.

"Be doers of the word," says St. James, "and not hearers alone so that you do not deceive yourselves." This exhortation is necessary because who can boast about the greatness of his faith and the gospel when their deeds, manners, behavior, and life oppose such faith and the teaching of the gospel? If a person is to be a good tree, that is, worthy of being called a believer, then good fruit, that is, an honorable Christian life and conduct, must follow, otherwise such a life is nothing but outward appearance and hypocrisy.

Whom does St. James call doers of the word? Those who actually demonstrate that they are Christians who not only hear the gospel with their ears or speak about it with their mouths, but who also grasp it in their hearts and then put it into practice, ordering their lives after it.

To whom does St. James compare a simple hearer of the word? He speaks thus: "If someone is a hearer of the word and not a doer of it, they are like someone who sees their face in a mirror and then an hour after they have seen themselves they forget how they look." This is a fine image because just as the reflection in a mirror quickly vanishes and is forgotten, so it is with mere hearers of the word who do not actually grasp its meaning nor have God's word constantly in their hearts and order their lives after the gospel. Epistle for the Fifth Sunday After Easter.[7]

The Kingdom of God Comes by Divine Power. Huldrych Zwingli: The position of this whole epistle is that those are vain and hypocritical who prattle much concerning faith, concerning God, and concerning virtues, while they are without the fruit of good works. For although the justification and salvation of all is by election and faith, nevertheless works of charity most certainly are signs of election and faith, so that if they are absent (which belongs to human judgment) it is certain that election and faith are not present, because the tree may be known by its fruits. Many are those who thus learn the gospel by heart, so that they even have it memorized, they speak splendidly concerning Christ, they sing sweetly, they read daily, they listen daily,

[6]CRR 6:207-208*; citing Mt 3:8; Acts 24:25; Jer 23:29.

[7]Spangenberg, *Postilla Teütsch*, 5:16v-18r; citing Mt 7:15-20.

they even teach others, but they never ponder the strength and spirit of the gospel. Christ is neither here nor there: he comes to those who love him; he dwells among those who keep his commands. The kingdom of God is not in speech but in power. The kingdom of God is righteousness, peace, and joy in the Holy Spirit. HULDRYCH ZWINGLI'S BRIEF AND EXCELLENT EXPOSITION OF THE EPISTLE OF BLESSED JAMES 1:22.[8]

CHRISTIANS ARE GOOD TREES THAT BEAR GOOD FRUIT. BALTHASAR HUBMAIER: Just as a good tree cannot be without fruit at the proper season, so it is also impossible for true faith to be without good works. Those who say they can do nothing good deceive themselves and there is no true faith in them. APOLOGY, JAMES 1:22-24.[9]

1:25 *Looking into the Perfect Law of Liberty*

THE GOSPEL IS THE PERFECT LAW OF FREEDOM. ANDREAS ALTHAMER: James names the gospel the perfect law of freedom because through this teaching of Christ we become righteous, pious, perfect, and free, as we are by nature unrighteous, evil, and captive. James does not speak about the law of Moses, which is no perfect law of freedom, because it brings no one to perfection, Hebrews 7, and does not make for a certain and free conscience, as the gospel does; rather, it makes us into slaves and sinners, but it cannot help us with sin. Therefore the words of James are to be understood according to the words of Christ in John 8 concerning the gospel. The one who perseveres in the gospel by faith will be blessed in his deeds, in his faith and endurance, according to the promise of Christ in Matthew 10: "The one who endures to the end shall be blessed." That is the deed (obedience to the divine word, namely, faith) that makes us blessed. THE EPISTLE OF ST. JAMES 1:25.[10]

BOASTING VERSUS BELIEVING THE GOSPEL. LUCAS OSIANDER: And James wanted to teach here (according to my judgment) that they ought not to promise salvation to themselves, who consider that it is enough if they hear the word of God and are able to speak and dispute concerning the same, even if meanwhile the gospel has no roots in their hearts, nor if any piety is detected in them. For it is one thing to boast concerning the gospel and another truly to believe the gospel. Commonly there are few of the latter and truly more of the former. THE EPISTLE . . . TO JAMES 1:25.[11]

WALKING IN THE WAY TO HEAVEN. DAVID DICKSON: The one who does these four things shall be blessed in their work: (1) the one who diligently looks into the word of God, studiously inquiring into the whole will of God, which is called the "law" or "the doctrine of liberty," because it teaches the true means of freedom from sin and wrath, and of serving God honestly, as it becomes God's free people, who are bound by love and thankfulness to please God; (2) the one who perseveres continuing in the study of the doctrine of holiness; (3) the one who takes care lest they forget the things they have learned; (4) the one who endeavors to practice that which God's word commands. Truly this person shall be blessed in their work, because although it is impossible they should deserve happiness by their works, yet it shall be declared by their works before all that they are blessed, and in the exercise of good works, as walking in the way to heaven, they shall certainly obtain the blessedness promised to the saints, and so shall be blessed in their work. AN EXPOSITION OF ALL ST. PAUL'S EPISTLES, JAMES 1:25.[12]

THE POISONOUS TONGUE OF A FALSE PREACHER. JOHANN SPANGENBERG: What is

[8]Zwingli, *Expositio in Epistolam beati Iacobi*, 15r-v; citing Mt 7:20; 24:23; Jn 14:23; 1 Cor 4:20; Rom 14:17.
[9]CRR 5:528; citing Mt 7:15-20.
[10]Althamer, *Die Epistel S. Jacobs*, F3v; citing Heb 7:19; Jn 8:31-36; Mt 10:22.
[11]Osiander, *Epistola ad . . . Iacobi*, 117.
[12]Dickson, *An Exposition of All St. Pauls Epistles*, 280*. Dickson's reference to "work" in this excerpt does not appear to mean vocation or job; rather, it seems to refer to good works. However, the alternative use of "work" and "works" is true to Dickson's original text.

more harmful in the church and Christian community than an evil, poisonous tongue of a false preacher who with false doctrine misleads and poisons the hearts of simple people and throws them to the devil in wrath? This is what all papists, spiritualists, and sects do, and no less evangelicals who can speak impressively and splendidly about the gospel and worship and yet who do not demonstrate their Christianity with a single small work or fruit of faith. EPISTLE FOR THE FIFTH SUNDAY AFTER EASTER.[13]

THE PERFECT LAW OF FREEDOM IS THE GOSPEL. JOHANN SPANGENBERG: What does St. James mean by the perfect law of freedom? This is what he calls the gospel because it is a perfect teaching that alone makes the human conscience free and joyful.

If I can be saved through works why did Christ die? . . . St. James is looking on the well from which such works flow [namely, faith], which Scripture also does in many places. EPISTLE FOR THE FIFTH SUNDAY AFTER EASTER.[14]

1:26-27 *Worthless Versus True Religion*

TRUE WORSHIPERS VERSUS HYPOCRITES. JOHN CALVIN: The object here, then, was to distinguish between the true worshipers of God and hypocrites, who are so swollen with Pharisaic pride, that they seek praise from the defects of others. . . . Rightly, then, has James, wishing to remove the effect, that is, the lust of evil-speaking, added the cause, even that hypocrites flatter themselves immoderately. For they would be ready to forgive, were they in turn to acknowledge themselves to be in need of forgiveness. Hence the flatteries by which they deceive themselves as to their own vices make them such supercilious censors of others. COMMENTARIES ON THE EPISTLE OF JAMES 1:26.[15]

[13]Spangenberg, *Postilla Teütsch*, 5:20r.
[14]Spangenberg, *Postilla Teütsch*, 5:18v-19r.
[15]CTS 42:288-89.

WE MUST "VISIT" ALL WHO ARE IN NEED. DAVID DICKSON: As for the works of charity, for example, he names compassion toward the fatherless and needy in their affliction. To "visit" is liberally and bountifully to succor the misery and necessity of others, under which duty he synecdochically comprehends the other duties towards our neighbor.

As for holy conversation, [James] comprehends that under the endeavor of preserving ourselves, through the grace of God, undefiled from the world, or from the defilements that are abroad in the world, and from the contagion of other people's sins, so that we pollute not ourselves with wickedness, nor have fellowship with those who pollute themselves in the mire of sin. AN EXPOSITION OF ALL ST. PAUL'S EPISTLES, JAMES 1:27.[16]

WE MUST SHOW MERCY TO ALL OF OUR NEIGHBORS IN NEED. JOHN CALVIN: As he passes by those things that are of the greatest moment in religion, he does not define generally what religion is, but reminds us that religion without the things he mentions is nothing. It is as when one given to wine and gluttony boasts that they are temperate, and another should object and say that the temperate person is the one who does not indulge in excess as to wine or eating; their object is not to express the whole of what temperance is, but to refer only to one thing, suitable to the subject in hand. For they are in vain religious of whom he speaks, as they are for the most part trifling pretenders.

James then teaches us that religion is not to be estimated by the pomp of ceremonies, but that there are important duties to which the servants of God ought to attend.

To "visit" in necessity is to extend a helping hand to alleviate those who are in distress. And as there are many others whom the Lord bids us to succor, in mentioning widows and orphans, he states a part for the whole. There is then no doubt but that under one particular thing he recommends to us every act of love, as though he had

[16]Dickson, *An Exposition of All St. Pauls Epistles*, 280*.

said, "Let the one who would be deemed religious, prove themselves to be such by self-denial and by mercy and benevolence toward their neighbor." COMMENTARIES ON THE EPISTLE OF JAMES 1:27.[17]

WE MUST HAVE COMPASSION ON OTHERS AS GOD HAS HAD COMPASSION ON US. DESIDERIUS ERASMUS: Do you want then to hear what true religion is in the eyes of God the Father, who does not judge you in the manner that human beings do? Pure and spotless religion consists in being both compassionate and kind toward our neighbor in the same way we have experienced God's compassion and kindness toward ourselves. We behave this way not from some expectation that a charitable act will be reciprocated, but from a pure and sincere love as we wait for the reward for our charity from no other source than from God. He allows the credit to be given to himself for whatever our love of him has caused us to place in a brother. PARAPHRASE ON JAMES 1:27.[18]

[17]CTS 42:299-300*.

[18]CWE 44:146.

2:1-13 Show No Partiality

My brothers,[a] show no partiality as you hold the faith
in our Lord Jesus Christ, the Lord of glory. 2 *For if a*
man wearing a gold ring and fine clothing comes into
your assembly, and a poor man in shabby clothing
also comes in, 3 *and if you pay attention to the one*
who wears the fine clothing and say, "You sit here in a
good place," while you say to the poor man, "You
stand over there," or, "Sit down at my feet," 4 *have you*
not then made distinctions among yourselves and
become judges with evil thoughts? 5 *Listen, my beloved*
brothers, has not God chosen those who are poor in
the world to be rich in faith and heirs of the kingdom,
which he has promised to those who love him? 6 *But*
you have dishonored the poor man. Are not the rich
the ones who oppress you, and the ones who drag you
into court? 7 *Are they not the ones who blaspheme the*
honorable name by which you were called?
8 *If you really fulfill the royal law according to the*
Scripture, "You shall love your neighbor as yourself,"
you are doing well. 9 *But if you show partiality, you*
are committing sin and are convicted by the law as
transgressors. 10 *For whoever keeps the whole law but*
fails in one point has become guilty of all of it. 11 *For*
he who said, "Do not commit adultery," also said,
"Do not murder." If you do not commit adultery but
do murder, you have become a transgressor of the law.
12 *So speak and so act as those who are to be judged*
under the law of liberty. 13 *For judgment is without*
mercy to one who has shown no mercy. Mercy
triumphs over judgment.

a Or *brothers and sisters*; also verses 5, 14

Overview: The statements in this section of James about the rich and the poor presented a challenge to the reformers, for on the one hand they wished to affirm all that the biblical text had to say on the subject, while on the other they desired to affirm what they saw as good, godly, and necessary distinctions between persons within the temporal sphere. Early modern society was marked more by fear of chaos than by fear of tyranny, and maintaining order was a paramount concern shared by nearly all. One sees the reformers wrestling with these twin desires in their comments on this section. One also sees them struggling with this section's statement about God's preference for the poor over the rich and the way it could—in the reformers' eyes—threaten election and justification by faith as the way to obtain God's favor. The reformers seek to solve this apparent conundrum by stressing that the elect poor are in view in this section of James. Still, the reformers do have sharp words about the rich and readily acknowledge that wealth is as much an impediment to salvation in their own day as in the past.

God Esteems the Poor Highly. Erasmus Sarcerius: Why should one not despise the poor? Because God has elected them and esteems them highly. . . . Who are these poor ones? They are people rich in faith, heirs of the kingdom, which God has promised to those who love him. Summaries and Brief Content, James 2:1-13.[1]

2:1-7 *Do Not Favor the Rich At the Poor's Expense*

Respect to the Rich Should Not Entail Reproach of the Poor. John Calvin: This reproof seems at first sight to be hard and unreasonable, for it is one of the duties of courtesy, not to be neglected, to honor those who are elevated in the world. Further, if respect of persons is vicious, servants are to be freed from all subjection, for freedom and servitude are deemed by Paul as conditions of life. The same must be thought of

[1] Sarcerius, *Summarien vnd kurtzer Jnhalt*, 4:KK1r-KK2r.

magistrates. But the solution for these questions is not difficult, if what James writes is not misunderstood. For he does not simply disapprove of honor being paid to the rich, but that this should not be done in a way so as to despise or reproach the poor; and this will appear more clearly when he proceeds to speak of the rule of love.

Let us therefore remember that the respect of persons here condemned is that by which the rich is so extolled that wrong is done to the poor, which also he shows clearly by the context. And surely the honor that is shown to the rich to the contempt of the poor is full of false ambition and vanity. Nor is there a doubt but that false ambition reigns and vanity also, when the masks of this world are alone in high esteem. Commentaries on the Epistle of James 2:1-4.[2]

Christians Should Not Measure Others by Their Wealth. Desiderius Erasmus: One who loves their neighbor because of God and loves God in their neighbor does not measure the neighbor by the extent of his power or the size of their wealth or the degree of their nobility, but by the extent to which they abound in divine goods. Measured by this standard a king or a rich person is no better than someone who is of low estate or poor. Christ died for all people equally, and all are equally called to the inheritance of immortality. Therefore, my brothers, if you really have faith in the promises of our Lord Jesus Christ, do not show partiality to persons according to the value of their worldly possessions. By the world's measure Christ was lowborn and poor, and yet the Father wanted him to be the prince of all glory. It was not to the rich but to the poor that he promised the kingdom of heaven. . . . Not everyone who is wealthy is impious of course; nevertheless, the rich of this world scarcely ever meet the demands of evangelical piety. Paraphrase on James 2:1-7.[3]

The Virtuous Poor Bear the Image of Christ. John Mayer: All sound expositors speak to the same effect, and that is, simply to give outward respect to the richer and to the more noble in this world, as God has differentiated them by outward dignity, wealth, or the office that they bear, is not a sin, but may and ought to be done, for it is commanded, "Honor father and mother," "Honor the king," and "Give honor to whom honor belongs." And servants are commanded to reverence their masters, and the younger to rise up before the gray-headed. A great rich person is in the office of a great steward in which they may do good to many, and therefore in civility they may be reverenced by the poor, and by all people they may so be preferred as regards their place in society. But if out of an interior estimation of such a person in the heart, thinking them to be better, because they are richer, and the poor more vile and worse, because they are outwardly more base; if in their mind, they with the gold ring and the colorful clothes are honored, and they that go in poor clothing are debased, this is a sinful accepting of persons, and such as ought not to be among Christians. Muckish earthworms indeed that know not wherein true worth stands are wont to measure their esteem of human beings by these things, thinking them a most excellent and happy person who has the wealth and dignities of this world. But he who has his eyes opened esteems in his mind only virtuous people, and thinks the vicious most base, though in civility, as they are bound, they give outward reverence to them as their place requires. Again, to reverence the rich that are vicious for their riches, and to show all contempt toward the virtuous poor is a great sin, because by those who do so riches are preferred before virtue, which is plain injustice. Since virtue is a thousand degrees beyond riches, it is to honor the image of the world before the image of Christ, for the vicious rich person bears the image of the world, the virtuous poor person, the image of Christ. A Commentary upon the New Testament, James 2:1-3.[4]

[2]CTS 42:300-301*.
[3]CWE 44:147-48; citing 1 Cor 2:8; Lk 6:20.
[4]Mayer, *A commentarie vpon the New Testament*, 3:23-24*; citing Eph 6:1; 1 Pet 2:17; Col 3:22; Eph 6:5; 1 Pet 2:18; Lev 19:32; Rom 13:7.

THERE ARE GRADES OF PERSONS IN CIVIL LIFE BUT NOT IN THE CHURCH. LUCAS OSIANDER: For although God has certainly constituted grades of persons in civil life, nevertheless, in the church it is proper neither for the impious rich to be flattered nor to condemn the pious poor. THE EPISTLE . . . TO JAMES 2:1.[5]

CHRISTIANS MUST AVOID JUDGING PERSONS ON THE BASIS OF WEALTH. DAVID DICKSON: The first vice that he admonishes them to avoid is respect of persons, which is committed when in the same cause more or less is attributed to anyone than is fitting by reason of something in their person, which has nothing to do with the cause. So those among the Hebrews committed an offense when they magnified faith in Christ among the richer sort but esteemed the same faith as nothing in the poorer sort, so that the rich, though unbelievers, were esteemed very highly, but the poor, though believers, were accounted of no value, but were instead condemned. AN EXPOSITION OF ALL ST. PAUL'S EPISTLES, JAMES 2:1.[6]

DO NOT HARM THE CHURCH. JOHN CALVIN: He means that the respect of persons is inconsistent with the faith of Christ, so that they cannot be united together, and rightly so; for we are by faith united into one body, in which Christ holds the primacy. When therefore the pomps of the world become preeminent so as to cover over what Christ is, it is evident that faith has but little vigor. . . . For so great is the brightness of Christ that it easily extinguishes all the glories of the world, if indeed it irradiates our eyes. It hence follows that Christ is little esteemed by us when the admiration of worldly glory lays hold on us. COMMENTARIES ON THE EPISTLE OF JAMES 2:1.[7]

CHRISTIANS BELONG TO A HOLY BROTHERHOOD. RICHARD TURNBULL: This evil cannot stand with Christian profession: the gospel teaches that with God is no respecter of persons, but that all those who fear God and work righteousness are accepted through the joyful tidings of salvation by Jesus Christ, in whom there is neither male nor female, bond nor free, neither rich nor poor, but they are all alike unto him. The sound of this gospel went not to the rich, noble, honorable, and mighty men of the world alone, but it was preached to the poor also. By this gospel are we united into a holy brotherhood, and this brotherhood implies equality in this case, so that if the rich are to be regarded and the poor neglected, this necessarily renders the spiritual brotherhood violate and broken. Through the gospel we become all of us members of one body, each of us members of each other and all members of Christ our head. If then for riches, honor, or worldly pomp, we esteem and account human beings, and not for their union with Christ and their incorporation with him, we fall away from Christian religion. Thus the respect of other's persons and esteeming religion by their outward appearance cannot stand with the faith of Christ, which teaches us to embrace Christians with brotherly love and not to regard one with the contempt of another, which is a thing unseemly to our calling, repugnant to love, and contrary to our profession. St. James in his proposition condemning respect of persons exhorts the brothers not to have faith in our glorious Lord Jesus Christ and at the same time to practice respect of persons. AN EXPOSITION UPON THE CANONICAL EPISTLE OF SAINT JAMES 2:1.[8]

THE RICH COME TO CHURCH TO DISPLAY THEIR LUXURY. LUCAS OSIANDER: Even today sometimes the rich occupy favorable places in the churches, which they also close off with a bolt, lest these places stand open to others. Meanwhile they themselves rarely attend sacred sermons, or they come more that they might show off the luxury of their clothes than listen attentively to the word of God. Such haughtiness of the rich deforms the church. THE EPISTLE . . . TO JAMES 2:2-4.[9]

[5]Osiander, *Epistola ad . . . Iacobi*, 118.
[6]Dickson, *An Exposition of All St. Pauls Epistles*, 280*.
[7]CTS 42:301*.
[8]Turnbull, *An Exposition upon the Canonical Epistle of Saint James*, 103r-10 v*; Gal 3:28; Is 61:1, Mt 11:5; 1 Cor 12:27.
[9]Osiander, *Epistola ad . . . Iacobi*, 119.

GOD MAKES ONE RICH IN FAITH THROUGH THE GIFTS OF THE SPIRIT. JOHN CALVIN: As God honors the poor, then everyone who repudiates them reverses the order of God. . . . "The rich in faith" are not those who abound in the greatness of faith, but such as God has enriched with the various gifts of his Spirit, which we receive by faith. For, doubtless, since the Lord deals bountifully with all, everyone becomes a partaker of his gifts according to the measure of their own faith. If, then, we are empty or needy, that proves the deficiency of our faith; for if we only enlarge the bosom of faith, God is always ready to fill it. . . . He says that a kingdom is "promised" to those who love God, not that the promise depends on love, but he reminds us that we are called by God to the hope of eternal life, on this condition and to this end, that we may love him. Then the end, and not the beginning, is here pointed out. COMMENTARIES ON THE EPISTLE OF JAMES 2:5.[10]

THE ELECT POOR ARE IN VIEW IN THIS PASSAGE. ANDREAS ALTHAMER: He does not speak here concerning all poor people, because one finds many godless rogues—both male and female—among the poor. He is referring to believers, the elect who have become God's children through faith, who are our brothers and who are poor in terms of temporal goods but rich in spiritual goods. And note: St. James says that God has chosen them so that no one can be of the opinion that it is earned; God chose and called them out of pure grace apart from all merit, just as they were created. THE EPISTLE OF ST. JAMES 2:5.[11]

THE RIGHTEOUS RICH MUST TAKE CARE LEST THEY GO THE WAY OF THE WORLD. JOHN CALVIN: There are, indeed, some of the rich who are just, and meek, and hate all unrighteousness; but few of such people are to be found. James, then, mentions what for the most part usually happens, and what daily experience proves true. For as people commonly exercise their power in doing what is wrong it hence happens that the more power any one has, the worse they are, and the more unjust toward their neighbors. The rich ought to be all the more careful, lest they should contract any of the contagion that everywhere prevails among those of their own rank. COMMENTARIES ON THE EPISTLE OF JAMES 2:6.[12]

WEALTH AS AN IMPEDIMENT TO SALVATION. LUCAS OSIANDER: As not all poor people are saved, thus not all rich people are damned. But nevertheless many rich people have been devoted to their own wealth and pleasures, so that they care not enough for true religion and eternal salvation. Truly many needs and miseries of this life drive the poor so that they seriously seek eternal goods. THE EPISTLE . . . TO JAMES 2:6.[13]

THE TYRANNOUS RICH. HULDRYCH ZWINGLI: When he speaks of the rich, he names those who exercise tyranny among the poor, who lead the poor into trials, who blaspheme the name of the Lord . . . and who serve money, those we now especially esteem and move into public offices. HULDRYCH ZWINGLI'S BRIEF AND EXCELLENT EXPOSITION OF THE EPISTLE OF BLESSED JAMES 2:7.[14]

2:8-13 *Love Fulfills the Royal Law*

A VAIN DESIRE WINS FAVOR WITH THE RICH. JOHN CALVIN: Now follows a plainer declaration, for he expressly points out the cause of the last reproof, for they were officiously attentive to the rich, not from love, but on the contrary, from a vain desire of attaining their favor. . . . I think there is an allusion here to the servile obedience that they rendered to the rich, when by serving their neighbors in sincerity they might not only be free but also live as kings. COMMENTARIES ON THE EPISTLE OF JAMES 2:8-11.[15]

[10]CTS 42:302-3*.
[11]Althamer, *Die Epistel S. Jacobs*, Gii r-v. Eph 1:4, 11; 2:8-10.
[12]CTS 42:304*.
[13]Osiander, *Epistola ad . . . Iacobi*, 119.
[14]Zwingli, *Expositio in Epistolam beati Iacobi*, 23v-24r.
[15]CTS 42:305-6*.

THE ROYAL LAW IS THE IMMORTAL KING'S LAW. RICHARD TURNBULL: This law of love here called the royal law is therefore called the royal law ... because it is from a king, not mortal but immortal, even the king of kings and Lord of Lords, even from God. This law then proceeding from this king is called the king's law, the royal law, the princely law. And it is clear that this law concerning love is from God, for when God informs his people, among other things, he prescribes this law to them: "love your neighbor as yourself." AN EXPOSITION UPON THE CANONICAL EPISTLE OF SAINT JAMES 2:8.[16]

THE LAW COMMON TO ALL. THE ENGLISH ANNOTATIONS: The law of loving our neighbor as ourselves is called the royal law as highways are called the king's, that is, because they are common to all. So this law should be extended to all, whether poor or rich, there is no limitation on the law. You shall love your neighbor, whosoever they be, without respect of persons. ANNOTATIONS ON HEBREWS 2:8.[17]

THE LAW OF LIBERTY IS THE MERCY OF GOD. JOHN CALVIN: This is a proof of the former verse, because the lawgiver is to be considered rather than each particular precept apart. The righteousness of God, as an indivisible body, is contained in the law. Whosoever, then, transgresses one article of the law destroys, as far as they can, the righteousness of God.... The sense [of "liberty"] is as though he had said, "Except you wish to undergo the rigor of the law, you must be less rigid toward your neighbors, for the law of liberty is the same as the mercy of God, which delivers us from the curse of the law." And so this verse ought to be read with what follows, where he speaks of the duty of bearing with infirmities. And doubtless the whole passage thus reads well: "Since none of us can stand before God, except we be delivered and freed from the strict rigor of the law, we ought so to act, that we may not through too much severity exclude the indulgence or mercy of God, of which we all have need to the last." ... It is indeed a singular commendation of kindness and benevolence that God promises he will be merciful to us, if we be so to our brothers, not that our mercy, however great it may be, shown toward others, merits the mercy of God, but that God would have those whom he has adopted, as he is to them a kind and indulgent Father, to bear and exhibit his image on the earth, according to the saying of Christ, "Be merciful as your heavenly Father is merciful." COMMENTARIES ON THE EPISTLE OF JAMES 2:11-13.[18]

TREAT ALL EQUALLY, AS GOD TREATS YOU. JOHN DONNE: And this is truly, most literally, the purpose of the apostle here, that you undervalue no one for their outward appearance; that you overvalue no one for their goodly apparel, or gold rings; that you say not to a poor person, "Stand thou there"; or of you admit them to sit, "Sit here under my footstool." But it is a precept of accessibleness, and of affability; affability that is, a civility of the city of God and a courtship of the court of heaven, to receive other people, the images of God, with the same easiness that God receives you. SERMON ON JAMES 2:12.[19]

CHRISTIANS ARE TO LIVE IN ACCORDANCE WITH THEIR PROFESSION. JOHN DONNE: This then is the Christian's case, and this is the abridgement of their religion, to speak aright and to do aright; to profess the truth and be not ashamed nor afraid of that; and to live according to that profession: for, no one can make God the author of sin, but that person comes as near it as they can that makes God's religion a cloak for his sin. To this God proceeds not merely and only by commandment, but by persuasion too, and, though he not be bound to do so, yet he does give a reason. The reason is, because he must give account of both, both of actions and of words; of both we shall be

[16]Turnbull, *An Exposition upon the Canonical Epistle of Saint James*, 113r*; citing Lev 19:18.
[17]Downame, ed., *Annotations*, OOO1r*.

[18]CTS 42:307-8*; citing Mt 5:7.
[19]Donne, *Works*, 5:399*.

judged, but judged by a law, a law that excludes on God's part, any secret ill purpose upon us if we keep his law; a law that excludes, on our part, all pretense of ignorance; for no one can plead ignorant of a law. And then, a law of liberty; of liberty to God; for God was not bound to save anyone because he made them; but of his own goodness, he vouchsafed them a law, by which they may be saved; a law of liberty to us: so that there is no epicurism, to do what we list; no such liberty as to make us libertines, for then there were no law; nor stoicism, nor fatality that constrains us to do what we would not do, for then there were no liberty. But the gospel is such a law of liberty, as delivers us, upon whom it works, from the necessity of falling into the bondage of sin before, and from the impossibility of recovering after, if we be fallen into bondage. And this is liberty enough: and of this liberty, our blessed God give us the right use, for his Son Christ Jesus' sake, by the operation of that Holy Ghost, that proceeds from both. SERMON ON JAMES 2:12.[20]

WE MUST SHARE THE GIFT OF MERCY. DESIDERIUS ERASMUS: You have been freely forgiven the sins of your past life. You have received freely the gift of the heavenly Spirit, through which you have not only been reconciled to God but have also been cemented together in mutual love. This gift was conferred, and conferred freely on you who did nothing to deserve it. All the more severe, therefore, will the punishment be of those who, having experienced so much mercy from God toward themselves, do not show themselves in turn gentle and merciful toward their neighbor. PARAPHRASE ON JAMES 2:12-13.[21]

[20]Donne, *Works*, 5:414*.
[21]CWE 44:150.

2:14-26 FAITH APART FROM WORKS IS DEAD

14 What good is it, my brothers, if someone says he has
faith but does not have works? Can that faith save him?
15 If a brother or sister is poorly clothed and lacking in
daily food, 16 and one of you says to them, "Go in peace,
be warmed and filled," without giving them the things
needed for the body, what good[a] *is that? 17 So also faith*
by itself, if it does not have works, is dead.
18 But someone will say, "You have faith and I have
works." Show me your faith apart from your works,
and I will show you my faith by my works. 19 You
believe that God is one; you do well. Even the demons
believe—and shudder! 20 Do you want to be shown,
you foolish person, that faith apart from works is
useless? 21 Was not Abraham our father justified by
works when he offered up his son Isaac on the altar?
22 You see that faith was active along with his works,
and faith was completed by his works; 23 and the
Scripture was fulfilled that says, "Abraham believed
God, and it was counted to him as righteousness"—
and he was called a friend of God. 24 You see that a
person is justified by works and not by faith alone.
25 And in the same way was not also Rahab the
prostitute justified by works when she received the
messengers and sent them out by another way? 26 For
as the body apart from the spirit is dead, so also faith
apart from works is dead.

a Or *benefit*

OVERVIEW: In this section, the magisterial Protestant reformers are at pains to demonstrate against their detractors that the faith that justifies is a lively and active faith that necessarily issues forth in good works. Reformed Protestants and some Lutherans also insist (against Luther) that Paul and James are not opposed in their teaching about justification; rather, they deal with two different kinds of justification, one before God and the other before human beings, because they were addressing two different problems: legalism and works righteousness versus lax Christianity. Catholic reformers place a similar emphasis on the necessarily lively nature of justifying faith. Radical reformers see in this section of James a warrant to criticize the alleged "mouth-faith" and "paper-faith" of magisterial Protestants and to argue instead for "hand-faith."

LOVE DOES NOT GO ON HOLIDAY. DESIDERIUS ERASMUS: But what is faith without love? Love moreover is a living thing; it does not go on holiday; it is not idle; it expresses itself in kind acts wherever it is present. . . . Someone will now appear perhaps who, eager to separate things that are by nature most closely joined together and cannot be split apart from each other, might say, "You have faith, I have deeds. Let each one of us be satisfied with their part. Let your faith be enough for you. I am content to have for my part good deeds." On the contrary, neither part is sufficient by itself. PARAPHRASE ON JAMES 2:14-26.[1]

THERE ARE TWO KINDS OF FAITH AND TWO KINDS OF WORKS. JOHN MAYER: From here to the end of the chapter there is only one point handled against those who were bearing themselves on their faith but who neglected the works of mercy. St. James undertakes here to argue for the latter. The main question here is what he means when he denies that a person is justified by faith only and affirms justification by works. Because St. Paul speaking of justification by faith says that it is by faith without the works of the law. Oecumenius considering these propositions of these two apostles, seeming to be so contrary (Oecumen. in Iac. 2.),[†] and yet that Abraham is brought for example by them both, said that the

[1] CWE 44:150-51.

word "faith" is taken two ways: first, for a simple consent to the thing preached that it is true; second, for a consent joined with the acquirement thereof out of an affection and with obedience. Of the first of these James affirms that a person is not justified hereby. But Paul speaking of the other ascribes justification to it. The word "works" is also to be understood in two ways, for there are works before baptism and works after: the one who dies immediately after baptism dies justified by their faith without works, because they had no time to do any; but the one who lives and has time to do them is not justified without good works, which is to be understood, not as though good works had a part in the act of our justification, but because they cannot but necessarily follow as fruits and effects in whomsoever there is a saving and justifying faith. Touching Abraham, whom Paul says was justified by faith, but James by works, both are truly said of him, and do indeed agree in one. He believed that he should be the father of many nations, he believed God's promise touching his seed, and this was counted to him for righteousness, and when he came to the work here spoken of, viz., the offering of his son, he did not fall from this faith, for he believed that God was able to raise him from the dead again. A Commentary upon the New Testament, James 2:14-26.[2]

The Righteousness of Life and Imperfect Righteousness. Erasmus Sarcerius: Objection. Can faith still be true if good works do not follow from it? No, because the works that follow from it are witnesses to true faith. James further distinguishes true faith from false or dead faith. . . . The latter does not make one righteousness or blessed; only the true believers have the former. The devil, hypocrites, and Turks have the latter. It is historical faith in which one believes that this or that in Scripture is true as with other worldly histories. The papists require and have such a faith, therefore they can become neither righteous nor blessed.

Here the apostle draws on the example of Abraham to prove that faith without works is dead, further, that good works are necessary to imperfect righteousness (*ad iustitiam inchoatam*), which consists of works.† Thus, after Abraham was justified through faith (the righteousness of life), he sacrificed his son Isaac (imperfect righteousness). Abraham is a model of all the godly, who must be clothed with two kinds of righteousness: the righteousness of life, which comes alone through faith from grace without works; and the righteousness that one calls unformed righteousness to which good works belong. Summaries and Brief Content, James 2:14-25.[3]

2:14-19 *Showing Faith with Works*

True Faith Versus Show Faith. Richard Turnbull: Here now begins the second part of this second chapter. It is concerned to the end to teach that good works must necessarily be joined with true faith in all the saints of God. . . . Now to proceed to these things as they lie in the apostle. The first is the apostle's proposition, "What does it avail a person who says they have faith, when they have no works? Can their faith save them?" It is as if he would say, "That faith that is void and destitute of good works, as fruits, effects, and tokens of faith, is not to be reputed and taken for a true, saving, and justifying faith, but rather for a show and shadow of faith than for faith indeed." For no one is justified and saved by faith before God, whose faith in due time, and in convenient manner, does not show itself in the fruits and duties of love. If our faith is

[2]Mayer, *A commentarie vpon the New Testament*, 3:28*; citing Rom 3:28; Gen 17:5; 22:1-19. †See Gerald Bray, ed., *James, 1–2 Peter, 1–3 John, Jude*, ACCS, NT XI (Downers Grove, IL: InterVarsity Press, 2000), 28, 31. Oecumenius was a sixth-century orator and philosopher.

[3]Sarcerius, *Summarien vnd kurtzer Jnhalt*, 4:KK2v. †On *iustitia inchoata* in the Lutheran tradition, see "Image of God," in *Christian Cyclopedia*, ed. Erwin L. Lueker, Luther Poellot, and Paul Jackson (St. Louis: Concordia, 2000), 4. Imperfect righteousness is analogous to Luther's concept of "actual righteousness," referring to the good works that flow from "alien righteousness" and that are necessary yet always incomplete or imperfect in this life owing to the power of indwelling sin. See Martin Luther, *Two Kinds of Righteousness* (1519), LW 31:293-306; WA 2:145-52.

therefore to be perfect in every way, it must be accompanied with the fruits of righteousness. For how can we believe the gospel unless we live after the gospel? . . . That faith, then, that is without good works is not such a faith by which we are justified and stand before God; it is rather a fruitless, dead, and barren faith, whereof we boast in vain. For outward profession without holy conversation is halting hypocrisy, and pretended religion without true sanctification is double iniquity. This is the doctrine of holy Scripture; this is the state of and proposition of this present treatise; this is the thing carefully and continually preached by the ministers and preachers of the gospel newly received. An Exposition upon the Canonical Epistle of Saint James 2:14-19.[4]

Faith Without Love Avails Nothing. John Calvin: He proceeds to commend mercy. And as he had threatened that God would be a severe judge to us, and at the same time very dreadful, except we be kind and merciful toward our neighbors, and as on the other hand hypocrites objected and said that faith is sufficient to us, in which the salvation of human beings consists, he now condemns this vain boasting. The sum, then, of what is said is that faith without love avails nothing, and that it is therefore wholly dead.

But here a question arises: Can faith be separated from love? It is indeed true that the exposition of this passage has produced that common distinction of the Sophists, between unformed and formed faith,† but of such a thing James knew nothing, for it appears from the first words that he speaks of false profession of faith. For he does not begin thus, "If anyone has faith," but, "If any says that they have faith," by which he certainly states that hypocrites boast of the empty name of faith, which really does not belong to them. . . . "Can that faith save them?" This is the same as though he had said that we do not attain salvation by a frigid and bare knowledge of God, which all confess to be most true, for salvation comes to us by faith for this reason, because it joins us to God. And this comes not in any other way than by being united to the body of Christ, so that, living through his Spirit, we are also governed by him. There is no such thing as this in the dead image of faith. There is then no wonder that James denies that salvation is connected with it. Commentaries on the Epistle of James 2:14.[5]

One Who Possesses True Faith Authenticates It. Martin Luther: Truly, if faith is there, one cannot hold back; one proves oneself, breaks out into good works, confesses and teaches this gospel before the people, and stakes one's life on it. . . . Seeing that Christ has done this for them, they thus follow Christ's example. Preface to the New Testament.[6]

We Must Love in Words and Deeds. Huldrych Zwingli: Those who speak of faith rightly certainly do not do less than these brothers who say to the hungry or the cold, "Go, be warmed, eat." But this is not sufficient unless they express this faith by deeds, which will happen if they have fed or made warm the needy. For then clearly the substance of faith may become an essence in the heart, with the result that the inner parts of the brother are moved within by necessity, so that not only by word but also by deed and truth we love. For the one who has worldly means and sees their brother in need and closes their own heart from them, how does the love of God remain in them? Huldrych Zwingli's Brief and Excellent Exposition of the Epistle of Blessed James 2:14-17.[7]

Faith Is Nourished by Good Works. Thomas Cranmer: Faith may not be naked without works, for then it is no true faith; and when

[4]Turnbull, *An exposition upon the Canonical Epistle of Saint James*, 126r-v, 127v*.

[5]CTS 42:309-10*. †Calvin here refers to the medieval distinction between faith that was formed by love and faith that was not; only the former was held to be salvific.

[6]LW 35:361.

[7]Zwingli, *Expositio in Epistolam beati Iacobi*, 30r; citing Heb 11:1; 1 Jn 3:17.

it is adjoined to works, yet it is above the works. For as people who are people indeed first have life, and after are nourished, so must our faith in Christ go before, and after be nourished with good works. And life may be without nourishment, but nourishment cannot be without life. A person must be nourished by good works, but first a person must have faith. Whoever does good deeds yet without faith has not life. I can show that a person by faith without works lived, and came to heaven, but without faith a person never had life. HOMILY OF GOOD WORKS.[8]

MOUTH-CHRISTIANS VERSUS HAND-CHRISTIANS. BALTHASAR HUBMAIER: Mere faith alone is not sufficient for salvation. . . . Therefore mere faith is like a green fig tree without fruit, like a cistern without water, like a cloud without rain. I have taught thus in my booklets. In them I bemoan with tears that people have in so many years not learned better than to say: "We believe, faith saves us"; while in this age brotherly love and loyalty have grown staler and colder in us than ever before. . . . We still claim to be Christians, truly evangelical, and boast of our great faith, and have never touched the works of the gospel and of faith with our little finger. We are, consequently, as said above, nothing but mouth-Christians, ear-Christians, paper Christians, but not hand-Christians. Concerning these, St. James speaks most rebukingly in his Christian and very profitable epistle. . . . Yea, I confess on the strength of this article that mere faith does not deserve to be called faith, for a true faith can never exist without deeds of love. APOLOGY, JAMES 2:14-19.[9]

FAITH MUST BE EFFECTIVE THROUGH LOVE. LUCAS OSIANDER: The priests err by the span of heaven who conclude from this saying that faith gains the strength to justify from love, and that love is the form of faith. But James says nothing concerning justification in this place, but he only demonstrates that faith that is not effective through love is not true but dead. This is what we ourselves also teach. THE EPISTLE . . . TO JAMES 2:17.[10]

LUTHERANS ARE LIKE THE EARLY TIMID BELIEVING SYNAGOGUE LEADERS. MELCHIOR HOFFMAN: Therefore let everyone be warned that they regard carefully how and what they believe in order that they deceive not themselves and go astray with the others. For the whole world [of Lutheranism] cries: Believe, believe; grace, grace; Christ Jesus. And therefore it does not choose the better part, for its hope is idle and a great deception. For such belief cannot justify them before God, as the holy apostle James writes: "Even so faith, if it has not fruits is in itself dead." Thus there were many of the leaders of the Jewish synagogue who believed in Christ Jesus, but nevertheless would not openly confess it, for they preferred the praise of human beings to the praise of God. What profited them such a faith? For all such timid ones will not inherit the kingdom of God, as the Holy Spirit of God testifies. And as the Lord Christ Jesus says: Those who deny him before humans, them will he deny before God, his Father, and before all the angels. For whoever wishes to save their life, they will lose it in eternity. THE ORDINANCE OF GOD, JAMES 2:17.[11]

TRUE FAITH IS NOT DEAD. LEUPOLD SCHARNSCHLAGER: This is what we have to say about faith in Jesus Christ. No one should claim that faith, which comes from the preaching of God's word, is merely a historical or dead faith, without effect or fruit. No doubt that is what people held at the time of James. According to his epistle, James replied with a demonstration of faith at work. Even today some understand Christ and Paul as ascribing righteousness and life to faith alone, as if a faith without deeds and fruit is enough for salvation. For how can it be a barren, that is, a dead faith, when life—and much more—comes forth from it? CONCERNING TRUE FAITH.[12]

[8]Cranmer, *Cranmer's Select Writings*, 34.
[9]CRR 5:526-27.
[10]Osiander, *Epistola ad . . . Iacobi*, 122-23.
[11]LCC 25:201; citing Mt 10:33; 16:25.
[12]CRR 12:537.

The Dispute Is Not About Faith but About Common Knowledge of God. John Calvin: "You believe that there is one God." From this one sentence it appears evident that the whole dispute is not about faith, but of the common knowledge of God, which can no more connect humanity with God than the sight of the sun carry them up to heaven; but it is certain that by faith we come near to God. Besides, it would be ridiculous were anyone to say that the devils have faith; and James prefers them in this respect to hypocrites. The devil *trembles*, he says, at the mention of God's name, because when he acknowledges his own judge he is filled with the fear of him. He then who despises an acknowledged God is much worse. Commentaries on the Epistle of James 2:19.[13]

Belief That There Is a God Versus Belief in God. Andreas Althamer: Believing that there is a God is nothing high, special, or of great significance. But to believe in God, that is spirit and life. To believe in God is to trust God, to ascribe all that is good to God, the call on God in necessity, to place all consolation and hope in God, to love, honor, call on, and confess him from the heart, and to know that he is our savior, protector, help, and life. Neither the godless nor the devils have this faith, rather only the elect. The Epistle of St. James 2:19.[14]

Permissible Doubt. John Mayer: Here is also a certainty not to be doubted, which is set forth as a property of true faith: for it is without all doubting assented to, that Jesus is the Savior of the world, and that whosoever rightly believes on him shall have everlasting life. But as for certainty of a person's own particular estate in grace, I suppose that is not so much a part of the essence of faith that they should be said to have no faith who is not able for the present to apply God's promises without doubting to themselves. If this were true then many true Christians would be in a woeful state, who in time of temptation find many fears and perplexities in themselves, so much so that they are ready to say with David that they are cast out of God's presence, though afterward they see their weakness and recover their hold again. Besides this, particular assurance is a thing that is to increase daily as people grow up in Christ, and therefore it is no marvel if in those that are yet children in the faith it is not so strong as it should be. A Commentary upon the New Testament, James 2:19.[15]

Christ Must Be Received, Not Just Known. Dirk Philips: It is not enough that we confess that Jesus Christ is the Son of the living God, conceived in Mary through the Holy Spirit, and born out of her as a true human being, etc. But we also receive him as the eternal Word, and the imperishable seed of God the heavenly Father, through the Holy Spirit, prove him and through this be preserved. If not, then all our boasting of knowledge and faith will not help. For the devil well knows and confesses that Jesus Christ is God's Son. But as little as such learning and knowledge helps the devil, so little shall the oral confession of faith help us without the living, discernible, and actual power of God, of which all pious Christians are participants. Therefore, Christ also says he "who believes in me" has eternal life. Why? Because he has received a divine power, yes, a quickening power of eternal life—creating life in their heart that so thoroughly penetrates, purifies, and renews, and finally drives, leads, and transposes to the origin from which it has sprung, namely, eternal divine life itself. The Enchiridion.[16]

2:20-26 *Faith Completed by Works*

Two Kinds of Righteousness. Andreas Althamer: It is important to note here that St. James did not use these examples of Abraham and Rahab to hold up the righteousness of works, that

[13]CTS 42:312-13*.
[14]Althamer, *Die Epistel S. Jacobs*, J v.

[15]Mayer, *A commentarie vpon the New Testament*, 3:30-31* citing Jas 1:5; Jn 3:16; Ps 51:11.
[16]CRR 6:149*; citing Jn 1:1; 1 Jn 1:1; 1 Pet 1:23; 1 Jn 3:9; Jn 3:16; 11:25.

one becomes pious and righteous before God by merit and works and receives salvation by the same. It is obvious that Abraham and Rahab were already pious and righteous before God on account of their faith before they performed the works that James here discusses. . . . Because there are two kinds righteousness, one that counts before God, namely, the righteousness of faith that occurs when God out of pure grace on account of faith forgives all of our misdeeds and accepts us as righteous, which St. Paul treats abundantly in Romans 3 and 4. The other righteousness is an external piety by which we walk blamelessly before people, who are not able to find anything punishable in our conduct but must instead confess that we are pious and blameless. The little word "to justify" is not always taken to mean the making of pious and righteous person out of an unrighteous person before God; rather, it is often used to refer to being held and regarded as pious and righteous before people, as in Isaiah 5 . . . Proverbs 17 . . . and Luke 7. THE EPISTLE OF ST. JAMES 2:20-26.[17]

FAITH IS COLD AND DEAD APART FROM LOVE. HULDRYCH ZWINGLI: He says, "You see therefore that a person is justified by works and not only by faith." Here James establishes that deeds operating by faith were accepted, and that faith operating as mere affectation was understood as a dead and empty faith, which many people were boasting of in his time. Therefore, he reproaches mere faith, while he accords faith having been confirmed by deeds the highest praise, and he bestows praise on this righteousness and salvation. . . . And Paul makes use of this example in his epistle to the Hebrews (Heb 11), approving the same that James does here: he commends the faith of those among the Jews were who famous among them, and he makes known this commendation from their excellent deeds and honors. Therefore, faith is declared to be true and effectual by deeds . . . and it is cold apart from love, nor does it deserve to be called faith, but it is dead and useless, just as a body destitute of life is dead and useless. HULDRYCH ZWINGLI'S BRIEF AND EXCELLENT EXPOSITION OF THE EPISTLE OF BLESSED JAMES 2:20-26.[18]

A CATHOLIC CARDINAL TEACHES JUSTIFICATION BY FAITH. RICHARD TURNBULL: Let us with Matthias Flacius Illyricus see that annotation and observation or note of Cardinal Cajetan, one of the Romish clergy, on these words: "Do you wish to understand, O you vain person, that faith without works is dead?" "Mark well reader," Cajetan says, "that James does not mean that faith without works is dead, because it is manifest that we are justified by faith even without works, as is the case with infants who are baptized, and in older people also who are baptized and then die; but he means faith without works, that is, faith refusing to work, is dead, vain, and not able to justify."† Thus even one of their own, who would here hence conclude the necessity of works in the matter of justification, spoke the same thing that we all speak and defend and for which we are wrongfully condemned of them, that faith that is not prepared to do well, when occasion is offered, but then refuses to work, is dead and profits nothing. For true faith always works (when matter, occasion, and opportunity is offered) through love, as St. Paul avows. If the Romanists would hold to this sense of St. James, if not with us yet with their own cardinal, then there should remain out of this place no such great controversy between us and them in the matter of justification. AN EXPOSITION UPON THE CANONICAL EPISTLE OF SAINT JAMES 2:20.[19]

JAMES AND PAUL ARE NOT OPPOSED ON JUSTIFICATION. LUCAS OSIANDER: James treats the term *justification* differently than Paul. For

[17]Althamer, *Die Epistel S. Jacobs*, J2v, J3v-J4r; citing Is 5:23; Prov 17:15; Lk 7:29. On the two kinds of righteousness, see Martin Luther, *Two Kinds of Righteousness* (1519), LW 31:293-306; WA 2:145-52.

[18]Zwingli, *Expositio in Epistolam beati Iacobi*, 33v-34r; citing Gal 5:6.

[19]Turnbull, *An Exposition upon the Canonical Epistle of Saint James*, 142v*; citing Gal 5:6. †Cardinal Cajetan, *Opera omnia qvotqvot in Sacrae Scripturae expositionem reperiuntur* (Lyons: Jean and Pierre Prost, 1639), 5:367. For Flacius's citation of Cajetan, see the former's *Glossa Compendaria* (Basel, 1570), 1209.

according to the apostle Paul, to be justified signifies to be absolved from sin. For James, to be justified denotes to be declared righteous: the good tree may be recognized by its good fruit, which will soon become manifest. Therefore, this saying of James need not be opposed to the teaching of Paul concerning justification. The Epistle . . . to James 2:20.[20]

The Design of the Writer Must Be Kept in View. John Calvin: We must understand the state of the question, for the dispute here is not respecting the cause of justification, but only what avails a profession of faith without works, and what opinion we are to form of it. Absurdly then do they act who strive to prove by this passage that human beings are justified by works, because James meant no such thing, for the proofs that he uses refer to this declaration, that no faith, or only a dead faith, is without works. No one will ever understand what is said, nor judge wisely of words, except he who keeps in view the design of the writer. Commentaries on the Epistle of James 2:20.[21]

Justification Before God and Human Beings. Richard Turnbull: As there is justifying before God, which is through faith, so there is justification before human beings, which is to be showed, declared, and known of human beings, to be just and righteous. And this justifying is by works, which only shows forth our faith to the knowledge of human beings and makes it known to the world that we are righteous and just indeed. Thus by his obedience (as the fruit of his faith) was Abraham justified in the offering of his son. This offering did not make him righteous before God, but his faith did. But the offering made him known to human beings to have been justified before God through faith, and so he was justified before human beings through works. Thus to be justified by works with human beings, is to be . . . known as righteous. . . . Seeing there is a double justifying, one before God, through faith alone, and the other before human beings, and that through works, of which kind does St. James speak? He speaks of being justified before human beings, not before God. An Exposition upon the Canonical Epistle of Saint James 2:21.[22]

The Twofold Meaning of "Justified." John Calvin: When, therefore, the Sophists set up James against Paul, they go astray through the ambiguous meaning of a term. When Paul says that we are justified by faith, he means no other thing than that by faith we are counted righteous before God. But James has quite another thing in view, even to show that the one who professes that they have faith must prove the reality of their faith by their works. Doubtless James did not mean to teach us here the ground on which our hope of salvation ought to rest; and it is this alone that Paul dwells on.

That we may not then fall into that false reasoning which has deceived the Sophists, we must take notice of the twofold meaning of the word "justified." Paul means by it the gratuitous imputation of righteousness before the tribunal of God; and James, the manifestation of righteousness by the conduct, and that before human beings, as we may gather from the preceding words, "Show to me your faith. . . ." In this sense we fully allow that humankind is justified by works, as when anyone says that a person is enriched by the purchase of a large and valuable estate, because their riches, before hidden and shut up in a chest, were thus made known. Commentaries on the Epistle of James 2:21.[23]

James and Paul Agree Concerning Faith and Works. David Dickson: Here James proves that faith without works is dead and consequently the profession of faith that is wanting in works is in vain. James does this from the example of Abraham, who in the foresaid matter concerning the demon-

[20]Osiander, *Epistola ad . . . Iacobi*, 123; citing Lk 6:42-44.
[21]CTS 42:314*.
[22]Turnbull, *An Exposition upon the Canonical Epistle of Saint James*, 150v-151r*; Gen 22:10.
[23]CTS 42:314-15*.

stration of his faith, whether it was alive or dead, is found and declared just by his works, and thus here by an interrogation James urges on the conscience of the hypocrite. Abraham the father of the faithful is justified before the whole world, because his faith was not dead but alive by his works, when he had offered Isaac his son on the altar in testimony of the sincerity of his faith; or that he by a lively faith believed in God and pleased not himself in the vain profession of an idle or dead faith, as many do. Therefore, faith that is without works is dead and vain. And so James agrees very well with Paul: For Paul argues thus in Romans 4:2: If Abraham was justified by works he has something whereof to glory, but not before God; therefore, he is not justified before God by works. But James argues thus: Abraham is justified by works before human beings, who might say to him, "Show me your faith by your works, or demonstrate to me that your faith is not dead, but alive." From this antecedent it does not only follow therefore that faith without works is dead but also, the conclusion agreeing with Paul's conclusion, that Abraham therefore is justified before God not by that dead faith that is void of works, but by a lively faith and efficacious in works, and so the apostles agree very well. AN EXPOSITION OF ALL ST. PAUL'S EPISTLES, JAMES 2:21.[24]

A MISREADING OF MOSES. JOHN CALVIN: They who seek to prove from this passage of James that the works of Abraham were imputed for righteousness must necessarily confess that Scripture is perverted by him, for however they may turn and twist, they can never make the effect to be its own cause. The passage is quoted from Moses. The imputation of righteousness that Moses mentions preceded more than thirty years the work by which they would have Abraham to have been justified. Since faith was imputed to Abraham fifteen years before the birth of Isaac, this could not surely have been done through the work of sacrificing him. I consider that all those are bound fast by an indissoluble knot who imagine that righteousness was imputed to Abraham before God because he sacrificed his son Isaac, who was not yet born when the Holy Spirit declared that Abraham was justified. It hence necessarily follows that something posterior is pointed out here. . . . A person is not justified by faith alone, that is, by a bare and empty knowledge of God; they are justified by works, that is, their righteousness is known and proved by its fruits. COMMENTARIES ON THE EPISTLE OF JAMES 2:23.[25]

THERE IS NO DISAGREEMENT BETWEEN PAUL AND JAMES ON FAITH AND WORKS. RICHARD TURNBULL: We must diligently consider and carefully weigh with what people, hearers, and persons these two [Paul and James] had to deal. St. Paul, as appears in many places of the New Testament, had to do with people who were persuaded that unless they observed the law of Moses they could not be saved. He confutes such people out of the law itself, out of the prophets, David, Habakkuk, and others; out of the gospel and the true end and use both of it and of the law of Moses. To this purpose he sets down a doctrine in words quite contrary to this matter, namely, that humans are justified by faith in Jesus Christ without the works of the law of Moses. In order to establish this assertion, the epistles to the Romans, Galatians, Ephesians, and Philippians seemed to have been penned and written. In process of time this assured doctrine was wrongly and wretchedly interpreted by some, who gathered that it was not needful for those who by faith in Jesus Christ were justified to be practice good works, but that to believe only barely, without care of holy conduct of life, was sufficient. To prevent this St. Paul in those forenamed epistles often joins to the doctrine of free justification by faith with God, sundry exhortations to proper conduct. St. James, seeing the carnal professors greatly abusing the gospel to the liberty and looseness of the flesh, in this epistle confronts them, testifying and protesting to all people that faith without works in those

[24]Dickson, *An Exposition of All St. Pauls Epistles*, 282*.

[25]CTS 42:316*; citing Gen 15:6.

pretending they are justified is but a dead carcass. And thus he writes not against Paul, but with him, against such as perverted St. Paul's most certain and true doctrine, and abused their liberty and free justification, to the wantonness of the flesh. As people now do also, who hearing justification by faith alone, think themselves thereby discharged and set at liberty from the practice of holiness, which is their error, in that they do not perceive that as we are freely justified before God through faith, without the help or respect of our works, so are we known to be just by works before human beings, whereby God for his mercy is glorified and therefore ought to be performed by us. AN EXPOSITION UPON THE CANONICAL EPISTLE OF SAINT JAMES 2:24.[26]

JUSTIFICATION THROUGH INFUSED FAITH. JACQUES LEFÈVRE D'ÉTAPLES: It is certainly impossible for anyone to be faithful who, having faith, has not the works of faith when the occasion for the operating of faith through love affords itself. . . . For faith is an infused charism from the Spirit of God, and it is the good tree. And every good tree, from the statement of the Savior, produces good fruit (Mt 7). By way of contrast, it is impossible for a person to have good works who does not have faith. . . . For all that is not from faith is sin (Rom 14). For the rest, if you do not have faith you are unfaithful and are an evil tree; you are a person of the flesh and an old person. . . . Hence James says, "I will show you my faith by my works." For good works are signs of faith. . . . And to have faith without works, as far as the Scriptures are concerned is to believe and to confess that one is not justified, except perhaps if the time had not yet come for exercising works of faith, as in young children, for whom faith alone suffices for righteousness. . . . And Abraham was justified because he believed, but not because he believed with a dead faith, but with a living one; not idle, but working, which always has with it the fear and love of God. . . . Therefore, his faith was manifested by his works. . . . And the one in whom this faith is present, this one is immediately righteous, both righteous and justified, God reckoning faith of this kind for righteousness, that is, God justifying. . . . Without faith Abraham certainly not would have worked in this way, but his faith was cooperating by means of works through love of God. COMMENTS ON THE CATHOLIC EPISTLES, JAMES 2:24.[27]

JAMES DOES NOT CONFLICT WITH PAUL. PHILIPP MELANCHTHON: It is evident that "faith" in this passage in James refers to the knowledge of the historical facts such as the damned also possess. For he says, "the devils believe and tremble." Furthermore it must be confessed, and we do clearly confess, that a person is not righteous by this knowledge. But Paul, when he is speaking of faith, understands confidence in God's mercy, which relies on the mediator and for his sake receives reconciliation. Therefore we must understand "faith" in one sense in Paul . . . and another way in James. . . . Therefore James is not in conflict with Paul but is speaking about something else and refuting the error of those who imagine that they are righteous on account of their profession of the dogmas, as this opinion can easily take over the minds of inexperienced people. In the same way the Jews imagined that they were righteous on account of their profession of their doctrine and their ceremonies. It is necessary to refute this error.

Nor does this refutation conflict with Paul, when James adds, "A person is justified by works," for he is speaking of the righteousness or works that Paul also proclaims with great emphasis as being necessary; but he denies that remission of sins is given on account of this righteousness. Therefore the word "to justify" should not be understood as the equivalent of reconciliation, but as we have often said elsewhere, it means "to be

[26]Turnbull, *An Exposition upon the Canonical Epistle of Saint James*, 153v-154r*; citing Acts 15:1; Phil 3:2; Gal 3:1; Rom 4:1-2; 1 Pet 2:16; Jude 4; Jn 13:35; Mt 5:16; 1 Pet 2:12.

[27]Lefèvre d'Étaples, *Commentarii in epistolas catholicas*, 9r-v; citing Mt 7:17-19; Rom 14:23.

approved." A person is justified by their works; that is, they have a righteousness of works that is approved and that pleases God. That obedience is necessary in the reconciled and how it is pleasing to God has been said above. A person is not righteous or pleasing or accepted if they lack this obedience and if sins against conscience remain. Therefore the statement that a person is obliged to have the righteousness of works must be confessed by us. But in the meantime the hearer must also learn some things, namely, that they do not receive the remission of sins because of their works, or that they are pleasing to God, for they do not satisfy the law, but they are only pleasing for the sake of the mediator. It is clear that he must add these points.

Thus it is very apparent that James is not disputing about the entire matter but has spoken about only one aspect; he is demanding the righteousness of works and refuting those who imagine that they are righteous merely on the basis of their profession. Loci Praecipui Theologici.[28]

[28]Melanchthon, *Loci Praecipui Theologici*, 201-2*; citing Rom 10:10.

3:1-18 TAMING THE TONGUE AND OBTAINING HEAVENLY WISDOM

Not many of you should become teachers, my
brothers, for you know that we who teach will be
judged with greater strictness. 2For we all stumble in
many ways. And if anyone does not stumble in what
he says, he is a perfect man, able also to bridle his
whole body. 3If we put bits into the mouths of horses
so that they obey us, we guide their whole bodies as
well. 4Look at the ships also: though they are so large
and are driven by strong winds, they are guided by a
very small rudder wherever the will of the pilot
directs. 5So also the tongue is a small member, yet it
boasts of great things.

How great a forest is set ablaze by such a small
fire! 6And the tongue is a fire, a world of unrighteous-
ness. The tongue is set among our members, staining
the whole body, setting on fire the entire course of life,[a]
and set on fire by hell.[b] *7For every kind of beast and*
bird, of reptile and sea creature, can be tamed and
has been tamed by mankind, 8but no human being
can tame the tongue. It is a restless evil, full of deadly
poison. 9With it we bless our Lord and Father, and
with it we curse people who are made in the likeness
of God. 10From the same mouth come blessing and
cursing. My brothers,[c] *these things ought not to be so.*
11Does a spring pour forth from the same opening
both fresh and salt water? 12Can a fig tree, my
brothers, bear olives, or a grapevine produce figs?
Neither can a salt pond yield fresh water.

13Who is wise and understanding among you? By
his good conduct let him show his works in the
meekness of wisdom. 14But if you have bitter jealousy
and selfish ambition in your hearts, do not boast and
be false to the truth. 15This is not the wisdom that
comes down from above, but is earthly, unspiritual,
demonic. 16For where jealousy and selfish ambition ex-
ist, there will be disorder and every vile practice. 17But
the wisdom from above is first pure, then peaceable,
gentle, open to reason, full of mercy and good fruits,
impartial and sincere. 18And a harvest of righteous-
ness is sown in peace by those who make peace.

a Or *wheel of birth* **b** Greek *Gehenna* **c** Or *brothers and sisters*; also verse 12

OVERVIEW: Perhaps the most significant interpretative issue to emerge in the reformers' comments on this section of James has to do with the simple word "teachers" in verse 1. Some take it to mean those who hold the preaching office and thus understand James to mean that those who seek out this office for themselves should be cautious because so much is at stake—the salvation of souls—in what a preacher teaches the flock. Others take "teachers" (or "masters") to refer to laypeople who take it on themselves to oversee and censure their fellow Christians without taking care as to how they employ their own tongues as they do so. In the commentary here, Lutheran and Catholic reformers adopt the former interpretation while Reformed pastor-theologians opt for the latter. Other reformers underscore the emphasis on peaceableness and spiritual wisdom in this section, juxtaposing it to the strife and carnal wisdom of the world.

THE COHERENCE OF CHAPTERS 1, 2, AND 3. JOHN MAYER: Even though there may seem to be no coherence between this chapter and those that went before, yet if we look back to 1:19 and 1:25 it will appear that it coheres very well with what precedes it. For having there begun an argument concerning speech and the abuse of the tongue, to which he joined an exhortation to do the word and not to hear it only, and especially by emptying out all maliciousness and filthiness, and putting on meekness and exercising mercy rather than contempt toward the poor, as we may well observe, he keeps within these bounds throughout the remainder of his epistle. First, in chapter 2 he treats more largely of treating the poor with contempt and of works of mercy. Second, in a similarly expansive manner he returns to speak of the misgovernment of the tongue in chapter 3, after which, third, in the same chapter, he also resumes his exhortation to meekness and against maliciousness (cf. verse 13 to the end of the chapter).... Here then are two points, first, against the abuse of the tongue; second, against the strife and contention arising from the want of meekness in the heart—such strife manifests itself by railing and cursed speaking. Touching the first, he reproves it first more obscurely in verse 1, then plainly in verses 2 and following. A COMMENTARY UPON THE NEW TESTAMENT, JAMES 3.[1]

A GODLY TEACHER. DESIDERIUS ERASMUS: The human tongue has great utility whenever someone is teaching the elements of true godliness, but to assume the task of the teacher is to assume an office encumbered with risk. It requires a person who is first of all eminently learned in the content of evangelical doctrine and second, has their emotions completely purged. It is not enough for them simply to teach what is correct; their one and only aim must be the glory of Christ. A teacher of this kind can have the greatest benefit if they are also in love with what they teach. Conversely, there is great loss to the people when someone occupies the position of teacher whose doctrine is corrupt or whose mind is corrupted and warped by passions like hatred, anger, revenge, greed, ambition, or lust. PARAPHRASE ON JAMES 3:1-12.[2]

WORDS ARE NOT WIND BUT FIRE AND DEADLY POISON. JOHN MAYER: Note of what great necessity it is to have a special care of the governing of the tongue, for as a person is in this respect, so are they accounted before God. Words are not wind, as the common saying is, but fire and deadly poison, if they are evil, to the destruction of the whole person. They come out of the heart, Mark 7, and defile indeed, Matthew 12:37.

Note again that an evil tongue works from fire to fire, from hell and the devil to the kindling of heart and fury and contention here, and to the bringing of a person to suffer in hellfire hereafter. The lewd-tongued person is on a wheel turned by the devil, till they are brought to the same destruction as the devil. He is more savage than the wildest and most savage beasts, which may be tamed, but he is unreclaimably barbarous.

Last note that the best speeches that an ill-tongued person can use are all corrupted and distasteful before God, by means of their ill language at other times, which is as bitter water that makes of all their water bitter, to the turning of them into a bramble, on which no figs grow. Let railers, and swearers, and cursers, and filthy speakers consider this and tremble. A COMMENTARY UPON THE NEW TESTAMENT, JAMES 3:1-12.[3]

3:1 *Not Too Many Should Be Teachers*

WARNING AGAINST ASSUMING THE PREACHING OFFICE LIGHTLY. ANDREAS ALTHAMER: In the third chapter St. James teaches and exhorts the Christians to bridle their tongues and neither quickly, lightly, nor sacrilegiously to intrude into the preaching office because they wish to be teachers, bishops, and masters of other people, as he also exhorted above in the first chapter. For those who want to be bishops, preachers, and pastors will have to give great account and will receive a severe judgment if they have not carried out their office industriously and faithfully. And although we are all sinners and often and in many ways err, fail, and sin (because there is no person who does not sin ...), but those mentioned above will certainly receive a great judgment when they fail, as Christ the Lord himself says. THE EPISTLE OF ST. JAMES 3:1.[4]

---

[1]Mayer, *A commentarie vpon the New Testament*, 3:33*.
[2]CWE 44:154.
[3]Mayer, *A commentarie vpon the New Testament*, 3:42-43*.
[4]Althamer, *Die Epistel S. Jacobs*, K1v; citing Eccles 7:20; Lk 12:48.

Masters of Morals. John Calvin: The common and almost universal interpretation of this passage is that the apostle discourages the desire for the office of teaching, and for this reason: because it is dangerous and exposes one to a heavier judgment in case one transgresses. And they think that he said, "Be not many masters," because there ought to have been some. But I take masters not to be those who performed a public duty in the church but such as took upon them the right of passing judgment upon others, for such reprovers sought to be accounted as masters of morals. And it was a mode of speaking usual among the Greeks as well as Latins; they were called masters who superciliously passed criticism on others.

And it was for this reason that he forbade them to be many, because many everywhere were thrusting themselves forward to be such masters, for it is, as it were, an innate disease in humankind to seek reputation by blaming others. Commentaries on the Epistle of James 3:1.[5]

Erudition Is Not Sufficient for Assuming the Office of Teaching. Lucas Osiander: With these words James did not want to deter suitable people from the ecclesiastical ministry, but he warns here, lest those fascinated by the vain conviction of erudition might seize the office of teaching, who neither have been instructed in the necessary gifts, nor have they been legitimately called. For many who are intoxicated and also swelled with the conviction of [their own] erudition think that it is an easy thing to teach the church concerning true religion. The Epistle . . . to James 3:1.[6]

Masters Are Those Who Judge Others Harshly. Richard Turnbull: Touching the exhortation itself, it teaches us not ambitiously, as commonly people do, neither too rigorously and austerely to judge, censure, and condemn our brothers. The apostle inserts this exhortation under this form of speech and words: "My brothers, be not many masters," that is, let not the saints usurp authority ambitiously to judge and censure their brothers with sharpness and rigor. Wherein, by masters are not understood such as are called to public place and office of reproving, but such as are private people, or as private people challenge and arrogate to themselves, in the ambition of their minds, an absolute authority as it were to judge, give sentence of, and censure their brothers in rigor and austerity of judgment, a vice and evil common to all times, and with hypocrites, most usual in St. James's days. An Exposition upon the Canonical Epistle of Saint James 3:1.[7]

3:2-4 *We All Stumble*

The Hypocrisy of the Censors. John Calvin: He then indirectly touches here on the hypocrisy of censors, because in examining themselves they omitted the chief thing, and what was of great moment, even their evil-speaking. For they who reproved others pretended a zeal for perfect holiness, but they ought to have begun with the tongue if they wished to be perfect. As they made no account of bridling the tongue but, on the contrary, bit and tore others, they exhibited only a fictitious sanctity. It is hence evident that they were the most reprehensible of all, because they neglected a primary virtue. This connection renders the meaning of the apostle plain to us. Commentaries on the Epistle of James 3:2.[8]

Perfection Among Sinful Mortals. Lucas Osiander: The person in view shall be able to control their tongue so that they speak nothing that may be worthy of reprehension; this one undoubtedly will also bridle and restrain their own body, so that they will commit no wickedness. (And James calls such a person perfect, not because the person has been perfected in the severe judgment of God,

[5]CTS 42:317-18*.
[6]Osiander, *Epistola ad . . . Iacobi*, 125-26.
[7]Turnbull, *An Exposition upon the Canonical Epistle of Saint James*, 156r*.
[8]CTS 42:319*.

but because the person has perfection of such a kind that is able to occur in a mortal person in whom sin still dwells.) The Epistle . . . to James 3:2.[9]

The Well-Ruled Tongue. Juan de Valdés: As God wishes us not to offend divine love by the lips, he lays down the second rule, which I have mentioned, speaking of the care you ought to take for the love of God, so also for the care of the love of our neighbor he lays down a rule over the tongue. . . . This is, that you keep the tongue well ruled and governed, and use it only for the glory of God, and for the religious or physical good of your neighbor and your own, taking away and removing from you every occasion that may lead or induce you to let anything escape from your lips that offends, or may offend, the most lowly or abject individual of all who are found in the world. And that you may see how important this is, I wish you to know that Saint James says: "If anyone offend not in word, the same is a perfect person." And notice, *signora*, that I do not tell you that in order to keep the commandment of love toward their neighbor perfectly, a person must do all these things precisely, for I do not say so; but that a person who wishes to be perfect must keep all their affections so obedient and well-regulated that when it may be needful for the honor of God to do so, they will not find in themselves a repugnance to them. The Christian Alphabet, James 3:2.[10]

3:5-12 *The Danger of the Tongue*

The Walled-In Tongue. Andreas Althamer: Blessed is the one who can bridle their tongue so that it does not slip out of the bridle. God has placed the tongue in the middle of the head and secured it with two walls, namely, the teeth and lips, that it may be enclosed and blocked and not always travel beyond these walls and thus cause misfortune with its unnecessary prattling. However, these two thick walls cannot always contain it so that it sometimes travels out and wishes to be free and unbridled. Yes, one can much sooner make a frightful, wild animal tame than an evil tongue. The Epistle of St. James 3:5-8.[11]

The Tongue Set on Fire by Hell. John Calvin: When he says that it is "set on fire by hell," it is the same as though he had said that the outrageousness of the tongue is the flame of the infernal fire. For as heathen poets imagined that the wicked are tormented by the torches of the Furies, so it is true that Satan by the fans of temptations kindles the fire of all evils in the world. But James means that fire sent by Satan is most easily caught by the tongue, so that it immediately burns; in short, that it is a material fitted for receiving, fostering, and increasing the fire of hell. Commentaries on the Epistle of James 3:6.[12]

Christians Should Be Free of All Stench and Bitterness. Lucas Osiander: Therefore it is fitting that as each tree or bush has its own proper fruit, and as from one source both sweet and bitter water do not emanate, so also from Christians (whose hearts ought to be imbued with true love) every bitterness and stench should be absent. The Epistle . . . to James 3:10.[13]

3:13-16 *Characteristics of Demonic Wisdom*

Wisdom in the Sight of God. John Calvin: Then the meaning is that supercilious censors, who largely indulge themselves, and at the same time spare none, seem to themselves to be very wise, but are greatly mistaken; for the Lord teaches his people far otherwise, even to be meek and to be courteous to others. They, then, are alone wise in the sight of God who connect this meekness with an honest conduct of life; for they who are severe and inexorable, though they may excel others in

[9]Osiander, *Epistola ad . . . Iacobi*, 126.
[10]LCC 25:380-81.
[11]Althamer, *Die Epistel S. Jacobs*, Kiii v.
[12]CTS 42:321*.
[13]Osiander, *Epistola ad . . . Iacobi*, 128.

many virtues, do not yet follow the right way of wisdom. Commentaries on the Epistle of James 3:16.[14]

Spiritual and Carnal Zeal. Lucas Osiander: There are two kinds of zeal, spiritual and carnal. The spiritual kind is kindled by the Spirit of God, and it sets right many crooked things. The carnal kind is inflamed by Satan, and in the church and the state, as well as in household affairs, it destroys many things. Therefore take care most studiously lest under the species of spiritual zeal carnal zeal creeps in among you. The Epistle . . . to James 3:16.[15]

3:17-18 *Characteristics of Heavenly Wisdom*

Physicians Who Seek to Heal Vices Should Not Be Executioners. John Calvin: "And the fruit of righteousness." This admits of two meanings—that fruit is sown by the peaceable, which afterward they gather—or that they themselves, though they meekly tolerate many things in their neighbors, do not yet cease to sow righteousness. It is, however, an anticipation of an objection; for they who are carried away to evil-speaking by the lust of slandering have always this excuse, "What! Can we then remove evil by our courteousness?" Hence James says that those who are wise according to God's will are so kind, meek, and merciful as yet not to cover vices nor favor them, but on the contrary in such a way as to strive to correct them, and yet in a peaceable manner, that is, in moderation, so that union is preserved. And thus he testifies that what he had hitherto said tends in no degree to do away with calm reproofs, but that those who wish to be physicians to heal vices ought not to be executioners. Commentaries on the Epistle of James 3:18.[16]

Reaping and Sowing to the Flesh or to the Spirit. Lucas Osiander: For the tranquil peace-loving soul proceeds by doing good and does many things to the glory of God and much that it useful for the salvation of the neighbor. Truly those who are living contentiously neglect the works of the Christian calling, and they merit from their neighbor not good but evil, and they use up the great part of life with quarrels and injuries given and received infelicitously. And the things a person will have sown, these things will they also reap. Because the one who sows according to their own flesh (that is, the one who sustains a habit of the corruption of their own flesh and lives impiously and carnally), this one reaps corruption concerning the flesh (that is, damnation or eternal ruin), but the one who sows in the Spirit (that is, the one who submits to the Holy Spirit, and works well), this one will reap eternal life from the Spirit. The Epistle . . . to James 3:18.[17]

Peaceable Wisdom. Richard Turnbull: And this reason is set down to persuade the saints to embrace peace against the corrupt judgment of the world, which judges them miserable, foolish, and wretched who live peaceably. But the Spirit of truth teaches here the contrary, that howsoever the world judges peaceable persons, yet shall they assuredly in due time reap and receive the reward of peaceable righteousness. This reward ought to allure all people to the meekness of wisdom, which ought to be followed by Christians and a good conscience retained, vice and iniquity suppressed, virtue and godliness promoted, love and charity in the holy fear of God cherished. And this is the peaceable wisdom commanded by the apostle. May Christ Jesus our Lord, who of God is for us made wisdom and righteousness, sanctification and redemption, grant us this wisdom, that in all peace and quietness of heart we may serve one another in love, and in one spirit and one truth, with one mind and one mouth, may glorify God the God of peace, to whom with Jesus Christ his Son our

[14]CTS 42:324*.
[15]Osiander, *Epistola ad . . . Iacobi*, 129.
[16]CTS 42:327-28 *.
[17]Osiander, *Epistola ad . . . Iacobi*, 130; citing Gal 6:7-8.

Savior and the Holy Spirit our comforter, be praise in the great congregation of the saints. Amen. An Exposition upon the Canonical Epistle of Saint James 3:18.[18]

Evangelical Philosophy. Desiderius Erasmus: Human-made philosophy produces professors who are captious, obstinate, and ferocious. But the more sincere, the more effective evangelical philosophy becomes, the less it is marked by arrogance. Its special force is located not in syllogistic subtleties or rhetorical trappings, but in sincerity of life and gentleness of character, which gives way to the contentious, attracts the docile, and has no other object than the salvation of its hearers. It is a heavenly wisdom. Paraphrase on James 3:13-18.[19]

[18]Turnbull, *An Exposition upon the Canonical Epistle of Saint James*, 186r*.

[19]CWE 44:158.

The Occasion of This Exhortation. Richard Turnbull: The occasion of this exhortation may be the sin that the apostle in the first place condemned, namely, that many took authority to themselves to reprove and check their brothers, and to be as censors over them, thereby seeking the opinion of wisdom among human beings, which (notwithstanding) were themselves envious and contentious.

St. James here (to abate their pride, to beat down the arrogance of their spirits, to assuage their malice, and to cool the heat of their madness and fury) tells them that to be contentious among human beings is not the way to be counted wise; but rather that wisdom consists in this, that they show themselves modest, quiet, meek, and gentle in their whole conduct of life. An Exposition upon the Canonical Epistle of Saint James 3:13-18.[20]

[20]Turnbull, *An Exposition upon the Canonical Epistle of Saint James*, 175r*.

4:1-17 Warning Against Friendship with the World

What causes quarrels and what causes fights among you? Is it not this, that your passions[a] *are at war within you?*[b] [2]*You desire and do not have, so you murder. You covet and cannot obtain, so you fight and quarrel. You do not have, because you do not ask.* [3]*You ask and do not receive, because you ask wrongly, to spend it on your passions.* [4]*You adulterous people!*[c] *Do you not know that friendship with the world is enmity with God? Therefore whoever wishes to be a friend of the world makes himself an enemy of God.* [5]*Or do you suppose it is to no purpose that the Scripture says, "He yearns jealously over the spirit that he has made to dwell in us"?* [6]*But he gives more grace. Therefore it says, "God opposes the proud but gives grace to the humble."* [7]*Submit yourselves therefore to God. Resist the devil, and he will flee from you.* [8]*Draw near to God, and he will draw near to you. Cleanse your hands, you sinners, and purify your hearts, you double-minded.* [9]*Be wretched and mourn and weep. Let your laughter be turned to mourning and your joy to gloom.* [10]*Humble yourselves before the Lord, and he will exalt you.*

[11]*Do not speak evil against one another, brothers.*[d] *The one who speaks against a brother or judges his brother, speaks evil against the law and judges the law. But if you judge the law, you are not a doer of the law but a judge.* [12]*There is only one lawgiver and judge, he who is able to save and to destroy. But who are you to judge your neighbor?*

[13]*Come now, you who say, "Today or tomorrow we will go into such and such a town and spend a year there and trade and make a profit"—* [14]*yet you do not know what tomorrow will bring. What is your life? For you are a mist that appears for a little time and then vanishes.* [15]*Instead you ought to say, "If the Lord wills, we will live and do this or that."* [16]*As it is, you boast in your arrogance. All such boasting is evil.* [17]*So whoever knows the right thing to do and fails to do it, for him it is sin.*

a Greek *pleasures;* also verse 3 **b** Greek *in your members* **c** Or *You adulteresses!* **d** Or *brothers and sisters*

Overview: The reformers give full rein to their emphasis on human depravity in their comments on this section of James, seeing in its warnings against spiritual adultery and friendship with the world evidence for their view that human nature is in utter bondage to sin. Two main exegetical issues arise in this section. The first has to do with the proper interpretation of "spirit/Spirit" in verse 5—does it refer to the fallen human spirit or the Holy Spirit? The reformers make cases for both interpretations. The second and related issue has to do with the authorship of James. Some interpreters assume that the quotation in verse 5 is from Paul (Gal 5:17) and that this proves that James was not an apostle but merely the disciple of the apostles, for he quotes Paul as Scripture.

4:1-3 *The Source of Quarrels and Fighting*

Two Clarifications. John Mayer: To come now to the resolving of the doubts concerning this passage:

1. Concerning "wars and fightings," it is clear, as all agree, that wars properly are not meant, for Christians were not then permitted to have weapons or armor, but private wranglings and strifes.
2. Concerning their "pleasures," Pareus† has also cleared this up sufficiently, and the members wherein they fight are the inward faculties of

the mind, acting the part of contention by the tongue, hands, feet, and the other members of the body.

A COMMENTARY UPON THE NEW TESTAMENT, JAMES 4:1-3.[1]

THE PLEASURES AT WAR WITHIN US. RICHARD TURNBULL: Either to enlarge their honor, either to increase their wealth, or to fulfill their desires and fleshly lusts, these pleasures are said to fight in our members, because these pleasures, these covetous, ambitious, voluptuous desires use both the powers of our mind and also the parts of our bodies as soldiers to fight with as instruments and weapons whereby sin accomplishes and finishes her work in us.

And this agrees with that saying of Saint Paul.... In some sense, these and all other evil pleasures and evil desires, as branches of the old tree and root of Adam, fight in the very elect of God, as St. Paul confessed of himself.... But here St. James seems to call that the fighting of pleasures in our members, not when the spirit strives against the flesh, but when we give over ourselves wholly to the following and obeying of our lusts and pleasures in following and seeking after wealth, honor, and fleshly lusts; when we bend all our force, when we employ all our labor, bestow all our time, spend all our wits and attention, when we make our bodies and souls servants of our wealth, honor, and desires, and strive for those by all possible means. Then do our pleasures fight in our members; then we use them as soldiers to fight for our covetousness and ambition. AN EXPOSITION UPON THE CANONICAL EPISTLE OF SAINT JAMES 4:1-3.[2]

HUMANITY'S INSATIABLE LUSTS. JOHN CALVIN: "You desire." ... He seems to indicate that the human soul is insatiable when it indulges wicked lusts, and truly it is so, for the one who suffers their sinful propensities to rule uncontrolled will know no end to their lust. Were even the world given to them, they would wish other worlds to be created for them....

Some copies have *phoneuete*, "you kill;" but I doubt not but that we ought to read, *phoneite*, "you envy," as I have rendered it; for the verb "to kill" does in no way suit the context. COMMENTARIES ON THE EPISTLE OF JAMES 4:2.[3]

4:4-6 *Friendship with the World Is Enmity Toward God*

NOTHING IS DIFFICULT FOR SOMEONE IN LOVE. DESIDERIUS ERASMUS: What husband is so patient as to put up with a hostile rival for his wife's companionship? Do you think it is possible to please both the world and God at the same time? Do you not understand that just as a wife immediately loses [her] husband's love if she sleeps with an adulterer, so a Christian immediately incurs the hostility of God who has nothing in common with the world, if they try to renew their friendship with the world? ... But just as he [i.e., God] requires from us a singular kind of love and one far more pure than that expected by the law of Moses, so does he confer a richer grace. It is extremely difficult to do what he requires, but he gives us the strength for this very purpose, to make us able to do it easily. Nothing is difficult for someone in love. This in fact is his gift to us, that we love him or rather that we return his love. He took the initiative in attracting us by his own love and won us over when we were hostile. He will increase his gifts in us if we will only empty ourselves wholly for him, if we depend on him alone, if we have nothing in common with this world and its prince, the devil. PARAPHRASE ON JAMES 4:4-6.[4]

WHICH SPIRIT DOES JAMES MEAN HERE? JOHN MAYER: Almost all expositors agree as to the sense of these words, except regarding the place of

[1]Mayer, *A commentarie vpon the New Testament,* 3:47*. †It has not been possible to locate this reference.
[2]Turnbull, *An Exposition upon the Canonical Epistle of Saint James,* 190r-191r*; citing Rom 6:12; 7:23.
[3]CTS 42:329*.
[4]CWE 44:161-62.

Scripture cited in verse 5. "You adulterers": this they expound as referring to spiritual adultery, as I have already touched, though I see no reason why he might not mean this vice properly . . . because he speaks so much of pleasure as well as of bitter envying and strife, for they altogether war against the soul, though I grant indeed that his main scope here is to impugn a malevolent and splenetic disposition. Still, there is nothing to hinder the interpretation that those were so were so sensual might be libidinous. . . . Of all these expositions [of verse 5] it is hard to say which is to be preferred. One must confess that the place is most intricate. But that exposition that says that the Spirit of God is here meant, though it be most commonly embraced, seems to me to be most improbable, because he, that is, God, who offers "more grace," verse 6, is opposed to the spirit here spoken of, for an adversative particle "but" is used, as he should have spoken of two contraries: thus is our spirit inclined, but God prescribes otherwise. Again, it would be a strange form of speech to say that the spirit lusts to envy, if the meaning were "is jealous" . . . seeing that envy is the corruption so much impugned in this epistle. Therefore, if he would have spoken a word that should carry a good sense, he would have chosen some other, and not have used this, which was never yet taken but in an ill sense. . . . I prefer therefore that exposition that interprets "the sprit that dwells in us" as that spirit that all people have in common, the spirit of natural life; for every person that lives, lives by a spirit, which is the soul. For when this departs out of the body, the spirit is said "to go to God" who gave it, and this is called the spirit of the world, and as it is now corrupt, since the fall of Adam, it is opposed to God's Spirit. A Commentary upon the New Testament, James 4:4-6.[5]

The Corrupt Human Spirit. Richard Turnbull: Now he says that the Scripture says that the spirit which dwells in us lusts after envy. By the spirit here the corrupt affection and human heart is understood; the crooked . . . and corrupt disposition of nature; the fancies, the natural inclination of our hearts. . . . The meaning of this place is that it is manifest by testimonies of Scripture tending thereunto, that the heart, spirit, and mind of humankind is naturally set on envy, evil, wickedness. An Exposition upon the Canonical Epistle of Saint James 4:5.[6]

The Spirit in Question Is the Holy Spirit. John Calvin: He seems to adduce from Scripture the next following sentence. Hence interpreters toil much, because none such, at least none exactly alike, is found in Scripture. . . . "The Spirit." . . . Some think that the human soul is meant, and therefore they read the sentence affirmatively, and according to this meaning—that the spirit of humankind, as it is malignant, is so infected with envy that it has ever a mixture of it. They, however, think better who regard the Spirit of God as intended; for it is he that is given to dwell in us. I then take the Spirit as that of God, and read the sentence as a question; for it was his object to prove that because they envied they were not ruled by the Spirit of God, because he teaches the faithful otherwise, and this he confirms in the next verse, by adding that he "gives more grace." . . . In short, James denies that the Spirit of God rules where depraved lusts prevail, which excite to mutual contention, because it is peculiarly the office of the Spirit to enrich people more and more continually with new gifts. Commentaries on the Epistle of James 4:5.[7]

The Holy Spirit Battles Against Hate. Andreas Althamer: Do you think Scripture says in vain "The Spirit seeks to overcome hate"; that is, the Spirit and hate cannot travel together. The Holy Spirit battles against envy as water against fire, and, on the other hand, hate battles

[5]Mayer, *A commentarie vpon the New Testament*, 3:49-51*; citing Eccles 12:1; 1 Cor 2:12.

[6]Turnbull, *An Exposition upon the Canonical Epistle of Saint James*, 204v-205r*; citing Ezek 13:3; Dan 5:20.
[7]CTS 42:332*.

against the Spirit. Where envy and hate are present there the Holy Spirit can have no place. Where the Holy Spirit dwells, there envy and hate cannot remain. The Holy Spirit drives out, purges, and purifies sin, and richly fills with grace and all spiritual goods, faith, and love. Thus St. Paul writes in Galatians 5. . . . Hate is a fruit of the flesh, and James take the part for the whole through synecdoche: if the Spirit battles against the flesh it also battles against envy, which is a work of the flesh.

That St. James cites the writings of the New Testament (for he here has in mind St. Paul's saying in Gal 5 . . .) is great proof that this epistle was written long after the apostolic age, because the writings of the holy apostles were already known among Christians and were accepted by the church. The Epistle of St. James 4:5-6.[8]

James Is Not an Apostolic Epistle. Lucas Osiander: James adduces this saying against envy, a work of the flesh, by the testimony of the apostle Paul in Galatians 5. And since James adduces the writings of Paul, not as a colleague, but expressly affirms, "Scripture here says," it is clear that James sets forth a great distance between himself and the writings of Paul. . . . From this place we can gather that the epistle of James is not apostolic. The Epistle . . . to James 4:5.[9]

4:7-10 *Submit Yourselves to God*

A Jewish Proverb and the Vanquishing of Satan. John Calvin: Many copies have introduced here the following sentence: "Wherefore he says, God resists the proud but gives grace to the humble." But in others it is not found. Erasmus suspects that it was first a note in the margin, and afterward crept into the text. It may have been so, though it is not unsuitable to the passage. For what some think, that it is strange that what is found only in Peter should be quoted as Scripture, may be easily disposed of. But I rather conjecture that this sentence, which accords with the common doctrine of Scripture, had become then a sort of proverbial saying common among the Jews. And, indeed, it is no more than what is found in Psalm 18. . . .

"Resist the devil." . . . However, the promise he adds, respecting the fleeing of Satan, seems to be refuted by daily experience; for it is certain that the more strenuously anyone resists, the more fiercely they are urged. For Satan, in a manner, acts playfully, when he is not in earnest repelled; but against those who really resist him, he employs all the strength he possesses. And further, he is never wearied with fighting, but when conquered in one battle, he immediately engages in another. To this I reply that fleeing is to be taken here for putting to flight, or routing. And doubtless, though he repeats his attacks continually, he yet always departs vanquished. Commentaries on the Epistle of James 4:7.[10]

On Drawing Near to God. Richard Turnbull: Does not the fact that we are commanded to draw near to God indicate to us that naturally we are estranged and alienated from him by sin originally drawn from Adam and actually committed by ourselves? As the prophet of the Lord declares to Israel, "Your iniquities have separated you and your God, and your sins have hid his face from you, that he will not hear you." . . . God finally draws near to us in a spiritual union with humankind through the incarnation of Jesus Christ, whereby God is united to us and we to him in the union of the two natures in the person of Jesus Christ, by which means God dwells among us and is made manifest in the flesh, as St. John and St. Paul speak, "And therefore Christ is Emmanuel." Thus, when the apostle says, "draw near to God, and he will draw near to you," he speaks chiefly of drawing near by his grace, favor, mercy, who enlarges his lovingkindness toward all those who with reverence and fear draw near unto him.

These things being thus set down, in the last place we are taught how we should draw near to God, which the apostle expresses in these words:

[8]Althamer, *Die Epistel S. Jacobs*, Mii v-Miii r; citing Gal 5:17.
[9]Osiander, *Epistola ad . . . Iacobi*, 132-33; citing Gal 5:17.
[10]CTS 42:333-34*; citing Ps 18:27.

"Cleanse your hands, you sinners, and purge your hearts, you double-minded." While some see these words as a new or additional exhortation, yet to me they seem to follow logically from what precedes them, as the manner by which we should draw near to God, namely, in purity and sincerity of life. . . . People draw near to God also by prayer, whereby we ascend (as it were) to heaven, and approach near to the presence of God, which is, as it were, a pair of wings to carry us to him. St. Augustine says of prayer that it is the key that opens the door of heaven (226 Serv. de tempo.),† and our prayer ascends to him and the mercy of God descends to us. . . . Thus Paul and Silas drew near to God, when at their prayer the very foundations of the earth shook and trembled. Thus the prayers of God's saints shake heaven and earth, and make a way for us, whereby we draw near to God. Thus we fly to God in our needs; thus we draw near to him; thus are we joined to God, to whom we draw near by prayer, which leads us to the presence of God, and of Christ. An Exposition upon the Canonical Epistle of Saint James 4:7-8.[11]

The Holy Spirit Enables Us to Draw Near To God. John Calvin: But if anyone concludes from this passage that the first part of the work belongs to us, and that afterward the grace of God follows, the apostle meant no such thing, for though we ought to do this, yet it does not immediately follow that we can. And the Spirit of God, in exhorting us to our duty, derogates nothing from himself, or from his own power, but the very thing he bids us to do he himself fulfills in us. Commentaries on the Epistle of James 4:8.[12]

4:11-12 *Do Not Slander One Another*

God Alone Is the Best Judge. Lucas Osiander: Therefore since God is the best judge, let us confide to him things requiring judgment, and in dubious things, where all of the circumstances are not sufficiently known to us, let us not judge concerning another servant of God rashly. For he himself stands or falls to his Lord. For those who judge hastily concerning the neighbor set up themselves in the place and throne of God, as if they were the inspectors of hearts and knew all things perfectly, which certainly is insane and impious arrogance. The Epistle . . . to James 4:11-12.[13]

4:13-17 *Boasting About Tomorrow*

We Have No Treaty with Death. Desiderius Erasmus: Life is in itself very, very short, and so many accidents, so many diseases make it thoroughly uncertain as well. And here you are, as if you had a treaty with death, speeding over land and sea to prepare some provision for your old age, which you will perhaps never reach since no one can guarantee even their own tomorrow. Why do you put such trust in this life as though it were something firm and stable? What is that life of yours in fact, which is your sole concern, the sole object of your toils and exertions? Mere vapor that appears for a brief moment and soon vanishes. Paraphrase on James 4:13-17.[14]

Christian Speech About the Future. John Calvin: It is a very insane thing to undertake to execute what we cannot pronounce with our tongue. James does not reprove the form speaking, but rather the arrogance of mind, that people should forget their own weakness and speak thus presumptuously; for even the godly, who think humbly of themselves, and acknowledge that their steps are guided by the will of God, may yet sometimes say, without any qualifying clause, that they will do this or that. It is indeed right and proper when we promise anything as to future time, to accustom ourselves to such words as these, "If it shall please the Lord," "If the Lord will permit." But no scruple ought to be entertained, as though it were a sin to

[11]Turnbull, *An Exposition upon the Canonical Epistle of Saint James*, 219v-222v*; citing Is 59:2; Jer 5:25; Jn 1:14; 1 Tim 3:16; Mt 1:23; Acts 16:25. †Augustine, *Sermo 47, De beato Tobia*, PL 39:1838.
[12]CTS 42:334*.

[13]Osiander, *Epistola ad . . . Iacobi*, 135.
[14]CWE 44:164-65.

omit them, for we read everywhere in the Scriptures that the holy servants of God spoke unconditionally of future things, when yet they had it as a principle fixed in their minds that they could do nothing without the permission of God. Then as to the practice of saying, "If the Lord will or permit," it ought to be carefully attended by all the godly. Commentaries on the Epistle of James 4:13.[15]

Humanity's Vain Confidence. Richard Turnbull: Are there not many in our time likewise culpable of similar pride and vanity? Do not princes say, "This will we do the next year, and the year following, and who shall hinder us?" Do not captains say, "We will besiege such and such a city, and such and such a time we will invade such and such a town, and what shall prevent us?" Do our merchants not say among themselves, "We will shortly go to Turkey, to Barbary, to Venice, to Constantinople, to Hamburg, to Nuremberg, to France, to Flanders, to Spain, to the East countries, and there will we stay for thus long and have our factors and agents in this place, and that place of the world"? Do not gentlemen and rich citizens say, "At such and such a time we will ride down into the country and there remain so many weeks, so many days, and then we will return and spend the winter in the city"? Do not all men and women in the confidence of their own life circumstances say, "This will we do, and that will we do," not looking to the will and providence of God, but determining their matters long before in the vanity and pride of their own mind? This is the vain confidence that humans conceive of to themselves, which the apostle here reproves. An Exposition upon the Canonical Epistle of Saint James 4:13-14.[16]

[15]CTS 42:340*.

[16]Turnbull, *An Exposition upon the Canonical Epistle of Saint James*, 256r-v*.

5:1-20 Patient Suffering and Faithful Prayer

Come now, you rich, weep and howl for the miseries that are coming upon you. [2]Your riches have rotted and your garments are moth-eaten. [3]Your gold and silver have corroded, and their corrosion will be evidence against you and will eat your flesh like fire. You have laid up treasure in the last days. [4]Behold, the wages of the laborers who mowed your fields, which you kept back by fraud, are crying out against you, and the cries of the harvesters have reached the ears of the Lord of hosts. [5]You have lived on the earth in luxury and in self-indulgence. You have fattened your hearts in a day of slaughter. [6]You have condemned and murdered the righteous person. He does not resist you.

[7]Be patient, therefore, brothers,[a] until the coming of the Lord. See how the farmer waits for the precious fruit of the earth, being patient about it, until it receives the early and the late rains. [8]You also, be patient. Establish your hearts, for the coming of the Lord is at hand. [9]Do not grumble against one another, brothers, so that you may not be judged; behold, the Judge is standing at the door. [10]As an example of suffering and patience, brothers, take the prophets who spoke in the name of the Lord. [11]Behold, we consider those blessed who remained steadfast. You have heard of the steadfastness of Job, and you have seen the purpose of the Lord, how the Lord is compassionate and merciful.

[12]But above all, my brothers, do not swear, either by heaven or by earth or by any other oath, but let your "yes" be yes and your "no" be no, so that you may not fall under condemnation.

[13]Is anyone among you suffering? Let him pray. Is anyone cheerful? Let him sing praise. [14]Is anyone among you sick? Let him call for the elders of the church, and let them pray over him, anointing him with oil in the name of the Lord. [15]And the prayer of faith will save the one who is sick, and the Lord will raise him up. And if he has committed sins, he will be forgiven. [16]Therefore, confess your sins to one another and pray for one another, that you may be healed. The prayer of a righteous person has great power as it is working.[b] [17]Elijah was a man with a nature like ours, and he prayed fervently that it might not rain, and for three years and six months it did not rain on the earth. [18]Then he prayed again, and heaven gave rain, and the earth bore its fruit.

[19]My brothers, if anyone among you wanders from the truth and someone brings him back, [20]let him know that whoever brings back a sinner from his wandering will save his soul from death and will cover a multitude of sins.

a Or *brothers and sisters;* also verses 9, 10, 12, 19 **b** Or *The effective prayer of a righteous person has great power*

Overview: In their comments on the final section of James, the reformers have sharp words for the wealthy in their own day, although they distinguish between the unrighteous wealthy, who place their trust in their riches and oppress the poor, and the righteous wealthy, who put their trust in God and use their God-given wealth to help others. Doubts about the apostolicity of James continue. Furthermore, the reformers stress the necessity of patience in the midst of suffering as they exhort Christians to have deep confidence in the goodness of the Lord's timing. In times of trial, Christians must have their eyes firmly fixed on Christ's return and also on their own death, through which they will experience of a kind personal second coming. The Protestant reformers urge Christians to invoke the name of Christ over the sick rather than seek recourse to pagan remedies and formulas. The Protestant reformers categorically reject the sacrament of unction, finding no support for it in James. Most insist that the age of miraculous healing ended with the apostles; they do allow that God may still heal in their own time, although usually through natural means, which are also gifts from God. Our Protestant commentators also reject the sacrament of penance, again finding no warrant for it in this letter, although they do urge Christians to seek out pastors in times of distress and need so that they can confess their sins to them and receive consolation.[1]

James Cannot Be an Apostolic Epistle. Andreas Althamer: The people to whom St. James writes do not behave very well. There was great [moral] deficit and great error among them, as we have seen in the foregoing chapter. Therefore, I maintain that this epistle could not have been written in the time of the apostles, for as one may deduce from the history and writings of the apostles, and the same from Tertullian and Eusebius, such perverse lives of the kind St. James registers and punishes here were not be found among believers during the time of the apostles. In the apostolic age Christians helped one another, the rich shared with the poor what they needed and sent them alms and what their bodily needs required by land, as St. Paul (Rom 15; 1 Cor 16; 2 Cor 8; 2 Cor 9; and St. Luke [Acts 11]) show. They did not treat one another unjustly, no one withheld wages earned from another, and they did not hate and quarrel with one another as in the times of our St. James. From this one may deduce that this St. James lived and wrote long after the apostles because Christian discipline and respectability had greatly decreased. The Epistle of St. James 5:1-6.[2]

[1]On Lutheran private confession, see Ronald K. Rittgers, "Private Confession in the German Reformation," in *Repentance in Christian Theology*, ed. Mark J. Boda and Gordon T. Smith (Collegeville, MN: Liturgical Press, 2006), 189-207, Rittgers, *The Reformation of the Keys: Confession, Conscience, and Authority in Sixteenth-Century Germany* (Cambridge, MA: Harvard University Press, 2004).

[2]Althamer, *Die Epistel S. Jacobs*, Nii v; citing Rom 15:25-29; 1 Cor 16:1-2; 2 Cor 8:1-15; 9:1-15; Acts 11:30.

5:1-6 *Woe to the Rich*

A Declaration of God's Judgment of the Prideful Rich. John Calvin: They are mistaken, as I think, who consider that James here exhorts the rich to repentance. It seems to me to be a simple declaration of God's judgment, by which he meant to terrify them without giving them any hope of pardon, for all that he says tends only to despair. He, therefore, does not address them in order to invite them to repentance; but, on the contrary, he has a regard to the faithful, that they, hearing of the miserable end of the rich, might not envy their fortune, and also that knowing that God would be the avenger of the wrongs they suffered, they might with a calm and resigned mind bear them.

He does not speak of the rich indiscriminately, but of those who, being immersed in pleasures and inflated with pride, thought of nothing but of the world, and who, like inexhaustible gulfs, devoured everything. For they, by their tyranny, oppressed others, as it appears from the whole passage. Commentaries on the Epistle of James 5:1-6.[3]

Ill-Gotten Wealth Will Redound to Judgment in Hell. Lucas Osiander: James now inveighs against the rich who were impious and nevertheless were mingling themselves with the church of God in external society and association. . . .

O you rich people, your worldly treasures are corruptible, which even today you are able to see: the grains are destroyed and vanish, your clothes are consumed by a gnawing worm, your money and precious goods perish either by rust or fire. Daily these things are able to teach you by experience, and thus these corruptible treasures shall speak a testimony against you in the last day, because you conducted yourself foolishly and impiously by placing your trust in uncertain riches rather than in the living God. And indeed your corruptible treasures shall torment you in hell. . . . Your evilly won goods and your shameful

[3]CTS 42:342-43*.

misuse of them shall burn upon you in hell, for the ones who provide for themselves in an unrighteous manner shall endure humiliation in proportion to their worldly greatness. The Epistle . . . to James 5:1-6.[4]

The Unrighteous Rich Are in View Here. Richard Turnbull: The rich of this world are those against whom the apostle issues this threat. What shall we say? Are all rich people under this denouncement and threat? Shall they all weep and howl for their miseries, which should come upon them? Was Abraham the noble patriarch, whose riches were great and his wealth exceeding, subject to this or the like judgment? Was Isaac his son, whom for his herds of cattle, flocks of sheep, and other riches the Philistines envied under this threat? Was David the king, a man according to the mind of God himself, greatly enriched by God, subject to this matter? . . . Were the centurions mentioned in the Gospel and story of the apostles (also men of wealth) condemned by this place of Scripture? No, assuredly. For these and many more mentioned in the book of God have been wealthy and rich, yet godly also. Neither does James denounce this against all people who are rich without any exception: for riches are the gifts of God . . . and often bestowed on the most elect and dear children of God, for the which they are not subject to this condemnation, threat, and threatening.

Wherefore as when Christ had told his disciples that it was easier for a camel to pass through the eye of needle than for a rich person to enter into the kingdom of heaven, he expounded his meaning, for he did not speak of all rich people in general, but of such as trusted in their riches, which he plainly protested to his disciples, who took an occasion thereby to doubt of the salvation of many. Even so when the apostle threatens rich people, whose utter destruction and calamity he denounces, he ought not to be understood to be speaking of all rich people without exception. For there are many rich who use their riches to God's glory and the comfort of their poor brethren, who are to be exempted from this threat of the apostle. An Exposition upon the Canonical Epistle of Saint James 5:1-3.[5]

Spiritual Laborers Must Also Not Be Denied Their Wages. Richard Turnbull: To conclude, this sin is mightily amplified, in that the cry thereof is said to ascend and come to the ears of the Lord of Hosts. This speech is used in heinous and horrible sins. For although there is sin that is judged little or small by human standards, it all still comes to the ears of the Lord . . . yet to note the horror and heinousness of some sins above others, the Holy Spirit in the sacred Scripture says of such that they cry unto the Lord. . . . To like purpose our apostle, setting forth the great iniquity and injury done to the poor laborers, in the detaining and keeping back of their wages by the rich of the world, assumes that the same cry to God, and that the cry thereof is gone up to the ears of the Lord of Hosts. . . . Now if the cries of the detained wages of those who work in our bodily and earthly harvest enter into the ears of the Lord of Hosts, wages that have been held back by wicked persons through fraud, and if they therefore hear so heavy a sentence of endless destruction against them, how much more fearful judgment shall be pronounced against them, under how woeful and wretched a condition are they, who by fraud or by force, detain, withhold, and keep back the hire and wages of those who labor in the heavenly and spiritual harvest of the Lord, who sow the furrows of your hearts with the divine seed of the word of truth, and should reap the increase of their labors with great joyfulness? These are God's laborers sent into the harvest of the world to gather in many souls into the Lord's barns and to fill his garners with the spirits of the saints.

---

[4]Osiander, *Epistola ad . . . Iacobi*, 137.

[5]Turnbull, *An Exposition upon the Canonical Epistle of Saint James*, 267r-v; citing Gen 13:2; 26:12-13; Mt 8:8; Acts 10:1; Mt 19:24; Mk 10:24-25.

People do not care for this in these days either, for not only do they withhold from the ministers and preachers of the word of God who labor in the spiritual harvest of the Lord those wages and that hire that are due to the Lord's laborers and the pastors of his church, but they also endeavor by all means to take that hire from them, which many years past for this end was given to them.† An Exposition upon the Canonical Epistle of Saint James 5:4-6.[6]

5:7-12 *Patience in Suffering*

We Must Patiently Await the Day of Our Redemption. John Calvin: "The precious fruit." He calls it precious because it is the nourishment of life and the means of sustaining it. And James implies that since the farmer suffers their life, so precious to them, to lie long deposited in the bosom of the earth, and calmly suspends their desire to gather the fruit, we ought not to be too hasty and fretful, but resignedly to wait for the day of our redemption. Commentaries on the Epistle of James 5:7.[7]

Death as Happy Exit from this Life into Immortality. Lucas Osiander: And although several hundreds of years have already elapsed, nevertheless let us just as much as they be daily prepared, for we do not know in which hour he might be going to come. And as much as we might wish for it, we may not all live until the Lord corrects all things by his glorious coming. Nevertheless, we are set free through the same our Lord Jesus Christ, when through the happy exit from this life we are introduced to blessed immortality. The Epistle ... to James 5:8.[8]

The Apostle's Similitude of Patience. Richard Turnbull: This virtue of patience is a most excellent ornament in the life of a Christian. Neither is there any other thing more seemly or more answerable to the condition of the professors of the gospel of Christ Jesus than with invincible courage and constancy to bear and suffer the manifold afflictions to which we are subject, whenever they come, through whatever means they come, and whatever for may take. There are manifold exhortations to this end in the holy and sacred Word of God.... Having set down this exhortation, the next and second thing in this discourse about patience is the similitude that the apostle uses to show them how they ought to be patient. And it seems to be added to prevent that which the poor who are afflicted might have objected: "We have been patient a long while and waited for deliverance from our oppressions and miseries, yet we see no remedy; we find no end of our troubles. It seems that the Lord defers his coming to avenge us of the prophane rich people who grievously afflict us; what shall we now do then?" James says, "You must imitate and follow the wise and skillful famer, who endures all weathers, patiently abides the appointed seasons, and is not discouraged by any means. They cast the seed into the ground, think not long for harvest, but weigh the appointed time until it will be ready, and in the meantime endure many things patiently. So must you, O my brothers, wait with patient minds upon the Lord's timing, who has preestablished and predetermined the day of your deliverance from these oppressions of your enemies. Until this time you must rest yourselves contented." And this is the sum of the apostle's similitude.... An Exposition upon the Canonical Epistle of Saint James 5:8-11.[9]

We Must Not Grumble Against Other Christians. John Calvin: "Grudge not, or, groan not." As the complaints of many were hard

[6]Turnbull, *An Exposition upon the Canonical Epistle of Saint James*, 280r-v, 282r-v*; citing Gen 4:10; 18:20; Ex 3:9; Is 5:9; 1 Kings 9:16; Job 34:28; Mt 9:38; 10:10; 20:1; Heb 13:7. †Turnbull is here thinking of church livings, that is, a benefice or means of providing for the material needs of the clergy of the Church of England. A church living might consist of a house and income from tithes and land (glebe) associated with the ecclesiastical office.

[7]CTS 42:348*.

[8]Osiander, *Epistola ad . . . Iacobi*, 139; citing Mt 24:32; 25:13.

[9]Turnbull, *An Exposition upon the Canonical Epistle of Saint James*, 293r-v, 296v*; citing Rom 12:12; Eph 4:2; 1 Pet 4:12; Jas 1:2; Rev 2:10; Heb 10:35-36; 2 Pet 1:6-8.

because they were more severely treated than others, this passage is so explained by some as though James bade each to be contented with their own lot, not to envy others, nor to begrudge them if the condition of others was more tolerable. But I take another view, for after having spoken of the unhappiness of those who distress good and quiet people by their tyranny, he now exhorts the faithful to be just toward one another and ready to pass by offenses. That this is real meaning may be gathered from the reason that is added: "Do not be not querulous against one another, lest you be condemned." We may indeed groan when any evil torments us; but he means an accusing groan, when one expostulates with the Lord against another. And he declares that thus they would all be condemned, because there is no one who does not offend their brothers and afford them an occasion of groaning. . . . God will be the common judge of all. What, then, will be the case, but that everyone who seeks to bring judgment on others must allow the same against themselves; and thus all will be given up to the same ruin. Let no one, then, ask for vengeance on others, except they wish to bring it on their own head. And lest they should be hasty in making complaints of this kind, he declares that the judge was at the door. COMMENTARIES ON THE EPISTLE OF JAMES 5:9.[10]

THE PATIENCE OF JOB. JOHN CALVIN: If, however, it be asked, "Why does the apostle so much commend the patience of Job, as he had displayed many signs of impatience, being carried away by a hasty spirit?" To this I reply that though he sometimes failed through the infirmity of the flesh, or murmured within himself, yet he ever surrendered himself to God, and was ever willing to be restrained and ruled by him. Though, then, his patience was somewhat deficient, it is yet deservedly commended. COMMENTARIES ON THE EPISTLE OF JAMES 5:11.[11]

[10]CTS 42:349*.

[11]CTS 42:351-52*. On Calvin's treatment of Job, see Susan E. Schreiner, *Where Shall Wisdom Be Found? Calvin's Exegesis of Job from the Medieval and Modern Perspectives* (Chicago: University of Chicago Press, 1994).

5:13-18 *The Prayer of Faith*

CHRISTIANS MUST NOT SEEK SUPERSTITIOUS MEANS OF HEALING. DESIDERIUS ERASMUS: Now if someone is suffering from bad health, they should not take refuge in magical remedies or spend huge sums of money on doctors, whose cures are often such that it is better to depart cheerfully from life. Let them summon to their side the elders of the Christian congregation. Let them pour out prayers to God for the sick person and anoint the sick person with oil, not employing the magical entreaties the pagans commonly employ, but invoking rather the name of our Lord Jesus Christ, which is more efficacious than any form of magic spell. Moreover, let confidence be present in their prayers, and God will hear and save the one who is sick. He will not only restore their physical health, assuming that this is to the sick person's advantage, but if they have been guilty of sins (diseases of the body generally arise from evils of the soul), they will be forgiven the sick person in response to the prayers of the elders, so long as their faith commends both those who pray and the person for whom the pray. . . . If heaven, as though under a spell, obeys the prayers of one godly man [Elijah], is it strange if God, who is very ready to forgive, is appeased by the prayers of many? PARAPHRASE ON JAMES 5:13-18.[12]

FAITH HEALS AND SAVES, NOT OIL. ERASMUS SARCERIUS: What should one do in time and need when one is sick? One should call the elders to oneself and have them pray over and anoint oneself with oil in the name of the Lord. The anointing with oil was used at the time for bodily health; people used it along with other remedies to reduce pain in the body and its members. Is the sick person helped by oil or by prayer to return to bodily health? The prayer of faith, which the Lord hears.

Does such prayer also serve the sick person with regard to the forgiveness of sin? Yes, where they believe this themselves, because the believer

[12]CWE 44:169.

lives by their own faith and Christ forgives the paralytic his sins on the basis of his faith. What the papists babble here about the false sacrament of unction is nonsense. Summaries and Brief Content, James 5:13-16.[13]

The Gift of Healing Was for the Apostolic Age Only. Richard Turnbull: Notwithstanding our adversaries the papists, by an apish and elfish imitation of the apostles, contrary to their meaning, retain the sign, the thing that has ceased. And although healing was taken away from the church long ago, yet they still anoint, which they also make a sacrament, and call it extreme unction. They minister it to the sick, not in sign of health and recovery, as the apostle did, but when there is no hope of life in them, then they anoint men and women as a goodly remedy and help against sin, Satan, death, and damnation. . . . The apostle in this place speaks accordingly as the gift of healing was in force in his time, and he binds men and women to this word for as long as this gift continued, nor for all times, as the papists do.

From this place we may learn the following: that as when in the apostles' time the gift of healing was in force, they were told to send for the elders of the church, that they might pray for the sick and anoint them with oil, so that they might recover; so now (the gift being taken away) in our great and extreme sickness, we are to send for the elders of the church, the pastors, the ministers, the preachers of the word, with the faithful brothers, so that by them we may be taught that the cause of our sickness is our sin and so that they may inform us in the doctrine of unfeigned repentance and may comfort and counsel us in our extreme need, and finally may pour out prayers to God for the assistance of his grace and the increase of all needful spiritual virtues in us, as well as for the removal of our pains and sickness, as shall seem best to God's heavenly wisdom. Once we have done this, we may use all other lawful means of medicine or the like for our recovery in the fear of God. An Exposition upon the Canonical Epistle of Saint James 5:13-18.[14]

James Does Not Speak of the Pope's Oil. Michael Sattler: We have not rejected the oil [of extreme unction]. For it is a creature of God, and what God has made is good and not be refused, but that the pope, bishops, monks, and priests can make it better we do not believe; for the pope never made anything good. That of which the epistle of James speaks is not the pope's oil. The Trial and Martyrdom of Michael Sattler, James 5:14.[15]

Elders Must Follow the Spirit's Lead in Anointing the Sick. David Dickson: Touching the sick in body, that before they fly to physicians they should turn themselves to God and call for the ministers of the church, who may stir up repentance, faith, and comfort in them; furthermore, that the elders should pray to God for the sick person. . . . That if anyone among the elders, of whatever order, has the gift of healing (which flourished in the church in the apostles' times), let them in the name and authority of the Lord Jesus Christ (who gave this gift) use it, and by the example of Christ's disciples (who in Mark 6:13, having received power from Christ, anointed many sick persons with oil and healed them), let them anoint the one who is sick, that is, the one whom the Holy Spirit wishes to restore to health, having confirmed this to the elder. For it is certain that the elders who were endued with the gift of healing only anointed the sick whom they knew the Holy Spirit wished to restore to health. An Exposition of All St. Paul's Epistles, James 5:14.[16]

[13]Sarcerius, *Summarien vnd kurtzer Jnhalt*, 4:KK5r-KK5v; citing Mt 9:1-8. In point of fact, Christ commends the friends' faith, not the paralytic's, of which there is no mention.

[14]Turnbull, *An Exposition upon the Canonical Epistle of Saint James*, 329r-330v*.

[15]LCC 25:140*.

[16]Dickson, *An Exposition of All St. Pauls Epistles*, 286*.

Anointing with Oil Is an External Ceremony, Not a Sacrament. Andreas Althamer: And because anointing with oil was common among the Jews . . . the disciples of Christ used it as a free thing. They anointed many sick people with oil and made them healthy, as Mark writes in the sixth chapter. The oil did not of itself make the sick well, because Christ commanded the disciples nothing concerning it. . . . Thus these ceremonies continued among the Jews but not among the Gentiles, because we do not read of the apostles anointing Gentile believers with oil. Because James writes to Jews he makes mention of oil. Otherwise oil and anointing refer to the Holy Spirit, as 1 John 2 proves. However, it cannot be proved with any holy Scripture that the anointing with oil or unction, as we call it, is therefore a sacrament, that is, a sign of grace or a necessary ceremony that one must hold. We let it remain an external ceremony that God neither commanded nor forbade. But we cannot hold it to be a sacrament, because a sacrament must have two things: first, a divine institution and promise, that Christ the Lord himself instituted such to be a sacrament with his word, and attached to it a gracious promise, as he established baptism and the Lord's Supper and sealed them with a gracious promise; second, a sacrament must have an external sign that has been named by Christ, as water in baptism and bread and wine in the Lord's Supper, of which unction has nothing—therefore it is not a divine sacrament. The Epistle of St. James 5:13-15.[17]

Prayers Obtain Forgiveness of Sins, Not Unction. Lucas Osiander: It was a custom in the primitive church that when Christians . . . still had the gift of healing, they would draw near to the sick and anoint them with oil, pray, and also thus restore them to health. This custom had begun with the apostles, concerning which Mark writes, "And going forth they were preaching that people should repent, and they were casting out many demons, and they were anointing many sick people with oil, and they were being healed," Mark 6. This custom of anointing was rightly observed in the church as long as it was gleaming with miracles. And with the cessation of miracles unction also had to cease. And thus today the priests erringly urge extreme unction as if it were necessary, and they do wrong, because they anoint those whom they think are certainly going to die. And they believe impiously because they reckon that through such unction sins are taken away, whereas James says this happens by the prayer of the pious, not by the bestowal of oil, because prayer obtains remission of sins, which has been accomplish by the blood of Christ. The Epistle . . . to James 5:13-15.[18]

The True Oil Is the Holy Spirit. Leonhard Schiemer: James also speaks about this oil [i.e., the Holy Spirit]. . . . James is not referring to olive oil here. The elect saints who in these days at Salzburg and other places praised God with their holy martyrdom† could have bathed in bathtubs full of olive oil and would still not necessarily have remained constant in their faith. But the comfort of the Holy Spirit made their torment bearable. This is the oil of anointing that the apostles used and also we today. Letter to the Church at Rattenberg, James 5:13-15.[19]

The Folly of the Sacrament of Extreme Unction. Martin Luther: To this rite of anointing the sick the theologians of our day have made two additions that are worthy of them: first, they call it a sacrament, and second, they make it the last sacrament. So it is now the sacrament of extreme unction, which is to be administered only to those who are at the point of death. Since they are such subtle dialecticians, perhaps they have done

[17]Althamer, *Die Epistel S. Jacobs*, Piii v-Piv r; citing Mt 6:17; Lk 7:46; 10:34; Mk 6:13; Mt 10:2; 1 Jn 2:20, 27.

[18]Osiander, *Epistola ad . . . Iacobi*, 142; citing Mk 6:12-13.

[19]Schiemer, *Letter to the Church at Rattenberg*, 80. †There had already been a number of Anabaptist martyrdoms in Salzburg at this time (1527). Walter Klaassen, Frank Friesen, and Werner O. Packull, trans., C. Arnold Snyder, ed., *Sources of South German/Austrian Anabaptism* (Kitchner, ON: Pandora Press; Scottdale, PA: Herald Press, 2001).

this in order to relate it to the first unction of baptism† and the two subsequent ones of confirmation and ordination. But here they are able to cast in my teeth that, in the case of this sacrament, there are on the authority of the apostle James both promise and sign, which, as I have maintained all along, do constitute a sacrament. For the apostle says, "Is any among you sick. . . ." There, they say, you have the promise of forgiveness of sins and the sign of the oil.

But I say: If ever folly has been uttered, it has been uttered especially on this subject: I will say nothing of the fact that many assert with much probability that this epistle is not by James the apostle, and that it is not worthy of an apostolic spirit; although, whoever was its author, it has come to be regarded as authoritative. But even if the apostle James did write it, I still would say that no apostle has the right on his own authority to institute a sacrament, that is, to give a divine promise with a sign attached. For this belongs to Christ alone. . . . And nowhere do we read in the Gospel of the sacrament of extreme unction. But let us pass over this point. Let us examine the words of the apostle, or whoever was the author of the epistle, and we shall see at once how little heed these multipliers of sacraments have given to them.

In the first place, if they believe the apostle's words to be true and binding, by what right do they change and contradict them? Why do they make an extreme and special kind of unction out of that which the apostle wished to be general? For the apostle did not desire it to be an extreme unction or administered only to the dying, but he says expressly: "Is anyone sick?" He does not say: "Is any one dying?" . . . Furthermore, if this unction is a sacrament, it must necessarily be (as they say) an "effective sign"‡ of that which it signifies and promises. Now it promises health and recovery to the sick, as the words plainly say: "The prayer of faith will save the sick man, and the Lord will raise him up." But who does not see that this promise is seldom, if ever, fulfilled? Scarcely one in a thousand is restored to health, and when one is restored nobody believes that it came about through the sacrament, but through the working of nature or medicine. Indeed, to the sacrament they ascribe the opposite effect. What shall we say then? Either the apostle lies in making this promise or else this unction is no sacrament. For the sacramental promise is certain; but this promise fails in the majority of cases. . . . Therefore, I take it that this unction is the same as that practiced by the apostles, of whom it is written in Mark 6: "They anointed with oil many that were sick and healed them." It was a rite of the early church, by which they worked miracles on the sick, and which has long since ceased. . . . I do not believe that was a counsel given to all sick persons, for the church's infirmity is her glory and death is gain; but it was given only to such as might bear their sickness impatiently and with little faith, those whom the Lord allowed to remain in order that miracles and the power of faith might be manifest in them. . . . There is no doubt at all that, even if today such a prayer [as in James 5:15] were made over a sick person, that is, made in full faith by older, graver, and saintly persons, as many as we wished would be healed. For what could not faith do? But we neglect this faith that the authority of the apostle demands above all else. THE BABYLONIAN CAPTIVITY OF THE CHURCH, JAMES 5:14-15.[20]

PROPER UNCTION AND CONFESSION. HULDRYCH ZWINGLI: He describes the entreaties and salvation of prayers of faith, not of unction or oil, so that it should not be possible to find here a defense of the oil of the pontiffs. The custom of these people was to anoint the body with oil, which also Christ anticipates with the disciples. And olive oil is a salubrious medicine for many infirmities. We understand by the name of oil or unction a service of charity that can be applied to the sick. Concerning the other presbyters, it has been said that they are the ones in the church who surpass others by both authority and prudence, and they have been placed in authority

[20]WA 6:567.33-570.25; LW 36:117-21; citing Mk 6:13; Phil 1:21. †LW editor's note (118 n. 212): "In the order for baptism, just after the Creed, the child was anointed with oil on chest and shoulders." ‡An effective sign accomplished what it signified.

over others by the sanctity of their life and innocence of their morals. . . .

The pontiffs distort this place to entail auricular confession, so that they leave nothing intact. But this place urges the sick person, with respect to those they have harmed, that they might frankly confess their own ignorance and error and ask for mercy. For it seems that this place should be understood as concerning the laboring and infirm who must be admonished in this duty, so that they might either forgive those have done harm to them, with the result that they might return to them in grace, or so that the guilty might obtain mercy from those they themselves have injured, and then they might help one another by mutual prayers. Huldrych Zwingli's Brief and Excellent Exposition of the Epistle of Blessed James 5:14-16.[21]

The Benefits of Mutual Confession. Richard Hooker: But the greatest thing which made people forward and willing, upon their knees to confess whatsoever they had committed against God, and in no wise to be withheld from the same with any fear of disgrace, contempt, or obloquy which might ensue, was their fervent desire to be helped and assisted with the prayers of God's saints, wherein St. James exhorts to mutual confession, alleging this only for a reason, that just as people's devout prayers are of great avail with God, so it has been heretofore the use of penitents for that intent to unburden their minds, even to private persons, and to crave their prayers. Laws of Ecclesiastical Polity, Book 6.[22]

The Sick Should Confess to a Minister of God. John Mayer: Touching confession of sins to the priest, we hold that there is no ground for it here, neither to prove that it ought to be made annually, or that it must be made to the priest in the time of sickness; it only teaches that one who is acquainted with the state of the sick may the better commend their case to the Lord in prayer and minister fitting instructions to them. . . . To conclude this point, it is certain that the popish auricular confession is not indicated here, and several papists confess that it is uncertain by what authority it is required that people should thus confess. . . . Yet it seems to me that in the time of sickness it is good and profitable for the sick person to confess their sins freely to the minister of God's word, so that by him, as by God's instrument appointed to speak comfort to him, in respect of the remission of their sins, he may be comfort to them . . . and that being well acquainted with their case, he may the better stir them up to repentance and the more effectually commend his case to God in his prayers. For I think that to "confess your sins to another" may be better expounded in this way, layperson to layperson, that is, to the elders, who are of yourselves and are appointed for your comfort, both bodily and spiritual. For of such he had spoken before, and it is most to the purpose to interpret this as . . . directing the sick not only to send for them, but to confess to them also, that knowing what sins in particular trouble their consciences, they may herein pray to God for them and obtain pardon. For, if you take this verse to mean other common Christians, this absurdity will follow, that those who are less able to advise and to comfort a distressed soul should have the sores of such people opened to them, and those to whom it properly belongs to apply medicines are neglected. . . . Confess your sins then first and chiefly to God, and confess in time of sickness "one to another," that is, the private Christian to the faithful minister of God, and "pray one for another," that is, the minister for the private person, being in extremity through sickness, being assured, that as Elijah by prayer prevailed mightily for the common good, so a godly minister shall prevail for the release and comfort of the one who is in distress. A Commentary upon the New Testament, James 5:16.[23]

[21]Zwingli, *Expositio in Epistolam beati Iacobi*, 49-50.
[22]Hooker, *The Works of Richard Hooker*, 3:31.
[23]Mayer, *A commentarie vpon the New Testament*, 3:60-61*.

5:19-20 *Bring Back the Wandering*

FORESTALLING THE DEATH OF SOULS THROUGH PRAYER. DESIDERIUS ERASMUS: Now, brothers, weigh the following point: If it is an act of piety and Christian charity to alleviate through communal prayer a disease in the body of another person, how much more right is it to aid those who suffer from a disease of the soul? There is nothing grand in bringing it about through prayer that death, which is going to come some day in any case, is postponed a little while for this or that person, but to have forestalled the death of the soul is something grand indeed. PARAPHRASE ON JAMES 5:19-20.[24]

TRUE CONFESSION AND TRUE PRAYER. JOHANN SPANGENBERG: What is the confession in search of counsel? It is when I seek out an ordained servant of the Christian community . . . and open my heart to him, bewail my sin and pressing need, and ask him to give me good counsel from the holy divine Scripture as to how I may gain peace for my conscience, and then help me to ask God for the forgiveness of my sin. This confession was ordained by Christ in Matthew 18 . . . and John 20. God has made a great promise with respect to such confession in Matthew 18. . . .

What is called prayer? Prayer is nothing other than speaking with God and pouring out one's sorrow and bringing them to him with a burning steadfast heart, with proper and earnest perseverance, with a humble and lowly heart and confession of sin.

What is prayer? Prayer is a lifting up of the soul and a heartfelt sighing and longing of the Spirit for God. It is a ladder on which we climb to heaven before the face of God and bear our need before him, as Jesus Sirach says in chapter 35. EPISTLE FOR CROSS WEEK.[25]

BRING BACK THE LOST AMONG GOD'S SHEEP. MENNO SIMONS: We would entreat all pious hearts for Jesus' sake to differentiate rightly between erring in ignorance and erring on purpose, between lying in death and walking into death, in order that the above saying of James may be scripturally explained and it may not be construed so as to become a false comfort and support to frivolous and erring sinners. For it is clear that they are already condemned to death by the Scriptures, as we have frequently observed. But when any of our Father's little ones, that is, Christ's sheep, stray in the direction of death so as to turn their ears to false doctrine adorned with fair words; if they should suffer themselves through their lusts, to be led from the truth; should begin to set their feet upon the broad way, and should seek the intimacy of their neighbor's wife, daughter, servant girls, or the company of frivolous people; if they should become cold and weak in their faith, calloused to the truth and erring grievously, and should nevertheless imagine that they are traveling on the right way, then we may not let such erring ones be lost. But we should seek with all our power and might to bring them back, not with one or two admonitions, as is done with sectaries, nor with three as in the case of a transgression between brother and brother, but as often as the Lord gives spirit and grace, till they again observe the truth and cease from their error and return to the right way; or until they become as ravening, biting dogs or unclean, filthy swine. . . . And covers from whose sight? From humans' or from God's? Not from humans, but from God. For it is impossible to hide from human beings that which they see happening before their eyes, such as open seduction of women, adultery, fornication, homicide, open idolatry, drunkenness, etc. . . . And of such covering of sin David testifies, "Blessed is he whose transgression is forgiven, whose sin is covered. Blessed is the man unto whom the Lord imputes not iniquity." INSTRUCTION ON EXCOMMUNICATION, JAMES 5:19-20.[26]

[24]CWE 44:169.

[25]Spangenberg, *Postilla Teütsch*, 5:22v, 23r; citing Mt 18:18; Jn 20:22-23; Mt 18:19; Sir 35:21-22.

[26]Simons, *Instruction on Excommunication*, 986-87; citing Ps 32:1-2.

Map of Europe at the Time of the Reformation

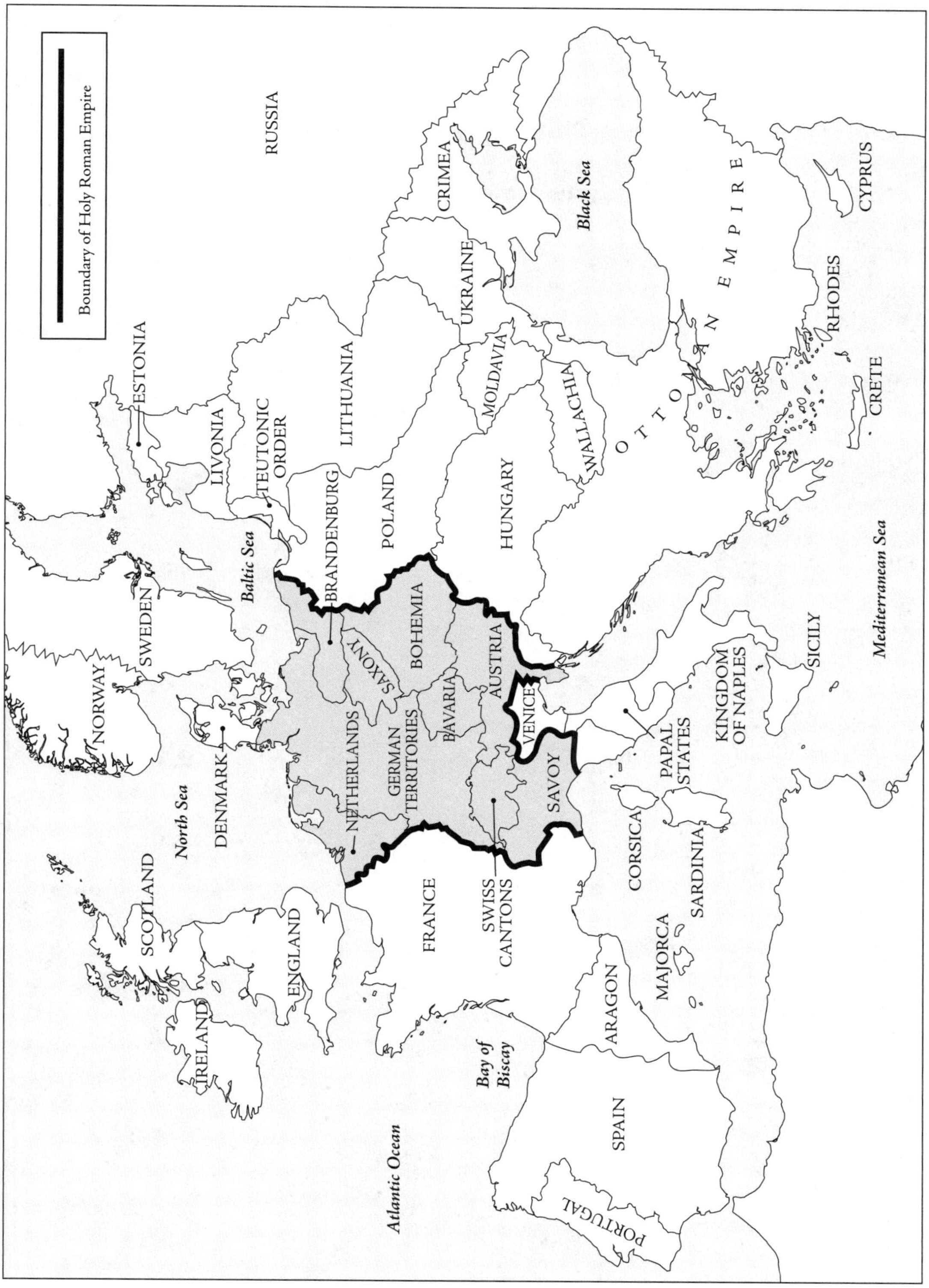

Timeline of the Reformation

	German Territories	France	Spain	Italy	Switzerland	Netherlands	British Isles
1309–1377		Babylonian Captivity of the Papacy					
1337–1453		d. Nicholas of Lyra Hundred Years' War	b. Paul of Burgos (Solomon ha-Levi)(d. 1435) Alonso Tostado (1400–1455)				Hundred Years' War
1378–1415		Western Schism (Avignon Papacy)		Western Schism			
1384							d. John Wycliffe
1414–1418					Council of Basel (1431–1437)		
1415				Council of Constance; d. Jan Hus; Martin V (r. 1417–1431); Council of Florence (1438–1445)			
1450	Invention of printing press						
1452				b. Leonardo da Vinci (d. 1519)			
1453				Fall of Constantinople			
1455–1485	b. Johannes Reuchlin (d. 1522)						War of Roses; rise of House of Tudor
1456	Gutenberg Bible						
1460				Pope Pius II issued *Execrabilis*			
1466		b. Jacques Lefèvre d'Étaples (d. 1536)					
1467						b. Desiderius Erasmus (d. 1536)	b. John Colet (d. 1519)
1469	b. Antoius Broickwy von Königstein (d. 541)						
1470				b. Santes Pagninus (d. 1541)			b. John (Mair) Major (d. 1550)
1475				b. Michelangelo (d. 1564)			
1478	b. Wolfgang Capito (d. 1541)		Ferdinand and Isabella	b. Jacopo Sadoleto (d. 1547)			b. Thomas More (d. 1535)

	German Territories	France	Spain	Italy	Switzerland	Netherlands	British Isles
1480	b. Balthasar Hubmaier (d. 1528); b. Andreas Bodenstein von Karlstadt (d. 1541)						
1481–1530			Spanish Inquisition				
1482					b. Johannes Oecolampadius (d. 1531)		
1483	b. Martin Luther (d. 1546)						
1484	b. Johann Spangenberg (d. 1550)				b. Huldrych Zwingli (d. 1531)		
1485	b. Johannes Bugenhagen (d. 1554)						b. Hugh Latimer (d. 1555)
1486	r. Frederick the Wise, Elector (d. 1525); b. Johann Eck (d. 1543)						
1488	b. Otto Brunfels (d. 1534)						b. Miles Coverdale (d. 1568)
1489	b. Thomas Müntzer (d. 1525); b. Kaspar von Schwenckfeld (d. 1561)						b. Thomas Cranmer (d. 1556)
1491	b. Martin Bucer (d. 1551)		b. Ignatius Loyola (d. 1556)				
1492			Defeat of Moors in Grenada; Columbus discovers America; expulsion of Jews from Spain	Alexander VI (r. 1492–1503)			
1493	b. Justus Jonas (d. 1555)						
1494							b. William Tyndale (d. 1536)
1496	b. Andreas Osiander (d. 1552)					b. Menno Simons (d. 1561)	
1497	b. Philipp Melanchthon (d. 1560); b. Wolfgang Musculus (d. 1563) b. Johannes (Ferus) Wild (d. 1554)						

	German Territories	France	Spain	Italy	Switzerland	Netherlands	British Isles
1498				d. Girolamo Savonarola	b. Conrad Grebel (d. 1526)		
1499	b. Johannes Brenz (d. 1570) b. Justus Menius (d. 1558)			b. Peter Martyr Vermigli (d. 1562)			
1500			b. Charles V (–1558)				
1501	b. Erasmus Sarcerius (d. 1559)						
1502	Founding of University of Wittenberg			Julius II (r. 1503–1513)		b. Frans Titelmans (d. 1537)	
1504					b. Heinrich Bullinger (d. 1575)		
1505	Luther joins Augustinian Order			b. Benedict Aretius (d. 1574)			
1506		b. Augustin Marlorat (d. 1562)		Restoration of St. Peter's begins			
1507				Sale of indulgences approved to fund building			
1508	b. Lucas Lossius (d. 1582)						
1509		b. John Calvin (d. 1564)					r. Henry VIII (–1547)
1510	Luther moves to Rome			b. Immanuel Tremellius (d. 1580)			b. Nicholas Ridley (d. 1555)
1511	Luther moves to Wittenberg						
1512				Sistine Chapel completed			
1512–1517				Fifth Lateran Council; rejection of conciliarism			
1513	Luther lectures on Psalms			r. Pope Leo X (–1521)			b. John Knox (d. 1572)
1515	Luther lectures on Romans	r. Francis I (–1547); b. Peter Ramus (d. 1572)					
1516		Est. French National Church (via Concordat of Bologna)		Concordat of Bologna		Publication of Erasmus's Greek New Testament	
1517	Tetzel sells indulgences in Saxony; Luther's Ninety-five Theses						

	German Territories	France	Spain	Italy	Switzerland	Netherlands	British Isles
1518	Heidelberg Disputation; Luther examined by Cajetan at Diet of Augsburg			Diet of Augsburg			
1519	Leipzig Disputation	b. Theodore Beza (d. 1605)	Cortés conquers Aztecs; Portuguese sailor Magellan circumnavigates the globe		Zwingli appointed pastor of Grossmünster in Zurich; b. Rudolf Gwalther (d. 1586)		
1520	Publication of Luther's "Three Treatises"; burning of papal bull in Wittenberg		Coronation of Charles V	Papal Bull v. Luther: *Exsurge Domine*			
1521	Luther excommunicated; Diet/Edict of Worms—Luther condemned; Luther in hiding; Melanchthon's *Loci communes*	French-Spanish War (–1526)	French-Spanish War; Loyola converts	Papal excommunication of Luther			Henry VIII publishes *Affirmation of the Seven Sacraments* against Luther; awarded title "Defender of the Faith" by Pope
1521–1522	Disorder in Wittenberg; Luther translates New Testament						
1521–1525		First and Second Habsburg–Valois War					
1522	Luther returns to Wittenberg; Luther's NT published; criticizes Zwickau prophets; b. Martin Chemnitz (d. 1586)		Publication of Complutensian Polyglot Bible under Cisneros		Sausage Affair and reform begins in Zurich under Zwingli		b. John Jewel (d. 1571)
1523	Knight's Revolt	Bucer begins ministry in Strasbourg	Loyola writes Spiritual Exercises	r. Pope Clement VII (–1534)	Iconoclasm in Zurich		
1524	Luther criticizes peasants; d. Johann von Staupitz					Erasmus's disputation on free will	
1524–1526	Peasants' War						
1525	Luther marries; execution of Thomas Müntzer; publication of Luther's *Bondage of the Will*				Abolition of mass in Zurich; disputation on baptism; first believers' baptism performed in Zurich		

	German Territories	France	Spain	Italy	Switzerland	Netherlands	British Isles
1526					Zurich council mandates capital punishment of Anabaptists	Publication of Tyndale's English translation of NT	
1527	d. Hans Denck (b. c. 1500) d. Hans Hut (b. 1490) b. Tilemann Hesshus (d. 1588)			Sack of Rome by mutinous troops of Charles V	First Anabaptist executed in Zurich; drafting of Schleitheim Confession		
1528	Execution of Hubmaier						
1529	Second Diet of Speyer; evangelical "protest"; publication of Luther's catechisms; Marburg Colloquy; siege of Vienna by Turkish forces	Abolition of mass in Strasbourg			d. Georg Blaurock (b. 1492)		Thomas More appointed chancellor to Henry VIII
1530	Diet of Augsburg; Confession of Augsburg	d. Francois Lambert (Lambert of Avignon) (b. 1487)	Charles V crowned Holy Roman Emperor				
1531	Formation of Schmalkaldic League				d. H. Zwingli; succeeded by H. Bullinger		
1532		Publication of Calvin's commentary on Seneca; conversion of Calvin	b. Francisco de Toledo (d. 1596)				
1533	b. Valentein Weigel (d. 1588)	Nicholas Cop addresses University of Paris; Cop and Calvin implicated as "Lutheran" sympathizers	b. Juan de Maldonado (d. 1583)				Thomas Cranmer appointed as Archbishop of Canterbury; Henry VIII divorces
1534	First edition of Luther's Bible published	Affair of the Placards; Calvin flees d. Guillame Briçonnet (b. 1470)		Jesuits founded; d. Cardinal Cajetan (Thomas de Vio) (b. 1469)			Act of Supremacy; English church breaks with Rome
1535	Bohemian Confession of 1535; Anabaptist theocracy at Münster collapses after eighteen months				b. Lambert Daneau (d. 1595)		d. Thomas More; d. John Fisher

	German Territories	France	Spain	Italy	Switzerland	Netherlands	British Isles
1536	Wittenberg Concord; b. Kaspar Olevianus (d. 1587)				First edition of Calvin's *Institutes* published; Calvin arrives in Geneva (–1538); First Helvetic Confession	Publication of Tyndale's translation of NT; d. W. Tyndale	d. A. Boleyn; Henry VIII dissolves monasteries (–1541)
1537					Calvin presents ecclesiastical ordinances to Genevan Council		
1538					Calvin exiled from Geneva; arrives in Strasbourg (–1541)		
1539		Calvin publishes second edition of *Institutes* in Strasbourg		d. Felix Pratensis			Statute of Six Articles; publication of Coverdale's Great Bible
1540				Papal approval of Jesuit order			d. Thomas Cromwell
1541	Colloquy of Regensburg	French translation of Calvin's *Institutes* published	d. Juan de Valdés (b. 1500/1510)		d. A. Karlstadt; Calvin returns to Geneva (–1564)		
1542	d. Sebastian Franck (b. 1499)			Institution of Roman Inquisition			War between England and Scotland; James V of Scotland defeated; Ireland declared sovereign kingdom
1543	Copernicus publishes *On the Revolutions of the Heavenly Spheres*; d. Johann Eck (Johann Maier of Eck) (b. 1486)						
1545–1547	Schmalkaldic Wars; d. Martin Luther			First session of Council of Trent			b. Richard Bancroft (d. 1610)
1546	b. Johannes Piscator (d. 1625)						
1547	Defeat of Protestants at Mühlberg	d. Francis I; r. Henri II (–1559)					d. Henry VIII; r. Edward VI (–1553)
1548	Augsburg Interim (–1552) d. Caspar Cruciger (b. 1504) b. David Pareus (d. 1622)						

	German Territories	France	Spain	Italy	Switzerland	Netherlands	British Isles
1549	d. Paul Fagius (b. 1504)	d. Marguerite d'Angoulême (b. 1492)			Consensus Tigurinus between Calvin and Bullinger		First Book of Common Prayer published
1550	b. Aegidius Hunnius (d. 1603)						
1551–1552				Second session of Council of Trent			
1552	d. Sebastian Münster (b. 1488) d. Friedrich Nausea (b. c. 1496)						Book of Common Prayer revised
1553	d. Johannes Aepinus (b. 1449)				Michael Servetus executed in Geneva		Cranmer's Forty-Two Articles; d. Edward VI; r. Mary I (d. 1558)
1554							Richard Hooker (d. 1600)
1555	Diet of Augsburg; Peace of Augsburg establishes legal territorial existence of Lutheranism and Catholicism b. Johann Arndt (d. 1621)	First mission of French pastors trained in Geneva				b. Sibbrandus Lubbertus (d. 1625)	b. Lancelot Andrewes (d. 1626) b. Robert Rollock (d. 1599); d. Hugh Latimer; d. Nicholas Ridley d. John Hooper
1556	d. Pilgram Marpeck (b. 1495) d. Konrad Pellikan (b. 1478) d. Peter Riedemann (b. 1506)		Charles V resigns			d. David Joris (b. c. 1501)	d. Thomas Cranmer
1557							Alliance with Spain in war against France
1558			d. Charles V				b. William Perkins (d. 1602); d. Mary I; r. Elizabeth I (–1603)
1559		d. Henry II; r. Francis II (–1560); first national synod of French reformed churches (1559) in Paris; Gallic Confession		First index of prohibited books issued	Final edition of Calvin's *Institutes*; founding of Genevan Academy	b. Jacobus Arminius (d. 1609)	Elizabethan Settlement

	German Territories	France	Spain	Italy	Switzerland	Netherlands	British Isles
1560	d. P. Melanchthon	d. Francis II; r. Charles IX (1574); Edict of Toleration created peace with Huguenots	d. Domingo de Soto (b. 1494)		Geneva Bible		Kirk of Scotland established; Scottish Confession
1561-1563				Third session of Council of Trent			
1561						Belgic Confession	
1562	d. Katharina Schütz Zell (b. 1497/98)	Massacre of Huguenots begins French Wars of Religion (–1598)					The Articles of Religion—in Elizabethan "final" form (1562/71); publication of Latin edition of Jewel's *Apology*
1563	Heidelberg Catechism						
1564				b. Galileo (d. 1642)	d. J. Calvin		b. William Shakespeare (d. 1616); publication of Lady Ann Bacon's English translation of Jewel's *Apology*
1566	d. Johann Agricola (b. 1494)			Roman Catechism	Second Helvetic Confession		
1567						Spanish occupation	Abdication of Scottish throne by Mary Stuart; r. James VI (1603–1625)
1568						d. Dirk Phillips (b. 1504) Dutch movement for liberation (–1645)	*Bishops' Bible*
1570		d. Johannes Mercerus (Jean Mercier)		Papal Bull *Regnans in Excelsis* excommunicates Elizabeth I			Elizabeth I excommunicated
1571	b. Johannes Kepler (d. 1630)		Spain defeats Ottoman navy at Battle of Lepanto				b. John Downame (d. 1652)
1572		Massacre of Huguenots on St. Bartholomew's Day		r. Pope Gregory XIII (1583–1585)		William of Orange invades	b. John Donne (d. 1631)
1574		d. Charles IX; r. Henri III (d. 1589)					

	German Territories	France	Spain	Italy	Switzerland	Netherlands	British Isles
1575	d. Georg Major (b. 1502); Bohemian Confession of 1575						
1576		Declaration of Toleration; formation of Catholic League		b. Giovanni Diodati (d. 1649)		Sack of Antwerp; Pacification of Ghent	
1577	Lutheran Formula of Concord						England allies with Netherlands against Spain
1578	Swiss Brethren Confession of Hesse d. Peter Walpot		Truce with Ottomans				Sir Francis Drake circumnavigates the globe
1579			Expeditions to Ireland			Division of Dutch provinces	
1580	Lutheran Book of Concord						
1581			d. Teresa of Avila				Anti-Catholic statutes passed
1582				Gregorian Reform of calendar			
1583							b. David Dickson (d. 1663)
1584		Treaty of Joinville with Spain	Treaty of Joinville; Spain inducted into Catholic League; defeats Dutch at Antwerp			Fall of Antwerp; d. William of Orange	
1585	d. Josua Opitz (b. c. 1542)	Henri of Navarre excommunicated		r. Pope Sixtus V (–1590)			
1586							Sir Francis Drake's expedition to West Indies; Sir Walter Raleigh in Roanoke
1587	d. Johann Wigand (b. 1523)	Henri of Navarre defeats royal army					d. Mary Stuart of Scotland
1588		Henri of Navarre drives Henri III from Paris; assassination of Catholic League Leaders	Armada destroyed				English Navy defeats Spanish Armada
1589		d. Henri III; r. Henri (of Navarre) IV (–1610)	Victory over England at Lisbon				Defeated by Spain in Lisbon
1590		Henri IV's siege of Paris		d. Girolamo Zanchi (b. 1516)			Alliance with Henri IV

	German Territories	France	Spain	Italy	Switzerland	Netherlands	British Isles
1592	d. Nikolaus Selnecker (b. 1530)						
1593		Henri IV converts to Catholicism					Books I-IV of Hooker's *Laws of Ecclesiastical Polity* published
1594		Henri grants toleration to Huguenots					
1595		Henri IV declares war on Spain; received into Catholic Church		Pope Sixtus accepts Henri IV into Church			Alliance with France
1596		b. René Descartes (d. 1650) b. Moïse Amyraut (d. 1664)					
1597							Book V of Hooker's *Laws of Ecclesiastical Polity* published
1598		Edict of Nantes; toleration of Huguenots; peace with Spain	Treaty of Vervins; peace with France				
1600	d. David Chytraeus (b. 1531)						
1601							b. John Trapp (d. 1669)
1602					d. Daniel Toussain (b. 1541)		
1603							d. Elizabeth I; r. James I (James VI of Scotland) (–1625)
1604	d. Cyriacus Spangenberg (b. 1528)						d. John Whitgift (b. 1530)
1605						b. Rembrandt (d. 1669)	Guy Fawkes and gunpowder plot
1606							Jamestown Settlement
1607							b. John Milton (d. 1674)
1608							
1610		d. Henri IV; r. Louis XIII (–1643)	d. Benedict Pererius (b. 1535)			The Remonstrance; Short Confession	

	German Territories	France	Spain	Italy	Switzerland	Netherlands	British Isles
1611							Publication of Authorized English Translation of Bible (AV/KJV); George Abbot becomes Archbishop of Canterbury (–1633)
1612							b. Richard Crashaw (d. 1649)
1616							b. John Owen (d. 1683)
1617							b. Ralph Cudworth (d. 1689)
1618–1619						Synod of Dordrecht	
1618–1648	Thirty Years' War						
1620							English Sepratists land in Plymouth, Massachusetts
1621							d. Andrew Willet (b. 1562)
1628							Puritans establish Massachusetts Bay colony
1633	d. Christoph Pelargus (b. 1565)						Laud becomes Archbishop of Canterbury
1637	d. Johann Gerhard (b. 1582)					*Statenvertaling*	
1638							d. Joseph Mede (b. 1638)
1640				Diodati's Italian translation of Bible published			
1642–1649							English civil wars; d. Charles I; r. Oliver Cromwell (1650)
1643		d. Louis XIII; r. Louis XIV (–1715)					
1643–1649							Westminster Assembly
1645							d. William Laud (b. 1573)

	German Territories	France	Spain	Italy	Switzerland	Netherlands	British Isles
1648		Treaty of Westphalia ends Thirty Years' War					Books VI and VIII of Hooker's *Laws of Ecclesiastical Polity* posthumously published
1656	d. Georg Calixtus (b. 1586)						
1658							d. Oliver Cromwell
1659							Richard Cromwell resigns
1660							English Restoration; r. Charles II (–1685)
1662							Act of Uniformity; Book VII of Hooker's *Laws of Ecclesiastical Polity* posthumously published
1664						d. Thieleman Jans van Braght (b. 1625)	d. John Mayer (b. 1583)
1671							d. William Greenhill (b. 1591)
1677							d. Thomas Manton (b. 1620)
1678						d. Anna Maria von Schurman (b. 1607)	
1688							Glorious Revolution; r. William and Mary (-1702); d. John Bunyan (b. 1628)
1691							d. Richard Baxter (b. 1615)

BIOGRAPHICAL SKETCHES OF REFORMATION-ERA FIGURES AND WORKS

For works consulted, see "Sources for Biographical Sketches," p. 321.

Thomas Adams (1583–1653). Anglican minister and author. He attended the University of Cambridge where he received his BA in 1601 and his MA in 1606. Following his ordination in 1604, Adams served as curate at Northill in Bedfordshire. In 1611, he became vicar of Willmington. Three years later he served the parish of Wingrave, Buckinghamshire, where he remained until 1618. From 1618 to 1623 Adams was preacher at St. Gregory by St. Paul's. He also served as chaplain to Henry Montague, First Earl of Manchester, and Lord Chief Justice of England. Among his most important works are the *Happiness of the Church* (1618) and an extensive commentary on 2 Peter (1638).

Johannes Aepinus (1499–1553). German Lutheran preacher and theologian. Aepinus studied under Martin Luther,* Philipp Melanchthon* and Johannes Bugenhagen* in Wittenberg. Because of his Lutheran beliefs, Aepinus lost his first teaching position in Brandenburg. He fled north to Stralsund and became a preacher and superintendent at Saint Peter's Church in Hamburg. In 1534, he made a diplomatic visit to England but could not convince Henry VIII to embrace the Augsburg Confession.* His works include sermons and theological writings. Aepinus became best known as leader of the Infernalists, who believed that Christ underwent torment in hell after his crucifixion.

Johann Agricola (c. 1494–1566). German Lutheran pastor and theologian. An early student of Martin Luther,* Agricola eventually began a controversy over the role of the law, first with Melanchthon* and then with Luther himself. Agricola claimed to defend Luther's true position, asserting that only the gospel of the crucified Christ calls Christians to truly good works, not the fear of the law. After this first controversy, Agricola seems to have radicalized his views to the point that he eliminated Luther's *simul iustus et peccator* ("at the same time righteous and sinful") paradox of the Christian life, emphasizing instead that believers have no need for the law once they are united with Christ through faith. Luther responded by writing anonymous pamphlets against antinomianism. Agricola later published a recantation of his views, hoping to assuage relations with Luther, although they were never personally reconciled. He published a commentary on Luke, a series of sermons on Colossians, and a massive collection of German proverbs.

Henry Ainsworth (1571–1622/1623). English Puritan Hebraist. In 1593, under threat of persecution, Ainsworth relocated to Amsterdam, where he served as a teacher in an English congregation. He composed a confession of faith for the community and a number of polemical and exegetical works, including annotations on the Pentateuch, the Psalms and Song of Songs.

Henry Airay (c. 1560–1616). English Puritan professor and pastor. He was especially noted for his preaching, a blend of hostility toward Catholicism and articulate exposition of English Calvinism. He was promoted to provost of Queen's College Oxford (1598) and then to vice chancellor of the university in 1606. He disputed with William Laud* concerning Laud's putative Catholicization of the Church of England, particularly over the practice of genuflection, which Airay vehemently opposed. He also opposed fellow Puritans who wished to separate from the Church of England. His lectures on Philippians were his only work published during his lifetime.

Alexander (Ales) Alesius (1500–1565). Scottish Lutheran theologian. Following the martyrdom of his theological adversary Patrick Hamilton (c. 1504–1528), Alesius converted to the Reformation and fled to Germany. In 1535 Martin Luther* and Philip Melanchthon* sent him as an emissary to Henry VIII and Thomas Cranmer.* He taught briefly at Cambridge, but after the Act of Six Articles reasserted Catholic sacramental theology he returned to Germany, where he lectured at Frankfurt an der Oder and Leipzig. Alesius composed many exegetical, theological and polemical works, including commentaries on John, Romans, 1–2 Timothy, Titus and the Psalms.

Andreas Althamer (c. 1500–1539). German Lutheran humanist and pastor. Forced from the chaplaincy at Schwäbisch-Gmünd for teaching evangelical ideas, Althamer studied theology at Wittenberg before serving as a pastor in Eltersdorf, Nuremberg, and Ansbach. A staunch Lutheran, he contended against Reformed theologians at the 1528 disputation at Bern and delivered numerous polemics against Anabaptism. He also composed an early Lutheran catechism, published at Nuremberg in 1528.

Moïse Amyraut (1596–1664). French Reformed pastor and professor. Originally intending to be a lawyer, Amyraut turned to theology after an encounter with several Huguenot pastors and having read Calvin's* *Institutes*. After a brief stint as a parish pastor, Amyraut spent the majority of his career at the Saumur Academy. He was well known for his irenicism and ecumenicism (for example, in advocating intercommunion with Lutherans). Certain aspects of his writings on justification, faith, the covenants and especially predestination proved controversial among the Reformed. His doctrine of election is often called hypothetical universalism or Amyraldianism, stating that Christ's atoning work was intended by God for all human beings indiscriminately, although its effectiveness for salvation depends on faith, which is a free gift of God given only to those whom God has chosen from eternity. Amyraut was charged with grave doctrinal error three times before the National Synod but was acquitted each time. Aside from his theological treatises, Amyraut published paraphrases of almost the entire New Testament and the Psalms, as well as many sermons.

Anabaptists of Trieste (1539). Following a meeting between Swiss Brethren and the Hutterites at Steinabrunn on December 6, 1536, around 140 radicals were arrested and imprisoned in Falkenstein Castle. After six weeks in captivity, the ninety men of the group were forced to march to Trieste to be sold as galley slaves. Twelve days after arrival, all but twelve prisoners managed to escape and return to Moravia, where they published a confession of their beliefs.

Jakob Andreae (1528–1590). German Lutheran theologian. Andreae studied at the University of Tübingen before being called to the diaconate in Stuttgart in 1546. He was appointed ecclesiastical superintendent of Göppingen in 1553 and supported Johannes Brenz's* proposal to place the church under civil administrative control. An ecclesial diplomat for the duke of Württemberg, Andreae debated eucharistic theology, the use of images and predestination with Theodore Beza* at the Colloquy of Montbéliard (1586) to determine whether French Reformed exiles would be required to submit to the Formula of Concord.* Andreae coauthored the Formula of Concord. He and his wife had eighteen children.

Lancelot Andrewes (1555–1626). Anglican bishop. A scholar, pastor and preacher, Andrews prominently shaped a distinctly Anglican identity between the poles of Puritanism and Catholicism.

He oversaw the translation of Genesis to 2 Kings for the Authorized Version.* His eight-volume collected works—primarily devotional tracts and sermons—are marked by his fluency in Scripture, the Christian tradition and classical literature.

Benedict Aretius (d. 1574). Swiss Reformed professor. Trained at the universities of Bern, Strasbourg and Marburg, Aretius taught logic and philosophy as well as the biblical languages and theology. He advocated for stronger unity and peace between the Lutheran and Reformed churches. Aretius joined others in denouncing the antitrinitarian Giovanni Valentino Gentile (d. 1566). He published commentaries on the New Testament, as well as various works on astronomy, botany and medicine.

Jacobus Arminius (1559–1609). Dutch Remonstrant pastor and theologian. Arminius was a vocal critic of high Calvinist scholasticism, whose views were repudiated by the Synod of Dordrecht. Arminius was a student of Theodore Beza* at the academy of Geneva. He served as a pastor in Amsterdam and later joined the faculty of theology at the university in Leiden, where his lectures on predestination were popular and controversial. Predestination, as Arminius understood it, was the decree of God determined on the basis of divine foreknowledge of faith or rejection by humans who are the recipients of prevenient, but resistible, grace.

Johann Arndt (1555–1621). German Lutheran pastor and theologian. After a brief time teaching, Arndt pastored in Badeborn (Anhalt) until 1590, when Prince Johann Georg von Anhalt (1567–1618) began introducing Reformed ecclesial policies. Arndt ministered in Quedlinberg, Brunswick, Eisleben and Celle. Heavily influenced by medieval mysticism, Arndt centered his theology on Christ's mystical union with the believer, out of which flows love of God and neighbor. He is best known for his *True Christianity* (1605–1609), which greatly influenced Philipp Jakob Spener (1635–1705) and later Pietists.

John Arrowsmith (1602–1659). English Puritan theologian. Arrowsmith participated in the Westminster Assembly, and later taught at Cambridge. His works, all published posthumously, include three sermons preached to Parliament and an unfinished catechism.

Articles of Religion (1562; revised 1571). The Articles underwent a long editorial process that drew from the influence of Continental confessions in England, resulting in a uniquely Anglican blend of Protestantism and Catholicism. In their final form, they were reduced from Thomas Cranmer's* Forty-two Articles (1539) to the Elizabethan Thirty-Nine Articles (1571), excising polemical articles against the Anabaptists and Millenarians as well as adding articles on the Holy Spirit, good works and Communion. Originating in a 1535 meeting with Lutherans, the Articles retained a minor influence from the Augsburg Confession* and Württemberg Confession (1552), but showed significant revision in accordance with Genevan theology, as well as the Second Helvetic Confession.*

Anne Askew (1521–1546). English Protestant martyr. Askew was forced to marry her deceased sister's intended husband, who later expelled Askew from his house—after the birth of two children—on account of her religious views. After unsuccessfully seeking a divorce in Lincoln, Askew moved to London, where she met other Protestants and began to preach. In 1546, she was arrested, imprisoned and convicted of heresy for denying the doctrine of transubstantiation. Under torture in the Tower of London she refused to name any other Protestants. On July 16, 1546, she was burned at the stake. Askew is best known through her accounts of her arrests and examinations. John Bale (1495–1563), a bishop, historian and playwright, published these manuscripts. Later John Foxe (1516–1587) included them in his *Acts and Monuments*, presenting her as a role model for other pious Protestant women.

Augsburg Confession (1530). In the wake of Luther's* stand against ecclesial authorities at the Diet of Worms (1521), the Holy Roman Empire splintered along theological lines. Emperor Charles V sought to ameliorate this—while also hoping to secure a united European front against Turkish invasion—by calling together another imperial diet in Augsburg in 1530. The Evangelical party was cast in a strongly heretical light at the diet by Johann Eck.* For this reason, Philipp Melanchthon* and Justus Jonas* thought it best to strike a conciliatory tone (Luther, as an official outlaw, did not attend), submitting a confession rather than a defense. The resulting Augsburg Confession was approved by many of the rulers of the northeastern Empire; however, due to differences in eucharistic theology, Martin Bucer* and the representatives of Strasbourg, Constance, Lindau and Memmingen drafted a separate confession (the Tetrapolitan Confession). Charles V accepted neither confession, demanding that the Evangelicals accept the Catholic rebuttal instead. In 1531, along with the publication of the Augsburg Confession itself, Melanchthon released a defense of the confession that responded to the Catholic confutation and expanded on the original articles. Most subsequent Protestant confessions followed the general structure of the Augsburg Confession.

Authorized Version (1611). In 1604 King James I* commissioned this new translation—popularly remembered as the King James Version—for uniform use in the public worship of the Church of England. The Bible and the Apocrypha was divided into six portions and assigned to six companies of nine scholars—both Anglicans and Puritans—centered at Cambridge, Oxford and Westminster. Richard Bancroft, the general editor of the Authorized Version, composed fifteen rules to guide the translators and to guard against overly partisan decisions. Rather than offer an entirely fresh English translation, the companies were to follow the Bishops' Bible* as closely as possible. "Truly (good Christian Reader)," the preface states, "we neuer thought from the beginning that we should need to make a new Translation, nor yet to make of a bad one a good one . . . but make a good one better, or out of many good ones, one principall good one, not iustly to be excepted against: that hath bene our endeauour, that our mark." Other rules standardized spelling, dictated traditional ecclesial terms (e.g., *church*, *baptize* and *bishop*), and allowed only for linguistic marginal notes and cross-references. Each book of the Bible went through a rigorous revision process: first, each person in a company made an initial draft, then the company put together a composite draft, then a supercommittee composed of representatives from each company reviewed these drafts, and finally two bishops and Bancroft scrutinized the final edits. The text and translation process of the Authorized Version have widely influenced biblical translations ever since.

Robert Bagnall (b. 1559 or 1560). English Protestant minister. Bagnall authored *The Steward's Last Account* (1622), a collection of five sermons on Luke 16.

John Ball (1585–1640). English Puritan theologian. Ball was a respected educator. He briefly held a church office until he was removed on account of his Puritanism. He composed popular catechisms and tracts on faith, the church and the covenant of grace.

Thomas Bastard (c. 1565–1618). English Protestant minister and poet. Educated at Winchester and New College, Oxford, Bastard published numerous works, including collections of poems and sermons; his most famous title is *Chrestoleros* (1598), a collection of epigrams. Bastard was alleged to be the author of an anonymous work, *An Admonition to the City of Oxford*, which revealed the carnal vices of many clergy and scholars in Oxford; despite denying authorship, he was dismissed from Oxford in 1591. Bastard was recognized as a skilled classical scholar and preacher. He died impoverished in a debtor's prison in Dorchester.

Jeremias Bastingius (1551–1595). Dutch Reformed theologian. Educated in Heidelberg and Geneva, Bastingius pastored the Reformed church in Antwerp for nearly a decade until the Spanish overran the city in 1585; he later settled in Dordrecht. He spent the last few years of his life in Leiden on the university's board of regents. He wrote an influential commentary on the Heidelberg Catechism that was translated into English, Dutch, German and Flemish.

Johann (Pomarius) Baumgart (1514–1578). Lutheran pastor and amateur playwright. Baumgart studied under Georg Major,* Martin

Luther* and Philipp Melanchthon* at the University of Wittenberg. Before becoming pastor of the Church of the Holy Spirit in 1540, Baumgart taught secondary school. He authored catechetical and polemical works, a postil for the Gospel readings throughout the church year, numerous hymns and a didactic play (*Juditium Salomonis*).

Richard Baxter (1615–1691). English Puritan minister. Baxter was a leading Puritan pastor, evangelist and theologian, known throughout England for his landmark ministry in Kidderminster and a prodigious literary output, producing 135 books in just over forty years. Baxter came to faith through reading William Perkins,* Richard Sibbes* and other early Puritan writers and was the first cleric to decline the terms of ministry in the national English church imposed by the 1662 Act of Uniformity; Baxter wrote on behalf of the more than 1700 who shared ejection from the national church. He hoped for restoration to national church ministry, or toleration, that would allow lawful preaching and pastoring. Baxter sought unity in theological, ecclesiastical, sociopolitical and personal terms and is regarded as a forerunner of Noncomformist ecumenicity, though he was defeated in his efforts at the 1661 Savoy Conference to take seriously Puritan objections to the revision of the 1604 Prayer Book. Baxter's views on church ministry were considerably hybrid: he was a paedo-baptist, Nonconformist minister who approved of synodical Episcopal government and fixed liturgy. He is most known for his classic writings on the Christian life, such as *The Saints' Everlasting Rest* and *A Christian Directory*, and pastoral ministry, such as *The Reformed Pastor*. He also produced *Catholick Theology*, a large volume squaring current Reformed, Lutheran, Arminian and Roman Catholic systems with each other.

Thomas Becon (1511/1512–1567). English Puritan preacher. Becon was a friend of Hugh Latimer,* and for several years chaplain to Archbishop Thomas Cranmer.* Becon was sent to the Tower of London by Mary I and then exiled for his controversial preaching at the English royal court. He returned to England upon Elizabeth I's accession. Becon was one of the most widely read popular preachers in England during the Reformation. He published many of his sermons, including a postil, or collection of sermon helps for undertrained or inexperienced preachers.

Belgic Confession (1561). Written by Guy de Brès (1523–1567), this statement of Dutch Reformed faith was heavily reliant on the Gallic Confession,* although more detailed, especially in how strongly it distances the Reformed from Roman Catholics and Anabaptists. The Confession first appeared in French in 1561 and was translated to Dutch in 1562. It was presented to Philip II (1527–1598) in the hope that he would grant toleration to the Reformed, to no avail. At the Synod of Dordrecht* the Confession was revised, clarifying and strengthening the article on election as well as sharpening the distinctives of Reformed theology against the Anabaptists, thus situating the Dutch Reformed more closely to the international Calvinist movement. The Belgic Confession in conjunction with the Heidelberg Catechism* and the Canons of Dordrecht were granted official status as the confessional standards (the Three Forms of Unity) of the Dutch Reformed Church.

Theodore Beza (1519–1605). French pastor and professor. Beza was compatriot and successor to John Calvin* as moderator of the Company of Pastors in Geneva during the second half of the sixteenth century. He was a noteworthy New Testament scholar whose *Codex Bezae* formed the basis of the New Testament section of later English translations. A leader in the academy and the church, Beza served as professor of Greek at the Lausanne Academy until 1558, at which time he moved to Geneva to become the rector of the newly founded Genevan Academy. He enjoyed an international reputation through his correspondence with key European leaders. Beza developed and extended Calvin's doctrinal thought on several important themes such as the nature of predestination and the real spiritual presence of Christ in the Eucharist.

Theodor Bibliander (1504?–1564). Swiss Reformed Hebraist and theologian. Professor of

Old Testament at the Zurich Academy from 1531, Bibliander published two Hebrew grammars, a collection of letters by Zwingli* and Oecolampadius*, commentaries on Isaiah, Ezekiel, and Nahum, a Latin translation of the Qur'an, and a tract warning Christians against the threat of Islam. He taught a universalist view of predestination, arguing that God saved all people unless they rejected divine grace. Following a dispute with double-predestinarian Peter Martyr Vermigli*, he was forced into retirement in 1560.

Hugh Binning (1627–1653). Scottish Presbyterian theologian. At the age of eighteen, Binning became a professor of philosophy at the University of Glasgow. In his early twenties he left this post for parish ministry, and died of consumption a few years later. His commentary on the Westminster Confession and a selection of his sermons were published after his death.

Samuel Bird (d. 1604). Anglican minister and author. A native of Essex, Bird matriculated at Queen's College, Cambridge, where he received his BA in 1570 and his MA in 1573, at which time he was also elected a fellow of Corpus Christi College, Cambridge. For reasons unknown, Bird resigned his fellowship sometime in 1576. He spent nearly the entirety of his post-university career as rector of St. Peter's in Ipswich until his death in 1604. Among Bird's major works are *A Friendlie Communication or Dialogue Betweene Paule and Demas, wherein is Disputed How We are to Use the Pleasures of This Life* (1580), *Lectures upon the 11. Chapter of Hebrews and upon the 38. Psalme* (1598), and *Lectures upon the 8 and 9 Chapters of the Second Epistle to the Corinthians* (1598).

Bishops' Bible (1568). Anglicans were polarized by the two most recent English translations of the Bible: the Great Bible (1539) relied too heavily on the Vulgate* and was thus perceived as too Catholic, while the Geneva Bible's* marginal notes were too Calvinist for many Anglicans. So Archbishop Matthew Parker (1504–1575) commissioned a new translation of Scripture from the original languages with marginal annotations (many of which, ironically, were from the Geneva Bible). Published under royal warrant, the Bishops' Bible became the official translation for the Church of England. The 1602 edition provided the basis for the King James Bible (1611).

Georg Blaurock (1492–1529). Swiss Anabaptist. Blaurock (a nickname meaning "blue coat," because of his preference for this garment) was one of the first leaders of Switzerland's radical reform movement. In the first public disputations on baptism in Zurich, he argued for believer's baptism and was the first person to receive adult believers' baptism there, having been baptized by Conrad Grebel* in 1525. Blaurock was arrested several times for performing mass adult baptisms and engaging in social disobedience by disrupting worship services. He was eventually expelled from Zurich but continued preaching and baptizing in various Swiss cantons until his execution.

Bohemian Confession (1535). Bohemian Christianity was subdivided between traditional Catholics, Utraquists (who demanded Communion in both kinds) and the *Unitas Fratrum*, who were not Protestants but whose theology bore strong affinities to the Waldensians and the Reformed. The 1535 Latin edition of this confession—an earlier Czech edition had already been drafted—was an attempt to clarify and redefine the beliefs of the *Unitas Fratrum*. This confession purged all earlier openness to rebaptism and inched toward Luther's* eucharistic theology. Jan Augusta (c. 1500–1572) and Jan Roh (also Johannes Horn; c. 1490–1547) presented the confession to King Ferdinand I (1503–1564) in Vienna, but the king would not print it. The *Unitas Fratrum* sought, and with slight amendments eventually obtained, Luther's advocacy of the confession. It generally follows the structure of the Augsburg Confession.*

Bohemian Confession (1575). This confession was an attempt to shield Bohemian Christian minorities—the Utraquists and the *Unitas Fratrum*—from the Counter-Reformation and Habsburg insistence on uniformity. The hope was that this umbrella consensus would ensure peace in the midst of Christian diversity; anyone who affirmed the 1575 Confession, passed by the Bohemian legislature, would be tolerated. This confession was, like the Bohemian Confession of 1535, patterned after the Augsburg Confession.* It emphasizes both justification by faith alone and good works as the fruit of salvation. Baptism and the Eucharist are the focus of the sacramental section, although the five traditional Catholic sacraments are also listed for the Utraquists. Though it was eventually accepted in 1609 by Rudolf II (1552–1612), the Thirty Years' War (1618–1648) rendered the confession moot.

Book of Common Prayer (1549; 1552). After the Church of England's break with Rome, it needed a liturgical manual to distinguish its theology and practice from that of Catholicism. Thomas Cranmer* drafted the Book of Common Prayer based on the medieval Roman Missal, under the dual influence of the revised Lutheran Mass and the reforms of the Spanish Cardinal Quiñones. This manual details the eucharistic service, as well as services for rites such as baptism, confirmation, marriage and funerals. It includes a matrix of the epistle and Gospel readings and the appropriate collect for each Sunday and feast day of the church year. The 1548 Act of Uniformity established the Book of Common Prayer as *the* authoritative liturgical manual for the Church of England, to be implemented everywhere by Pentecost 1549. After its 1552 revision, Queen Mary I banned it; Elizabeth reestablished it in 1559, although it was rejected by Puritans and Catholics alike.

The Book of Homilies (1547; 1563; 1570). This collection of approved sermons, published in three parts during the reigns of Edward VI and Elizabeth I, was intended to inculcate Anglican theological distinctives and mitigate the problems raised by the lack of educated preachers. Addressing doctrinal and practical topics, Thomas Cranmer* likely wrote the majority of the first twelve sermons, published in 1547; John Jewel* added another twenty sermons in 1563. A final sermon, *A Homily Against Disobedience*, was appended to the canon in 1570. Reprinted regularly, the *Book of Homilies* was an important resource in Anglican preaching until at least the end of the seventeenth century.

Martin (Cellarius) Borrhaus (1499–1564). German Reformed theologian. After a dispute with his mentor Johann Eck,* Borrhaus settled in Wittenberg, where he was influenced by the radical Zwickau Prophets. He travelled extensively, and finally settled in Basel to teach philosophy and Old Testament. Despite his objections, many accused Borrhaus of Anabaptism; he argued that baptism was a matter of conscience. On account of his association with Sebastian Castellio (1515–1563) and Michael Servetus (1511–1553), some scholars posit that Borrhaus was an antitrinitarian. His writings include a treatise on the Trinity and commentaries on the Torah, historical books, Ecclesiastes and Isaiah.

John Boys (1571–1625). Anglican priest and theologian. Before doctoral work at Cambridge, Boys pastored several parishes in Kent; after completing his studies he was appointed to more prominent positions, culminating in his 1619 appointment as the Dean of Canterbury by James I. Boys published a popular four-volume postil of the Gospel and epistle readings for the church year, as well as a companion volume for the Psalms.

Thieleman Jans van Braght (1625–1664). Dutch Radical preacher. After demonstrating great ability with languages, this cloth merchant was made preacher in his hometown of Dordrecht in 1648. He served in this office for the next sixteen years, until his death. This celebrated preacher had a reputation for engaging in debate wherever an opportunity presented itself, particularly concerning infant baptism. The publication of his book of martyrs, *Het Bloedigh Tooneel of Martelaersspiegel* (1660; *Martyrs' Mirror*), proved to be his lasting contribution to the Mennonite tradition. *Martyrs' Mirror* is heavily indebted to the earlier martyr book *Offer des Heeren* (1562), to which Braght added many early church martyrs who rejected infant baptism, as well as over 800 contemporary martyrs.

Johannes Brenz (1499–1570). German Lutheran theologian and pastor. Brenz was converted to the reformation cause after hearing Martin Luther* speak; later, Brenz became a student of Johannes Oecolampadius.* His central achievement lay in his talent for organization. As city preacher in Schwäbisch-Hall and afterward in Württemberg and Tübingen, he oversaw the introduction of reform measures and doctrines and new governing structures for ecclesial and educational communities. Brenz also helped establish Lutheran orthodoxy through treatises, commentaries and catechisms. He defended Luther's position on eucharistic presence against Huldrych Zwingli* and opposed the death penalty for religious dissenters.

Guillaume Briçonnet (1470–1534). French Catholic abbot and bishop. Briçonnet created a short-lived circle of reformist-minded humanists in his diocese under the sponsorship of Marguerite d'Angoulême. His desire for ecclesial reform developed throughout his prestigious career (including positions as royal chaplain to the queen, abbot at Saint-Germain-des-Prés and bishop of Meaux), influenced by Jacques Lefèvre d'Étaples.* Briçonnet encouraged reform through ministerial visitation, Scripture and preaching in the vernacular and active study of the Bible. When this triggered the ire of the theology faculty at the Sorbonne in Paris, Briçonnet quelled the activity and departed, envisioning an ecclesial reform that proceeded hierarchically.

Thomas Brightman (1562–1607). English Puritan pastor and exegete. Under alleged divine inspiration, Brightman wrote a well known commentary on Revelation, influenced by Joachim of Fiore (d. 1202). In contrast to the putatively true churches of Geneva and Scotland, he depicted the Church of England as a type of the lukewarm Laodicean church. He believed that the Reformation would result in the defeat of the Vatican and the Ottoman Empire and that all humanity would be regenerated through the spread of the gospel before Christ's final return and judgment.

Otto Brunfels (c. 1488–1534). German Lutheran botanist, teacher and physician. Brunfels joined the Carthusian order, where he developed interests in the natural sciences and became involved with a humanist circle associated with Ulrich von Hutten and Wolfgang Capito.* In 1521, after coming into contact with Luther's* teaching, Brunfels abandoned the monastic life, traveling and spending time in botanical research and pastoral care. He received a medical degree in Basel and was appointed city physician of Bern in 1534. Brunfels penned defenses of Luther and Hutten, devotional biographies of biblical figures, a prayer book, and annotations on the Gospels and the Acts of the Apostles. His most influential contribution, however, is as a Renaissance botanist.

Martin Bucer (1491–1551). German Reformed theologian and pastor. A Dominican friar, Bucer was influenced by Desiderius Erasmus* during his doctoral studies at the University of Heidelberg, where he began corresponding with Martin Luther.* After advocating reform in Alsace, Bucer was excommunicated and fled to Strasbourg, where he became a leader in the city's Reformed ecclesial and educational communities. Bucer sought concord between Lutherans and Zwinglians and Protestants and Catholics. He emigrated to England, becoming a professor at Cambridge. Bucer's greatest theological concern was the centrality of Christ's sacrificial death, which achieved justification and sanctification and orients Christian community.

Johannes Bugenhagen (1485–1558). German Lutheran pastor and professor. Bugenhagen, a priest and lecturer at a Premonstratensian monastery, became a city preacher in Wittenberg during the reform efforts of Martin Luther* and Philipp Melanchthon.* Initially influenced by his reading of Desiderius Erasmus,* Bugenhagen grew in evangelical orientation through Luther's works; later, he studied under Melanchthon at the University of Wittenberg, eventually serving as rector and faculty member there. Bugenhagen was a versatile commentator, exegete and lecturer on Scripture. Through these roles and his development of lectionary and devotional material, Bugenhagen facilitated rapid establishment of church order throughout many German provinces.

Heinrich Bullinger (1504–1575). Swiss Reformed pastor and theologian. Bullinger succeeded

Huldrych Zwingli* as minister and leader in Zurich. The primary author of the First and Second Helvetic Confessions,* Bullinger was drawn toward reform through the works of Martin Luther* and Philipp Melanchthon.* After Zwingli died, Bullinger was vital in maintaining adherence to the cause of reform; he oversaw the expansion of the Zurich synodal system while preaching, teaching and writing extensively. One of Bullinger's lasting legacies was the development of a federal view of the divine covenant with humanity, making baptism and the Eucharist covenantal signs.

John Bunyan (1628–1688). English Puritan preacher and writer. His *Pilgrim's Progress* is one of the best-selling English-language titles in history. Born to a working-class family, Bunyan was largely unschooled, gaining literacy (and entering the faith) through reading the Bible and such early Puritan devotional works as *The Plain Man's Pathway to Heaven* and *The Practice of Piety*. Following a short stint in Oliver Cromwell's parliamentary army, in which Bunyan narrowly escaped death in combat, he turned to a preaching ministry, succeeding John Gifford as pastor at the Congregational church in Bedford. A noted preacher, Bunyan drew large crowds in itinerant appearances and it was in the sermonic form that Bunyan developed his theological outlook, which was an Augustinian-inflected Calvinism. Bunyan's opposition to the Book of Common Prayer and refusal of official ecclesiastical licensure led to multiple imprisonments, where he wrote many of his famous allegorical works, including *Pilgrim's Progress, The Holy City, Prison Meditations* and *Holy War*.

Jeremiah Burroughs (c. 1600–1646). English Puritan pastor and delegate to the Westminster Assembly. Burroughs left Cambridge, as well as a rectorate in Norfolk, because of his nonconformity. After returning to England from pastoring an English congregation in Rotterdam for several years (1637–1641), he became one of only a few dissenters from the official presbyterianism of the Assembly in favor of a congregationalist polity. Nevertheless, he was well known and respected by presbyterian colleagues such as Richard Baxter* for his irenic tone and conciliatory manner. The vast majority of Burroughs's corpus was published posthumously, although during his lifetime he published annotations on Hosea and several polemical works.

Cardinal Cajetan (Thomas de Vio) (1469–1534). Italian Catholic cardinal, professor, theologian and biblical exegete. This Dominican monk was the leading Thomist theologian and one of the most important Catholic exegetes of the sixteenth century. Cajetan is best-known for his interview with Martin Luther* at the Diet of Augsburg (1518). Among his many works are polemical treatises, extensive biblical commentaries and most importantly a four-volume commentary (1508–1523) on the *Summa Theologiae* of Thomas Aquinas.

Georg Calixtus (1586–1656). German Lutheran theologian. Calixtus studied at the University of Helmstedt where he developed regard for Philipp Melanchthon.* Between his time as a student and later as a professor at Helmstedt, Calixtus traveled through Europe seeking a way to unite and reconcile Lutherans, Calvinists and Catholics. He attempted to fuse these denominations through use of the Scriptures, the Apostles' Creed, and the first five centuries, interpreted by the Vincentian canon. Calixtus's position was stamped as syncretist and yielded further debate even after his death.

John Calvin (1509–1564). French Reformed pastor and theologian. In his *Institutes of the Christian Religion*, Calvin provided a theological dogmatics for the Reformed churches. Calvin's gradual conversion to the cause of reform occurred through his study with chief humanist scholars in Paris, but he spent most of his career in Geneva (excepting a three-year exile in Strasbourg with Martin Bucer*). In Geneva, Calvin reorganized the structure and governance of the church and established an academy that became an international center for theological education. He was a tireless writer, producing his *Institutes*, theological treatises and Scripture commentaries.

Wolfgang Capito (1478?–1541). German Reformed humanist and theologian. Capito, a Hebrew scholar, produced a Hebrew grammar and published several Latin commentaries on books of the Hebrew Scriptures. He corresponded with Desiderius Erasmus* and fellow humanists. Capito translated Martin Luther's* early works into Latin for the printer Johann Froben. On meeting Luther, Capito was converted to Luther's vision, left Mainz and settled in Strasbourg, where he lectured on Luther's theology to the city clergy. With Martin Bucer,* Capito reformed liturgy, ecclesial life and teachings, education, welfare and government. Capito worked for the theological unification of the Swiss cantons with Strasbourg.

Thomas Cartwright (1535–1606). English Puritan preacher and professor. Cartwright was educated at St. John's College, Cambridge, although as an influential leader of the Presbyterian party in the Church of England he was continually at odds with the Anglican party, especially John Whitgift.* Cartwright spent some time as an exile in Geneva and Heidelberg as well as in Antwerp, where he pastored an English church. In 1585, Cartwright was arrested and eventually jailed for trying to return to England despite Elizabeth I's refusal of his request. Many acknowledged him to be learned but also quite cantankerous. His publications include commentaries on Colossians, Ecclesiastes, Proverbs and the Gospels, as well as a dispute against Whitgift on church discipline.

Mathew Caylie (unknown). English Protestant minister. Caylie authored *The Cleansing of the Ten Lepers* (1623), an exposition of Luke 17:14-18.

John Chardon (d. 1601). Irish Anglican bishop. Chardon was educated at Oxford. He advocated Reformed doctrine in his preaching, yet opposed those Puritans who rejected Anglican church order. He published several sermons.

Martin Chemnitz (1522–1586). German Lutheran theologian. A leading figure in establishing Lutheran orthodoxy, Chemnitz studied theology and patristics at the University of Wittenburg, later becoming a defender of Philipp Melanchthon's* interpretation of the doctrine of justification. Chemnitz drafted a compendium of doctrine and reorganized the structure of the church in Wolfenbüttel; later, he led efforts to reconcile divisions within Lutheranism, culminating in the Formula of Concord*. One of his chief theological accomplishments was a modification of the christological doctrine of the *communicatio idiomatium*, which provided a Lutheran platform for understanding the sacramental presence of Christ's humanity in the Eucharist.

David Chytraeus (1531–1600). German Lutheran professor, theologian and biblical exegete. At the age of eight Chytraeus was admitted to the University of Tübingen. There he studied law, philology, philosophy, and theology, finally receiving his master's degree in 1546. Chytraeus befriended Philipp Melanchthon* while sojourning in Wittenberg, where he taught the *Loci communes*. While teaching exegesis at the University of Rostock Chytraeus became acquainted with Tilemann Heshusius,* who strongly influenced Chytraeus away from Philippist theology. As a defender of Gnesio-Lutheran theology Chytraeus helped organize churches throughout Austria in accordance with the Augsburg Confession.* Chytraeus coauthored the Formula of Concord* with Martin Chemnitz,* Andreas Musculus (1514–1581), Nikolaus Selnecker* and Jakob Andreae.* He wrote commentaries on most of the Bible, as well as a devotional work titled *Regula vitae* (1555) that described the Christian virtues.

David Clarkson (1622–1686). English Puritan theologian. After his dismissal from the pastorate on account of the Act of Uniformity (1662), little is known about Clarkson. At the end of his life he ministered with John Owen* in London.

Robert Cleaver (1571–1613). English Puritan pastor. Cleaver served as rector at Drayton in Oxfordshire until silenced by Archbishop Richard Bancroft for advocating Nonconformity. Despite opposition from ecclesiastical authorities, Cleaver enjoyed a reputation as an excellent preacher. His published works include sermons on Hebrews 4 and Song of Songs 2 as well as one on the last chapter of Proverbs. Cleaver also authored *The Parsimony of Christian Children*, which contained a defense of infant baptism against Baptist criticisms.

John Colet (1467–1519). English Catholic priest, preacher and educator. Colet, appointed dean of Saint Paul's Cathedral by Henry VII, was a friend of Desiderius Erasmus,* on whose classical ideals Colet reconstructed the curriculum of Saint Paul's school. Colet was convinced that the foundation of moral reform lay in the education of children. Though an ardent advocate of reform, Colet, like Erasmus, remained loyal to the Catholic Church throughout his life. Colet's agenda of reform was oriented around spiritual and ethical themes, demonstrated in his commentaries on select books of the New Testament and the writings of Pseudo-Dionysius the Areopagite.

Gasparo Contarini (1483–1542). Italian statesman, theologian and reform-minded cardinal. Contarini was an able negotiator and graceful compromiser. Charles V requested Contarini as the papal legate for the Colloquy of Regensburg (1541), where Contarini reached agreement with Melanchthon* on the doctrine of justification (although neither the pope nor Luther* ratified the agreement). He had come to a similar belief in the priority of faith in the work of Christ rather than works as the basis for Christian life in 1511, though unlike Luther, he never left the papal church over the issue; instead he remainied within it to try to seek gentle reform, and he adhered to papal sacramental teaching. Contarini was an important voice for reform within the Catholic Church, always seeking reconciliation rather than confrontation with Protestant reformers. He wrote many works, including a treatise detailing the ideal bishop, a manual for lay church leaders, a political text on right governance and brief commentaries on the Pauline letters.

John Cosin (1594–1672). Anglican preacher and bishop. Early in his career Cosin was the vice chancellor of Cambridge and canon at the Durham cathedral. But as a friend of William Laud* and an advocate for "Laudian" changes, he was suspected of being a crypto-Catholic. In 1640 during the Long Parliament a Puritan lodged a complaint with the House of Commons concerning Cosin's "popish innovations." Cosin was promptly removed from office. During the turmoil of the English Civil Wars, Cosin sojourned in Paris among English nobility but struggled financially. Cosin returned to England after the Restoration in 1660 to be consecrated as the bishop of Durham. He published annotations on the Book of Common Prayer* and a history of the canon.

Council of Constance (1414–1418). Convened to resolve the Western Schism, root out heresy and reform the church in head and members, the council asserted in *Sacrosancta* (1415) the immediate authority of ecumenical councils assembled in the Holy Spirit under Christ—even over the pope. Martin V was elected pope in 1417 after the three papal claimants were deposed; thus, the council ended the schism. The council condemned Jan Hus,* Jerome of Prague (c. 1365–1416) and, posthumously, John Wycliffe. Hus and Jerome, despite letters of safe conduct, were burned at the stake. Their deaths ignited the Hussite Wars, which ended as a result of the Council of Basel's concessions to the Bohemian church. The council fathers sought to reform the church through the regular convocation of councils (*Frequens*; 1417). Martin V begrudgingly complied by calling the required councils, then immediately disbanding them. Pius II (r. 1458–1464) reasserted papal dominance through *Execrabilis* (1460), which condemned any appeal to a future council apart from the pope's authority.

Council of Trent (1545–1563) Convoked by Pope Paul III (r. 1534–1549) with the support of Charles V*, the nineteenth ecumenical council was convened in the northern Italian city of Trent. Attended primarily by Italian clerics, it met in three distinct phases. Beginning in December 1545, during its first eight sessions, the council issued doctrinal decrees, asserting the authority of tradition alongside Scripture, the authenticity of the Vulgate, the prerogative of the church in interpretation, and the necessity of human cooperation in the work of salvation. Ecclesial abuses were also addressed, as attempts were made to eliminate absenteeism and pluralism and devolve power from Rome to bishoprics and parishes. The council was suspended following the outbreak of the plague in Trent in March 1547. A number of Protestant delegates were present during the second phase of the council, which met between May 1551 and April 1552 under the supervision of Pope Julius III (r. 1550–1555). The primary achievement of this period of the council was the clarification of teachings on the seven sacraments, with transubstantiation, the objective efficacy of the Eucharist, and the necessity of auricular confession confirmed as dogma. Reconvened by Pope Pius IV (r. 1559–1565) in 1561, the third phase of the council addressed the relationship between bishops and Rome, resulting in affirmations of the divine appointment of the church hierarchy and the obligation of bishops to reside in their dioceses. Clerical education, the regulation of marriage, and teachings on purgatory, indulgences, the use of images, and the saints were also addressed.

Miles Coverdale (1488–1568). Anglican bishop. Coverdale is known for his translations of the Bible into English, completing William Tyndale's* efforts and later producing the Great Bible commissioned by Henry VIII (1539). A former friar, Coverdale was among the Cambridge scholars who met at the White Horse Tavern to discuss Martin Luther's* ideas. During Coverdale's three terms of exile in Europe, he undertook various translations, including the Geneva Bible*. He was appointed bishop of Exeter by Thomas Cranmer* and served as chaplain to Edward VI. Coverdale contributed to Cranmer's first edition of the Book of Common Prayer.*

William Cowper (Couper) (1568–1619). Scottish Puritan bishop. After graduating from the University of St. Andrews, Cowper worked in parish ministry for twenty-five years before becoming bishop. As a zealous Puritan and advocate of regular preaching and rigorous discipline, Cowper championed Presbyterian polity and lay participation in church government. Cowper published devotional works, sermon collections and a commentary on Revelation.

Thomas Cranmer (1489–1556). Anglican archbishop and theologian. Cranmer supervised church reform and produced the first two editions of the Book of Common Prayer.* As a doctoral student at Cambridge, he was involved in the discussions at the White Horse Tavern. Cranmer contributed to a religious defense of Henry VIII's divorce; Henry then appointed him Archbishop of Canterbury. Cranmer cautiously steered the course of reform, accelerating under Edward VI. After supporting the attempted coup to prevent Mary's assuming the throne, Cranmer was convicted of treason and burned at the stake. Cranmer's legacy is the splendid English of his liturgy and prayer books.

Richard Crashaw (1612–1649). English Catholic poet. Educated at Cambridge, Crashaw was fluent in Hebrew, Greek and Latin. His first volume of poetry was *Epigrammatum sacrorum liber* (1634). Despite being born into a Puritan family, Crashaw was attracted to Catholicism, finally converting in 1644 after he was forced to resign his fellowship for not signing the Solemn League and Covenant (1643). In 1649, he was made a subcanon of Our Lady of Loretto by Cardinal Palotta.

Herbert Croft (1603–1691). Anglican bishop. As a boy Croft converted to Catholicism; he returned to the Church of England during his studies at Oxford. Before the English Civil Wars, he served as chaplain to Charles I. After the Restoration, Charles II appointed him as bishop. Croft ardently opposed Catholicism in his later years.

John Crompe (d. 1661). Anglican priest. Educated at Cambridge, Crompe published a commentary on the Apostles' Creed, a sermon on Psalm 21:3 and an exposition of Christ's passion.

Caspar Cruciger (1504–1548). German Lutheran theologian. Recognized for his alignment with the theological views of Philipp Melanchthon,* Cruciger was a scholar respected among both Protestants and Catholics. In 1521, Cruciger came Wittenberg to study Hebrew and remained there most of his life. He became a valuable partner for Martin Luther* in translating the Old Testament and served as teacher, delegate to major theological colloquies and rector. Cruciger was an agent of reform in his birthplace of Leipzig, where at the age of fifteen he had observed the disputa-

tion between Luther and Johann Eck.*
Ralph Cudworth (d. 1624) English Protestant minister. Father of noted Cambridge Platonist Ralph Cudworth (1617–1688), the elder Cudworth was a fellow of Emanuel College, Cambridge and rector of Aller in Somersetshire.
Marguerite d'Angoulême (1492–1549). French Catholic noblewoman. The elder sister of King Francis I of France, Marguerite was the Queen of Navarre and Duchess of Alençon and Berry. She was a poet and author of the French Renaissance. She composed *The Mirror of a Sinful Soul* (1531)—condemned by the theologians of the Sorbonne for containing Lutheran ideas—and an unfinished collection of short stories, the *Heptaméron* (1558). A leading figure in the French Reformation, Marguerite was at the center of a network of reform-minded individuals that included Guillame Briçonnet,* Jacques Lefèvre d'Etaples,* Gérard Roussel (1500–1550) and Guillame Farel (1489–1565).
Jakob Dachser (1486–1567). German Anabaptist theologian and hymnist. Dachser served as a Catholic priest in Vienna until he was imprisoned and then exiled for defending the Lutheran understanding of the Mass and fasting. Hans Hut* rebaptized him in Augsburg, where Dachser was appointed as a leader of the Anabaptist congregation. Lutheran authorities imprisoned him for nearly four years. In 1531 he recanted his Radical beliefs and began to catechize children with the permission of the city council. Dachser was expelled from Augsburg as a possible insurrectionist in 1552 and relocated to Pfalz-Neuberg. He published a number of poems, hymns and mystical works, and he versified several psalms.
Jean Daillé (1594–1670). French Reformed pastor. Born into a devout Reformed family, Daillé studied theology and philosophy at Saumur under the most influential contemporary lay leader in French Protestantism, Philippe Duplessis-Mornay (1549–1623). Daillé held to Amyraldianism—the belief that Christ died for all humanity inclusively, not particularly for the elect who would inherit salvation (though only the elect are in fact saved). He wrote a controversial treatise on the church fathers that aggravated many Catholic and Anglican scholars because of Daillé's apparent demotion of patristic authority in matters of faith.
Lambert Daneau (1535–1595). French Reformed pastor and theologian. After a decade of pastoring in France, following the St. Bartholomew's Day Massacre, Daneau fled to Geneva to teach theology at the Academy. He later taught in the Low Countries, finishing his career in southern France. Daneau's diverse works include tracts on science, ethics and morality as well as numerous theological and exegetical works.
John Davenant (1576–1641). Anglican bishop and professor. Davenant attended Queen's College, Cambridge, where he received his doctorate and was appointed professor of divinity. During the Remonstrant controversy, James I sent Davenant as one of the four representatives for the Church of England to the Synod of Dordrecht.* Following James's instructions, Davenant advocated a *via media* between the Calvinists and the Remonstrants, although in later years he defended against the rise of Arminianism in England. In 1621, Davenant was promoted to the bishopric of Salisbury, where he was generally receptive to Laudian reforms. Davenant's lectures on Colossians are his best-known work.
Defense of the Augsburg Confession (1531). See *Augsburg Confession.*
Hans Denck (c. 1500–1527). German Radical theologian. Denck, a crucial early figure of the German Anabaptist movement, combined medieval German mysticism with the radical sacramental theology of Andreas Bodenstein von Karlstadt* and Thomas Müntzer.* Denck argued that the exterior forms of Scripture and sacrament are symbolic witnesses secondary to the internally revealed truth of the Sprit in the human soul. This view led to his expulsion from Nuremberg in 1525; he spent the next two years in various centers of reform in the German territories. At the time of his death, violent persecution against Anabaptists was on the rise throughout northern Europe.
Stephen Denison (unknown). English Puritan

pastor. Denison received the post of curate at St. Katherine Cree in London sometime in the 1610s, where he ministered until his ejection from office in 1635. During his career at St. Katherine Cree, Denison waded into controversy with both Puritans (over the doctrine of predestination) and Anglicans (over concerns about liturgical ceremonies). He approached both altercations with rancor and rigidity, although he seems to have been quite popular and beloved by most of his congregation. In 1631, William Laud* consecrated the newly renovated St. Katherine Cree, and as part of the festivities Denison offered a sermon on Luke 19:27 in which he publicly rebuked Laud for fashioning the Lord's house into a "den of robbers." Aside from the record of his quarrels, very little is known about Denison. In addition to *The White Wolf* (a 1627 sermon against another opponent), he published a catechism for children (1621), a treatise on the sacraments (1621) and a commentary on 2 Peter 1 (1622).

Marie Dentière (1495–1561). Belgian Reformed theologian. Dentière relinquished her monastic vows and married Simon Robert (d.1533), a former priest, in Strasbourg. After Robert died, she married Antoine Froment (1508–1581), a reformer in Geneva, and became involved in the reform of that city. Her best-known writings are a tract addressed to Marguerite d'Angoulême,* the *Very Useful Epistle* (1539), in which she espoused the evangelical faith and the right of women to interpret and teach scripture, and a preface to Calvin's sermon on 1 Timothy 2:8-12. Dentière is the only woman to have her name inscribed on the International Monument to the Reformation in Geneva.

David Dickson (1583?–1663). Scottish Reformed pastor, preacher, professor and theologian. Dickson defended the Presbyterian form of ecclesial reformation in Scotland and was recognized for his iteration of Calvinist federal theology and expository biblical commentaries. Dickson served for over twenty years as professor of philosophy at the University of Glasgow before being appointed professor of divinity. He opposed the imposition of Episcopalian measures on the church in Scotland and was active in political and ecclesial venues to protest and prohibit such influences. Dickson was removed from his academic post following his refusal of the oath of supremacy during the Restoration era.

Veit Dietrich (1506–1549). German Lutheran preacher and theologian. Dietrich intended to study medicine at the University of Wittenberg, but Martin Luther* and Philipp Melanchthon* convinced him to study theology instead. Dietrich developed a strong relationship with Luther, accompanying him to the Marburg Colloquy (1529) and to Coburg Castle during the Diet of Augsburg (1530). After graduating, Dietrich taught on the arts faculty, eventually becoming dean. In 1535 he returned to his hometown, Nuremberg, to pastor. Later in life, Dietrich worked with Melanchthon to reform the church in Regensburg. In 1547, when Charles V arrived in Nuremberg, Dietrich was suspended from the pastorate; he resisted the imposition of the Augsburg Interim to no avail. In addition to transcribing some of Luther's lectures, portions of the Table Talk and the very popular *Hauspostille* (1544), Dietrich published his own sermons for children, a manual for pastors and a summary of the Bible.

Giovanni Diodati (1576–1649). Italian Reformed theologian. Diodati was from an Italian banking family who fled for religious reasons to Geneva. There he trained under Theodore Beza;* on completion of his doctoral degree, Diodati became professor of Hebrew at the academy. He was an ecclesiastical representative of the church in Geneva (for whom he was a delegate at the Synod of Dordrecht*) and an advocate for reform in Venice. Diodati's chief contribution to the Italian reform movement was a translation of the Bible into Italian (1640–1641), which remains the standard translation in Italian Protestantism.

John Dod (c. 1549–1645). English Puritan pastor. Over the course of his lengthy pastoral career (spanning roughly sixty years), Dod was twice suspended for nonconformity and twice reinstated. A popular preacher, he published many sermons as well as commentaries on the Ten Commandments and the Lord's Prayer; collections of his sayings and anecdotes were compiled after his death.

John Donne (1572–1631). Anglican poet and preacher. Donne was born into a strong Catholic family. However, sometime between his brother's death from the plague while in prison in 1593 and the publication of his *Pseudo-Martyr* in 1610, Donne joined the Church of England. Ordained to the Anglican priesthood in 1615 and already widely recognized for his verse, Donne quickly rose to prominence as a preacher—some have deemed him the best of his era. His textual corpus is an amalgam of erotic *and* divine poetry (e.g., "Batter My Heart"), as well as a great number of sermons.

Dordrecht Confession (1632). Dutch Mennonite confession. Adriaan Cornelisz (1581–1632) wrote the Dordrecht Confession to unify Dutch Mennonites. This basic statement of Mennonite belief and practice affirms distinctive doctrines such as nonresistance, shunning, footwashing and the refusal to swear oaths. Most continental Mennonites subscribed to this confession during the second half of the seventeenth century.

John Downame (c. 1571–1652). English Puritan pastor and theologian. See *English Annotations*.

Charles Drelincourt (1595–1669). French Reformed pastor, theologian and controversialist. After studying at Saumur Academy, Drelincourt pastored the Reformed Church in Paris for nearly fifty years. He was well known for his ministry to the sick. In addition to polemical works against Catholicism, he published numerous pastoral resources: catechisms, three volumes of sermons and a five-volume series on consolation for the suffering.

The Dutch Annotations (1657). See *Statenvertaling*.

Daniel Dyke (d. 1614). English Puritan preacher. Born of nonconformist stock, Dyke championed a more thorough reformation of church practice in England. After the promulgation of John Whitgift's* articles in 1583, Dyke refused to accept what he saw as remnants of Catholicism, bringing him into conflict with the bishop of London. Despite the petitions of his congregation and some politicians, the bishop of London suspended Dyke from his ministry for refusing priestly ordination and conformity to the Book of Common Prayer.* All of his work was published posthumously; it is mostly focused on biblical interpretation.

Johann Eck (Johann Maier of Eck) (1486–1543). German Catholic theologian. Though Eck was not an antagonist of Martin Luther* until the dispute over indulgences, Luther's Ninety-five Theses (1517) sealed the two as adversaries. After their debate at the Leipzig Disputation (1519), Eck participated in the writing of the papal bull that led to Luther's excommunication. Much of Eck's work was written to oppose Protestantism or to defend Catholic doctrine and the papacy; his *Enchiridion* was a manual written to counter Protestant doctrine. However, Eck was also deeply invested in the status of parish preaching, publishing a five-volume set of postils. He participated in the assemblies at Regensburg and Augsburg and led the Catholics in their rejection of the Augsburg Confession.

Elizabeth I of England (1533–1603) English monarch. The daughter of Henry VIII (r. 1509–1547) and Anne Boleyn (c. 1501–1536), Elizabeth outwardly conformed to Catholicism during the reign of her sister Mary I (r. 1553–1558), but her Protestant upbringing encouraged the hopes of many reformers upon her accession in 1558. With the 1559 Elizabethan Settlement, Elizabeth redefined England as a Protestant country, with the Act of Supremacy asserting the monarch as the head of the English church, and the Act of Uniformity establishing the 1559 *Book of Common Prayer** as the valid order of service within the realm. However, Elizabeth resisted the aggressive persecution of Catholics for political reasons, while also allowing some traditional vestments, furniture and ceremonies to be retained. Her moderate and pragmatic reforms frustrated many who wished for more thorough change and led to the emergence of the Puritan movement. Elizabeth faced numerous threats during her reign, including the machinations of Scottish Catholics and claims to the throne of

Mary Stuart (1542–1547), leading to her rival's imprisonment and execution in 1587; the attempted invasion of England by Spain, which culminated in the celebrated defeat of the Spanish Armada in 1588; and a Catholic rebellion in Ireland that was suppressed during the Nine Years War (1594–1603). Elizabeth never married, and was succeeded on the throne by James I* following her death in 1603.

English Annotations (1645; 1651; 1657). Under a commission from the Westminster Assembly, the editors of the English Annotations—John Downame* along with unnamed colleagues—translated, collated and digested in a compact and accessible format several significant Continental biblical resources, including Calvin's* commentaries, Beza's* *Annotationes majores* and Diodati's* *Annotations.*

Desiderius Erasmus (1466–1536). Dutch Catholic humanist and pedagogue. Erasmus, a celebrated humanist scholar, was recognized for translations of ancient texts, reform of education according to classical studies, moral and spiritual writings and the first printed edition of the Greek New Testament. A former Augustinian who never left the Catholic Church, Erasmus addressed deficiencies he saw in the church and society, challenging numerous prevailing doctrines but advocating reform. He envisioned a simple, spiritual Christian life shaped by the teachings of Jesus and ancient wisdom. He was often accused of collusion with Martin Luther* on account of some resonance of their ideas but hotly debated Luther on human will.

Paul Fagius (1504–1549). German Reformed Hebraist and pastor. After studying at the University of Heidelberg, Fagius went to Strasbourg where he perfected his Hebrew under Wolfgang Capito.* In Isny im Allgäu (Baden-Württemberg) he met the great Jewish grammarian Elias Levita (1469–1549), with whom he established a Hebrew printing press. In 1544 Fagius returned to Strasbourg, succeeding Capito as preacher and Old Testament lecturer. During the Augsburg Interim, Fagius (with Martin Bucer*) accepted Thomas Cranmer's* invitation to translate and interpret the Bible at Cambridge. However, Fagius died before he could begin any of the work. Fagius wrote commentaries on the first four chapters of Genesis and the deuterocanonical books of Sirach and Tobit.

Guillaume Farel (1489–1565) French Reformed preacher and theologian. At the vanguard of the French Reformation, Farel was a student of Jacques Lefèvre d'Étaples* and member of Archbishop Briçonnet's* circle in Meaux until his desire for more rapid change saw him depart in 1523 to preach the Protestant message in Basel, Montbéliard, Strasbourg, Bern, and Aigle. During this period of his ministry, he composed the first French Protestant book, an evangelical commentary on the Lord's Prayer and the Apostle's Creed, as well as the first French Confession of Faith. A catalyst in Geneva's acceptance of the Reformation in 1536, it was Farel who persuaded Calvin* to settle in the city. After he and Calvin were banished from Geneva in 1538, Farel accepted the pastorate in Neuchâtel, a position he held until his death while continuing to travel and support the Reformation in the French-speaking lands.

John Fary (unknown). English Puritan pastor. Fary authored *God's Severity on Man's Sterility* (1645), a sermon on the fruitless fig tree in Luke 13:6-9.

William Fenner (1600–1640). English Puritan pastor. After studying at Cambridge and Oxford, Fenner ministered at Sedgley and Rochford. Fenner's extant writings, which primarily deal with practical and devotional topics, demonstrate a zealous Puritan piety and a keen interest in Scripture and theology.

First Helvetic Confession (1536). Anticipating the planned church council at Mantua (1537, but delayed until 1545 at Trent), Reformed theologians of the Swiss cantons drafted a confession to distinguish themselves from both Catholics and the churches of the Augsburg Confession.* Heinrich Bullinger* led the discussion and wrote the confession itself; Leo Jud, Oswald Myconius, Simon Grynaeus and others were part of the assembly. Martin Bucer* and Wolfgang Capito* had desired to draw the Lutheran and Reformed communions closer together through this document, but Luther* proved unwilling after Bullinger refused to accept the Wittenberg Concord (1536). This confession was largely eclipsed by Bullinger's Second Helvetic Confession.*

John Fisher (1469–1535). English Catholic bishop and theologian. This reputed preacher defended Catholic orthodoxy and strove to reform abuses in the church. In 1521 Henry VIII honored Fisher with the title *Fidei Defensor* ("defender of the faith"). Nevertheless, Fisher opposed the king's divorce of Catherine of Aragon (1485–1536) and the independent establishment of the Church of England; he was convicted for treason and executed. Most of Fisher's works are polemical and occasional (e.g., on transubstantiation, against Martin Luther*); however, he also published a series of sermons on the seven penitential psalms. In addition to his episcopal duties, Fisher was the chancellor of Cambridge from 1504 until his death.

Matthias Flacius (1520–1575). Lutheran theologian. A native of Croatia, Matthias Flacius commenced his studies at the University of Tubingen, and completed them at Wittenberg, where through Luther's influence, he embraced the university's evangelical theology. Flacius began his career as instructor of Hebrew at the University of Wittenberg in 1544, and remained in this post until 1549. As a devoted follower of Luther's teachings, Flacius sought to defend them in their purity which drove him and Nikolaus von Amsdorf as leaders of the Gnesio-Lutherans to oppose the more moderate positions of Philip Melanchthon and his sympathizers, the Philippists, in several controversies concerning the role of free will and good works in justification as well as relations with Calvinism. After serving as a professor at the University of Jena (1557–1561), Flacius spent the remainder of his life as an independent scholar, frequently moving from one city to another to escape persecution. Flacius died in Frankfurt am Main in 1575. His important exegetical works are *De vocabula Dei* (1549), *Clavis Scripturae Sacrae* (1567), and *Glossa Novi Testamenti* (1570). Flacius also published two historical works, *Catalogus Testium Veritatis* (1556) and the *Magdeburg Centuries*.

John Flavel (c. 1630–1691). English Puritan pastor. Trained at Oxford, Flavel ministered in southwest England from 1650 until the Act of Uniformity in 1662, which reaffirmed the compulsory use of the Book of Common Prayer. Flavel preached unofficially for many years, until his congregation was eventually allowed to build a meeting place in 1687. His works were numerous, varied and popular.

Giovanni Battista Folengo (1490–1559). Italian Catholic exegete. In 1528 Folengo left the Benedictine order, questioning the validity of monastic vows; he returned to the monastic life in 1534. During this hiatus Folengo came into contact with the Neapolitan reform-minded circle founded by Juan de Valdés.* Folengo published commentaries on the Psalms, John, 1–2 Peter and James. Augustin Marlorat* included Folengo's comment in his anthology of exegesis on the Psalms. In 1580 Folengo's Psalms commentary was added to the Index of Prohibited Books.

Formula of Concord (1577). After Luther's* death, intra-Lutheran controversies between the Gnesio-Lutherans (partisans of Luther) and the Philippists (partisans of Melanchthon*) threatened to cause a split among those who had subscribed to the Augsburg Confession.* In 1576, Jakob Andreae,* Martin Chemnitz,* Nikolaus Selnecker,* David Chytraeus* and Andreas Musculus (1514–1581) met with the intent of resolving the controversies, which mainly regarded the relationship between good works and salvation, the third use of the law, and the role of the human will in accepting God's grace. In 1580, celebrating the fiftieth anniversary of the presentation of the Augsburg Confession to Charles V (1500–1558), the *Book of Concord* was printed as the authoritative interpretation of the Augsburg Confession; it included the three ancient creeds, the Augsburg Confession, its Apology (1531), the Schmalkald Articles,* Luther's *Treatise on the Power and Primacy of the Pope* (1537) and both his Small and Large Catechisms (1529).

Sebastian Franck (1499–1542). German Radical theologian. Franck became a Lutheran in 1525, but by 1529 he began to develop ideas that distanced him from Protestants and Catholics. Expelled from Strasbourg and later Ulm due to his controversial writings, Franck spent the end of his life in Basel. Franck emphasized God's word as a divine internal spark that cannot be adequately expressed in outward forms. Thus he criticized religious institutions and dogmas. His work consists mostly of commentaries, compilations and translations. In his sweeping historical *Chronica* (1531), Franck supported numerous heretics condemned by the Catholic Church and criticized political and church authorities.

Leonhard Frick (d. 1528). Austrian Radical martyr. See *Kunstbuch*.

Gallic Confession (1559). This confession was accepted at the first National Synod of the Reformed Churches of France (1559). It was intended to be a touchstone of Reformed faith but also to show to the people of France that the Huguenots—who faced persecution—were not seditious. The French Reformed Church presented this confession to Francis II (1544–1560) in 1560, and to his successor, Charles IX (1550–1574), in 1561. The later Genevan draft, likely written by Calvin,* Beza* and Pierre Viret (1511–1571), was received as the true Reformed confession at the seventh National Synod in La Rochelle (1571).

Geneva Bible (originally printed 1560). During Mary I's reign many English Protestants sought safety abroad in Reformed territories of the Empire and the Swiss Cantons, especially in Calvin's* Geneva. A team of English exiles in Geneva led by William Whittingham (c. 1524–1579) brought this complete translation to press in the course of two years. Notable for several innovations—Roman type, verse numbers, italics indicating English idiom and not literal phrasing of the original languages, even variant readings in the Gospels and Acts—this translation is most well known for its marginal notes, which reflect a strongly Calvinist theology. The notes explained Scripture in an accessible way for the laity, also giving unlearned clergy a new sermon resource. Although controversial because of its implicit critique of royal power, this translation was wildly popular; even after the publication of the Authorized Version (1611) and James I's 1616 ban on its printing, the Geneva Bible continued to be the most popular English translation until after the English Civil Wars.

Johann Gerhard (1582–1637). German Lutheran theologian, professor and superintendent. Gerhard is considered one of the most eminent Lutheran theologians, after Martin Luther* and Martin Chemnitz.* After studying patristics and Hebrew at Wittenberg, Jena and Marburg, Gerhard was appointed superintendent at the age of twenty-four. In 1616 he was appointed to a post at the University of Jena, where he reintroduced Aristotelian metaphysics to theology and gained widespread fame. His most important work was the nine-volume *Loci Theologici* (1610–1625). He also expanded Chemnitz's harmony of the Gospels (*Harmonia Evangelicae*), which was finally published by Polykarp Leyser (1552–1610) in 1593. Gerhard was well-known for an irenic spirit and an ability to communicate clearly.

George Gifford (c. 1548–1600). English Puritan pastor. Gifford was suspended for nonconformity in 1584. With private support, however, he was able to continue his ministry. Through his published works he wanted to help develop lay piety and biblical literacy.

Anthony Gilby (c. 1510–1585). English Puritan translator. During Mary I's reign, Gilby fled to Geneva, where he assisted William Whittingham (c. 1524–1579) with the Geneva Bible.* He returned to England to pastor after Elizabeth I's accession. In addition to translating numerous continental Reformed works into English—especially those of John Calvin* and Theodore Beza*—Gilby also wrote commentaries on Micah and Malachi.

Bernard Gilpin (1517–1583). Anglican theologian and priest. In public disputations, Gilpin defended Roman Catholic theology against John Hooper (c. 1495-1555) and Peter Martyr Vermigli.* These debates caused Gilpin to reexamine his faith. Upon Mary I's accession, Gilpin resigned his benefice. He sojourned in Belgium and France, returning to pastoral ministry in England in 1556. Gilpin dedicated himself to a preaching circuit in northern England, thus earning the moniker "the Apostle to the North." His zealous preaching and almsgiving roused royal opposition and a warrant for his arrest. On his way to the queen's commission, Gilpin fractured his leg, delaying his arrival in London until after Mary's death and thus likely saving his life. His only extant writing is a sermon on Luke 2 confronting clerical abuses.

Glossa ordinaria. This standard collection of biblical commentaries consists of interlinear and marginal notes drawn from patristic and Carolingian exegesis appended to the Vulgate*; later editions also include Nicholas of Lyra's* *Postilla*. The *Glossa ordinaria* and the *Sentences* of Peter Lombard (c. 1100–1160) were essential resources for all late medieval and early modern commentators.

Simon Goulart (1543–1628) French Reformed pastor, translator, and theologian. Goulart spent most of his career as a pastor in Geneva and its surrounds, particularly at the city parish of St. Gervais, and was the leader of the Company of Pastors during the last decades of his life. A prolific translator, he published numerous French editions of classical, patristic, and contemporary works from diverse authors including Plutarch, Seneca, Chrysostom, Cyprian, Tertullian, Beza*, Perkins* and Vermigli*. He also composed numerous devotional writings, important histories of early French Protestantism, and polemical treatises supporting the Huguenot cause.

Conrad Grebel (c. 1498–1526). Swiss Radical theologian. Grebel, considered the father of the Anabaptist movement, was one of the first defenders and performers of believers' baptism, for which he was eventually imprisoned in Zurich. One of Huldrych Zwingli's* early compatriots, Grebel advocated rapid, radical reform, clashing publicly with the civil authorities and Zwingli. Grebel's views, particularly on baptism, were influenced by Andreas Bodenstein von Karlstadt* and Thomas Müntzer.* Grebel advocated elimination of magisterial involvement in governing the church; instead, he envisioned the church as lay Christians determining their own affairs with strict adherence to the biblical text, and unified in volitional baptism.

William Greenhill (1591–1671). English Puritan pastor. Greenhill attended and worked at Magdalen College. He ministered in the diocese of Norwich but soon left for London, where he preached at Stepney. Greenhill was a member of the Westminster Assembly of Divines and was appointed the parliament chaplain by the children of Charles I. Oliver Cromwell included him among the preachers who helped draw up the Savoy Declaration. Greenhill was evicted from his post following the Restoration, after which he pastored independently. Among Greenhill's most significant contributions to church history was his *Exposition of the Prophet of Ezekiel*.

Catharina Regina von Greiffenberg (1633–1694). Austrian Lutheran poet. Upon her adulthood her guardian (and half uncle) sought to marry her; despite her protests of their consanguinity and her desire to remain celibate, she relented in 1664. After the deaths of her mother and husband, Greiffenberg abandoned her home to debtors and joined her friends Susanne Popp (d. 1683) and Sigmund von Birken (1626–1681) in Nuremberg. During her final years she dedicated herself to studying the biblical languages and to writing meditations on Jesus' death and resurrection, which she never completed. One of the most important and learned Austrian poets of the Baroque period, Greiffenberg published a collection of sonnets, songs and poems (1662) as well as three sets of mystical meditations on Jesus' life, suffering and death (1672; 1683; 1693). She participated in a society of poets called the Ister Gesellschaft.

Argula von Grumbach (c. 1490–c. 1564) German Lutheran noblewoman. Grumbach, an attendant of Queen Kunigunde of Austria (1465–1520), was one of the first women to publish in support of the Reformation. She is best known for letters from 1523 and 1524 written in defense of Arsacius Seehofer (1503–1545), a lecturer at the university of Ingolstadt accused of Lutheranism. For unknown reasons, Grumberg ceased to publish after 1524, although her private correspondence after this time demonstrates a continued effort to support evangelical reform.

Rudolf Gwalther (1519–1586). Swiss Reformed preacher. Gwalther was a consummate servant of the Reformed church in Zurich, its chief religious officer and preacher, a responsibility fulfilled previously by Huldrych Zwingli* and Heinrich Bullinger.* Gwalther provided sermons and commentaries and translated the works of Zwingli into Latin. He worked for many years alongside Bullinger in structuring and governing the church in Zurich. Gwalther also strove to strengthen the connections to the Reformed churches on the Continent and England: he was a participant in the Colloquy of Regensburg (1541) and an opponent of the Formula of Concord.*

Hans Has von Hallstatt (d. 1527). Austrian Reformed pastor. See *Kunstbuch*.

Henry Hammond (1605–1660). Anglican priest. After completing his studies at Oxford, Hammond was ordained in 1629. A Royalist, Hammond helped recruit soldiers for the king; he was chaplain to Charles I. During the king's captivity, Hammond was imprisoned for not submitting to Parliament. Later he was allowed to pastor again, until his death. Hammond published a catechism, numerous polemical sermons and treatises as well as his *Paraphrase and Annotations on the New Testament* (1653).

Jörg Haug (Unknown) German Anabaptist leader. Haug was a radical preacher during the 1525 Peasant's Revolt and composed a tract entitled *A Christian Order of a True Christian* (1524) enumerating seven degrees of faith reached by Christians.

Peter Hausted (d. 1645). Anglican priest and playwright. Educated at Cambridge and Oxford, Hausted ministered in a number of parishes and preached adamantly and vehemently against Puritanism. He is best known for his play *The Rival Friends*, which is filled with invective against the Puritans; during a performance before the king and queen, a riot nearly broke out. Haustead died during the siege of Banbury Castle.

Heidelberg Catechism (1563). This German Reformed catechism was commissioned by the elector of the Palatinate, Frederick III (1515–1576) for pastors and teachers in his territories to use in instructing children and new believers in the faith. It was written by theologian Zacharias Ursinus (1534–1583) in consultation with Frederick's court preacher Kaspar Olevianus* and the entire theology faculty at the University of Heidelberg. The Heidelberg Catechism was accepted as one of the Dutch Reformed Church's Three Forms of Unity—along with the Belgic Confession* and the Canons of Dordrecht—at the Synod of Dordrecht,* and became widely popular among other Reformed confessional traditions throughout Europe.

Niels Hemmingsen (1513–1600). Danish Lutheran theologian. Hemmingsen studied at the University of Wittenberg, where he befriended Philipp Melanchthon.* In 1542, Hemmingsen returned to Denmark to pastor and to teach Greek, dialectics and theology at the University of Copenhagen. Foremost of the Danish theologians, Hemmingsen oversaw the preparation and publication of the first Danish Bible (1550). Later in his career he became embroiled in controversies because of his Philippist theology, especially regarding the Eucharist. Due to rising tensions with Lutheran nobles outside of Denmark, King Frederick II (1534–1588) dismissed Hemmingsen from his university post in 1579, transferring him to a prominent but less internationally visible Cathedral outside of Copenhagen. Hemmingsen was a prolific author, writing commentaries on the New Testament and Psalms, sermon collections and several methodological, theological and pastoral handbooks.

King Henry VIII of England (1491–1547). English monarch. The second son of Henry VII (r. 1485–1509) and Elizabeth of York (1466–1503), Henry VIII succeeded his father to the English throne, his elder brother Edward having died in 1502. Soon after accession, he married his brother's widow, Catherine of Aragon (1485–

1536). Following several stillbirths and the birth of a daughter, Mary, Henry, who was desperate for a male heir to head off dynastic challenges, wished separation from Catherine in order to marry Anne Boleyn (c. 1501–1536). Believing his marriage cursed as it transgressed the commands in Leviticus against marrying a brother's widow, Henry sought dispensation from the church for his annulment and remarriage. While the case was first heard by a papal legate in England, it was transferred to Rome upon the order of Pope Clement VII*, who wished to placate Charles V, Catherine's nephew, whose troops had recently sacked Rome and held the pope under house arrest. Henry asserted praemunire, arguing that as king, he was supreme in his own kingdom. With the formation of the Reformation Parliament in 1529, the legislative process to disentangle the English Church from the Roman was begun. The issue of Henry's divorce was finalized in 1533, after Thomas Cranmer* became Archbishop of Canterbury and declared his marriage to Catherine invalid. While Henry's divorce, assertion of royal supremacy, and subversion of Catholic institutions gave impetus to English Protestantism, Henry's beliefs remained essentially Catholic, and these continued to be enforced by law. He ultimately married six times, and was succeeded by Edward VI*, his son by his third wife, Jane Seymour (1508–1537). Elizabeth I*, Henry's daughter by Anne Boleyn, later became Queen and with the Elizabethan Settlement in 1559, redefined England as a Protestant country.

Tilemann Hesshus (1527–1588). German Lutheran theologian and pastor. Hesshus studied under Philipp Melanchthon* but was a staunch Gnesio-Lutheran. With great hesitation—and later regret—he affirmed the Formula of Concord.* Heshuss ardently advocated for church discipline, considering obedience a mark of the church. Unwilling to compromise his strong convictions, especially regarding matters of discipline, Hesshus was regularly embroiled in controversy. He was expelled or pressed to leave Goslar, Rostock, Heidelberg, Bremen, Magdeburg, Wesel, Königsberg and Samland before settling in Helmstedt, where he remained until his death. He wrote numerous polemical tracts concerning ecclesiology, justification, the sacraments and original sin, as well as commentaries on Psalms, Romans, 1–2 Corinthians, Galatians, Colossians and 1–2 Timothy, and a postil collection.

Cornelis Hoen (c. 1460–1524). Dutch humanist, jurist, and theologian. A lawyer at the Court of Holland at the Hague, Hoen was prosecuted in 1523 over his sympathy for the evangelical message. He proposed a symbolic interpretation of Christ's presence in the Eucharist justified with reference to Matthew 24:23 in an influential, posthumously-published treatise.

Melchior Hoffman (1495?–1543). German Anabaptist preacher. First appearing as a Lutheran lay preacher in Livonia in 1523, Hoffman's claim to direct revelation, his perfectionist teachings and his announcements that the end of the world would occur in 1533 saw him alienated from both Lutheran and Reformed circles. After converting to Anabaptism in Strasbourg in 1530, a city he claimed would rise as the spiritual Jerusalem, Hoffman escaped brief arrest and fled to the Netherlands, where his preaching made him the first to bring the radical faith to the Low Countries. Believing himself to be Elijah, Hoffman gathered numerous followers, including future Anabaptist leaders Obbe Philips* and Jan Mathijs (d. 1534), until his arrest in Strasbourg in 1533, whereupon he was imprisoned for the final decade of his life. A tendency toward mystical allegory and apocalyptic exegesis supported by direct revelation is found in his writings, which include commentaries on Romans, Revelation, and Daniel 12 alongside numerous tracts, pamphlets, and letters.

Christopher Hooke (unknown). English Puritan physician and pastor. Hooke published a treatise promoting the joys and blessings of childbirth (1590) and a sermon on Hebrews 12:11-12. To support the poor, Hooke proposed a bank funded by voluntary investment of wealthy households.

Richard Hooker (c. 1553–1600). Anglican priest. Shortly after graduating from Corpus Christi College Oxford, Hooker took holy orders as a priest in 1581. After his marriage, he struggled to find work and temporarily tended sheep until Archbishop John Whitgift* appointed him to the Temple Church in London. Hooker's primary work is *The Laws of Ecclesiastical Polity* (1593), in which he sought to establish a philosophical and logical foundation for the highly controversial Elizabethan Religious Settlement (1559). The Elizabethan Settlement, through the Act of Supremacy, reasserted the Church of England's independence from the Church of Rome, and, through the Act of Uniformity, constructed a common church structure based on the reinstitution of the Book of Common Prayer.* Hooker's argumentation strongly emphasizes natural law and anticipates the social contract theory of John Locke (1632–1704).

John Hooper (d. 1555). English Protestant bishop and martyr. Impressed by the works of Huldrych Zwingli* and Heinrich Bullinger,* Hooper joined the Protestant movement in England. However, after the Act of Six Articles was passed, he fled to Zurich, where he spent ten years. He returned to England in 1549 and was appointed as a bishop. He stoutly advocated a Zwinglian reform agenda, arguing against the use of vestments and for a less "popish" Book of Common Prayer.* Condemned as a heretic for denying transubstantiation, Hooper was burned at the stake during Mary I's reign.

Rudolf Hospinian (Wirth) (1547–1626). Swiss Reformed theologian and minister. After studying theology at Marburg and Heidelberg, Hospinian pastored in rural parishes around Zurich and taught secondary school. In 1588, he transferred to Zurich, ministering at Grossmünster and Fraumünster. A keen student of church history, Hospinian wanted to show the differences between early church doctrine and contemporary Catholic teaching, particularly with regard to sacramental theology. He also criticized Lutheran dogma and the Formula of Concord*. Most of Hospinian's corpus consists of polemical treatises; he also published a series of sermons on the Magnificat.

Caspar Huberinus (1500–1553). German Lutheran theologian and pastor. After studying theology at Wittenberg, Huberinus moved to Augsburg to serve as Urbanus Rhegius's* assistant. Huberinus represented Augsburg at the Bern Disputation (1528) on the Eucharist and images. In 1551, along with the nobility, Huberinus supported the Augsburg Interim, so long as communion of both kinds and regular preaching were allowed. Nevertheless the people viewed him as a traitor because of his official participation in the Interim, nicknaming him "Buberinus" (i.e., scoundrel). He wrote a number of popular devotional works as well as tracts defending Lutheran eucharistic theology against Zwinglian and Anabaptist detractions.

Balthasar Hubmaier (1480/5–1528). German Radical theologian. Hubmaier, a former priest who studied under Johann Eck,* is identified with his leadership in the peasants' uprising at Waldshut. Hubmaier served as the cathedral preacher in Regensberg, where he became involved in a series of anti-Semitic attacks. He was drawn to reform through the early works of Martin Luther*; his contact with Huldrych Zwingli* made Hubmaier a defender of more radical reform, including believers' baptism and a memorialist account of the Eucharist. His involvement in the Peasants' War led to his extradition and execution by the Austrians.

Aegidius Hunnius (1550–1603). German Lutheran theologian and preacher. Educated at Tübingen by Jakob Andreae (1528–1590) and Johannes Brenz,* Hunnius bolstered and advanced early Lutheran orthodoxy. After his crusade to root out all "crypto-Calvinism" divided Hesse into Lutheran and Reformed regions, Hunnius joined the Wittenberg theological faculty, where with Polykarp Leyser (1552–1610) he helped shape the university into an orthodox stronghold. Passionately confessional, Hunnius developed and nuanced the orthodox doctrines of predestination, Scripture, the church and Christology (more explicitly Chalcedonian), reflecting their codification in the Formula of Concord.* He was unafraid to engage in confessional polemics from the pulpit. In addition to his many treatises (most notably *De persona Christi*, in which he defended Christ's ubiquity), Hunnius published commentaries on Matthew, John, Ephesians and Colossians; his notes on Galatians, Philemon and 1 Corinthians were published posthumously.

Jan Hus (d. 1415). Bohemian reformer and martyr. This popular preacher strove for reform in the church, moral improvement in society, and an end to clerical abuses and popular religious superstition. He was branded a heretic for his alleged affinity for John Wycliffe's writings; however, while he agreed that a priest in mortal sin rendered the sacraments inefficacious, he affirmed the doctrine of transubstantiation. The Council of Constance* convicted Hus of heresy, banned his books and teaching, and, despite a letter of safe conduct, burned him at the stake.

Hans Hut (1490–1527). German Radical leader. Hut was an early leader of a mystical, apocalyptic strand of Anabaptist radical reform. His theological views were shaped by Andreas Bodenstein von Karlstadt,* Thomas Müntzer* and Hans Denck,* by whom Hut had been baptized. Hut rejected society and the established church and heralded the imminent end of days, which he perceived in the Peasants' War. Eventually arrested for practicing believers' baptism and participating in the Peasants' War, Hut was tortured and died accidentally in a fire in the Augsburg prison. The next day, the authorities sentenced his corpse to death and burned him.

George Hutcheson (1615–1674). Scottish Puritan pastor. Hutcheson, a pastor in Edinburgh, published commentaries on Job, John and the Minor Prophets, as well as sermons on Psalm 130.

Roger Hutchinson (d. 1555). English reformer. Little is known about Hutchinson except for his controversies. He disputed against the Mass while at Cambridge and debated with Joan Bocher (d. 1550), who affirmed the doctrine of the celestial flesh. During the Marian Restoration he was deprived of his fellowship at Eton because he was married.

Andreas Hyperius (1511–1564). Dutch Protestant theologian. A peripatetic student, Hyperius moved through Germany, France, Italy and England until settling in Marburg as professor of theology in 1541. Alongside commentaries on Romans and Hebrews, he composed texts on homiletics, the use of the church fathers, practical piety, and church administration.

Abraham Ibn Ezra (1089–c. 1167). Spanish Jewish rabbi, exegete and poet. In 1140 Ibn Ezra fled his native Spain to escape persecution by the Almohad Caliphate. He spent the rest of his life as an exile, traveling through Europe, North Africa and the Middle East. His corpus consists of works on poetry, exegesis, grammar, philosophy, mathematics and astrology. In his commentaries on the Old Testament, Ibn Ezra restricts himself to *peshat* (see *quadriga*).

Valentin Ickelshamer (c. 1500–1547). German Radical teacher. After time at Erfurt, he studied under Luther,* Melanchthon,* Bugenhagen* and Karlstadt* in Wittenberg. He sided with Karlstadt against Luther, writing a treatise in Karlstadt's defense. Ickelshamer also represented the Wittenberg guilds in opposition to the city council. This guild committee allied with the peasants in 1525, leading to Ickelshamer's eventual exile. His poem in the Marpeck Circle's *Kunstbuch** is an expansion of a similar poem by Sebastian Franck.*

Thomas Jackson (1579–1640). Anglican theologian and priest. Before serving as the president of Corpus Christi College at Oxford for the final decade of his life, Jackson was a parish priest and chaplain to the king. His best known work is a twelve-volume commentary on the Apostles' Creed.

King James I of England (VI of Scotland) (1566–1625). English monarch. The son of Mary, Queen of Scots, James ascended to the Scottish throne in 1567 following his mother's abdication. In the Union of the Crowns (1603), he took the English and Irish thrones after the death of his cousin, Elizabeth I. James's reign was tumultuous and tense: Parliament and the nobility often opposed him, church factions squabbled over worship forms and ecclesiology, climaxing in the Gunpowder Plot. James wrote treatises on the divine right of kings, law, the evils of smoking tobacco and demonology. His religious writings include a versification of the Psalms, a paraphrase of Revelation and meditations on the Lord's Prayer and passages from Chronicles, Matthew and Revelation. He also sponsored the translation of the Authorized Version*—popularly remembered as the King James Version.

John Jewel (1522–1571). Anglican theologian and bishop. Jewel studied at Oxford where he met Peter Martyr Vermigli.* After graduating in 1552, Jewel was appointed to his first vicarage and became the orator for the university. Upon Mary I's accession, Jewel lost his post as orator because of his Protestant views. After the trials of Thomas Cranmer* and Nicholas Ridley,* Jewel affirmed Catholic teaching to avoid their fate. Still he had to flee to the continent. Confronted by John Knox,* Jewel publicly repented of his cowardice before the English congregation in Frankfurt, then reunited with Vermigli in Strasbourg. After Mary I's death, Jewel returned to England and was consecrated bishop in 1560. He advocated low-church ecclesiology, but supported the Elizabethan Settlement against Catholics and Puritans. In response to the Council of Trent, he published the *Apoligia ecclesiae Anglicanae* (1562), which established him as the apostle for Anglicanism and incited numerous controversies.

Justus Jonas (1493–1555). German Lutheran theologian, pastor and administrator. Jonas studied law at Erfurt, where he befriended the poet Eobanus Hessus (1488–1540), whom Luther* dubbed "king of the poets"; later, under the influence of the humanist Konrad Muth, Jonas focused on theology. In 1516 he was ordained as a priest, and in 1518 he became a doctor of theology and law. After witnessing the Leipzig Disputation, Jonas was converted to Luther's* cause. While traveling with Luther to the Diet of Worms, Jonas was appointed professor of canon law at Wittenberg. Later he became its dean of theology, lecturing on Romans, Acts and the Psalms. Jonas was also instrumental for reform in Halle. He preached Luther's funeral sermon but had a falling-out with Melanchthon* over the Leipzig Interim. Jonas's most influential contribution was translating Luther's *The Bondage of the Will* and Melanchthon's *Loci communes* into German.

William Jones (1561–1636). Anglican minister and theologian. After teaching at Cambridge, Jones ministered at East Bergholt in Suffolk for forty-four years, publishing a commentary on Philemon and Hebrews and tracts on suffering, the nativity, and arrangements to be made before one's death.

David Joris (c. 1501–1556). Dutch Radical pastor and hymnist. This former glass painter was one of the leading Dutch Anabaptist leaders after the fall of Münster (1535), although due to his increasingly radical ideas his influence waned in the early 1540s. Joris came to see himself as a "third David," a Spirit-anointed prophet ordained to proclaim the coming third kingdom of God, which would be established in the Netherlands with Dutch as its *lingua franca*. Joris's interpretation of Scripture, with his heavy emphasis on personal mystical experience, led to a very public dispute with Menno Simons* whom Joris considered a teacher of the "dead letter." In 1544 Joris and about one hundred followers moved to Basel, conforming outwardly to the teaching of the Reformed church there. Today 240 of Joris's books are extant, the most important of which is his *Twonder Boek* (1542/43).

Andreas Bodenstein von Karlstadt (Carlstadt) (1486–1541). German Radical theologian. Karlstadt, an early associate of Martin Luther* and Philipp Melanchthon* at the University of Wittenberg, participated alongside Luther in the dispute at Leipzig with Johann Eck.* He also influenced the configuration of the Old Testament canon in Protestantism. During Luther's captivity in Wartburg Castle in Eisenach, Karlstadt oversaw reform in Wittenberg. His acceleration of the pace of reform brought conflict with Luther, so Karlstadt left Wittenberg, eventually settling at the University of Basel as professor of Old Testament (after a sojourn in Zurich with Huldrych Zwingli*). During his time in Switzerland, Karlstadt opposed infant baptism and repudiated Luther's doctrine of Christ's real presence in the Eucharist.

Edward Kellett (d. 1641). Anglican theologian and priest. Kellett published a sermon concerning the reconversion of an Englishman from Islam, a tract on the soul and a discourse on the Lord's Supper in connection with Passover.

David Kimchi (Radak) (1160–1235). French Jewish rabbi, exegete and philosopher. Kimchi wrote an important Hebrew grammar and dictionary, as well as commentaries on Genesis, 1–2 Chronicles, the Psalms and the Prophets. He focused on *peshat* (see *quadriga*). In his Psalms commentary he attacks Christian interpretation as forced, irrational and inadmissible. While Sebastian Münster* censors and condemns these arguments in his *Miqdaš YHWH* (1534–1535), he and many other Christian commentators valued Kimchi's work as a grammatical resource.

Moses Kimchi (Remak) (1127–1190). French Jewish rabbi and exegete. He was David Kimchi's* brother. He wrote commentaries on Proverbs and Ezra-Nehemiah. Sebastian Münster* translated Kimchi's concise Hebrew grammar into Latin; many sixteenth-century Christian exegetes used this resource.

John Knox (1513–1572). Scottish Reformed preacher. Knox, a fiery preacher to monarchs and zealous defender of high Calvinism, was a leading figure of reform in Scotland. Following imprisonment in the French galleys, Knox went to England, where he became a royal chaplain to Edward VI. At the accession of Mary, Knox fled to Geneva, studying under John Calvin* and serving as a pastor. Knox returned to Scotland after Mary's death and became a chief architect of the reform of the Scottish church (Presbyterian), serving as one of the authors of the Book of Discipline and writing many pamphlets and sermons.

Antonius Broickwy von Königstein (1470–1541). German Catholic preacher. Very little is known about this important cathedral preacher in Cologne. Strongly opposed to evangelicals, he sought to develop robust resources for Catholic homilies. His postils were bestsellers, and his biblical concordance helped Catholic preachers to construct doctrinal loci from Scripture itself.

Kunstbuch. In 1956, two German students rediscovered this unique collection of Anabaptist works. Four hundred years earlier, a friend of the recently deceased Pilgram Marpeck*—the painter Jörg Probst—had entrusted this collection of letters, tracts and poetry to a Zurich bindery; today only half of it remains. Probst's redaction arranges various compositions from the Marpeck Circle into a devotional anthology focused on the theme of the church as Christ incarnate (cf. Gal 2:20).

Osmund Lake (c. 1543–1621). English Pastor who ministered at Ringwood in Hampshire.

François Lambert (Lambert of Avignon) (1487–1530). French Reformed theologian. In 1522, after becoming drawn to the writings of Martin Luther* and meeting Huldrych Zwingli,* Lambert left the Franciscan order. He spent time in Wittenberg, Strasbourg, and Hesse, where Lambert took a leading role at the Homberg Synod (1526) and in creating a biblically based plan for church reform. He served as professor of theology at Marburg University from 1527 to his death. After the Marburg Colloquy (1529), Lambert accepted Zwingli's symbolic view of the Eucharist. Lambert produced nineteen books, mostly biblical commentaries that favored spiritual interpretations; his unfinished work of comprehensive theology was published posthumously.

Hugh Latimer (c. 1485–1555). Anglican bishop and preacher. Latimer was celebrated for his sermons critiquing the idolatrous nature of Catholic practices and the social injustices visited on the underclass by the aristocracy and the individualism of Protestant government. After his support for Henry's petition of divorce he served as a court preacher under Henry VIII and Edward VI. Latimer became a proponent of reform following his education at Cambridge University and received license as a preacher.

Following Edward's death, Latimer was tried for heresy, perishing at the stake with Nicholas Ridley* and Thomas Cranmer.*

William Laud (1573–1645). Anglican archbishop, one of the most pivotal and controversial figures in Anglican church history. Early in his career, Laud offended many with his highly traditional, anti-Puritan approach to ecclesial policies. After his election as Archbishop of Canterbury in 1633, Laud continued to strive against the Puritans, demanding the eastward placement of the Communion altar (affirming the religious centrality of the Eucharist), the use of clerical garments, the reintroduction of stained-glass windows, and the uniform use of the Book of Common Prayer.* Laud was accused of being a crypto-Catholic—an ominous accusation during the protracted threat of invasion by the Spanish Armada. In 1640 the Long Parliament met, quickly impeached Laud on charges of treason, and placed him in jail for several years before his execution.

Ludwig Lavater (1527–1586). Swiss Reformed pastor and theologian. Under his father-in-law Heinrich Bullinger,* Lavater became an archdeacon in Zurich. In 1585 he succeeded Rudolf Gwalther* as the city's Antistes. He authored a widely disseminated book on demonology, commentaries on Chronicles, Proverbs, Ecclesiastes, Nehemiah and Ezekiel, theological works, and biographies of Bullinger and Konrad Pellikan.*

John Lawson (unknown). Seventeenth-century English Puritan. Lawson wrote *Gleanings and Expositions of Some of Scripture* (1646) and a treatise on the sabbath in the New Testament.

Jacques Lefèvre d'Étaples (Faber Stapulensis) (1460?–1536). French Catholic humanist, publisher and translator. Lefèvre d'Étaples studied classical literature and philosophy, as well as patristic and medieval mysticism. He advocated the principle of *ad fontes*, issuing a full-scale annotation on the corpus of Aristotle, publishing the writings of key Christian mystics, and contributing to efforts at biblical translation and commentary. Although he never broke with the Catholic Church, his views prefigured those of Martin Luther,* for which he was condemned by the University of Sorbonne in Paris. He then found refuge in the court of Marguerite d'Angoulême, where he met John Calvin* and Martin Bucer.*

Edward Leigh (1602–1671). English Puritan biblical critic, historian and politician. Educated at Oxford, Leigh's public career included appointments as a Justice of the Peace, an officer in the parliamentary army during the English Civil Wars and a member of Parliament. Although never ordained, Leigh devoted himself to the study of theology and Scripture; he participated in the Westminster Assembly. Leigh published a diverse corpus, including lexicons of Greek, Hebrew and juristic terms, and histories of Roman, Greek and English rulers. His most important theological work is *A Systeme or Body of Divinity* (1662).

John Lightfoot (1602–1675). Anglican priest and biblical scholar. After graduating from Cambridge, Lightfoot was ordained and pastored at several small parishes. He continued to study classics under the support of the politician Rowland Cotton (1581–1634). Siding with the Parliamentarians during the English Civil Wars, Lightfoot relocated to London in 1643. He was one of the original members of the Westminster Assembly, where he defended a moderate Presbyterianism. His best-known work is the six-volume *Horae Hebraicae et Talmudicae* (1658–1677), a verse-by-verse commentary illumined by Hebrew customs, language and the Jewish interpretive tradition.

Wenceslaus Linck (1482–1547). German Lutheran theologian and preacher. As dean of the theology faculty at the University of Wittenberg and successor to Johannes von Staupitz* as the prior of the Augustinian Monastery, Linck worked closely with Martin Luther* and attended the Heidelberg Disputation with him. He replaced Staupitz as vicar-general of the Augustinian order in 1520 in Germany, a capacity in which he pronounced all members free from their vows before renouncing the order himself. After periods of ministry in Munich and Altenburg, Linck settled in Nuremberg, where he became known as an exemplary preacher and an advisor to cities undertaking Protestant reform. He published a significant number of sermons and practical tracts as well as a paraphrase and annotations on the Old Testament.

Lucas Lossius (1508–1582). German Lutheran teacher and musician. While a student at Leipzig and Wittenberg, Lossius was deeply influenced by Melanchthon* and Luther,* who found work for him as Urbanus Rhegius's* secretary. Soon after going to work for Rhegius, Lossius began teaching at a local gymnasium (or secondary school), *Das Johanneum*, eventually becoming its headmaster. Lossius remained at *Das Johanneum* until his death, even turning down appointments to university professorships. A man of varied interests, he wrote on dialectics, music and church history, as well as publishing a postil and a five-volume set of annotations on the New Testament.

Sibrandus Lubbertus (c. 1555–1625). Dutch Reformed theologian. Lubbertis, a key figure in the establishment of orthodox Calvinism in Frisia, studied theology at Wittenburg and Geneva (under Theodore Beza*) before his appointment as professor of theology at the University of Franeker. Throughout his career, Lubbertis advocated for high Calvinist theology, defending it in disputes with representatives of Socinianism, Arminianism and Roman Catholicism. Lubbertis criticized the Catholic theologian Robert Bellarmine and fellow Dutch reformer Jacobus Arminius*; the views of the latter he opposed as a prominent participant in the Synod of Dordrecht.*

Martin Luther (1483–1546). German Lutheran priest, professor and theologian. While a professor in Wittenberg, Luther reinterpreted the doctrine of justification. Convinced that righteousness comes only from God's grace, he disputed the sale of indulgences with the Ninety-five Theses. Luther's positions brought conflict with Rome; his denial of papal authority led to excommunication. He also challenged the Mass, transubstantiation and communion under one kind. Though Luther was condemned by the Diet of Worms, the Elector of Saxony provided him safe haven. Luther returned to Wittenberg with public order collapsing under Andreas Bodenstein von Karlstadt;* Luther steered a more cautious path of reform. His rendering of the Bible and liturgy in the vernacular, as well as his hymns and sermons, proved extensively influential.

Georg Major (1502–1574). German Lutheran theologian. Major was on the theological faculty of the University of Wittenberg, succeeding as dean Johannes Bugenhagen* and Philipp Melanchthon.* One of the chief editors on the Wittenberg edition of Luther's works, Major is most identified with the controversy bearing his name, in which he stated that good works are necessary to salvation. Major qualified his statement, which was in reference to the totality of the Christian life. The Formula of Concord* rejected the statement, ending the controversy. As a theologian, Major further refined Lutheran views of the inspiration of Scripture and the doctrine of the Trinity.

John (Mair) Major (1467–1550). Scottish Catholic philosopher. Major taught logic and theology at the universities of Paris (his alma mater), Glasgow and St Andrews. His broad interests and impressive work drew students from all over Europe. While disapproving of evangelicals (though he did teach John Knox*), Major advocated reform programs for Rome. He supported collegial episcopacy and even challenged the curia's teaching on sexuality. Still he was a nominalist who was critical of humanist approaches to biblical exegesis. His best-known publication is *A History of Greater Britain, Both England and Scotland* (1521), which promoted the union of the kingdoms. He also published a commentary on Peter Lombard's *Sentences* and the Gospel of John.

Juan de Maldonado (1533–1583). Spanish Catholic biblical scholar. A student of Francisco de Toledo,* Maldonado taught philosophy and theology at the universities of Paris and Salamanca. Ordained to the priesthood in Rome, he revised the Septuagint under papal appointment. While Maldonado vehemently criticized Protestants, he asserted that Reformed baptism was valid and that mixed confessional marriages were acceptable. His views on Mary's immaculate conception proved controversial among many Catholics who conflated his statement that it was not an article of faith with its denial. He was intrigued by demonology (blaming demonic influence for the Reformation). All his work was published posthumously; his Gospel commentaries were highly valued and important.

Thomas Manton (1620–1677). English Puritan minister. Manton, educated at Oxford, served for a time as lecturer at Westminster Abbey and rector of St. Paul's, Covent Garden, and was a strong advocate of Presbyterianism. He was known as a rigorous evangelical Calvinist who preached long expository sermons. At different times in his ecclesial career he worked side-by-side with Richard Baxter* and John Owen.* In his later life, Manton's Nonconformist position led to his ejection as a clergyman from the Church of England (1662) and eventual imprisonment (1670). Although a voluminous writer, Manton was best known for his preaching. At his funeral in 1677, he was dubbed "the king of preachers."

Augustin Marlorat (c. 1506–1562). French Reformed pastor. Committed by his family to a monastery at the age of eight, Marlorat was also ordained into the priesthood at an early age in 1524. He fled to Geneva in 1535, where he pastored until the Genevan Company of Pastors sent him to France to shepherd the nascent evangelical congregations. His petition to the young Charles IX (1550–1574) for the right to public evangelical worship was denied. In response to a massacre of evangelicals in Vassy (over sixty dead, many more wounded), Marlorat's congregation planned to overtake Rouen. After the crown captured Rouen, Marlorat was arrested and executed three days later for treason. His principle published work was an anthology of New Testament comment modeled after Thomas Aquinas's *Catena aurea in quatuor Evangelia*. Marlorat harmonized Reformed and Lutheran comment with the church fathers, interspersed with his own brief comments. He also wrote such anthologies for Genesis, Job, the Psalms, Song of Songs and Isaiah.

Pilgram Marpeck (c. 1495–1556). Austrian Radical elder and theologian. During a brief sojourn in Strasbourg, Marpeck debated with Martin Bucer* before the city council; Bucer was declared the winner, and Marpeck was asked to leave Strasbourg for his views concerning paedobaptism (which he compared to a sacrifice to Moloch). After his time in Strasbourg, Marpeck traveled throughout southern Germany and western Austria, planting Anabaptist congregations. Marpeck criticized the strict use of the ban, however, particularly among the Swiss brethren. He also engaged in a christological controversy with Kaspar von Schwenckfeld.*

Johannes Mathesius (1504–1565). German Lutheran theologian and pastor. After reading Martin Luther's* *On Good Works*, Mathesius left his teaching post in Ingolstadt and traveled to Wittenberg to study theology. Mathesius was an important agent of reform in the Bohemian town of Jáchymov, where he pastored, preached and taught. Over one thousand of Mathesius's sermons are extant, including numerous wedding and funeral sermons as well as a series on Luther's life. Mathesius also transcribed portions of Luther's Table Talk.

John Mayer (1583–1664). Anglican priest and biblical exegete. Mayer dedicated much of his life to biblical exegesis, writing a seven-volume commentary on the entire Bible (1627–1653). Styled after Philipp Melanchthon's* *locus* method, Mayer's work avoided running commentary, focusing instead on textual and theological problems. He was a parish priest for fifty-five years. In the office of priest Mayer also wrote a popular catechism, *The English Catechisme, or a Commentarie on the Short Catechisme* (1621), which went through twelve editions in his lifetime.

Joseph Mede (1586–1638). Anglican biblical scholar, Hebraist and Greek lecturer. A man of encyclopedic knowledge, Mede was interested in numerous fields, varying from philology and history to mathematics and physics, although millennial thought and apocalyptic prophesy were clearly his chief interests. Mede's most important work was his *Clavis Apocalyptica* (1627, later translated into English as *The Key of the Revelation*). This work examined the structure of Revelation as the key to its interpretation. Mede saw the visions as a connected and chronological sequence hinging around Revelation 17:18. He is remembered as an important figure in the history of millenarian theology. He was respected as a mild-mannered and generous scholar who avoided controversy and debate, but who had many original thoughts.

Philipp Melanchthon (1497–1560). German Lutheran educator, reformer and theologian. Melanchthon is known as the partner and successor to Martin Luther* in reform in Germany and for his pioneering *Loci communes*, which served as a theological textbook. Melanchthon participated with Luther in the Leipzig disputation, helped implement reform in Wittenberg and was a chief architect of the Augsburg Confession.* Later, Melanchthon and Martin Bucer* worked for union between the reformed and Catholic churches. On account of Melanchthon's more ecumenical disposition and his modification of several of Luther's doctrines, he was held in suspicion by some.

Justus Menius (1499–1558). German Lutheran pastor and theologian. Menius was a prominent reformer in Thuringia. He participated in the Marburg Colloquy and, with others, helped Martin Luther* compose the Schmalkald Articles.* Throughout his career Menius entered into numerous controversies with Anabaptists and even fellow Lutherans. He rejected Andreas Osiander's (d. 1552) doctrine of justification—that the indwelling of Christ's divine nature justifies, rather than the imputed alien righteousness of Christ's person, declared through God's mercy. Against Nikolaus von Amsdorf (1483–1565) and Matthias Flacius (1520–1575), Menius agreed with Georg Major* that good works are necessary to salvation. Osiander's view of justification was censored in Article 3 of the Formula of Concord*; Menius's understanding of the relationship between good works and salvation was rejected in Article 4. Menius translated many of Luther's Latin works into German. He also composed a handbook for Christian households and an influential commentary on 1 Samuel.

Johannes Mercerus (Jean Mercier) (d. 1570). French Hebraist. Mercerus studied under the first Hebrew chair at the Collège Royal de Paris, François Vatable (d. 1547), whom he succeeded in 1546. John Calvin* tried to recruit Mercerus to the Genevan Academy as professor of Hebrew, once in 1558 and again in 1563; he refused both times. During his lifetime Mercerus published grammatical helps for Hebrew and Chaldean, an aid to the Masoretic symbols in the Hebrew text, and translated the commentaries and grammars of several medieval rabbis. He himself wrote commentaries on Genesis, the wisdom books, and most of the Minor Prophets. These commentaries—most of them only published after his death—were philologically focused and interacted with the work of Jerome, Nicholas of Lyra,* notable rabbis and Johannes Oecolampadius.*

Ambrose Moibanus (1494–1554). German Lutheran bishop and theologian. Moibanus helped reform the church of Breslau (modern Wroclaw, Poland). He revised the Mass, bolstered pastoral care and welfare for the poor, and wrote a new evangelical catechism.

Thomas More (1478–1535). English Catholic lawyer, politician, humanist and martyr. More briefly studied at Oxford, but completed his legal studies in London. After contemplating the priesthood for four years, he opted for politics and was elected a member of Parliament in 1504. A devout Catholic, More worked with church leaders in England to root out heresy while he also confronted Lutheran teachings in writing. After four years as Lord Chancellor, More resigned due to heightened tensions with Henry VIII over papal supremacy (which More supported and Henry did not). Tensions did not abate. More's steadfast refusal to accept the Act of Supremacy (1534)—which declared the King of England to be the supreme ecclesial primate not the pope—resulted in his arrest and trial for high treason. He was found guilty and beheaded with John Fisher (1469–1535). Friends with John Colet* and Desiderius Erasmus,* More was a widely respected humanist in England as well as on the continent. Well-known for his novel *Utopia* (1516), More also penned several religious treatises on Christ's passion and suffering during his imprisonment in the Tower of London, which were published posthumously.

Sebastian Münster (1488–1552). German Reformed Hebraist, exegete, printer, and geographer. After converting to the Reformation in 1524, Münster taught Hebrew at the universities of Heidelberg and Basel. During his lengthy tenure in Basel he published more than seventy books, including Hebrew dictionaries and rabbinic commentaries. He also produced an evangelistic work for Jews titled *Vikuach* (1539). Münster's *Torat ha-Maschiach* (1537), the Gospel of Matthew, was the first published Hebrew translation of any portion of the New Testament. Despite his massive contribution to contemporary understanding of the Hebrew language, Münster was criticized by many of the reformers as a Judaizer.

Thomas Müntzer (c. 1489–1525). German Radical preacher. As a preacher in the town of Zwickau, Müntzer was influenced by German mysticism and, growing convinced that Martin Luther* had not carried through reform properly, sought to restore the pure apostolic church of the New Testament. Müntzer's radical ideas led to expulsions from various cities; he developed a highly apocalyptic theology, in which he heralded the last days that would establish the pure community out of suffering, prompting Müntzer's proactive role in the Peasants' War, which he perceived as a crucial apocalyptic event. Six thousand of Müntzer's followers were annihilated by magisterial troops; Müntzer was executed.

John Murcot (1625–1654). English Puritan pastor. After completing his bachelor's at Oxford in 1647, Murcot was ordained as a pastor, transferring to several parishes until in 1651 he moved to Dublin. All his works were published posthumously.

Simon Musaeus (1521–1582). German Lutheran theologian. After studying at the universities of Frankfurt an der Oder and Wittenberg, Musaeus began teaching Greek at the Cathedral school in Nuremberg and was ordained. Having returned to Wittenberg to complete a doctoral degree, Musaeus spent the rest of his career in numerous ecclesial and academic administrative posts. He opposed Matthias Flacius's (1505–1575) view of original sin—that the formal essence of human beings is marred by original sin—even calling the pro-Flacian faculty at Wittenberg "the devil's latrine." Musaeus published a disputation on original sin and a postil.

Wolfgang Musculus (1497–1563). German Reformed pastor and theologian. Musculus produced translations, biblical commentaries and an influential theological text, *Loci communes Sacrae Theologiae* (*Commonplaces of Sacred Theology*), outlining a Zwinglian theology. Musculus began to study theology while at a Benedictine monastery; he departed in 1527 and became secretary to Martin Bucer* in Strasbourg. He was later installed as a pastor in Augsburg, eventually performing the first evangelical liturgy in the city's cathedral. Displaced by the Augsburg Interim, Musculus ended his career as professor of theology at Bern. Though Musculus was active in the pursuit of the reform agenda, he was also concerned for ecumenism, participating in the Wittenberg Concord (1536) and discussions between Lutherans and Catholics.

Friedrich Nausea (c. 1496–1552). German Catholic bishop and preacher. After completing his studies at Leipzig, this famed preacher was appointed priest in Frankfurt but was run out of town by his congregants during his first sermon. He transferred to Mainz as cathedral preacher. Nausea was well connected through the German papal hierarchy and traveled widely to preach to influential ecclesial and secular courts. Court preacher for Ferdinand I (1503–1564), his reform tendencies fit well with royal Austrian theological leanings, and he was enthroned as the bishop of Vienna. Nausea thought that rather than endless colloquies only a council could settle reform. Unfortunately he could not participate in the first session of Trent due to insufficient funding, but he arrived for the second session. Nausea defended the laity's reception of the cup and stressed the importance of promulgating official Catholic teaching in the vernacular.

Melchior Neukirch (1540–1597). German Lutheran pastor and playwright. Neukirch's pastoral career spanned more than thirty years in several northern German parishes. Neukirch published a history of the Braunschweig church since the Reformation and a dramatization of Acts 4–7. He died of the plague.

Nicholas of Lyra (1270–1349). French Catholic biblical exegete. Very little is known about this influential medieval theologian of the Sorbonne aside from the works he published, particularly the *Postilla litteralis super totam Bibliam* (1322–1333). With the advent of the printing press this work was regularly published alongside the Latin Vulgate and the *Glossa ordinaria*. In this running commentary on the Bible Nicholas promoted literal interpretation as the basis for theology. Despite his preference for literal interpretation, Nicholas also published a companion volume, the *Postilla moralis super totam Bibliam* (1339), a commentary on the spiritual meaning of the biblical text. Nicholas was a major conversation partner for many reformers though many of them rejected his exegesis as too literal and too "Jewish" (not concerned enough with the Bible's fulfillment in Jesus Christ).

Johannes Oecolampadius (Johannes Huszgen) (1482–1531). Swiss-German Reformed humanist, reformer and theologian. Oecolampadius (an assumed name meaning "house light") assisted with Desiderius Erasmus's* Greek New Testament, lectured on biblical languages and exegesis and completed an influential Greek grammar. After joining the evangelical cause through studying patristics and the work of Martin Luther,* Oecolampadius went to Basel, where he lectured on biblical exegesis and participated in ecclesial reform. On account of Oecolampadius's effort, the city council passed legislation restricting preaching to the gospel and releasing the city from compulsory Mass. Oecolampadius was a chief ally of Huldrych Zwingli,* whom he supported at the Marburg Colloquy (1529).

Kaspar Olevianus (1536–1587). German Reformed theologian. Olevianus is celebrated for composing the Heidelberg Catechism and producing a critical edition of Calvin's *Institutes* in German. Olevianus studied theology with many, including John Calvin,* Theodore Beza,* Heinrich Bullinger* and Peter Martyr Vermigli.* As an advocate of Reformed doctrine, Olevianus oversaw the shift from Lutheranism to Calvinism throughout Heidelberg, organizing the city's churches after Calvin's Geneva. The Calvinist ecclesial vision of Olevianus entangled him in a dispute with another Heidelberg reformer over the rights of ecclesiastical discipline, which Olevianus felt belonged to the council of clergy and elders rather than civil magistrates.

Josua Opitz (c. 1542–1585). German Lutheran pastor. After a brief stint as superintendent in Regensburg, Opitz, a longtime preacher, was dismissed for his support of Matthias Flacius's (1520–1575) view of original sin. (Using Aristotelian categories, Flacius argued that the formal essence of human beings is marred by original sin, forming sinners into the image of Satan; his views were officially rejected in Article 1 of the Formula of Concord.*) Hans Wilhelm Roggendorf (1533–1591) invited Opitz to lower Austria as part of his Lutheranizing program. Unfortunately Roggendorf and Opitz never succeed in getting Lutheranism legal recognition, perhaps in large part due to Opitz's staunch criticism of Catholics, which resulted in his exile. He died of plague.

Lucas Osiander (1534–1604). German Lutheran pastor. For three decades, Osiander— son of the controversial Nuremberg reformer Andreas Osiander (d. 1552)—served as pastor and court preacher in Stuttgart, until he fell out of favor with the duke in 1598. Osiander produced numerous theological and exegetical works, as well as an influential hymnal.

John Owen (1616–1683). English Puritan theologian. Owen trained at Oxford University, where he was later appointed dean of Christ Church and vice chancellor of the university, following his service as chaplain to Oliver Cromwell. Although Owen began his career as a Presbyterian minister, he eventually departed to the party of Independents. Owen composed many sermons, biblical commentaries (including seven volumes on the book of Hebrews), theological treatises and controversial monographs (including disputations with Arminians, Anglicans, Catholics and Socinians).

Santes Pagninus (c. 1470–1541). Italian Catholic biblical scholar. Pagninus studied under Girolamo Savonarola* and later taught in Rome, Avignon and Lyons. He translated the Old Testament into Latin according to a tight, almost wooden, adherence to the Hebrew. This translation and his Hebrew lexicon *Thesaurus linguae sanctae* (1529) were important resources for translators and commentators.

David (Wängler) Pareus (1548–1622). German Reformed pastor and theologian. Born at Frankenstein in Lower Silesia, Pareus studied theology at Heidelberg under Zacharias Ursinus (1534–1583), the principal author of the Heidelberg Catechism.* After reforming several churches, Pareus returned to Heidelberg to teach at the Reformed seminary. He then joined the theological faculty at the University of Heidelberg, first as a professor of Old Testament and later as a professor of New Testament. Pareus edited the *Neustadter Bibel* (1587), a publication of Martin Luther's* German translation with Reformed annotations—which was strongly denounced by Lutherans, especially Jakob Andreae* and Johann Georg Sigwart (1554–1618). In an extended debate, Pareus defended the orthodoxy of Calvin's exegesis against Aegidius Hunnius,* who accused Calvin of "judaizing" by rejecting many traditional Christological interpretations of Old Testament passages. Towards the end of his career, Pareus wrote commentaries on Genesis, Hosea, Matthew, Romans, 1 Corinthians, Galatians, Hebrews and Revelation.

Catherine Parr (1512–1548). The last of King Henry VIII's* six wives, Catherine Parr was Queen Consort to Henry from 1543 until his death in 1547. She enjoyed a close relationship with two of her step children, Elizabeth and Edward (the future Queen Elizabeth I and King Edward VI), involving herself extensively in their education. Having married three more times after the death of Henry VIII, Catherine died in 1548. Her published works are *Psalms or Prayers* (1543) and a *Lamentation of a Sinner* (1548).

Paul of Burgos (**Solomon ha-Levi**) (c. 1351–1435). Spanish Catholic archbishop. In 1391 Solomon ha-Levi, a rabbi and Talmudic scholar, converted to Christianity, receiving baptism with his entire family (except for his wife). He changed his name to Paul de Santa Maria. Some have suggested that he converted to avoid persecution; he himself stated that Thomas Aquinas's (1225–1274) work persuaded him of the truth of Christian faith. After studying theology in Paris, he was ordained bishop in 1403. He actively and ardently persecuted Jews, trying to compel them to convert. In order to convince Jews that Christians correctly interpret the Hebrew Scriptures, Paul wrote *Dialogus Pauli et Sauli contra Judaeos, sive Scrutinium Scripturarum* (1434), a book filled with vile language toward the Jews. He also wrote a series of controversial marginal notes and comments on Nicholas of Lyra's* *Postilla*, many of which criticized Nicholas's use of Jewish scholarship.

Christoph Pelargus (1565–1633). German Lutheran pastor, theologian, professor and superintendent. Pelargus studied philosophy and theology at the University of Frankfurt an der Oder, in Brandenburg. This irenic Philippist was appointed as the superintendent of Brandenburg and later became a pastor in Frankfurt, although the local authorities first required him to condemn Calvinist theology, because several years earlier he had been called before the consistory in Berlin under suspicion of being a crypto-Calvinist. Among his most important works were a four-volume commentary on *De orthodoxa fide* by John of Damascus (d. 749), a treatise defending the breaking of the bread during communion, and a volume of funeral sermons. He also published commentaries on the Pentateuch, the Psalms, Matthew, John and Acts.

Konrad Pellikan (1478–1556). German Reformed Hebraist and theologian. Pellikan attended the University of Heidelberg, where he mastered Hebrew under Johannes Reuchlin. In 1504 Pellikan published one of the first Hebrew grammars that was not merely a translation of the work of medieval rabbis. While living in Basel, Pellikan assisted the printer Johannes Amerbach, with whom he published some of Luther's* early writings. He also worked with Sebastian Münster* and Wolfgang Capito* on a Hebrew Psalter (1516). In 1526, after teaching theology for three years at the University of Basel, Huldrych Zwingli* brought Pellikan to Zurich to chair the faculty of Old Testament. Pellikan's magnum opus is a seven-volume commentary on the entire Bible (except Revelation) and the Apocrypha; it is often heavily dependent upon the work of others (esp. Desiderius Erasmus* and Johannes Oecolampadius*).

Benedict Pererius (1535–1610). Spanish Catholic theologian, philosopher and exegete. Pererius entered the Society of Jesus in 1552. He taught philosophy, theology, and exegesis at the Roman College of the Jesuits. Early in his career he warned against neo-Platonism and astrology in his *De principiis* (1576). Pererius wrote a lengthy commentary on Daniel, and five volumes of exegetical theses on Exodus, Romans, Revelation and part of the Gospel of John (chs. 1–14). His four-volume commentary on Genesis (1591–1599) was lauded by Protestants and Catholics alike.

William Perkins (1558–1602). English Puritan preacher and theologian. Perkins was a highly regarded Puritan Presbyterian preacher and biblical commentator in the Elizabethan era. He studied at Cambridge University and later became a fellow of Christ's Church college as a preacher and professor, receiving acclaim for his sermons and lectures. Even more, Perkins gained an esteemed reputation for his ardent exposition of Calvinist reformed doctrine in the style of Petrus Ramus,* becoming one of the first English reformed theologians to achieve international recognition. Perkins influenced the federal Calvinist shape of Puritan theology and the vision of logical, practical expository preaching.

François Perrault (1577–1657). French Reformed pastor for over fifty years. His book on demonology was prominent, perhaps because of the intrigue at his home in 1612. According to his account, a poltergeist made a commotion and argued points of theology; a few months later Perrault's parishioners slew a large snake slithering out of his house.

Dirk Philips (1504–1568). Dutch Radical elder and theologian. This former Franciscan monk, known for being severe and obstinate, was a leading theologian of the sixteenth-century Anabaptist movement. Despite the fame of Menno Simons* and his own older brother Obbe, Philips wielded great influence over Anabaptists in the Netherlands and northern Germany where he ministered. As a result of Philips's understanding of the apostolic church as radically separated from the children of the world, he advocated a very strict interpretation of the ban, including formal shunning. His writings were collected and published near the end of his life as *Enchiridion oft Hantboecxken van de Christelijcke Leere* (1564).

Obbe Philips (1500–1568) Dutch radical leader. Trained as a physician, Philips was drawn to mystical Anabaptism, as taught by Melchior Hoffman (1495–1543) in his hometown of Leewarden. After adult rebaptism and ordination, he preached in Amsterdam, Delft, Appingedam, and Grongen, and he ordained other leaders including his brother Dirk Philips*, David Joris*, and Menno Simmons*. Disillusioned with the growth of revolutionary, enthusiastic, and apocalyptic elements within Anabaptism and unable to reconcile any visible church with the church of God, Philips withdrew from the radical movement in 1540, after which nothing is known of his life. His only extant writing, entitled *The Confession of Obbe Philips*, was published after his death and recounts elements of the history of the

Anabaptist movement and defends his departure from the movement.

Johannes Piscator (1546–1625). German Reformed theologian. Educated at Tübingen (though he wanted to study at Wittenberg), Piscator taught at the universities of Strasbourg and Heidelberg, as well as academies in Neustadt and Herborn. His commentaries on both the Old and New Testaments involve a tripartite analysis of a given passage's argument, of scholia on the text and of doctrinal loci. Some consider Piscator's method to be a full flowering of Beza's* "logical" scriptural analysis, focused on the text's meaning and its relationship to the pericopes around it.

Felix Pratensis (d. 1539). Italian Catholic Hebraist. Pratensis, the son of a rabbi, converted to Christianity and entered the Augustinian Hermits around the turn of the sixteenth century. In 1515, with papal permission, Pratensis published a new translation of the Psalms based on the Hebrew text. His *Biblia Rabbinica* (1517–1518), printed in Jewish and Christian editions, included text-critical notes in the margins as well as the Targum and rabbinic commentaries on each book (e.g., Rashi* on the Pentateuch and David Kimchi* on the Prophets). Many of the reformers consulted this valuable resource as they labored on their own translations and expositions of the Old Testament.

Quadriga. The *quadriga*, or four senses of Scripture, grew out of the exegetical legacy of Paul's dichotomy of letter and spirit (2 Cor 3:6), as well as church fathers like Origen (c. 185–254), Jerome (c. 347–420) and Augustine (354–430). Advocates for this method—the primary framework for biblical exegesis during the medieval era—assumed the necessity of the gift of faith under the guidance of the Holy Spirit. The literal-historical meaning of the text served as the foundation for the fuller perception of Scripture's meaning in the three spiritual senses, accessible only through faith: the allegorical sense taught what should be believed, the tropological or moral sense taught what should be done, and the anagogical or eschatological sense taught what should be hoped for. Medieval Jewish exegesis also had a fourfold interpretive method—not necessarily related to the *quadriga*—called *pardes* ("grove"): *peshat*, the simple, literal sense of the text according to grammar; *remez*, the allegorical sense; *derash*, the moral sense; and *sod*, the mystic sense related to Kabbalah. Scholars hotly dispute the precise use and meaning of these terms.

Petrus Ramus (1515–1572). French Reformed humanist philosopher. Ramus was an influential professor of philosophy and logic at the French royal college in Paris; he converted to Protestantism and left France for Germany, where he came under the influence of Calvinist thought. Ramus was a trenchant critic of Aristotle and noted for his method of classification based on a deductive movement from universals to particulars, the latter becoming branching divisions that provided a visual chart of the parts to the whole. His system profoundly influenced Puritan theology and preaching. After returning to Paris, Ramus died in the Saint Bartholomew's Day Massacre.

Rashi (**Shlomo Yitzchaki**) (1040–1105). French Jewish rabbi and exegete. After completing his studies, Rashi founded a yeshiva in Troyes. He composed the first comprehensive commentary on the Talmud, as well as commentaries on the entire Old Testament except for 1–2 Chronicles. These works remain influential within orthodox Judaism. Late medieval and early modern Christian scholars valued his exegesis, characterized by his preference for peshat (see quadriga).

Remonstrance (1610). See *Synod of Dordrecht*.

Johannes Reuchlin (1455–1522). German Catholic lawyer, humanist and Hebraist. Reuchlin held judicial appointments for the dukes of Württemberg, the Supreme Court in Speyer and the imperial court of the Swabian League. He pioneered the study of Hebrew among Christians in Germany, standing against those who, like Johannes Pfefferkorn (1469–1523), wanted to destroy Jewish literature. Among his many works he published a Latin dictionary, an introductory Greek grammar, the most important early modern Hebrew grammar and dictionary (*De rudimentis* *hebraicis*; 1506), and a commentary on the penitential psalms.

Edward Reynolds (1599–1676). Anglican bishop. Reynolds succeeded John Donne* as the preacher at Lincoln's Inn before entering parish ministry in Northamptonshire. During the English Civil Wars, he supported the Puritans because of his sympathy toward their simplicity and piety—despite believing that Scripture demanded no particular form of government; later he refused to support the abolition of the monarchy. Until the Restoration he ministered in London; afterward he became the bishop of Norwich. He wrote the general thanksgiving prayer which is part of the morning office in the *Book of Common Prayer.**

Urbanus Rhegius (1489–1541). German Lutheran pastor. Rhegius, who was likely the son of a priest, studied under the humanists at Freiburg and Ingolstadt. After a brief stint as a foot soldier, he received ordination in 1519 and was made cathedral preacher in Augsburg. During his time in Augsburg he closely read Luther's* works, becoming an enthusiastic follower. Despite his close friendship with Zwingli* and Oecolampadius,* Rhegius supported Luther in the eucharistic debates, later playing a major role in the Wittenberg Concord (1536). He advocated for peace during the Peasants' War and had extended interactions with the Anabaptists in Augsburg. Later in his career he concerned himself with the training of pastors, writing a pastoral guide and two catechisms. About one hundred of his writings were published posthumously.

Lancelot Ridley (d. 1576). Anglican preacher. Ridley was the first cousin of Nicholas Ridley,* the bishop of London who was martyred during the Marian persecutions. By Cranmer's* recommendation, Ridley became one of the six Canterbury Cathedral preachers. Upon Mary I's accession in 1553, Ridley was defrocked (as a married priest). Ridley returned to Canterbury Cathedral after Mary's death. He wrote commentaries on Jude, Ephesians, Philippians and Colossians.

Nicholas Ridley (c. 1502–1555). Anglican bishop. Ridley was a student and fellow at Cambridge University who was appointed chaplain to Archbishop Thomas Cranmer* and is thought to be partially responsible for Cranmer's shift to a symbolic view of the Eucharist. Cranmer promoted Ridley twice: as bishop of Rochester, where he openly advocated Reformed theological views, and, later, as bishop of London. Ridley assisted Cranmer in the revisions of the Book of Common Prayer.* Ridley's support of Lady Jane Grey against the claims of Mary to the throne led to his arrest; he was tried for heresy and burned at the stake with Hugh Latimer.*

Peter Riedemann (1506–1556). German Radical elder, theologian and hymnist. While traveling as a Silesian cobbler, Riedemann came into contact with Anabaptist teachings and joined a congregation in Linz. In 1529 he was called to be a minister, only to be imprisoned soon after as part of Archduke Ferdinand's efforts to suppress heterodoxy in his realm. Once he was released, he moved to Moravia in 1532 where he was elected as a minister and missionary of the Hutterite community there. His *Account of Our Religion, Doctrine and Faith* (1542), with its more than two thousand biblical references, is Riedemann's most important work and is still used by Hutterites today.

John Robinson (1576–1625). English Puritan pastor. After his suspension for nonconformity, Robinson fled to the Netherlands with his congregation, eventually settling in Leiden in 1609. Robinson entered into controversies over Arminianism, separation and congregationalism. Most of his healthy congregants immigrated to Plymouth in 1620; Robinson remained in Leiden with those unable to travel.

Nehemiah Rogers (1593–1660). Anglican priest. After studying at Cambridge, Rogers ministered at numerous parishes during his more than forty-year career. In 1643, he seems to have been forced out of a parish on account of being a Royalist and friend of William Laud.* Rogers published a number of sermons and tracts, including a series of expositions on Jesus' parables in the Gospels.

Robert Rollock (c. 1555–1599). Scottish Reformed pastor, educator and theologian. Rollock was deeply influenced by Petrus Ramus's* system of logic, which he implemented as a tutor and (later) principal of Edinburgh University and in his expositions of the Bible. Rollock, as a divinity professor and theologian, was instrumental in diffusing a federalist Calvinism in the Scottish church; he lectured on theology using the texts of Theodore Beza* and articulated a highly covenantal interpretation of the biblical narratives. He was a prolific writer of sermons, expositions, commentaries, lectures and occasional treatises.

Jacopo Sadoleto (1477–1547). Italian Catholic Cardinal. Sadoleto, attaché to Leo X's court, was appointed bishop in 1517, cardinal in 1536. He participated in the reform commission led by Gasparo Contarini.* However, he tried to reconcile with Protestants apart from the commission, sending several letters to Protestant leaders in addition to his famous letter to the city of Geneva, which John Calvin* pointedly answered. Sadoleto published a commentary on Romans that was censored as semi-Pelagian. His insufficient treatment of prevenient grace left him vulnerable to this charge. Sadoleto emphasized grammar as the rule and norm of exegesis.

Heinrich Salmuth (1522–1576). German Lutheran theologian. After earning his doctorate from the University of Leipzig, Salmuth served in several coterminous pastoral and academic positions. He was integral to the reorganization of the University of Jena. Except for a few disputations, all of Salmuth's works—mostly sermons—were published posthumously by his son.

Robert Sanderson (1587–1663). Anglican bishop and philosopher. Before his appointment as professor of divinity at Oxford in 1642, Sanderson pastored in several parishes. Because of his loyalty to the Crown during the English Civil Wars, the Parliamentarians stripped Sanderson of his post at Oxford. After the Restoration he was reinstated at Oxford and consecrated bishop. He wrote an influential textbook on logic.

Edwin Sandys (1519–1588). Anglican bishop. During his doctoral studies at Cambridge, Sandys befriended Martin Bucer.* Having supported the Protestant Lady Jane Grey's claim to the throne, Sandys resigned his post at Cambridge upon Mary I's accession. He was then arrested and imprisoned in the Tower of London. Released in 1554, he sojourned on the continent until Mary's death. On his return to England he was appointed to revise the liturgy and was consecrated bishop. Many of his sermons were published, but his most significant literary legacy is his work as a translator of the Bishop's Bible (1568), which served as the foundational English text for the translators of the King James Bible (1611).

Erasmus Sarcerius (1501–1559). German Lutheran superintendent, educator and pastor. Sarcerius served as educational superintendent, court preacher and pastor in Nassau and, later, in Leipzig. The hallmark of Sarcerius's reputation was his ethical emphasis as exercised through ecclesial oversight and family structure; he also drafted disciplinary codes for regional churches in Germany. Sarcerius served with Philipp Melanchthon* as Protestant delegates at the Council of Trent, though both withdrew prior to the dismissal of the session; he eventually became an opponent of Melanchthon, contesting the latter's understanding of the Eucharist at a colloquy in Worms in 1557.

Michael Sattler (c. 1490–1527). Swiss Radical leader. Sattler was a Benedictine monk who abandoned the monastic life during the upheavals of the Peasants' War. He took up the trade of weaving under the guidance of an outspoken Anabaptist. It seems that Sattler did not openly join the Anabaptist movement until after the suppression of the Peasants' War in 1526. Sattler interceded with Martin Bucer* and Wolfgang Capito* for imprisoned Anabaptists in Strasbourg. Shortly before he was convicted of heresy and executed, he wrote the definitive expression of Anabaptist theology, the Schleitheim Articles.*

Girolamo Savonarola (1452–1498). Italian Catholic preacher and martyr. Outraged by clerical corruption and the neglect of the poor, Savonarola traveled to preach against these abuses and to prophesy impending judgment—a mighty king would scourge and reform the church. Savonarola thought that the French invasion of Italy in 1494 confirmed his apocalyptic visions. Thus he pressed to purge Florence of vice and institute public welfare, in order to usher in a new age of Christianity. Florence's refusal to join papal resistance against the French enraged Alexander VI (r. 1492–1503). He blamed Savonarola, promptly excommunicating him and threatening Florence with an interdict. After an ordeal by fire turned into a riot, Savonarola was arrested. Under torture he admitted to charges of conspiracy and false prophecy; he was hanged and burned. In addition to numerous sermons and letters, he wrote meditations on Psalms 31 and 51 as well as *The Triumph of the Cross* (1497).

Leupold Scharnschlager (d. 1563). Austrian Radical elder. See *Kunstbuch*.

Leonhard Schiemer (d. 1528) Austrian radical martyr. Troubled by the hypocrisies he experienced, Scheimer left the Franciscan order and spent a period of time wandering. Attracted to the teachings of Hans Hut* after hearing him debate Balthasar Hubmaier* in Moravia, he was rebaptized and traveled widely throughout Austria and Southern Germany, spreading the Anabaptist message until he was arrested in Rattenberg, where he was condemned to death and beheaded. A number of his essays and hymns survive, dispersed among the *Kunstbuch** and other collections of radical writings.

Hans Schlaffer (c. 1490–1528). Austrian Radical martyr. See *Kunstbuch*.

Schleitheim Articles (1527). After the death of Conrad Grebel* in 1526 and the execution of Felix Manz (born c. 1498) in early 1527, the young Swiss Anabaptist movement was in need of unity and direction. A synod convened at Schleitheim under the chairmanship of Michael Sattler,* which passed seven articles of Anabaptist distinctives—likely defined against both magisterial reformers and other Anabaptists with less orthodox and more militant views (e.g., Balthasar Hubmaier*). Unlike most confessions, these articles do not explicitly address traditional creedal interests; they explicate instead the Anabaptist view of the sacraments, church discipline, separatism, the role of ministers, pacifism and oaths. Throughout the document there is a resolute focus on Christ's example. Also referred to as the Schleitheim Confession and the Schleitheim Brotherly Union, the Schleitheim Articles are considered the definitive statement of Anabaptist theology, particularly regarding separatism.

Schmalkald Articles (1537). In response to Pope Paul III's (1468–1549) 1536 decree ordering a general church council to solve the Protestant crisis, Elector John Frederick (1503–1554) commissioned Martin Luther* to draft the sum of his teaching. Intended by Luther as a last will and testament—and composed with advice from well-known colleagues Justus Jonas,* Johann Bugenhagen,* Caspar Cruciger,* Nikolaus von Amsdorf (1483–1565), Georg Spalatin (1484–1545), Philipp Melanchthon* and Johann Agricola*—these articles provide perhaps the briefest and most systematic summary of Luther's teaching. The document was not adopted formally by the Lutheran Schmalkald League, as was hoped, and the general church council was postponed for several years (until convening at Trent in 1545). Only in 1580 were the articles officially received, by being incorporated into the *Book of Concord* defining orthodox Lutheranism.

Anna Maria van Schurman (1607–1678). Dutch Reformed polymath. Van Schurman cultivated talents in art, poetry, botany, linguistics and theology. She mastered most contemporary European languages, in addition to Latin, Greek, Hebrew, Arabic, Farsi and Ethiopian. With the encouragement of leading Reformed theologian Gisbertus Voetius (1589–1676), van Schurman attended lectures at the University of Utrecht—although she was required to sit behind a wooden screen so that the male students could not see her. In 1638 van Schurman published her famous treatise advocating female scholarship, *Amica dissertatio . . . de capacitate ingenii muliebris ad scientias*. In addition to these more polemical works, van Schurman also wrote hymns and poems, including a paraphrase of Genesis 1–3. Later in life she became a devotee of Jean de Labadie (1610–1674), a former Jesuit who was also expelled from the Reformed church for his separatist leanings. Her *Eucleria* (1673) is the most well known defense of Labadie's theology.

Kaspar von Schwenckfeld (1489–1561). German Radical reformer. Schwenckfeld was a Silesian nobleman who encountered Luther's* works in 1521. He traveled to Wittenberg twice: first to meet Luther and Karlstadt,* and a second time to convince Luther of his doctrine of the "internal word"—emphasizing inner revelation so strongly that he did not see church meetings or the sacraments as necessary—after which Luther considered him heterodox. Schwenckfeld won his native territory to the Reformation in 1524 and later lived in Strasbourg for five years until Bucer* sought to purify the city of less traditional theologies. Schwenckfeld wrote numerous polemical and exegetical tracts.

Scots Confession (1560). In 1560, the Scottish Parliament undertook to reform the Church of Scotland and to commission a Reformed confession of faith. In the course of four days, a committee—which included John Knox*—wrote this confession, largely based on Calvin's* work, the Confession of the English Congregation in Geneva (1556) and the Gallic Confession.* The articles were not ratified until 1567 and were displaced by the Westminster Confession (1646), adopted by the Scottish in 1647.

Second Helvetic Confession (1566). Believing he would soon die, Heinrich Bullinger* penned a personal statement of his Reformed faith in 1561 as a theological will. In 1563, Bullinger sent a copy of this confession, which blended Zwingli's and Calvin's theology, to the elector of the Palatinate, Frederick III (1515–1576), who had asked for a complete explication of the Reformed faith in order to defend himself against aggressive Lutheran attacks after printing the Heidelberg Confession.* Although not published until 1566, the Second Helvetic Confession became the definitive sixteenth-century Reformed statement of faith. Theodore Beza* used it as the organizing confession for his *Harmonia Confessionum* (1581), which sought to emphasize the unity of the Reformed churches. Bullinger's personal confession was adopted by the Reformed churches of Scotland (1566), Hungary (1567), France (1571) and Poland (1571).

Obadiah Sedgwick (c. 1600–1658). English Puritan minister. Educated at Oxford, Sedgwick pastored in London and participated in the Westminster Assembly. An ardent Puritan, Sedgwick was appointed by Oliver Cromwell (1599–1658) to examine clerical candidates. Sedgwick published a catechism, several sermons and a treatise on how to deal with doubt.

Nikolaus Selnecker (1530–1592). German Lutheran theologian, preacher, pastor and hymnist. Selnecker taught in Wittenberg, Jena and Leipzig, preached in Dresden and Wolfenbüttel, and pastored in Leipzig. He was forced out of his post at Jena because of suspicions that he was a crypto-Calvinist. He sought refuge in Wolfenbüttel, where he met Martin Chemnitz* and Jakob Andreae.* Under their influence Selnecker was drawn away from Philippist theology. Selnecker's shift in theology can be seen in his *Institutio religionis christianae* (1573). Selnecker coauthored the Formula of Concord* with Chemnitz, Andreae, Andreas Musculus (1514–1581), and David Chytraeus.* Selnecker also published lectures on Genesis, the Psalms, and the New Testament epistles, as well as composing over a hundred hymn tunes and texts.

Short Confession (1610). In response to some of William Laud's* reforms in the Church of England—particularly a law stating that ministers who refused to comply with the Book of Common Prayer* would lose their ordination—a group of English Puritans immigrated to the Netherlands in protest, where they eventually embraced the practice of believer's baptism. The resulting Short Confession was an attempt at union between these Puritans and local Dutch Anabaptists ("Waterlanders"). The document highlights the importance of love in the church and reflects optimism regarding the freedom of the will while explicitly rejecting double predestination.

Richard Sibbes (1577–1635). English Puritan preacher. Sibbes was educated at St. John's College, Cambridge, where he was converted to reforming views and became a popular preacher. As a moderate Puritan emphasizing interior piety and brotherly love, Sibbes always remained within the established Church of England, though opposed to some of its liturgical ceremonies. His collected sermons constitute his main literary legacy.

Menno Simons (c. 1496–1561). Dutch Radical leader. Simons led a separatist Anabaptist group in the Netherlands that would later be called Mennonites, known for nonviolence and renunciation of the world. A former priest, Simons rejected Catholicism through the influence of Anabaptist disciples of Melchior Hoffmann and based on his study of Scripture, in which he found no support for transubstantiation or infant baptism. Following the sack of Anabaptists at Münster, Simons committed to a nonviolent way of life. Simons proclaimed a message of radical discipleship of obedience and inner purity, marked by voluntary adult baptism and communal discipline.

Henry Smith (c. 1550–1591). English Puritan minister. Smith stridently opposed the Book of Common Prayer* and refused to subscribe to the Articles of Religion,* thus limiting his pastoral opportunities. Nevertheless he gained a reputation as an eloquent preacher in London. He published sermon collections as well as several treatises.

Domingo de Soto (1494–1560). Spanish Catholic theologian. Soto taught philosophy for four years at the University in Alcalá before entering the Dominican order. In 1532 he became chair of theology at the University of Salamanca; Soto sought to reintroduce Aristotle in the curriculum. He served as confessor and spiritual advisor to Charles V, who enlisted Soto as imperial theologian for the Council of Trent. Alongside commentaries on the works of Aristotle and Peter Lombard (c. 1100–1160), Soto commented on Romans and wrote an influential treatise on nature and grace.

Cyriacus Spangenberg (1528–1604). German Lutheran pastor, preacher and theologian. Spangenberg was a staunch, often acerbic, Gnesio-Lutheran. He rejected the Formula of Concord* because of concerns about the princely control of the church, as well as its rejection of Flacian language of original sin (as constituting the "substance" of human nature after the fall). He published many commentaries and sermons, most famously seventy wedding sermons (*Ehespiegel* [1561]), his sermons on Luther* (*Theander Luther* [1562–1571]) and Luther's hymns (*Cithara Lutheri* [1569–1570]). He also published an analysis of the Old Testament (though he only got as far as Job), based on a methodology that anticipated the logical bifurcations of Peter Ramus.*

Johann Spangenberg (1484–1550). German Lutheran pastor and catechist. Spangenberg studied at the University of Erfurt, where he was welcomed into a group of humanists associated with Konrad Muth (1470–1526). There he met the reformer Justus Jonas,* and Eobanus Hessius (1488–1540), whom Luther* dubbed "king of the poets." Spangenberg served at parishes in Stolberg (1520–1524), Nordhausen (1524–1546) and, by Luther's recommendation, Eisleben (1546–1550). Spangenberg published one of the best-selling postils of the sixteenth century, the *Postilla Teütsch*, a six-volume work meant to prepare children to understand the lectionary readings. It borrowed the question-answer form of Luther's *Small Catechism* and was so popular that a monk, Johannes Craendonch, purged overt anti-Catholic statements from it and republished it under his own name. Among Spangenberg's other pastoral works are *ars moriendi* ("the art of dying") booklets, a postil for the Acts of the Apostles and a question-answer version of Luther's *Large Catechism*. In addition to preaching and pastoring, Spangenberg wrote pamphlets on controversial topics such as purgatory, as well as textbooks on music, mathematics and grammar.

Georg Spindler (1525–1605). German Reformed theologian and pastor. After studying theology under Caspar Cruciger* and Philipp Melanchthon,* Spindler accepted a pastorate in Bohemia.

A well-respected preacher, Spindler published postils in 1576 which some of his peers viewed as crypto-Calvinist. To investigate this allegation Spindler read John Calvin's* *Institutes*, and subsequently converted to the Reformed faith. After years of travel, he settled in the Palatinate and pastored there until his death. In addition to his Lutheran postils, Spindler also published Reformed postils in 1594 as well as several treatises on the Lord's Supper and predestination.

Statenvertaling (1637). The Synod of Dordrecht* commissioned this new Dutch translation of the Bible ("State's Translation"). The six theologians who undertook this translation also wrote prefaces for each biblical book, annotated obscure words and difficult passages, and provided cross-references; they even explained certain significant translation decisions. At the request of the Westminster Assembly, Theodore Haak (1605–1690) translated the *Statenvertaling* into English as *The Dutch Annotations Upon the Whole Bible* (1657).

Johann von Staupitz (d. 1524). German Catholic theologian, professor and preacher. Frederick the Wise summoned this Augustinian monk to serve as professor of Bible and first dean of the theology faculty at the University of Wittenberg. As Vicar-General of the Reformed Augustinian Hermits in Germany, Staupitz sought to reform the order and attempted unsuccessfully to reunite with the conventional Augustinians. While in Wittenberg, Staupitz was Martin Luther's* teacher, confessor and spiritual father. He supported Luther in the early controversies over indulgences, but after releasing Luther from his monastic vows (to protect him), he distanced himself from the conflict. He relocated to Salzburg, where he was court preacher to Cardinal Matthäus Lang von Wellenburg (d. 1540) and abbot of the Benedictine monastery. Staupitz wrote treatises on predestination, faith and the love of God. Many of his sermons were collected and published during his lifetime.

Michael Stifel (1486–1567). German Lutheran mathematician, theologian and pastor. An Augustinian monk, Stifel's interest in mysticism, apocalypticism and numerology led him to identify Pope Leo X as the antichrist. Stifel soon joined the reform movement, writing a 1522 pamphlet in support of Martin Luther's* theology. After Luther quelled the fallout of Stifel's failed prediction of the Apocalypse—October 19, 1533 at 8 a.m.—Stifel focused more on mathematics and his pastoral duties. He was the first professor of mathematics at the University of Jena. He published several numerological interpretations of texts from the Gospels, Daniel and Revelation. However, Stifel's most important work is his *Arithmetica Integra* (1544), in which he standardized the approach to quadratic equations. He also developed notations for exponents and radicals.

Viktorin Strigel (1524–1569). German Lutheran theologian. Strigel taught at Wittenberg, Erfurt, Jena, Leipzig and Heidelberg. During his time in Jena he disputed with Matthias Flacius (1520–1575) over the human will's autonomy. Following Philipp Melanchthon,* Strigel asserted that in conversion the human will obediently cooperates with the divine will through the Holy Spirit and the Word of God. In the Weimar Disputation (1560), Strigel elicited Flacius's opinion that sin is a substance that mars the formal essence of human beings. Flacius's views were officially rejected in Article 1 of the Formula of Concord*; Strigel's, in Article 2. In 1567 the University of Leipzig suspended Strigel from teaching on account of suspicions that he affirmed Reformed Eucharistic theology; he acknowledged that he did and joined the Reformed confession on the faculty of the University of Heidelberg. In addition to controversial tracts, Strigel published commentaries on the entire Bible (except Lamentations) and the Apocrypha.

Johann Sutell (1504–1575). German Lutheran pastor. After studying at the University of Wittenberg, Sutell received a call to a pastorate in Göttingen, where he eventually became superintendent. He wrote new church orders for Göttingen (1531) and Schweinfurt (1543), and expanded two sermons for publication, *The Dreadful Destruction of Jerusalem* (1539) and *History of Lazarus* (1543).

Swiss Brethren Confession of Hesse (1578). Anabaptist leader Hans Pauly Kuchenbecker penned this confession after a 1577 interrogation by Lutheran authorities. This confession was unusually amenable to Lutheran views—there is no mention of pacifism or rejection of oath taking.

Synod of Dordrecht (1618–1619). This large Dutch Reformed Church council—also attended by English, German and Swiss delegates—met to settle the theological issues raised by the followers of Jacobus Arminius.* Arminius's theological disagreements with mainstream Reformed teaching erupted into open conflict with the publication of the *Remonstrance* (1610). This "protest" was based on five points: that election is based on foreseen faith or unbelief; that Christ died indiscriminately for all people (although only believers receive salvation); that people are thoroughly sinful by nature apart from the prevenient grace of God that enables their free will to embrace or reject the gospel; that humans are able to resist the working of God's grace; and that it is possible for true believers to fall away from faith completely. The Synod ruled in favor of the Contra-Remonstrants, its Canons often remembered with a TULIP acrostic—total depravity, unconditional election, limited atonement, irresistible grace, perseverance of the saints—each letter countering one of the five Remonstrant articles. The Synod also officially accepted the Belgic Confession,* Heidelberg Catechism* and the Canons of Dordrecht as standards of the Dutch Reformed Church.

Arcangela Tarabotti (1604–1652). Italian Catholic nun. At the age of eleven, Tarabotti entered a Benedictine convent as a student-boarder; three years later her father forced her to take monastic vows. The dignity of women and their treatment in the male-controlled institutions of early modern Venice concerned Tarabotti deeply. She protested forced cloistering, the denial of education to women, the exclusion of women from public life and the double standards by which men and women were judged. Tarbotti authored numerous polemical works and an extensive correspondence.

Johannes Tauler (c. 1300–1361) German mystical theologian. A Dominican friar and disciple of Meister Eckhart (c. 1260–c. 1328), Tauler spent most of his career as a mendicant preacher in Strasburg and Basel. Known through a collection of about eighty German sermons, Tauler taught a practical spirituality, accessible to those outside the cloister and intended to draw his audience to deeper contemplation of the divine nature.

Richard Taverner (1505–1575). English Puritan humanist and translator. After graduating from Oxford, Taverner briefly studied abroad. When he returned to England, he joined Thomas Cromwell's (1485–1540) circle. After Cromwell's beheading, Taverner escaped severe punishment and retired from public life during Mary I's reign. Under Elizabeth I, Taverner served as justice of the peace, sheriff and a licensed lay preacher. Taverner translated many important continental Reformation works into English, most notably the Augsburg Confession* and several of Desiderius Erasmus's* works. Some of these translations—John Calvin's* 1536 catechism, Wolfgang Capito's* work on the Psalms and probably Erasmus Sarcerius's* postils—he presented as his own work. Underwritten by Cromwell, Taverner also published an edited version of the Matthew Bible (1537).

Thomas Thorowgood (1595–1669). English Puritan pastor. Thorowgood was a Puritan minister in Norfolk and the chief financier of John Eliot (1604–1690), a Puritan missionary among the Native American tribes in Massachusetts. In 1650, under the title *Jews in America, or, Probabilities that Americans be of that Race,* Thorowgood became one of the first to put forward the thesis that Native Americans were actually the ten lost tribes of Israel.

Frans Titelmans (1502–1537). Belgian Catholic philosopher. Titelmans studied at the University of Leuven, where he was influenced by Petrus Ramus.* After first joining a Franciscan monastery, Titelmans realigned with the stricter Capuchins and moved to Italy. He is best known for his advocacy for the Vulgate and his debates with Desiderius Erasmus* over Pauline theology (1527–1530)—he was deeply suspicious of the fruits of humanism, especially regarding biblical studies. His work was published posthumously by his brother, Pieter Titelmans (1501–1572).

Francisco de Toledo (1532–1596). Spanish Catholic theologian. This important Jesuit taught philosophy at the universities of Salamanca and Rome. He published works on Aristotelian philosophy and a commentary on Thomas Aquinas's work, as well as biblical commentaries on John, Romans and the first half of Luke. He was also the general editor for the Clementine Vulgate (1598).

Alonso Tostado (1400–1455). Spanish Catholic bishop and exegete. Tostado lectured on theology, law and philosophy at the University of Salamanca, in addition to ministering in a local parish. Tostado entered into disputes over papal supremacy and the date of Christ's birth. Tostado's thirteen-volume collected works include commentaries on the historical books of the Old Testament and the Gospel of Matthew.

Daniel Toussain (1541–1602). Swiss Reformed pastor and professor. Toussain became pastor at Orléans after attending college in Basel. After the third War of Religion, Toussain was exiled, eventually returning to Montbéliard, his birthplace. In 1571, he faced opposition there from the strict Lutheran rulers and was eventually exiled due to his influence over the clergy. He returned to Orléans but fled following the Saint Bartholomew's Day Massacre (1572), eventually becoming pastor in Basel. He relocated to Heidelberg in 1583 as pastor to the new regent, becoming professor of theology at the university, and he remained there until his death.

John Trapp (1601–1669). Anglican biblical exegete. After studying at Oxford, Trapp entered the pastorate in 1636. During the English Civil Wars he sided with Parliament, which later made it difficult for him to collect tithes from a congregation whose royalist pastor had been evicted. Trapp published commentaries on all the books of the Bible from 1646 to 1656.

Immanuel Tremellius (1510–1580). Italian Reformed Hebraist. Around 1540, Tremellius received baptism by Cardinal Reginald Pole (1500–1558) and converted from Judaism to Christianity; he affiliated with evangelicals the next year. On account of the political and religious upheaval, Tremellius relocated often, teaching Hebrew in Lucca; Strasbourg, fleeing the Inquisition; Cambridge, displaced by the Schmalkaldic War; Heidelberg, escaping Mary I's persecutions; and Sedan, expelled by the new Lutheran Elector of the Palatine. Many considered Tremellius's translation of the Old Testament as the most accurate available. He also published a Hebrew grammar and translated John Calvin's* catechism into Hebrew.

Richard Turnbull (d. 1593). English minister. A preacher in London, Richard Turnbull published sermons on James, Jude, and Psalm 15.

William Tyndale (Hychyns) (1494–1536). English reformer, theologian and translator. Tyndale was educated at Oxford University, where he was influenced by the writings of humanist thinkers. Believing that piety is fostered through personal encounter with the Bible, he asked to translate the Bible into English; denied permission, Tyndale left for the Continent to complete the task. His New Testament was the equivalent of a modern-day bestseller in England but was banned and ordered burned. Tyndale's theology was oriented around justification, the authority of Scripture and Christian obedience; Tyndale emphasized the ethical as a concomitant reality of justification. He was martyred in Brussels before completing his English translation of the Old Testament, which Miles Coverdale* finished.

Juan de Valdés (1500/10–1541). Spanish Catholic theologian and writer. Although Valdés adopted an evangelical doctrine, had Erasmian affiliations and published works that were listed on the Index of Prohibited Books, Valdés rebuked the reformers for creating disunity and never left the Catholic Church. His writings included translations of the Hebrew Psalter and various biblical books, a work on the Spanish language and several commentaries. Valdés fled to Rome in 1531 to escape the Spanish Inquisition and worked in the court of Clement VII in Bologna until the pope's death in 1534. Valdés subsequently returned to Naples, where he led the reform- and revival-minded Valdesian circle.

Peter Martyr Vermigli (1499–1562). Italian Reformed humanist and theologian. Vermigli was one of the most influential theologians of the era, held in common regard with such figures as Martin Luther* and John Calvin.* In Italy, Vermigli was a distinguished theologian, preacher and advocate for moral reform; however, during the reinstitution of the Roman Inquisition Vermigli fled to Protestant regions in northern Europe. He was eventually appointed professor of divinity at Oxford University, where Vermigli delivered acclaimed disputations on the Eucharist. Vermigli was widely noted for his deeply integrated biblical commentaries and theological treatises.

Vulgate. In 382 Pope Damasus I (c. 300–384) commissioned Jerome (c. 347–420) to translate the four Gospels into Latin based on Old Latin and Greek manuscripts. Jerome completed the translation of the Gospels and the Old Testament around 405. It is widely debated how much of the rest of the New Testament was translated by Jerome. During the Middle Ages, the Vulgate became the Catholic Church's standard Latin translation. The Council of Trent recognized it as the official text of Scripture.

Thomas Walkington (d. 1621). Anglican minister and author. Born in Lincoln, he was educated at Cambridge, graduating with his BA in 1597 and his MA in 1600. Walkington was elected a fellow at St. John's College, Cambridge, in 1602. Later, he received a BD from Oxford and a DD from Cambridge. He served as rector of parishes in Northamptonshire, Lincolnshire, and Middlesex. A prolific author, Walkington published works on diverse subjects. Among his biblical works are *An Exposition of the First Two Verses of the Sixth Chapter to the Hebrews in form of a Dialogue* (1609) and *Theologicall Rules to Guide Us in the Understanding and Practice of Holy Scripture* (1615).

Peter Walpot (d. 1578). Moravian Radical pastor and bishop. Walpot was a bishop of the Hutterite community after Jakob Hutter, Peter Riedemann* and Leonhard Lanzenstiel. Riedemann's *Confession of Faith* (1545; 1565) became a vital authority for Hutterite exegesis, theology and morals. Walpot added his own *Great Article Book* (1577), which collates primary biblical passages on baptism, communion, the community of goods, the sword and divorce. In keeping with Hutterite theology, Walpot defended the community of goods as a mark of the true church.

Valentin Weigel (1533–1588). German Lutheran pastor. Weigel studied at Leipzig and Wittenberg, entering the pastorate in 1567. Despite a strong anti-institutional bias, he was recognized by the church hierarchy as a talented preacher and compassionate minister of mercy to the poor. Although he signed the Formula of Concord,* Weigel's orthodoxy was questioned so openly that he had to publish a defense. He appears to have tried to synthesize several medieval mystics with the ideas of Sebastian Franck,* Thomas Müntzer* and others. His posthumously published works have led some recent scholars to suggest that Weigel's works may have deeply influenced later Pietism.

Hieronymus Weller von Molsdorf (1499–1572). German Lutheran theologian. Originally intending to study law, Weller devoted himself to theology after hearing one of Martin Luther's* sermons on the catechism. He boarded with Luther and tutored Luther's son. In 1539 he moved to Freiburg, where he lectured on the Bible and held theological disputations at the Latin school. In addition to hymns, works of practical theology and a postil set, Weller published commentaries on Genesis, 1–2 Samuel, 1–2 Kings, Job, the Psalms, Christ's passion, Ephesians, Philippians, 1–2 Thessalonians and 1–2 Peter.

John Whitgift (1530–1604). Anglican archbishop. Though Whitgift shared much theological common ground with Puritans, after his election as Archbishop of Canterbury (1583) he moved decisively to squelch the political and ecclesiastical threat they posed during Elizabeth's reign. Whitgift enforced strict compliance to the Book of Common Prayer,* the Act of Uniformity (1559) and the Articles of Religion.* Whitgift's policies led to a large migration of Puritans to Holland. The bulk of Whitgift's published corpus is the fruit of a lengthy public disputation with Thomas Cartwright,* in which Whitgift defines Anglican doctrine against Cartwright's staunch Puritanism.

Johann Wigand (1523–1587). German Lutheran theologian. Wigand is most noted as one of the compilers of the *Magdeburg Centuries*, a German ecclesiastical history of the first thirteen centuries of the church. He was a student of Philipp Melanchthon* at the University of Wittenburg and became a significant figure in the controversies dividing Lutheranism. Strongly opposed to Roman Catholicism, Wigand lobbied against innovations in Lutheran theology that appeared sympathetic to Catholic thought. In the later debates, Wigand's support for Gnesio-Lutheranism established his role in the development of confessional Lutheranism. Wigand was appointed bishop of Pomerania after serving academic posts at the universities in Jena and Königsburg.

Thomas Wilcox (c. 1549–1608). English Puritan theologian. In 1572, Wilcox objected to Parliament against the episcopacy and the Book of Common Prayer,* advocating for presbyterian church governance. He was imprisoned for sedition. After his release, he preached itinerantly. He was brought before the courts twice more for his continued protest against the Church of England's episcopal structure. He translated some of Theodore Beza* and John Calvin's* sermons into English, and he wrote polemical and occasional works as well as commentaries on the Psalms and Song of Songs.

Johann (Ferus) Wild (1495–1554). German Catholic pastor. After studying at Heidelberg and teaching at Tübingen, this Franciscan was appointed as lector in the Mainz cathedral, eventually being promoted to cathedral preacher—a post for which he became widely popular but also controversial. Wild strongly identified as Catholic but was not unwilling to criticize the curia. Known for an irenic spirit—criticized in fact as *too* kind—he was troubled by the polemics between all parties of the Reformation. He preached with great lucidity, integrating the liturgy, Scripture and doctrine to exposit Catholic worship and teaching for common people. His sermons on John were pirated for publication without his knowledge; the Sorbonne banned them as heretical. Despite his popularity among clergy, the majority of his works were on the Roman Index until 1900.

Andrew Willet (1562–1621). Anglican priest, professor, and biblical expositor. Willet was a gifted biblical expositor and powerful preacher. He walked away from a promising university career in 1588 when he was ordained a priest in the Church of England. For the next thirty-three years he served as a parish priest. Willet's commentaries summarized the present state of discussion while also offering practical applications for preachers. They have been cited as some of the most technical commentaries of the early seventeenth century. His most important publication was *Synopsis Papismi, or a General View of Papistrie* (1594), in which he responded to many of Robert Bellarmine's critiques. After years of royal favor, Willet was imprisoned in 1618 for a month after presenting to King James I his opposition to the "Spanish Match" of Prince Charles to the Infanta Maria. While serving as a parish priest, he wrote forty-two works, most of which were either commentaries on books of the Bible or controversial works against Catholics.

Thomas Wilson (d. 1586). English Anglican priest. A fellow of St John's, Cambridge, Wilson fled to Frankfurt to escape the Marian Persecution. After his return to England, he served as a canon and Dean of Worcester.

John Woolton (c. 1535–1594). Anglican bishop. After graduating from Oxford, Woolton lived in Germany until the accession of Elizabeth I. He was ordained as a priest in 1560 and as a bishop in 1578. Woolton published many theological, devotional and practical works, including a treatise on the immortality of the soul, a discourse on conscience and a manual for Christian living.

Girolamo Zanchi (1516–1590). Italian Reformed theologian and pastor. Zanchi joined an Augustinian monastery at the age of fifteen, where he studied Greek and Latin, the church fathers and the works of Aristotle and Thomas Aquinas. Under the influence of his prior, Peter Martyr Vermigli,* Zanchi also imbibed the writings of the Swiss and German reformers. To avoid the Inquisition, Zanchi fled to Geneva where he was strongly attracted to the preaching and teaching of John Calvin.* Zanchi taught biblical theology and the *locus* method at academies in Strasbourg, Heidelberg, and Neustadt. He also served as pastor of an Italian refugee congregation. Zanchi's theological works, *De tribus Elohim* (1572) and *De natura Dei* (1577), have received more attention than his commentaries. His commentaries comprise about a quarter of his literary output, however, and display a strong typological and christological interpretation in conversation with the church fathers, medieval exegetes, and other reformers.

Katharina Schütz Zell (1497/98–1562). German Reformed writer. Zell became infamous in Strasbourg and the Empire when in 1523 she married the priest Matthias Zell, and then published an apology defending her husband against charges of impiety and libertinism. Longing for a united church, she called for toleration of Catholics and Anabaptists, famously writing to Martin Luther* after the failed Marburg Colloquy of 1529 to exhort him to check his hostility and to be ruled instead by Christian charity. Much to the chagrin of her contemporaries, Zell published diverse works, ranging from polemical treatises on marriage to letters of consolation, as well as editing a hymnal and penning an exposition of Psalm 51.

Huldrych Zwingli (1484–1531). Swiss Reformed humanist, preacher and theologian. Zwingli, a parish priest, was influenced by the writings of Desiderius Erasmus* and taught himself Greek. While a preacher to the city cathedral in Zurich, Zwingli enacted reform through sermons, public disputations and conciliation with the town council, abolishing the Mass and images in the church. Zwingli broke with the lectionary preaching tradition, instead preaching serial expository biblical sermons. He later was embroiled in controversy with Anabaptists over infant baptism and with Martin Luther* at the Marburg Colloquy (1529) over their differing views of the Eucharist. Zwingli, serving as chaplain to Zurich's military, was killed in battle.

SOURCES FOR BIOGRAPHICAL SKETCHES

General Reference Works

Allgemeine Deutsche Biographie. 56 vols. Leipzig: Duncker & Humblot, 1875–1912; reprint, 1967–1971. Accessible online via deutsche-biographie.de/index.html.

Baskin, Judith R., ed. *The Cambridge Dictionary of Judaism and Jewish Culture.* New York: Cambridge University Press, 2011.

Benedetto, Robert, ed. *The New Westminster Dictionary of Church History.* Vol. 1. Louisville: Westminster John Knox Press, 2008.

Bettenson, Henry and Chris Maunder, eds. *Documents of the Christian Church.* 3rd ed. Oxford: Oxford University Press, 1999.

Betz, Hans Dieter, Don Browning, Bernd Janowski and Eberhard Jüngel, eds. *Religion Past & Present: Encyclopedia of Theology and Relgion.* 13 vols. Leiden: Brill, 2007–2013.

Bremer, Francis J. and Tom Webster, eds. *Puritans and Puritanism in Europe and America: A Comprehensive Encyclopedia.* 2 vols. Santa Barbara, CA: ABC-CLIO, 2006.

Gritsch, Eric W. *A History of Lutheranism.* Minneapolis: Fortress Press, 2002.

Haag, Eugene and Émile Haag. *La France protestante ou vies des protestants français.* 2nd ed. 6 vols. Paris: Sandoz & Fischbacher, 1877–1888.

Hillerbrand, Hans J., ed. *Oxford Encyclopedia of the Reformation.* 4 vols. New York: Oxford University Press, 1996.

Kolb, Robert, and Timothy J. Wengert, eds. *The Book of Concord: The Confessions of the Evangelical Lutheran Church.* Translated by Charles Arand et al. Minneapolis: Fortress, 2000.

McKim, Donald K., ed. *Dictionary of Major Biblical Interpreters.* Downers Grove, IL: InterVarsity Press, 2007.

Müller, Gerhard, et al., ed. *Theologische Realenzyklopädie.* Berlin: Walter de Gruyter, 1994.

Neue Deutsche Biographie. 28 vols. projected. Berlin: Duncker & Humblot, 1953–. Accessible online via deutsche-biographie.de/index.html.

New Catholic Encyclopedia. 15 vols. New York: McGraw-Hill, 1967; 2nd ed., Detroit: Thomson-Gale, 2002.

Oxford Dictionary of National Biography. 60 vols. Oxford: Oxford University Press, 2004.

Pelikan, Jaroslav. *The Christian Tradition.* 5 vols. Chicago: University of Chicago Press, 1971–1989.

Stephen, Leslie, and Sidney Lee, eds. *Dictionary of National Biography.* 63 vols. London: Smith, Elder and Co., 1885–1900.

Terry, Michael, ed. *Reader's Guide to Judaism.* New York: Routledge, 2000.

Wordsworth, Christopher, ed. *Lives of Eminent Men connected with the History of Religion in England.* 4 vols. London: J. G. & F. Rivington, 1839.

Additional Works for Individual Sketches

Akin, Daniel L. "An Expositional Analysis of the Schleitheim Confession." *Criswell Theological Review* 2 (1988): 345-70.

Bald, R. C. *John Donne: A Life.* Oxford: Oxford University Press, 1970.

Bireley, Robert, *The Refashioning of Catholicism, 1450–1700,* Washington, DC: Catholic University of America Press, 1999.

Burke, David G. "The Enduring Significance of the KJV." *Word and World* 31, no. 3 (2011): 229-44.

Campbell, Gordon. *Bible: The Story of the King James Version, 1611–2011.* Oxford: Oxford University Press, 2010.

Doornkaat Koolman, J ten. "The First Edition of Peter Riedemann's 'Rechenschaft.'" *Mennonite Quarterly Review* 36, no. 2 (1962): 169-70.

Fischlin, Daniel and Mark Fortier, eds. *Royal Subjects: Essays on the Writings of James VI and I.* Detroit: Wayne State University Press, 2002.

Fishbane, Michael A. "Teacher and the Hermeneutical Task: A Reinterpretation of Medieval Exegesis." *Journal of the American Academy of Religion* 43, no. 4 (1975): 709-21.

Friedmann, Robert. "Second Generation Anabaptism as Illustrated by the Walpot Era of the Hutterites." *Mennonite Quarterly* 44, no. 4 (1970): 390-93.

Frymire, John M. *The Primacy of the Postils: Catholics, Protestants, and the Dissemination of Ideas in Early Modern Germany.* Leiden: Brill, 2010.

Furcha, Edward J. "Key Concepts in Caspar von Schwenckfeld's Thought, Regeneration and the New Life." *Church History* 37, no. 2 (1968): 160-73.

Gordon, Bruce, *The Swiss Reformation.* Manchester: Manchester University Press, 2002.

Greaves, Richard L. *Society and Religion in Elizabethan England.* Minneapolis: University of Minnesota, 1981.

Greiffenberg, Catharina Regina von. *Meditations on the Incarnation, Passion and Death of Jesus Christ.* Edited and translated by Lynne Tatlock. The Other Voice in Early Modern Europe. Chicago: University of Chicago Press, 2009.

Grendler, Paul. "Italian biblical humanism and the papacy, 1515-1535." In *Biblical Humanism and Scholasticism in the Age of Erasmus.* Edited by Erika Rummel, 225-76. Leiden: Brill, 2008.

Heiden, Albert van der. "Pardes: Methodological Reflections on the Theory of the Four Senses." *Journal of Jewish Studies* 34, no. 2 (1983): 147-59.

Hendrix, Scott H., ed. and trans. *Early Protestant Spirituality.* New York: Paulist Press, 2009.

Hvolbek, Russell H. "Being and Knowing: Spiritualist Epistelmology and Anthropology from Schwenckfeld to Böhme." *Sixteenth Century Journal* 22, no. 1 (1991): 97-110.

Kahle, Paul. "Felix Pratensis—a Prato, Felix. Der Herausgeber der Ersten Rabbinerbibel, Venedig 1516/7." *Die Welt des Orients* 1, no. 1 (1947): 32-36.

Kelly, Joseph Francis. *The Ecumenical Councils of the Catholic Church: A History.* Collegeville, MN: Liturgical Press, 2009.

Lake, Peter. *The Boxmaker's Revenge: "Orthodoxy", "Heterodox" and the Politics of the Parish in Early Stuart London.* Stanford, CA: Stanford University Press, 2001.

Lockhart, Paul Douglas. *Frederick II and the Protestant Cause: Denmark's Role in the Wars of Religion, 1559–1596.* Leiden: Brill, 2004.

Lubac, Henri de. *Medieval Exegesis: The Four Senses of Scripture.* 3 vols. Translated by Mark Sebanc and E. M. Macierowski. Grand Rapids: Eerdmans, 1998–2009.

Manetsch, Scott, *Calvin's Company of Pastors: Pastoral Care and the Emerging Reformed Church, 1536–1609.* Oxford: Oxford University Press, 2013.

Matheson, Peter, *Argula von Grumbach: A Woman's Voice in the Reformation.* Edinburgh: T&T Clark, 1995.

McKinley, Mary B. "Volume Editor's Introduction." In *Epistle to Marguerite of Navarre and Preface to a Sermon by John Calvin,* edited and translated by Mary B. McKiney. Chicago: University of Chicago Press, 2004.

Norton, David. *A Textual History of the King James Bible.* New York: Cambridge University Press, 2005

Packull, Werner O. "The Origins of Peter Riedemann's Account of Our Faith." *Sixteenth Century Journal* 30, no. 1 (1999): 61-69.

Papazian, Mary Arshagouni, ed. *John Donne and the Protestant Reformation: New Perspectives.* Detroit: Wayne State University Press, 2003.

Paulicelli, Eugenia. "Sister Arcangela Tarabotti: Hair, Wigs and Other Vices." In *Writing Fashion in Early Modern Italy: From Sprezzatura to Satire,* by idem, 177-204. Farnham, Surrey, UK: Ashgate, 2014.

Pragman, James H. "The Augsburg Confession in the English Reformation: Richard Taverner's Contribution." *Sixteenth Century Journal* 11, no. 3 (1980): 75-85.

Rashi. *Rashi's Commentary on Psalms.* Translated by Mayer I. Gruber. Atlanta: Scholars Press, 1998.

Reid, Jonathan A. *King's Sister—Queen of Dissent: Marguerite of Navarre (1492–1549) and her Evangelical Network.* Leiden: Brill, 2009.

Schmidt, Josef, "Introduction" in Johannes Tauler, *Sermons.* New York: Paulist Press, 1985, 1-34.

Spinka, Matthew. *John Hus: A Biography.* Princeton, NJ: Princeton University Press, 1968.

———. *John Hus at the Council of Constance.* New York: Columbia University Press, 1968.

———. *John Hus and the Czech Reform.* Hamden, CT: Archon Books, 1966.

Steinmetz, David C. *Reformers in the Wings: From Geiler von Kayserberg to Theodore Beza.* Oxford: Oxford University Press, 2000.

———. "The Superiority of Pre-Critical Exegesis." *Theology Today* 37, no. 1 (1980): 27-38.

Synder, C. Arnold. "The Confession of the Swiss Brethren in Hesse, 1578." In *Anabaptism Revisited: Essays on Anabaptist/Mennonite Studies in Honor of C. J. Dyck*. Edited by Walter Klaassen, 29-49. Waterloo, ON; Scottdale, PA: Herald Press, 1992.

———. "The Schleitheim Articles in Light of the Revolution of the Common Man: Continuation or Departure?" *Sixteenth Century Journal* 16, no. 4 (1985): 419-30.

Todd, Margo. "Bishops in the Kirk: William Cowper of Galloway and the Puritan Episcopacy of Scotland." *Scottish Journal of Theology*, 57 (2004): 300-312.

Van Liere, Frans. *An Introduction to the Medieval Bible*. New York: Cambridge University Press, 2014.

Voogt, Gerrit. "Remonstrant-Counter-Remonstrant Debates: Crafting a Principled Defense of Toleration after the Synod of Dordrecht (1619–1650)." *Church History and Religious Culture* 89, no. 4 (2009): 489-524.

Wallace, Dewey D. Jr. "George Gifford, Puritan Propaganda and Popular Religion in Elizabethan England." *Sixteenth Century Journal* 9, no. 1 (1978): 27-49.

Wengert, Timothy J. "'Fear and Love' in the Ten Commandments." *Concordia Journal* 21, no. 1 (1995): 14-27.

———. "Philip Melanchthon and John Calvin against Andreas Osiander: Coming to Terms with Forensic Justification." In *Calvin and Luther: The Continuing Relationship*, edited by R. Ward Holder, 63-87. Göttingen: Vandenhoeck & Ruprecht, 2013.

Wilkinson, Robert J. *Tetragrammaton: Western Christians and the Hebrew Name of God*. Leiden: Brill, 2015.

BIBLIOGRAPHY

The Epistle to the Hebrews

Adams, Thomas. *The Happines of the Church. Or, a Description of Those Spirituall Prerogatiues wherewith Christ hath endowed her Considered in some contemplations upon part of the 12. chapter to the Hebrewes. Together with certain other meditations and discourses . . . Being the summe of diuerse sermons preached in S. Gregories London*. London: G. Purslowe, 1618. Digital copy online at ebbo.chadwyck.com.

Bird, Samuel. *The Lectures of Samuel Bird of Ipswidge upon the 11th Chapter of the Epistle unto the Hebrews, and upon the 38th Psalm*. Cambridge: John Legare, 1598. Digital copy online at ebbo.chadwyck.com.

Bugenhagen, Johannes. *Annotationes . . . in epistolas Pauli ad Galatas, Ephesios, Philippenses, Coloßenses, Thessalonicenses primam et secundam, Timotheum primam et secundam, Titum, Philemonem, Hebraeos*. Strasbourg: Johann Knobloch, 1525. Digital copy online at www.gateway-bayern.de.

Bullinger, Heinrich. *In piam et eruditam Pauli ad Hebraeos epistolam Heinrychi Bullingeri commentarius*. Zurich: Christoph Froschauer, 1532). Digital copy online at www.e-rara.ch.

———. *Die rechten opffer der Christenheit: Ein predig usz dem XIII. Cap. S. Pauli zuo den Hebreern*. Zurich: Christoph Froschauer, 1551. Digital copy online at www.e-rara.ch.

Cajetan, Cardinal (Thomas de Vio). *Epistolae Pavli et aliorvm apostolorvm ad graecam veritatem castigatae*. Venice: Luca-Antonio Giunta, 1531. Digital copy online at books.google.com.

Calvin, John. *Commentaries on the Epistle of Paul the Apostle to the Hebrews* (1549). Translated and edited by John Owen. CTS 40. Edinburgh: Calvin Translation Society, 1853; reprint, Grand Rapids: Baker, 2005. Digital copy online at archive.org.

Cleaver, Robert. *Four Sermons: The Two First, of Godly Feare, on Hebrews 4, Verse 1 by Robert Cleaver; The Two Last, of Christian Love and Life, on Canticles 2, Verse 10 by Richard Webb*. London: Thomas Snodham, 1613. Digital copy online at ebbo.chadwyck.com.

Contarini, Gasparo. *Gasparis Contareni Cardinalis Opera*. Paris: Sebastian Nivellium, 1571. Digital copy online at books.google.com.

Cranmer, Thomas. *Cranmer's Selected Writings*. Edited by Carl S. Meyer. London: SPCK, 1961.

Dering, Edward. *XXVII Lectures or readings upon part of the Epistle written to the Hebrues*. London: Thomas Woodcocke, 1590. Digital copy online at books.google.com.

Dietrich, Veit. *Summaria vber das newe Testament, Darin auffs kürtzste angezeigt wird was am nötigsten vnd nützsten ist dem jungen Volck vnd gemeinem Man aus allen Capiteln zu wissen vnd zu lernen, Darnach sie jr Leben richten zu jrer Seelen seligkeit brauchen können*. Wittenberg: Veit Kreutzer, 1544. Digital copy online at www.gateway-bayern.de.

Erasmus, Desiderius. *Paraphrases on the Epistle to the Hebrews*. Translated and annotated by John J. Bateman. CWE 44. Toronto: University of Toronto Press, 1993.

Hemmingsen, Niels. *Commentaria in Omnes Epistolas Apostolorvm, Pavli, Petri, Ivdae, Iohannis, Iacobi, et in eam qave ad Hebraeos inscribitur, scripta, recognita, emendata et alicubi aucta à Nicolao Hemmingio*. Leipzig: Ernst Vögelin, 1571. Digital copy online at www.gateway-bayern.de.

Hubmaier, Balthasar, *Balthasar Hubmaier: Theologian of Anabaptism*. Translated and edited by H. Wayne Pipkin and John H. Yoder. CRR 5. Scottdale, PA: Herald Press, 1989.

Illyricus, Matthias Flacius. *Novum Testamentum Jesu Christi Fili Dei, Ex Versione Erasmi, Innumerus In Locis ad Graecum Veritatem Genuinumque Sensum Emendata. Glossa Compendaria M. Matthiae Flacii Illyrici Albonensis in Novum Testamentum*. Basel, 1570. Digital copy online at books.google.com.

Jones, William. *A Commentary upon the Epistles of St Paul to Philemon and to the Hebrewes, together with a compendious explication of the second and third epistles of Saint John*. London: Robert Allot, 1636. Digital copy online at books.google.com.

Lefèvre d'Étaples, Jacques. *Epistola ad Hebraeos*. Paris: Estienne, 1512. Digital copy online at www.gateway-bayern.de.

Linck, Wenzeslaus. *Das zwölfft Capitel der Epistel an die Ebreer/mit kurtzer einfeltiger ausslegung/wie man sich im leiden soll trösten/vnd den glauben beweisen durch bestendigkeit/bey Christo vnd dem Euangelio.* Magdeburg: Christian Rödinger, 1544. Digital copy online at www.gateway-bayern.de.

Luther, Martin. *D. Martin Luthers Werke, Kritische Gesamtausgabe: Deutsche Bibel*. 12 vols. Weimar: Böhlaus Nachfolger, 1906–1961. Digital copy online at archive.org.

———. *D. Martin Luthers Werke, Kritische Gesamtausgabe: [Schriften]*. 73 vols. Weimar: Hermann Böhlaus Nachfolger, 1883–2009. Digital copy online at archive.org.

———. *Luther's Works [American Edition]*. 82 vols. planned. St. Louis: Concordia; Philadelphia: Fortress, 1955–1986; 2009–.

Marguerite of Navarre. *The Mirror of the Sinful Soul*. Translated by Queen Elizabeth I. London: Asher and Company, 1897. Digital copy online at archive.org

Melanchthon, Philip. *The Chief Theological Topics: Loci Praecipui Theologici 1559*. Translated by J. A. O. Preus. St Louis: Concordia, 2011.

Oecolampadius, Johannes. *In Epistolam ad Hebraeos*. Strasbourg: Mathias Apiarius, 1534. Digital copy online at books.google.com.

Osiander, Lucas. *Epistola ad Hebraeos, Iacobi, Prima et Secunda Petri, Prima, Secunda, et tertia Ioannis, Iudae & Apocalypsis Ioannis*. Tübingen: Gruppenbach, 1584. Digital copy online at books.google.com.

Parr, Catherine. *A Lamentation of a Sinner*. London, 1548. Digital copy online at ebbo.chadwyck.com.

Perkins, William. *The Workes of that Famovs and Worthy Minister of Christ in the Universitie of Cambridge, Mr. William Perkins*. 3 vols. London: John Legatt; London: John Haviland, 1626–1631. Digital copy online at www.digitalpuritan.net.

Sarcerius, Erasmus. *Summarien und kurtzer Jnhalt sampt einer zimlichen und völligen Auslegung: Uber alle Capitel aller Biblischen Bücher des Alten und newen Testaments*. 4 vols. Leipzig: Berwalt, 1559. Digital copy online at books.google.com and www.gateway-bayern.de.

Spangenberg, Johann. *[Postilla Teütsch:] Auslegung der Episteln, so auff die fürnemeste Feste in der Kirchen gelesen werden*. Postilla Teütsch 6. Wittenberg: Peter Seitz, 1553. Digital copy online at www.gateway-bayern.de.

———. *[Postilla Teütsch:] Auslegung der Episteln, so auff die Sonntage vom Advent biß auff Ostern in der Kirchen gelesen werden*. Postilla Teütsch 4. Magdeburg: Michael Lotter, 1544. Digital copy online at www.gateway-bayern.de.

Walkington, Thomas. *An Exposition of the First Two Verses of the Sixth Chapter to the Hebrews in the Forme of a Dialogue, Wherein You Have A Commendation of Catechizing, Also a Declaration of the Six Fundamental Principles, Wherein the Christians of the Primitive Apostolicall Church Were Catechized*. London: Joseph Bulkley, 1609. Digital copy online at ebbo.chadwyck.com.

Williams, George H., and Angel M. Megal, eds. *Spiritual and Anabaptist Writers*. LCC 25. Philadelphia: Westminster, 1957.

Zwingli, Huldrych. *In Evangelicam Historiam de Domino Nostro Iesv Christo, per Matthaevm, Marcvm, Lucam, et Ioannem conscriptam, Epistolasque aliquot Pauli, Annotationes . . . Adiecta est Epistola Pauli ad Hebraeos, et Ioannis Apostoli Epistola*. Edited by Leo Jud and Kaspar Megander. Zurich: Christoph Froschauer, 1539. Digital copy online at books.google.com.

The Epistle to James

Althamer, Andreas. *Die Epistel S. Jacobs mit newer auslegung Andree Althamers: Wie sie gepredigt worden zu Onolzbach*. Wittenberg: Georg Rhau, 1533. Digital copy online at books.google.com.

Cajetan, Cardinal (Thomas de Vio). *Opera omnia qvotqvot in Sacrae Scripturae expositionem reperiuntur*. 5 vols. Lyons: Jean and Pierre Prost, 1639. Digital copy online at books.google.com.

Calvin, John. *Commentaries on the Catholic Epistles* (1551). Translated and edited by John Owen. CTS 42. Edinburgh: Calvin Translation Society, 1855; reprint, Grand Rapids: Baker, 2005. Digital copy online at archive.org.

Contarini, Gasparo. *Gasparis Contareni Cardinalis Opera*. Paris: Sebastian Nivellium, 1571. Digital copy online at books.google.com.

Cranmer, Thomas. *Cranmer's Selected Writings*. Edited by Carl S. Meyer. London: SPCK, 1961.

Dickson, David. *An expositon of all St. Pauls epistles together with an explanation of those other epistles of the apostles St. James, Peter, John and Jude*. London: R. I. for Francis Eglesfield, 1659. Accessed digitally via EEBO.

Dietrich, Veit. *Summaria vber das newe Testament/ Darin auffs kürtzste angezeigt wird/ was am nötigsten vnd nützsten ist/dem jungen Volck vnd gemeinem Man/aus allen Capiteln/zu wissen vnd zu lernen/Darnach sie jr Leben richten zu jrer Seelen seligkeit brauchen können*. Wittenberg: Veit Kreutzer, 1544. Digital copy online at www.gateway-bayern.de.

Erasmus, Desiderius. *Paraphrase on James*. Translated and annotated by John J. Bateman. CWE 44. Toronto: University of Toronto Press, 1993.

Hooker, Richard. *The Folger Library Edition of the Works of Richard Hooker*. Vol. 3. Edited by W. Speed Hill. Cambridge, MA: Harvard University Press, 1981.

Hubmaier, Balthasar. *Balthasar Hubmaier: Theologian of Anabaptism*. Translated and edited by H. Wayne Pipkin and John H. Yoder. CRR 5. Scottdale, PA: Herald Press, 1989.

Lefèvre d'Étaples, Jacques. *Commentarii in Epistolas Catholicas, Iacobi, Petri, Ioannis, Iudae*. Basel: Andreas Cratander, 1527. Digital copy online at www.e-rara.ch.

Luther, Martin. *D. Martin Luthers Werke, Kritische Gesamtausgabe: Deutsche Bibel*. 12 vols. Weimar: Böhlaus Nachfolger, 1906–1961. Digital copy online at archive.org.

———. *D. Martin Luthers Werke, Kritische Gesamtausgabe: [Schriften]*. 73 vols. Weimar: Hermann Böhlaus Nachfolger, 1883–2009. Digital copy online at archive.org.

———. *Luther's Works [American Edition]*. 82 vols. planned. St. Louis: Concordia; Philadelphia: Fortress, 1955–1986; 2009–.

Mayer, John. *A commentarie vpon the New Testament*. 3 vols. London: Iohn Hauiland for Iohn Grismond, 1631. Accessed digitally via EEBO.

Osiander, Lucas. *Epistola ad Hebraeos, Iacobi, Prima et Secunda Petri, Prima, Secunda, et tertia Ioannis, Iudae & Apocalypsis Ioannis*. Tübingen: Gruppenbach, 1584. Digital copy online at books.google.com.

Pellikan, Konrad. *Commentaria bibliorum*. 7 vols. Zurich: Christoph Froschauer, 1539. Digital copy online at books.google.com.

Sarcerius, Erasmus. *Summarien und kurtzer Jnhalt sampt einer zimlichen und völligen Auslegung: Uber alle Capitel aller Biblischen Bücher des Alten und newen Testaments*. 4 vols. Leipzig: Berwalt, 1559. Digital copy online at books.google.com and www.gateway-bayern.de.

Simons, Menno. *The Complete Writings of Menno Simons, c. 1496–1561*. Translated Leonard Verduin. Edited by J. C. Wenger. Scottdale, PA: Herald Press, 1984.

Snyder, C. Arnold. *Sources of South German/Austrian Anabaptism*. Translated by Walter Klaassen, Frank Friesen, and Werner O. Packull. CRR 10. Kitchener, ON: Pandora Press, 2001.

Spangenberg, Johann. [*Postilla Teütsch:*] *Auslegung der Episteln, so auff die Sonntage von Ostern biß auff das Advent in der Kirchen gelesen werden*. Postilla Teütsch 5. Augsburg: Valentein Othmar, 1545. Digital copy online at www.gateway-bayern.de.

Turnbull, Richard. *An exposition upon the canonicall Epistle of Saint Iames*. London: John Windet, 1591. Accessed digitally via EEBO.

Zwingli, Huldrych. *Brevis et luculenta Huldrychi Zvinglii in Epistolam beati Iacobi Expositio*. Edited by Leo Jud. Zurich: Christoph Froschauer, 1533. Digital copy online at www.e-rara.ch.

Other Works Consulted

Adeney, Joel D. "The Same Yesterday and Today and Forever: The Ongoing Priestly Ministry of the Exalted Christ in Reformation Commentaries on Hebrews, 1517–1539." MA Thesis, Trinity Evangelical Divinity School, 2011.

Angel, Silvert. *The Confessionalist Homiletics of Lucas Osiander: A Study of a South-German Lutheran Preacher in the Age of Confessionalization*. Tübingen: Mohr Siebeck, 2014.

Attridge, Harold. *A Commentary on the Epistle to the Hebrews*. Hermeneia. Philadelphia: Fortress Press, 1989.

Augustine, John, ed. *A Commentary on Hebrews 11 (1609 edition)/William Perkins*. New York: Pilgrim Press, 1991.

Bagchi, David, and David C. Steinmetz, eds. *The Cambridge Companion to Reformation Theology*. Cambridge: Cambridge University Press, 2004.

Bayer, Oswald. *Promissio: Geschichte der reformatorischen Wende in Luthers Theologie*. Göttingen: Vandenhoeck & Ruprecht, 1971.

Bizer, Ernst. *Fides Ex Auditu: Eine Untersuchung über die Entdeckung der Gerechtigkeit Gottes durch Martin Luther*. 3rd ed. Neukirchen-Vluyn: Neukirchener Verlag, 1966.

Cameron, Euan. *The European Reformation*. 2nd ed. Oxford: Oxford University Press, 2012.

Cyprian. *The Lapsed; The Unity of the Church*. Translated and annotated by Maruice Bévenot. ACW 25. New York: Newman Press, 1957.

Dibelius, Martin. *A Commentary on the Epistle of James*. Hermeneia. Revised by Heinrich Greeven. Translated by Michael A. Williams. Philadelphia: Fortress Press, 1976.

Fisher, Jeff. *A Christoscopic Reading of Scripture: Johannes Oecolampadius on Hebrews*. Göttingen: Vandenhoeck & Ruprecht, 2016.

George, Timothy. *Theology of the Reformers*. Rev. ed. Nashville: B & H, 2013.

Greenslade, S. L. *The Cambridge History of the Bible*. 3 vols. Cambridge: Cambridge University Press, 1975.

Hagen, Kenneth. "The First Translation of Luther's *Lectures on Hebrews:* A Review Article." *Church History* 34 (1965): 204-13.

———. *Hebrews Commenting from Erasmus to Bèze, 1516–1598*. Tübingen: Mohr Siebeck, 1981. Reprint, Eugene, OR: Wipf and Stock, 2011

———. *A Theology of Testament in the Young Luther: The Lectures on Hebrews*. Leiden: Brill, 1974.

Hamm, Berndt. *The Early Luther: Stages in a Reformation Reorientation*. Translated by Martin J. Lohrmann. Grand Rapids: Eerdmans, 2014.

———. *The Reformation of Faith in the Context of Late Medieval Theology and Piety*. Edited by Robert J. Bast. Leiden: Brill, 2004.

Hansen, Gary Neal. "Calvin as Commentator on Hebrews and the Catholic Epistles." In *Calvin and the Bible*, edited by Donald K. McKim, 257-81. New York: Cambridge University Press, 2006.

Holmes, Michael W. *The Apostolic Fathers in English*. 3rd ed. Grand Rapids: Baker Academic, 2006.

Johnson, Luke Timothy. *The Letter of James: A New Translation with Introduction and Commentary*. Anchor Bible 37a. New York: Doubleday, 1995.

Koester, Craig R. *Hebrews: A New Translation with Introduction and Commentary*. Anchor Bible 36. New York: Doubleday, 2001.

Lane, Jason Daniel. "The Lutheran Interpretation of the Epistle of James in the Sixteenth and Seventeenth Centuries." PhD diss., Hamburg University, 2015.

———. "Luther's Criticism of James as a Key to His Biblical Hermeneutic." In *Auslegung und Hermeneutik der Bibel in der Reformationszeit*, edited by Christine Christ-von Wedel and Sven Grosse, 111-24. Berlin: de Gruyter, 2017.

Lane, William L. *Hebrews 1–8*. Word Biblical Commentary 47a. Dallas: Word, 1991.

———. *Hebrews 9–13*. Word Biblical Commentary 47b. Dallas: Word, 1991.

Lea, Henry Charles. *A History of Auricular Confession and Indulgences in the Latin Church*. 3 vols. Philadelphia: Lea Brothers & Company, 1896.

Lohse, Bernhard, ed. *Der Durchbruch der Reformatorischen Erkenntnis bei Luther*. Darmstadt: Wissenschaftliche Buchgesellschaft, 1968.

———. *Der Durchbruch der Reformatorischen Erkenntnis bei Luther: Neuere Untersuchungen*. Stuttgart: Franz Steiner Verlag, 1988.

Lueker, Erwin L., Luther Poellot, and Paul Jackson, eds. *Christian Cyclopedia*. St. Louis: Concordia, 2000. Accessible digitally via cyclopedia.lcms.org.

Martin, Ralph. *James*. Word Biblical Commentary 28. Waco: Word, 1988.

McGrath, Alister E. *Iustitia Dei: A History of the Christian Doctrine of Justification*. 3rd ed. Cambridge: Cambridge University Press, 2005.

———. *Luther's Theology of the Cross: Martin Luther's Theological Breakthrough*. Oxford: Blackwell, 1985.

———. *Reformation Thought: An Introduction*. 4th ed. Wiley Blackwell, 2012.

McKim, Donald K, ed. *Calvin and the Bible*. New York: Cambridge University, 2006.

McNutt, Jennifer Powell. "James, 'The Book of Straw,' in Reformational Biblical Exegesis: A Comparison of Luther and the Radicals." In *Reconsidering the Relationship Between Biblical and Systematic Theology in the New Testament*, edited by Benjamin E. Reynolds, Brian Lugioyo, and Kevin J. Vanhoozer, 157-76. Tübingen: Mohr Siebeck, 2014.

Muller, Richard A. *Dictionary of Latin and Greek Theological Terms: Drawn Principally from Protestant Scholastic Theology*. Grand Rapids: Baker, 1985.

Muller, Richard, and John L. Thompson, eds. *Biblical Interpretation in the Era of the Reformation: Essays Presented to David C. Steinmetz in Honor of His Sixtieth Birthday*. Grand Rapids: Eerdmans, 1996.

Ozment, Steven. *The Age of Reform, 1250–1550: An Intellectual and Religious History of Late Medieval and Reformation Europe*. New Haven, CT: Yale University Press, 1980.

Parker, T. H. L. "Calvin's Commentary on Hebrews." In *Church, Word and Spirit: Historical and Theological Essays in Honor of Geoffrey W. Bromiley*, edited by James E. Bradley and Richard A. Muller, 135-40. Grand Rapids: Eerdmans, 1987.

Pelikan, Jaroslav. *The Christian Tradition*. 5 vols. Chicago: University of Chicago Press, 1971–1989.

Rittgers, Ronald K. "Embracing the 'True Relic' of Christ: Suffering, Penance, and Private Confession in the Thought of Martin Luther." In *The New History of Penance*, edited by Abigail Firey, 377-93. Leiden: Brill, 2008.

———. "Private Confession in the German Reformation." In *Repentance in Christian Theology*, edited by Mark J. Boda and Gordon T. Smith, 189-207. Collegeville, MN: Liturgical Press, 2006.

———. *The Reformation of Suffering: Pastoral Theology and Lay Piety in Late Medieval and Early Modern Germany*. New York: Oxford University Press, 2012.

———. *The Reformation of the Keys: Confession, Conscience, and Authority in Sixteenth-Century Germany*. Cambridge, MA: Harvard University Press, 2004.

Rummel, Erika, ed. *The Erasmus Reader*. Toronto: University of Toronto Press, 1990.

Schreiner, Susan. *Where Shall Wisdom Be Found? Calvin's Exegesis of Job from the Medieval and Modern Perspectives*. Chicago: University of Chicago Press, 1994.

Shelling, F. W. J. *Historical-Critical Introduction to the Philosophy of Mythology*. Translated by M. Richey and M. Zisselsberger. Albany: State University of New York Press, 2007.

Smalley, Beryl. *The Study of the Bible in the Middle Ages*. Oxford: Oxford University Press, 1952.

Steinmetz, David, ed. *The Bible in the Sixteenth Century*. Durham, NC: Duke University Press, 1990.

———. "The Superiority of Pre-critical Exegesis." *Theology Today* 37, no. 1 (1980): 27-38.

———. *Taking the Long View: Christian Theology in Historical Perspective*. New York: Oxford University Press, 2011.

Stephens, W. P. "Bullinger's Commentaries on Hebrews: In Comparison with the Commentaries of Luther and Calvin." *Bible Translator* 55 (2004): 401-8.

Stützinger, Sarah. "Die Auslegung des Hebräerbriefs bei Luther und lutherischen Theologen des sechzehnten Jahrhunderts am Beispiel von Hebr 9." In *Auslegung und Hermeneutik der Bibel in der Reformationszeit*, edited by Christine Christ-von Wedel and Sven Grosse, 125-46. Berlin: de Gruyter, 2017.

Tentler, Thomas N. *Sin and Confession on the Eve of the Reformation*. Princeton, NJ: Princeton University Press, 1977.

Tertullian. *Treatises on Penance: On Penitence and On Purity*. Translated and annotated by William P. Le Saint. ACW 28. New York: Newman Press, 1959.

Author and Writings Index

Subject Index

Scripture Index